Edexcel GCSE (9-1)

Combined Science

Mark Levesley Penny Johnson Sue Kearsey Iain Brand Nigel Saunders John Ling
Sue Robilliard Carol Tear

PEARSON

Contents

Teaching and learning   vi

CB1	**Key Concepts in Biology** (Paper 1 and Paper 2)	1
CB1a	Microscopes	2
CB1b	Plant and animal cells	4
CB1b	Core practical – Using microscopes	6
CB1c	Specialised cells	8
CB1d	Inside bacteria	10
CB1e	Enzymes and nutrition	12
CB1f	Enzyme action	14
CB1g	Enzyme activity	16
CB1g	Core practical – pH and enzymes	18
CB1h	Transporting substances	20
CB1h	Core practical – Osmosis in potato slices	22
CB1	Preparing for your exams	24

CB2	**Cells and Control** (Paper 1)	25
CB2a	Mitosis	26
CB2b	Growth in animals	28
CB2c	Growth in plants	30
CB2d	Stem cells	32
CB2e	The nervous system	34
CB2f	Neurotransmission speeds	36
CB2	Preparing for your exams	38

CB3	**Genetics** (Paper 1)	39
CB3a	Meiosis	40
CB3bi	DNA	42
CB3bii	DNA extraction	44
CB3c	Alleles	46
CB3d	Inheritance	48
CB3e	Gene mutation	50
CB3f	Variation	52
CB3	Preparing for your exams	54

CB4	**Natural Selection and Genetic Modification** (Paper 1)	55
CB4a	Evidence for human evolution	56
CB4b	Darwin's theory	58
CB4c	Classification	60
CB4d	Breeds and varieties	62
CB4e	Genes in agriculture and medicine	64
CB4	Preparing for your exams	66

CB5	**Health, Disease and the Development of Medicines** (Paper 1)	67
CB5a	Health and disease	68
CB5b	Non-communicable diseases	70
CB5c	Cardiovascular disease	72
CB5d	Pathogens	74
CB5e	Spreading pathogens	76
CB5f	Physical and chemical barriers	78
CB5g	The immune system	80
CB5h	Antibiotics	82
CB5	Preparing for your exams	84

CB6	**Plant Structures and their Functions** (Paper 2)	85
CB6a	Photosynthesis	86
CB6b	Factors that affect photosynthesis	88
CB6b	Core practical – Light intensity and photosynthesis	90
CB6c	Absorbing water and mineral ions	92
CB6d	Transpiration and translocation	94
CB6	Preparing for your exams	96

CB7	**Animal Coordination, Control and Homeostasis** (Paper 2)	97
CB7a	Hormones	98
CB7b	Hormonal control of metabolic rate	100
CB7c	The menstrual cycle	102
CB7d	Hormones and the menstrual cycle	104
CB7e	Control of blood glucose	106
CB7f	Type 2 diabetes	108
CB7	Preparing for your exams	110

CB8	**Exchange and Transport in Animals** (Paper 2)	111
CB8a	Efficient transport and exchange	112
CB8b	The circulatory system	114
CB8c	The heart	116
CB8d	Cellular respiration	118
CB8d	Core practical – Respiration rates	120
CB8	Preparing for your exams	122

CB9	**Ecosystems and Material Cycles** (Paper 2)	123
CB9a	Ecosystems	124
CB9b	Abiotic factors and communities	126
CB9b	Core practical – Quadrats and transects	128
CB9c	Biotic factors and communities	130
CB9d	Parasitism and mutualism	132
CB9e	Biodiversity and humans	134
CB9f	Preserving biodiversity	136
CB9g	The water cycle	138
CB9h	The carbon cycle	140
CB9i	The nitrogen cycle	142
CB9	Preparing for your exams	144

CC1 CC2	**States of Matter** **Methods of Separating and Purifying Substances** (Paper 3)	145
CC1a	States of matter	146
CC2a	Mixtures	148
CC2b	Filtration and crystallisation	150
CC2c	Paper chromatography	152
CC2d	Distillation	154
CC2d	Core practical – Investigating inks	156
CC2e	Drinking water	158
CC1–2	Preparing for your exams	160

CC3	**Atomic Structure** (Paper 3 and Paper 4)	161
CC3a	Structure of an atom	162
CC3b	Atomic number and mass number	164
CC3c	Isotopes	166
CC3	Preparing for your exams	168

CC4	**The Periodic Table** (Paper 3 and Paper 4)	169
CC4a	Elements and the periodic table	170
CC4b	Atomic number and the periodic table	172
CC4c	Electronic configurations and the periodic table	174
CC4	Preparing for your exams	176

CC5 CC6 CC7	**Ionic Bonding** **Covalent Bonding** **Types of Substance** (Paper 3 and Paper 4)	177
CC5a	Ionic bonds	178
CC5b	Ionic lattices	180
CC5c	Properties of ionic compounds	182
CC6a	Covalent bonds	184
CC7a	Molecular compounds	186
CC7b	Allotropes of carbon	188
CC7c	Properties of metals	190
CC7d	Bonding models	192
CC5–7	Preparing for your exams	194

CC8	**Acids and Alkalis** (Paper 3)	195
CC8a	Acids, alkalis and indicators	196
CC8b	Looking at acids	198
CC8c	Bases and salts	200
CC8c	Core practical – Preparing copper sulfate	202
CC8d	Alkalis and balancing equations	204
CC8d	Core practical – Investigating neutralisation	206
CC8e	Alkalis and neutralisation	208
CC8f	Reactions of acids with metals and carbonates	210
CC8g	Solubility	212
CC8	Preparing for your exams	214

CC9	**Calculations Involving Masses** (Paper 3 and Paper 4)	215
CC9a	Masses and empirical formulae	216
CC9b	Conservation of mass	218
CC9c	Moles	220
CC9	Preparing for your exams	222

CC10	**Electrolytic Processes**	
CC11	**Obtaining and Using Metals**	
CC12	**Reversible Reactions and Equilibria** (Paper 3)	223
CC10a	Electrolysis	224
CC10a	Core practical – Electrolysis of copper sulfate solution	226
CC10b	Products from electrolysis	228
CC11a	Reactivity	230
CC11b	Ores	232
CC11c	Oxidation and reduction	234
CC11d	Life cycle assessment and recycling	236
CC12a	Dynamic equilibrium	238
CC10–12	Preparing for your exams	240

CC13	**Groups in the Periodic Table**	
CC14	**Rates of Reaction**	
CC15	**Heat Energy Changes in Chemical Reactions** (Paper 4)	241
CC13a	Group 1	242
CC13b	Group 7	244
CC13c	Halogen reactivity	246
CC13d	Group 0	248
CC14a	Rates of reaction	250
CC14b	Factors affecting reaction rates	252
CC14b	Core practical – Investigating reaction rates	254
CC14c	Catalysts and activation energy	256
CC15a	Exothermic and endothermic reactions	258
CC15b	Energy changes in reactions	260
CC13–15	Preparing for your exams	262

CC16	**Fuels**	
CC17	**Earth and Atmospheric Science** (Paper 4)	263
CC16a	Hydrocarbons in crude oil and natural gas	264
CC16b	Fractional distillation of crude oil	266
CC16c	The alkane homologous series	268
CC16d	Complete and incomplete combustion	270
CC16e	Combustible fuels and pollution	272
CC16f	Breaking down hydrocarbons	274
CC17a	The early atmosphere	276
CC17b	The changing atmosphere	278
CC17c	The atmosphere today	280
CC17d	Climate change	282
CC16–17	Preparing for your exams	284

CP1	**Motion** (Paper 5)	285
CP1a	Vectors and scalars	286
CP1b	Distance/time graphs	288
CP1c	Acceleration	290
CP1d	Velocity/time graphs	292
CP1	Preparing for your exams	294

CP2	**Forces and Motion** (Paper 5)	295
CP2a	Resultant forces	296
CP2b	Newton's First Law	298
CP2c	Mass and weight	300
CP2d	Newton's Second Law	302
CP2d	Core practical – Investigating acceleration	304
CP2e	Newton's Third Law	306
CP2f	Momentum	308
CP2g	Stopping distances	310
CP2h	Crash hazards	312
CP2	Preparing for your exams	314

CP3	**Conservation of Energy** (Paper 5)	315
CP3a	Energy stores and transfers	316
CP3b	Energy efficiency	318
CP3c	Keeping warm	320
CP3d	Stored energies	322
CP3e	Non-renewable resources	324
CP3f	Renewable resources	326
CP3	Preparing for your exams	328

CP4	**Waves** (Paper 5)	329
CP4a	Describing waves	330
CP4b	Wave speeds	332
CP4b	Core practical – Investigating waves	334
CP4c	Refraction	336
CP4	Preparing for your exams	338

CP5	**Light and the Electromagnetic Spectrum** (Paper 5)	339
CP5a	Electromagnetic waves	340
CP5a	Core practical – Investigating refraction	342
CP5b	The electromagnetic spectrum	344
CP5c	Using the long wavelengths	346
CP5d	Using the short wavelengths	348
CP5e	EM radiation dangers	350
CP5	Preparing for your exams	352

CP6	**Radioactivity** (Paper 5)	353
CP6a	Atomic models	354
CP6b	Inside atoms	356
CP6c	Electrons and orbits	358
CP6d	Background radiation	360
CP6e	Types of radiation	362
CP6f	Radioactive decay	364
CP6g	Half-life	366
CP6h	Dangers of radioactivity	368
CP6	Preparing for your exams	370

CP7 CP8	**Energy – Forces Doing Work Forces and their Effects** (Paper 6)	371
CP7a	Work and power	372
CP8a	Objects affecting each other	374
CP8b	Vector diagrams	376
CP7–8	Preparing for your exams	378

CP9	**Electricity and Circuits** (Paper 6)	379
CP9a	Electric circuits	380
CP9b	Current and potential difference	382
CP9c	Current, charge and energy	384
CP9d	Resistance	386
CP9e	More about resistance	388
CP9e	Core practical – Investigating resistance	390
CP9f	Transferring energy	392
CP9g	Power	394
CP9h	Transferring energy by electricity	396
CP9i	Electrical safety	398
CP9	Preparing for your exams	400

CP10 CP11	**Magnetism and the Motor Effect Electromagnetic Induction** (Paper 6)	401
CP10a	Magnets and magnetic fields	402
CP10b	Electromagnetism	404
CP10c	Magnetic forces	406
CP11a	Transformers	408
CP11b	Transformers and energy	410
CP10–11	Preparing for your exams	412

CP12 CP13	**Particle Model Forces and Matter** (Paper 6)	413
CP12a	Particles and density	414
CP12a	Core practical – Investigating densities	416
CP12b	Energy and changes of state	418
CP12c	Energy calculations	420
CP12c	Core practical – Investigating water	422
CP12d	Gas temperature and pressure	424
CP13a	Bending and stretching	426
CP13a	Core practical – Investigating springs	428
CP13b	Extension and energy transfers	430
CP12–13	Preparing for your exams	432

Glossary	433
Index	445
The periodic table of the elements	450

Teaching and learning

The **topic reference** tells you which part of the course you are in. 'CP2b' means, 'Combined Science, Physics, unit 2, topic b'.

The **specification reference** allows you to cross reference against the specification criteria so you know which parts you are covering.

If you see an **H** icon that means that content will be assessed on the Higher Tier paper only.

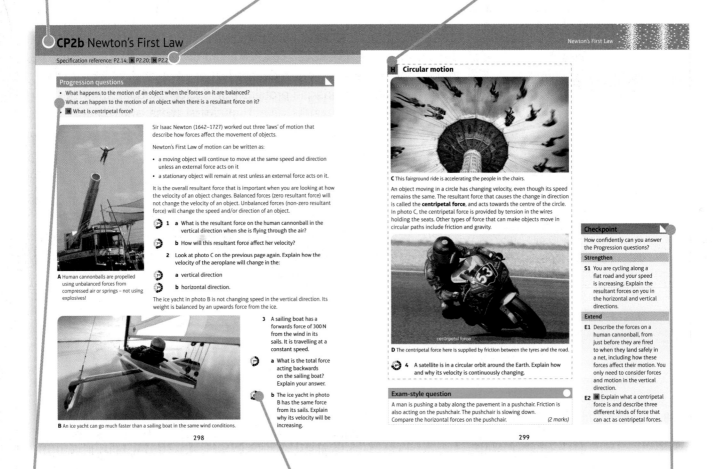

CP2b Newton's First Law

Newton's First Law

Specification reference: P2.14; **H** P2.20; **H** P2.2

Progression questions

- What happens to the motion of an object when the forces on it are balanced?
- What can happen to the motion of an object when there is a resultant force on it?
- **H** What is centripetal force?

Sir Isaac Newton (1642–1727) worked out three 'laws' of motion that describe how forces affect the movement of objects.

Newton's First Law of motion can be written as:

- a moving object will continue to move at the same speed and direction unless an external force acts on it
- a stationary object will remain at rest unless an external force acts on it.

It is the overall resultant force that is important when you are looking at how the velocity of an object changes. Balanced forces (zero resultant force) will not change the velocity of an object. Unbalanced forces (non-zero resultant force) will change the speed and/or direction of an object.

1 **a** What is the resultant force on the human cannonball in the vertical direction when she is flying through the air?

   b How will this resultant force affect her velocity?

2 Look at photo C on the previous page again. Explain how the velocity of the aeroplane will change in the:

   a vertical direction

   b horizontal direction.

The ice yacht in photo B is not changing speed in the vertical direction. Its weight is balanced by an upwards force from the ice.

A Human cannonballs are propelled using unbalanced forces from compressed air or springs – not using explosives!

3 A sailing boat has a forwards force of 300 N from the wind in its sails. It is travelling at a constant speed.

   a What is the total force acting backwards on the sailing boat? Explain your answer.

   b The ice yacht in photo B has the same force from its sails. Explain why its velocity will be increasing.

B An ice yacht can go much faster than a sailing boat in the same wind conditions.

298

H Circular motion

C This fairground ride is accelerating the people in the chairs.

An object moving in a circle has changing velocity, even though its speed remains the same. The resultant force that causes the change in direction is called the **centripetal force**, and acts towards the centre of the circle. In photo C, the centripetal force is provided by tension in the wires holding the seats. Other types of force that can make objects move in circular paths include friction and gravity.

D The centripetal force here is supplied by friction between the tyres and the road.

4 A satellite is in a circular orbit around the Earth. Explain how and why its velocity is continuously changing.

Exam-style question

A man is pushing a baby along the pavement in a pushchair. Friction is also acting on the pushchair. The pushchair is slowing down. Compare the horizontal forces on the pushchair.   *(2 marks)*

Checkpoint

How confidently can you answer the Progression questions?

Strengthen

S1 You are cycling along a flat road and your speed is increasing. Explain the resultant forces on you in the horizontal and vertical directions.

Extend

E1 Describe the forces on a human cannonball, from just before they are fired to when they land safely in a net, including how these forces affect their motion. You only need to consider forces and motion in the vertical direction.

E2 **H** Explain what a centripetal force is and describe three different kinds of force that can act as centripetal forces.

299

By the end of the topic you should be able to confidently answer the **Progression questions**. Try to answer them before you start and make a note of your answers. Think about what you know already and what more you need to learn.

Each question has been given a **Pearson Step** from 1 to 12. This tells you how difficult the question is. The higher the step the more challenging the question.

When you've worked through the main student book questions, answer the **Progression questions** again and review your own progress. Decide if you need to reinforce your own learning by answering the **Strengthen question**, or apply, analyse and evaluate your learning in new contexts by tackling the **Extend question**.

Paper 1 and Paper 2

CB1 Key Concepts in Biology

The bone-eating snot-flower worm (*Osedax mucofloris*) has no digestive system but still manages to feed on one of the hardest substances produced by vertebrate animals – their bones. These worms are a type of zombie worm, so-called because they have no eyes or mouth, and were discovered in the North Sea in 2005 feeding on a whale skeleton. Enzymes in the 'foot' of the worm cause the production of an acid, which attacks bone and releases lipids and proteins from inside the bone. Enzymes in bacteria on the foot of the worm then digest these large organic molecules into smaller molecules that the worms absorb (using processes such as diffusion).

In this unit you will learn about some of the central ideas in biology, including ideas about cells, microscopy, enzymes, nutrition, diffusion, osmosis and active transport.

The learning journey

Previously you will have learnt at KS3:

- how to use a microscope
- about the differences between cells from different organisms
- how some cells are specialised and adapted to their functions
- how enzymes help to digest food in the digestive system
- how substances can move by diffusion.

In this unit you will learn:

- how developments in microscopy have allowed us to find out more about the sub-cellular structures found in plant, animal and bacterial cells
- about the importance of enzymes in nutrition, growth and development
- how enzymes are affected by pH and temperature and why each enzyme only works on a certain type of molecule
- how substances are carried by diffusion, osmosis and active transport.

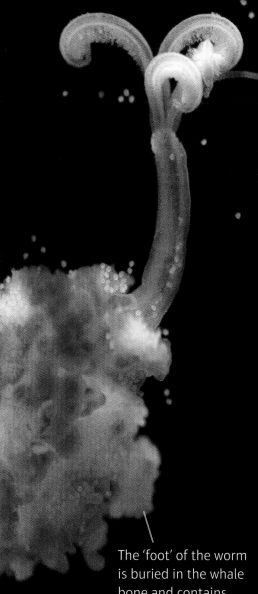

The 'foot' of the worm is buried in the whale bone and contains many bacteria.

CB1a Microscopes

Specification reference: B1.3; B1.4; B1.5

Progression questions

- What determines how good a microscope is at showing small details?
- What has the development of the electron microscope allowed us to do?
- What units are used for very small sizes?

eyepiece lens

focusing wheel – adjusts the focus to make the image clearer

objective lens

specimen holder

A Hooke's microscope

The most common microscope used today contains two lenses and was invented at the end of the 16th century. Robert Hooke (1635–1703) used a microscope like this to discover cells in 1665.

Hooke's microscope had a **magnification** of about ×30 (it made things appear about 30 times bigger). A person magnified 30 times would be roughly the size of the Statue of Liberty in New York.

1 **a** A photo of a water flea says it is magnified ×50. What does this mean?

 b On the photo, the flea is 5 cm long. Calculate the unmagnified length of the water flea.

To work out a microscope's magnification, you *multiply* the magnifications of its two lenses together. So, the magnification of a microscope with a ×5 **eyepiece lens** and ×10 **objective lens** is:

$$5 \times 10 = \times 50$$

2 A microscope has a ×5 eyepiece lens with ×5, ×15 and ×20 objective lenses. Calculate its three total magnifications.

Hooke's microscope was not very powerful because the glass lenses were of poor quality. Antonie van Leeuwenhoek (1632–1723) found a way of making much better lenses, although they were very small. He used these to construct microscopes with single lenses, which had magnifications of up to ×270. In 1675, he examined a drop of rainwater and was surprised to find tiny organisms, which he called 'animalcules'. Fascinated by his discovery, he searched for 'animalcules' in different places.

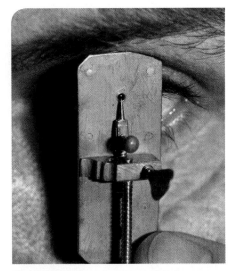

B replica of a van Leeuwenhoek microscope

3 The top bacterium in photo C is 0.002 mm long in real life. At what magnification is the drawing?

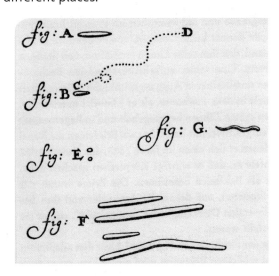

C These are van Leeuwenhoek's drawings of 'animalcules' found in scrapings from his teeth. We call them bacteria.

Did you know?

Van Leeuwenhoek examined his semen and discovered sperm cells.

2

The detail obtained by a microscope also depends on its **resolution**. This is the smallest distance between two points that can still be seen as two points. Van Leeuwenhoek's best microscopes had a resolution of 0.0014 mm. Two points that were 0.0014 mm or further apart could be seen as two points, but two points closer together than this appeared as a single point.

D These images of tiny beads have the same magnification but different resolutions.

 4 Hooke's microscope had a resolution of about 0.002 mm. What does this mean?

With the development of **stains** for specimens, and better lenses and light sources, today's best light microscopes magnify up to ×1500 with resolutions down to about 0.0001 mm.

The electron microscope was invented in the 1930s. Instead of light, beams of electrons pass through a specimen to build up an image. These microscopes can magnify up to ×2 000 000, with resolutions down to 0.0000002 mm. They allow us to see cells with great detail and clarity.

 5 Explain why electron microscope images show more detail than light microscopes.

SI units

The measurements on these pages are in millimetres. Adding the 'milli' prefix to a unit divides it by 1000. One metre (m) contains 1000 millimetres (mm). There are other prefixes that often make numbers easier to understand.

Table E

Prefix	Effect on unit	Example
milli-	÷ 1000	millimetres (mm)
micro-	÷ 1 000 000	micrometres (µm)
nano-	÷ 1 000 000 000	nanometres (nm)
pico-	÷ 1 000 000 000 000	picometres (pm)

× 1000 ↻
× 1000 ↻
× 1000 ↻

⤳ ÷ 1000
⤳ ÷ 1000
⤳ ÷ 1000

 6 Give the highest resolution of electron microscopes in micro-, nano- and picometres.

Checkpoint

How confidently can you answer the Progression questions?

Strengthen

S1 Compare today's light microscopes with Hooke's.

Extend

E1 Diatoms are algae, 20–120 µm in length and with 1 µm diameter 'pores' in their outer coats. Van Leeuwenhoek described diatom shapes but not their pores. Explain why.

Exam-style question

State two advantages of using an electron microscope to view cells, rather than a light microscope. *(2 marks)*

CB1b Plant and animal cells

Specification reference: B1.1; B1.4; B1.6

Progression questions

- How are animal cells different to plant cells?
- What do the sub-cellular structures in eukaryotic cells do?
- How can we estimate the sizes of cells and their parts?

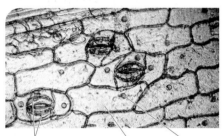

two guard cells (form a stoma in the surface of a leaf)   leaf surface cell   nucleus

A This micrograph ('microscope picture') was taken using Brown's original microscope, of the same cells in which he discovered nuclei (magnification ×67).

As microscopes improved, scientists saw more details inside cells. In 1828, Robert Brown (1773–1858) examined cells from the surface of a leaf and noticed that each cell contained a small, round blob. He called this the **nucleus** (meaning 'inner part' in Latin).

1 Photo A is at a magnification of 67. State what this means.

Brown wrote a **scientific paper** about his discovery. Matthias Schleiden (1804–1881) read the paper and thought that the nucleus must be the most important part of a plant cell. He mentioned this idea to Theodor Schwann (1810–1882), who then wondered if he could find cells with nuclei in animals. He did. And so the idea of cells being the basic building blocks of all life was born.

A cell with a nucleus is described as **eukaryotic**. We have now discovered many other sub-cellular ('smaller than a cell') structures in eukaryotic cells and worked out what they do.

The **cell membrane** is like a very thin bag. It controls what enters and leaves, and separates one cell from another.

The **cytoplasm** contains a watery jelly and is where most of the cell's activities occur.

One of these blobs is a **mitochondrion** (see photo C). Mitochondria are jelly-bean shaped structures in which **aerobic respiration** occurs. Mitochondria are very difficult to see with a light microscope.

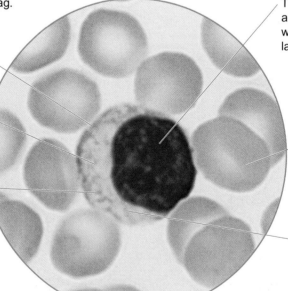

The **nucleus** controls the cell and its activities. Inside it are **chromosomes**, which contain **DNA**. It is especially large in white blood cells.

red blood cell

The cytoplasm also contains tiny round structures called **ribosomes**. These make new proteins for a cell. It is impossible to see them with a light microscope.

2 Draw a table to show the parts of an animal cell and the function of each part.

B The labelled central cell is a human white blood cell, which has been stained to make its features show up clearly (magnification ×2500).

3 Estimate the diameter of the labelled red blood cell in photo B. Show your working.

The circular area you see in a light microscope is the **field of view**. If we know its diameter, we can estimate sizes. The diameter of the field of view in photo B is 36 µm. We can imagine that three white blood cells will roughly fit across the field of view. So the cell's diameter is about $\frac{36}{3}$ = 12 µm.

Electron micrographs

Photo C shows many parts inside a white blood cell that you cannot see with a light microscope. However, you still cannot see ribosomes because they are only about 25 nm in diameter.

 4 a Look at photo C. What part has been coloured purple?

 b Use the magnification to estimate the width of the cell.

 5 State the diameter of a ribosome in micrometres.

Scale bars are often shown on micrographs and these are also used to estimate sizes. The scale bar on photo C shows how long 4 μm is at this magnification. About three of these bars could fit across the cell at its widest point; the cell is about 3 × 4 = 12 μm wide.

Plant cells may have some additional structures compared with animal cells, as shown in diagram D.

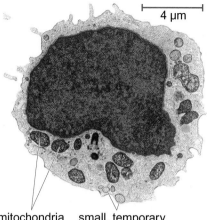

mitochondria small, temporary vacuoles

C electron micrograph of a white blood cell (magnification ×4200)

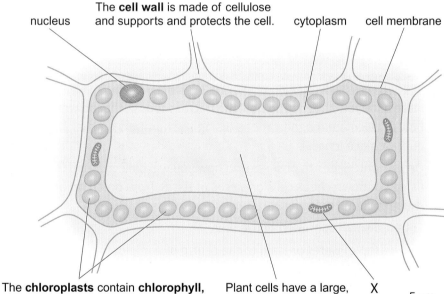

nucleus — The **cell wall** is made of cellulose and supports and protects the cell. cytoplasm cell membrane

The **chloroplasts** contain **chlorophyll**, which traps energy transferred from the Sun. The energy is used for photosynthesis.

Plant cells have a large, permanent **vacuole** which stores **cell sap** and helps to keep the cell firm and rigid. X 5 μm

D a cell from inside a plant leaf

 7 Look at diagram D. What is part X?

 8 Cells on leaf *surfaces* contain vacuoles and carry out aerobic respiration but are not green. Suggest what part they lack. Explain your reasoning.

Did you know?

The pigment in human skin is made in sub-cellular structures called melanosomes.

6 Use the scale bar on photo C to estimate the:

 a width of the nucleus at its widest point

 b length of the longest mitochondrion (coloured red).

Checkpoint

How confidently can you answer the Progression questions?

Strengthen

S1 Draw a plant cell and label its parts, describing what each part does.

Extend

E1 An 'organelle' is a structure inside a cell with a specific function. Compare the organelles found in plant and animal cells.

Exam-style question

Describe the function of chloroplasts in a leaf palisade cell. *(3 marks)*

CB1b Core practical – Using microscopes

Specification reference: B1.6

Aim

Investigate biological specimens using microscopes, including magnification calculations and labelled scientific drawings from observations.

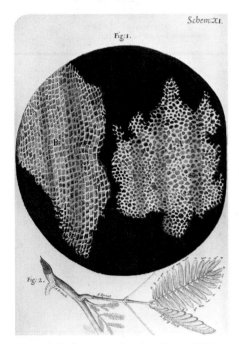

A Hooke's drawing of cork cells, published in 1665 in his book *Micrographia*

One of the first people to examine cells using a microscope was Robert Hooke. He examined bark from a cork oak tree and saw little box shapes. He called them 'cells' because he thought the boxes looked like the small rooms (or cells) found in monasteries at the time. Hooke also realised the importance of making accurate drawings of what he saw to help explain his work to others.

Your task

You are going to make a slide of some plant or animal tissue and examine it using a microscope. You will then make an accurate drawing of one or more of the cells that you see, and add information to help people understand your drawing (e.g. labelling the cell, adding a scale bar).

Method

Wear eye protection.

A Make sure you understand how the microscopes in the lab work, and how to calculate magnifications (using the numbers on the objective and eyepiece lenses).

B Decide which cells to observe and how you will collect them. Consider using your own cheek cells or pieces of tissue from onion bulbs, rhubarb stems or leaves.

C Collect a small specimen of the cells.

D Add a drop of water or stain to the centre of a microscope slide. Record the name of any stain that you use.

E Place your specimen on the drop of water or stain.

F Use a toothpick to slowly lower a coverslip onto the specimen, as shown in diagram B. The coverslip keeps the specimen flat, holds it in place and stops it drying out.

G Examine your specimen under a microscope. Start with the lowest magnification and work up to higher magnifications.

H Draw one or more of the cells that you see and annotate your drawing appropriately.

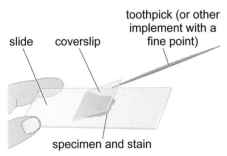

B Lowering a coverslip slowly and carefully means a slide is less likely to contain air bubbles.

Exam-style questions

1 State the name of the part of a microscope where you would place the slide. *(1 mark)*

2 Photo C shows a light microscope.
   a Give the letter of the part that is an objective lens. *(1 mark)*
   b Give the letter of a part that is used to focus an image. *(1 mark)*

3 State why the lowest power magnification is used when first examining a specimen. *(1 mark)*

4 A microscope is fitted with three objective lenses (of ×2, ×5 and ×10).
   a State what ×2 on a lens means. *(1 mark)*
   b The microscope has a ×7 eyepiece lens. Calculate the possible total magnifications. Show your working. *(3 marks)*

5 Luka has made a slide of some onion tissue. When he examines the specimen with a light microscope, he sees large, thick-walled circles that make it difficult to observe the cells.
   a Give the reason for Luka's observation. *(1 mark)*
   b State how he could prepare a better slide. *(1 mark)*

6 When looking at plant root tissue under a microscope, Jenna notices that about 10 cells fit across the field of view. She calculates the diameter of the field of view as 0.2 mm. Estimate the diameter of one cell. Show your working. *(2 marks)*

7 Photo D shows a certain type of white blood cell called a neutrophil. The image was taken using an electron microscope.
   a State one advantage of using an electron microscope rather than a light microscope. *(1 mark)*
   b Calculate the diameter of the cell to the nearest whole micrometre using the scale bar. *(1 mark)*
   c Give your answer to part b in mm. *(1 mark)*
   d Draw the cell and label the nucleus, cell membrane and cytoplasm. *(2 marks)*

8 Sasha draws a palisade cell from a star anise plant. The cell has a length of 0.45 mm.
   a Sasha's drawing is magnified ×500. Calculate the length of the cell in Sasha's drawing. *(1 mark)*
   b Sasha adds a scale bar to show 0.1 mm. Calculate the length of the scale bar. *(1 mark)*

9 A heart muscle cell is 20 μm wide. It has been drawn 1 cm wide. Calculate the magnification of the drawing. *(2 marks)*

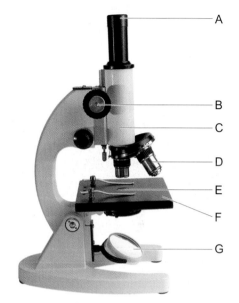

C a light microscope

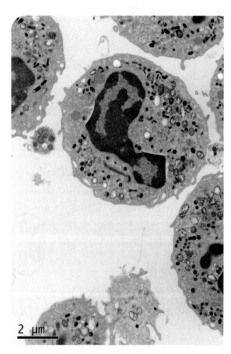

2 μm

D human neutrophils

CB1c Specialised cells

Specification reference: B1.2; B1.4; B1.6

Progression questions

- How are some specialised cells adapted to their functions?
- What is the function of a gamete?
- What is the function of cilia?

Did you know?

Human nerve cells (neurones) carry information very quickly. Many are adapted by being extremely long, with some reaching lengths of about 1.4 m.

5th 2 a Draw a small intestine cell and label its parts.

7th b These cells are 20 µm long. Add a 10 µm scale bar to your drawing.

6th c Explain why a cell with microvilli absorbs substances more quickly than one without.

7th 3 Cells called hepatocytes make a lot of a substance called serum albumin. These cells contain many ribosomes. Suggest what type of substance serum albumin is. Explain your reasoning.

8th 4 Nerve cells require a lot of energy. Suggest the adaptation that allows them to get enough energy.

6th 5 a State whether a sperm cell is haploid or diploid.

7th b Explain why it needs to be like this.

Specialised cells have a specific function (job). There are about 200 different types of specialised cells in humans. All human cells have the same basic design, but their sizes, shapes and sub-cellular structures can be different so that specialised cells are **adapted** to their functions.

5th 1 List three specialised human cells and state their functions.

Specialised cells for digestion

The cells that line the small intestine absorb small food molecules produced by **digestion**. They are adapted by having membranes with many tiny folds (called **microvilli**). These **adaptations** increase the surface area of the cell. The more area for molecules to be absorbed, the faster absorption happens.

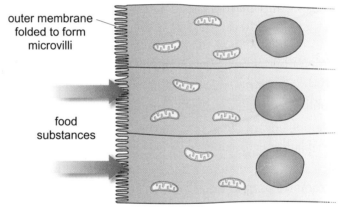

outer membrane folded to form microvilli

food substances

A small intestine cells

Cells in an organ called the pancreas make **enzymes** needed to digest certain foods in the small intestine. The enzymes are proteins and so these cells are adapted by having a lot of ribosomes.

The wall of the small intestine has muscles to squeeze food along. The muscle cells require a lot of energy and are adapted by having many mitochondria.

Specialised cells for reproduction

During sexual reproduction, two specialised cells (**gametes**) fuse to create a cell that develops into an **embryo**. Human gametes are the **egg cell** and the **sperm cell**.

Most human cell nuclei contain two copies of the 23 different types of chromosome. Gametes contain just *one* copy of each. This means that the cell produced by **fertilisation** has two copies. Cells with two sets of chromosomes are **diploid** and those with one copy of each chromosome are **haploid**.

The cell membrane fuses with the sperm cell membrane. After fertilisation, the cell membrane becomes hard to stop other sperm cells entering.

The jelly coat protects the egg cell. It also hardens after fertilisation, to ensure that only one sperm cell enters the egg cell.

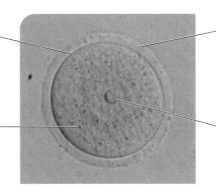

The cytoplasm is packed with nutrients, to supply the fertilised egg cell with energy and raw materials for the growth and development of the embryo.

haploid nucleus

B adaptations of a human female gamete

streamlined shape

The tip of the head contains a small vacuole called the **acrosome.** It contains enzymes that break down the substances in the egg cell's jelly coat. This allows the sperm cell to burrow inside.

nucleus

A large number of mitochondria are arranged in a spiral around the top of the tail, to release lots of energy to power the tail.

The tail waves from side to side, allowing the sperm cell to swim.

cell surface membrane

10 μm

C adaptations of a human male gamete

Fertilisation occurs in the **oviducts** of the female reproductive system. Cells in the lining of the oviduct transport egg cells (or the developing embryos after fertilisation) towards the uterus. The oviduct cells are adapted for this function by having hair-like **cilia**. These are like short sperm cell tails and wave from side to side to sweep substances along. Cells that line structures in the body are called **epithelial cells**, and epithelial cells with cilia are called **ciliated epithelial cells**.

egg cell

Cilia are covered in cell membrane and contain strands of a substance that can contract and cause wavy movement.

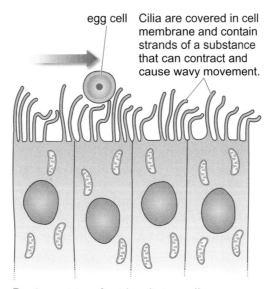

D adaptations of oviduct lining cells

 7 Compare and contrast microvilli and cilia.

 8 Explain why an egg cell does not need a tail but a sperm cell does.

 6 **a** Make a drawing of a human egg cell and label its parts.

 b Describe how an egg cell is adapted to prevent more than one sperm cell entering.

 c A human egg cell has a diameter of 0.1 mm. Calculate the magnification of your drawing.

Checkpoint

How confidently can you answer the Progression questions?

Strengthen

S1 List the steps that occur between an egg cell entering an oviduct and it becoming an embryo, and explain how adaptations of specialised cells help each step.

Extend

E1 Explain how both human gametes are adapted to ensure that the cell produced by fertilisation can grow and develop.

Exam-style question

Explain how cells that line the oviduct are adapted to their function of moving the egg cell. *(2 marks)*

Progression questions

- What are the functions of the sub-cellular structures in bacteria?
- What are the differences between prokaryotic and eukaryotic cells?
- How do we change numbers to and from standard form?

Bacteria are difficult to see with light microscopes because they are very small and mostly colourless. Stains are often used to make them show up.

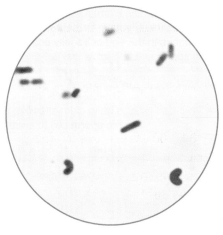

 1 a Estimate the size of the longest bacterium in photo A. Explain your reasoning.

 b The length of the bacterium in photo B is 4.5 cm (without its tail). Calculate its size in real life. Show all your working.

A light micrograph of *Vibrio cholerae* bacteria stained with safranin (field of view = 20 μm)

B electron micrograph of *Vibrio cholerae* bacterium, with colours added by a computer (magnification ×22 500)

The extra magnification and resolution of an electron microscope allow scientists to see bacteria in more detail. Photo B shows that this bacterium has a **flagellum**, which spins round like a propeller so the bacterium can move. The yellow colour shows its **DNA**.

Bacteria are **prokaryotic**, which means that their cells do not have nuclei or chromosomes. Instead, the cytoplasm contains one large loop of **chromosomal DNA**, which controls most of the cell's activities. There are also smaller loops of DNA, called **plasmids** (shown in photo C). **Plasmid DNA** controls a few of the cell's activities. Prokaryotic cells do not have mitochondria or chloroplasts.

2 a Describe the location of the plasmid in photo B.

b Give the name of the substance it is made from.

c Where is this substance mainly found in a eukaryotic cell?

3 Describe the function of a bacterium's flagellum.

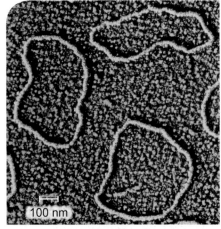

100 nm

C electron micrograph of plasmids from a bacterium (magnification ×50 000)

Information from microscope images and other work has allowed scientists to discover more about the parts of bacterial cells and their functions, as shown in diagram D.

flagellum (is not covered in a membrane and not all bacteria have them, but some have many flagella)

plasmids   chromosomal DNA

slime coat (for protection – not all bacteria have this)

flexible cell wall (for support – not made out of cellulose)

cell membrane

cytoplasm (contains ribosomes, which are smaller than eukaryotic ribosomes)

D Different bacteria are different shapes and sizes but usually have these parts.

H Standard form

A prokaryotic ribosome is 20 nm in diameter and a football is 0.22 m in diameter. It is hard to compare these sizes because they have different units.

1 m is 1 000 000 000 nm, so a football is 220 000 000 nm in diameter. The units are now the same but figures with so many zeros can be difficult to read and use. To solve this problem, we can show figures in the form of a number between 1 and 10 multiplied by a power of 10.

$$A \times 10^n$$

where A is between 1 and 10 and n is the power of 10; n is also called the **index** number. This is **standard form**. The index number tells you how many place values to move the digit.

For numbers greater than 0, count how many times you need to move the unit to the right until you form a number between 1 and 10.

Write this number as the power of 10, insert the decimal point and remove the zeros.

$$1150000 = 1.15 \times 10^6$$

For numbers less than 0, count how many times you need to move the unit to the left until you form a number between 1 and 10.

This becomes a negative power.

$$0.0000007 = 7 \times 10^{-8}$$

E writing numbers in standard form

Make sure you know how to input numbers in standard form on your calculator.

---

 4 Draw a table to show the functions of the different parts of a bacterial cell.

 5 Estimate the diameter of one plasmid shown in photo C.

6 Suggest why ribosomes are not shown on diagram D.

Did you know?

Your body contains more bacterial cells than human cells. Most of these are found in the digestive system.

7 Make a copy of table E from CB1a, adding another column to show in standard form the effect of adding each prefix. For example, 'milli-' divides a number by a thousand, which in standard form is the same as multiplying by 10^{-3}.

8 Write the diameters of a ribosome and a football in metres in standard form.

Checkpoint

How confidently can you answer the Progression questions?

Strengthen

S1 Draw a bacterium and label its parts, describing what each part does.

Extend

E1 Compare eukaryotic and prokaryotic cells.

Exam-style question

State two sub-cellular parts that bacterial cells may have but animal cells never have. *(2 marks)*

CB1e Enzymes and nutrition

Specification reference: B1.12

Progression questions

- What are enzymes made out of?
- What do enzymes do?
- Why are enzymes important for life?

Most animals get substances for energy, growth and development by digesting food inside their bodies. Bacteria, on the other hand, release digestive enzymes into their environments and then absorb digested food into their cells. Starfish use a similar trick for large items of food.

In humans, digestive enzymes turn the large molecules in our food into the smaller subunits they are made of. The digested molecules are then small enough to be absorbed by the small intenstine.

A To eat large items of food, a starfish pushes its stomach out of its mouth and into the food. The stomach surface releases enzymes to break down the food, which can then be absorbed.

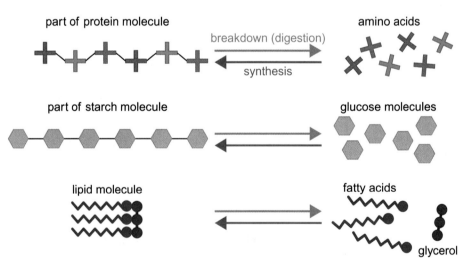

B Large molecules such as complex carbohydrates, proteins and lipids (fats and oils) are built from smaller molecules.

1 Which small molecules make up the following large molecules?

 a carbohydrates

 b proteins

 c lipids

 2 When you chew a piece of starchy bread for a while it starts to taste sweet. Suggest a reason for this.

3 Which monomers make up:

a proteins

b carbohydrates?

Once the small molecules are absorbed into the body, they can be used to build the larger molecules that are needed in cells and tissues. Building larger molecules from smaller subunits is known as **synthesis**. Complex carbohydrates and proteins are both **polymers** because they are made up of many similar small molecules, or **monomers**, joined in a chain.

The breakdown of large molecules happens incredibly slowly and only if the bonds between the smaller subunits have enough energy to break. Synthesis also happens very slowly, since the subunits rarely collide with enough force or in the right orientation to form a bond. These reactions happen much too slowly to supply all that the body needs to stay alive and be active.

Many reactions can be speeded up using a **catalyst**. In living organisms, the catalysts that speed up breakdown (e.g. digestion) and synthesis reactions are enzymes. So enzymes are **biological catalysts** that increase the rate of reactions. Enzymes are a special group of proteins that are found throughout the body. The substances that enzymes work on are called **substrates**, and the substances that are produced are called **products**.

 4 Define the term 'biological catalyst'.

 5 a Which type of smaller molecule are enzymes built from?

 b Explain your answer.

Enzyme name	Where found	Reaction catalysed
amylase	saliva and small intestine	breaking down starch to small sugars, such as maltose
catalase	most cells, but especially liver cells	breaking down hydrogen peroxide made in many cell reactions to water and oxygen
starch synthase	plant	synthesis of starch from glucose
DNA polymerase	nucleus	synthesis of DNA from its monomers

C examples of enzymes, where they are found and what they do

 6 Name the substrate of amylase, and the products of the reaction it catalyses.

 7 Give two examples of processes that are controlled by enzymes in the human body.

 8 Suggest what will happen in the cells of someone who does not make phenylalanine hydroxylase. Explain your answer.

 9 Sketch a diagram or flowchart to explain how the starfish in photo A absorbs food molecules into its body.

Exam-style question

Explain why the role of enzymes as catalysts in digestion is important for life.

(3 marks)

Did you know?

The heel prick test takes a small amount of blood to test for several factors, including the enzyme phenylalanine hydroxylase. This enzyme catalyses the breakdown of an amino acid called phenylalanine. A few babies are born without the ability to make the enzyme, which can result in nerve and brain damage as they grow older.

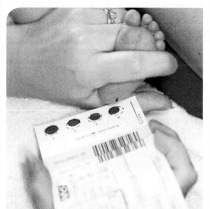

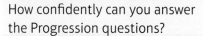

D Babies are given the heel prick test before they are a week old.

Checkpoint

How confidently can you answer the Progression questions?

Strengthen

S1 Draw a concept map that includes all the important points on these pages. Link words to show how they are related.

Extend

E1 Many bacteria have flexible cell walls made by linking together chains of a polymer. The links are formed in reactions catalysed by an enzyme. Penicillin stops this enzyme from working. Explain how penicillin causes bacteria to be weakened.

CB1f Enzyme action

Specification reference: B1.7; B1.8

Progression questions

- What is the function of the active site of an enzyme?
- Why do enzymes only work on specific substrates?
- How are enzymes denatured?

Did you know?

There are about 3000 different enzymes in the human body, catalysing reactions that would otherwise not occur. For example, an enzyme called OMP decarboxylase helps to produce a substance used to make DNA in 18 milliseconds. Without the enzyme, this reaction would take 78 million years!

A The bombardier beetle repels attackers by releasing a very hot, foul liquid. The liquid is made by enzymes that rapidly break down substances (including hydrogen peroxide) in a reaction chamber at the end of the beetle's body.

A protein is a large three-dimensional (3D) molecule formed from a chain of amino acids. The 3D shape is caused by folding of the chain, which depends on the sequence of the amino acids in the chain. The 3D shape of enzymes is important in how they work, because within that shape is a small pocket called the **active site**.

The active site is where the substrate of the enzyme fits at the start of a reaction. Different substrates have different 3D shapes, and different enzymes have active sites of different shapes. This explains why every enzyme can only work with **specific** substrates that fit the active site.

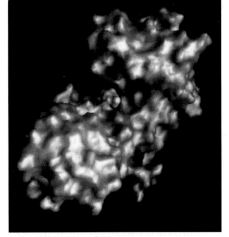

B Glucose is the substrate for the enzyme hexokinase (blue). The substrate (yellow) fits neatly within the enzyme's active site.

 1 What is the active site of an enzyme?

 2 Why is the active site a different shape in different enzymes?

 3 What is meant by 'enzyme specificity'?

One model of how enzymes work is called the **lock-and-key model**, because of how the enzyme and substrate fit together.

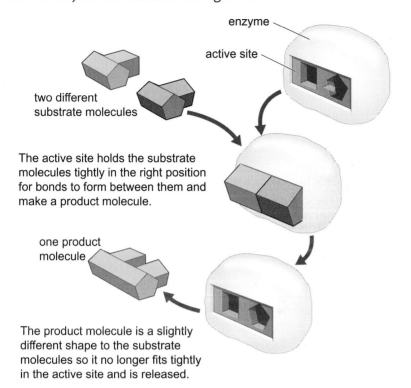

The active site holds the substrate molecules tightly in the right position for bonds to form between them and make a product molecule.

The product molecule is a slightly different shape to the substrate molecules so it no longer fits tightly in the active site and is released.

C When substrate molecules are held in the right position in the active site, the bonds between them are more easily broken and formed.

Changes in pH or temperature can affect how the protein folds up, and so can affect the shape of the active site. If the shape of the active site changes too much, the substrate will no longer fit neatly in it. If the active site changes shape too much, the enzyme will no longer catalyse the reaction. We say that the enzyme has been **denatured**.

 6 Explain what denaturing of an enzyme means.

7 Systems in humans keep our body temperatures constant. Using your knowledge of enzymes, explain why this is important.

 4 Explain why amylase does not break down proteins.

5 Use the lock-and-key model to suggest how an amylase enzyme catalyses the breakdown of starch to small sugar molecules.

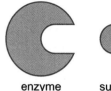
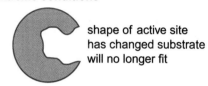

D Changes in an enzyme's environment can change the shape of the active site.

Checkpoint

How confidently can you answer the Progression questions?

Strengthen

S1 Sketch one flowchart to show how an enzyme normally works, and another to show what happens when the enzyme is denatured.

Extend

E1 Sketch labelled diagrams to show the following:

a why enzymes have a particular shape

b why enzymes are specific to a particular substrate

c what happens when an enzyme is denatured.

Exam-style question

Describe how the active site works in an enzyme. *(2 marks)*

CB1g Enzyme activity

Specification reference: B1.9; B1.11

Progression questions

- How is enzyme activity affected by temperature, pH and substrate concentration?
- How do you calculate the rate of enzyme activity?
- Why is enzyme activity affected by temperature, pH and substrate concentration?

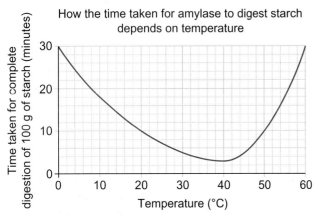

How the time taken for amylase to digest starch depends on temperature

A results from experiments at different temperatures combined on to one graph

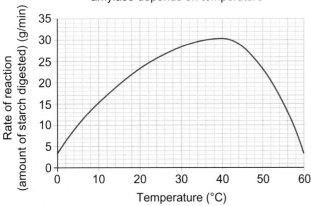

How the rate of starch breakdown using amylase depends on temperature

B the data in graph A shown as a rate of reaction graph

 3 a Identify the optimum temperature for the enzyme shown in graph B.

 b Explain your answer.

4 Explain why enzymes work more slowly when the temperature is:

 a below the optimum

 b above the optimum.

Enzymes are affected by the conditions in their surroundings. The results of a series of experiments that measure the time taken for an enzyme to complete the breakdown of a substrate at different temperatures can be combined to produce a graph.

 1 Use graph A to identify how long it took for the complete breakdown of starch at the following temperatures:

    a 10 °C   **b** 40 °C   **c** 50 °C.

 2 Suggest an explanation for the difference in reaction rates at 40 °C and 50 °C.

Graph A can be converted to a graph showing the rate of reaction by calculating the amount of substrate broken down or product formed in a given time. For example, graph A shows that, at 30 °C, 100 g of starch was broken down in 5 min. The mean rate of reaction was:

$$\frac{100}{5} = 20 \text{ g/min}$$

Converting the values in graph A in this way gives graph B.

Why does graph B have this shape?

- As the temperature increases, molecules move faster. Higher speeds increase the chance of substrate molecules bumping into enzyme molecules and slotting into the active site.
- However, when the temperature gets too high, the shape of the enzyme molecule starts to change. The amount of change increases as the temperature increases. So it becomes more and more difficult for a substrate molecule to fit into the active site.

The temperature at which an enzyme works fastest is called its **optimum temperature**.

Did you know?

Many human enzymes have an optimum temperature of around 37 °C.

Enzymes are now used in many processes in industry. Some industrial processes take place at high temperatures, so the search for new enzymes that have a high optimum temperature is important.

Some other factors that affect the rate of an enzyme-controlled reaction are pH and the concentration of the substrate, as shown in graphs D and E.

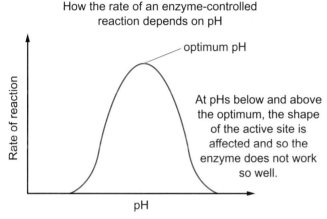

D the effect of pH on the rate of an enzyme-controlled reaction

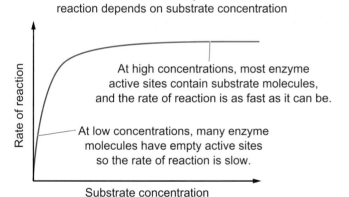

E the effect of substrate concentration on the rate of an enzyme-controlled reaction

6 Explain the effect of substrate concentration on the rate of an enzyme-controlled reaction.

7 The pH in the stomach is about 2, but in the small intestine it is about 6. Explain why different protease enzymes are found in the two digestive organs.

C The bacterium *Thermus aquaticus* was discovered growing in this hotspring pool, which is at about 70 °C.

 5 **a** Sketch a graph to show the effect of pH on the enzyme pepsin, which has an **optimum pH** of 2.

 b Annotate your sketch to explain the shape.

Checkpoint

How confidently can you answer the Progression questions?

Strengthen

S1 Close the book, then sketch and annotate a graph to show how temperature affects the rate of an enzyme-controlled reaction.

Extend

E1 A manufacturer is testing several high-temperature cellulase enzymes to break down plant cell walls in plant waste used for making biofuels. Suggest how the manufacturer might carry out the test and how they would decide which is the best enzyme for this process.

Exam-style question

The enzyme pepsin digests proteins. Pepsin is denatured at pH 8. Explain what this means. *(2 marks)*

Specification reference: B1.10

Aim

Investigate the effect of pH on enzyme activity.

A Only microorganisms that can tolerate highly acidic conditions can live in the water from some mine workings.

Metal ores are rocks that contain valuable metal compounds. Waste water from metal ore mines is often highly acidic and contains small amounts of toxic metals. Mining companies are looking for microorganisms that can live in this water and remove the metals (a process called bioleaching). This will not only reduce pollution, but also help to recover more metal from a mine. Organisms that can live in these environments must have enzymes with an optimum pH that is highly acidic.

Your task

You are going to find the optimum pH of an enzyme. In this case, you are going to use the enzyme amylase, which digests starch. You are going to measure the time taken for the enzyme to break down its substrate at different pHs. Then you will plot the results on a graph. The shortest time taken to digest the substrate indicates the optimum pH for the enzyme.

Method

Wear eye protection.

A blue/black colour indicates the presence of starch.

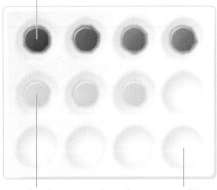

A yellow/orange colour that no longer changes indicates that the reaction is complete.   well tray

B iodine solution is used to indicate the presence of starch

A Set up heating apparatus using a tripod, gauze, heat-resistant mat, Bunsen burner and large beaker half-filled with water. Heat the water to a temperature of 40 °C, and then use the collar on the Bunsen burner to produce a flame that keeps the water at this temperature. Check that the temperature is being kept constant for a couple of minutes before you start step D.

B Place one drop of iodine solution into each depression of a well tray (dimple tile).

C Measure 2 cm³ of amylase solution into a tube.

D Add 1 cm³ of a solution with a particular pH into the tube.

E Add 2 cm³ of starch solution to the tube and place it carefully into the water bath. Start the stop clock. Stir the mixture.

F Every 20 seconds, take a small amount of mixture and place one drop of it into a fresh drop of iodine solution. Stop testing when the iodine solution stops changing colour.

G Repeat the experiment using a different pH solution in step D.

Exam-style questions

1   State what is meant by the substrate of an enzyme. *(1 mark)*

2   State what is meant by the optimum pH of an enzyme. *(1 mark)*

3   Explain why an enzyme catalyses the reaction of only one particular substrate. *(2 marks)*

4   Explain why changing the pH affects the activity of an enzyme. *(2 marks)*

5   State the colour of iodine solution before and after it is in contact with starch. *(2 marks)*

6   In the experiment described on the previous page, explain why the iodine solution eventually stops changing colour when mixed with the solution. *(2 marks)*

7   a   Explain why the enzyme reaction is carried out in a water bath in step A of the method on the previous page. *(2 marks)*

   b   Describe an alternative way of doing this. *(1 mark)*

   c   Explain whether your alternative suggestion would improve the experiment. *(2 marks)*

8   Catalase is an enzyme that breaks down hydrogen peroxide into water and oxygen. Some students are investigating the effect of pH on this enzyme-controlled reaction by collecting the oxygen. One suggestion is to bubble the gas through water and collect it in an upturned measuring cylinder full of water. Another suggestion is to collect the gas in a gas syringe.

   a   Explain which method of gas collection you would use. *(2 marks)*

   b   Explain how the students should measure the pH in their investigation. *(2 marks)*

   c   Table C shows the results from the students' investigation. Draw a graph to display the results. *(3 marks)*

   d   Identify the anomalous result and suggest a reason for the error. *(2 marks)*

   e   Calculate the average rate of reaction (average volume of oxygen produced per minute) at pH 6. *(1 mark)*

9   Scientists working on bioleaching are interested in an enzyme called glucose oxidase, which is found in many microorganisms. Graph D shows the results from an investigation into the effect of pH on the rate of activity of glucose oxidase from two different types of bacteria.

   a   What is the optimum pH for glucose oxidase from each type of bacterium? *(2 marks)*

   b   Explain which enzyme is more active at pH 5. *(1 mark)*

   c   Explain which bacterium might be more useful for bioleaching mine water. *(2 marks)*

Time (min)	Volume of O_2 released (cm^3)	
	at pH 3	at pH 6
1	1.4	1.6
2	2.7	3.2
3	4.2	5.6
4	5.9	5.7
5	6.6	8.4
6	8.4	10.6

C results for an investigation of the effect of pH on an enzyme-controlled reaction

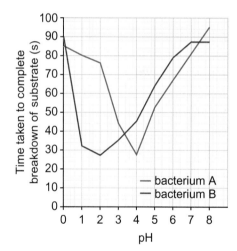

D Graph to show the effect of pH on glucose oxidase. This enzyme catalyses a reaction in which glucose is broken down to form hydrogen peroxide. Hydrogen peroxide can help obtain metals from mine waste.

CB1h Transporting substances

Specification reference: B1.15; B1.17

Progression questions

- What is the difference between diffusion and osmosis?
- How do cells move substances against a concentration gradient?
- How do you calculate a percentage change in mass?

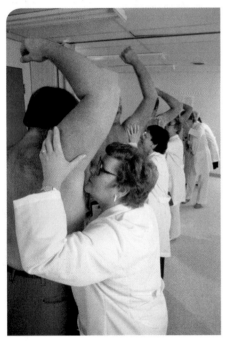

A an experiment to assess body odour

Bacteria living on your body cause body odour. The smelly substances they produce are released into the air and reach our noses.

Smells spread by **diffusion**. Particles in gases and liquids are constantly moving past each other in random directions. This causes an overall movement of particles from where there are more of them (a higher **concentration**) to where there are fewer (a lower concentration).

A difference between two concentrations forms a **concentration gradient**. Particles diffuse *down* a concentration gradient. The bigger the difference between concentrations, the steeper the concentration gradient and the faster diffusion occurs.

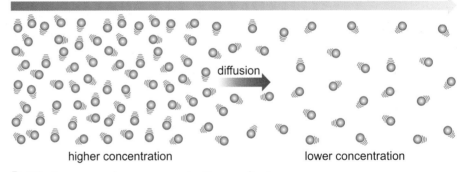

The number of particles *decreases* as you go *down* a concentration gradient.

higher concentration   lower concentration

B diffusion occurs down a concentration gradient

Diffusion allows small molecules (such as oxygen and carbon dioxide) to move into and out of cells.

Osmosis

A membrane that allows some molecules through it and not others is **partially permeable** (or **semi-permeable**).

Cell membranes are semi-permeable and trap large soluble molecules inside cells, but water molecules can diffuse through the membrane. If there are more water molecules in a certain volume on one side of the membrane than the other, there will be an overall movement of water molecules from the side where there are more water molecules (a more dilute **solute** concentration) to the side where there are fewer water molecules (a more concentrated solution of solute). This diffusion of small molecules of a **solvent**, such as water, through a semi-permeable membrane is called **osmosis**. The overall movement of solvent molecules will stop when the concentration of solutes is the same on both sides of a membrane.

 1 Explain why smells spread.

 2 a A dish of perfume is put at the front of a lab. Describe the perfume's concentration gradient after 5 minutes.

b Describe the overall movement of the perfume molecules.

 3 Muscle cells in the leg use up oxygen but are surrounded by a fluid containing a lot of oxygen. Explain why oxygen moves into the cells.

4 a In diagram C, in which direction will water flow, X to Y or Y to X?

 b Explain why this flow occurs.

 5 Red blood cells contain many solute molecules. Explain why red blood cells burst if put in pure water.

Osmosis can cause tissues to gain or lose mass. To calculate the mass change:

* work out the difference between the mass of tissue at the start and at the end (final mass – initial mass)
* divide this difference by the initial mass
* multiply by 100.

So, percentage change in mass = $\dfrac{\text{(final mass – initial mass)}}{\text{initial mass}} \times 100$

A negative answer is a percentage *loss* in mass.

 6 An 8 g piece of potato is left in water for an hour. Its mass becomes 8.5 g. Calculate the percentage change in mass.

Active transport

Cells may need to transport molecules *against* a concentration gradient or transport molecules that are too big to diffuse through the cell membrane. They can do this using **active transport**.

This process is carried out by transport proteins in cell membranes. The transport proteins capture certain molecules and carry them across the cell membrane. This is an active process and so requires energy. Osmosis and diffusion are **passive** processes, so do not require an input of energy.

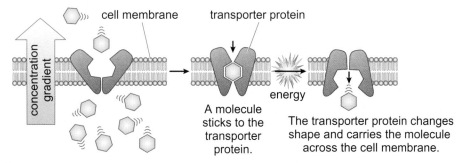

cell membrane   transporter protein

concentration gradient

A molecule sticks to the transporter protein.

energy

The transporter protein changes shape and carries the molecule across the cell membrane.

D active transport

 8 Explain how cells that carry out a lot of active transport would be adapted to their function.

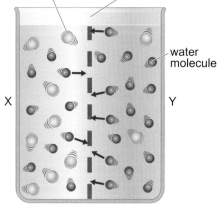

soluble molecule that is too large to pass through the membrane (e.g. sucrose)

partially permeable membrane allows molecules to pass through if they are small enough

water molecule

X   Y

more concentrated solution

more dilute solution

C In osmosis, a solvent flows from a dilute solution of a solute to a more concentrated one.

 7 Look at diagram D. Explain why active transport is needed to move the molecules.

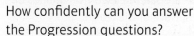

Checkpoint

How confidently can you answer the Progression questions?

Strengthen

S1 A small number of sugar molecules are in your small intestine. Describe how they will be absorbed into cells in the small intestine and why they need to be absorbed in this way.

Extend

E1 Sorbitol is a sweet-tasting substance that is not broken down or absorbed by the body. It is used in some sugar-free sweets. Explain why eating too many of these sweets can cause diarrhoea.

Exam-style question

Explain why a slice of potato will decrease in mass if it is placed in a concentrated sugar solution. *(2 marks)*

Specification reference: B1.16

Aim

Investigate osmosis in potatoes.

A The tiny white crystals on this cord grass are salt released from glands on the surface of the leaves.

Most land plants die if flooded with sea water. Usually the concentration of mineral salts in the soil is less than inside the roots, so water moves into the root from the soil by osmosis. If the soil contains a high concentration of salts then osmosis occurs out of the root, into the soil. Without sufficient water, plants die. Some plants, called halophytes, are adapted to live in salty areas. Their roots take in large amounts of salts from the soil, which helps osmosis to continue from the soil into the plant. Halophytes get rid of the extra salt they absorb in various ways.

Your task

You are going to measure osmosis in plant tissue, by comparing the mass of the tissue before and after soaking in sucrose solution. Sucrose is used because the molecules are too large to diffuse through cell membranes. The change in the mass of the tissue shows how much water is absorbed or lost. You can work out the solute concentration of the plant tissue from repeating the experiment with solutions of different concentrations.

When comparing different pieces of tissue, remember to calculate the percentage change in mass of each piece.

Method

A Label a separate boiling tube with the sucrose concentration of each solution you will test. Place all the tubes in a rack.

B Cut similar-sized pieces of potato, enough for one per tube. (Make sure they fit in a tube.)

C Blot each potato piece dry, measure and record its mass, and put it in an empty tube.

D Fill each tube with the solution of the appropriate concentration. Ensure you cover the potato with the solution.

E After at least 15 minutes, remove each potato piece and blot it dry. Measure and record its mass again.

Exam-style questions

1 Define the term 'osmosis'. *(1 mark)*

2 Use the idea of osmosis to explain why most plants in salty soil would have problems absorbing water through their roots. *(2 marks)*

3 Explain how halophyte roots are adapted to help them absorb water from salty soil. *(2 marks)*

4 a State which variables have been kept the same in the method on the previous page. *(1 mark)*

   b Explain the importance of controlling these variables. *(2 marks)*

5 Write an equipment list for the method shown on the previous page. *(2 marks)*

6 Explain how you would work out a suitable range of sucrose concentrations for the solutions in the potato experiment. *(2 marks)*

7 Give a reason why you should calculate percentage change in mass when comparing results. *(1 mark)*

8 State one way to improve the method for the potato experiment so that you could be more certain of the results. *(1 mark)*

9 Table B shows the results from an experiment similar to the one described in the method.

   a For each solution, calculate the gain or loss in mass of the potato piece. *(2 marks)*

   b For each solution, calculate the percentage change in mass of the potato. *(2 marks)*

   c Give a reason for the result from tube A. *(1 mark)*

   d Explain the results from tubes B–D. *(2 marks)*

   e Use the results to give the possible solute concentration of potato tissue, giving a reason for your answer. *(2 marks)*

   f Describe how the method could be adapted to give a more accurate answer to part **e**. *(1 mark)*

10 Graph C shows the results of an experiment comparing osmosis in tissue from a halophyte plant and a potato in the same solution.

   a Identify, with a reason, which tissue lost water fastest over the first five minutes. *(2 marks)*

   b Explain why it lost water faster than the other tissue. *(2 marks)*

   c Calculate the average rate of change in mass over the first four minutes for the potato. *(1 mark)*

Tube	A	B	C	D
Sucrose concentration (%)	0	10	30	50
Mass of potato at start (g)	4.81	5.22	4.94	4.86
Mass of potato at end (g)	4.90	4.96	4.39	3.69

B the effect of sucrose concentration on the change in mass of potato (concentration 0 is distilled water)

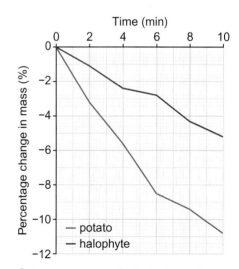

C change in mass of a halophyte plant and potato in the same solution

23

Arginase

Unused amino acids are broken down into a waste substance called urea. One enzyme involved in the process is called arginase, which catalyses this reaction:

arginine + water → ornithine + urea

In an experiment, the activity of arginase was tested at different pHs. The graph below shows the results. Explain the effect of pH on arginase.

(6 marks)

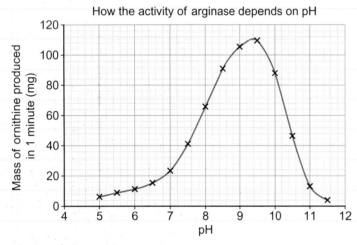

A

Student answer

The pH affects arginine [1] and makes it make the reaction faster or slower. It shows that the enzyme is best in high pH [2].

[1] The name of the enzyme is arginase (the substrate is arginine). It is very important to use the correct scientific names.

[2] The answer correctly says that the enzyme is more active at higher pHs.

Verdict

This is a weak answer. It only contains one correct fact and there is no explanation about why pH has an effect on the enzyme.

The key word in the question is 'explain'. The answer could be improved by explaining the link between the shape of the graph and how the enzyme works (i.e. the enzyme works best at the optimum pH because this is when the active site has the best shape for the substrate to fit into it). A really good answer would also have used data from the graph (e.g. pointing out that the optimum pH is 9.4).

Exam tip

It may help to note down some key facts that you know about the topic before you write your answer. Cross out your notes when you have finished writing.

Paper 1

CB2 Cells and Control

The blue whale (*Balaenoptera musculus*) is the largest animal ever to have lived on Earth – larger than the biggest dinosaurs. Blue whales grow to over 30 m in length and have masses of over 150 tonnes. The mass of a whale is, however, not just made up of trillions of different whale cells but also thousands of other organisms (such as 'whale lice' that live on their bodies, and tonnes of bacteria in their digestive systems).

In this unit you will discover how plants and animals develop from single cells the size of full stops to become complex organisms made of many different types of cells, which all need to be controlled and coordinated.

The learning journey

Previously you will have learnt at KS3:

- that cells divide
- about the structure of plant and animal cells (including the chromosomes in their nuclei)
- that your nervous system helps to coordinate your actions.

In this unit you will learn:

- about mitosis and its importance in growth, repair and asexual reproduction
- how cells become specialised, and the importance of stem cells
- to identify different specialised cells in the nervous system and explain how the system works.

CB2a Mitosis

Specification reference: B2.1; B2.2; B2.3; B2.4

Progression questions

- Why is mitosis important?
- What happens in the different stages of mitosis?
- How do cancer tumours occur?

Every living thing needs to be able to grow and to repair itself in order to stay alive. In organisms that are made of many cells (**multicellular organisms**) the processes of growth and repair require new cells. These are produced in a process called the **cell cycle**.

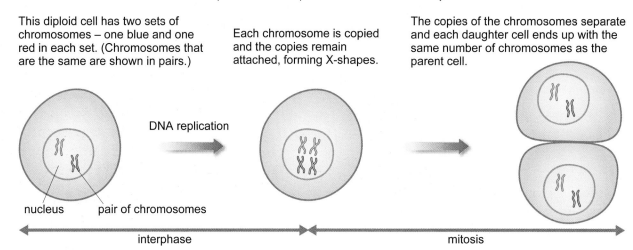

This diploid cell has two sets of chromosomes – one blue and one red in each set. (Chromosomes that are the same are shown in pairs.)

Each chromosome is copied and the copies remain attached, forming X-shapes.

The copies of the chromosomes separate and each daughter cell ends up with the same number of chromosomes as the parent cell.

DNA replication

nucleus   pair of chromosomes

interphase   mitosis

A During the cell cycle two identical daughter cells are formed from a parent cell.

The nuclei of human body cells contain two copies of each of 23 types of chromosome, making 46 in all. Cells with two copies of each chromosome (two sets of chromosomes) are **diploid**. Gametes (sex cells) contain one copy of each type of chromosome and are **haploid**.

There are two phases in the cell cycle, the first of which is **interphase**. In this phase the cell makes extra sub-cellular cell parts (e.g. mitochondria). **DNA replication** (copying) also occurs, to make copies of all the chromosomes. The copies of the chromosomes stay attached to each another, making the chromosomes look like Xs.

The next phase of the cell cycle is cell division or **mitosis**. The cell splits to form two **daughter cells**, which are both identical to the parent cell. Mitosis occurs in a series of continuous stages, shown in diagram B.

1 Give the name of one diploid and one haploid cell in the body of a mammal.

2 Alligators have eight types of chromosome. How many chromosomes are in a diploid alligator cell?

3 Why is DNA replication important in interphase?

4 Why must the number of mitochondria double in a cell during interphase?

5 Draw a table to show what happens in each stage of mitosis.

Did you know?

Damaged human organs cannot regrow ... apart from the liver. Liver transplants are often done using part of a liver because the transplanted piece of liver grows by mitosis to form a full-sized liver. The liver pieces for transplants can be taken from living donors because livers grow back.

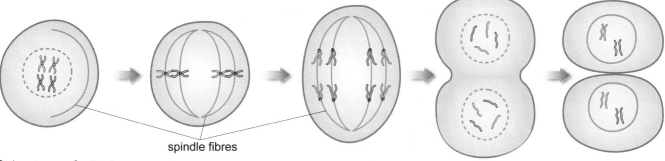

In **prophase** the nucleus starts to break down and **spindle fibres** appear.

By the end of **metaphase**, the chromosomes are lined up on the spindle fibres across the middle of the cell.

The chromosome copies are separated and moved to either end of the cell on the spindle fibres. This is **anaphase**.

In **telophase** a membrane forms around each set of chromosomes to form nuclei.

A cell surface membrane forms to separate the two cells during **cytokinesis.** Cell walls form in plant cells.

spindle fibres

B the stages of mitosis

Asexual reproduction

Some organisms can reproduce using just one parent. This **asexual reproduction** produces offspring that are **clones**, which means that their cells have the same chromosomes as the parent (they are genetically identical). So, asexual reproduction relies on mitosis. Strawberry plants, for example, reproduce asexually using stems that grow along the ground, called runners, and potatoes use tubers. Some animals, such as aphids, can also reproduce asexually. Asexual reproduction is much faster than sexual reproduction because organisms do not need others for reproduction. However, sexual reproduction produces variation and asexual reproduction does not.

C Asexual reproduction is rare in larger animals, but female Komodo dragons can reproduce asexually.

D plantlets produced by asexual reproduction growing on the leaf margins of *Kalanchöe* plant

Growth of cancer tumours

Normal cells only divide when they need to. Changes in cells can, however, sometimes turn them into **cancer cells**, which means that they undergo uncontrollable cell division. This rapid cell division produces growing lumps of cells called **tumours** that can damage the body and can result in death.

---

 6 Why is each plantlet in photo D a clone?

 7 Daughter cells produced by mitosis are said to be 'genetically identical' to the parent cell. Explain what this means.

 8 Why does asexual reproduction rely on mitosis?

9 A rose plant has a 'crown gall tumour' on its stem.

 a What would you expect this to look like?

 b Explain how this occurs.

Checkpoint

How confidently can you answer the Progression questions?

Strengthen

S1 Draw a flow chart to show mitosis.

Extend

E1 Explain why mitosis is important for the reproduction of organisms if there are very few members of the opposite sex in an area.

Exam-style question

Explain why sperm cells cannot be produced using the cell cycle. *(2 marks)*

Progression questions

- Which processes in animals result in growth and development?
- How are percentile charts used to monitor growth in children?
- Why is cell differentiation important in animals?

caterpillar

preparing to pupate

pupa

adult

A During the pupal stage, a caterpillar digests itself! Only some cells remain, but using cell division and differentiation these cells produce all the specialised cells in the adult butterfly.

Growth is an increase in size as a result of an increase in number or size of cells. The number of cells increases due to cell division by mitosis. Growth can be recorded by taking measurements over time, such as of length or mass.

 1 **a** Suggest how you could measure the growth of a kitten.

 b Explain your answer.

 2 **a** Your mass increases when you take in food and drink. Is this an example of growth?

 b Explain your answer.

The growth of human babies is regularly checked by measuring them, including mass and length. The measurements are checked on charts to show how well a baby is growing compared to others at the same age.

These charts were created by measuring a very large number of babies. The measurements were divided into 100 groups. When divided like this we can find out what percentage of readings are below a certain value, or **percentile**. For example, 25 per cent of babies will have masses below the 25th percentile line, whereas 75 per cent of babies will be below the 75th percentile line. So, if the 25th percentile for an 8-month-old baby's mass is 8 kg then 25 per cent of 8-month-old babies have a mass below this value.

The curved lines (see graph B) show the rate of growth of a baby who stays at exactly the same percentile within the population. Most babies don't grow at the same rate all the time, so plotting their mass helps to identify whether they are growing normally. Although rate of growth may vary from week to week, a baby should remain near the same percentile curve as it gets older.

Did you know?

Growth is not charted for the first two weeks of life because babies often lose weight as they adjust to feeding from the breast or bottle rather than getting their nutrients from the placenta.

The 50th percentile curve shows the growth of a baby of the median (average) size of the population. Half (50%) of all babies will have a mass above this curve and half equal to or below the curve.

B Percentile growth curves for UK baby boys from 2 weeks to 1 year, for mass. The red line that has been plotted on the curves shows the growth of one baby.

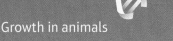

Cell differentiation

Although all animals develop from a single cell, not all the cells in their bodies are the same. Cells produced by mitosis are the same as the cell from which they were formed. However, the new cells may then change in different ways, so they become specialised for different functions. The process that changes less specialised cells into more specialised ones is called **differentiation**.

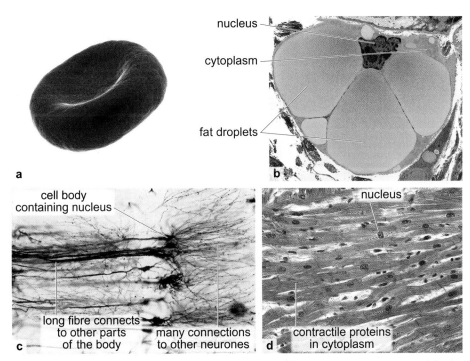

C Here are some specialised human cells. (a, top left) A red blood cell has no nucleus, allowing more space for red haemoglobin molecules (which carry oxygen). It also has a large surface area (allowing oxygen to diffuse in and out more quickly). (b, top right) The cytoplasm of fat cells is filled with large fat droplets. The fat is stored until the body needs energy. (c, bottom left) Nerve cells (neurones) have a long fibre that carries electrical impulses around the body and many connections to other neurones. (d, bottom right) Muscle cells contain special contractile proteins that can shorten the cell.

5   **a**   Describe a special feature of a fat cell.

      b   Explain how a red blood cell is specialised for its function of carrying oxygen around the body.

6   **a**   Describe two kinds of specialised cells you would expect to find in a butterfly.

      b   Explain your choices and predict the adaptations that the cells have.

Exam-style question

Explain why percentile curves are used to measure the growth of babies.

(2 marks)

3   Look at graph B.

   a   What is the value of the 50th percentile for mass in a 6-month-old baby boy?

   b   How much should the mass of a baby boy in the 50th percentile increase between 3 and 9 months of age?

4   Does the baby plotted on graph B (the red line) show healthy growth? Explain your answer.

Checkpoint

How confidently can you answer the Progression questions?

Strengthen

S1 Describe how a single fertilised human egg cell develops into the billions of different cells in a human adult.

Extend

E1 What are the advantages and disadvantages of using percentile curves to assess the growth and development of a young baby?

CB2c Growth in plants

Specification reference: B2.5; B2.6

Progression questions

- How do plants grow?
- How are some specialised plant cells adapted to their function?
- Why is cell differentiation important in plants?

A El Árbol del Tule is a Montezuma cypress. In 1998, its girth was 36 m round the trunk at 1.5 m above the ground.

Guinness World Records has two entries for 'the world's largest living tree'. El Árbol del Tule has the largest girth (the length around its trunk) and General Sherman has the greatest volume.

A group of cells near the end of each shoot and root allows plants to continue growing throughout their lives. These groups of cells are called **meristems**. The cells in meristems divide rapidly by mitosis. Many of the cells produced then increase in length (**elongation**), and **differentiate** into specialised cells that have different functions.

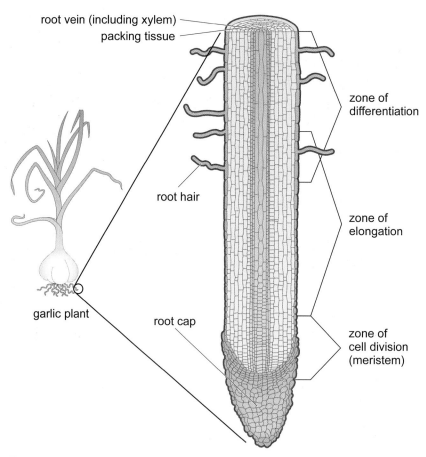

B The zones of an onion root tip where cells divide, elongate and differentiate into specialised cells. (Note: colour has been added to help identify different tissues.)

1 What is a plant meristem?

2 Describe what happens in the following zones of a plant shoot.

  a zone of division

  b zone of elongation

  c zone of differentiation

3 a Are the dividing cells in a plant meristem all similar to or different from each other?

  b Explain your answer.

4 Diagram B shows root hair cells, which absorb water and mineral salts from the soil.

  a How are the cells adapted for this function?

  b Explain how their adaptation helps them to carry out their function well.

There are many kinds of specialised plant cell, such as **root hair cells** and **xylem cells**. Each kind of cell has certain features so that it is adapted to its function. The many different kinds of specialised cell in a plant allow the plant to carry out many different processes effectively.

 5 Photo C shows xylem vessels that carry water throughout the plant. Describe how xylem vessels are specialised to carry out this function well.

 6 Explain why plants need root hair cells and xylem vessels.

Did you know?

About 400 dm³ of water is absorbed from the soil, passes through the xylem and evaporates from the leaves of a large oak tree every day.

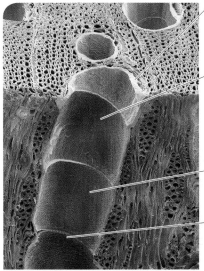

- thickened wall to withstand water pressure
- tiny pores in wall allow water and mineral salts to enter and leave the vessel
- no cytoplasm, so vessel is empty
- loss of cell walls of two xylem cells to form a tube

C A xylem vessel is a long tube formed from many dead xylem cells.

There are many different ways of measuring growth in plants, including height, leaf surface area and mass. Percentage changes are often worked out for these values and can be calculated using this formula:

$$\frac{\text{final value} - \text{starting value}}{\text{starting value}} \times 100\%$$

 7 Use the definition of 'growth' on page 22 to explain why increases in height, leaf surface area, tree girth and mass can all be used as measures of growth.

8 Look at diagram D.

 a Calculate the increase in mass of the tree during the experiment.

 b Calculate the percentage increase in mass of the tree over the five years.

 9 Palisade cells are plant cells found inside leaves, near the top surface. Their main function is photosynthesis. Suggest how these cells are adapted for this function, and explain your reasoning.

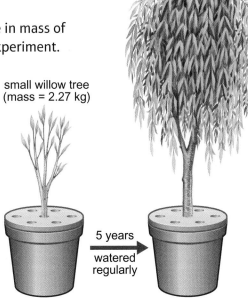

willow tree (mass = 76.74 kg)

small willow tree (mass = 2.27 kg)

5 years watered regularly

D the results of a growth experiment carried out by Jan Baptista Van Helmont (1580–1644)

Checkpoint

How confidently can you answer the Progression questions?

Strengthen

S1 The tree in photo A grew from a small seedling. Use bullet points to describe how the seedling increased in size and developed into the tree.

Extend

E1 In the bottom surface of leaves are tiny pores that allow gases to diffuse into and out of the leaf. Each pore is controlled by two guard cells, which can change shape. At night the guard cells lose water to close the pore. During the day they fill with water to open the pore. Suggest one adaptation you would expect to see in guard cells and explain your answer.

Exam-style question

Explain why plant meristem cells contain many ribosomes. *(2 marks)*

CB2d Stem cells

Specification reference: B2.8; B2.9

Progression questions

- Where are stem cells found?
- What is the function of stem cells?
- What are the advantages and risks of using stem cells in medicine?

A Geckos are reptiles that are able to grow a whole new tail if it is cut off. Regrowth of many different tissues to make a new organ is rare in adult animals.

Cells that can divide repeatedly over a long period of time to produce cells that then differentiate are called **stem cells**. In plants, these cells are found in meristems (and are sometimes called **meristem cells**).

Plant stem cells are usually able to produce any kind of specialised cell throughout the life of the plant. This is not true for most animals, especially vertebrates.

Animals start life as a fertilised egg cell, which then divides to form an embryo. The cells of an early-stage embryo are **embryonic stem cells** that can produce any type of specialised cell. As the cells continue to divide, the embryo starts to develop different areas that will become the different organs. The stem cells in these areas become more limited in the types of specialised cell they can produce.

 1 a State where you can find stem cells in two different plant organs.

 b Describe the function of the stem cells in these two plant organs.

 2 Stem cells are unspecialised cells. Define the term 'unspecialised'.

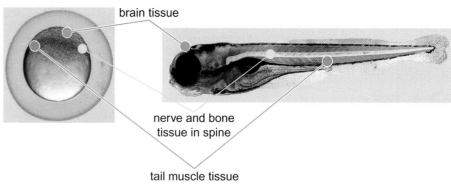

B Stem cells in different parts of a zebrafish embryo (on the left) form different tissues as it develops into a young fish.

By the time the young animal is fully developed, the stem cells can usually only produce the type of specialised cell that is in the tissue around them. These are called **adult stem cells** (even if they are in a young animal). The adult stem cells in human tissues allow the tissues to grow and to replace old or damaged cells.

Did you know?

Zebrafish are able to regenerate many parts of their body using stem cells. They can replace their fins, skin, heart tissue, and even brain cells when they are young. This has made them the most important organism in stem cell research.

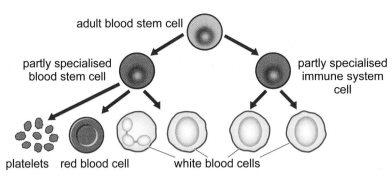

C Blood stem cells are found in marrow in the middle of long bones (such as the femur). They continue to divide throughout life to produce new blood cells.

Stem cells offer a way of treating many different diseases caused by damaged cells. The first successful human bone marrow transplant was carried out in the late 1950s. Healthy bone marrow from one identical twin was given to the other twin who had a blood disease. Since then, scientists have studied other ways to use adult and embryonic stem cells to treat diseases such as type I diabetes, or to replace damaged cells. This is done by stimulating stem cells to make them produce the specialised cells that are needed and then injecting them into the places they are needed.

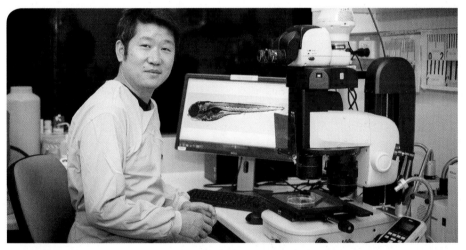

D Young zebrafish are transparent. This makes them useful for studying how vertebrate stem cells work and finding out which drugs or treatments might affect stem cells in the body. Successful treatments might then be tried on humans.

There are problems with using stem cells, which scientists are still trying to solve. For example, if stem cells continue to divide inside the body after they have replaced damaged cells, they can cause **cancer**. Another problem is that stem cells from one person are often killed by the immune system of other people that they are put into. This is called **rejection**.

 7 Describe two risks of using stem cells to treat disease.

Exam-style question

Describe the role of meristems in plant growth. *(2 marks)*

 3 What is the function of stem cells in bone marrow?

 4 Explain why blood stem cells only produce blood cells.

9th 5 Compare adult and embryonic stem cells in terms of what they can do, and their functions.

 6 Explain how stem cells could be used to help repair damaged heart muscle cells in someone who has had a heart attack.

Checkpoint

How confidently can you answer the Progression questions?

Strengthen

S1 a Describe the functions of the different kinds of stem cell in animals and plants.

    b Describe one benefit and one risk of using stem cells in medicine.

Extend

E1 In 2014, scientists studying zebrafish discovered that 'buddy' cells are needed to help one type of stem cell become blood stem cells.

    a Suggest how this research could lead to new treatments for people with diseases.

    b Suggest what risks must be overcome before these treatments can be given to patients.

CB2e The nervous system

Specification reference: B2.13

Progression questions

- What is the nervous system?
- How does the nervous system allow the body to respond to stimuli?
- How is a sensory neurone adapted to its function?

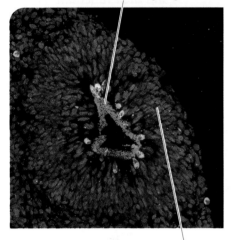

stem cells undergoing mitosis

cells differentiating into nerve cells (neurones)

A This clump of living brain cells was produced from stem cells and grown in the lab. These clumps can be up to 5 mm in diameter.

6ᵗʰ 1 Name the organs in the central nervous system.

To study how a human brain works, it is useful for scientists to experiment on living brain tissue. This cannot be done with living people, but in 2015 scientists from Stanford University in the USA managed to grow brain tissue in their lab by using stem cell techniques.

The brain and **spinal cord** form the **central nervous system** (**CNS**), which controls your body. Nerves make up the rest of the **nervous system**. This organ system allows all the parts of your body to communicate, using electrical signals called **impulses**.

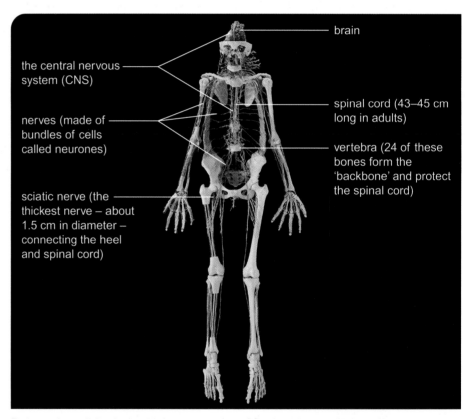

the central nervous system (CNS)

brain

spinal cord (43–45 cm long in adults)

vertebra (24 of these bones form the 'backbone' and protect the spinal cord)

nerves (made of bundles of cells called neurones)

sciatic nerve (the thickest nerve – about 1.5 cm in diameter – connecting the heel and spinal cord)

B dissection of the human nervous system, including some of the thicker nerves

Anything your body is sensitive to, including changes inside your body and in your surroundings, is called a **stimulus**. **Sense organs** (such as eyes, ears and skin) contain **receptor cells** that detect stimuli. For example, skin contains receptor cells that detect the stimulus of temperature change.

Receptor cells create impulses, which usually travel to the brain. The brain then processes this information and can send impulses to other parts of the body to cause something to happen (a **response**).

Did you know?

Lined up end to end, all the neurones in your body would stretch for 1000 km. You would not, however, see this line, because it would be only 10 μm wide.

 2 In which sense organ would you find receptor cells that detect changes in light?

 3 How will the person in diagram C know that she has picked up the pencil?

 4 You hear a track you like on a playlist and turn up the volume. Describe what happens in your nervous system when you do this.

The travelling, or transmission, of impulses is called **neurotransmission** and happens in **neurones** (**nerve cells**). Neurones have a cell body and long extensions to carry impulses.

There are different types of neurone. Diagram D shows a **sensory neurone**. Its function is to carry impulses from receptor cells towards the CNS. A receptor cell impulse passes into a tiny branch called a **dendrite**. It is then transmitted along the **dendron** and the **axon**. A series of **axon terminals** allow impulses to be transmitted to other neurones.

Dendrons and axons are frequently long, to allow fast neurotransmission over long distances. There is also a fatty layer surrounding these parts, called the **myelin sheath**. This electrically insulates a neurone from neighbouring neurones (e.g. in a nerve), stopping the signal losing energy. It also makes an impulse 'jump' along the cell between the gaps in the myelin, and so speeds up neurotransmission.

1 Impulses from receptor cells in the eye are transmitted by sensory neurones in the optic nerve to the brain. The brain processes these impulses and 'sees' the pencil.

2 The brain can send more impulses to tell parts of the body to do something (the response).

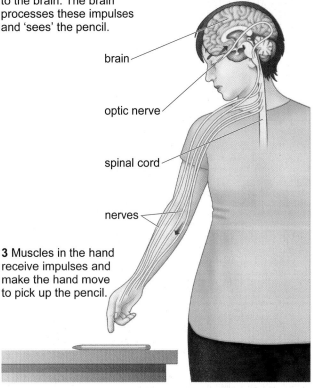

3 Muscles in the hand receive impulses and make the hand move to pick up the pencil.

C This is what happens in the nervous system when someone picks up a pencil.

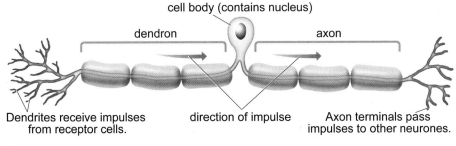

D a sensory neurone

 5 a Suggest the name of a cell that a dendrite might receive an impulse from.

 b Draw a flow chart to show the route of an impulse along a sensory neurone.

 6 Explain the ways in which a sensory neurone is adapted to its function.

 7 Explain what is meant by a 'response to a stimulus'.

Exam-style question

Describe how you detect the stimulus of temperature change. *(3 marks)*

Checkpoint

How confidently can you answer the Progression questions?

Strengthen

S1 Draw a flow chart to show how information about something touching the heel of your foot gets to your brain.

Extend

E1 You pick up an ice cube. Explain how your nervous system allows you to do this.

CB2f Neurotransmission speeds

Specification reference: B2.13; B2.14

Progression questions

- How is a motor neurone adapted to its function?
- How do neurotransmitters allow a connection between neurones?
- How does the structure of a reflex arc allow faster reactions to stimuli?

A Lance Corporal Craig Lundberg was blinded by a grenade but gets around unaided using the BrainPort®.

The device in photo A allows blind people to see … with their tongues! The image from the camera is sent to a 'lollipop' that contains hundreds of small electrodes. Each electrode produces pulses of electricity depending on how much light is in that part of the image. By putting the lollipop on the tongue, the user can feel these pulses and build up an idea of basic shapes and movement. This allows some blind people to react and respond to visual stimuli.

When the brain coordinates a response to a stimulus, impulses are sent to **effectors** and these carry out an action. Effectors include muscles and glands (e.g. sweat glands).

1 Imagine you see a lion and run away.

 a Where are the receptor cells that receive the stimulus?

 b What effectors carry out the response?

 c Suggest another effector triggered by seeing the lion.

Different neurones

Motor neurones carry impulses to effectors. **Relay neurones** are short neurones that are found in the spinal cord, where they link motor and sensory neurones. They also make up a lot of the nerve tissue in the brain. Neither of these types of neurone has a dendron, and the dendrites are on the cell body.

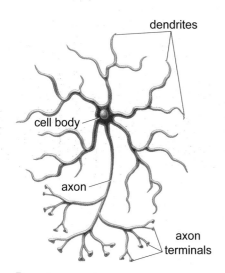

B a relay neurone

2 Do the following carry information to or away from the central nervous system?

 a motor neurones

 b sensory neurones

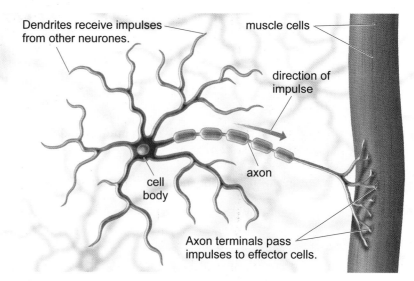

C a motor neurone

Synapses

One neurone meets another at a **synapse**, which contains a tiny gap. When an impulse reaches an axon terminal, a **neurotransmitter** substance is released into the gap. This is detected by the next neurone, which generates a new impulse. Synapses slow down neurotransmission. They are, however, useful because neurotransmitters are only released from axon terminals and so impulses only flow in one direction. They also allow many fresh impulses to be generated in many neurones connected to one neurone – the original impulse does not need to be split and lose 'strength'.

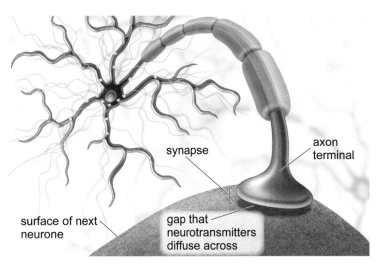

 3 Give two reasons why synapses are used in the nervous system.

D The gap in a synapse is only about 20 nm (0.00002 mm) wide.

The reflex arc

If you touch a very hot object you need to pull your finger away very quickly to stop it burning you. You don't want to have to waste time thinking about this and so a **reflex** is used. Reflex actions are responses that are automatic, extremely quick and protect the body. They use neurone pathways called **reflex arcs**, which bypass the parts of the brain involved in processing information and so are quicker than responses that need processing.

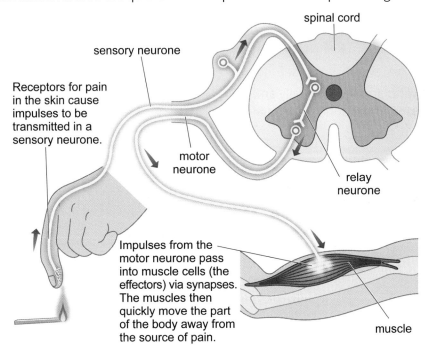

Receptors for pain in the skin cause impulses to be transmitted in a sensory neurone.

sensory neurone

spinal cord

motor neurone

relay neurone

Impulses from the motor neurone pass into muscle cells (the effectors) via synapses. The muscles then quickly move the part of the body away from the source of pain.

muscle

E a reflex arc

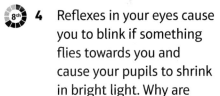 **4** Reflexes in your eyes cause you to blink if something flies towards you and cause your pupils to shrink in bright light. Why are these responses useful?

 5 Draw a table to compare and contrast reflex actions with processed responses.

 6 Suggest why there are very few synapses between the receptor and effector in a reflex arc.

 7 You kick a football. Describe how this response occurs.

Checkpoint

How confidently can you answer the Progression questions?

Strengthen

S1 Draw a flow chart to show how an impulse in a relay neurone causes an impulse in a motor neurone.

Extend

E1 Explain how response times are decreased in reflex actions.

Exam-style question

Describe how the arrival of an impulse at the end of one neurone can cause an impulse in a neighbouring neurone. *(3 marks)*

Reflex arc

Describe how impulses are transmitted in a reflex arc in order to reduce the chance of getting burnt when someone touches a hot object.

(6 marks)

Student answer

If you touch a hot object, receptor cells in the hand detect this. Impulses travel into a sensory neurone, and then into a relay neurone in the spinal cord. After [1] this, the impulses pass to motor neurones, which cause muscles (the effectors) to move the hand quickly out of the way [2]. This pathway is called a reflex arc, and it is shorter than if the impulses had to go to the brain to be processed. This means that the response is much quicker than usual [3]. This means that the hand is moved away from the hot object as quickly as possible, meaning that there is less chance of it being burnt [4].

[1] The answer shows good use of prepositions such as 'then' and 'after' to show order.

[2] The neurones are described in the correct order.

[3] A good explanation of why the hand moves away so quickly.

[4] The answer relates back to the question, which was about the chance of being burnt.

Verdict

This is a strong answer. The answer is arranged logically and written clearly. It shows good linking of scientific knowledge to the context of the question.

The answer first describes the reflex arc in the correct order, and uses the correct scientific names for the neurones. The answer then links the description to the speed of response, and then to the reduced chance of being burnt. This was the original point of the question.

Exam tip

When you have to write about a sequence of events, it is a good idea to write out bullet points of the facts that you will use, and then number them to show the order in which you will use the points. When you have written your answer, neatly cross out your bullet points.

Paper 1

CB3 Genetics

This image was made by splicing together a photograph of a mother (aged 52) and her son (aged 30). It is one of a number of 'genetic portraits' created by Canadian graphic designer Ulric Collette to illustrate how closely members of the same family resemble one another. In this unit you will learn about the DNA code that produces our features and the processes that allow features to be passed on from parents to their offspring.

The learning journey

Previously you will have learnt at KS3:

- about the differences between environmental and inherited (or genetic) variation
- how two gametes fuse during fertilisation to produce a single zygote
- how the nuclei of eukaryotic cells contain chromosomes, which contain DNA.

In this unit you will learn:

- how gametes are produced by meiosis
- about the structure of DNA
- about mutations and how genes cause genetic variation
- why certain characteristics are passed down through families.

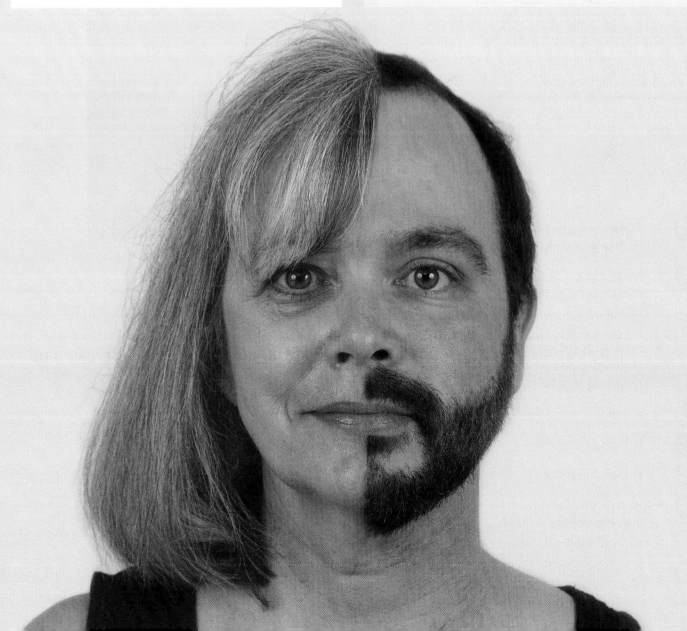

Specification reference: B3.3; B3.5

Progression questions

- What happens in meiosis?
- Why is meiosis necessary for sexual reproduction?
- What is the role of the genome in the manufacture of proteins?

You started off life smaller than this.

A A human zygote is 0.1 mm in diameter, which is even smaller than this tiny dot.

Did you know?

There are about 37 million million cells in an adult human.

Humans start life as a single fertilised egg cell, a **zygote**. This is formed when two **gametes** (sex cells) fuse during **fertilisation**. The zygote then forms a ball of cells using a type of cell division called **mitosis** (see CB2a).

Almost all human cells carry exactly the same instructions. These instructions control each individual cell, and also shape, coordinate and control our bodies. So, it's amazing that all the instructions fit into the nucleus of the zygote (the nucleus is about 6 µm or 0.006 mm in diameter).

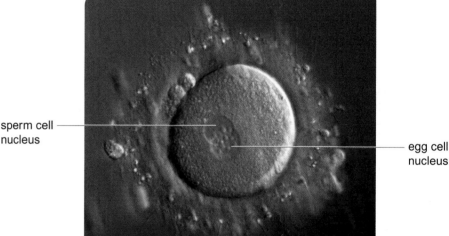

sperm cell nucleus

egg cell nucleus

B a human **sperm cell** nucleus and an **egg cell** nucleus fusing during fertilisation

The instructions for an organism are found as code in a molecule called **DNA**. The DNA of an organism is its **genome**, and most cells contain a complete copy of an organism's genome.

The human genome is found on 46 very long molecules of DNA, and each molecule is inside a **chromosome**. Along the length of a DNA molecule are sections that each contain a code for making a protein. These DNA sections are **genes**. Proteins are **polymers**, made by linking different amino acids together in a chain. The order of amino acids is controlled by a gene. Humans have about 20 000 genes.

There are 23 different chromosomes in humans and most nuclei contain two of each type. So, a human body cell contains two sets of 23 chromosomes, making 46 in all. A cell like this is **diploid** (from the Greek for 'double'). The shorthand for this is 2n. If two diploid cells joined in fertilisation, the **zygote** would have four sets of chromosomes, so gametes need to have just one set of chromosomes. They have to be **haploid**. The shorthand for a haploid cell is 1n.

 1 State the names of the human gametes.

 2 Name the process that turns the zygote into a ball of cells.

3 How many individual chromosomes do the following cells have?

 a human sperm cell

b human liver cell

c human zygote

 4 How much of an organism's genome does a gamete contain?

 5 Define the term 'gene'.

40

Gamete production

Mitosis produces diploid cells, and so a different process is used to produce gametes – **meiosis**.

Each chromosome **replicates** – makes a copy of itself. The two copies remain attached, making each chromosome look like an X. The two sets of chromosomes 'pair up', forming 23 pairs, and the pairs then separate into two new cells. Next, the two copies of a chromosome in each X-shape split into two more new cells. Meiosis therefore produces four haploid **daughter cells**, which is how gametes are produced.

Each chromosome in a pair contains different versions of the same genes. They are 'genetically different'. So, gametes are all different because they contain genetically different chromosomes. This explains why brothers and sisters often look similar but not identical (unless they are identical twins).

C Brothers and sisters have different selections of chromosomes passed down from their parents and so look different to one another.

The gamete-making cell has two sets of chromosomes. It is diploid (2n).

The chromosomes replicate (and the copies stay stuck to one another).

The cell divides into two and then into two again. Each of the final four daughter cells has a copy of one chromosome from each pair. They are haploid (1n).

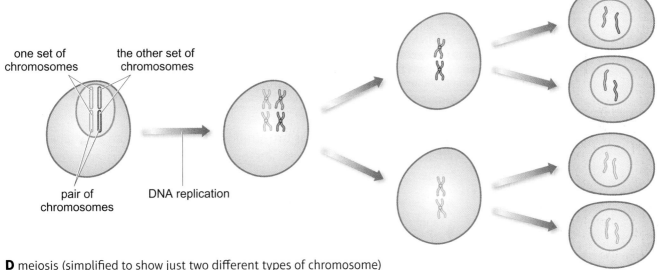

one set of chromosomes · the other set of chromosomes

pair of chromosomes · DNA replication

D meiosis (simplified to show just two different types of chromosome)

 6 Explain why chromosomes look X-shaped at the start of meiosis.

7 Name the process in which the following cells are made.

 a zygote

 b embryo cell

 c sperm cell

 8 'Triploid syndrome' is a rare human disease. What do you think the cells of someone with this disease are like?

Exam-style question

Compare and contrast mitosis and meiosis.　　　　　*(3 marks)*

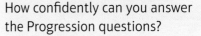

Checkpoint

How confidently can you answer the Progression questions?

Strengthen

S1 Draw a diagram to explain how a zygote's genome is created.

Extend

E1 Explain why a brother and sister do not look identical.

CB3bi DNA

Specification reference: B3.4

Progression questions

- What are DNA bases?
- What is the structure of DNA?
- How are DNA strands held together?

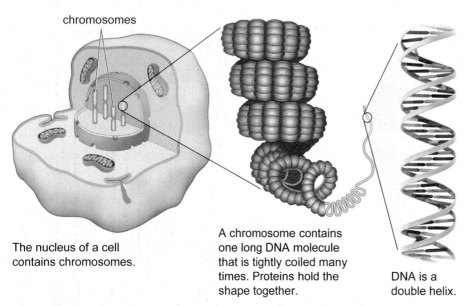

chromosomes

The nucleus of a cell contains chromosomes.

A chromosome contains one long DNA molecule that is tightly coiled many times. Proteins hold the shape together.

DNA is a double helix.

A DNA is packaged up tightly with proteins in a chromosome.

The nuclei of your cells contain very long molecules of **DNA**. Each molecule is tightly coiled and packaged up with proteins to form **chromosomes**.

1 How many molecules of DNA would you expect to find in one of your liver cells?

2 What parts of a DNA molecule contain the instructions for making chromosome packaging proteins?

A molecule of DNA contains two strands, each of which forms a shape called a helix. The two strands are joined together by pairs of substances called **bases**, to form a **double helix**.

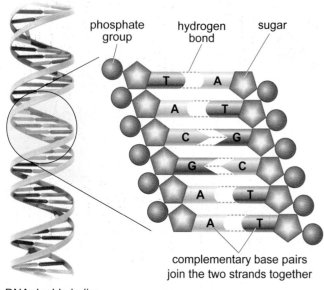

phosphate group   hydrogen bond   sugar

complementary base pairs join the two strands together

DNA double helix

B the structure of DNA

There are four bases in DNA: **adenine**, **thymine**, **cytosine** and **guanine**. To make things simpler, we often call them A, T, C and G. Diagram B shows how they are arranged. Notice that A always pairs with T and C always pairs with G. The matching bases are **complementary base pairs**.

Each base is attached to a sugar and each sugar is attached to a phosphate group. The sugars and phosphate groups form the backbone of the DNA strands. DNA is therefore made of many similar units joined in a chain, and so it is a polymer.

3 Describe the shape of a DNA molecule.

4 If cytosine is found on one strand of DNA, which base will it join with on the other strand?

5 One part of a DNA strand contains this order of bases: ATTTCGC. Copy the letters and write the letters for the complementary base pairs underneath.

Hydrogen bonding

Parts of DNA bases have very slight electrical charges. A slightly negatively charged part of one base attracts a slightly positively charged part of another base. This forms a weak force of attraction called a **hydrogen bond**. Cytosine and guanine form three hydrogen bonds between them. Adenine and thymine form two hydrogen bonds. This helps to explain why C only pairs with G, and A pairs with T.

The DNA code

The order of bases in a **gene** contains the coded instructions for a protein. However, we all have slight differences in our genes caused by slightly different orders of bases in our DNA. In fact, everyone except identical twins has different DNA. This allows scientists to match DNA from cells to specific people. And, since DNA is passed down through families, analysing DNA allows scientists to find out if or how people are related.

C the skeleton of Richard III

DNA analysis helped to solve the identity of a skeleton found under a car park in Leicester in 2012. The skeleton looked like it was that of King Richard III, who died in 1485. DNA tests on the bones and on cells from a living relative of the king supported this idea.

D a model of Richard III with one of his living relatives, Michael Ibsen

Exam-style question

Describe the nature of the genetic code found in a gene. *(2 marks)*

 6 Describe a hydrogen bond.

 7 What makes genes slightly different from person to person?

8 If you are arrested by the police in the UK, a sample of your cells can be taken. Explain why this is done.

Checkpoint

How confidently can you answer the Progression questions?

Strengthen

S1 Describe how complementary base pairs help to form the structure of DNA.

Extend

E1 In some types of DNA analysis, the two strands of a small length of DNA are pulled apart to allow copies of the DNA to be made. Draw a labelled diagram to explain how this process works.

CB3bii DNA extraction

Specification reference: B3.6

Aim

Explain how DNA can be extracted from fruit.

A Some meat products were withdrawn from sale when it was discovered they had been mislabelled.

At the beginning of 2013, food scientists in Ireland and the UK found that some brands of beefburger contained horsemeat. Horsemeat is safe to eat, but it is illegal to label foods with the wrong ingredients. More tests were carried out on meat products in many countries, and it soon became clear that horsemeat was being used in a variety of 'beef' products throughout Europe. Eventually, people were identified who had mislabelled horsemeat as beef and they were arrested.

During testing, DNA was first extracted from cells in the foods. The DNA was then analysed to work out the order of some of the bases. Different organisms have different orders of bases in certain genes, and so these tests can identify which organisms have been used to make a food. One method of extracting DNA is given below.

Method

Wear eye protection.

A Dissolve 3 g of salt in 100 cm³ of water in a large beaker. Add 10 cm³ of washing-up liquid and stir gently until the salt dissolves. Do not make the mixture foamy! The detergent in this solution breaks down cell surface membranes and the membranes around nuclei. The salt makes the DNA more likely to clump together, which is important in step G.

B Thoroughly mash 50 g of peas. Put the mashed peas into an empty beaker and add the solution made in step A. Stir slowly for one minute.

C Place the beaker in a water bath at 60 °C for 15 minutes.

D Filter the mixture and collect the filtrate in a small beaker.

E Measure 10 cm³ of the filtrate and pour it into a boiling tube.

F Add two drops of protease enzyme solution. (Proteases break down proteins.)

G Tilt the boiling tube slightly and pour in ice-cold ethanol, letting the ethanol run down the inside of the tube very slowly. Stop when as much ethanol has been added as there is filtrate. DNA is insoluble in ethanol and so it forms a precipitate.

H Leave the tube for a few minutes. A white layer forms between the filtrate and the ethanol. This is DNA, and it can be wound around a glass stirring rod and lifted out of the tube.

B Ethanol causes DNA to precipitate, so you can see it.

Exam-style questions

1 **a** State the reason why food scientists analyse the DNA from meat products. *(1 mark)*

   b Suggest an explanation for why DNA is so useful for this purpose. *(2 marks)*

2 State which substance is used to precipitate DNA? *(1 mark)*

3 Most of the 'meat' in a food is made of muscle proteins called actin and myosin. State where the instructions for making these proteins are found in an animal. *(1 mark)*

4 Make a list of the apparatus needed to carry out the method on the previous page. *(2 marks)*

5 Draw a labelled diagram to show the apparatus used in step D. *(2 marks)*

6 Explain two safety precautions that should be used when carrying out the experiment on the previous page. *(4 marks)*

7 Explain how the following steps in the method on the previous page allow a good sample of DNA to be extracted in:

   a step B *(2 marks)*

   b step F. *(2 marks)*

8 The pea DNA produced in step H of the method was put into a new test tube. Twice the volume of ammonia solution as the DNA sample was added, followed by a few drops of silver nitrate. The solution turned cloudy white, indicating the presence of adenine and/or guanine. Explain why this test should be done on the sample of DNA. *(2 marks)*

9 DNA is often analysed by chopping it up into small pieces. Where the cuts occur in the DNA is due to the order of the bases. The sizes of the pieces produced are different for different organisms. A form of chromatography is then used to separate the pieces of DNA, with smaller pieces travelling further than larger pieces. The results can then be examined. Diagram C shows the results of one of these tests on the meat in three pre-packed foods.

   a State what substance would be added to the DNA samples to chop them into smaller pieces. *(1 mark)*

   b Explain which meat produced the smallest size pieces of DNA. *(2 marks)*

   c Explain which food(s) contain(s) only the meat they should. *(2 marks)*

   d Identify the meats in the illegal food(s). *(2 marks)*

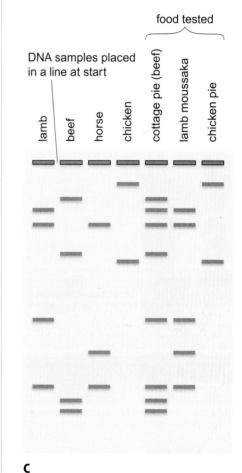

C

CB3c Alleles

Specification reference: B3.12; B3.13; B3.14

Progression questions

- What is the difference between a gene and an allele?
- Why will a recessive allele not affect the phenotype of an organism that is heterozygous for that gene?
- Why are genetic diagrams useful?

This book contains instructions for eye colour, height and nose shape.

A The human genome is contained on two sets of 23 chromosomes.

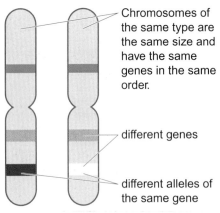

Chromosomes of the same type are the same size and have the same genes in the same order.

different genes

different alleles of the same gene

B Each gene can exist in a number of different forms called alleles.

You can think of chromosomes as a set of books. Each book (chromosome) contains a set of sentences giving instructions (genes). All of the books together contain all of the instructions needed to produce a certain organism (its genome).

1 List these terms in order of size, largest first: base, chromosome, gene, genome.

Genes for the same characteristic (e.g. eye colour) can contain slightly different instructions that create variations (e.g. brown, blue). Different forms of the same gene are called **alleles**.

Since there are two copies of every chromosome in a body cell nucleus, a body cell contains two copies of every gene. Each copy of a gene may be a different allele. There are many alleles for most of the 20 000 human genes, and the different combination of alleles in each person gives each of us slightly different characteristics (**genetic variation**).

2 Define the term 'allele'.

3 How does the idea of alleles help to explain why we all look different?

If both alleles for one gene are the same, an organism is **homozygous** for that gene. If the alleles are different, an organism is **heterozygous**. The plants on the far left and far right of diagram C are homozygous.

Gametes have only one copy of each chromosome and so only contain one copy of each gene. In diagram C, gametes from the purple and white flowers fertilise and form a **zygote** that is heterozygous. However, in the offspring plant only the allele for purple flowers has an effect. It is said to be **dominant**. The white flower allele has no effect if the purple flower allele is there. This white flower allele is **recessive**.

gametes contain the purple allele

gametes contain the white allele

The flower colour alleles are both the same. They contain the instructions for purple flowers.

All the offspring have both alleles. However, all the flowers are purple. This is because purple is the dominant allele.

The flower colour alleles are both the same. They contain the instructions for white flowers.

C

A recessive characteristic is only seen if *both* alleles are recessive. This can be shown in a **genetic diagram** (diagram D).

A dominant allele is shown by a capital letter (e.g. R for purple). The recessive allele has the lower case version of the *same* letter (e.g. r for *not* purple). The letter for the dominant allele is always written before the recessive one (e.g. Rr and never rR). The alleles in an organism are its **genotype**. What the organism looks like is its **phenotype**.

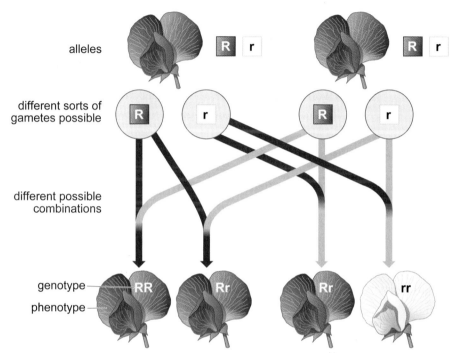

D A genetic diagram shows the possible combinations of alleles when two organisms breed. We use diagrams like this to explain the inheritance of one gene (**monohybrid inheritance**). We can also use these diagrams to predict the **ratios** of the phenotypes (purple and white phenotypes are in a 3:1 ratio in this example).

 6   When will a recessive allele affect a phenotype?

 7   Draw a table to show the three genotypes in diagram D and their matching phenotypes.

 8   The pea plant gene for height has two alleles: T (dominant, causing tall plants) and t (recessive, causing short plants). A homozygous tall plant is crossed (bred) with a homozygous short plant. Draw a genetic diagram to show the pattern of monohybrid inheritance of the height gene.

Exam-style question

ADWH is a condition in which people have curly hair that looks like sheep's wool. It is caused by a dominant allele (D). Calculate the ratio of children with and without the condition if one parent is heterozygous and the other is homozygous for the recessive allele. *(4 marks)*

 4   How would you add to the book analogy (in diagram A) to include alleles?

 5   **a** Is the plant in the centre of diagram C heterozygous or homozygous for the flower colour allele?

   b Explain your reasoning.

Did you know?

The ability to taste a bitter substance called PTC (phenylthiocarbamide) is controlled by one gene. People with a dominant allele of the gene can taste PTC. People with two recessive alleles cannot taste it.

Checkpoint

How confidently can you answer the Progression questions?

Strengthen

S1 Two pea plants are bred together. One has two dominant alleles for purple flowers (R) and one has two recessive alleles for white flowers (r). Draw a diagram to explain why none of the offspring will have white flowers.

Extend

E1 The pea plant gene for seed shape has two alleles: N (causing smooth peas) and n (causing wrinkled peas). Use a genetic diagram to work out the ratio of offspring with smooth and wrinkled peas if the parent plants are both heterozygous.

CB3d Inheritance

Specification reference: B3.14; B3.15; B3.16

Progression questions

- How is the sex of offspring determined in humans?
- How do we use genetic diagrams, Punnett squares and family pedigrees to show inheritance?
- How are the probable outcomes of offspring phenotypes calculated, using information about alleles?

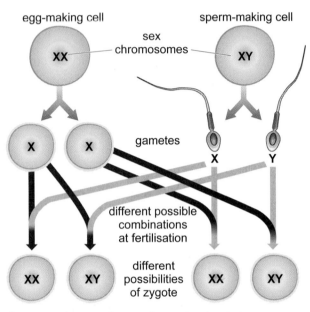

A genetic diagram for sex determination in humans

Two of your chromosomes determine what sex you are. They are your **sex chromosomes** and there are two types: X and Y. Females have two X sex chromosomes and males have one X and one Y.

A woman's gametes (egg cells) all contain an X sex chromosome but male sperm cells contain either an X or a Y. Diagram A shows the ways in which sex chromosomes can combine.

 1 In humans, which gamete is responsible for determining the sex of the offspring?

Punnett squares (such as diagram B) are another way to demonstrate inheritance. The boxes show the possible genotypes. Two boxes contain XX and two contain XY, so the ratio of the outcomes is 2:2 (simplified to 1:1). This means that there should be equal numbers of offspring born with XX sex chromosomes as are born with XY.

The likelihood of an event happening is its **probability**. Punnett squares are used to work out the theoretical probability of offspring inheriting certain genotypes. Probabilities can be shown as fractions, decimals or percentages. The probability of an impossible event is 0 or 0 per cent. The probability of an event that is certain to happen is 1 or 100 per cent.

B Punnett square for human sex determination

The boxes show the possible combinations in the offspring.

Worked example

In diagram B, two out of four boxes are XX. So the probability of a child being XX is:

$$\frac{2}{4} = \frac{1}{2} = 0.5$$

Or as a percentage: 50%

Did you know?

Birds have Z and W sex chromosomes and it is the egg cell that determines the sex; the females are ZW and males are ZZ.

 2 Explain why about half the population of the UK is female.

Punnett squares are used to work out the probabilities of different phenotypes caused by alleles. Diagram C shows an example for a genetic disorder called cystic fibrosis (CF), caused by a recessive allele. People with CF have problems with their lungs and digestive systems.

People who inherit two recessive CF alleles (f) have the disorder. People who inherit at least one dominant allele (F) do not have CF. The Punnett square shows that if heterozygous parents have children, the ratio of children without CF to those with CF is predicted to be 3:1.

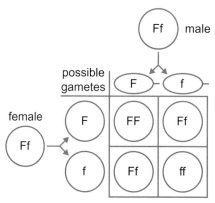

C Punnett square for parents that are heterozygous for the CF gene

 3 Draw a Punnett square for the plants shown in CB3c diagram D.

4 Look at diagram C.

 a What is the ratio of the phenotypes of the offspring?

 b If the parents had four children, how many are predicted to have CF?

c Calculate the probability of a child being born without CF. Show your answer as a fraction, a decimal and as a percentage, and show all your working.

A **family pedigree chart** (such as diagram D, below) shows how genotypes and their resulting phenotypes are inherited in families.

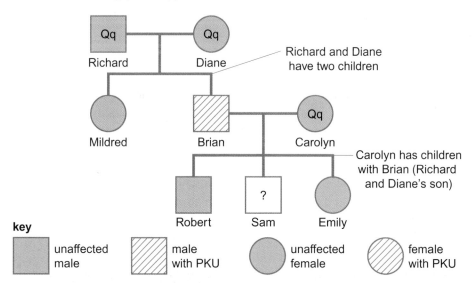

D Phenylketonuria (PKU) is a disorder caused by a recessive allele. People with PKU lack an enzyme called phenylalanine hydroxylase and can develop nerve problems unless they stick to a special diet.

5 Look at diagram D.

 a Which letter shows the recessive allele?

 b Why doesn't Carolyn have PKU?

 c What is Brian's genotype?

 d Calculate the probability that Sam has PKU. Show your working.

Checkpoint

How confidently can you answer the Progression questions?

Strengthen

S1 Look at diagram D. Draw a Punnett square for Richard and Diane.

S2 Work out the probability that a child of theirs will have PKU. Show all of your working.

Extend

E1 The pea plant gene for unripe pod colour has two alleles: G (green pods) and g (yellow pods). Two homozygous plants are crossed (bred together), one with green pods and one with yellow pods. Two of the offspring are crossed. Work out the probability that an offspring plant from this second crossing will have yellow pods. Show all of your working.

Exam-style question

Explain how the sperm cell is responsible for the determination of sex in humans. *(4 marks)*

CB3e Gene mutation

Specification reference: B3.19; B3.20; B3.21; B3.22; B3.23

Progression questions

- Why is it difficult to identify how most inherited characteristics are controlled?
- What is a mutation?
- How can mutations cause variation?

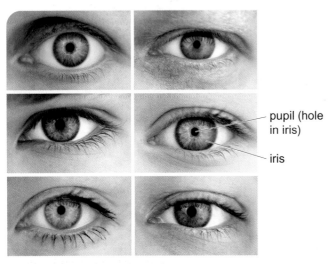

pupil (hole in iris)

iris

A Human eye colour is caused by the amount of melanin (a dark-coloured protein) and how light is scattered by the iris.

Most human characteristics are controlled by many genes, not just one. For example, several genes affect eye colour in humans. However, most **variation** in eye colour is caused by the OCA2 gene, which controls the amount of melanin produced. Melanin is a protein that makes hair, eyes and skin darker in colour. A blue iris contains little melanin, while a brown iris contains a lot of melanin.

1 Suggest two alleles for the OCA2 gene, and explain your answer.

2 It is sometimes said that brown eyes are dominant to blue eyes. Use this information, and your answer to question 1, to draw a Punnett square that describes the inheritance of eye colour from heterozygous brown-eyed parents. Describe the outcomes in terms of genotype and phenotype.

Did you know?

A baby has about 70 mutations that neither of its parents have. These mutations occur during gamete production and during growth.

3 Which kind of cell division could produce a mutation in:

a a gamete

b a body cell?

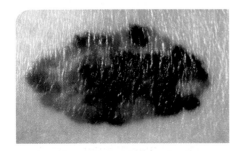

B Sunlight contains ultraviolet radiation that can cause mutations in skin cells, which can result in skin cancer.

It is thought that early humans had brown eyes. As our ancestors moved north from Africa, changes in the alleles for melanin production in some people resulted in blue eyes and fair skin. A change in a gene that creates a new allele is called a **mutation**. Mutations often occur during cell division.

Mutations happen when there is a mistake in copying DNA during cell division. For example, one base in a DNA sequence might be replaced with another, rather like typing the wrong letter in a word. This can happen naturally, but is more likely to happen if there is damage to the DNA caused by radiation or certain substances.

Sometimes a mutation produces an allele that causes a big change in the protein that is produced. This will affect how the body works. However, mutations can occur in different parts of a gene and so may only have a small effect on the protein that is produced. Many other mutations will not change the protein at all and so have no effect on the phenotype.

 4 Explain why the risk of developing skin cancer can increase with the amount of sunlight your skin receives.

 5 Explain why a mutation does not always produce a change in a characteristic.

The Human Genome Project

In 2003, the first complete human genome was decoded. This was the result of the **Human Genome Project** and involved scientists in many different countries. The project produced a map of 3.3 billion complementary base pairs in one set of 46 human chromosomes. Further work has found many sections of DNA that are the genes. Now other human genomes have also been mapped. This has shown that there are variations between people, but that over 99 per cent of the DNA bases in different people are the same.

Mapping a person's genome can indicate their risk of developing diseases that are caused by different alleles of genes. It can also help identify which medicines might be best to treat a person's illness, because the alleles we have can affect how medicines work in the body.

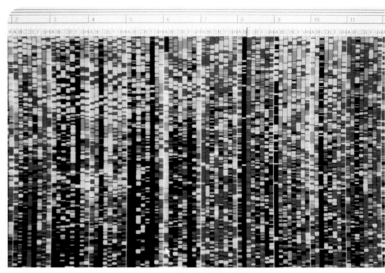

C A map of part of one human genome. Each coloured band represents a different base in the DNA sequence. Some of the bases in this part of the genome will be different in different people.

Clopidogrel is a drug used to prevent blood clots in people at risk of heart attack or stroke. Some people have particular alleles that mean the drug does not protect them.

Drug response	Status
Clopidogrel effectiveness	reduced
Simvastatin-induced myopathy	typical risk
Warfarin sensitivity	increased

The drug simvastatin is used to reduce high levels of cholesterol in the blood. Some people suffer a side effect of myopathy (weak muscles) if they take the drug.

Warfarin is given to people to reduce the risk of blood clots. Some people are more sensitive to the drug than others, due to their alleles, and so need to take a smaller dose than others, otherwise it can cause dangerous bleeding.

D Genome analysis for one person showing how they might respond to some drugs as a result of the alleles they have for particular genes.

 7 Give two ways in which information about a person's genome could be useful in medicine.

 8 a Suggest how a doctor might use the information in table D to identify which drugs to use with that particular person.

 b Explain why the information in table D can be different for different people.

Exam-style question

Explain how mutation can lead to variation in the phenotype.   *(3 marks)*

 6 Look at photo C. Explain why some colour bands would be different in this part of the genome from another person.

Checkpoint

How confidently can you answer the Progression questions?

Strengthen

S1 Different people have different eye colours. Explain why there is variation in human eye colour.

Extend

E1 The RHO gene controls the production of a protein in the retina of the eye that helps with vision in low light. The gene is 6705 bases long, and over 150 different variations in some of the bases have been found. Some variations have no obvious effect, but some lead to night blindness by the age of 40. Explain this variation in vision in different people.

CB3f Variation

Specification reference: B3.20

Progression questions

- How is genetic variation caused?
- How can the environment affect characteristics?
- What are discontinuous and continuous variation?

A These plants are all the same species, *Begonia rex*. X-ray radiation was used to produce mutations that led to many new varieties of the species with different shapes and colours of leaves.

Some of the variation between individuals of the same species is the result of variation in their genes. **Genetic variation** is caused by the different alleles inherited during sexual reproduction. Different alleles are produced by mutations, some of which cause changes in the phenotype. However, many characteristics also show **environmental variation**, because they are affected by their surroundings. For example, how well a plant grows is affected by how much light, water and nutrients it gets.

 1 a i Look at photo A. Identify one characteristic in *Begonia rex* plants that is caused by genetic variation.

 ii Explain your answer.

 b i Suggest one characteristic in these plants that shows variation caused by the environment.

 ii Explain your answer.

In a few cases, a characteristic shows variation that is caused only by the environment, such as the loss of a limb in an accident. Characteristics that are changed by the environment during the life of the individual are called **acquired characteristics**.

B These bushes have acquired different shapes due to pruning by the gardener.

Variation can be grouped into two types:

- **discontinuous variation** is where the data can only take a limited set of values
- **continuous variation** is where the data can be any value in a range.

Charts C and D show how to display these different types of variation.

2 For each of these human characteristics, state whether they are controlled only by genes, only by the environment, or by both genes and environment. Explain each of your answers.

 a length of hair

 b blood group

 c height

 3 Explain why the shapes of the bushes in photo B are acquired characteristics.

52

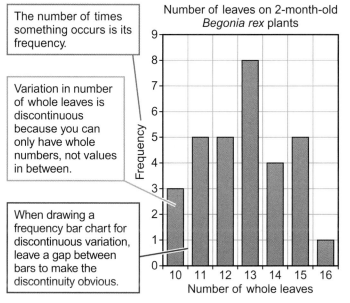

The number of times something occurs is its frequency.

Variation in number of whole leaves is discontinuous because you can only have whole numbers, not values in between.

When drawing a frequency bar chart for discontinuous variation, leave a gap between bars to make the discontinuity obvious.

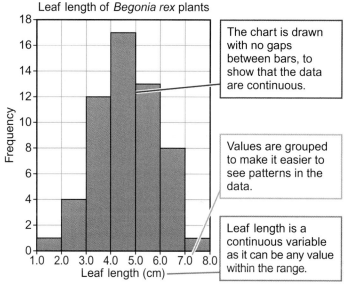

The chart is drawn with no gaps between bars, to show that the data are continuous.

Values are grouped to make it easier to see patterns in the data.

Leaf length is a continuous variable as it can be any value within the range.

C This bar chart shows variation in numbers of leaves on a plant. Since the variable on the *y*-axis is frequency, it is also called a frequency diagram.

D This bar chart is also a frequency diagram, and shows variation in leaf length from several *Begonia rex* plants.

4 Look at charts C and D. Which type of chart would you use for these human characteristics? Explain your answers.

 a length of hand

 b presence or absence of freckles

Continuous data for variation often forms a bell-shaped curve, known as a **normal distribution** (see graph E). It is called this because it is what is expected for a large amount of data for a characteristic where:

• the most common value is the middle value in the whole **range**

• the further a value is from the median, the fewer individuals have that value.

E In a normal distribution curve, the **mean** value is the same as the **mode** (most common value) and the **median** (the middle value).

5 Look at chart D.

 a What is the range of leaf lengths shown in the chart?

 b What is the modal class for leaf length shown in the chart?

 c Does leaf length in *Begonia* plants show a normal distribution? Explain your answer.

Checkpoint

How confidently can you answer the Progression questions?

Strengthen

S1 A child has long, wavy blonde hair, but his mother has short, straight brown hair. Give as many reasons as you can for these differences, explaining your answers.

Extend

E1 Is the DNA in each of your cells exactly the same? Explain your answer.

Exam-style question

A group of humans will show variation in height. Describe how this variation is caused. *(2 marks)*

Mitosis and meiosis

Compare the roles of mitosis and meiosis in reproduction.

(6 marks)

Student answer

Mitosis is the cell division that produces two diploid daughter cells from one parent cell. During mitosis each daughter cell receives a copy of every chromosome in the parent cell, which means that [1] they are genetically identical. Mitosis is used in asexual reproduction and produces offspring that are genetically identical to the one parent [2].

In meiosis, four daughter cells are produced from one parent cell. Each daughter cell is haploid [3], and has copies of only half the chromosomes of the diploid parent cell. This produces gametes that are genetically different to each other [4]. Meiosis occurs before sexual reproduction, in which two gametes fuse to form a fertilised egg cell that is diploid. The variation in the gametes means that the offspring differ genetically from each other and from the two parents [5].

[1] The student uses a linking phrase ('which means that') to identify cause and effect. This helps to structure the answer and provide links to reasoning.

[2] This part of the answer clearly links mitosis to reproduction – which was one aim of the question.

[3] The answer correctly uses (and correctly spells) scientific terms, such as haploid.

[4] This part of the answer clearly links meiosis to cell division – which was the other aim of the question.

[5] The answer is logically divided into two paragraphs – one about mitosis and one about meiosis. Each of the paragraphs is structured in the same order. This makes the differences between mitosis and meiosis very clear.

Verdict

This is a strong answer. It contains detail about both types of cell division, and uses appropriate scientific terminology.

The answer also clearly links the description of each type of cell division with what this means for reproduction. The answer is well organised and makes it easy to compare the differences between each process.

Exam tip

The answer to a 'compare' question should describe the similarities *or* differences between **all** the subjects of the question (in this case the answer includes differences between *both* types of cell division). A 'compare' question does not need a conclusion.

Paper 1

CB4 Natural Selection and Genetic Modification

The green glow from this cat is not the result of some terrible nuclear accident! The cat has been genetically modified by scientists who are trying to stop cats getting a form of AIDS (from a virus like HIV). The cats were modified to contain a gene that helps prevent certain monkeys getting a form of AIDS. This gene was attached to another xgene that makes the cats glow green under ultraviolet light. If the cat glows green, the scientists know that the modification has worked and that the cat also contains the anti-AIDS gene. In this unit you will find out more about how organisms are changed genetically by natural selection and by humans.

The learning journey

Previously you will have learnt at KS3:

- that organisms change over time (evolution)
- that Charles Darwin came up with a theory to explain this
- about how DNA contains instructions for the characteristics of organisms.

In this unit you will learn:

- about Darwin's theory of evolution by natural selection
- how different methods, including genetic analysis, are being used to investigate evolution
- how organisms are classified
- about selective breeding
- how genetic modification is done.

Progression questions

- What is evolution?
- How do fossils provide evidence for human evolution?
- How do stone tools provide evidence for human evolution?

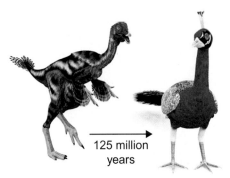

125 million years

Caudipteryx species dinosaur

Indian peafowl (*Pavo cristatus*)

A Scientists think that birds evolved from dinosaurs.

Until the 17th century, most Europeans did not think humans were animals. Ideas started to change when Carl Linnaeus (1707–1778) published his system of classification and suggested that humans were related to apes and monkeys. His **binomial system**, using two Latin words for naming **species**, is still used today.

 1 Give the binomial name for a peafowl.

Later, James Burnett, Lord Monboddo (1714–1799), proposed that humans had evolved from monkeys or apes. However, most people thought he was mad, and he had an obsession for searching for humans with tails! Now, fossil evidence suggests he was on the right track.

Fossil evidence

Evolution is a gradual change in the characteristics of a species over time. Scientists use fossils to find out about human evolution. They work out how old the fossils are and put them in age order. The fossils, though, do not show smooth changes over time because some have not been discovered.

In 1992 scientists discovered some 4.4-million-year-old fossilised bones from a female of an extinct human-like species. More fossils of this species were found and named *Ardipithecus ramidus*. The most complete set of these fossils is nicknamed **Ardi**.

 2 Define the term 'evolution'.

3 Describe two differences between Ardi and a modern human.

Ardi was about 1.2 m tall and 50 kg. Her leg bones show that she may have been able to walk upright. She had very long arms, though, and very long big toes that stuck out to the sides of her feet and would have allowed her to climb trees.

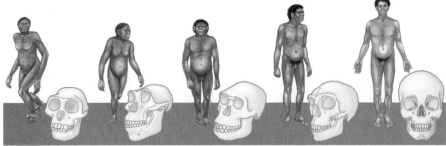

Ardipithecus ramidus ('Ardi') Skull volume: 350 cm³

Australopithecus afarensis ('Lucy') Skull volume: 400 cm³

Homo habilis Skull volume: 500–600 cm³

Homo erectus Skull volume: 850 cm³

Homo sapiens Skull volume: 1450 cm³

B These species are arranged in age order (oldest on the left). Although there are trends, gaps in fossil evidence mean that scientists cannot be certain that these species evolved into each other.

Australopithecus afarensis (nickname **Lucy**) was discovered in 1974. She lived 3.2 million years ago and was about 1.07 m tall. She could probably walk upright, but although her toe bones were arranged in the same way as those of modern humans, they were much more curved.

 4 Describe one difference between Lucy and Ardi.

 5 Identify two trends in the evolution of humans.

In the 1960s, Mary Leakey (1913–1996) and Louis Leakey (1903–1972) found a more recent human-like species. They decided it was closely related to modern humans (*Homo sapiens*) and so gave it the same first word for its binomial name. It is called *Homo habilis*, which translates as 'handy man'.

Homo habilis fossils are 2.4–1.4 million years old. The animals were quite short with long arms but walked upright.

Homo erectus was discovered in Asia in the late 19th century and so many scientists thought that modern humans evolved in Asia. However, an almost complete 1.6-million-year-old skeleton was found by Richard Leakey (1944–) in 1984 in Kenya, providing evidence that humans evolved in Africa. This species was tall (1.79 m) and strongly built.

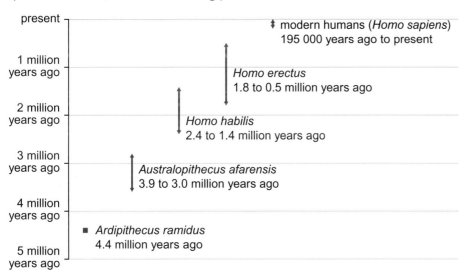

C ages of human-like species fossils

Stone tools

The earliest evidence of human-like animals using stone tools dates to about 3.3 million years ago. Scientists can work out the ages of different layers of rock. They then assume that a stone tool is about the same age as that layer of rock.

The oldest stone tools are very simple, but would have helped with skinning an animal or cutting up meat. Tools found in more recent rocks are more sophisticated.

 6 a Describe how stone tools developed over time.

 b Suggest a conclusion we could draw from this evidence.

 7 Some scientists suggest that there is direct evolution from *Homo habilis* to *Homo erectus* to *Homo sapiens*. Discuss arguments for and against this idea.

Exam-style question

Explain why scientists cannot be sure that human-like animals, such as Ardi, evolved into modern humans. *(2 marks)*

Did you know?

In 2015, scientists in Ethiopia found a species of human-like animal with a thick jaw and small front teeth. They think it lived alongside Lucy and have called it *Australopithecus deyiremeda*.

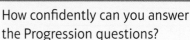

D The stone tool in the upper photo is about 2 million years old. The lower one is about 13 000 years old.

Checkpoint

How confidently can you answer the Progression questions?

Strengthen

S1 Describe how scientists try to show human evolution by placing fossils in order.

Extend

E1 One explanation for the appearance of more sophisticated tools is that larger or more complex brains were evolving. Suggest another hypothesis to explain this.

CB4b Darwin's theory

Specification reference: B4.2; B4.3

Progression questions

- What is natural selection?
- How does natural selection lead to evolution?
- How is Darwin's theory supported by evidence?

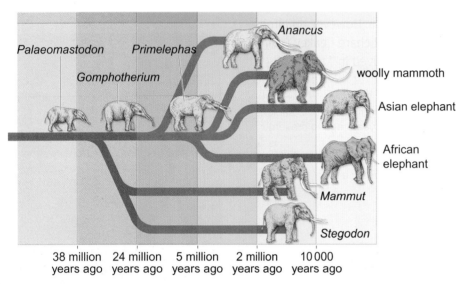

A An idea about elephant evolution, based on fossil evidence. Evolution rarely happens in one neat line – there are usually many branches.

During the 18th century, people started to accept that organisms slowly evolve into others. Two scientists, Charles Darwin (1809–1882) and Alfred Russel Wallace (1823–1913) came up with essentially the same idea about how this happened. The first book about this idea was written by Darwin and published in 1859.

1 Describe how one characteristic of African elephants has evolved.

We can think about Darwin's idea as a series of stages, as follows.

- **Genetic variation**: the characteristics of individuals vary (due to differences in genes).
- Environmental change: conditions in an area change. For example, the lack of a resource (such as food) causes more **competition** between organisms.
- **Natural selection**: by chance, the variations of some individuals make them better at coping with the change than others, and more likely to survive (also called 'survival of the fittest').
- Inheritance: the survivors breed and pass on their variations to their offspring. So the next generation contains more individuals with the 'better-adapted variations'.
- Evolution: if the environmental conditions remain changed, natural selection occurs over and over again, and a new species evolves with all the individuals having the 'better-adapted variations'.

2 Suggest a characteristic that shows genetic variation in elephants.

Temperature range over which *Primelephas* individuals survived

1. Most *Primelephas* were best adapted to medium temperatures. However, in conditions of medium temperature and ample resources, *all* the animals in the population could survive and reproduce.	2. Some *Primelephas* were better adapted to colder temperatures because they had more hair. When the area in which they were living became colder, more of these animals survived and reproduced.

B When conditions change, some individuals are better adapted to cope than others.

Woolly mammoths and elephants evolved from the same animal; they share a common **ancestor**. Scientists think that an area in which this ancestor lived started getting colder. Due to genetic variation, some animals by chance had hairier skin. They were more likely to survive the cold than less hairy animals, especially when food was scarce. More of these individuals survived and bred. Over time the animals became hairier and hairier, forming a new species.

 3 Suggest why elephants with longer trunks survive better than others when there is not much food.

 4 Give the name of the common ancestor of elephants and woolly mammoths.

 5 Large ears help animals to cool down. Suggest an explanation for how African elephants evolved large ears.

Faster evolution

In the 1940s and 1950s, a substance called warfarin was used to poison rats. When it was first used, most rats died, but within 10 years most rats were **resistant** to (not affected by) warfarin. Due to genetic variation there had always been some rats that were resistant. As the poison killed the non-resistant rats, the only ones left to breed were resistant.

The same thing has happened with bacteria and **antibiotics** (drugs that kill bacteria). In a population of bacteria, some bacteria are more resistant than others and take longer to be killed. People who take an antibiotic to treat an infection often stop taking it too early, because they feel better. This leaves resistant bacteria still alive. They reproduce and spread, causing infections that cannot be treated with the antibiotic because all the bacteria are now resistant.

This problem of resistance in bacteria was not present when antibiotics were first used.

 7 Explain how antibiotic resistance in bacteria provides evidence to support Darwin's theory.

Bacteria in a population show variation in the amount of resistance to an antibiotic.

With time, the antibiotic kills more and more of the bacteria. The most resistant bacteria take the longest to die.

course of antibiotics is started

course of antibiotics is finished too early

The resistant bacteria survive and reproduce. The new population of bacteria are all now resistant to the antibiotic.

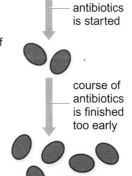

key

low resistance   high resistance

D Stopping an antibiotic early can cause resistance to develop in a species of bacterium.

Did you know?

There are many ideas for why elephants evolved trunks. One idea is that trunks act like snorkels, allowing elephants to swim in deep water or hide underwater from predators on land.

C

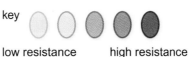 **6 a** What environmental change in the 1940s and 1950s caused rats to evolve?

b What allowed the rats to evolve?

Checkpoint

How confidently can you answer the Progression questions?

Strengthen

S1 List the stages of evolution and use each stage to show how bacteria develop antibiotic resistance.

Extend

E1 Ground finches have large, powerful beaks to crush seeds. A closely related species has a narrow beak for probing in small holes for insect larvae. Suggest how this species could have evolved from the seed-eating species.

Exam-style question

Wolbachia bacteria kill male blue moon butterflies. The bacteria arrived in the Samoan Islands in the late 1990s and, by 2001, only 1 per cent of the butterflies were male. Today, 50 per cent of the butterflies are male, as expected. Explain what has happened.   *(3 marks)*

CB4c Classification

Specification reference: B4.7

Progression questions

- How are organisms classified as five kingdoms?
- How has genetic analysis changed our understanding of evolution?
- How are organisms classified as three domains?

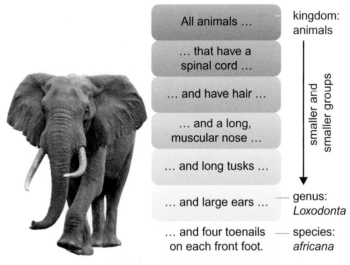

A Classification today is still based on Linnaeus' original system.

In 1735, Carl Linnaeus published his **classification** system, dividing organisms into groups based on what they looked like. His largest groups (**kingdoms**) were plants and animals, which were divided into ever smaller and smaller groups. The characteristics of the organisms in a group got more and more similar as the groups got smaller and smaller. The last group contained one type of organism. Linnaeus used the two last groups (**genus** and **species**) to give each organism its binomial name.

Using characteristics for classification causes problems for organisms that have evolved similar characteristics but which are not closely related. Once scientists accepted the idea of evolution, they started to work out how different organisms had evolved and to alter the classification system so that the smaller groups contained organisms that had all evolved from recent common ancestors.

 1 **a** What kingdom do African elephants belong to?

 b What genus do they belong to?

 c What is their scientific name?

 2 Suggest why some people used to think that bats should be classified in the same group as birds.

 3 **a** Look at photo B. Suggest why the fossa was originally grouped with cats.

 b Suggest a piece of evidence that might have been used to show that the fossa should not be in this group.

B The fossa (from Madagascar) was classified with cats in the past. We now know that it evolved from a different ancestor to cats.

Together with an understanding of evolution, scientists since Linnaeus' time have been able to look at organisms in much greater detail, which has also helped to improve classification. Linnaeus had two kingdoms, but today we often use five kingdoms based on what the cells of organisms look like.

4 Green seaweeds do not have cellulose cell walls but do photosynthesise.

   a Suggest why seaweeds were once thought to be plants.

   b Give one reason why seaweeds are no longer classified as plants.

In the 1970s, scientists started to find examples of a new group of single-celled organisms. The cells had no nuclei, and so scientists put them into the prokaryote kingdom, as a group called Archaea.

However, scientists later found that certain Archaea genes were more similar to the genes of plants and animals than those of prokaryotes. The development of genetic analysis also showed that all organisms *apart from* prokaryotes have unused sections of DNA in their genes. Most of a gene is used to make a protein, but these 'unused' sections do not help with this. Archaea were found to have genes containing unused sections. This led Carl Woese (1928–2012) to propose that all organisms should be divided into three **domains**:

- Archaea (cells with no nucleus, genes contain unused sections of DNA)
- Bacteria (cells with no nucleus, no unused sections in genes)
- Eukarya (cells with a nucleus, unused sections in genes).

DNA changes slowly over time and so, by looking at these changes, scientists can work out how closely related two organisms are. The more DNA two organisms have in common, the more recently they evolved from a common ancestor and the more closely related they are. As DNA analysis gets faster and more precise, our classification system is updated to reflect new discoveries.

Kingdom	Main charateristics
animals	multicellular (with cells arranged as tissues and organs), cells have nuclei, no cell walls
plants	multicellular (with cells arranged as tissues and organs), have chloroplasts for photosynthesis, cells have nuclei, cellulose cell walls
fungi	multicellular (apart from yeasts), live in or on the dead matter on which they feed, cells have nuclei, cell walls contain chitin (not cellulose)
protists	mostly unicellular (a few are multicellular), cells have nuclei, some have cell walls (made of different substances but not chitin)
prokaryotes	unicellular, cells do not have nuclei, flexible cell walls

C the five-kingdom system of classification

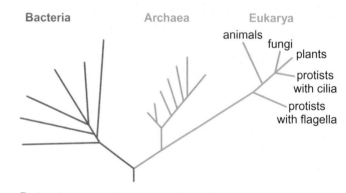

D the three-domain system of classification

 5 Which is more recent, the common ancestor of Eukarya and Archaea, or of Eukarya and Bacteria? Explain your answer with reference to diagram D.

 6 What is meant by 'genetic analysis'?

 7 Explain why all members of the animal kingdom are in the Eukarya domain.

 8 Explain why Archaea are no longer grouped with other bacteria.

Exam-style question

Explain how advances in technology have changed the classification of organisms.   *(2 marks)*

Checkpoint

How confidently can you answer the Progression questions?

Strengthen

S1 State two things that scientists examine in order to put organisms into groups.

Extend

E1 Explain why Archaea were placed in their own domain only after genetic analysis became available.

CB4d Breeds and varieties

Specification reference: B4.8; B4.10

Progression questions

- What are the ways in which we create new breeds and varieties?
- How is selective breeding carried out?
- Why do we genetically engineer organisms?

A a mouflon – the ancestor of domestic sheep

By chance, some individuals inherit characteristics that allow them to survive better than others in a certain area. This is natural selection. **Artificial selection** is when humans choose certain organisms because they have useful characteristics, such as sheep with thick wool.

About 8000 years ago, people started to look for wild sheep that were naturally hairier than others and to breed them together. They then selected the most hairy offspring and used them to breed. By repeating this over and over again, they eventually ended up with woolly sheep. Breeding organisms in this way is called **selective breeding**. It is still done today to produce new **breeds** of animal species and new **varieties** of plant species.

 1 Suggest two characteristics a cattle breeder might select for.

 2 Explain how a goat that produces more milk could be selectively bred.

One of the first plants to be selectively bred was wheat, about 12 000 years ago. Wild wheat plants produce few grains (seeds), and the grains fall off the plant when ripe. So early farmers selectively bred new varieties of wheat that had more grains that stayed on the plants, making them easier to harvest.

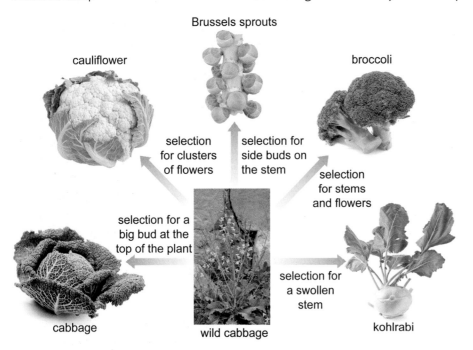

B Selective breeding of wild cabbage has produced many vegetables – all varieties of the same species.

Plants and animals are often selectively bred for:

- **disease resistance** (how well they cope with diseases)
- **yield** (how much useful product they make)
- coping with certain environmental conditions
- fast growth
- flavour.

 3 Suggest two characteristics a wheat breeder might select for.

 4 Explain how kohlrabi has been selectively bred.

Genetic engineering

Genetic engineering involves changing the DNA of one organism (its **genome**), often by inserting **genes** from another. This creates **genetically modified organisms** (**GMOs**). The process is much faster than artificial selection but much more expensive.

Golden Rice is a GMO with two genes inserted into its genome, one from a daffodil and one from a bacterium. They allow the rice to produce beta-carotene in its grains. Humans need beta-carotene to make vitamin A, a lack of which can cause blindness. The scientists who created Golden Rice hope that it can be grown by farmers in poorer parts of the world where vitamin A deficiency is a problem.

C Beta-carotene makes Golden Rice yellower than normal rice.

Some GMOs are resistant to disease-causing organisms, and others grow larger and faster than normal. Scientists are developing GM goats and sheep to produce proteins in their milk that can treat human diseases. GM pigs are being developed with human-like organs to use in organ transplants.

 5 Explain how Golden Rice could help reduce blindness in poorer parts of the world.

D The AquAdvantage salmon grow much faster than normal.

GM bacteria make a range of useful substances, including antibiotics and other medicines.

 6 Explain why some farmers want to grow GM crops.

 7 Milk contains lysozyme – an enzyme that prevents harmful bacteria growing in the intestines. Human breast milk contains 2500 times more lysozyme than cow's milk. Describe two ways of producing cows that make milk containing a lot of lysozyme.

 8 Explain why genetic engineering changes a species' genome but artificial selection does not.

Exam-style question

Scientists have created a goat that produces spider silk in its milk. Explain how the scientists would have done this. *(2 marks)*

Did you know?

Most cheese is made using enzymes produced by GM bacteria.

Checkpoint

How confidently can you answer the Progression questions?

Strengthen

S1 People with haemophilia lack a blood protein called Factor VIII, so their blood does not clot properly. They can be treated with Factor VIII from donated blood, but this is expensive. Describe how another organism could be used to make Factor VIII more cheaply.

Extend

E1 Compare and contrast the use of selective breeding and genetic engineering in agriculture.

CB4e Genes in agriculture and medicine

Specification reference: **H** B4.11; B4.14

Progression questions

- What are the benefits and risks of selective breeding?
- What are the benefits and risks of genetic engineering?
- **H** How is genetic engineering carried out?

A Merino sheep have been bred to grow lots of fine wool. This one was found wearing a 40 kg fleece.

B Nearly half of all banana plants are one variety. A fungus is now threatening to destroy them.

Did you know?

Scottish scientist Helen Sang has produced GM chickens that lay eggs containing proteins that can be used to treat cancer.

Organisms are selectively bred or genetically engineered to grow faster, cope with environmental conditions, increase yields or make new products. However, there are drawbacks.

 1 Define the term 'GMO'.

Selective breeding risks

Genes exist in different forms, called **alleles**, which cause variation in characteristics. For example, the different alleles in wild wheat plants cause different seed sizes. In selective breeding, only certain alleles are selected. Others become rare or disappear. So, alleles that might be useful in the future are no longer available.

Farming huge numbers of the same breed or variety is also a problem. All the organisms are very similar and so if a change in conditions (e.g. a new disease) affects one organism, all the others are affected.

Animal welfare is a further concern. For example, some selectively bred chickens produce so much breast meat they can hardly stand up.

 2 **a** What is an allele?

 b Why does it matter if alleles are lost from a species?

 3 In the 1840s, many Irish families grew one variety of potato for food. Suggest why a disease (potato blight) caused mass starvation in Ireland at this time.

 4 Suggest why scientists now save the seeds of thousands of different plant varieties in seed banks.

Genetic engineering issues

GM crops have been produced to be resistant to some insects (so less insecticide is needed). Others are resistant to certain herbicides (weed killers) which then kill weeds but not the crop. These herbicides do not affect animals and are very effective against weeds, so less herbicide is used. However, the seeds for many GM plants are expensive. Some people think that GM crops will reproduce with wild plant varieties and pass on their resistance genes, and these genes may also have unknown consequences in wild plants. Others think that eating GM organisms may be bad for health (but there is not evidence to support this).

GM bacteria produce many useful substances, such as **insulin** (needed to treat **type 1 diabetes**). Insulin used to be extracted from dead pigs and cows, but insulin from GM bacteria is cheaper and suitable for vegans or people who do not eat pork or beef for religious reasons. However, it is slightly different to insulin from mammals and so not all diabetics can use it.

 5 a State a benefit of Golden Rice (see *CB4d Breeds and varieties*).

 b Suggest why some people are against growing Golden Rice.

 6 Suggest a problem of wild plants becoming resistant to a herbicide.

C Campaigners often destroy GM crops during trials.

H Genetic engineering of bacteria

A bacterium has one large loop of DNA (containing most of its genes) and some small circles of DNA, called **plasmids**. To genetically engineer bacteria, additional genes are added to a plasmid. The plasmid is made of DNA combined in a new way and so it is an example of **recombinant DNA**.

Scientists use **restriction enzymes** to cut a useful gene out of an organism's DNA. This cutting leaves strands of DNA with jagged ends, called **sticky ends**. If two sticky ends match, they can be joined together using an enzyme called **ligase**. Diagram D shows the process.

Any DNA molecule used to carry new DNA into another cell is called a **vector**.

1 Restriction enzymes make staggered cuts in DNA molecules, producing sections with a few unpaired **bases** at each end – 'sticky ends'. A section of DNA containing the gene for making insulin is cut from a human chromosome in this way.

2 Restriction enzymes are also used to cut plasmids open. By using the same restriction enzyme as was used on the human chromosome DNA, the cut plasmids have the same sticky ends.

3 Sections of DNA containing the insulin gene are mixed with the cut plasmids. The complementary bases on the sticky ends pair up. An enzyme called ligase is used to join the ends together.

4 The plasmids are then inserted back into bacteria, which are then grown in huge tanks. The insulin they now make can easily be extracted.

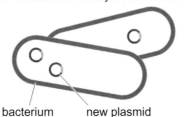

bacterium   new plasmid

D genetic engineering of a bacterium

 7 a Draw a flow chart to describe how to genetically engineer a bacterium.

 b What vector is used in this process?

Checkpoint

How confidently can you answer the Progression questions?

Strengthen

S1 Discuss how a farmer might decide whether or not to plant a large area with one variety of wheat that is suited to that area.

Extend

E1 **H** Explain the importance of using just one type of restriction enzyme in genetic engineering.

Exam-style question

Describe the advantages of making insulin using genetically modified bacteria rather than extracting it from animals. *(2 marks)*

Genetic engineering

The European corn borer damages maize crops in the south of the UK. Discuss whether farmers should be allowed to grow genetically modified corn that is resistant to this insect in the UK.

(6 marks)

Student answer

There are advantages and disadvantages to GM corn [1]. The GM corn is resistant to European corn borers [2]. This GM corn is good because it kills a pest and so less pesticide is needed, but there are other pests and so some pesticide will still be needed [3]. Some people think GM will be bad for them [4].

[1] For a discussion question, first think about the problem that is being addressed in the question. This is a good start since there are pros and cons that need to be thought about when reaching a decision.

[2] Avoid repeating information given in the question.

[3] Excellent point, stating an advantage and explaining why it is an advantage and then going on to balance that up with a disadvantage.

[4] Another disadvantage, but why people think GM will be bad for them is not explained (e.g. may cause allergies).

Verdict

This is an acceptable answer. It gives both an advantage and a disadvantage of the GM corn.

It would be better if there were a few more advantages and disadvantages, and if there was more scientific detail. For example, the answer could contain more detail on why people do not want to eat GM crops. The answer talks about the fact that less pesticide is needed if the GM crops are grown, but it could also then go on to explain that pesticides can be harmful. This would show that the student can link scientific ideas.

Exam tip

A question that says 'Discuss …' really means 'What do you think about … ?'. Write down a couple of points 'for' and a couple of points 'against'. Then build an argument around these. Don't be scared to say what you think, but you need to back up your ideas with scientific information.

Paper 1

CB5 Health, Disease and the Development of Medicines

Hidekichi Miyazaki set a record of 42.22 seconds for the 100 m sprint at the age of 105. Miyazaki put his success down to daily exercise and eating healthily.

In the UK, between 2002 and 2012 there was a 73 per cent increase in the number of people living beyond 100 years. There are similar increases in other parts of the world. Although governments are concerned that the cost of looking after older people will also increase, people are living healthily and are active to a much older age than before. Maybe one day we will see sporting competitions just for those over 100.

The learning journey

Previously you will have learnt at KS3:

- that imbalances in the diet can lead to obesity and deficiency diseases
- that recreational drugs (such as alcohol) can affect behaviour, health and life processes.

You will also have learnt in *CB1 Key Concepts in Biology*:

- about the structure of bacteria
- about the use of microscopes to study cells.

In this unit you will learn:

- about how we define health
- about some pathogens and the diseases they cause
- how the spread of pathogens can be reduced or prevented
- how the body is protected against infection
- about the immune system
- how antibiotics work
- how new medicines are developed.

CB5a Health and disease

Specification reference: B5.1; B5.2; B5.3

Progression questions

- What is health?
- How do communicable and non-communicable diseases differ?
- Why can having one disease increase the chance of getting another disease?

A Physical fitness improves physical well-being. Exercising as part of a group can also improve your social and mental well-being.

 1 Use your own words to define the term 'good health'.

The World Health Organization (WHO) is responsible for coordinating ways to improve **health** across the world. According to the organisation, good health means more than simply feeling well; it is a state of 'complete physical, social and mental well-being'.

- Physical well-being includes being free from **disease**, eating and sleeping well, getting regular activity, and limiting the intake of harmful substances such as alcohol and drugs.
- Social well-being includes how well you get on with other people, and also how your surroundings affect you.
- Mental well-being includes how you feel about yourself.

These three categories of well-being are not separate – improving one category can also improve the others.

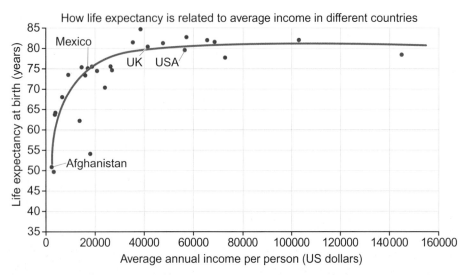

B Graph showing a link (correlation) between income and the average age of death (life expectancy) for people living in different countries.

Graph B shows a **correlation** between health and income: the smaller someone's income, the less likely they are to live for a long time. However, we cannot be entirely sure of the **cause** of this correlation. It may be because poorer people cannot afford as healthy a diet, or access to the same medical care, as those with more money. In regions where there are disasters such as floods or wars, people are also more likely to have poor health because it is likely there will be more disease and fewer doctors and hospitals.

 3 Explain what is meant by a correlation between two factors.

 4 a Describe what the shape of the curve in graph B shows.

 b Suggest a reason for the correlation shown in graph B. Explain your answer.

A disease is a problem with a structure or process in the body that is not the result of injury. A disease might be due to microorganisms getting into the body and changing how it works. For example, the flu virus can cause a high temperature, sneezing and aches and pains. Microorganisms that cause diseases are called **pathogens**. Diseases caused by pathogens are **communicable diseases**, as they can be passed from an infected person to other people.

Some diseases are **non-communicable**, because they are not passed from person to person. They are caused by a problem in the body, such as a fault in the genes (as in cystic fibrosis) or as a result of the way we live – our **lifestyle**.

Diseases may be correlated, so that having one disease means a person is more likely to have another disease. Possible causes of these correlations include:

- one disease damages the **immune system**, making it easier for other pathogens to cause disease (the immune system protects the body from communicable diseases; one pathogen that attacks the immune system is the HIV virus)
- a disease damages the body's natural barriers and defences, allowing pathogens to get into the body more easily
- a disease stops an organ system from working effectively, making other diseases more likely to occur.

 5 a Periodontal disease is correlated with heart disease. Describe this correlation.

 b Suggest a cause of this correlation.

Exam-style question

Describe the difference between communicable and non-communicable diseases. Use an example of each in your description. *(2 marks)*

 2 Suggest how exercising regularly as part of a group can improve:

 a your physical well-being

b your social well-being

 c your mental well-being.

Did you know?

Brushing your teeth well protects against periodontal disease, caused by bacteria stuck in plaque between teeth. It can also help protect against other diseases such as heart disease.

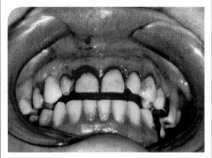

C Periodontal disease causes bleeding gums. Pathogens in the mouth can enter the blood and circulatory system where gums are bleeding.

Checkpoint

How confidently can you answer the Progression questions?

Strengthen

S1 Suggest why somebody infected with the HIV virus is more likely than people without the virus to get other communicable diseases.

Extend

E1 Suggest why where you live might affect how long you live for.

CB5b Non-communicable diseases

Progression questions

- What do non-communicable diseases have in common?
- How can diet affect malnutrition?
- Why does alcohol cause problems for people and for society?

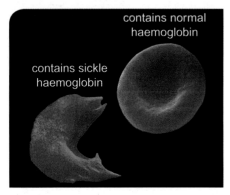

A Sickle-shaped red blood cells are caused by a mutation in a gene that codes for haemoglobin. A person with two sickle mutant alleles suffers from sickle cell disease.

 2 Suggest how scurvy should be treated. Explain your answer.

 3 Suggest why kwashiorkor is usually only seen in people living in very poor parts of the world.

 4 Explain why deficiency diseases are examples of malnutrition.

Did you know?

Rickets used to be thought of as a disease of the past in the UK, but studies show it is increasing again, particularly in the under-fives. A poor diet may be only part of the problem. Rickets can also be caused by a lack of sunlight because vitamin D is produced naturally in the skin when in sunshine.

There are several different types of non-communicable disease. One type is **genetic disorder** (genetic disease) caused by faulty alleles of genes. Genetic disorders can be passed to offspring but not to any other person.

 1 Explain why sickle cell disease is a non-communicable disease.

Other non-communicable diseases occur as a result of poor diet or **malnutrition**. Malnutrition occurs when you get too little or too much of particular nutrients from your food. The lack of a certain nutrient can cause a specific **deficiency disease**.

Nutrient	Disease caused by deficiency of nutrient	Symptoms of disease	Good sources in diet
protein	kwashiorkor	enlarged belly, small muscles, failure to grow properly	meat, fish, dairy, eggs, pulses (e.g. lentils)
vitamin C	scurvy	swelling and bleeding gums, muscle and joint pain, tiredness	citrus fruits (e.g. oranges) and some vegetables (e.g. broccoli)
vitamin D and/or calcium	rickets or osteomalacia	soft bones, curved leg bones	vitamin D: oily fish calcium: dairy products
iron	anaemia	red blood cells that are smaller than normal and in reduced number, tiredness	red meat, dark green leafy vegetables, egg yolk

B some diseases caused by lack of particular nutrients

Alcohol and disease

Some diseases are caused by how we choose to live – our lifestyle. This includes whether we take enough exercise and whether we take drugs. Ethanol, found in alcoholic drinks, is a **drug** because it changes the way the body works. Ethanol is broken down by the liver, and a large amount of ethanol taken over a long period can lead to liver disease, including **cirrhosis**.

A cirrhotic liver does not function well and can result in death. Liver disease is the fifth largest cause of death in the UK. Deaths from alcohol-related liver disease have increased by 450 per cent in the last 30 years in the UK. The cost of treating people with liver disease is more than £500 million each year and is still rising.

5 Explain why liver disease is a non-communicable disease.

6 Explain why there is a Drink Awareness campaign in the UK aimed at limiting the amount of alcohol people drink.

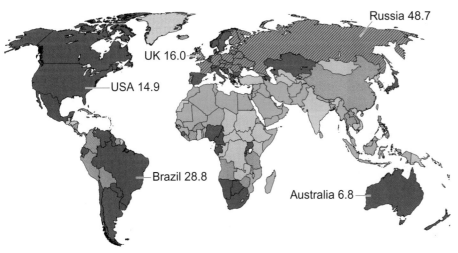

Alcohol (dm³) per person per year

- <2.50
- 2.50–4.99
- 5.00–7.49
- 7.50–9.99
- 10.00–12.49
- ≥12.50
- Data not available

D Global map of alcohol consumption in different countries. Death rates (number per 100 000 people) from liver disease are labelled for five countries.

7 Look at map D.

a Put the named countries in order (starting with the highest value) of:

i deaths from liver disease

ii consumption of alcohol per year.

b What do your lists from part **a** suggest about the correlation between deaths from liver disease and alcohol consumption? Explain your answer.

Exam-style question

Explain how a person's diet can cause anaemia. *(2 marks)*

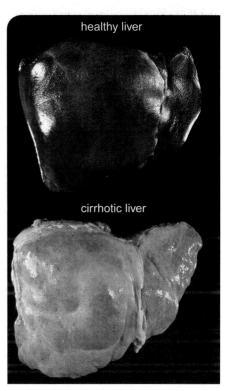

C A healthy liver is dark red, smooth and soft. A liver that has cirrhosis may be paler and larger, rough and much harder.

Checkpoint

How confidently can you answer the Progression questions?

Strengthen

S1 Give one reason why too much alcohol over a long time is a problem for each of the following.
- the person who drinks it
- their family
- the society they live in

Extend

E1 The UK Department of Health recommends that all children from six months to five years should take vitamin D drops every day to supplement their diet. Discuss the advantages and disadvantages of this advice.

CB5c Cardiovascular disease

Specification reference: B5.24; B5.25

Progression questions

- What is cardiovascular disease?
- What effect do smoking and obesity have on the risk of developing cardiovascular disease?
- Why are there a range of treatments for cardiovascular disease?

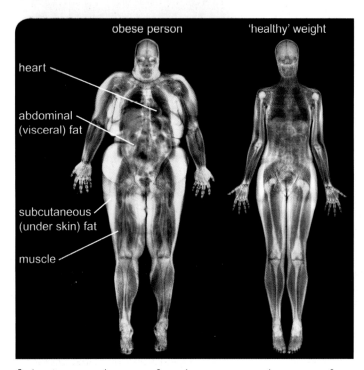

A the tissues and organs of an obese person and a person of healthy mass ('weight')

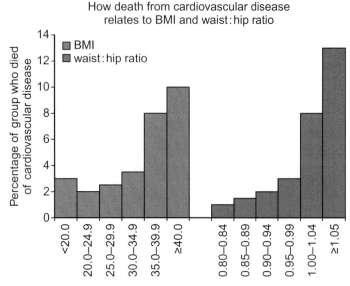

B correlation between BMI and waist:hip ratio with death caused by cardiovascular disease for over 4000 Australian men

Malnutrition caused by a diet that is high in sugars and fats can lead to **obesity**, where large amounts of fat are formed under the skin and around organs such as the heart and kidneys.

We need some fat to cushion organs when we move, to store some vitamins, and to provide a store of energy. Too much fat can increase the risk of many diseases, including **cardiovascular disease**. Cardiovascular disease is a result of the circulatory system functioning poorly. One sign of this is high blood pressure, which can lead to heart pain or even a **heart attack**.

 1 Define the term 'obesity'.

Measuring the amount of fat on the body is difficult, so it is estimated using other measures. **Body mass index (BMI)** for adults uses height (in metres) and mass (in kilograms) in the formula:

$$BMI = \frac{mass}{height^2}$$

When BMI is used to predict the amount of fat, it assumes that the mass of other body tissues is in proportion to height. An adult who has a BMI of 30 or more is usually considered obese.

 2 Explain why a BMI of 30 or more is used as a predictor of cardiovascular disease.

 3 Explain why BMI is not a good predictor of body fat for a weightlifter with large muscles.

The fat that seems to be most closely linked with cardiovascular disease is abdominal fat. Dividing waist measurement by hip measurement to get **waist-to-hip (waist:hip) ratio** gives a better method of measuring abdominal fat than BMI.

4 Use the evidence in chart B to explain why waist:hip ratio is better than BMI when looking at death caused by cardiovascular disease.

Smoking and disease

Tobacco smoke contains many harmful substances that can damage the lungs when they are breathed in. Some of these substances are absorbed from the lungs into the blood and are transported around the body. These substances can damage blood vessels (diagram C), increase blood pressure, make blood vessels narrower and increase the risk of blood clots forming in blood vessels. All of these can lead to cardiovascular disease.

Substances from tobacco smoke damage the artery lining.

Fat builds up in the artery wall at the site of damage, making the artery narrower.

A blood clot may block the artery here, or break off and block an artery in another part of the body – causing a heart attack or **stroke**.

C Damage to blood vessels by substances from tobacco smoke can cause the build-up of fat in an artery.

Treating cardiovascular disease

High blood pressure increases the risk of cardiovascular disease. A doctor may advise a patient with high blood pressure to exercise more and give up smoking. If blood pressure is very high, then the patient may be given medicines to reduce it.

A narrowed blood vessel can be widened by inserting a small mesh tube (**stent**) at the narrowest part to hold it open. Blocked arteries in the heart can be bypassed by inserting other blood vessels so that the heart tissue is supplied with oxygen and nutrients again. Patients who have these operations may have to take medicines for the rest of their lives to help prevent a heart attack or stroke.

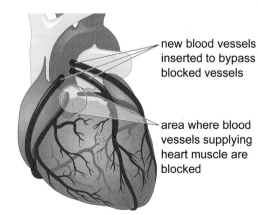
new blood vessels inserted to bypass blocked vessels

area where blood vessels supplying heart muscle are blocked

D Blocked blood vessels can be bypassed by inserting new blood vessels.

Exam-style question

State and explain two methods of treating cardiovascular disease. *(2 marks)*

Did you know?

Nicholas Culpeper's book *Complete Herbal* (published in 1653) recommended eating garlic to 'provoke urine' and to treat digestive problems caused by 'drinking stinking waters'. Current research suggests eating garlic can help reduce fat in arteries and so reduce blood pressure.

5 Sketch a flowchart to show how smoking can lead to cardiovascular disease.

6 Heart muscle has its own blood supply through coronary arteries. Explain why narrowed or blocked coronary arteries must be bypassed to avoid cardiovascular disease.

Checkpoint

How confidently can you answer the Progression questions?

Strengthen

S1 Explain why a doctor may advise a patient with a high BMI to give up smoking and to exercise more.

Extend

E1 Explain why 'prevention is better than cure' is a good approach to the problem of cardiovascular disease.

CB5d Pathogens

Specification reference: B5.4; B5.5

Progression questions

- Which groups of organisms include pathogens?
- Which pathogens cause some common infections?
- What are the symptoms of some common infections?

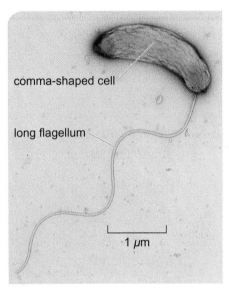

A The bacterium *Vibrio cholerae* is the pathogen that causes cholera.

comma-shaped cell

long flagellum

1 µm

B Visible symptoms of chalara ash dieback include lesions on the trunk and branches, leaves dying earlier than usual and dieback of the crown (top branches) of the tree.

lesion caused by chalara dieback fungus

In 1854, there was a major outbreak of a disease called **cholera** in Florence, Italy. Cholera causes severe **diarrhoea** (watery faeces). Filippo Pacini (1812–1883) was the first person to isolate a bacterium from people with cholera, and to suggest that the bacterium caused the disease.

Pacini's work was not well known, but in 1883 Robert Koch (1843–1910) proved that *Vibrio cholerae* caused the disease. Koch showed that the bacterium was always found in the diarrhoea from people with cholera but not in the diarrhoea from people with other diseases.

Koch also showed that the disease **tuberculosis** (**TB**) is caused by a different bacterium, which was called *Mycobacterium tuberculosis*. This bacterium infects and damages the lungs, resulting in blood-specked mucus after coughing, fever (high body temperature) and weight loss.

 1 What is the general term for a microorganism that causes a disease?

 2 Why are diseases caused by microorganisms called communicable diseases?

 3 What symptoms are shown by someone infected with the TB bacterium?

Both cholera and TB are communicable diseases of humans. We say that humans are their **host**. However, every kind of organism may be infected by microorganisms. Plants are often infected by fungi. **Chalara dieback** is a disease of ash trees caused by a fungus. Chalara was first spotted in the UK in early 2012, and woodlands are being closely surveyed to monitor its spread.

One of the greatest causes of human death through infection is **malaria**. Every year there are between 124 million and 283 million cases of malaria, and up to 755 000 people die of the disease. Malaria is caused by a **protist**, called *Plasmodium*, which multiplies inside red blood cells and liver cells. When new protists break out of these cells, it causes fever, weakness and sickness.

Did you know?

Until antibiotics were developed, people with TB were isolated in specialist TB hospitals for up to a year, to help them recover and to protect others from infection.

 4 a Calculate the lowest and highest possible percentage of deaths worldwide from malaria each year.

 b Describe the signs of malaria.

Viruses

Viruses are not true organisms, because they do not have a cellular structure. They multiply by infecting a cell and taking over the cell's DNA-copying processes to make new viruses. Different viruses infect different organisms, including bacteria.

Virus infections often affect many parts of the body at the same time. For example, the Ebola virus causes the breakdown of blood vessels and liver and kidney cells. This leads to internal bleeding (haemorrhaging) and fever, so causing **haemorrhagic fever**.

The **human immunodeficiency virus** (**HIV**) attacks and destroys **white blood cells** in the immune system. People infected with HIV often develop **AIDS** (**acquired immune deficiency syndrome**) because their immune systems cannot protect them from **secondary infections**. Many people die from these other infections, including TB.

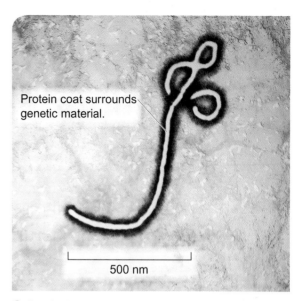

Protein coat surrounds genetic material.

500 nm

C The Ebola virus particle is an unusually large virus.

 5 Calculate how many times longer a *Vibrio* bacterium is than an Ebola virus.

6 Look at diagram D.

 a Calculate the percentage of people with TB who are also infected with HIV.

 b Explain why people infected with HIV may also suffer from TB.

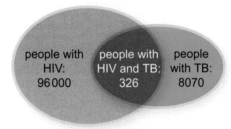

people with HIV: 96 000 | people with HIV and TB: 326 | people with TB: 8070

D Venn diagram showing cases of HIV and TB in the UK in 2011

Hidden pathogens

Many types of bacteria live in our bodies. Some are essential for our health, but others may not affect us most of the time. For example, over 50 per cent of people have *Helicobacter pylori* bacteria in their stomachs. Over 80 per cent of these people never show symptoms of disease caused by these bacteria, but others may develop sore areas, called **ulcers**, where the bacteria attack the stomach lining.

 7 Describe a negative effect of *Helicobacter pylori* on humans.

Exam-style question

Describe a communicable disease caused by **(a)** a fungus, **(b)** a protist, and describe the symptoms of each disease. Use one example for each answer.

(2 marks)

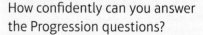

Checkpoint

How confidently can you answer the Progression questions?

Strengthen

S1 Draw up a table with the following headings: Name of disease, Name of pathogen, Type of pathogen, Host organism, Symptoms of disease. Complete the table with all the examples of diseases on these two pages.

Extend

E1 Explain how Koch's evidence to support the idea that *Vibrio cholerae* was the cause of cholera was better than Pacini's.

CB5e Spreading pathogens

Specification reference: B5.6

Progression questions

- How can pathogens spread?
- What is a vector of disease?
- How can the spread of pathogens be reduced or prevented?

A The 'catch it, bin it, kill it' slogan encourages people to use tissues and wash their hands when infected with a disease such as flu. The idea is to stop the spread of many pathogens that are spread through the air.

 2 Explain why it was difficult to prevent the spread of chalara ash dieback into the UK.

Most pathogens cannot grow outside their host, and so must spread from one host to another so they can increase in number. If we know how pathogens are spread, then we can find ways of stopping that spread.

Infections such as colds, flu and tuberculosis (TB) cause a person to sneeze or cough. This sends droplets containing pathogens into the air. Once in the air, flu viruses can survive for about a day. However, TB bacteria can survive for months in air, and mix with dust that can blow around and infect another person. Fungi, such as that causing chalara ash dieback, can also spread in the air, as tiny tough spores (cells that can grow into new organisms). Strong winds can carry chalara spores over long distances, such as to the southern UK from nearby Europe.

 1 **a** Look at photo A. Explain how the 'catch it, bin it, kill it' idea could help to reduce the spread of TB bacteria.

 b Suggest one other method that could be used to reduce the number of TB bacteria in the environment.

Some pathogens spread in water, such as the bacteria that cause cholera, typhoid and dysentery (which all cause severe diarrhoea). These diseases are normally rare in developed countries, because the water that we use for drinking, cooking and washing is treated to kill pathogens. Keeping things clean to remove or kill pathogens is known as good **hygiene**. Outbreaks of these diseases occur when hygiene is difficult, such as in very poor areas, after major environmental disasters, or in refugee camps.

Did you know?

At the time that Pacini identified the cholera bacterium, John Snow was mapping the outbreaks of cholera in parts of London. The map he produced showed how cholera infections and water supply were linked.

B After a major earthquake in Haiti in 2010, pipes carrying clean water were broken, and people had to get their drinking water from polluted wells and rivers.

Pathogens of the digestive system can spread in food as well as water. They enter the body through the mouth, which is described as the **oral route**. *Helicobacter* bacteria are thought to be spread when people touch other people's food after touching their mouths, or after going to the toilet (oral-faecal transmission). The bacteria may also spread on the feet of flies that have fed on infected faeces and then landed on food.

 4 Suggest two ways in which the spread of *Helicobacter* could be reduced, and explain your answers.

A few pathogens, such as the Ebola virus, require extreme hygiene practices to control them. The virus very easily enters people's bodies through broken skin or the eyes, nose or mouth. The 2014–15 Ebola outbreak, which mainly affected West Africa, became an **epidemic** because many people became infected when burying those who had died from Ebola.

 5 Explain why normal hygiene practices, such as cleaning hands thoroughly, do not prevent the spread of Ebola.

Some pathogens cannot survive in the environment and so must spread in other ways. For example, the malaria protist is carried in blood by mosquitoes that sucked blood from an infected person. The mosquito injects the protist directly into the blood of the next person it feeds on. Organisms that carry pathogens from one person to the next are called **vectors** of disease. Controlling the spread of the pathogen may involve controlling the spread of the vector.

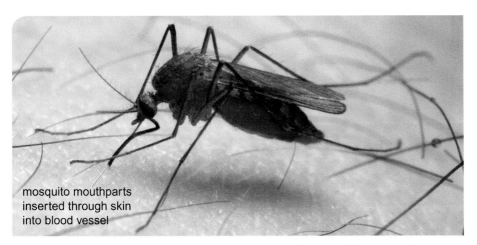

mosquito mouthparts inserted through skin into blood vessel

D Female *Anopheles* mosquitoes feed on human blood by piercing the skin with their mouthparts. The blood may also carry malaria protists.

 6 Explain why killing mosquitoes could help control the spread of malaria.

Exam-style question

Explain two ways that the spread of cholera in a refugee camp could be prevented. *(2 marks)*

 3 a Suggest why cholera spread after the 2010 Haiti earthquake.

 b Suggest hygiene practices that could have prevented this spread of cholera.

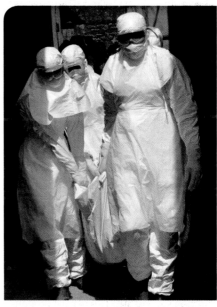

C The best way to avoid infection with the Ebola virus is by wearing full body protection, because the virus is present in all body fluids of infected people, even after death.

Checkpoint

How confidently can you answer the Progression questions?

Strengthen

S1 Explain why it is important to wash your hands thoroughly after going to the toilet.

Extend

E1 Explain how isolating infected people and wearing full-body protective clothing helped to bring the 2014–15 Ebola epidemic under control.

CB5f Physical and chemical barriers

Specification reference: B5.8; B5.12

Progression questions

- How do physical barriers of the body protect against infection?
- How do chemical barriers of the body protect against infection?
- How can the spread of sexually transmitted infections be reduced or prevented?

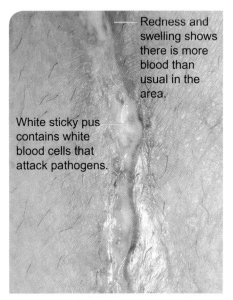

Redness and swelling shows there is more blood than usual in the area.

White sticky pus contains white blood cells that attack pathogens.

A Although blood clotting quickly blocks an open wound, infection by pathogens can cause swelling and the formation of pus as the body attacks the pathogen.

The body has many ways of defending against the attack of pathogens in the environment. The most obvious barrier is the skin, which is very thick over most of the body. Pathogens can usually only cross this barrier through wounds or by an animal vector that pierces the skin. The skin is a **physical barrier**, because pathogens have difficulty getting past it.

 1 Name one protist pathogen that is able to get through the skin barrier, and explain how it does this.

The skin has additional defences, because it contains glands that secrete substances onto the skin surface. These substances include **lysozyme**, which is an enzyme that breaks down the cell walls of some types of bacteria. Lysozyme is a **chemical defence**, because it reacts with substances in the pathogen and this kills the pathogens or makes them inactive.

Did you know?

Alexander Fleming named lysozyme in 1922, when he found mucus from the nose of a person with a cold killed bacterial colonies on an agar plate. Later work on lysozyme identified the way all enzymes work as biological catalysts.

 2 Explain why lysozyme is said to be a chemical defence of the body.

Lysozyme is secreted in tears (from the eyes), saliva (in the mouth), and in **mucus**, where it helps to protect the thinner surfaces of the body. Mucus is a sticky secretion produced by cells lining the many openings, such as the mouth and nose, that pathogens could use to enter the body. Dust and pathogens get trapped in the mucus.

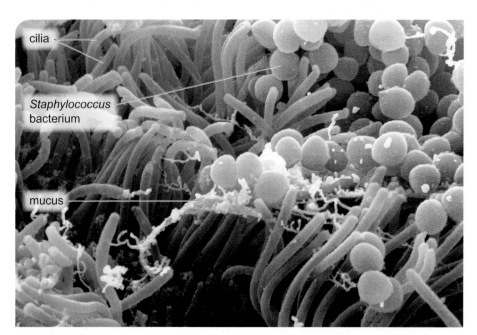

cilia

Staphylococcus bacterium

mucus

B *Staphylococcus* bacteria are trapped in mucus in the nose (magnification × 12 500). The mucus is then wafted by movement of the cilia to the back of the throat, where it can be swallowed.

 3 Is mucus a physical barrier or chemical defence of the body? Explain your answer.

Some of the cells that line the inside of the nose and tubes in the breathing system have cilia. **Ciliated cells** are specialised to move substances such as mucus across their surfaces. This helps to carry dust and pathogens away, either out of the body or into the throat, where they enter the digestive system.

Food, drink and mucus from the respiratory system all pass down the oesophagus (gullet) into the stomach. Some of the cells lining the stomach secrete **hydrochloric acid**, reducing the pH of the stomach contents to about 2. At this acidity, many pathogens are destroyed. Only a few types of bacteria, such as *Helicobacter pylori*, are adapted to survive in the stomach.

Sexually transmitted infections

The reproductive system has natural defences, such as lysozyme in vaginal fluid and mucus. However, some pathogens can overcome these defences. These pathogens are usually transmitted through sexual activity and are called **sexually transmitted infections (STIs)**. These include the HIV virus and the *Chlamydia* bacterium. Both of these pathogens can be spread by contact with sexual fluids (semen or vaginal fluid). This method of transmission can be reduced or prevented by avoiding direct contact with sexual fluids, such as by using a condom as an artificial barrier during sexual intercourse. Both of these pathogens may also be passed from a pregnant mother to her unborn baby, which can harm the baby. HIV may also be passed from an infected person to others in blood, such as through sharing needles when injecting drugs.

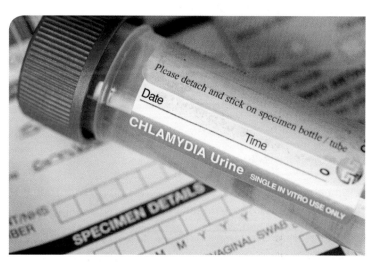

C A small sample of urine or a swab of sexual fluids can be used to screen for *Chlamydia*.

Many people with STIs are not aware that they are infected. **Screening** helps to identify an infection so that people can be treated for the disease. For example, there is a nationwide *Chlamydia* screening programme in the UK for people under 25. As a result, over 200 000 people are being diagnosed with *Chlamydia* each year, and the number of diagnosed new cases is rising. However, this may be due to more people being screened than before.

Blood given to people who have lost a lot of blood, such as during an operation, is first screened (checked) to make sure it does not contain HIV particles or other pathogens.

 6 Explain how screening for an STI can help to reduce spread of the infection.

 4 Explain how cilia help cells lining tubes in the lungs to carry out their function well.

 5 Explain why the stomach is a good defence against pathogens entering the body.

Checkpoint

How confidently can you answer the Progression questions?

Strengthen

S1 Millions of pathogens are breathed into the nose and mouth every day. Describe all the barriers and defences that the body has to prevent those pathogens causing disease.

Extend

E1 Almost 70 per cent of all *Chlamydia* diagnoses are in people under 25 years old. Suggest reasons for this, and explain your answers.

Exam-style question

Explain how one natural physical barrier and one chemical defence stop pathogens from entering the body. *(2 marks)*

CB5g The immune system

Specification reference: B5.13; B5.14

Progression questions

- What is the function of the immune system?
- What are the stages of response by the immune system to infection?
- How does immunisation protect the body from disease?

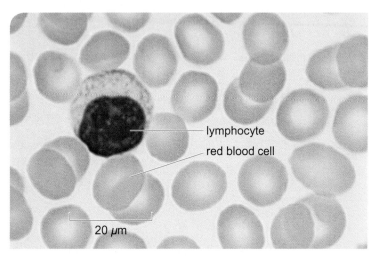

A Lymphocytes are one type of white blood cell. Their function in the immune system is to make antibodies. Different lymphocytes make different antibodies.

Sometimes pathogens manage to get through all the physical barriers and chemical defences of the body. Then the immune system becomes active, attacking the pathogens and trying to prevent them causing harm.

All cells and virus particles have molecules on their outer surface, called **antigens**. Cells from different organisms have different antigens. The immune system uses these antigens to identify if something inside the body is a cell of the body or has come from outside.

1 What is an antigen?

2 Explain why the immune system attacks pathogens but not other cells in the body.

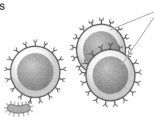

1 Pathogens have antigens on their surface that are unique to them.

These lymphocytes are not activated.

2 A lymphocyte with an antibody that perfectly fits the antigen is activated.

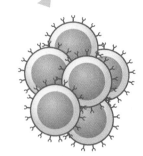

3 This lymphocyte divides over and over again to produce clones of identical lymphocytes.

4 Some of the lymphocytes secrete large amounts of antibodies. The antibodies stick to the antigens and destroy the pathogen.Other lymphocytes remain in the blood as memory lymphocytes, ready to respond immediately if the same antigen ever turns up again.

B how the immune system attacks a pathogen

White blood cells called **lymphocytes** have other molecules on their surface, called **antibodies**. A lymphocyte with antibodies on its surface that match the shape of the antigens on a pathogen will attach to the pathogen. This stops the pathogen from working. The lymphocyte is **activated** and will divide rapidly to produce many identical lymphocytes with the same antibodies. Some of these cells release large amounts of identical antibody molecules into the blood. The antibodies attach to pathogens with the matching antigens. This may kill the pathogens or cause other parts of the immune system to destroy them.

3 Explain why only some lymphocytes are activated by a pathogen.

When all the pathogens have been killed, some of the lymphocytes with antibodies that match that pathogen's antigens remain in the blood. These cells are **memory lymphocytes**. If the same kind of pathogen tries to infect you again, the memory lymphocytes cause a much faster **secondary response** that will stop you becoming ill. This means you are **immune** to that pathogen. Immunity to one pathogen does not make you immune to a different pathogen, because different pathogens need different antibodies to attack them.

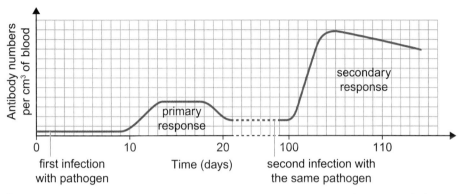

 4 a Use graph C to identify two ways in which the response to the first infection and the response to second infection by the same pathogen differ.

b Suggest how the differences in response explain why you may feel ill on the first infection but not the second.

C The immune responses to the first and second infection by a pathogen are different.

Immunisation

Immunity to a pathogen (**immunisation**) can be triggered artificially, by using a **vaccine**. The vaccine contains weakened or inactive pathogens, or bits of the pathogen that include the antigens. The vaccine may be injected into the body or be taken by mouth, and usually causes little reaction. Most vaccines will protect against particular diseases for many years.

 5 What is a vaccine?

 6 Explain why immunisation against one pathogen does not produce immunity to a different pathogen.

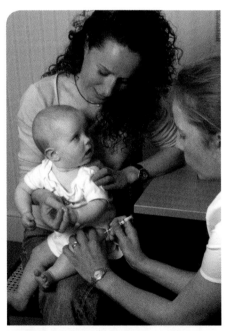

D Many childhood diseases that were once common, such as diphtheria and measles, are now rare in the UK because most children are immunised against the diseases.

Checkpoint

How confidently can you answer the Progression questions?

Strengthen

S1 How does the body respond if a pathogen gets past the body's natural defences?

Extend

E1 Compare the body's natural response to infection with immunisation.

Exam-style question

Explain why being given a vaccine for measles makes you immune to measles.   *(2 marks)*

CB5h Antibiotics

Specification reference: B5.16; B5.20

Progression questions

- What are antibiotics?
- Why are antibiotics useful?
- How are new medicines developed?

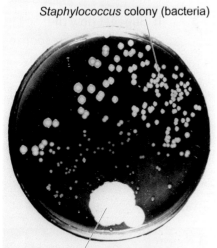

Staphylococcus colony (bacteria)

Penicillium mould (fungus)

A The bacterial plate that helped Fleming discover penicillin. Each bacterial **colony** contains large numbers of bacteria.

In 1928, Alexander Fleming noticed something strange on an agar plate covered in bacteria that he had left for several weeks. Where a mould had grown, the bacteria had been killed. He had discovered that the mould made **penicillin**.

Further work was needed to extract and purify the penicillin and to make it in large quantities, but it became the first antibiotic. **Antibiotics** are substances that either kill bacteria or **inhibit** their cell processes, which stops them growing or reproducing. Antibiotics do not have this effect on human cells. This makes them useful for attacking bacterial infections that the immune system cannot control.

 1 What evidence in photo A suggests the mould is releasing a substance that kills bacteria?

 2 Explain why giving penicillin to people with serious wounds could help save their lives.

 3 Explain why antibiotics have no effect on diseases such as flu and HIV.

Many kinds of antibiotic have been developed that work in different ways. This is important because different types of bacteria have different structures and they do not all respond in the same way to a particular antibiotic.

Did you know?

Penicillin was first used on a large scale during the Second World War. It saved thousands of soldiers from agonising deaths due to infected wounds.

 4 Explain how ceftazidime works as an antibiotic.

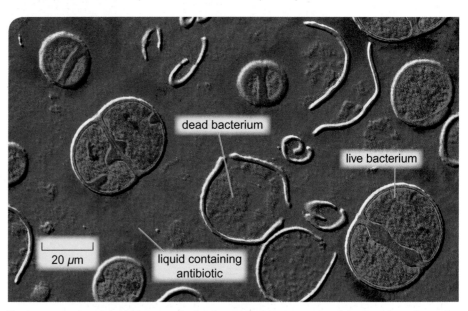

dead bacterium

live bacterium

20 µm

liquid containing antibiotic

B The antibiotic ceftazidime works by damaging bacteria that have a particular cell wall structure, so that they break open.

A major problem with using antibiotics is that many kinds of bacteria are evolving **resistance**, so they are no longer harmed by the antibiotic. New antibiotics and other medicines must be developed to help control infection.

The first step in the development of a possible new medicine is when it is tested on cells or tissues in the lab. This is the first **pre-clinical** stage of testing. This stage shows if the medicine can get into the cells and have the required effect. Although we take medicines to make us better, all medicines have **side effects**, causing unintended changes that may be harmful. So testing tries to make sure that harmful side effects are limited.

If this first stage is successful, the new medicine may then be tested on animals to see how it works in a whole body (without risk to humans). If that stage is successful, the medicine is tested in a small **clinical trial**, on a small number of healthy people, to check that it is safe and that side effects are small.

If that stage is successful, the medicine is then used in a large clinical trial, on many people who have the disease that the medicine will be used to treat. This helps to work out the correct amount to give (the **dose**), and to check for different side effects in different people. Only if a new medicine passes all these tests can a doctor prescribe it for treating patients.

liquid containing one possible new medicine

containers of cells for testing

C Many cell cultures can be automatically tested with several possible new medicines at the same time. This increases the rate of discovery of new medicines.

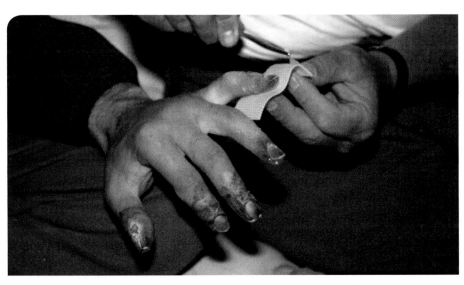

D Clinical trials do not always go according to plan. In one case, six men were injected with a trial leukaemia drug called TGN1412. It caused organ failures and fingers and toes to turn black (some of which had to be amputated).

 5 a List the stages of developing a new medicine, from discovery to prescription.

 b Explain why each stage is needed.

Checkpoint

How confidently can you answer the Progression questions?

Strengthen

S1 A new antibiotic has been made. Describe how the antibiotic will be tested before doctors are allowed to use it on their patients.

Extend

E1 A new medicine can only move to the next stage of testing when it has been successful in the previous stage. Describe the advantages and disadvantages of this, including time and cost of development.

Exam-style question

Describe two stages of pre-clinical testing in the development of a new antibiotic. *(2 marks)*

Immunisation

Young children are immunised against a range of infectious diseases. Explain how immunisation protects them from these diseases.

(6 marks)

Student answer

Immunisation means making someone immune to a disease by giving them a vaccine [1]. The vaccine contains an inactive form of the pathogen [2] that causes the disease. As these are not active pathogens, it won't make the person suffer from the disease.

The vaccine contains pathogen antigens. Putting these antigens into a child's body causes an immune response, which means that [3] lymphocytes that match these particular antigens become activated and produce many matching lymphocytes and antibodies. Some of the lymphocytes become memory lymphocytes and remain in the blood for a long time.

If the live pathogen gets into the body at a later time, the memory lymphocytes are already there to recognise the antigens on the pathogen and cause an immune response. This response is large and rapid because a large amount of antibodies is produced very quickly. The antibodies attack the pathogens and kill them before they can make the child ill [4].

[1] The student has explained a key scientific term from the question. This is often a good way to introduce an answer.

[2] There is good use of correct scientific terms (e.g. pathogen, vaccine, antigen and lymphocyte) and these have all been spelt correctly, which is important.

[3] The answer contains clear links between ideas by using linking words or phrases, such as 'because' or 'which means that'.

[4] The question has been fully answered and explains how immunised children are protected against infectious diseases.

Verdict

This is a strong answer. It explains what immunisation is, and then clearly sets out the steps by which a vaccine causes an immune response, leading to protection from a particular disease. The answer also uses proper scientific terms in a way that makes their meanings clear.

Exam tip

The effect of immunisation has a clear sequence, so it is important to make sure this is ordered in a logical way and linked back to the question being asked. To plan an answer like this, write out key words and phrases and then put them in order by using numbers. Also, write some key linking words and phrases that you will use, then cross these notes out as you include them in your answer.

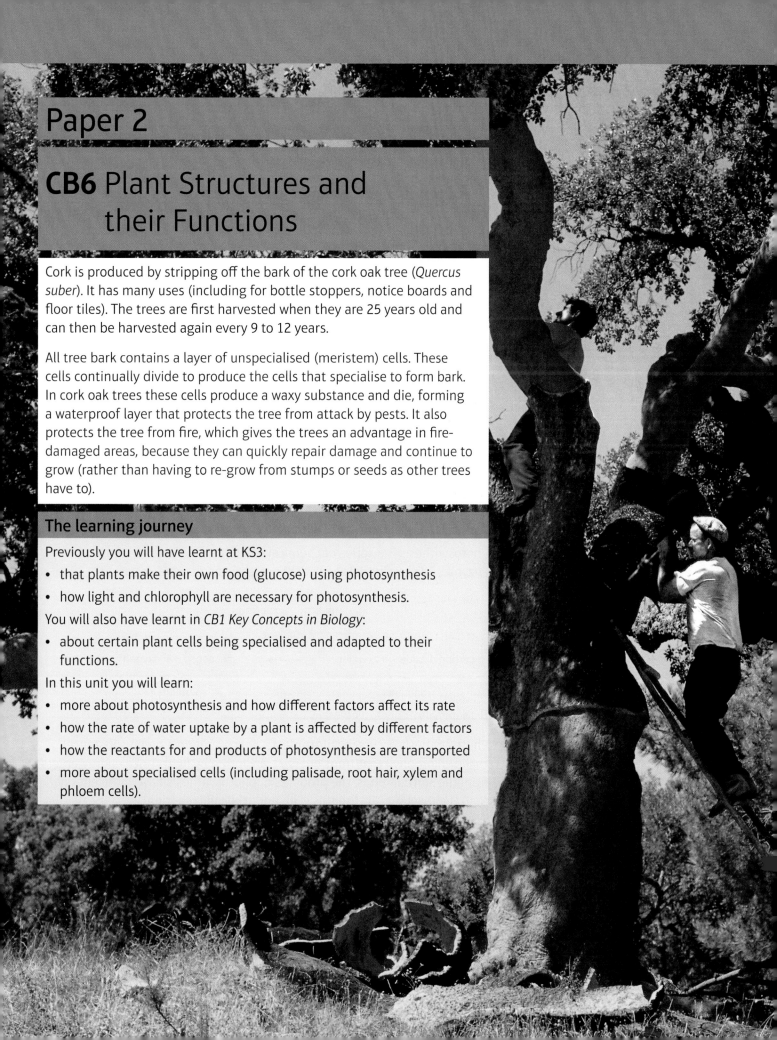

Paper 2

CB6 Plant Structures and their Functions

Cork is produced by stripping off the bark of the cork oak tree (*Quercus suber*). It has many uses (including for bottle stoppers, notice boards and floor tiles). The trees are first harvested when they are 25 years old and can then be harvested again every 9 to 12 years.

All tree bark contains a layer of unspecialised (meristem) cells. These cells continually divide to produce the cells that specialise to form bark. In cork oak trees these cells produce a waxy substance and die, forming a waterproof layer that protects the tree from attack by pests. It also protects the tree from fire, which gives the trees an advantage in fire-damaged areas, because they can quickly repair damage and continue to grow (rather than having to re-grow from stumps or seeds as other trees have to).

The learning journey

Previously you will have learnt at KS3:

- that plants make their own food (glucose) using photosynthesis
- how light and chlorophyll are necessary for photosynthesis.

You will also have learnt in *CB1 Key Concepts in Biology*:

- about certain plant cells being specialised and adapted to their functions.

In this unit you will learn:

- more about photosynthesis and how different factors affect its rate
- how the rate of water uptake by a plant is affected by different factors
- how the reactants for and products of photosynthesis are transported
- more about specialised cells (including palisade, root hair, xylem and phloem cells).

CB6a Photosynthesis

Specification reference: B6.1; B6.2; B6.9

Progression questions

- What happens during photosynthesis?
- Why is photosynthesis so important for almost all life on Earth?
- How is a leaf adapted for photosynthesis?

A Plant biomass feeds impalas. In turn, impala biomass feeds cheetahs.

All organisms need energy. Plants and algae (a type of **protist**) can trap energy transferred by light from the Sun. This energy is then transferred to molecules of a sugar called **glucose**, in a process called **photosynthesis**. Glucose and substances made from glucose are stores of energy. When animals eat plants, they get the energy from these stores.

The materials in an organism are its **biomass**. Plants and algae produce their own biomass and so produce the food for almost all other life on Earth. They are the **producers** in **food chains**.

1 Explain why most animals depend directly or indirectly on plants and algae.

2 Outline how plants produce biomass.

Photosynthesis is a series of chemical reactions, catalysed (speeded up) by enzymes. We can model the overall process using a word equation.

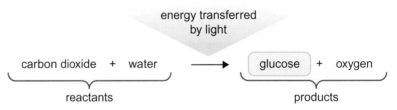

B a summary of photosynthesis

3 What are the reactants in photosynthesis?

4 Explain why the products of photosynthesis have more energy than the reactants.

Photosynthesis occurs in **chloroplasts**, which contain a green substance called chlorophyll that traps energy transferred by light. Since energy enters from the surroundings, the products of photosynthesis have more energy than the reactants and so this is an **endothermic reaction**.

5 Which product of photosynthesis is needed to make starch?

As glucose molecules are made, they are linked together to form a **polymer** called **starch**. This stays in the chloroplasts until photosynthesis stops. The starch is then broken down into simpler substances, which are moved into the cytoplasm and used to make **sucrose** (another type of sugar molecule). Sucrose is transported around the plant and may be used to make:

6 At what time of day would the amount of starch in chloroplasts be at its highest? Explain your reasoning.

- starch (in a **storage organ** such as a potato)
- other molecules for the plant (such as **cellulose**, **lipids** or **proteins**)
- glucose for **respiration** (to release energy).

Leaf adaptations

Leaves are often broad and flat, giving them a large surface area. The **palisade cells** near the top of a leaf are packed with chloroplasts. These adaptations allow a leaf to absorb a great deal of light.

Carbon dioxide for photosynthesis comes from the air. Leaves contain microscopic pores called **stomata** (singular **stoma**). Stomata allow carbon dioxide to diffuse into the leaf. The stomata are opened and closed by specialised **guard cells**. In the light, water flows into pairs of guard cells making them rigid. This opens the stoma. At night, water flows out of the guard cells. They lose their rigidity and the stoma shuts.

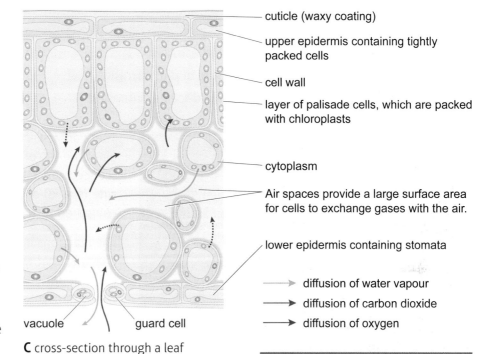

- cuticle (waxy coating)
- upper epidermis containing tightly packed cells
- cell wall
- layer of palisade cells, which are packed with chloroplasts
- cytoplasm
- Air spaces provide a large surface area for cells to exchange gases with the air.
- lower epidermis containing stomata

→ diffusion of water vapour
→ diffusion of carbon dioxide
→ diffusion of oxygen

vacuole   guard cell

C cross-section through a leaf

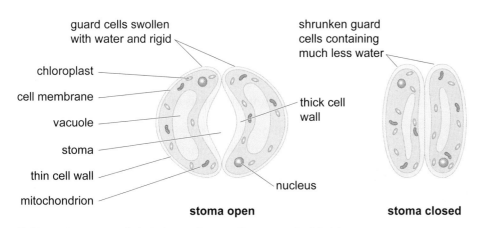

- guard cells swollen with water and rigid
- shrunken guard cells containing much less water
- chloroplast
- cell membrane
- vacuole
- stoma
- thin cell wall
- mitochondrion
- thick cell wall
- nucleus

stoma open   **stoma closed**

D Stomata open and shut depending on the amount of light.

Leaves are thin, so carbon dioxide does not have far to diffuse into the leaf before reaching cells that need it. Stomata also allow the oxygen produced by photosynthesis to escape into the air, as well as water vapour. The flow of different gases into and out of a leaf is an example of **gas exchange**.

7 Explain how stomata open when it is light and close when it is dark.

8 Water lily leaves float on the surface of ponds and lakes. Suggest how their leaves might be different to the leaf in diagram C. Explain your reasoning.

Exam-style question

Explain how palisade cells are adapted for photosynthesis. *(2 marks)*

Did you know?

At the bottom of the oceans, some microorganisms produce biomass without light. They use the energy transferred by some chemical reactions to drive the production of glucose.

Checkpoint

How confidently can you answer the Progression questions?

Strengthen

S1 Explain why carbon dioxide is vital for your life.

S2 List three adaptations of oak tree leaves for photosynthesis.

Extend

E1 A question on an 'ask a scientist' website reads: 'If plants need energy from light, how do they get their energy when it is dark?' Write an answer to this question.

CB6b Factors that affect photosynthesis

Specification reference: B6.3; H B6.4; H B6.6

Progression questions

- What are the limiting factors of photosynthesis?
- How do the limiting factors change the rate of photosynthesis?
- H How is the rate of photosynthesis related to light intensity?

A Mountain plants, such as edelweiss, are small partly because photosynthesis is slower higher up.

B These plants are being grown in water ('hydroponically') so that water is never a limiting factor. Being in a greenhouse means that the temperature, light intensity and carbon dioxide concentration can be controlled to maximise photosynthesis.

3 Explain why each of the following can be a limiting factor for photosynthesis.

 a temperature

 b carbon dioxide concentration

 c light intensity

 4 How would you test the idea that temperature is the limiting factor in graph C?

There are fewer molecules in each cubic centimetre of air at the top of a mountain than at the bottom. This reduced **concentration** of air molecules causes a lower **rate** (speed) of photosynthesis in high mountains compared with sea level.

The reactions in photosynthesis are catalysed by enzymes that work better at warmer temperatures. High mountain areas are cold, which is another reason why photosynthesis is slower at the top of a mountain than at the bottom.

 1 What gas from the air is needed for photosynthesis?

 2 **a** What is meant by the 'rate' of photosynthesis?

 b State two factors that affect the rate of photosynthesis in mountain areas.

A factor that prevents a rate increasing is a **limiting factor**. Carbon dioxide concentration, temperature and light intensity can all be limiting factors for photosynthesis. The maximum rate of photosynthesis is controlled by the factor in shortest supply.

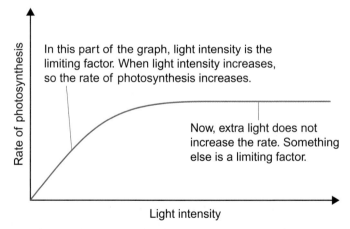

C An increase in light intensity increases the rate of photosynthesis until a limiting factor stops further increases.

Once a factor is limiting, changing its supply changes the rate of photosynthesis. In graph D, the lower line levels off because temperature is a limiting factor. Increasing the temperature allows higher rates of photosynthesis (upper line).

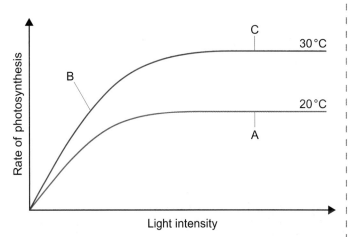

D The rate of photosynthesis can be increased by increasing the temperature if it is a limiting factor.

 5 In graph C, carbon dioxide concentration is the limiting factor. Sketch a copy of the graph and add another line to predict the effect of increasing carbon dioxide concentration by a set amount.

 6 Look at graph D. Explain what factors might be limiting at each stage (A–C).

A straight line on a graph shows a **linear relationship** between two variables. If the line goes through the origin (0, 0) it shows two variables that are in **direct proportion**. This means that if one variable increases, the other increases by the same percentage. The straight sloping parts of the lines in graphs C and D show that the rate of photosynthesis is directly proportional to light intensity until the limiting factor starts to have an effect.

Inverse square law

To calculate a new light intensity (I_{new}) when the distance of a light source changes (from d_{orig} to d_{new}), we use:

$$I_{new} = \frac{I_{orig} \times d^2_{orig}}{d^2_{new}}$$

I_{new} is **inversely proportional** to d^2_{new} (light intensity is inversely proportional to the new distance squared). Light intensity varies with distance according to the **inverse square law**.

So, if you double (×2) the distance from a light source, the light intensity is $1/2^2$ or ¼ times the original (it reduces to a quarter of the original). If you halve (÷ 2) the distance from a light source, light intensity is $1/(½)^2 = 1 ÷ ¼ = 4$ times the original.

 7 a The light intensity on a plant increases by 3 times and there are no limiting factors. What is the effect on the rate of photosynthesis? Explain your reasoning.

 b How can this increase be achieved by moving the light source?

Did you know?

A square metre of rainforest at sea level produces about 2200 g of new biomass per year. New biomass production in a square metre of high mountain vegetation is about 140 g/year.

Checkpoint

How confidently can you answer the Progression questions?

Strengthen

S1 In a forest, some plants grow in the shade and have very large, dark green leaves. Explain this, using the term 'limiting factor' in your answer.

Extend

E1 **H** A light source provides a light intensity of 2000 lux at a distance of 13 cm. Calculate the light intensity when the source is at a distance of 20 cm.

Exam-style question

In a commercial greenhouse, lights switch on at 17:00 in winter. Heating comes on if the inside temperature is below 21 °C. Explain these features.

(2 marks)

CB6b Core practical – Light intensity and photosynthesis

Specification reference: B6.5

Aim

Investigate the effect of light intensity on the rate of photosynthesis.

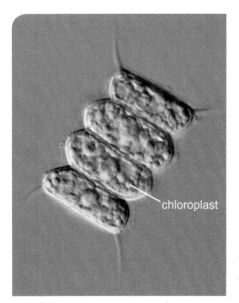

A a small group of *Scenedesmus* algae

Algae are single-celled protists and their cells contain chloroplasts. They photosynthesise in the same way as plants.

Your task

You are going to use balls of jelly containing algal cells to investigate photosynthesis in different light intensities. You can vary the light intensity by altering the distance between a lamp and the algae. You are going to use hydrogen carbonate indicator to monitor the change in pH of the solution in which you placed the balls.

Method

Wear eye protection.

A Decide on the different distances between the algae and the lamp you are going to use.

B For each distance you will need one clear glass bottle. You will also need one extra bottle.

C Add 20 of the algal balls to each bottle.

D Add the same amount of indicator solution to each bottle, and put on the bottle caps.

E Your teacher will have a range of bottles showing the colours of the indicator at different pHs. Compare the colour in your tubes with this pH range to work out the pH at the start.

F Set up a tank of water between the lamp and the area where you will place your tubes. Take extreme care not to spill water near electrical apparatus (such as a lamp).

G Cover one bottle in kitchen foil, so that it is in the dark.

H Measure the different distances from the lamp. Place your bottles at those distances. Put the bottle covered in kitchen foil next to the bottle that is closest to the lamp.

I Turn on the lamp and wait until you can see obvious changes in the colours in your bottles. The longer you can wait, the more obvious your results are likely to be.

J Compare the colours of all your bottles with the pH range bottles. Write down the pHs of the solutions in your bottles.

K For each bottle, calculate the 'change in pH/hour'.

L Plot a suitable graph or chart of your results.

B As the algae photosynthesise, the pH of the solution surrounding them changes. You can add hydrogen carbonate indicator to the solution to detect these changes.

Exam-style questions

1 Explain why the indicator changes colour in the bottles. *(2 marks)*

2 What is 'change in pH/hour' a measure of? *(1 mark)*

3 a State the dependent variable in the experiment. *(1 mark)*

   b State the independent variable. *(1 mark)*

   c One of the control variables is temperature. Explain why this is a control variable. *(2 marks)*

   d Explain whether or not you think this control variable has been adequately controlled. *(1 mark)*

   e List two more variables that have been controlled in this experiment. *(2 marks)*

4 The hydrogen carbonate indicator also ensures that there is plenty of carbon dioxide dissolved in the solution around the algal balls. Explain the purpose of making sure that there is a good supply of carbon dioxide. *(1 mark)*

5 a Describe how you would change this experiment to investigate the effect of temperature on the rate of photosynthesis. *(2 marks)*

   b What temperatures would you choose for your highest and lowest values? Explain your reasoning. *(4 marks)*

6 Explain the point of the tube wrapped in kitchen foil. *(2 marks)*

7 An experiment was carried out using pondweed, as shown in diagram C. When illuminated, the pondweed produced bubbles of gas, which were counted as they rose up the inverted funnel. The number of bubbles was counted for one minute at different distances from a lamp. Table D shows the results of the experiment.

   a Name the gas in the bubbles. *(1 mark)*

   b Plot the results on a scatter graph and draw a curve of best fit. *(3 marks)*

   c Explain the shape of your graph. *(2 marks)*

   d Explain one way in which this experiment could be improved. *(2 marks)*

   e **H** Plot a scatter graph to show that the rate of photosynthesis is proportional to the inverse of the distance squared. *(4 marks)*

   f **H** Explain why there is this relationship between the rate of photosynthesis and the distance in this experiment. *(2 marks)*

Distance (cm)	Rate of photosynthesis (bubbles per minute)
10	100
15	60
20	30
30	10
40	6
50	4

D

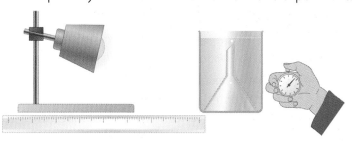

C measuring the rate of photosynthesis in pondweed

Specification reference: B1.15; B6.7

Progression questions

- How are diffusion and osmosis different?
- How do plant roots use diffusion, osmosis and active transport?
- How are root hair cells adapted to their functions?

A This giant buttress-rooted tree grows in Ghana.

Some trees are adapted to living in rainforests by having huge buttress roots. Like all roots, they absorb water and dissolved mineral ions from the soil. However, buttress roots help stop the tall trees falling over in thin rainforest soils, by acting as props. They also trap leaves and other dead vegetation, which then rot to provide additional minerals for the tree.

The water absorbed by plant roots is used for:

- carrying dissolved mineral ions
- keeping cells rigid (otherwise the plants **wilt** – their leaves and stems droop)
- cooling the leaves (when it evaporates from them)
- photosynthesis.

 1 Describe how plants lose water.

 2 For what chemical process do plants need water?

Root hair cells

The outer surfaces of many roots are covered with root hair cells. The 'hairs' are extensions of the cell that provide a large surface area so that water and **mineral ions** can be quickly absorbed. The 'hairs' also have thin cell walls so that the flow of water into the cells is not slowed down.

 3 Suggest two ways in which roots are adapted to absorb a lot of water.

Diffusion and osmosis

A certain volume containing more molecules of a substance than another identical volume has a greater concentration of the molecules. If the two spaces are connected, there will be a **concentration gradient** from higher concentration to lower concentration (see topic *CB1h Transporting substances*).

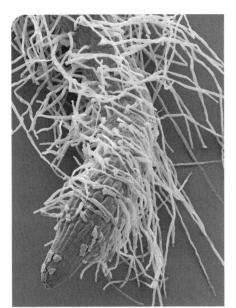

B root hair cells on a newly germinated poppy seedling root (magnification x66)

Particles constantly move in random directions and so particles in a **fluid** spread *down* a concentration gradient. This is **diffusion**. Inside plant roots, the cell walls have an open structure allowing water particles to diffuse towards the middle of the root (from where there are more of them to where there are fewer).

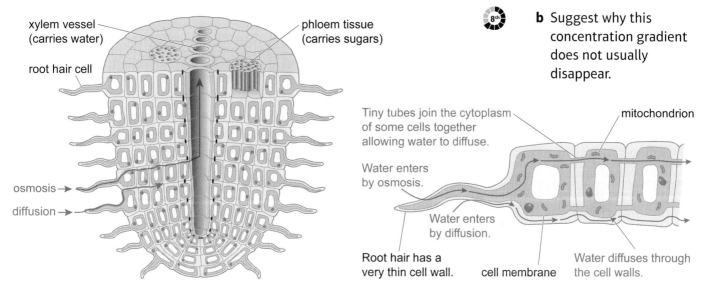

C pathways that water can take through a plant root

Osmosis is when solvent molecules (such as water) diffuse through a **semi-permeable membrane**. They diffuse from where there are more of them (a dilute solution of solutes) to where there are fewer (a more concentrated solution). Cell membranes are semi-permeable and so water passes into the cytoplasm of **root hair cells** by osmosis.

 6   Near the centre of a root is a layer of cells that have a waxy strip running through their cell walls (shown in black on diagram C). This strip stops the diffusion of water. Describe how water diffusing through cell walls gets to the xylem.

Active transport

Mineral salts are naturally occurring ionic compounds. Plants need ions from these compounds to produce new substances. For example, **nitrate** ions are needed to make **proteins**.

The concentration of ions inside a root hair cell is greater than in the soil. Mineral ions cannot diffuse against this concentration gradient. So, proteins in the cell membrane pump the ions into the cell. This is an example of **active transport** (see topic *CB1h Transporting substances*).

 7   Explain why mineral ions do not diffuse into root hair cells.

Exam-style question

Explain how water flows from soil into the cytoplasm of a root hair cell.
(2 marks)

 4   **a** Describe the concentration gradient for water molecules in root cell walls.

   b Suggest why this concentration gradient does not usually disappear.

5   By what process does water:

   a enter the cytoplasm of root hair cells

   b flow through root cells towards the xylem?

Checkpoint

How confidently can you answer the Progression questions?

Strengthen

S1 Explain how water enters a root hair cell by osmosis.

Extend

E1 Deciduous trees lose their leaves in winter. In the spring, before their leaves emerge, their roots suddenly start to grow and produce new root hair cells. Explain why this happens.

CB6d Transpiration and translocation

Specification reference: B6.8; B6.9; B6.10; B6.12; B6.13

Progression questions

- How do different factors affect the rate of transpiration?
- How is sucrose translocated around a plant?
- How are xylem and phloem adapted to their functions?

Did you know?

A large oak tree loses about 700 litres of water on a hot, sunny day.

 1 From what structures does water evaporate from leaves?

 2 Explain why a tree does not lose much water at night.

 3 Why should leaves be kept cool on a hot day? (*Hint:* think about enzymes.)

 4 State two ways in which transpiration helps a plant.

The evaporation of water from leaves keeps them cool and helps move water (and dissolved mineral ions) up the plant. The flow of water into a root, up the stem and out of the leaves is called **transpiration**.

Xylem vessels form tiny continuous pipes leading from a plant's roots up into its leaves. Inside the vessels is an unbroken chain of water, due to the weak forces of attraction between water molecules. Water is pulled up the xylem vessels in the stem as water evaporates from the xylem vessels in the leaves. As the water vapour diffuses out of a leaf, more water evaporates from the xylem inside the leaf.

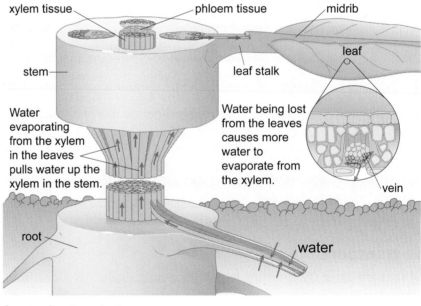

A water flow in a plant

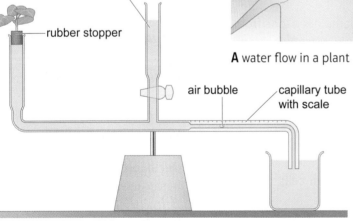

reservoir for pushing air bubble back to right-hand end of capillary tube

rubber stopper

air bubble

capillary tube with scale

B We can investigate the factors affecting transpiration using a **potometer**. The air bubble moves along the tube as the plant loses water. The speed of the bubble gives a measure of the rate of transpiration (e.g. in mm/min).

The concentration of water vapour in the air spaces inside a leaf is greater than outside it. So, water molecules diffuse down the concentration gradient, out of the leaf. A bigger difference between the concentrations makes the gradient steeper, which makes diffusion faster. So, any factor that reduces the concentration of water molecules outside the stomata will increase transpiration. Factors include:

- wind – moves water molecules away from stomata
- low humidity (little water vapour in the air).

Other factors that increase transpiration are:

- higher temperatures – particles move faster and so diffuse faster
- greater light intensity – makes the stomata wider.

 5 a Explain why water vapour diffuses more quickly out of a leaf on a windy day than on a calm day.

 b Explain why water moves out of the xylem inside leaves during the day.

 6 Explain why, during summer, trees lose more water at midday than at the end of the day.

Xylem

During their development, xylem cells die and their top and bottom cell walls disintegrate. This creates long empty vessels (tubes) through which water can move easily. Xylem vessels are rigid because they have thick side walls and rings of hard **lignin**, and so water pressure inside the vessels does not burst or collapse them. The rigid xylem vessels also help to support the plants.

 7 Describe how xylem cells are adapted to allow water to flow through them easily.

Phloem

Plants make sucrose from the glucose and starch made by photosynthesis. Sucrose is **translocated** (transported) in the **sieve tubes** of the **phloem tissue**. The large central channel in each sieve cell is connected to its neighbours by holes, through which sucrose solution flows.

Companion cells actively pump sucrose into or out of the sieve cells that form the sieve tubes. As sucrose is pumped into sieve tubes (e.g. in a leaf), the increased pressure causes the sucrose solution to flow up to growing shoots or down to storage organs.

 8 Explain why sieve cells have little cytoplasm.

 9 Explain why companion cells in a leaf contain so many mitochondria.

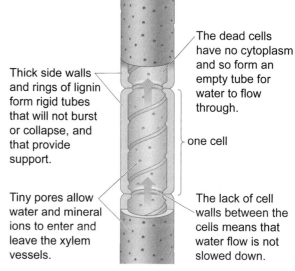

Thick side walls and rings of lignin form rigid tubes that will not burst or collapse, and that provide support.

The dead cells have no cytoplasm and so form an empty tube for water to flow through.

one cell

Tiny pores allow water and mineral ions to enter and leave the xylem vessels.

The lack of cell walls between the cells means that water flow is not slowed down.

C xylem adaptations

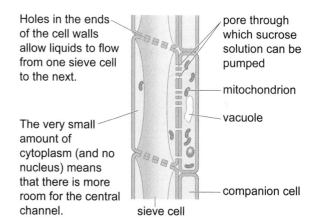

Holes in the ends of the cell walls allow liquids to flow from one sieve cell to the next.

pore through which sucrose solution can be pumped

mitochondrion

vacuole

The very small amount of cytoplasm (and no nucleus) means that there is more room for the central channel.

companion cell

sieve cell

D phloem adaptations

Checkpoint

How confidently can you answer the Progression questions?

Strengthen

S1 Design a table to compare transpiration and translocation.

Extend

E1 Explain why water enters sieve tubes from neighbouring xylem vessels as sucrose is pumped into the sieve tubes.

Exam-style question

In an experiment with a potometer, a faster wind speed causes the air bubble to move more quickly than a slower wind speed. Explain this observation.

(2 marks)

Mineral ions

Mineral ions are needed by plants in small quantities in order to make certain substances. For example, magnesium ions are an important part of chlorophyll molecules. Explain how magnesium ions are taken into a plant and transported to where they are needed.

(6 marks)

Student answer

The soil contains a lower concentration of magnesium ions than the cells in the roots [1]. Root hair cells pump the magnesium ions into the roots against this concentration gradient using active transport [2]. The ions dissolve in the water in the root cells and are carried along in the water by diffusion [3] into the xylem. The water evaporating from the leaves pulls more water up the xylem [4] and so carries the magnesium ions up the plant to the leaves where it is needed.

[1] A good place to start – at the beginning of the process in the soil.

[2] An excellent point that clearly states why active transport is needed.

[3] There is good use of scientific terms, such as diffusion, active transport and xylem.

[4] There is a clear demonstration that the student understands how the processes of water and mineral ion movement work.

Verdict

This is a strong answer. It has a logically ordered set of sentences that explain the processes that are occurring and makes good use of scientific terms.

Exam tip

While planning your answer, make a list of the important scientific words that you will use. Cross out your list when you have finished writing your answer.

Paper 2

CB7 Animal Coordination, Control and Homeostasis

When a child is hurt, parents and carers will often 'kiss it better'. Many people think this just helps the child to feel better. However, research has shown that this action releases a substance called oxytocin in the person receiving the kiss.

Oxytocin is an example of a hormone and has many effects in the body. It is sometimes called the 'cuddle' hormone because it is released when we are close to people who we are happy being with. One of its other effects, though, is to increase the speed of healing. So 'kissing it better' might really work!

The learning journey

Previously you will have learnt at KS3:

- how obesity is caused
- about the structure and function of human reproductive systems
- about the menstrual cycle.

You will also have learnt in *CB1 Key Concepts in Biology*:

- about the structure of sperm cells and egg cells
- how enzymes help digest food molecules.

In this unit you will learn:

- about endocrine glands
- how hormones are transported to their target organs
- how the menstrual cycle is controlled by hormones and how hormones are used in contraception
- about diabetes and how blood glucose concentration is controlled
- **H** how the hormones thyroxine and adrenalin affect the body
- **H** what a negative feedback mechanism is.

Progression questions

- What are hormones?
- Where are hormones produced?
- What are the names of some target organs?

A Response to fear involves the fast responses of the nervous system and the slower responses of the hormonal system, including dilated pupils in the eyes and a faster heart rate.

Your nervous system enables you to respond quickly to changes in your surroundings. However, humans have another response system, called the **hormonal system**. It works more slowly than the nervous system but can cause responses in many parts of the body.

The hormonal system uses chemical messengers called **hormones**, which are carried by the blood and so take time to get around the body. Different hormones are released by a range of **endocrine glands**, including the **pituitary**, **thyroid**, **adrenals**, **ovaries**, **testes** and **pancreas**.

1 The dog in photo A is responding to a threat.

   a Describe as fully as you can how the nervous system has helped the dog identify and respond to the threat.

   b Describe the responses caused by the dog's hormonal system.

   c Compare the speed of response of the nervous and hormonal systems.

2 Define the term 'hormone'.

3 Name one hormone produced in:

   a the ovaries

   b the pancreas.

The pituitary gland releases many hormones, including ACTH, FSH, LH and growth hormone.

The thyroid gland produces several hormones, including thyroxine.

The adrenal glands release several hormones, including adrenalin.

The pancreas contains some cells that produce insulin and others that produce glucagon.

The testes release the sex hormone testosterone.

The ovaries produce the sex hormones oestrogen and progesterone.

B The hormonal system consists of endocrine glands that produce and release hormones.

An organ that is affected by a specific hormone is called its **target organ**. Organs in different parts of the body may be target organs of the same hormone. The hormone affects the organ by changing what the organ is doing. For example, growth hormone stimulates cells in muscles and bones to divide. It also stimulates the digestive system to absorb calcium ions (used to help make strong bones).

C In 2014, Sultan Kösen, the world's tallest man, met Chandra Dangi, the world's shortest man. Kösen was 2.51 m tall while Dangi was 0.55 m. Both had problems with the production of growth hormone in their bodies.

Some endocrine glands are the target organs for other hormones. For example, the **sex hormones** oestrogen and testosterone, which are released by reproductive organs, stimulate the release of growth hormone. The release of sex hormones increases during puberty, which helps to explain the increase in growth rate at this time.

 5 Describe how a change in the amount of sex hormones produced during puberty leads to an increase in growth. Include the names of endocrine glands and target organs for the hormones you mention.

 4 a Name the endocrine gland that produces growth hormone.

 b Name two target organs of growth hormone.

 c Describe how growth hormone reaches its target organs from where it is produced.

 d Suggest why Sultan Kösen is so tall and Chandra Dangi so short.

e Use your knowledge of how growth hormone works to explain your answer to part **d**.

Checkpoint

How confidently can you answer the Progression questions?

Strengthen

S1 Using a hormone of your choice, state where it is made in the body and where it has its effect.

Extend

E1 Using examples, write definitions of the following terms for a web dictionary: hormone, endocrine gland, target organ.

Exam-style question

Describe how endocrine glands communicate with organs around the body. *(2 marks)*

CB7b Hormonal control of metabolic rate

Specification reference: H B7.2; H B7.3

Progression questions

- H What is a negative feedback mechanism?
- H How does thyroxine affect metabolic rate?
- H How does adrenalin prepare the body for 'fight or flight'?

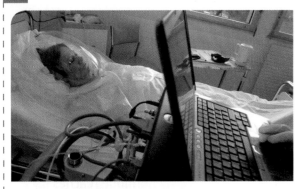

A measuring resting metabolic rate

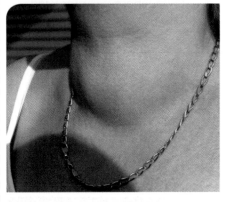

B A goitre is an enlarged thyroid gland. It may be caused by disease or by deficiency of iodine in the diet, because iodine is needed to make thyroxine.

 3 Suggest an effect on the body caused by the thyroid producing too little thyroxine.

 4 a Define the term 'negative feedback'.

 b Explain why negative feedback is important in controlling thyroxine release.

Your **metabolic rate** is the rate at which the energy stored in your food is transferred by all the reactions that take place in your body to keep you alive. **Resting metabolic rate** is measured with the body at rest, in a warm room and long after the person last had a meal.

 1 a Name two processes that require the transfer of energy when the body is fully at rest.

 b Explain why these processes need a source of energy.

 2 Explain why resting metabolic rate is measured in a warm room and not in a cold room.

One hormone that affects metabolic rate is **thyroxine**, which is released by the thyroid gland. Thyroxine is taken into, and affects, many different kinds of cell. It causes heart cells to contract more rapidly and strongly, and it also increases the rate at which proteins and carbohydrates are broken down inside cells.

The amount of thyroxine produced by the thyroid gland is controlled by hormones released by two other glands, as shown in diagram C. The control of thyroxine concentration in the blood is an example of **negative feedback**. This is because an *increase* in thyroxine concentration directly causes changes that bring about a *decrease* in the amount of thyroxine released into the blood, and vice versa.

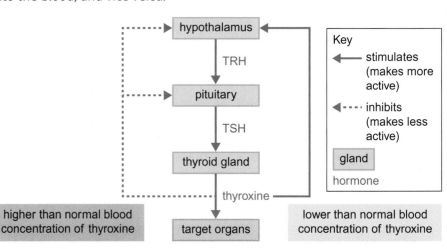

C Negative feedback of the blood concentration of thyroxine involves two other hormones. TRH is thyrotropin-releasing hormone, and TSH is thyroid-stimulating hormone.

H

Adrenalin is a hormone that is released from the adrenal glands. In normal conditions, very little adrenalin is released into the blood. However, in frightening or exciting situations, an increase in impulses from neurones reaching the adrenal glands from the spinal cord triggers the release of large amounts of adrenalin into the blood.

Adrenalin has many target organs, including the liver in which it causes the breakdown of a storage substance called **glycogen**. Glycogen is a polymer made of glucose molecules. When glycogen is broken down, the glucose molecules can be released into the blood providing additional glucose for respiration.

Some of the other target organs and effects of adrenalin are shown in diagram D. Together, these effects prepare the body to fight or run away from danger (the so-called **'fight-or-flight' response**).

Heart muscle cells contract:
• more rapidly, which increases the heart rate
• more strongly, which increases the blood pressure.

Diameter of blood vessels leading to muscles widens, which increases blood flow to muscles.

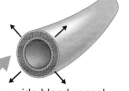

heart

wide blood vessel

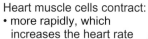

adrenalin

blood vessels

liver

Liver cells change glycogen to glucose and release it into the blood, which increases blood sugar concentration.

Diameter of blood vessels leading to other organs narrows, which reduces blood flow to those organs and increases blood pressure.

narrow blood vessel

D the effect of adrenalin on some of its target organs

 5 a Name three target organs of adrenalin.

  b Explain how the effects of adrenalin on different parts of the body help prepare the body for action.

Checkpoint

How confidently can you answer the Progression questions?

Strengthen

S1 Identify the endocrine gland and target organ(s) for each hormone mentioned on these two pages.

Extend

E1 Compare and contrast how thyroxine and adrenalin are released into the blood, and suggest an explanation for any differences.

Exam-style question

Describe how negative feedback can control the amount of a hormone in the blood.   *(2 marks)*

CB7c The menstrual cycle

Specification reference: B7.4; B7.6; B7.7

Progression questions

- What is the menstrual cycle?
- What are the roles of oestrogen and progesterone in the menstrual cycle?
- How can hormones and barrier methods be used as contraception?

A Many women experience symptoms before a period starts, such as abdominal pain, mood swings, breast tenderness and tiredness. These symptoms are caused by changes in hormone concentrations.

The **menstrual cycle** is a cycle of changes in a woman's reproductive system that takes about 28 days. The cycle continues from **puberty** (at around 12 years) to **menopause** (in early 50s), and prepares the woman's body for the **fertilisation** of an egg cell, leading to **pregnancy**.

Diagram B shows the menstrual cycle. Day 1 is set at the start of **menstruation**, when the thickened part of the uterus lining and an unfertilised egg cell are lost during a 'bleed' or **period**. During the cycle, the lining of the uterus thickens again and **ovulation** takes place, when an egg cell is released from an ovary.

Did you know?

Usually only one egg cell is released from one ovary during ovulation. However, sometimes two or more egg cells are released at the same time. If all the egg cells are fertilised, this can lead to multiple pregnancies, such as non-identical twins or triplets.

5th **1** On which days of the menstrual cycle is an egg cell most likely to be released from an ovary?

5th **2** How long does a menstrual period usually last for?

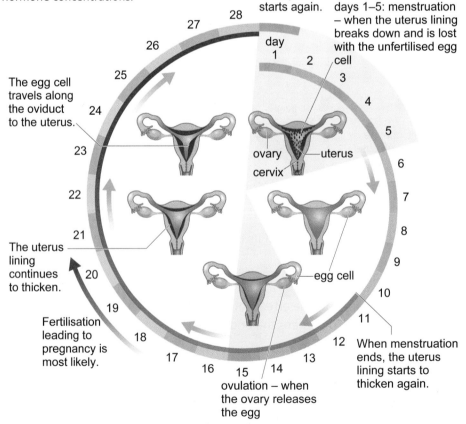

B one menstrual cycle

The cycle is controlled by the sex hormones **oestrogen** and **progesterone**, which are released by the ovaries into the blood.

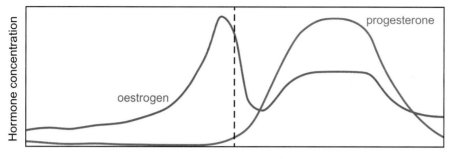

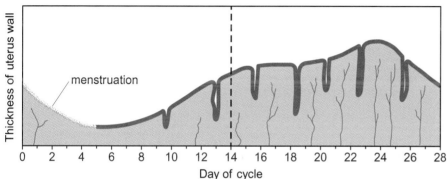

C Changes in the concentrations of hormones in the blood cause changes in the thickness of the uterus wall during the menstrual cycle.

During sexual intercourse, sperm cells are deposited in the vagina. They then pass through the cervix to the uterus and into the oviducts. If a sperm cell meets an egg cell, fertilisation can occur. **Contraception** is the prevention of fertilisation. There are many contraceptive methods, including some that use hormones and some that are physical barriers. Table D shows some examples.

Method and success rate (% of pregnancies prevented)	How it prevents fertilisation
male condom (98% success rate)	placed over erect penis, prevents sperm entering the vagina
diaphragm or cap (92–96% success rate)	placed over the cervix (entrance to the uterus), prevents sperm in the vagina entering the uterus
hormone pill or implant placed under the skin (>99% success rate)	release hormones to prevent ovulation and thickens mucus at the cervix, making it difficult for sperm cells to pass through

D different contraceptive methods and their success rates if used correctly

Exam-style question

A plastic 'vaginal' cap can be placed inside the vagina, over the cervix, during sexual intercourse. Explain how this can prevent pregnancy. *(2 marks)*

3 Use diagram C to answer these questions.

 a What happens to the concentration of oestrogen at ovulation?

 b Suggest the function of oestrogen in the first part of the menstrual cycle. Explain your answer.

 c Suggest what causes menstruation to begin? Explain your answer.

 4 What does 98 per cent success mean in terms of the number of pregnancies prevented?

 5 Explain which of the methods of contraception for preventing pregnancy shown in the table is the most effective.

 6 Suggest an explanation for how hormone methods of contraception work.

Checkpoint

How confidently can you answer the Progression questions?

Strengthen

S1 How do barrier and hormone methods of contraception prevent fertilisation?

Extend

E1 Suggest why the success rates at preventing pregnancy shown in table D are maximum values.

CB7d Hormones and the menstrual cycle

Specification reference: H B7.5; H B7.8

Progression questions

- H How do hormones control the menstrual cycle?
- H How do hormones in contraceptive pills interact with hormones in the body to prevent pregnancy?
- H How can hormones increase the chance of pregnancy?

 H

A The most babies born at the same time who all survived is eight. They were born to Nadya Suleman on 26 January 2009, after IVF treatment in which 12 embryos were placed in her uterus at the same time.

1 For each of the following hormones, identify where it is released and its target organ(s).

 a oestrogen

 b progesterone

 c FSH

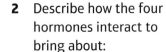 **d** LH

2 Describe how the four hormones interact to bring about:

 a ovulation

 b menstruation.

FSH (follicle-stimulating hormone) and **LH** (luteinising hormone) are released from the pituitary gland. The release of these hormones is controlled by the concentration of oestrogen (which increases as the **egg follicle** matures) and of progesterone (which is released after ovulation when the follicle becomes a structure called the **corpus luteum**). Diagram B shows how the four hormones interact to control the menstrual cycle.

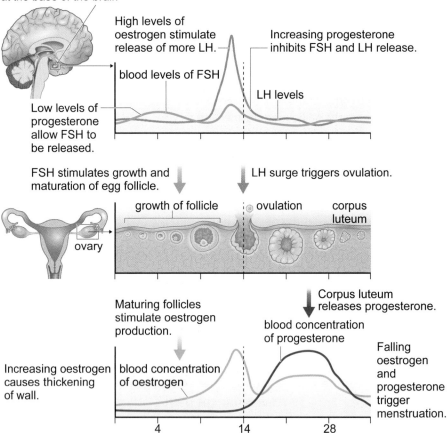

B Many hormones interact to control the menstrual cycle.

Hormonal contraception uses a progesterone-like hormone either on its own or with oestrogen. Raising hormone concentrations in this way prevents the natural fall of concentrations at the end of the menstrual cycle.

 3 Explain how the effect of hormonal contraception on FSH and LH can help to prevent pregnancy.

There are many possible reasons why some couples are unable to have a child. Some problems can be overcome using **Assisted Reproductive Technology (ART)**, which uses hormones and other techniques to increase the chance of pregnancy.

Clomifene therapy is useful for women who rarely or never release an egg cell during their menstrual cycles. Clomifene is a drug that helps to increase the concentration of FSH and LH in the blood.

 4 Explain how clomifene works to increase the chance of pregnancy for some women.

Another ART technique is **IVF** (in vitro fertilisation). This can overcome problems such as blocked oviducts in the woman, or if the man produces very few healthy sperm cells. Diagram C shows how IVF is carried out. Any healthy embryos not used in the first attempt at pregnancy may be frozen and stored for use another time.

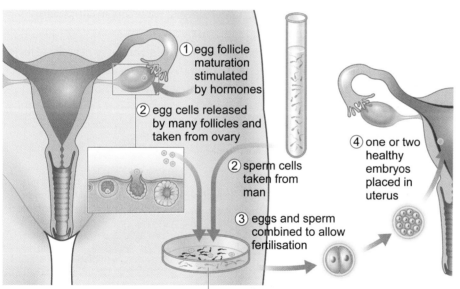

① egg follicle maturation stimulated by hormones

② egg cells released by many follicles and taken from ovary

② sperm cells taken from man

③ eggs and sperm combined to allow fertilisation

④ one or two healthy embryos placed in uterus

The technique is called 'in vitro' (which means 'in glass') because glass dishes were used originally.

C how IVF is carried out

 5 a Explain why the woman's ovaries are stimulated with hormones at the start of IVF treatment.

 b Suggest which of the hormones that normally control the menstrual cycle is given to stimulate the release of egg cells in IVF treatment. Explain your reasoning.

Exam-style question

Explain how a hormonal treatment using progesterone can prevent pregnancy. *(3 marks)*

Did you know?

During the IVF procedure, a cell can be removed from an embryo before the embryo is placed in the uterus. The cell can then be tested for genetic disorders or other problems.

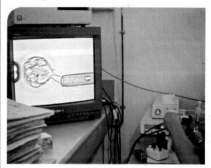

D removing a cell from an embryo to test for genetic disorders

Checkpoint

How confidently can you answer the Progression questions?

Strengthen

S1 If an egg cell is fertilised, the corpus luteum remains large and active. Explain why a missed period is often the first sign of pregnancy.

Extend

E1 Clomifene therapy works by blocking the negative feedback effect of oestrogen on a pituitary hormone involved in the control of the menstrual cycle. Explain what this means.

CB7e Control of blood glucose

Specification reference: B7.9; B7.13; H B7.14; B7.15

Progression questions

- What is homeostasis?
- How is blood glucose concentration regulated?
- How can type 1 diabetes be controlled?

A A 15th century urine colour chart helped doctors to diagnose illnesses in their patients.

Urine tests are a simple way of testing for pregnancy or for many diseases including **diabetes**. The substances in urine can provide important clues. However, while a doctor in the Middle Ages might have tasted the urine to test for diabetes, doctors today can use simple chemical tests.

During digestion in the gut, glucose is released from carbohydrates in our food. Glucose is easily absorbed from the small intestine into the blood and then into cells, where it is broken down during respiration.

It takes time for cells to take in the glucose released by digestion, so there is a risk that glucose may reach a very high concentration in the blood. This is dangerous because it can damage organs. However, in most people this does not happen, because blood glucose concentration is carefully controlled. As blood glucose concentration rises, it stimulates certain cells in the pancreas to release the hormone **insulin**. Insulin causes cells in the liver and other organs to take in glucose, which causes a fall in blood glucose concentration.

 1 a What happens to glucose during respiration?

 b Explain why glucose is important for the body.

 2 a What will happen to the concentration of glucose in the blood soon after a meal?

 b Explain your answer to part a.

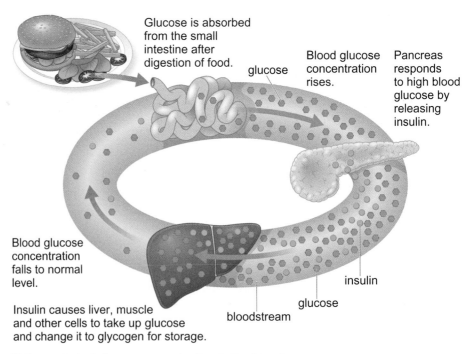

Glucose is absorbed from the small intestine after digestion of food.

glucose

Blood glucose concentration rises.

Pancreas responds to high blood glucose by releasing insulin.

insulin

glucose

bloodstream

Blood glucose concentration falls to normal level.

Insulin causes liver, muscle and other cells to take up glucose and change it to glycogen for storage.

B the control of glucose concentration in the blood

 3 Describe how the body responds when blood glucose concentration rises above normal.

As blood glucose concentration falls, the insulin-releasing cells in the pancreas release less and less insulin. If blood glucose concentration falls below a certain level, the cells stop releasing insulin altogether.

H

When glucose is absorbed by the liver, it is converted to glycogen, which is stored in the liver cells. If blood glucose concentration falls too low, another hormone is released from other pancreatic cells. This hormone is called **glucagon**. Glucagon causes liver cells to convert glycogen back to glucose, which is released into the blood. As blood glucose concentration increases, the amount of glucagon released from the pancreas falls.

 4 Compare the roles of glucagon and insulin in the control of blood glucose concentration.

 5 Explain why the control of blood glucose concentration is an example of negative feedback. It may help to draw a diagram.

The effects of hormones help to keep blood glucose concentration within limits that are safe. Maintaining constant conditions inside the body is called **homeostasis**. Other examples of homeostasis in the body include temperature control and the control of water content. All the processes involved in homeostasis help to prevent damage to the body as internal and external conditions change.

 6 Explain how the homeostatic control of blood glucose concentration helps to protect the body.

Type 1 diabetes

In a few people, the pancreatic cells that should produce insulin do not. This is because the cells have been destroyed by the body's immune system. These people have **type 1 diabetes**, and it means that they cannot control rising blood glucose concentration.

When blood glucose concentration is too high, some glucose can be detected in the urine. Therefore, glucose in the urine is often the first test for type 1 diabetes.

People with type 1 diabetes have to inject insulin into the fat layer below the skin, where it can enter the blood, causing blood glucose concentration to fall.

7 Explain how the following may affect how much insulin someone with type 1 diabetes should inject.

 a time since last meal

 b the types of food eaten in a meal

 c the amount of recent exercise

Exam-style question

Explain why people with type 1 diabetes must control their blood glucose concentration with injections of insulin. *(2 marks)*

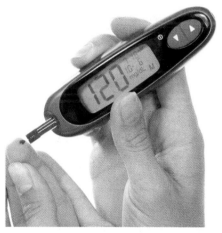

C In order to decide on the right amount of insulin to inject, a person with type 1 diabetes often does a simple blood test to check their blood glucose concentration.

Checkpoint

How confidently can you answer the Progression questions?

Strengthen

S1 Using an example, explain why homeostasis is important.

Extend

E1 **H** The control of blood glucose concentration involves two hormones. Suggest how this can provide better control of concentration than using just one hormone.

CB7f Type 2 diabetes

Specification reference: B7.16; B7.17

- How is type 2 diabetes caused?
- How can type 2 diabetes be controlled?
- How are body mass and type 2 diabetes correlated?

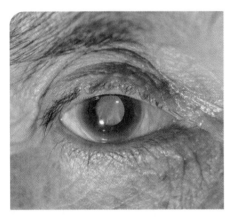

A Diabetes increases the risk of developing several eye problems, including cataracts where the lens becomes cloudy and makes it difficult to see clearly.

 3 Compare the treatment of people who have type 1 diabetes with that of people who have type 2 diabetes.

Year	Number of people in UK with type 2 diabetes (millions)	Total UK population (millions)
2010	2.63	62.3
2014	6.5	64.7

B

 5 Explain the difference in making comparisons using BMI rather than body mass.

There is a second kind of diabetes, called **type 2 diabetes**. This is caused either by insulin-releasing cells not producing enough insulin, or by target organs not responding properly to the hormone.

 1 Which are the target organs of insulin, and how do they respond to the hormone?

 2 Predict the effect of type 2 diabetes on blood glucose concentration. Explain your reasoning.

People with type 2 diabetes may have some response to insulin, so they are treated in a different way to people with type 1 diabetes. For some, just eating healthily and keeping the amount of sugar in the diet low can control their diabetes. Being physically active can also help, because it takes glucose out of the blood. People with more severe type 2 diabetes may be given medicines to reduce the amount of glucose that the liver releases into the blood, or to increase the sensitivity of the cells in target organs that respond to insulin.

Many countries are showing a rapid change in the number of people with type 2 diabetes. This includes the UK (as shown in table B).

 4 a Calculate the percentage of people with type 2 diabetes in the UK in 2010 and in 2014.

 b Describe what you would need to do to be more sure of the trend suggested by your answer to part a.

As the number of people with type 2 diabetes has increased, so has the average body mass. We say that the two factors are **correlated**. Scientists think that the more fat someone has in their body, the more likely they are to develop type 2 diabetes. Taller people have a larger mass than shorter people, so scientists need to take height into account and work out whether a person has the right mass for their height. They do this by calculating **body mass index (BMI)** using the equation:

$$BMI = \frac{mass\ (kg)}{height\ (m)^2}$$

adult BMI categories:
- underweight: below 18.5
- normal: 18.5–24.9
- overweight: 25.0–29.9
- **obese**: ≥30.0

There is a correlation between BMI categories and the percentages of UK adults with type 2 diabetes, as shown in chart C.

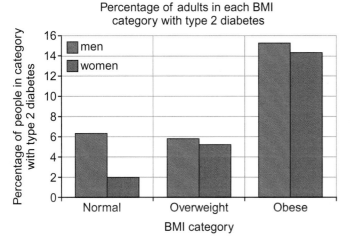

Percentage of adults in each BMI category with type 2 diabetes

C This study of UK adults shows that BMI category and type 2 diabetes are correlated.

An alternative to BMI is **waist:hip ratio**, calculated as the waist measurement divided by the hip measurement. As people increase in mass, they tend to develop more fat on their waists compared with their hips. This increases their waist:hip ratio. Waist:hip ratio also correlates with the risk of developing type 2 diabetes.

 6 a Use the evidence in chart C to analyse the correlation between BMI category and the proportion of people who have type 2 diabetes.

 b Suggest what a chart showing the percentage of people with type 2 diabetes against waist:hip ratio might look like.

 7 The average body mass of people in the UK is increasing. Explain what effect this may have on the percentage of people who develop type 2 diabetes.

Did you know?

About one-third of people who have type 2 diabetes do not know they have the disease, because they have no obvious symptoms.

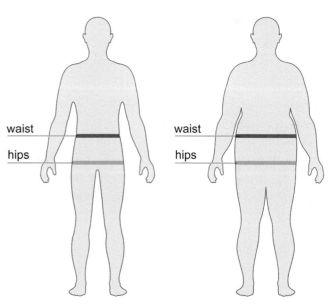

D taking waist and hip measurements

Checkpoint

How confidently can you answer the Progression questions?

Strengthen

S1 Describe the correlation between body mass, BMI, waist:hip ratio and type 2 diabetes.

Extend

E1 Explain why type 1 diabetes and type 2 diabetes are treated differently.

Exam-style question

Explain why doctors are concerned about the increase in obesity in the UK. *(2 marks)*

Risk of type 2 diabetes

A Swedish study investigated waist:hip ratios and type 2 diabetes. The waist:hip ratios of 792 54-year-old men in Gothenburg, Sweden were recorded. Thirteen years later, the scientists recorded whether or not these men had developed type 2 diabetes.

The waist:hip ratio values were arranged in order of size and then split into three groups: small, medium and large waist:hip ratios.

The mean probability of developing type 2 diabetes was calculated for each group. The chart shows the results.

Evaluate the relationship between waist:hip ratio and the risk of developing type 2 diabetes, using the results shown in the chart. **(6 marks)**

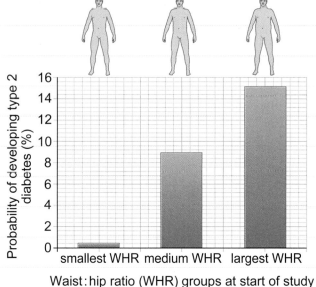

Waist:hip ratio (WHR) groups at start of study

Student answer

Between the smallest and the medium WHRs the probability of developing type 2 diabetes goes up to 8.6% and then goes up another 6.2% between the medium WHR and the largest WHR. So it looks like the higher someone's WHR, the more likely they are to develop type 2 diabetes [1].

The study included 792 men, which is a large number. This reduces the possibility that the results have happened by chance, and so suggests they could be repeated in similar studies [2].

The study only included men from one Swedish city who were 54 years old at the start of the study. Different groups of people, of different ages, gender or place might show different results [3].

This means that you cannot judge if the trend shown in the chart is true for everyone or just for the men who took part in the study [4].

[1] It is essential that you quote and use actual data from a graph or chart in questions of this type. This student has done this here, and used the data to then state the overall pattern shown.

[2] This part of the answer clearly identifies a strength of the study, and explains why it is a strength.

[3] This part of the answer clearly identifies a weakness of the study, and explains why it is a weakness.

[4] The answer finishes well with a conclusion based on the strength and weakness identified.

Verdict

This is a strong answer. It clearly explains what the chart shows. Some strengths and weaknesses of the study are set out in a logical and well-structured way, making it easy to follow the discussion, and to understand the conclusion.

Exam tip

'Evaluate' questions require you to consider the strengths and weaknesses of information and form a conclusion that takes those into account. It is a good idea to plan these questions by listing 'strengths' and 'weaknesses' before you start writing your answer.

Paper 2

CB8 Exchange and Transport in Animals

This shark has had all its skin and flesh removed. What you can see is just the dense network of capillaries, arteries and veins that forms its circulatory system. There are so many blood vessels because the system needs to ensure that every single cell in the shark's body gets an adequate supply of oxygen and food. The same is true for all large animals, including humans. In this unit you will find out about the importance of the circulatory system and how it works.

The learning journey

Previously you will have learnt at KS3:

- how the digestive system gets glucose and other food molecules into the blood
- how the respiratory (breathing) system gets oxygen into the blood
- about aerobic and anaerobic respiration.

You will also have learnt in *CB1 Key Concepts in Biology*:

- about diffusion
- about different animal cells and their adaptations.

In this unit you will learn:

- more about diffusion, gas exchange and the surface area : volume ratio
- more about the different types of respiration
- how the lungs, heart, blood vessels and blood are adapted for their functions
- how to calculate cardiac output.

CB8a Efficient transport and exchange

Specification reference: B8.1; B8.2; B8.3

Progression questions

- What substances need to be transported into and out of the body?
- Why is the surface area:volume ratio important for exchange of substances?
- How are lungs adapted for gas exchange?

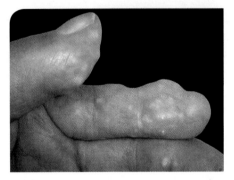

A Waste DNA is broken down into uric acid and excreted by your kidneys. If it builds up in the blood it can cause gout, in which uric acid crystals form and cause painful swellings.

All the chemical reactions in your body (your **metabolism**) produce wastes, which must be **excreted** so they do not cause problems. Your kidneys remove **urea**, which is a poison produced by breaking down amino acids. Your lungs get rid of carbon dioxide produced in **aerobic respiration**.

 1 Name two human excretory organs.

Your body also moves substances into it. Oxygen and glucose are needed for aerobic respiration. Dissolved food molecules (e.g. glucose, amino acids) and mineral ions are needed to produce new substances for your body.

 2 a What large molecules are made using amino acids?

 b When these molecules are broken down again, what waste do they form?

 c How is this waste excreted from the body?

 3 What organs take the substances needed for aerobic respiration into the body?

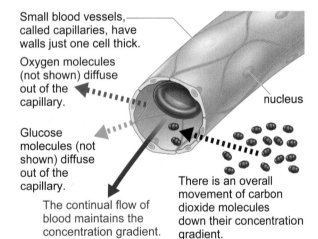

Small blood vessels, called capillaries, have walls just one cell thick.

Oxygen molecules (not shown) diffuse out of the capillary.

Glucose molecules (not shown) diffuse out of the capillary.

nucleus

The continual flow of blood maintains the concentration gradient.

There is an overall movement of carbon dioxide molecules down their concentration gradient.

B Substances diffuse down their concentration gradients into and out of narrow blood vessels called capillaries.

Many substances move into and out of parts of the body by **diffusion**. To make sure a lot of particles diffuse quickly, the surfaces through which they move:

- are thin – so that particles do not need to diffuse very far
- have a large surface area – so that there is more room for particles to diffuse.

 4 a In diagram B, is the glucose concentration highest inside or outside the vessel? Explain your reasoning.

 b Why do oxygen molecules diffuse out of the capillary?

 5 Describe one way in which a capillary is adapted so that substances diffuse quickly in and out.

Did you know?

Capillaries are 5–10 μm in diameter, with walls that are about 0.6 μm thick.

Surface area:volume ratio

It would take too long for materials to diffuse through cells on the outside of a tissue to reach cells on the inside. So, **multicellular organisms** have transport systems. In humans, a fine network of **capillaries** in the **circulatory system** uses blood to transport substances to and from all cells.

The larger a cell's surface area, the more of a substance can diffuse into (and out of) it in a certain time. However, if a cell's volume is too big, the cell cannot fill up with all the materials it needs quickly enough.

The **surface area:volume ratio** (**SA:V**) is the surface area divided by the volume, or

$$\frac{\text{surface area}}{\text{volume}}$$

The bigger this ratio, the more surface area something has per unit volume. Diagram C shows that as cells get bigger, their SA:V ratio gets smaller. If the ratio is too small, a cell cannot get enough raw materials fast enough. So, there is a limit to the size of cells.

Organs that move substances into and out of the body have large SA:V ratios. For example, a human lung has about the same volume as a football, but its surface area is about 250 times greater. This is because lungs are packed with millions of **alveoli**, which increase the surface area and so increase the speed and amount of **gas exchange**.

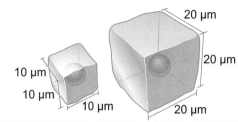

surface area = 6 × (10 × 10) = 600 μm²	surface area = 6 × (20 × 20) = 2400 μm²
volume = 10 × 10 × 10 = 1000 μm³	volume = 20 × 20 × 20 = 8000 μm³
SA:V = $\frac{600}{1000}$ = 0.6	SA:V = $\frac{2400}{8000}$ = 0.3

C Cells of different sizes have different SA:V ratios.

6 A skin cell is a cube with sides of 3 μm. Calculate:

 a its volume

 b its surface area

 c its SA:V ratio.

 7 Why is there a limit to cell size in a multicellular organism?

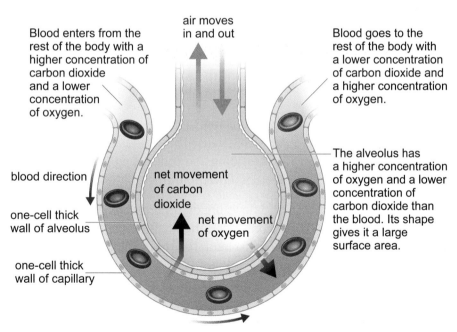

D The drawing shows an alveolus, which is adapted for fast gas exchange (swapping of gases). An adult lung contains about 500 million alveoli, which are grouped together in clusters at the ends of tiny tubes.

 8 Explain how alveoli are adapted for fast gas exchange.

Checkpoint

How confidently can you answer the Progression questions?

Strengthen

S1 List two gases that enter or leave muscle cells. For each, describe how it enters or leaves cells and why it needs to enter or leave.

S2 Compare the SA:V ratios of two cube-shaped cells, one with sides of 15 μm and the other with sides of 25 μm.

Extend

E1 Explain how oxygen and carbon dioxide in the air get to and from a muscle cell. Include details of how the lungs are adapted for this.

Exam-style question

Explain why humans need a circulatory system. *(2 marks)*

CB8b The circulatory system

Specification reference: B8.6; B8.7

Progression questions

- What are the components of the circulatory system?
- How are blood vessels adapted to their functions?
- How is blood adapted to its function?

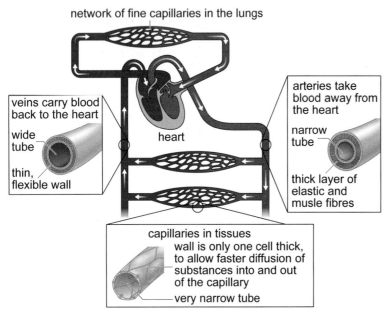

A the human circulatory system

network of fine capillaries in the lungs

veins carry blood back to the heart
wide tube
thin, flexible wall

heart

arteries take blood away from the heart
narrow tube
thick layer of elastic and musle fibres

capillaries in tissues
wall is only one cell thick, to allow faster diffusion of substances into and out of the capillary
very narrow tube

Did you know?

There are nearly 100 000 km of blood vessels in your body.

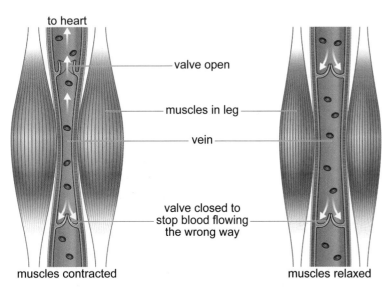

to heart
valve open
muscles in leg
vein
valve closed to stop blood flowing the wrong way
muscles contracted
muscles relaxed

B Valves ensure that blood flows in one direction.

In the circulatory system, **blood** flows away from the **heart** into **arteries**. These divide into narrow **capillaries**, which form fine networks running through tissues. Blood returns to the heart in **veins**.

1 List the parts of the circulatory system.

2 a Describe how the surface area for the exchange of substances is made so large in tissues.

b Explain why this is necessary.

With each beat, the heart squirts blood into arteries under high pressure. Artery walls are thick to withstand this sudden increase in pressure, but it makes them stretch. A wave of stretching then passes along the artery walls. You feel this wave as a **pulse** (the pulse is not your blood moving).

After stretching, muscle and elastic fibres in the artery walls cause the arteries to contract again. The stretching and contracting of arteries makes the blood flow more smoothly.

Blood flows under low pressure in veins and so they only need thin walls. As you move, muscles in your skeleton help to push blood along the veins. Veins contain **valves** to prevent blood flowing the wrong way (as shown in diagram B).

3 Draw a table to show one way in which each type of blood vessel is adapted for its function.

4 Explain why your pulse rate is the same as the rate at which your heart beats.

5 Some people have a disease in which the vein valves in their legs do not work properly. Suggest one symptom of this disease.

Blood

In each cubic millimetre (mm³) of blood there are about 5 000 000 **erythrocytes** (**red blood cells**), 7000 **white blood cells** and 250 000 **platelets**. The cells are suspended in a straw-coloured liquid called **plasma**, which carries dissolved substances such as glucose, carbon dioxide and urea.

Red blood cells are packed with **haemoglobin**. This substance binds with oxygen in the lungs and releases it again in tissues. When a lot of oxygen is bound to haemoglobin molecules, the cells are bright red. When there is less oxygen attached to the molecules, the cells are dark red.

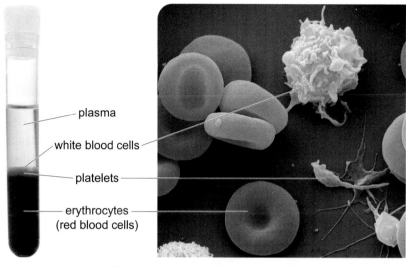

- plasma
- white blood cells
- platelets
- erythrocytes (red blood cells)

C the components of blood

Erythrocytes have no nucleus, so there is more space for haemoglobin. The cells are shaped like discs with a dimple in each side. This 'biconcave' shape allows a large surface area : volume ratio for oxygen to diffuse in and out.

There are different types of white blood cells, including **phagocytes** and **lymphocytes**, which remove foreign cells that get inside you. Lymphocytes produce proteins called **antibodies** that stick to foreign cells and help to destroy them. Phagocytes surround foreign cells and digest them.

Platelets are tiny fragments of cells that have no nuclei. Platelets produce substances needed to clot the blood at the site of an injury, for example when the skin is cut.

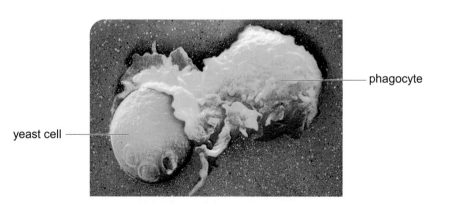

- phagocyte
- yeast cell

D White blood cells protect the body.

 8 Write a better caption for photo D to describe what the photo shows.

 9 Look at diagram D on *CB8a Efficient transport and exchange*. Explain why the erythrocytes are not all the same colour.

Exam-style question

Explain how oxygen is transported from the lungs to a tissue. *(3 marks)*

 6 State the difference between the way urea and oxygen are carried in the blood.

 7 Explain how erythrocytes are adapted to their function.

Checkpoint

How confidently can you answer the Progression questions?

Strengthen

S1 Draw a table to contrast arteries and veins. Include their structures and the substances in the blood inside them.

Extend

E1 In a condition called atherosclerosis, fatty substances build up inside arteries. This makes the arteries narrower and their walls harder. Explain the effects that this condition might have on someone.

CB8c The heart

Specification reference: B8.8; B8.12

Progression questions

- What is the structure of the heart like?
- How does the heart pump blood?
- How do you calculate cardiac output?

A This prototype drone can quickly reach a heart attack patient and deliver a defibrillator.

 1 Suggest why heart muscle dies if it does not get blood.

Someone has a **heart attack** in the UK every three minutes. A heart attack occurs when blood stops flowing to muscles in part of the heart, damaging them and stopping the heart pumping properly. If the heart stops completely, it can often be started again by putting an electric shock through it (using a defibrillator).

Heart structure

There are four **chambers** in the heart. Blood from most of the body enters the right **atrium** through the **vena cava** (a large vein). At the same time, blood from the lungs enters the left atrium through the **pulmonary vein**. When these top chambers are full, the muscles around them **contract** to push blood into the **ventricles**. The muscles in the ventricle walls then contract, forcing blood out of the heart. As this is happening, the muscles in the atria walls relax and these chambers refill with blood.

Heart valves stop blood flowing the wrong way. It is the sound of these valves shutting that you hear as 'lub-dub' when listening to a heart.

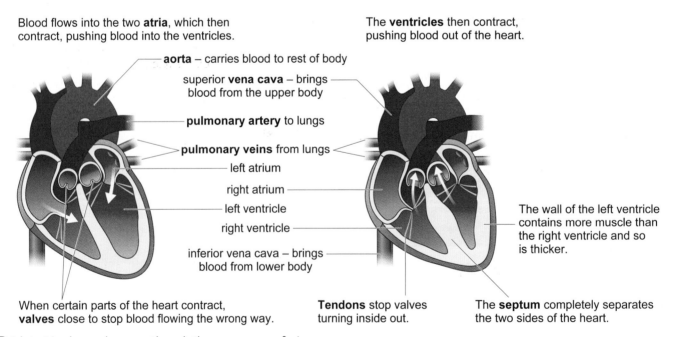

Blood flows into the two **atria**, which then contract, pushing blood into the ventricles.

The **ventricles** then contract, pushing blood out of the heart.

aorta – carries blood to rest of body

superior **vena cava** – brings blood from the upper body

pulmonary artery to lungs

pulmonary veins from lungs

left atrium

right atrium

left ventricle

right ventricle

inferior vena cava – brings blood from lower body

When certain parts of the heart contract, **valves** close to stop blood flowing the wrong way.

Tendons stop valves turning inside out.

The wall of the left ventricle contains more muscle than the right ventricle and so is thicker.

The **septum** completely separates the two sides of the heart.

B A heart is always drawn as though the person were facing you.

Heart muscle is all the same colour, but in diagram B the parts containing blood with little oxygen (**deoxygenated blood**) are coloured dark red. The parts that pump **oxygenated** blood are coloured bright red.

2 a How many atria does the heart contain?

 b Why is the left ventricle on the right of the heart in diagram B?

 3 List in order the parts through which blood flows from the vena cava to the aorta.

 4 Explain why blood in the vena cava is dark red but blood in the aorta is bright red.

 5 The left ventricle has a thicker muscle wall, and so contracts more strongly than the right. Explain why this is needed.

 6 What do the heart valves do?

Cardiac output

The contraction and relaxation of muscles during each heartbeat is controlled by **impulses** from the nervous system. The **heart rate** is the number of times the heart beats in a minute. The volume of blood pushed into the aorta in each beat is the **stroke volume**. It is measured in litres. The **cardiac output** is the volume of blood pushed into the aorta each minute, and can be calculated using the equation:

cardiac output = stroke volume × heart rate
(litres/min)   (litres/beat)   (beats/min)

Regular exercise increases the strength of heart muscle and ventricle size. So, fitter people often have bigger stroke volumes, and their hearts can beat more slowly to achieve the same cardiac output as a less fit person.

 7 a Calculate the cardiac output of a heart that pumps 0.07 litres of blood 55 times per minute.

 b Calculate the stroke volume for a cardiac output of 5 litres/min and a heart rate of 50 beats/min.

 8 Explain why people who take regular exercise often have slower heart rates than those who do not.

Exam-style question

Suggest an explanation for why the heart is sometimes called a 'double pump'. *(2 marks)*

Did you know?

Coronary arteries on the surface of the heart supply materials to the network of capillaries in the heart muscles. Heart attacks are often caused by a coronary artery becoming blocked.

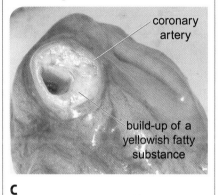

coronary artery

build-up of a yellowish fatty substance

C

D This triangle can help you rearrange the equation for cardiac output. Cover up the quantity you want to calculate and write what you see on the right of the = sign.

Checkpoint

How confidently can you answer the Progression questions?

Strengthen

S1 Explain two ways in which the heart is adapted to its function.

Extend

E1 George has a leak in the valve between his right atrium and right ventricle. Suggest an explanation for why his breathing rate is fast.

CB8d Cellular respiration

Specification reference: B8.9; B8.10

- Why do organisms need to respire?
- Why is respiration an exothermic process?
- What are the differences between aerobic and anaerobic respiration?

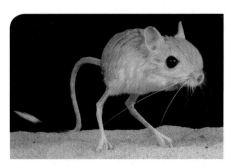

A This is a jerboa. Small mammals lose heat more quickly than larger mammals and so have higher rates of respiration.

Your body requires a constant supply of energy for:

- moving
- keeping warm
- producing and breaking down substances.

Cellular respiration is a series of chemical reactions that release energy from **glucose**. Some energy is transferred out of the cells by heating, which helps keep many animals warm. Respiration is therefore **exothermic** (a process in which energy transfer increases the temperature of the surroundings).

The main type of cellular respiration is **aerobic respiration**, which needs oxygen. Most of the reactions in this process occur in the **mitochondria** of cells and can be summarised in this word equation:

glucose + oxygen → carbon dioxide + water

The circulatory system makes sure that cells have a good supply of oxygen (taken in by the lungs) and glucose (taken in by the small intestine). It also ensures that wastes are carried away from cells.

 1 Explain why your body needs a constant supply of energy.

 2 Explain why cellular respiration helps keep your body warm.

 3 Hummingbird muscle uses twice the amount of oxygen as mammal muscle. Describe a feature you would expect to find in hummingbird muscle cells.

 4 Which substance in the equation for aerobic respiration stores the most energy?

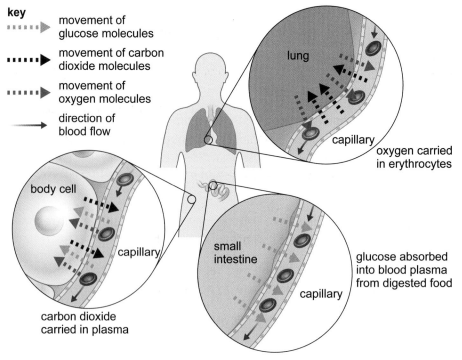

B The circulatory system transports the reactants for respiration to cells and carries away waste products.

Exercise and anaerobic respiration

During exercise your muscles need more energy. The rate of aerobic respiration increases and your muscle cells take more oxygen and glucose from the blood. Your heart beats faster to get more blood to your muscle cells. You breathe faster and deeper to increase the amount of oxygen diffusing into the blood in your lungs. Faster breathing also allows your lungs to excrete more carbon dioxide.

During very strenuous exercise, oxygen is used up faster than it is replaced. When this happens, the amount of **anaerobic respiration** occurring in the cytoplasm of cells greatly increases. This form of cellular respiration does not require oxygen and produces **lactic acid**:

glucose → lactic acid

 5 Explain why your muscles need more energy when you exercise.

Did you know?

There are different types of anaerobic respiration in different organisms. The holes in some cheeses are caused by gases released by a form of anaerobic respiration that occurs in some bacteria. The ethanol in alcoholic drinks is produced by yeast using another form of anaerobic respiration.

D

Anaerobic respiration releases less energy from glucose than aerobic respiration. In animals, it also causes muscles to tire quickly. However, anaerobic respiration can release bursts of energy without needing a sudden increase in oxygen supply. This is important for animals that may need to move fast and suddenly, such as when sprinting away from a predator.

Heart and breathing rates can remain high after exercise, because extra oxygen is needed to replace the oxygen lost from blood and muscles. Extra oxygen is also needed to release the extra energy required to get rid of lactic acid.

 7 What are the waste product(s) of anaerobic respiration?

 8 a Explain why people continue to have high pulse rates after strenuous exercise.

 b Suggest why a fit person's pulse rate decreases more quickly after exercise than an unfit person's.

Exam-style question

State an advantage of anaerobic respiration for humans. *(1 mark)*

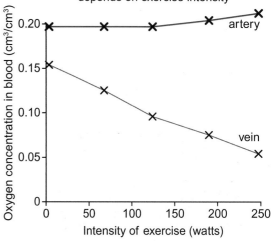

How the concentration of blood oxygen depends on exercise intensity

C Increasing exercise intensity affects the concentrations of gases dissolved in blood. Adapted from Carbon dioxide pressure-concentration relationship in arterial and mixed venous blood during exercise, Journal of Applied Physiology, Vol. 90, no. 5 (Sun, X-G, Hansen, J.E., Stringer, W.W., Ting, H., Wasserman, K.).

6 Look at graph C.

 a Suggest why the amount of oxygen in the artery increases as exercise intensity increases.

 b Explain why the line for the vein slopes downwards.

Checkpoint

How confidently can you answer the Progression questions?

Strengthen

S1 Design a table to compare and contrast aerobic and anaerobic respiration.

Extend

E1 Explain why small mammals lose heat more quickly than larger mammals.

E2 Explain how this affects their rate of respiration.

CB8d Core practical – Respiration rates

Specification reference: B8.11

Aim

Investigate the rate of respiration in living organisms.

A astronaut Kathryn Hire using a respirometer as part of an experiment in space

Many experiments are being done to find out the effects of space travel on human respiration. These experiments allow scientists to predict possible problems that astronauts might have while on space missions and to work out how much oxygen they will need. Scientists measure respiration rates using a respirometer, which measures the amount of oxygen used, the amount of carbon dioxide produced, or both.

Your task

You are going to use a simple respirometer to measure the oxygen consumption of some small organisms (e.g. mealworms) and to find out how the rate of respiration depends on temperature.

Method

Wear eye protection.

A Collect a tube with some soda lime, held in place with cotton wool. The soda lime absorbs carbon dioxide. Soda lime is corrosive, so do not handle it. The cotton wool is there to protect you and the organisms.

B Carefully collect some of the small organisms in a weighing boat.

C Gently shake the organisms out of the container and into the tube.

D Insert the bung and capillary tube, as shown in diagram B.

E Set up a control tube.

F Place both tubes into a rack in a water bath at a set temperature. It is best to tilt the rack slightly so that the capillary tubes hang over the side of the water bath at an angle.

G Wait for five minutes to let the organisms adjust to the temperature of the water bath.

H Hold a beaker of coloured liquid to the ends of the capillary tubes, so that liquid enters.

I Mark the position of the coloured liquid in the tube and time for five minutes.

J Mark the position of the coloured liquid again, and measure the distance it has travelled.

K Repeat the experiment at different temperatures.

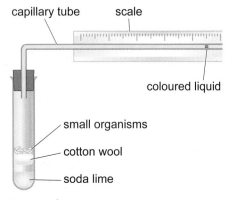

B a simple respirometer

Exam-style questions

1 a State the gas produced by aerobic respiration in the organisms.
(1 mark)

b Explain fully why the blob of coloured liquid moves in the capillary tube. *(3 marks)*

2 Describe one way in which the risk of harm is reduced in this experiment. *(1 mark)*

3 A student suggests using a small paintbrush to move the small organisms from a tray into her weighing boat. State why this would be a good idea. *(1 mark)*

4 a Describe how you would set up a control tube. *(1 mark)*

b Explain why a control tube is necessary. *(2 marks)*

5 The experiment was set up using three large tubes at 25 °C. One tube was a control, one contained 20 g of active mealworms, and the other contained 20 g of slow-moving waxworms.

a State the two control variables in this experiment. *(2 marks)*

b State the independent variable. *(2 marks)*

c In five minutes, the blob of coloured liquid moved 10 mm for the mealworms. Predict what would happen in the other two tubes. *(2 marks)*

d Explain your predictions. *(2 marks)*

e The moving of the liquid by 10 mm corresponds to a total change in volume of 5 mm³. Calculate the rate of respiration in terms of the volume of oxygen used up per gram of organism per minute. Show your working. *(2 marks)*

6 State the lowest and the highest temperature at which you would test the respiration rate in small organisms. Give reasons for your choices. *(2 marks)*

7 Table C shows the results of one experiment to measure the effect of temperature on the respiration rate of waxworms.

a Explain why the measurements were repeated for each temperature. *(1 mark)*

b Plot all the results on a scatter graph. *(2 marks)*

c Identify the anomalous result. *(1 mark)*

d Suggest an explanation for this anomalous result. *(1 mark)*

e Draw a line of best fit through the remaining points. *(1 mark)*

f Describe the correlation shown in your graph. *(1 mark)*

g Suggest an explanation for this correlation. *(2 marks)*

Temperature (°C)	Distance moved by the blob in 5 min (mm)
10	9
10	9
10	10
15	12
15	15
15	13
20	17
20	20
20	18
25	25
25	25
25	28
30	10
30	33
30	38

C

The heart

Explain why a change in heart and breathing rates is an advantage when exercising strenuously.　　(6 marks)

Student answer

Muscles need energy to make them work, and they need more energy when they work harder (like when you do exercise). Energy is released during respiration. As exercise gets harder, more and more energy is needed and so more and more respiration occurs. Aerobic respiration is the main type of respiration and needs oxygen and glucose:

glucose + oxygen → carbon dioxide + water [1]

The heart pumps faster to get more of the reactants for aerobic respiration to cells [2]. The breathing rate increases to get more oxygen into the blood [3]. A greater blood flow also helps to remove the carbon dioxide waste. If exercise is very strenuous, then anaerobic respiration increases. This uses up glucose but produces lactic acid, which is carried away faster by the increased flow of blood.

[1] This is an excellent start, clearly explaining what the body needs when exercising.

[2] This is a correct explanation for the first part of the question about heart rate.

[3] This is a correct explanation of the second part of the question about breathing rate. A small criticism here is that this sentence could have come first in this paragraph. Then all the information about the heart and increased blood flow would be together.

Verdict

This is a strong answer. It clearly makes the link between respiration, exercise and the increase in breathing and heart rates. The answer correctly mentions both aerobic and anaerobic respiration and links them both to the increase in blood flow and breathing rates. The answer is well organised and uses scientific words correctly.

Exam tip

There are two things to consider in the question, 'heart rate' and 'breathing rate'. When you have finished writing your answer, ensure you look back at the question so you know you have covered everything.

Paper 2

CB9 Ecosystems and Material Cycles

Many flowers produce a scent that mimics the smell of a female insect. This attracts males of that insect species to visit the flower. During their visit, pollen from the flower attaches to the male. The pollen is taken to the next flower that the male visits. The orchid plant in the photo goes one step further by having flowers that mimic the shape and colour of a female digger wasp. Male wasps are so convinced by the deception, they try to mate with the flower. The orchid is dependent on the males of this one species of wasp to carry out their pollination.

The learning journey

Previously you will have learnt at KS3:

- how almost all life on Earth depends on photosynthesis in plants and algae
- about the interdependence of organisms, including food webs and insect pollination
- how organisms affect and are affected by their environment, including the accumulation of toxic materials.

In this unit you will learn:

- how ecosystems are organised
- how communities are affected by abiotic and biotic factors
- how the abundance and distribution of organisms are measured
- about parasitism and mutualism
- how humans can affect ecosystems
- about the benefits of maintaining biodiversity
- how materials cycle through ecosystems
- about the importance of the carbon cycle, water cycle and nitrogen cycle.

CB9a Ecosystems

Specification reference: B9.1; B9.3; B9.6

Progression questions

- What is a community of organisms?
- How are ecosystems structured?
- Why is interdependence in communities important?

A Plants interact with each other both above and below ground.

Organisms need **resources** to stay alive. Plants need space in which to get light, water, carbon dioxide, oxygen, warmth and mineral ions. Animals need oxygen, food and water. They may also need somewhere to shelter from the weather or avoid predation from other animals. This means that organisms are continually interacting with each other and with their environments.

1 Give reasons for each of the following.

 a Plants and animals need oxygen.

 b Plants need light and water.

c Plants need mineral ions.

 2 a State why plants have root systems.

 b Use photo A to explain how plants interact with each other both above and below ground.

All the organisms and the environment in which they live form an **ecosystem**. An ecosystem may be large, such as a rainforest, or small, such as a pond.

All the organisms that live and interact in an ecosystem form a **community**. The community is made up of **populations** of different species. These species depend on each other for resources, so we say they are **interdependent**. Each population lives in a particular **habitat** within the ecosystem. A habitat includes the other organisms that affect the population and the local environment.

 3 a Sketch a diagram to show the relationship between the terms population, community and ecosystem.

 b Add an example of each term to your diagram, using the information from these pages.

B Coral reefs are the calcium carbonate outer skeletons built by tiny coral animals of different species. The reefs are also home to many other organisms, such as fish, starfish, sponges and turtles.

Abundance is a measure of how common something is in an area, such as its population size. Measuring population size by counting all the organisms in an area is often impossible. However, you can estimate population size by taking **samples** using a **quadrat**. Quadrats are placed randomly in the area, and the number of individuals in each quadrat is counted. The population size is estimated as:

$$\text{population size} = \text{number of organisms in all quadrats} \times \frac{\text{total size of area where organism lives}}{\text{total area of quadrats}}$$

A **food web** shows the feeding relationships between the organisms in a community. We can use a food web to help predict what will happen if there are changes in the ecosystem. For example, in diagram D, if all the herons die out, fewer frogs would be eaten. However, if the population of frogs increases, then more sticklebacks might be eaten.

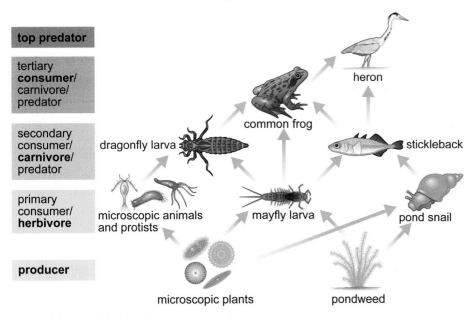

D a highly simplified food web for a pond ecosystem

top predator

tertiary **consumer/** carnivore/ predator

secondary consumer/ **carnivore/** predator

primary consumer/ **herbivore**

producer

heron

common frog

dragonfly larva

stickleback

microscopic animals and protists

mayfly larva

pond snail

microscopic plants

pondweed

C This quadrat has been placed on a school field. This sample includes two dandelion plants (long leaves) inside the large square. The square frame is divided into smaller squares to help count smaller plants, e.g. grass.

4 In a 1 m² quadrat on a rocky shore there are 50 limpet shells. The total area of rocks is 450 m².

a Estimate the total population size of limpets on the rocks.

b Explain why it would be better to estimate the population size from a mean number of limpets from several randomly placed quadrats.

5 Use diagram D to answer these questions.

a Name one herbivore in a pond ecosystem.

b What is the top predator in this ecosystem?

c What do frogs eat?

d What is a producer?

6 Use diagram D to predict the effect on other organisms if all the pond snails died out. Explain your answer.

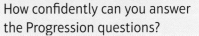

Checkpoint

How confidently can you answer the Progression questions?

Strengthen

S1 Define the terms: population, community, ecosystem, interdependence.

Extend

E1 Explain why diagram D is highly simplified and how this affects how correct your answer for question 6 might be.

Exam-style question

Describe two ways in which organisms in a community are interdependent. *(2 marks)*

Specification reference: B9.2; B9.6

Progression questions

* What are abiotic factors?
* How do natural abiotic factors affect communities?
* How can pollution affect communities?

A The brown areas in these fields show where plants have died due to waterlogged soils caused by floods.

The **distribution** of organisms is where they are found in an ecosystem. Distribution can be affected by physical and chemical factors, such as temperature, rainfall and substances in the soil. These non-living factors are called **abiotic factors**. The effect of abiotic factors on the distribution of organisms can be measured using a **belt transect**. Quadrats are placed along a line in a habitat, and the abundance of organisms is measured as well as the abiotic factors in each quadrat position. Changes in abundance can show which abiotic factor has the greatest effect on the organisms.

 1 Name two abiotic factors related to climate.

Each species of organism has certain **adaptations** that mean the organism is suited to particular conditions. If abiotic factors change, then the distribution of organisms may also change.

Few organisms can survive a **drought** (lack of water) for long. Most land plants cannot survive if their roots are under water for long. If the climate changes resulting in more flooding or more drought, then many species in different communities may die out.

Temperature also affects the distribution of organisms. For example, polar bears are adapted to living in cold regions, while cacti are adapted to living in hot deserts. However, all organisms have adaptations that make them suited to life at particular temperatures. A long-term rise or fall in temperature in an ecosystem will change the distribution of some organisms and so affect the whole community.

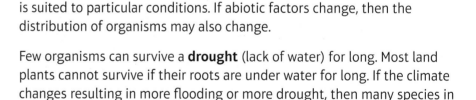

B Many sea birds such as the puffin, and predator fish such as haddock, depend on sandeels for food. Rising sea temperatures in the North Sea have reduced the numbers of microscopic animals that sandeels feed on.

 2 Explain why flooding may affect a whole community, not just the plants.

 3 **a** Sketch a food web involving sandeels in the North Sea.

 b Use your food web to explain why rising sea temperatures are linked to fewer haddock for us to eat and decreased numbers of puffins.

Light is essential for plants and algae to grow. In the oceans, most algae can only get enough light within 30 m of the surface. On land, light is limited within forests. In dense forests, few plants can grow on the forest floor.

 4 Suggest an explanation for where you would expect to find herbivores in the ocean.

 5 Explain why tree seedlings in a dense forest can start growing rapidly only when a mature tree has fallen.

Substances that cause harm in the environment are **pollutants** and cause **pollution**. Many human activities release pollutants. These can poison organisms or cause harm to organisms in other ways (such as plastics being eaten by fish and other organisms).

C In dense forests, tree seedlings can start growing to full height only when a mature tree has fallen and allowed light to reach the forest floor.

D In 2015 a dam collapsed at an iron mine on the River Doce in Brazil, releasing polluted muddy water into the river. High levels of poisonous mercury and arsenic killed fish and other river organisms.

Did you know?

The phrase 'mad as a hatter' refers to people who made hats in the 18th and 19th centuries. Mercury was used in the process. Long-term exposure to mercury damages the nervous system as well as many organs.

 6 State what is meant by pollution.

 7 Suggest how pollution from the collapsed dam in Brazil (see photo D) might have affected the whole community of organisms living beside the river.

Exam-style question

Explain why drought in an ecosystem can have long-term effects on the animals in a community. *(3 marks)*

Checkpoint

How confidently can you answer the Progression questions?

Strengthen

S1 A woodland is thinned by removing half the trees. Explain what effect this may have on low-growing plants in the following year.

Extend

E1 Plants that live in polar communities are generally much smaller than those living in tropical communities. Suggest an explanation for this.

CB9b Core practical – Quadrats and transects

Specification reference: B9.5

Aim

Investigate the relationship between organisms and their environment using field-work techniques, including quadrats and belt transects.

A Quadrats must be placed carefully on a coral reef to avoid damaging organisms and the scientists being cut by sharp corals.

Pollution, due to high concentrations of nitrates and other substances from rivers flowing into the oceans, is damaging large areas of many coral reefs. The effect of pollution on coral reefs can be studied using a **belt transect**, from a point on the reef close to the river to a point further away. These two points mark the ends of the transect line, which may be many kilometres in length. Quadrats are placed at regular intervals along the transect. Measurements of the species and the abiotic factors within each quadrat are recorded. The distribution of the organisms is then compared with the abiotic factors to see which populations are most affected by changes in abiotic factors. This method can also be used on land, for example to identify the effect of waterlogging or shade on the growth of plants.

Your task

You will use a belt transect to study the effect of abiotic factors on the abundance of low-growing plants. The transect will stretch between open ground and heavy shade under a large tree. Several abiotic factors will vary along the transect. Before you start, you will need to decide which abiotic factors to measure and how to measure them. You will also need to decide which plants to record and how you will record their abundance within a quadrat.

Method

A Peg out a long tape measure (at least 20 m) on the ground, starting where there is no shade and ending in heavy shade. This is the transect line.

B You will need to make measurements at regular intervals along the transect line (see diagram B). Decide on your measurement intervals, which may depend on how long the line is and how much time you have to record information.

C Place the top left-hand corner of the quadrat at a measurement point on the transect line.

D Measure the abiotic factors at that point and record them.

E Record the abundance of your selected plants in the quadrat.

F Repeat steps C to E at each measurement point along the transect.

B Quadrats are placed at regular intervals along a transect line.

Exam-style questions

1 Describe how a quadrat is used to measure distribution in the shade investigation. *(1 mark)*

2 What are abiotic factors? *(1 mark)*

3 Explain how two abiotic factors will change between the open ground and close to the tree. *(2 marks)*

4 Explain why the abundance of a plant species might change between the open ground and close to the tree. *(2 marks)*

5 Describe a disadvantage of:

   a measuring at short intervals along a long transect *(1 mark)*

   b measuring at long intervals. *(1 mark)*

6 Give a reason why the quadrats are placed at regular intervals along a transect and not randomly (as when estimating population size). *(1 mark)*

7 Describe how you would identify the plants in the investigation. *(1 mark)*

8 **a** Explain how some measurements of abiotic factors would vary if taken in the afternoon rather than in the morning. *(2 marks)*

   b Explain how these variations could affect the conclusion drawn from data taken at just one time of day. *(2 marks)*

9 Describe how you could adjust the method on the previous page to study the effect of pollution on a coral reef. Explain your changes. *(2 marks)*

10 Describe one way in which damage to the coral reef can be avoided while carrying out a transect survey. *(1 mark)*

11 Table C shows the results of a transect survey beginning on dry land, moving through marsh and swamp and ending in open water.

   a Name the abiotic factor measured in this survey. *(1 mark)*

   b Describe how this abiotic factor affects the distribution of each of the plants surveyed. *(5 marks)*

   c Use the table to predict which species would be most affected by flooding, giving a reason for your answer. *(2 marks)*

	dry land	marsh	swamp	open water
water depth (cm)	0–1	1–5	5–15	15–65
hazel bush	✓			
willow tree		✓		
meadowsweet		✓	✓	
duckweed			✓	✓
water lily				✓

C A tick indicates the species is present.

CB9c Biotic factors and communities

Specification reference: B9.2

Progression questions

- What are biotic factors?
- How can competition affect communities?
- How can predation affect communities?

A Grey wolves hunt together to bring down elk.

Biotic factors are the organisms in an ecosystem that affect other living organisms. Yellowstone National Park is a huge area of protected land in northern USA. The Yellowstone ecosystem had included grey wolves until 1926, when they became extinct in the area due to hunting. The wolves had been the top predator in the community.

 1 What is meant by a top predator?

 2 Explain why Yellowstone Park is an ecosystem.

After 1926, the number of elk in the park increased rapidly. Their huge numbers caused overgrazing of many tree species. This left little food for other large herbivores, including beavers. Elk and beavers **compete** for food from trees. The numbers of coyotes (a kind of wild dog) also increased, because there was less **competition** from wolves for food such as young elk.

In 1995, grey wolves were reintroduced to Yellowstone Park. The aim was to increase **predation** of elk, whose numbers were out of control.

3 Use the information on this page to give two examples of competition, naming the resource that is being competed for.

4 Explain how lack of competition from wolves could lead to an increase in the number of coyotes.

B Wolves are larger than coyotes and chase them away, making it more difficult for coyotes to get food.

In large communities such as Yellowstone, many biotic factors may affect predator and prey numbers. However, in small communities, the numbers of a predator and its prey may be closely related in a **predator–prey cycle**. Graph C shows an example.

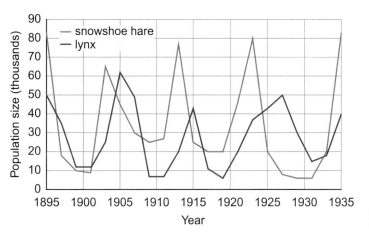

C Snowshoe hares are almost the only prey of lynxes in some areas of northern Canada. Their numbers are correlated in a predator–prey cycle.

The reintroduction of wolves to Yellowstone rapidly reduced the numbers of elk. This led to an increase in beaver numbers. Beavers change their surroundings by building dams, creating large pools and muddy areas. These new habitats allowed new species to grow in the area, increasing the **biodiversity** (the number of different species).

D Pools created by beaver dams allow the growth of species adapted to boggy areas, such as willow trees.

 6 Explain how the reintroduction of wolves to Yellowstone changed abiotic and biotic factors in that ecosystem.

 7 Explain why biodiversity in Yellowstone Park increased after wolves were reintroduced.

Exam-style question

Describe how introducing a new predator can affect a community through predation and competition. *(2 marks)*

 **5** Look at graph C.

 a Describe how the hare and lynx numbers are correlated.

 b Suggest an explanation for this correlation.

Did you know?

In the 19th century, humans hunted sea otters almost to extinction off western North America. This led to an increase in sea urchins, which sea otters eat. As a result, huge areas of kelp (seaweed) that sheltered many fish were destroyed as they were eaten by the sea urchins.

Checkpoint

How confidently can you answer the Progression questions?

Strengthen

S1 Explain why elk and beavers compete with each other in Yellowstone Park.

Extend

E1 Sketch a copy of graph C to show the snowshoe hare line. Add a line to your graph to show the population size of the hare's food (lichen). Explain the shape of your line.

CB9d Parasitism and mutualism

Specification reference: B9.4

Progression questions

- How are some organisms dependent on other species?
- How does parasitism affect the survival of some organisms?
- How does mutualism help the survival of some organisms?

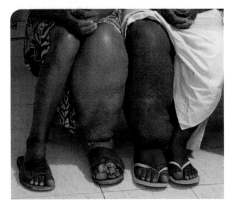

A Elephantiasis is caused by infection with roundworms. The roundworms absorb nutrients from human body fluids and become a problem when they block the flow of fluids in the body.

In most feeding relationships, a predator kills and eats its prey then moves on to find more prey. **Parasitism** is a different kind of feeding relationship in which one organism (the **parasite**) benefits by feeding off a **host** organism, causing harm to the host. The parasite lives in or on the host. The host may survive for a long time and continue to provide food for the parasite if the parasite causes limited harm.

1 Look at photo A.

 a Which is the parasite and which is the host organism?

 b Explain how the parasite benefits from its relationship with the host.

 c Explain how the host organism is harmed by its relationship with the parasite.

 2 In your own words, define the term parasite.

Some parasites, such as lice, live on the outside of their hosts. Others, such as tapeworms, live inside. All parasites have adaptations that help them survive in or on their host.

 3 How are lice adapted to feeding from their host?

 4 a Explain how a tapeworm could cause malnutrition in its host.

 b If malnutrition causes the tapeworm's host to die, explain why tapeworms do not all die out.

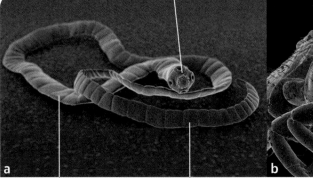

Hooks and suckers attach the worm's head firmly to the host's intestine wall.

Sharp mouthparts can pierce skin and suck blood.

Segments contain male and female sex organs so fertilisation can occur.

A flattened body allows absorption of nutrients over whole surface without need for digestive or circulatory systems.

Sharp claws grip on to hair and skin.

Eggs are glued to hairs to prevent them falling off.

B Two examples of parasites. **a** Tapeworms are adapted to living inside their host's intestines. **b** Head lice are adapted to living on hair and skin.

Mutualism

Some organisms that live together both benefit from the relationship. These relationships are said to be **mutualistic**. For example, many flowers depend on insects for pollination. The flower benefits by being able to produce fertilised egg cells, and the insect benefits by collecting nectar or pollen from the flower, which it uses for food.

 5 a How does the clownfish benefit from its relationship with a sea anemone?

 a How does the sea anemone benefit from its relationship with a clownfish?

C A sea anemone's stinging tentacles protect clownfish from predators. Clownfish chase off the predators of the anemone and provide nutrients in their faeces, which help the anemone to grow.

Coral polyps form a special relationship with single-celled algae. The algae can live in the water surrounding corals, but are better protected inside a polyp. The algae photosynthesise and share the food they make with the coral animal.

coral polyp

green algae inside polyp

D Single-celled algae live inside the coral animals that build coral reefs.

 6 Describe how the relationship between a coral animal and algae is mutualistic.

 7 Explain the difference between parasitic and mutualistic relationships.

Exam-style question

Scientists discover a close relationship between two organisms. Explain how scientists would decide whether this is mutualism or parasitism. *(2 marks)*

Checkpoint

How confidently can you answer the Progression questions?

Strengthen

S1 Using a suitable example, describe how a parasite is dependent on its host.

Extend

E1 One treatment for curing someone with elephantiasis is an antibiotic that kills *Wolbachia*. Explain why this works.

Progression questions

- How does fish farming affect ecosystems?
- How does the introduction of new species affect biodiversity?
- How does eutrophication affect ecosystems?

A Salmon are farmed in pens, where they are better fed and grow faster than in the wild. They are also protected against predators and disease.

Many of the ways in which humans affect ecosystems can reduce biodiversity.

Fish farming

About 17 per cent of the protein eaten by people globally comes from fish. As the human population increases, we will need more fish. However, **overfishing** of wild fish stocks has damaged some aquatic (water) ecosystems. **Fish farming** aims to produce more fish and so reduce overfishing of wild fish.

 1 What is fish farming?

 2 Give two reasons why farming fish may be a better way to provide food for humans than catching wild fish.

 3 Describe two harmful effects that fish farming can have on an environment.

Fish farming causes problems because so many fish are kept in a relatively small space. Uneaten food, and faeces from the fish, sinks to the bottom of the water. This can change conditions, which may harm the wild organisms that live there. Parasites and disease spread more easily between fish in pens, so the fish need to be treated to keep them healthy.

Introducing species

Introducing new species to ecosystems can affect the **indigenous**, or **native**, species (organisms that have always been there). For example, sheep, cattle and soybeans are **native** to Asia but are farmed for food in many parts of the world where they are **non-indigenous**.

Did you know?

In the 2000s, sea lice from farmed salmon killed over 90 per cent of young wild salmon on one Canadian coast. Timing of treatment to kill the lice on farmed salmon was changed to just before the wild salmon passed through the area, reducing deaths of wild salmon to 4 per cent.

B Ring-necked parakeets are escaped pets that are now common in parts of the UK. Some smaller native birds are unable to compete for food with the parakeets.

Some species are introduced in order to affect an ecosystem, such as to reduce the numbers of another species that has got out of control. This often happens after humans have changed ecosystems and affected the food web. For example, cane toads from South America were introduced to Australia to control the numbers of cane beetles, which were eating sugar cane crops. Now the numbers of cane toads are a problem; the toads are poisonous and kill native animals.

Eutrophication

Eutrophication is the addition of more nutrients to an ecosystem than it normally has. For example, this can happen when too much fertiliser is added to a field. Fertilisers help crop plants grow better, but will also increase the growth of other plants and algae. Diagram D shows how this can harm an ecosystem, causing a form of pollution.

native Australian frog

C Cane toads eat a wide range of indigenous species.

4 State three ways in which humans might introduce non-indigenous species into an ecosystem.

5 Give two ways in which introduced species can affect a native food web.

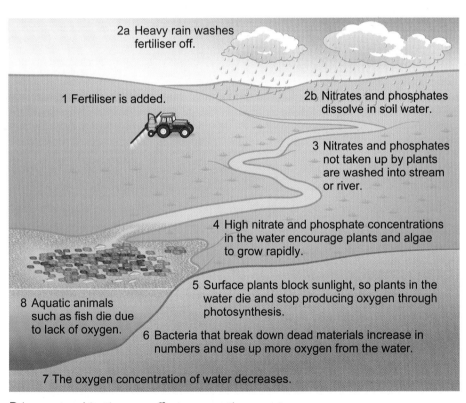

2a Heavy rain washes fertiliser off.

1 Fertiliser is added.

2b Nitrates and phosphates dissolve in soil water.

3 Nitrates and phosphates not taken up by plants are washed into stream or river.

4 High nitrate and phosphate concentrations in the water encourage plants and algae to grow rapidly.

5 Surface plants block sunlight, so plants in the water die and stop producing oxygen through photosynthesis.

8 Aquatic animals such as fish die due to lack of oxygen.

6 Bacteria that break down dead materials increase in numbers and use up more oxygen from the water.

7 The oxygen concentration of water decreases.

D how eutrophication can affect an aquatic ecosystem

6 a How does adding fertiliser benefit a farmer's field?

b Explain how eutrophication can change biodiversity in an aquatic ecosystem.

Did you know?

Lake Erie, a large lake on the border of Canada and the USA, became choked with algae in the 1960s and 70s due to fertiliser from fields and other nitrate sources. Strict pollution control has since reduced the problem.

Checkpoint

How confidently can you answer the Progression questions?

Strengthen

S1 Explain how too much fertiliser on a field can lead to the death of fish in a nearby river.

Extend

E1 American signal crayfish were introduced into the UK in the 1970s and bred for restaurants. Some escaped, and the wild population increased. Draw up a list of questions that need to be asked before a control programme is introduced to limit their numbers.

Exam-style question

Describe one benefit to biodiversity and one problem caused by farming fish rather than collecting them from the wild. *(2 marks)*

CB9f Preserving biodiversity

Specification reference: B9.10

Progression questions

- How can animal species be conserved?
- How can animal conservation protect biodiversity?
- How can reforestation affect biodiversity?

Northern England was once covered by forest. By 100 years ago, the trees had gone and it was mostly open moorland, where animals such as deer and grouse lived. Then a major **reforestation** project began. Kielder Forest was originally planted with conifer trees (e.g. pines) to provide wood. Today, both conifers and broad leaved trees are planted and some areas are left open, to increase the range of habitats and increase the number of species living in the area.

 1 What does reforestation mean?

 2 a Explain why the biodiversity of plants has increased in the Kielder area in the last 100 years.

 b Suggest a reason why increasing biodiversity of plants has affected the biodiversity of animals.

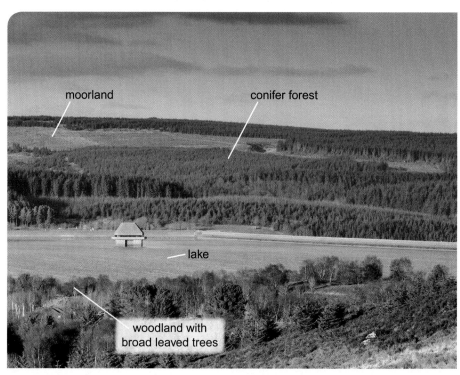

A The 250-square-mile Kielder Forest today is a mixture of habitats created by different tree species, moorland, grassland, a large artificial lake and many pools.

B Red squirrels are indigenous to the UK. Their numbers have decreased due to loss of their preferred conifer woodland habitat, and competition for food by introduced grey squirrels in broad leaved woodlands.

Kielder Forest is now home to species that are rare in other parts of the UK, including the osprey, goshawk and red squirrel. **Conservation** is when an effort is made to protect a rare or **endangered** species or habitat. For example, in Kielder, nesting platforms have been built in tall trees to encourage ospreys to nest. Also, any grey squirrels in the area are caught and killed, to help protect the red squirrels.

 3 Why are grey squirrels a threat to red squirrels?

 4 Explain how planting Kielder Forest has helped to conserve red squirrels.

Conservation of a species is easier if the species habitat is also protected. However, the habitats of many rare species are being damaged or destroyed. For example, tigers live in dense forests which are being cut down for wood and to create space for people to live. Also, people hunt tigers for fur and other body parts, and to reduce attacks on farm animals. Tigers are being bred in **captivity** (e.g. in zoos) to increase their numbers, but their habitats need to be rebuilt and protected too. These habitats also need to be linked so that tigers can roam more widely and find mates.

Preserving biodiversity is not just important for conserving individual species or communities. Areas with greater biodiversity can recover faster from natural disasters such as flooding. We also use plants and animals for food and as a source of medicines and other products. As conditions change, we may need new varieties of plants and animals to provide what we need. So it is important that we try to preserve as many species as we can.

D Angkor Wat temple in Malaysia was abandoned in 1431. Even now, the forest that has regrown around it is not the same as the original indigenous forest, due to lack of seeds from some species in the soil.

Did you know?

Rainforests are incredibly biodiverse ecosystems. Rainforests contain about 500 species of tree per hectare (compared with about 6 to 12 per hectare in a UK forest). Many rainforest plants could be used to develop new medicines, and there are still many plants to discover.

 7 Suggest, with reasons, how the biodiversity of land cleared of rainforest could be increased more quickly than by leaving the area to recover naturally.

Exam-style question

Explain the benefits to wildlife of the reforestation of the Kielder area.

(2 marks)

C The South China tiger has not been seen in the wild for over 25 years and there are only about 70 in zoos.

 5 a Give two reasons why tigers need conservation.

 b Explain why tiger conservation is being carried out in captivity.

 c Suggest what else needs to be done before tigers can be returned to the wild.

 6 Give three reasons why preserving rainforests should be encouraged.

Checkpoint

How confidently can you answer the Progression questions?

Strengthen

S1 How can planting an area of grassland with different kinds of trees increase biodiversity?

Extend

E1 A local landowner plans to develop a 5-hectare field. Write a letter outlining the advantages of replanting the area as mixed woodland.

CB9g The water cycle

Specification reference: B9.12, B9.14

Progression questions

- Which materials cycle through ecosystems?
- How does water cycle through ecosystems?
- How is potable drinking water produced?

Living organisms need different substances from their environment to stay alive, such as water and carbon and nitrogen compounds. There are only limited amounts of these substances on Earth, so they must be recycled through organisms and the environment in order to support life.

Diagram A shows the **water cycle**. It illustrates how water moves through the abiotic parts of an ecosystem.

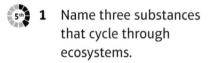 **1** Name three substances that cycle through ecosystems.

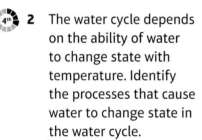 **2** The water cycle depends on the ability of water to change state with temperature. Identify the processes that cause water to change state in the water cycle.

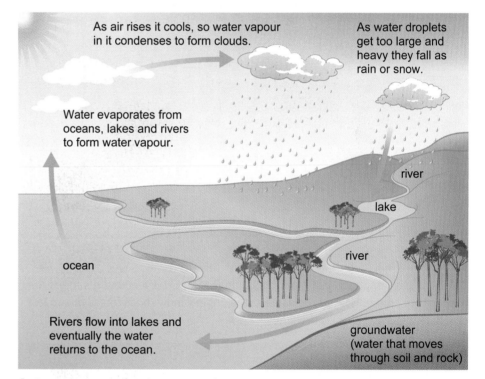

As air rises it cools, so water vapour in it condenses to form clouds.

As water droplets get too large and heavy they fall as rain or snow.

Water evaporates from oceans, lakes and rivers to form water vapour.

river

lake

river

ocean

Rivers flow into lakes and eventually the water returns to the ocean.

groundwater (water that moves through soil and rock)

A physical processes in the water cycle

3 Describe two ways in which we take water into our bodies.

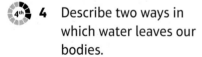 **4** Describe two ways in which water leaves our bodies.

5 Suggest how you could label diagram A to describe how water cycles through the biotic parts of an ecosystem.

6 Draw a flowchart to show how water from the environment is made potable.

Water makes up the majority of most organisms' body mass. For example, around 60 per cent of your body is water. Much of the cell cytoplasm is water, and reactions of substances often take place there. We are continually losing water to the environment, so we need to take in more water to replace it. Humans can only survive a few days without water.

There is plenty of fresh water in the environment, such as in rivers, lakes and underground. We can use this water for washing. To make it **potable** (safe for drinking), the water must be treated with chemicals and filtered, to remove dirt, pathogens and any toxic substances (such as some metal ions). The water may also be treated to improve the taste, by removing other non-toxic substances.

In places where there is drought, drinking water must either be collected from the air or extracted from sea water.

 7 Explain why water caught from clouds or mist is usually potable.

Obtaining fresh water from the sea or salty water is known as **desalination**. Several methods are used to do this, including **distillation** where the water is evaporated and then condensed and collected.

B Nets are used to catch droplets of water from clouds or mist in some desert areas. As long as equipment is clean, the water needs no treatment to make it potable.

Dirty water is put into the still here.

Water evaporates as it gets hotter inside the still.

Clean water is collected from the still here.

Water condenses under the cover and trickles to the bottom of the slope.

C A small solar still can supply fresh drinking water from dirty water where it is hot and sunny.

 8 Explain how distillation can produce potable water from dirty water.

 9 Explain why desalination is an important source of potable water in Saudi Arabia.

Water for desalination is taken from the nearby sea.

drinking water storage tanks

D Saudi Arabia is mostly desert. Over half the country's drinking water comes from desalination plants like this one at Shoaiba, though it requires a lot of energy for the process.

Checkpoint

How confidently can you answer the Progression questions?

Strengthen

S1 Explain why water is treated in the UK to make it suitable for drinking.

Extend

E1 Describe an advantage and a disadvantage of producing drinking water by desalination.

Exam-style question

Describe how water is cycled in the water cycle. *(3 marks)*

CB9h The carbon cycle

Specification reference: B9.13

Progression questions

- What is a decomposer?
- How is carbon cycled through an ecosystem?
- What is the role of decomposers in the carbon cycle?

Did you know?

We are made of stardust. All the carbon on Earth was originally formed in supergiant stars that exploded, scattering stardust across space. Carbon is the second-most abundant substance in the human body after water.

Pilobolus, the 'dung cannon' fungus, grows inside cow **faeces**, digesting the carbon compounds. The fungus produces capsules that contain spores (tiny new fungi). The capsule explodes off the top of the stalk onto fresh grass. When the cow eats the grass, the fungus is not digested and grows on the faeces when it leaves the cow. The fungus plays a key role in the **carbon cycle**.

A The stalks of *Pilobolus* are less than 4 cm high, but can throw their capsules over 2 m away.

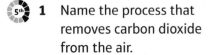 **1** Name the process that removes carbon dioxide from the air.

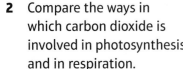 **2** Compare the ways in which carbon dioxide is involved in photosynthesis and in respiration.

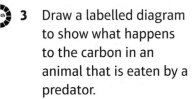 **3** Draw a labelled diagram to show what happens to the carbon in an animal that is eaten by a predator.

Carbon dioxide molecules in the atmosphere diffuse into plant leaves. Inside a leaf, photosynthesis may cause the carbon atom in the molecule to become part of another carbon compound, called glucose.

If glucose is used by the plant for respiration, the carbon atom will become part of carbon dioxide again and be released back into the atmosphere. Alternatively, the glucose may be changed into other carbon compounds and used to make more plant **biomass**.

Carbohydrates, fats and proteins in plants all contain carbon atoms. When an animal eats a plant, some of these compounds are digested and taken into its body. The rest will leave the animal's body in faeces.

Some of the absorbed carbon compounds are used for respiration and some form waste products that are excreted in urine. The rest are used to build more complex compounds in the animal's tissue, making more animal biomass. If the animal is eaten by a predator, the same process happens again.

If plants and animals are not eaten and just die, their bodies are broken down by **decay**. Decay is caused by microorganisms that we call **decomposers**. Decomposers include fungi and bacteria, which also break down the carbon compounds in animal waste (e.g. faeces and urine).

Decomposers use some of the carbon compounds they absorb for respiration and to make more complex compounds in their cells. When they die, they will be decayed by other decomposers. If many large dead plants are buried so quickly that decomposers cannot feed on them, then over millions of years they may be changed into peat or coal by heat and pressure from the Earth. In the same way, oil and natural gas are formed from dead microscopic sea plants and animals.

Coal, peat, oil and natural gas are **fossil fuels**, as they contain carbon compounds that were in living organisms millions of years ago. Burning fossil fuels releases the carbon back into the atmosphere as carbon dioxide.

The movement of carbon through the biotic and abiotic components of the environment is called the **carbon cycle**.

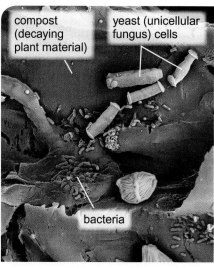

B Decomposers release enzymes into their surroundings to digest complex carbon compounds into smaller molecules that they can absorb. Magnification ×1500.

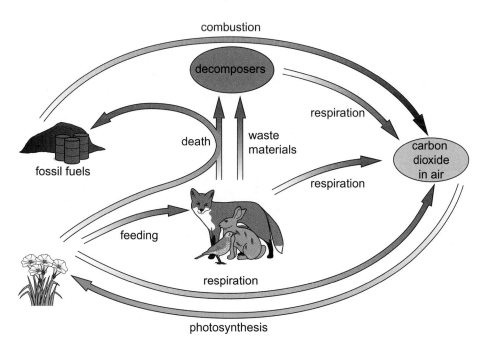

C the carbon cycle

 4 Which processes in the carbon cycle release carbon dioxide into the air?

 5 The natural carbon cycle does not include combustion of fossil fuels. Explain how the natural cycle usually keeps the amount of carbon dioxide in the air fairly constant.

Exam-style question

What is the role of decomposers in the carbon cycle? *(2 marks)*

Checkpoint

How confidently can you answer the Progression questions?

Strengthen

S1 Explain why *Pilobolus* (photo A) is important in the carbon cycle.

Extend

E1 Large areas of the Amazon rainforest have been cut down or burnt and replaced with grassland for cattle. Suggest what effect this has had on the local and global carbon cycle.

CB9i The nitrogen cycle

Specification reference: B9.15

Progression questions

- Why do plants need nitrates?
- How do farmers increase the amount of nitrates in the soil?
- What is the role of bacteria in the nitrogen cycle?

Nitrogen is an unreactive gas that makes up around 80 per cent of the atmosphere. However, around 3 per cent of your body is composed of nitrogen compounds.

A Energy released during lightning storms can cause unreactive nitrogen in the air to form reactive nitrogen compounds that are added to the soil when it rains.

 1 a Describe the effect on plant growth of a lack of nitrogen.

 b Explain why nitrogen deficiency has this effect.

 2 A farmer plants a crop in a field. Suggest a reason why the nitrate concentration of the soil will change during the growing season in that field.

Nitrogen in plants

Plants contain nitrogen compounds in proteins and DNA. To grow well, plants need nitrogen to make more of these compounds. They cannot use unreactive nitrogen from the air. Instead they absorb nitrogen compounds such as **nitrates** that are dissolved in soil water.

B These plants were planted at the same time. The one on the left is deficient in (has too little) nitrogen.

Bacteria and nitrates

Soil fertility is maintained by decomposers such as bacteria in the soil. These organisms release nitrogen compounds together with carbon compounds when they decompose dead plants and animals and their wastes.

 3 What is meant by soil fertility?

 4 Explain how digging manure into a field can increase soil fertility.

Farmers make use of this decay process when they add **manure** (which includes animal waste) to their fields. Farmers may also spread artificial fertilisers onto fields to increase the soil fertility. The nitrogen compounds in fertilisers are soluble and dissolve in soil water.

Did you know?

Some plants that live on nitrogen-poor soils have adaptations that help them get their nitrogen from animals. Carnivorous plants include the sundew, which has sticky leaves, and the Venus flytrap, which has hinged leaves to catch insects.

Some soil bacteria can convert nitrogen gas into nitrogen compounds in the soil. They are called **nitrogen-fixing bacteria**. Some plants such as peas and beans have a mutualistic relationship with these bacteria. The bacteria are protected inside nodules in the plant roots, and the plant gets nitrogen compounds directly from the bacteria.

 5 Explain why the relationship between nitrogen-fixing bacteria and pea plants is described as mutualistic.

Farmers can also make use of this relationship to keep their soil fertile, by planting a crop of peas (or related plants) and then digging in the roots after the crop has been harvested. The following year, a different crop will benefit from the additional nitrogen compounds in the soil. Planting a sequence of crops in different years, such as wheat followed by potatoes followed by peas, is called **crop rotation**.

Diagram D shows how nitrogen cycles through the biotic and abiotic components of an ecosystem in the **nitrogen cycle**.

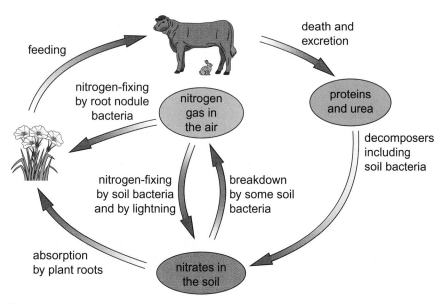

D the nitrogen cycle

C The root nodules of a pea plant contain nitrogen-fixing bacteria.

 6 Explain the purpose of crop rotation.

 7 Describe how the nitrogen compounds in your body come from nitrogen in the air.

Checkpoint

How confidently can you answer the Progression questions?

Strengthen

S1 Explain why farmers use manure, fertilisers and crop rotation in their fields.

Extend

E1 Until the early 1990s farmers used to burn the remains of crop plants after harvest and before planting a new crop. Now they usually plough in the remains. Explain why this change has helped to improve soil fertility.

Exam-style question

Explain how bacteria help make nitrates available for plant growth.

(2 marks)

Using fertilisers

Over the past 50 years, the use of fertilisers in the world has increased from about 30 million tonnes each year to over 160 million tonnes each year. Discuss the use of fertilisers in agriculture.

(6 marks)

Student answer

Farmers use fertilisers on their crops because fertilisers add mineral ions to the soil, which plants need for healthy growth [1]. The benefit of using fertilisers is that crop yields are higher. This means that we have been able to grow more food over the past 50 years [2]. The human population of the world has been growing, so growing more food is necessary to avoid food shortages or starvation [3].

Using large amounts of fertilisers can cause problems [4]. They can be expensive for a farmer to buy. Fertilisers can also harm the environment if the mineral ions escape into surrounding water. This can cause eutrophication [5], leading to pollution that kills plants and animals living in the water.

[1] Starting with a description of what fertilisers do makes it easier to follow the arguments in the rest of the answer.

[2] This is a good example of linking ideas. The answer links why plants need fertilisers to what happens to crop yields when fertilisers are used, and then why we need more food.

[3] This last sentence gives a reason why fertiliser use has increased, and so a benefit for using fertilisers.

[4] The second paragraph clearly discusses problems using fertilisers.

[5] This is a good use of a scientific term.

Verdict

This is a strong answer. It covers both benefits and problems of fertilisers and explains why there has been an increase in the use of fertilisers. The answer has been arranged clearly so that each paragraph covers one part of the discussion, making it obvious that benefits and problems have both been explored.

The answer could have also talked about whether some of the problems caused by using fertilisers can be reduced, for example by crop rotation. The answer could have also included some information about the sustainable use of fertilisers.

Exam tip

'Discuss' questions expect you to explore as many aspects of the issue or argument as you can. Don't focus on one aspect of the question, for example why fertilisers cause pollution, but try to give an answer that covers lots of different points.

Paper 3

CC1 States of Matter /
CC2 Methods of Separating and Purifying Substances

Millions of tonnes of tiny bits of plastic are floating in the oceans, and they harm wildlife. Water currents cause the plastic to collect in certain areas. The biggest of these is the 'Great Pacific Garbage Patch' in the Pacific Ocean, which could be three times the area of the UK. At the age of 19, Dutch student Boyan Slat came up with the idea of using giant floating booms to direct the plastic pieces into a mechanism that would filter the plastic out of the water. The idea relies on two properties of the plastic – it floats and it is insoluble in water. Not everyone agrees that it will work, and think that the system would not survive in the oceans. In this unit you will learn about how materials can be separated from one another using their properties.

The learning journey

Previously you have learnt at KS3:

- how particles are arranged in solids, liquids and gases and how their energy changes with changes of state
- how mixtures differ from pure substances
- how to separate some mixtures using filtration, distillation and chromatography.

In this unit you will learn:

- how to use information to predict the state of a substance
- how the arrangement, movement and energy of particles change during changes of state
- how to use melting points to tell the difference between mixtures and pure substances
- how to identify substances using melting points and chromatography
- how different methods of separation work
- how to choose a separation method based on the properties of the substances in a mixture.

CC1a States of matter

Specification reference: C2.1; C2.2; C2.3; C2.4

Progression questions

• What are particles like in substances in the solid, liquid and gas states?
• What changes happen to particles during the different changes of state?
• How do you decide what state a substance will be in at a given temperature?

A This 'ice hotel' is made entirely from ice and snow – these are both water in the solid state.

The three **states of matter** are solid, liquid and gas. For example, water can exist in the solid state as ice, or in the familiar liquid state, or in the gas state as steam or water vapour.

The particle model

Some **particles** are large enough to see, like the dust on a computer screen. Others, like **atoms** and **molecules**, are far too small for you to see. When chemists discuss particles, they usually mean these very small particles.

The **particle model** explains state changes in a substance in terms of the arrangement, movement and energy stored in its particles.

State	Particle diagram	Arrangement of particles	Movement of particles
Gas		random far apart	fast in all directions
Liquid		random close together	move around each other
Solid		regular close together	vibrate about fixed positions

B Particles in the solid state contain the smallest amount of stored energy; particles in the gas state contain the most.

Did you know?

Science recognises 16 different types of ice, depending on the arrangement of the water molecules. A type called amorphous ice is found in space (such as on comets). A type called Ice IV is what you'll find in a kitchen freezer, here on Earth.

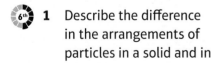 **1** Describe the difference in the arrangements of particles in a solid and in a liquid.

2 Describe the difference in the movement of particles in a liquid and in a gas.

State changes

State changes are **physical changes**. They can be reversed, and the **chemical properties** of the substance do not change. This is because the particles themselves do not change – only their arrangement, movement and amount of stored energy.

 3 State the meaning of the terms 'sublimation' and 'deposition'.

Particles are attracted to one another by weak forces of attraction. There are many of these forces in a solid. Some of these are overcome during melting. The remaining **attractive forces** between particles in a liquid are overcome during evaporation and boiling (when a substance is evaporating as fast as it can). For this to happen, energy must be transferred from the surroundings to the particles. This is why you heat ice to melt it, and why you boil water in a kettle. Diagram D shows how the temperature changes when water in the solid state is heated until it reaches the gas state.

Some attractive forces form between particles during condensing, and many attractive forces are formed during freezing. For this to happen, energy must be transferred from the particles to the surroundings. This is why water vapour turns into water droplets on a cold window, and why you put water in a freezer to make ice.

You can predict the state of a substance if you know its temperature, and its **melting point** and **boiling point**. If the temperature is:

- below the melting point, the substance is solid
- between the melting point and boiling point, the substance is liquid
- above the boiling point, the substance is gas.

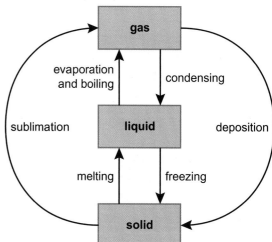

C the interconversions between the three states of matter

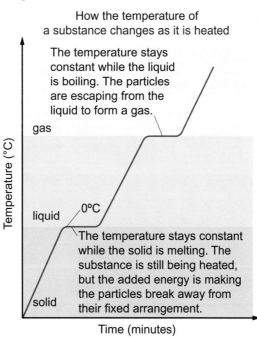

D a heating curve for water

 4 Describe how you can see from a 'heating curve' (such as diagram D) that a substance is changing state.

 5 Explain what happens to the particles when a substance melts.

 6 The melting point of gallium is 29.8 °C and its boiling point is 2204 °C. Predict its state at 25 °C, 100 °C and at 2205 °C.

Checkpoint

How confidently can you answer the Progression questions?

Strengthen

S1 Draw a diagram to show the states of matter. On your diagram, name each state change and describe what happens to the particles as it happens.

Extend

E1 Explain why the arrangement, movement and energy of particles change during changes of state.

Exam-style question

Camping gas is used by campers and hikers. It is a mixture of propane and butane. Explain, in terms of the arrangement of fuel particles, why camping gas is stored in cylinders as a liquid rather than as a gas. *(2 marks)*

Specification reference: C2.5; C2.6

Progression questions

- What is the difference between a pure substance and a mixture?
- What happens to its particles when a solid melts?
- How do melting points allow you to spot the differences between pure substances and mixtures?

A You can tell this gold bar is very nearly pure because of the '999.9' stamped on it. A number lower than 1000 on this 'fineness' scale means it is impure.

The composition (make-up) of a **pure** substance:

- cannot be changed
- is the same in all parts of a piece of the substance.

So, for example, pure gold contains only gold atoms.

 1 Which type of atoms are found in a piece of pure silver?

 2 State what is meant be the term 'impure'. Explain what the term 'impure' means.

Gold is an **element** and can be pure, but **compounds** can also be pure. The sugar we use at home is a compound called sucrose. It contains carbon, hydrogen and oxygen atoms chemically bonded together to form sucrose molecules. You cannot change the composition of pure sucrose.

Did you know?

The purest gold ever was produced in 1957 and was 999.999 on the fineness scale.

Gold purity is still often measured on the older carat scale, where 24 carat gold is pure gold.

B Pure sucrose is always sucrose, no matter how finely it is ground down.

A pure substance has the same fixed composition in all its parts and so we can't separate it into other substances using physical methods (such as filtering or picking bits out).

A **mixture** contains elements and/or compounds that are not chemically joined together. You *can* use physical processes to separate mixtures into different substances.

A mixture does not have a fixed composition. For example, air is a mixture of gases. When students sit in a classroom, they use up oxygen and breathe out carbon dioxide and so the composition of the air in the room changes. We still call it 'air', but because air is a mixture its composition can change.

 3 a Describe what a mixture of carbon, hydrogen and oxygen might look like.

 b Describe how you would separate marbles from sand.

 4 Oxygen can be removed from air by cooling. Explain why this would not be possible if air were not a mixture.

Melting points

When a solid melts, its particles gain enough energy to overcome the weak forces of attraction between them. They move further away from one another and the solid becomes a liquid. The temperature at which this happens is the **melting point**. This is an example of a **physical property** (how a substance responds to forces and energy).

A pure substance has the same composition in every part of it, and so its physical properties are the same in every part. So, all of a pure substance will melt at the same temperature until all the substance has changed state. The melting point of pure gold is 1063 °C and the melting point of oxygen is –218 °C.

 5 What is the freezing point of pure oxygen?

C this sweet is a mixture and so does not have a sharp melting point

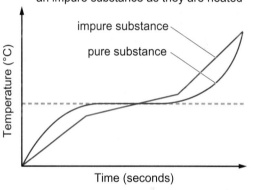

How temperature changes in a pure substance and an impure substance as they are heated

D heating curves for a pure substance and a mixture

The sweet shown in photo C has a liquid centre. The whole sweet melts over a *range* of temperatures and not all the parts melt and become liquid at the same time. This is what happens in mixtures – they do not have fixed, sharp melting points.

Substance	Melting temperatures (°C)
lead–tin alloy	183 to 258
argon	–189
carbon monoxide	–205

6 The table shows some melting temperatures.

 a Identify which substances are mixtures and which are pure.

 b Sketch a cooling curve for each of the three examples and explain their shapes.

Exam-style question

Explain why mixtures melt over a range of temperatures but pure substances have precise melting points. *(2 marks)*

Checkpoint

How confidently can you answer the Progression questions?

Strengthen

S1 List the ways in which pure substances are different from mixtures.

Extend

E1 A piece of gold jewellery is 750 on the fineness scale. Would you expect the jewellery to have a sharp melting temperature? Explain your answer.

CC2b Filtration and crystallisation

Specification reference: C0.6; C2.7

Progression questions

- How can filtration be used to separate mixtures?
- How can crystallisation be used to separate mixtures?
- What are the hazards and risks when separating mixtures by filtration and crystallisation?

A Some whales filter sea water with bristles (called baleen plates) to separate krill from the water.

 1 a Give one example of a mixture that can be separated by filtration.

 b Explain how this mixture is separated by filtration.

 c Describe another type of mixture that can be separated by filtration.

Did you know?

Nearly 4 million tonnes of salt are solution mined in the UK each year.

C Salt can be produced by the evaporation of sea water.

Filters can be used to separate some mixtures. They let smaller pieces or liquids through but trap bigger pieces or **insoluble** substances.

Examples of **filtration** are to be seen all around us. Cars, vacuum cleaners and air-conditioning systems all have filters. Some whales use filters to feed. They open their mouths and take in water. When they close their mouths, they push out the water through filters. Small animals (such as krill) get stuck in the filters and are swallowed.

Crystallisation

A **solution** is a mixture made of **solutes** (dissolved substances) in a liquid called the **solvent**. Solutes can be separated from a solution by evaporating the solvent to leave the solutes behind. This is called **crystallisation**. The process forms solid crystals of various sizes. If the crystals form slowly, the particles have longer to form an ordered pattern and will make larger crystals.

B Crystals in the Giant Crystal Cave in Mexico took over 500 000 years to form.

Table salt is produced from sea water, or is dug out of the ground or extracted using 'solution mining'. In this process water is pumped into layers of salt underground. The resulting salt solution is then heated, which evaporates the solvent and makes the solution more and more salty. Eventually it reaches a point where there is as much salt in the water as can possibly dissolve. This is a **saturated solution** and it contains the maximum amount of solute that can dissolve in that amount of solvent at that temperature. If more water evaporates and/or the solution cools, then some solute leaves the solution and salt crystals form.

Filtration and crystallisation in the lab

To filter a solution in the laboratory, a filter funnel is lined with filter paper that has fine holes in it. The solvent and solute(s) pass through the fine holes to form the **filtrate**. Bits of insoluble substances cannot fit through the holes and so leave a **residue** in the filter paper. A Bunsen burner is then used to evaporate the filtrate carefully. Care must be taken not to overheat the solution once it is saturated, because hot crystals may spit out. Further heating may also cause crystals to change chemically.

i

ii

 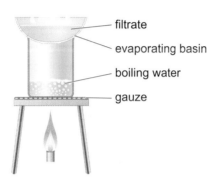

water vapour

filter paper
suspension
solid residue
filter funnel
filtrate

filtrate
evaporating basin
boiling water
gauze

D Laboratory apparatus for (i) filtration and (ii) crystallisation.

In a **risk assessment**, the **hazards** of doing an experiment are identified. A hazard is something that could cause harm. Then ways of reducing the **risk** (chance) of a hazard causing harm are considered.

During crystallisation, the risks from spitting can be reduced by wearing eye protection, removing the Bunsen burner before the solution is completely dry and/or using steam to heat the evaporating basin gently (as above).

7 When a mixture of rock pieces, salt and water is filtered, what will be found as the:

    a filtrate

    b residue?

8 a List two of the hazards when carrying out filtration and crystallisation.

    b Explain how the risks from each of your hazards can be reduced.

2 Give the names of two mixtures that can be separated by crystallisation.

3 In the solution mining of salt, give the names of the:

    a solvent

    b solution

    c solute.

4 When is a solution said to be 'saturated'?

5 Explain why crystals form during crystallisation.

6 Explain why the crystals in photo B are so big.

Checkpoint

How confidently can you answer the Progression questions?

Strengthen

S1 Explain how you would separate sand *and* salt from a mixture of the two.

Extend

E1 Scientists looking for new substances in plants grind up the plants with methanol. This solvent dissolves many plant compounds. However, methanol is flammable and toxic (especially if the vapour is inhaled). Large crystals can be made to help scientists work out what the compounds are made of. Explain how you would make plant-compound crystals using methanol.

Exam-style question

Explain the difference between a risk and a hazard. *(2 marks)*

CC2c Paper chromatography

Specification reference: C2.7; C2.9; C2.10

Progression questions

- How can chromatography be used to separate mixtures?
- What are the differences between mixtures and pure substances on a chromatogram?
- How do you calculate an R_f value?

A Experts restoring an old painting – they need to know what substances were mixed together to produce the paints used by the original artist.

Inks, paints and foods often contain mixtures of coloured compounds. **Chromatography** can be used to find out which coloured compounds the mixture contains. The type of chromatography used to analyse the substances in old oil paintings requires expensive machinery.

Paper chromatography is a simpler technique that works because some compounds dissolve better in a solvent than others. When a solvent moves along a strip of paper, it carries the different substances in the mixture at different speeds, so they are separated. The solvent is called the **mobile phase**. The paper contains the **stationary phase**, through which the solvent and dissolved substances move. The paper with the separated components on it is called a **chromatogram**.

 1 a How many different compounds are in substance X in diagram B?

 b For mixture Y, explain why the green spot is higher than the red spot.

2 Look at diagram B again. Explain why:

 a the labels for substances X, Y and Z are written in pencil, not ink

 b the starting positions for the different substances are above the level of solvent in the container.

 3 One of the coloured compounds in diagram B has an R_f value of 0.1. Explain which compound this is likely to be.

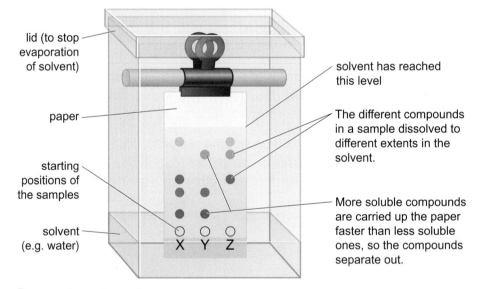

B paper chromatography

The **R_f value** is the distance the compound has risen divided by the distance the solvent has risen. Both measurements are made from the starting positions of the samples on the paper.

$$R_f = \frac{\text{distance moved by the spot}}{\text{distance moved by the solvent}}$$

The R_f value of a particular compound does not change if the chromatography conditions used remain the same.

Worked example

In diagram B, the pink spots have moved 4 cm and the solvent has moved 10 cm along the paper. Calculate the R_f value of this pink compound:

$R_f = \dfrac{4}{10} = 0.4$

A compound never rises as fast as the solvent, so R_f values are always less than 1. If you calculate an R_f value bigger than 1, you've made a mistake.

Paper chromatography can be used to:

- distinguish between pure and impure substances
- identify substances by comparing the pattern on the chromatogram with the patterns formed by known substances
- identify substances by calculating their R_f values.

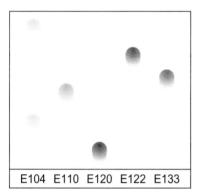

E104 E110 E120 E122 E133

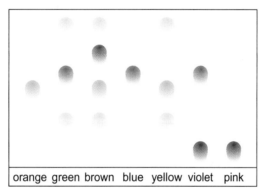

orange green brown blue yellow violet pink

C The chromatogram on the left was done using known substances. The chromatogram on the right shows that the orange and blue sweets contain single dyes.

4 In diagram B, the yellow spots have moved 9 cm and the solvent has moved 10 cm. Calculate the R_f value of the yellow substance.

5 In diagram C, the chromatogram on the left shows some food dyes found in sweets. The chromatogram on the right shows the results for some sweets.

    a Which sweets contain just one dye?

    b Which dyes are in the yellow sweets?

    c What is the colour of the most soluble dye?

Did you know?

In 1983, many national newspapers paid a lot of money to publish diaries allegedly written by Adolf Hitler. However, scientists used chromatography to analyse the inks in the diaries and found that they were not available during Hitler's lifetime – the diaries were fake.

D Chromatography can be used to help identify substances at crime scenes.

Checkpoint

How confidently can you answer the Progression questions?

Strengthen

S1 The police have taken four orange lipsticks from suspects. Explain the steps needed to find out if one of the lipsticks could have made a mark at a crime scene.

Extend

E1 A laboratory produces a list of R_f values for food colourings. Explain why R_f values are used and what other information is needed for these R_f values to be useful.

Exam-style question

Two dyes have the same R_f values when tested using chromatography. Explain whether this means they are the same dye or not. *(3 marks)*

CC2d Distillation

Specification reference: C0.6; C2.7

Progression questions

- What is distillation?
- How do simple distillation and fractional distillation differ?
- How would you reduce risks when carrying out a distillation experiment?

A a steam iron

Tap water contains dissolved minerals, especially in hard water areas – tap water is a **mixture**. For some jobs it is best to use pure water (such as for chemical analysis, in car-cooling systems and older steam irons). To make water pure we need to separate it from the dissolved solids. This is done by **distillation**.

 1 a What happens to the water in a steam iron when you turn the iron on?

 b Explain why some irons may not work well if you use ordinary tap water.

 2 In diagram B, what is the hazard if steam escapes from the tube?

 3 Suggest a way of improving a simple still so that more of the steam condenses back to water.

When mineral water **evaporates**, only the water turns to a gas (vapour). The solid minerals, which have much higher boiling points, are left behind. The water vapour (steam) is pure. If the vapour is then **condensed**, it turns back to liquid water again – the liquid water will now be pure. This combination of evaporation followed by condensation is called distillation. The apparatus used is called a **still**.

Diagram B shows a simple method for distilling. Water is heated in the conical flask and the vapour travels along the delivery tube, where it condenses. This method is not very efficient because much of the vapour is lost.

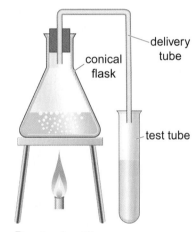

B a simple still

The type of still shown in diagram C is more efficient. The condenser keeps the tube cool, so that almost all of the vapour condenses and turns into a liquid.

 4 Explain how the still in diagram C can be used to purify water.

5 Explain how:

 a the condenser reduces the risk of hot vapour escaping

 b the safety of the method is improved by using anti-bumping granules.

thermometer

anti-bumping granules (to make the liquid boil more smoothly – small bubbles of vapour form on the corners of the granules and reduce the risk of the liquid boiling over.)

cooling water out

condenser (a central tube surrounded by a jacket of cold water)

distillation flask

solution (e.g. salty water)

cooling water in

distillate (e.g. pure water)

C distillation apparatus

Fractional distillation

Distillation can also be used to separate two or more liquids. This works because some liquids boil more easily than others. Liquids with lower boiling points evaporate more easily than others, and will turn into a vapour first. This is called **fractional distillation**, because the original mixture will be split into several parts, or fractions. The first fraction to be collected contains the liquid with the lowest boiling point. The fractions could be pure liquids, or may still be mixtures.

Fractional distillation can be used:

- to separate the different products in crude oil
- to make alcoholic drinks such as whisky and vodka
- to separate out the gases in the air, after the air has been cooled and turned into a liquid at −200 °C.

Diagram D shows how to separate liquids more efficiently. A column is fixed above the distillation flask. The hot vapour rises up the column. At first, the vapour condenses when it hits the cool glass and drips back down into the flask. As the column gradually heats up, there will be a temperature gradient – it will be hottest at the bottom and the temperature will drop as you go further up the column. The fraction with the lowest boiling point will reach the top of the column first and the vapour will then pass into the condenser. If you keep heating, fractions with higher boiling points will then rise up the column and can be collected later.

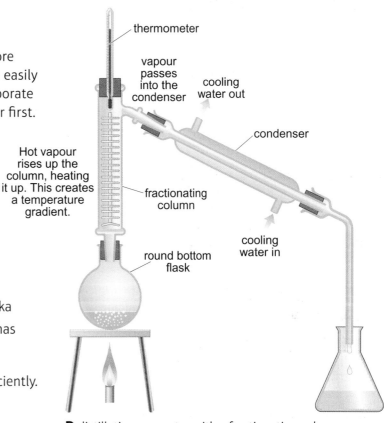

D distillation apparatus with a fractionating column

- thermometer
- vapour passes into the condenser
- cooling water out
- condenser
- Hot vapour rises up the column, heating it up. This creates a temperature gradient.
- fractionating column
- cooling water in
- round bottom flask

 6 Compare and contrast simple and fractional distillation.

 7 Explain why a liquid with a lower boiling point will reach the top of a fractionating column more quickly than one with a higher boiling point.

Did you know?

The vacuum flask that we now use to keep drinks hot was originally used to keep liquid air *cold*. It was designed by James Dewar in 1892.

Exam-style question

A student is asked to separate two liquids. Liquid A boils at 100 °C and liquid B boils at 65 °C. The student sets up a fractional distillation experiment, and after a few minutes a clear liquid is collected from the condenser. Explain which of the two liquids will be collected first. *(2 marks)*

Checkpoint

How confidently can you answer the Progression questions?

Strengthen

S1 Explain what distillation is and how the distillation apparatus (the still) works. Use a labelled diagram to make your explanation clear.

S2 Explain the safety precautions you need to take when carrying out distillation in a laboratory.

Extend

E1 Pure ethanol ('alcohol') boils at 78.5 °C. Explain how a 50:50 mixture of ethanol and water can be separated by fractional distillation.

E2 Suggest why the boiling point of the starting liquid will change with time.

CC2d Core practical – Investigating inks

Specification reference: C2.11

Aim

Investigate the composition of inks using simple distillation and paper chromatography.

A Fountain pen ink is available as a washable ink.

Ink is a mixture of coloured substances dissolved in a liquid solvent. Ink that appears to be a single colour, such as black, may contain two or more substances with different colours. Permanent inks do not run if the paper becomes wet, a useful property if you drop your homework in a puddle. Washable inks separate into their different colours if the paper gets wet, but may be removed if spilt on clothing.

Your task

You are going to use simple distillation to separate a sample of the solvent in some ink. You will also use paper chromatography to separate the coloured substances in samples of ink.

Method

Simple distillation

Wear eye protection.

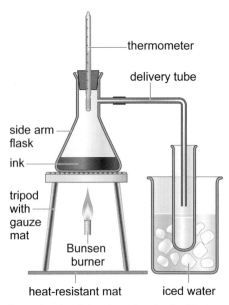

B separating ink using simple distillation

A Set up your apparatus so that the ink is in a flask, and its vapours can be led away to be condensed. Diagram B shows some typical apparatus but yours may be different.

B Heat the flask of ink using a Bunsen burner, making sure the ink simmers gently and does not boil over into the delivery tube.

C Continue heating until you have collected a few cm³ of distillate (distilled solvent).

D Note the maximum temperature obtained.

Paper chromatography

E Draw a pencil line on a piece of chromatography paper, about 2 cm from the bottom.

F Add a small spot of ink to the pencil line.

G Add water to a container to a depth of about 1 cm.

H Place the paper into the container. Make sure the paper is supported so that it does not slump into the water when it becomes damp. Allow the water to travel through the paper.

I Take the paper out before the water reaches the top. Immediately mark the position of the solvent front using a pencil, then leave the paper to dry.

J Measure the distance travelled by the water from the pencil line, and the distances travelled by each coloured substance.

K Calculate the R_f value for each coloured substance.

Exam-style questions

1 Explain the function of the beaker of iced water in diagram B.
(2 marks)

2 A student carries out simple distillation on a sample of blue ink.
   a Predict how the appearance of the ink changes, and give a
      reason for your answer. *(2 marks)*
   b During the experiment, hot liquid solvent drips from the bulb
      of the thermometer. Suggest an explanation for a temperature
      rise from 83 °C to 100 °C as this happens. *(1 mark)*

3 Explain why simple distillation allows a pure solvent to be
   separated from a solution. *(3 marks)*

4 A student distils a sample of ink. Devise a simple method to show
   that the liquid collected is pure water. Include the expected results
   in your answer. *(3 marks)*

5 Propanone is a flammable solvent. A student carries out paper
   chromatography of ink using propanone.
   a Identify the mobile phase and the stationary phase in her
      experiment. *(2 marks)*
   b Explain one precaution necessary to control the risk of harm in
      her experiment. *(1 mark)*
   c Suggest an explanation for why the level of the propanone
      should be below the ink spot on the paper at the start. *(1 mark)*

6 Explain how paper chromatography separates coloured
   substances in ink. *(3 marks)*

7 A student uses paper chromatography to analyse four samples of
   ink (X, A, B and C). Diagram C shows his results.
   a Describe what the results tell you about ink sample X. *(2 marks)*
   b Calculate the R_f value of the substance in ink B. *(2 marks)*

8 A student uses paper chromatography to analyse the dyes present
   in a sample of ink. She adds a sample of the ink and four dyes
   (1, 2, 3 and 4) to the paper. Table D shows her results for the dyes.
   a Explain which dye is the most soluble in the solvent used by
      the student. *(2 marks)*
   b Explain whether each dye is a pure substance. *(2 marks)*
   c Suggest an explanation for why a mixture of dyes 1 and 4 may
      appear as a single green spot in a paper chromatogram. *(2 marks)*

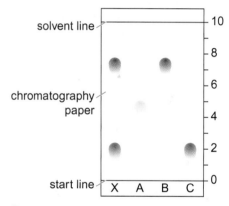

C

Dye	Spot colour	R_f
1	yellow	0.10
2	red	0.35
3	green	0.67
4	blue	0.12

D

Progression questions

- How would you choose which method to use to separate a mixture?
- How is drinking water produced?
- Why must water used in chemical analysis be pure?

A Personal water purifiers filter water to make it safer to drink.

About 97% of the Earth's water is in the oceans. The concentration of dissolved salts in sea water is far too high for us to drink safely. Producing pure water from sea water is called **desalination** and can be achieved using **simple distillation**.

Purifying sea water

Water is separated from dissolved salts using simple distillation. Sea water is heated so that water vapour leaves it quickly. This vapour is then cooled and condensed, forming water without the dissolved salts.

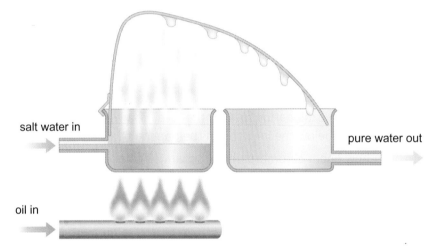

salt water in

oil in

pure water out

B Simple distillation of sea water using oil as a fuel.

 1 Explain how pure water is produced using the apparatus shown in diagram B.

 2 Suggest why the simple distillation of sea water may be used to provide drinking water in oil-rich coastal countries.

A lot of energy must be transferred to sea water during simple distillation, so it is not usually a suitable method for producing large volumes of drinking water. It is mainly carried out on a large scale where energy resources are cheap or plentiful, and where there is an abundant supply of sea water.

Water for chemical analysis

Chemical analysis involves using chemical reactions or sensitive machines to identify and measure the substances in a sample. The water used for chemical analysis should not contain any dissolved salts, otherwise incorrect results will be obtained. Tap water contains small amounts of dissolved salts, which may react to form unexpected cloudy **precipitates**. These may hide the correct result of the analysis. Also, the machines used for analysis may detect the salts, again leading to an incorrect conclusion.

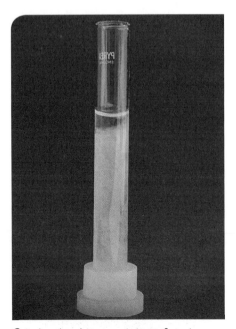

C A cloudy white precipitate forming during a chemical analysis.

 3 Explain why distilled water is more suitable than tap water for doing a chemical analysis.

Water for drinking

In the UK, the raw material for producing drinking water comes from rivers, lakes or **aquifers** (underground rocks containing groundwater). The water in these sources is often stored in reservoirs, which are artificial lakes produced by building a dam across a valley. Fresh water from these sources contains:

- objects such as leaves and twigs
- small insoluble particles such as grit and silt
- soluble substances, including salts, pesticides and fertilisers
- bacteria and other microorganisms that may be harmful to health.

Different steps are needed to deal with these impurities. They include screening using a sieve, **sedimentation** (in which small particles are allowed to settle out) and filtration using tanks containing beds of sand and gravel. Chlorine is added in a process called **chlorination**. Chlorine kills microorganisms in the treated water.

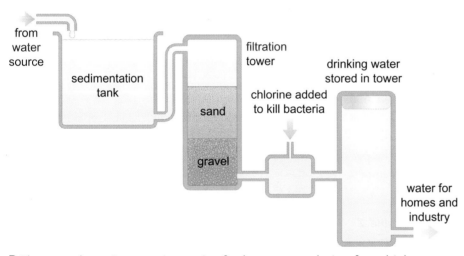

D These are the main stages in treating fresh water to make it safe to drink.

 5 a Describe how water is treated to deal with leaves and twigs, grit and silt, and with microorganisms.

 b Identify the stage missing from diagram D and draw a labelled diagram to show it.

 6 Suggest why chemical reactions, rather than separation methods, are used to remove harmful substances dissolved in drinking water in the UK.

Exam-style question

Fresh water is treated to make it safe to drink. Soluble and insoluble substances are removed during this treatment, and chlorine is added to kill harmful microorganisms. State two reasons why samples of the treated water are tested regularly. *(2 marks)*

 4 Explain why it may not be safe to drink water straight from a river.

Did you know?

Only about 2.5% of the Earth's water is fresh water. Of that, only 0.3% is in rivers and lakes – the rest is in icecaps, glaciers and ground water.

Checkpoint

How confidently can you answer the Progression questions?

Strengthen

S1 Draw flowcharts to describe two ways in which water can be made fit to drink.

Extend

E1 A bottle of water has a label saying 'Suitable for chemical analysis'. Describe how this water has been produced.

E2 Explain how you would check to see if this water really is suitable for analysis.

Methods of separating and purifying substances

A runny green mixture contains three compounds (**X**, **Y** and **Z**).

Compound	Melting point (°C)	Boiling point (°C)	State at room temperature	Notes
X	2435	4000	solid	not soluble in **Y** or **Z**
Y	−126	97.4	liquid	soluble in **Z**
Z	−114	78.4	liquid	soluble in **Y**

Plan a method to separate out **X**, **Y** and **Z**. Use the information in the table above and explain why you have suggested each step. **(6 marks)**

Student answer

Compound X is solid, and it is insoluble in the two liquids (Y and Z). This means it can be separated from them by filtration [1]. When X is collected in the filter paper it will be wet with the two liquids, so it should be dried in a warm oven. The boiling points of the two liquids are well below the melting point of compound X, so compound X will not melt in the oven [2].

The filtrate will be a mixture of compounds Y and Z. These can be separated using fractional distillation because their boiling points are different [3]. When the mixture is heated, compound Z will distil off first because it has the lower boiling point [4], leaving compound Y behind.

[1] This explains *why* compound X can be separated by filtration.

[2] The answer uses information from the table to explain why drying compound X will work.

[3] This makes it clear which physical property fractional distillation depends on.

[4] It is clear which liquid will be collected first, and why.

Verdict

This is a strong answer. It shows good knowledge and understanding of separation methods and uses correct scientific language.

The answer is organised logically, in the order that the practical would be carried out. Each step of the practical is linked to a scientific explanation.

Exam tip

If you are given a table of data or a graph in a question, make sure you use information from it in your answer.

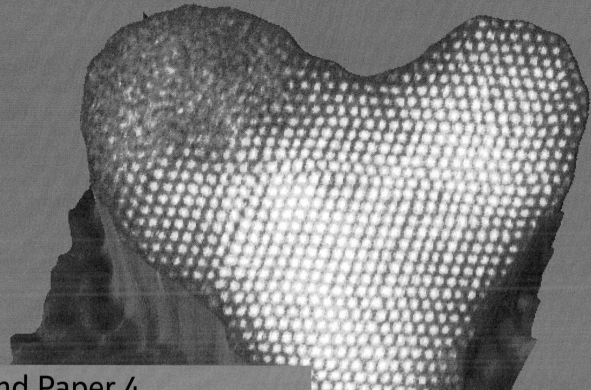

Paper 3 and Paper 4

CC3 Atomic Structure

This image shows palladium atoms on a base of carbon. According to the scientists who produced it, Zhiwei Wand and David Pearmain, although they had watched with love, they had nothing to do with the spontaneous formation of the heart shape. Unfortunately this atomic valentine, being only 8 nanometres (0.000000008 metres) across, is far too small to see even with the strongest light microscope. It may, however, help to explain the nature of matter, which is central to understanding the properties of materials and the chemical reactions that form new substances. In this unit you will find out more about atoms and their structure.

The learning journey

Previously you will have learnt at KS3:

- about the particle model of matter
- how Dalton's ideas about atoms helped to explain the properties of matter
- how elements are arranged in the periodic table.

In this unit you will learn:

- how our ideas about atoms have changed
- what a relative atomic mass is
- **H** how to calculate relative atomic mass for an element.

CC3a Structure of an atom

Specification reference: C1.1; C1.2; C1.3; C1.4; C1.5

Progression questions

- How has the model of the atom changed over the last 200 years?
- How do the parts of atoms compare with each other?
- Why do atoms have no overall charge?

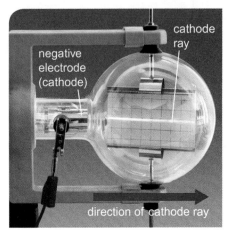

A a cathode ray tube

 1 What are atoms?

2 Which of Dalton's ideas about particles is supported by the image of palladium atoms on the previous page?

In 1805 the English chemist John Dalton (1766–1844) published his atomic theory that said:

- all matter is made up of tiny particles called **atoms**
- atoms are tiny, hard spheres that cannot be broken down into smaller parts
- atoms cannot be created or destroyed
- the atoms in an **element** are all identical (but each element has its own type of atom).

Dalton's ideas helped to explain some of the properties of matter. However, experiments towards the end of the nineteenth century suggested that atoms contain even smaller particles.

When a high voltage is applied to a glass tube that has most of the air removed, glowing rays are seen. Some scientists thought that these 'cathode rays' were atoms leaving the negative electrode. In 1897, JJ Thomson (1856–1940) investigated the mass of the particles in the rays and found that they were about 1800 times lighter than the lightest atom (hydrogen). Cathode rays, therefore, did not contain atoms but **subatomic particles**, which we now call **electrons**.

The structure of atoms

Scientists have now worked out that atoms are made up of electrons together with heavier subatomic particles called **protons** and **neutrons**. All these particles have very, very small masses and electric charges. So, rather than use their actual masses and charges, it is easier to describe them by looking at their **relative masses** and **relative charges** compared to a proton. For example, if we say the mass of a proton is '1' then anything else that has the same mass is also '1'.

Did you know?

The actual mass of a proton is 0.000 000 000 000 000 000 000 001 67 g (1.67×10^{-24} g).

Subatomic particle	Relative charge	Relative mass
proton	+1 (positive)	1
electron	−1 (negative)	1/1835 (negligible)
neutron	0 (no charge)	1

B relative masses and relative charges of subatomic particles

 3 Which subatomic particle has the lowest mass?

At the centre of all atoms is a tiny **nucleus** containing protons and neutrons. This is surrounded by fast moving electrons arranged in **electron shells** at different distances from the nucleus.

Atoms in elements always have equal numbers of protons and electrons and so have no overall charge, because the charges cancel out.

Diagram C shows two ways of modelling a beryllium atom. The three-dimensional model attempts to show how we imagine electrons to move.

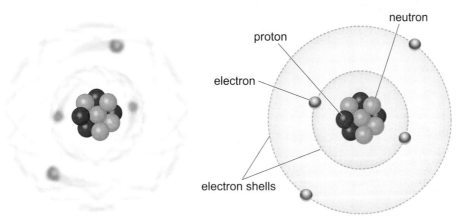

proton

neutron

electron

electron shells

C The 'target diagram' on the right shows the arrangement of the electrons more clearly.

Models of atoms help us to understand their structure – but most models don't really give a correct impression of scale. The overall diameter of an atom can be 100 000 times the diameter of its nucleus.

D If an atom could be made the size of the Lord's cricket ground, its nucleus would be about the size of this dot ●. Most of an atom is empty space.

 4 How many protons, neutrons and electrons are in a beryllium atom?

5 A lithium atom has 3 protons, 4 neutrons and 3 electrons.

 a Draw a diagram of this atom.

 b Why is this atom neutral?

 c How many electrons would be in an atom that has 17 protons?

Checkpoint

How confidently can you answer the Progression questions?

Strengthen

S1 Draw an atom and label it to describe the arrangement and properties of its subatomic particles.

Extend

E1 Figure E (below) shows what happens when the three subatomic particles are fired through an electric field.

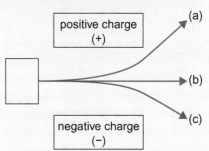

Name each particle a, b and c. Explain your answer.

Exam-style question

Compare the modern model of an atom to the atomic model proposed by John Dalton in 1805.   *(2 marks)*

CC3b Atomic number and mass number

Specification reference: C1.6; C1.7; C1.8; C1.10

Progression questions

- Why is most of the mass of an atom found in its nucleus?
- What does the atomic number tell you about an element?
- How can you calculate the numbers of protons, neutrons and electrons in atoms?

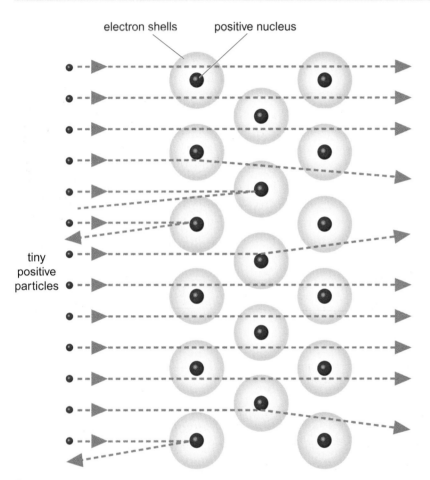

electron shells   positive nucleus

tiny positive particles

A Rutherford's scattering experiments suggested a nuclear atomic model.

The nuclear atom

In 1909, Ernest Rutherford (1871–1937) was working with others to investigate the structure of atoms. In one experiment, tiny positive particles were fired at a thin gold foil. To everyone's surprise most of the particles passed straight through the gold foil, with a few being deflected and a very small number bouncing back. Rutherford explained this by suggesting that atoms are mostly empty space, with a small positive central nucleus that contains most of the mass.

 1 a Where is most of the mass of an atom?

 b Explain how the experiment in diagram A suggests that atoms are mostly empty space.

Atomic number

The elements in the **periodic table** were originally placed in order of the masses of their atoms. However, this caused some elements to be grouped with others that had very different properties. So a few elements were swapped round to make sure that those with similar properties were grouped together, even if it meant that they were no longer in the correct order of mass.

Experiments by Henry Moseley (1887–1915) in 1913 confirmed that the rearranged order of elements in the table was actually correct. He showed that they were in order of the amount of positive charge in the nucleus. The proton was discovered about five years later. The modern periodic table places the elements in order of the number of protons in their atoms. This is the **atomic number** and it is this that defines an element – all the atoms of a particular element have the same unique atomic number.

Did you know?

Henry Moseley was killed during the First World War. As a result of Moseley's death, other important scientists were restricted from serving in front-line roles.

 2 Carbon has an atomic number of 6. How many protons does it have?

3 Use a periodic table to find:

     a the number of protons and electrons in atoms of:

       i nitrogen   **ii** potassium

     b two elements whose atomic mass order does not match their atomic number order.

4 In terms of structure, what do all atoms of a certain element have in common?

Mass number

The mass of an electron is described as 'negligible' – it is so small that it can be ignored. This explains why the nucleus of any atom contains nearly all its mass. For this reason the total number of protons and neutrons in an atom is called its **mass number**.

A mass number is represented by the symbol *A* and an atomic number by the symbol *Z*. These numbers are written next to an element's symbol as shown in diagram B.

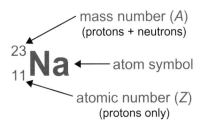

mass number (*A*) (protons + neutrons)

$$^{23}_{11}\text{Na}$$

atom symbol

atomic number (*Z*) (protons only)

B This is how scientists write the atomic number and the mass number for a sodium atom. It shows that the atom contains 11 protons and 12 neutrons in its nucleus.

 5 How many protons, neutrons and electrons are in the atom $^{27}_{13}\text{Al}$? Explain how you worked out your answer.

 6 A manganese atom has 25 protons, 30 neutrons and 25 electrons. Show this information using the form shown in diagram B.

 7 Look at the 'Did you know?' box on this page. Which subatomic particle does a hydrogen atom *not* have? Explain your reasoning.

Exam-style question

Complete the table below   *(2 marks)*

Atom	atomic number	mass number	number of protons	number of neutrons	number of electrons
X	90	222	90	132	(i)
Y	88	(ii)	88	134	88

Did you know?

Just two elements make up most of our Universe – about 74% is hydrogen $^{1}_{1}\text{H}$ and 24% is helium $^{4}_{2}\text{H}$. These are also the two simplest atoms in the periodic table. The Sun releases energy by converting hydrogen atoms into helium atoms. Every second, over 600 million tonnes of hydrogen is converted to helium.

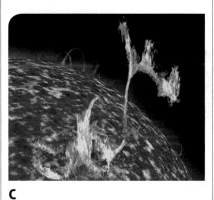

C

Checkpoint

How confidently can you answer the Progression questions?

Strengthen

S1 An atom can be represented in the form $^{65}_{29}\text{Cu}$. What does this tell you about this atom?

Extend

E1 Formulae can be written to connect the atomic number, mass number, and numbers of protons, electrons and neutrons in atoms.

For example:

atomic number = protons

Write formulae that connect the other four numbers.

CC3c Isotopes

Specification reference: C1.9; C1.10; C1.11; H C1.12

Progression questions

- How can you describe and identify isotopes of elements?
- Why are the relative atomic masses for some elements not whole numbers?
- H How do you calculate the relative atomic mass of an element?

 1 a Write the name of each of the three lithium isotopes in diagram A.

 b Describe each isotope in the format $_Z^A X$ (X is the element's symbol).

In 1932, James Chadwick (1891–1974) discovered the neutron. His discovery explains why some atoms of the same element have different masses. These atoms are known as **isotopes** – they have the same atomic number but different mass numbers. We refer to a specific isotope by adding its mass number to the element's name. The isotope on the left of diagram A is lithium-6.

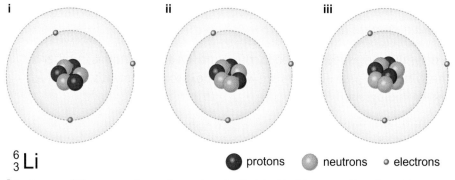

$_3^6$Li   ● protons   ○ neutrons   • electrons

A Isotopes of the same element are chemically identical because they have the same number of protons and electrons.

Did you know?

In 1945, at the end of the Second World War, two 'atomic bombs' were dropped on the Japanese cities of Hiroshima and Nagasaki. The bombs used nuclear fission and killed at least 129 000 people.

B

Understanding neutrons led to the discovery of nuclear energy. By firing neutrons at a uranium isotope, $_{92}^{235}$U, it was discovered that a nucleus can be split (**nuclear fission**). This produces new elements and transfers large amounts of energy. Nuclear power stations use the energy from nuclear fission to produce electricity.

 2 a State the numbers of protons and neutrons in an atom of uranium-235.

 b State the number of protons, neutrons and electrons in the barium isotope formed in diagram C.

c Identify the other product. Give your answer using the format $_Z^A X$.

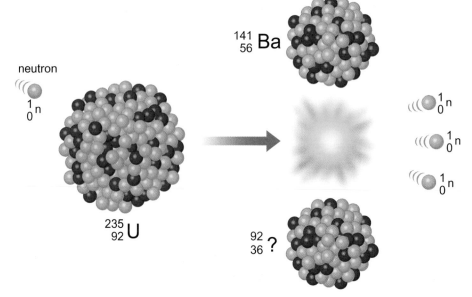

neutron
$_0^1$n
$_{92}^{235}$U
$_{56}^{141}$Ba
$_{36}^{92}$?
$_0^1$n
$_0^1$n
$_0^1$n

C Nuclear fission can be started by firing neutrons at atoms of uranium-235.

Relative atomic masses

The mass of an atom is incredibly small, so we measure their masses *relative to* (compared to) an atom of carbon-12. This isotope is used as a standard and given a mass of exactly 12. The masses of all other atoms are compared to this. For example, the mass of helium-4 is one-third of that of carbon-12 and so its relative mass is 4.

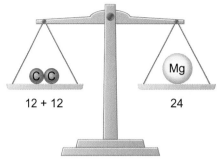

D An atom of the isotope $^{24}_{12}Mg$ has twice the mass of $^{12}_{6}C$ and so has a relative mass of 24.

 3 How many ^4_2He atoms would be needed to balance the mass of the $^{24}_{12}Mg$ atom in diagram D?

4 Use the list of isotopes to answer the questions that follow.

^4_2He $^{20}_{10}Ne$ $^{40}_{18}Ar$ ^5_2He $^{40}_{20}Ca$

Which two isotopes have the same:

 a mass   **b** chemical properties?

5 Write the mass ratios, in their simplest form, for the isotopes:

 a $^{20}_{10}Ne$ and $^{40}_{18}Ar$ **b** ^4_2He and $^{20}_{10}Ne$

The relative mass of an isotope is its mass number. For example, chlorine has two isotopes, $^{35}_{17}Cl$ and $^{37}_{17}Cl$, and their relative masses are 35 and 37, respectively.

All elements exist as mixtures of isotopes. We use this idea to calculate an element's **relative atomic mass** (**RAM**) – the symbol is **A_r**. A relative atomic mass is the **mean** mass of an atom of an element compared with carbon-12. It takes into account all the isotopes of the element and the amounts of each. RAMs are not whole numbers (for example the A_r of chlorine is 35.5) but most values are commonly rounded to whole numbers. The RAM of an element and its atomic number are shown on the periodic table.

 6 What does the relative atomic mass of an element tell you?

 7 **H** Copper has two isotopes – 69% is $^{63}_{29}Cu$ and 31% is $^{65}_{29}Cu$. Calculate the RAM of copper. Give your answer to 1 decimal place.

H

The abundances (overall proportions) of the two isotopes of chlorine are 75% of $^{35}_{17}Cl$ and 25% of $^{37}_{17}Cl$. We calculate the relative atomic mass of chlorine as follows.

If we take 100 atoms,
the relative atomic mass $= \dfrac{\text{total mass of the atoms}}{\text{the number of atoms}} = \dfrac{(75 \times 35) + (25 \times 37)}{100}$

$= \dfrac{2625 + 925}{100} = \dfrac{3550}{100}$

$A_r = 35.5$

Checkpoint

How confidently can you answer the Progression questions?

Strengthen

S1 Describe, with examples, the similarities and differences between isotopes of the same element.

Extend

E1 **H** Describing each step, work out the relative atomic mass of magnesium – it has the composition 79% ^{24}Mg, 10% ^{25}Mg and 11% ^{26}Mg.

Exam-style question

Neon gas has a relative atomic mass of 20.2 and is made up of two atoms: $^{20}_{10}Ne$ and $^{22}_{10}Ne$. Explain which of these isotopes is the most abundant.

(3 marks)

Isotopes

The diagram below shows the structure of two isotopes of lithium.

lithium-6

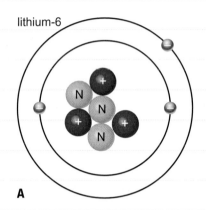

lithium-7

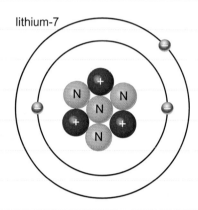

A

Using these lithium atoms as examples, explain the similarities and differences in the properties of different isotopes of the same element.

(6 marks)

Student answer

Atoms that are isotopes of the same element have the same atomic numbers but different mass numbers [1]. This means they have the same number of protons and electrons but different numbers of neutrons [2].

Atoms that are isotopes will chemically react in the same way [3] but be different in structure [4].

[1] The answer gives a basic definition of isotopes.

[2] This is a good description of the similarities and differences in the number of subatomic particles, but it doesn't use the lithium isotopes to illustrate the examples.

[3] This would be better if the answer explained *why* atoms of different isotopes react in the same way.

[4] This just repeats the earlier statement about differences, without adding any further detail.

Verdict

This is an acceptable answer. It contains a basic definition of isotopes, and a description of their similarities and differences in terms of structure. The answer also notes that the isotopes will have the same chemical properties. There is some linking of scientific ideas and a basic logical structure.

This answer could be improved by referring to the examples given in the question. It would have been better if the answer had included clearer definitions of 'atomic number' and 'mass number'. The answer should also link together some more scientific ideas. For example, it could have linked reactivity with electron configuration (to explain why isotopes of the same element have the same reactivity).

Exam tip

If an exam question asks you to use examples that are given, you must include them in your answer.

Paper 3 and Paper 4

CC4 The Periodic Table

There are over 100 known elements. The modern periodic table is a chart that arranges these elements in a way that is useful to chemists. Thanks to the periodic table, chemists can make sense of patterns and trends, which lets them predict the properties of elements. This works even if only a few atoms of an element exist. The periodic table shown here includes photos of most of the elements. If an element is very rare or difficult to obtain, it shows a photo of the relevant scientist or research laboratory involved in discovering or naming the element, or a diagram representing the arrangement of its electrons.

The learning journey

Previously you will have learnt at KS3:

- about chemical symbols for elements
- that Dmitri Mendeleev designed an early periodic table
- about periods and groups in the periodic table
- about metals and non-metals, their properties and their positions in the periodic table.

In this unit you will learn:

- how Mendeleev arranged the elements known at the time in a periodic table
- how Mendeleev predicted the existence and properties of undiscovered elements
- how Henry Moseley helped to confirm Mendeleev's ideas
- how the elements are arranged in the modern periodic table
- how to use the periodic table to predict and model the arrangement of electrons in atoms.

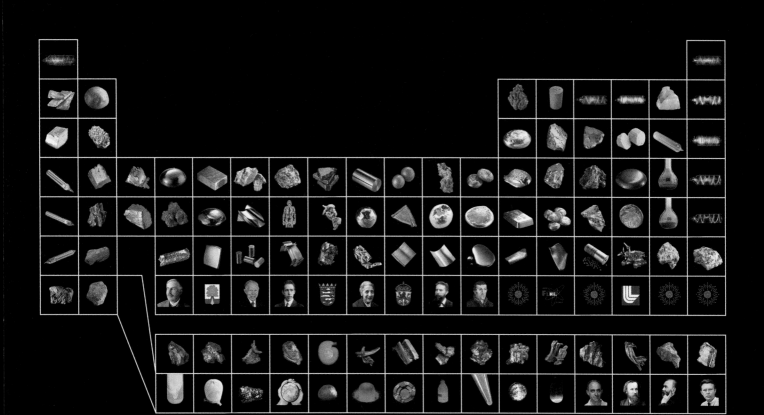

CC4a Elements and the periodic table

Specification reference: C0.1; C1.13; C1.14

Progression questions

- What are the symbols of some common elements?
- How did Mendeleev arrange elements into a periodic table?
- How did Mendeleev use his table to predict the properties of undiscovered elements?

A Towels come in all sorts of sizes, colours and patterns, just as the elements have different properties. How would you organise them?

The Russian chemist Dmitri Mendeleev (1834–1907) faced a problem early in 1869. He was busy writing the second volume of his chemistry textbook and could not decide which elements it made sense to write about next. His solution was to construct a table that led to the **periodic table** we know today.

Organising elements

Chemists had discovered 63 elements by 1869, and they were keen to organise them in a helpful way. Mendeleev arranged these elements in order of increasing **relative atomic masses** (called atomic weights then). Unlike other chemists who had tried this before, Mendeleev did not always keep to this order, and he left gaps in his table.

Mendeleev sometimes swapped the positions of elements if he thought that better suited their **chemical properties** and those of their compounds. For example, fluorine, chlorine, bromine and iodine are non-metals that do not easily react with oxygen, whereas tellurium is a metal that burns in air to form tellurium dioxide. Iodine has a lower relative atomic mass than tellurium, so Mendeleev should have placed it before tellurium according to this **physical property**. Instead, he placed iodine after tellurium so that it lined up with fluorine, chlorine and bromine (elements with similar chemical properties to iodine). Even though Mendeleev used the most accurate relative atomic masses then available, he justified this swap by stating that the value for tellurium must be incorrect.

Mendeleev assumed that elements would continue to be discovered, so he left gaps for them. This helped him to position the existing elements so that vertical columns contained elements with increasing relative atomic mass, and horizontal rows contained elements with similar chemical properties.

ОПЫТЪ СИСТЕМЫ ЭЛЕМЕНТОВЪ,
ОСНОВАННОЙ НА ИХЪ АТОМНОМЪ ВѢСѢ И ХИМИЧЕСКОМЪ СХОДСТВѢ.

		Ti=50	Zr=90	?=180.
		V=51	Nb=94	Ta=182.
		Cr=52	Mo=96	W=186.
		Mn=55	Rh=104,4	Pt=197,1.
		Fe=56	Ru=104,4	Ir=198.
		Ni=Co=59	Pd=106,6	Os=199.
H=1		Cu=63,4	Ag=108	Hg=200.
	Be= 9,4 Mg=24	Zn=65,2	Cd=112	
	B=11 Al=27,3	?=68	Ur=116	Au=197?
	C=12 Si=28	?=70	Sn=118	
	N=14 P=31	As=75	Sb=122	Bi=210?
	O=16 S=32	Se=79,4	Te=128?	
	F=19 Cl=35,5	Br=80	I=127	
Li=7 Na=23	K=39	Rb=85,4	Cs=133	Tl=204.
	Ca=40	Sr=87,6	Ba=137	Pb=207.
	?=45	Ce=92		
	?Er=56	La=94		
	?Yt=60	Di=95		
	?In=75,6	Th=118?		

B Mendeleev's published 1869 table. The question mark after the relative atomic mass of tellurium, Te, shows that he thought this was incorrect. He swapped the positions of iodine and tellurium so that iodine ended up in the same line as other elements with similar properties.

 1 What information about the elements did Mendeleev use to produce his first table?

 2 Explain why Mendeleev swapped the positions of iodine and tellurium in his table.

Making predictions

Mendeleev continued to work on his table. By 1871, he had settled on a table in which elements with similar properties were arranged into vertical columns, just as today.

Series	Group 1	Group 2	Group 3	Group 4	Group 5	Group 6	Group 7	Group 8
1	H 1							
2	Li 7	Be 9.4	B 11	C 12	N 14	O 16	F 19	
3	Na 23	Mg 24	Al 27.3	Si 28	P 31	S 32	Cl 35.5	
4	K 39	Ca 40	? 44	Ti 48	V 51	Cr 52	Mn 55	Fe 56 Co 59 Ni 59 Cu 63
5	(Cu 63)	Zn 65	? 68	? 72	As 75	Se 78	Br 80	
6	Rb 85	Sr 87	Y 88	Zr 90	Nb 94	Mo 96	? 100	Ru 104 Rh 104 Pd 106 Ag 108
7	(Ag 108)	Cd 112	In 113	Sn 118	Sb 122	Te 125	I 127	
8	Cs 133	Ba 137	Di 138	Ce 140				
9								
10			Er 178	La 180	Ta 182	W 184		Os 195 Ir 197 Pt 198 Au 199
11	(Au 199)	Hg 200	Tl 204	Pb 207	Bi 208			
12				Th 231		U 240		

C Mendeleev's 1871 table with his relative atomic masses. The red boxes are gaps left for elements not known at the time. Di, 'didymium', was later shown to be a mixture of two elements, neodymium and praseodymium.

Mendeleev used the gaps in his table to make **predictions** about the properties of undiscovered elements, based on the properties of nearby elements. One set of predictions was for an element he called eka-aluminium. When gallium was discovered shortly afterwards in 1875, its properties closely fitted those Mendeleev had predicted for eka-aluminium.

Property	Eka-aluminium, Ea	Gallium, Ga
relative atomic mass	about 68	70
density of element (g/cm³)	about 6.0	5.9
melting point of element (°C)	low	29.8
formula of oxide	Ea_2O_3	Ga_2O_3
density of oxide (g/cm³)	about 5.5	5.88
reacts with acids and alkalis?	yes	yes

D Mendeleev's predicted properties of eka-aluminium and the properties of gallium. He also successfully predicted the properties of scandium (discovered in 1879), germanium (1886) and polonium (1898).

Exam-style question

Suggest *two* reasons why other scientists did not accept Mendeleev's periodic table when it was first published. *(2 marks)*

 3 Mendeleev amended the relative atomic masses of some elements between 1869 and 1871. Give the symbol of one element for which its value was approximately doubled.

 4 Explain how Mendeleev's 1871 table shows he was unsure where to place three elements.

 5 Explain why the discovery of gallium was seen as a successful test of Mendeleev's periodic table.

Checkpoint

How confidently can you answer the Progression questions?

Strengthen

S1 What were the key features of Mendeleev's periodic table?

Extend

E1 How did Mendeleev think creatively to produce his table?

E2 What evidence supported Mendeleev's ideas?

CC4b Atomic number and the periodic table

Specification reference: C1.15; C1.16; C1.17; C1.18

Progression questions

- Why was Mendeleev right to alter the order of some elements in his table?
- What is an element's atomic number?
- How are the elements arranged in the modern periodic table?

A The modern periodic table is easily recognised. There are many fun versions including this one advertising a science park.

Development of the periodic table continued after Mendeleev's first tables. An entire group of **inert** or very unreactive elements was discovered near the end of the 19th century. Even though chemists had not predicted their existence, they were easily fitted into the periodic table as group 0. However, pair reversals such as iodine and tellurium were not properly explained, and there were still gaps. This began to change in 1913 due to a physicist called Henry Moseley.

1 Suggest why chemists in Mendeleev's time did not predict the existence of group 0 elements such as neon.

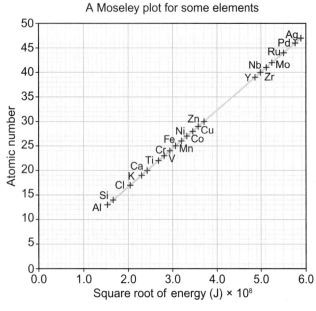

B There is a linear relationship between atomic number and the square root of the energy of emitted X-rays.

Atomic number

When scientists were beginning to accept the periodic table, an element's atomic number was just its position in the table. Moseley showed instead that it is a physical property of an element's atoms. He fired high-energy electrons at different elements, which made them give off **X-rays**. Moseley discovered that for every step increase in atomic number there was a step change in the energy of these X-rays.

Moseley realised that an atomic number was equal to the number of positive charges in the nucleus of an atom. The particle that carries this charge, the proton, was discovered a few years later. So the **atomic number** must be the number of protons in a nucleus.

2 Describe the difference between Mendeleev's atomic numbers and Moseley's modern atomic numbers.

Pair reversals

The elements in the modern periodic table are arranged in order of increasing atomic number, Z. When this is done:

- elements in a row or **period** are in order of increasing atomic number
- elements with similar properties are in the same column or **group**
- non-metals are on the right of the table (the other elements are metals)
- the iodine–tellurium pair reversal is explained.

Iodine exists naturally as ^{127}I but tellurium has several different isotopes. About 20% of its atoms are ^{126}Te but nearly two-thirds of its atoms are ^{128}Te or ^{130}Te, so its **relative atomic mass** is greater than that of iodine.

all (except oxygen) react with oxygen	group 6	group 7	none of them react with oxygen
	oxygen, O colourless gas $A_r = 16.0$ $Z = 8$	fluorine, F pale yellow gas $A_r = 19.0$ $Z = 9$	
none of them react with water	sulfur, S yellow solid $A_r = 32.1$ $Z = 16$	chlorine, Cl green-yellow gas $A_r = 35.5$ $Z = 17$	all react with water
	selenium, Se metallic grey solid $A_r = 79.0$ $Z = 34$	bromine, Br red-brown liquid $A_r = 79.9$ $Z = 35$	
all form compounds containing hydrogen: H_2O, H_2S, H_2Se, H_2Te	tellurium, Te silvery-white solid $A_r = 127.6$ $Z = 52$	iodine, I purple-black solid $A_r = 126.9$ $Z = 53$	all form compounds containing hydrogen: HF, HCl, HBr, HI

C These are the elements in groups 6 and 7, each with its relative atomic mass, A_r, and atomic number, Z.

Filling gaps

More X-ray analysis showed that just seven elements between hydrogen ($Z = 1$) and uranium ($Z = 92$) were left to be discovered. These were all discovered between 1917 and 1945. Neptunium, the first element with an atomic number above 92, was discovered in 1940. Other such 'transuranium' elements continue to be discovered, and all can be placed in the periodic table.

 6 Suggest why there is a gap between calcium, Ca, and titanium, Ti, in graph B.

Exam-style question

a Give an example, other than iodine and tellurium, of a pair of elements that would be in the wrong places if ordered by relative atomic mass. Use a periodic table to help you. *(1 mark)*

b Suggest why ordering by relative atomic mass would be incorrect. *(1 mark)*

---

 3 Give the relative atomic masses of tellurium and iodine to the nearest whole numbers.

 4 Use information from diagram C to explain fully why Mendeleev was correct after all to place tellurium before iodine.

 5 Use the periodic table at the back of the book to find the metals rubidium to tin, and the non-metals in groups 6 and 7. Describe the general positions of metals and non-metals.

CC4c Electronic configurations and the periodic table

Specification reference: C1.18; C1.19; C.1.20

Progression questions

- What information does an electronic configuration give?
- How do you work out and show the electronic configuration of an element?
- How is the electronic configuration of an element related to its position in the periodic table?

A There are many pairs of empty seats on this bus. Where would *you* sit?

You have many choices where to sit on an empty bus but fewer choices when other people are already seated. **Electrons** fill shells in an atom, rather like filling a bus one seat at a time from the front.

Electron shells

In an atom, electrons occupy **electron shells** arranged around the nucleus. The shells can be modelled in diagrams as circles, with the electrons drawn as dots or crosses on each circle. The way in which an atom's electrons are arranged is called its **electronic configuration**. Sodium atoms each contain 11 electrons, and diagram B shows the electronic configuration for sodium.

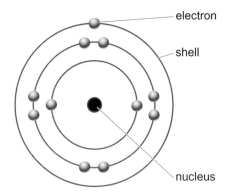

B The electronic configuration of sodium shows three occupied shells.

Each shell can contain different numbers of electrons. For the first 20 elements (hydrogen to calcium):

- the first shell can contain up to two electrons
- the second and third shells can contain up to eight electrons.

Electrons occupy the shells, starting with the innermost shell and working outwards as each one becomes full. This is why, in a sodium atom, the first shell contains two electrons, the second shell contains eight electrons and the third shell contains one electron.

 1 State what is meant by the term 'electronic configuration'.

 2 Explain why the electrons in a sodium atom do not all occupy one shell.

Working out configurations

Electronic configurations can also be written out rather than drawn. For example, the electronic configuration for sodium is 2.8.1 – the numbers show how many electrons occupy a shell, and the full stops separate each shell.

You can work out the electronic configuration of an element from its atomic number, *Z*. The atomic number of chlorine is 17 – each chlorine atom contains 17 protons and so also contains 17 electrons.

To fill a chlorine atom's shells:

- 2 electrons occupy the first shell (leaving 15 electrons)
- 8 electrons occupy the second shell (leaving 7 electrons)
- 7 electrons occupy the third shell.

The electronic configuration of chlorine is therefore 2.8.7 (diagram C shows this).

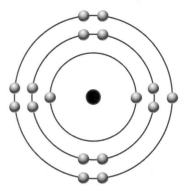

C The electronic configuration of chlorine shows three occupied shells.

 3 Describe how you can determine the atomic number, Z, of an element from its electronic configuration.

4 Write the electronic configuration of phosphorus, $Z = 15$.

Connections with the periodic table

Diagram D shows the electronic configurations for the first 20 elements in the periodic table. The electronic configuration of an element is related to its position:

- the number of occupied shells is equal to the period number
- the number of electrons in the outer shell is equal to the group number (except for group 0 elements, which all have full outer shells).

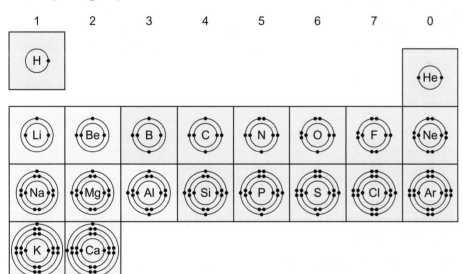

D These are the electronic configurations of the first 20 elements.

 5 What do the electronic configurations of sodium and the other elements in group 1 have in common?

 6 Explain how you can tell from their electronic configurations that sodium and chlorine are in the same period.

Exam-style question

Explain, in terms of electrons, why magnesium and calcium are in the same group in the periodic table. *(2 marks)*

Did you know?

After calcium, the third and fourth electron shells can actually contain up to 18 electrons. For this reason the International Union of Pure and Applied Chemistry (IUPAC) now recommends the use of group numbers in the range 1 to 18. In this newer numbering system, group numbers 3 to 12 refer to the block of elements between calcium and gallium. Group numbers 13 to 17 refer to the older group numbers 3 to 7, and 18 refers to group 0.

Checkpoint

How confidently can you answer the Progression questions?

Strengthen

S1 How do you work out the electronic configuration of an element?

Extend

E1 How is the electronic configuration of an element determined, and related to its position in the periodic table?

Atomic structure and the periodic table

The table shows information about tellurium and iodine.

Element	Atomic number	Relative atomic mass, A_r
tellurium	52	127.6
iodine	53	126.9

A

Describe how Mendeleev arranged the elements known to him into a periodic table, and compare this with the arrangement in the modern periodic table.

In your answer, use information from the table above to provide examples.

(6 marks)

Student answer

Mendeleev arranged the elements in order of relative atomic mass [1]. He also used the properties of elements and their compounds, so he sometimes had to swap elements. For example, the A_r of iodine is 126.9, so he should have put iodine first [2], but he put it second. He did this so it went into the same column as similar elements [3].

In the modern periodic table, elements are arranged in order of increasing atomic number (the number of protons in the nucleus) [4]. This explains why Mendeleev was correct when he placed tellurium before iodine.

[1] This shows knowledge of how Mendeleev ordered the elements, but it should say 'in order of *increasing* relative atomic mass'.

[2] The answer should be supported by comparing the A_r values for the two elements.

[3] An element in the same group, such as chlorine, could be identified using the periodic table.

[4] It is a good idea to give clear definitions like this.

Verdict

This is an acceptable answer. It shows good knowledge and understanding of the periodic table and the answer is organised in a logical way. The student has linked their knowledge of atomic structure with an understanding of Mendeleev's periodic table.

The answer could be improved by clearly quoting examples from the information given in the table. For example, in the last paragraph the answer could have included the atomic numbers for each of the elements.

Exam tip

If you are asked to use information from the question as part of your answer then make sure you include the information. It is important to make sure you *use* the information in your answer – don't just repeat what you have been given.

Paper 3 and Paper 4

CC5 Ionic Bonding /
CC6 Covalent Bonding /
CC7 Types of Substance

Using an extremely powerful 'atomic force microscope' scientists at the Berkeley Lab in California produced this amazing image showing the positions of the bonds holding the atoms of a small molecule together. Using this technique, the scientists were also able to examine the breaking and reforming of bonds during a chemical reaction. Bonds are the fundamental forces of attraction that hold our universe together. Understanding how bonds are formed and broken is essential in helping us explain even the simplest physical change or chemical reaction.

The learning journey

Previously you will have learnt at KS3:

- about the particle model of matter
- how Dalton's ideas about atoms and molecules helped to explain the properties of matter
- how elements are arranged in the periodic table.

In this unit you will learn:

- how ionic, covalent and metallic bonds are formed
- about the formation of lattice and molecular structures
- how the physical properties of a substance are linked to its bonding and structure.

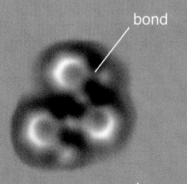

bond

1 nm

CC5a Ionic bonds

Specification reference: C0.1; C1.21;C1.22; C1.23; C1.24

Progression questions

- How are ions formed?
- How can the numbers of subatomic particles in an ion be calculated?
- What is an ionic bond?

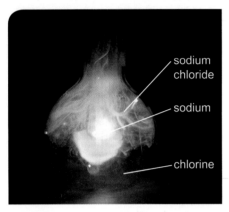

A Explosions can occur when new bonds form between sodium and chlorine atoms to form sodium chloride.

Bonds are forces of attraction that hold atoms together. When bonds form between atoms, energy is released from the atoms, making them more stable (less reactive). The most stable atoms are those of the noble gases, and scientists have found that this is because they have outer electron shells that contain as many electrons as possible – the outer shell of a noble gas atom is full.

Noble gas	Electronic configuration
He	2
Ne	2.8
Ar	2.8.8

B Atoms of all of the elements in group 0 have a stable electronic configuration (arrangement of electrons) with a complete outer shell of electrons.

The dots (●) and crosses (✗) represent electrons from different atoms.

The circles represent electron shells.

sodium atom (Na):
electronic configuration 2.8.1

chlorine atom (Cl):
electronic configuration 2.8.7

loses one electron

gains one electron

sodium ion (Na⁺):
electronic configuration 2.8

chloride ion (Cl⁻):
electronic configuration 2.8.8

Both ions have stable electronic configurations with full outer shells.

C Dot and cross diagrams can be used to show what happens when ions are formed.

Atoms are more stable if they have an outer electron shell that is full, like a noble gas. This can happen by the transfer of electrons between atoms, forming charged particles called **ions**.

Metal atoms tend to lose electrons and form positive ions, called **cations**. Cations have more protons than electrons. Non-metal atoms tend to gain electrons and form negative ions, called **anions**. Anions have more electrons than protons. The formation of sodium (Na^+) and chloride (Cl^-) ions is shown in diagram C. Note that when non-metals form negative ions the end of the name changes to –ide.

 1 a What are ions?

 b State the difference between a cation and an anion.

There are forces of attraction between all positively and negatively charged objects. These are called **electrostatic forces**. These forces hold the oppositely charged ions together, and form an **ionic bond** between them.

 2 a What is happening to the atoms when they form ions?

 b What holds the ions together in an ionic bond?

178

Atoms that easily form ions will have either a nearly full or a nearly empty outer electron shell. Most ionic bonds are formed between a metal and a non-metal. Table D shows the number of electrons lost or gained and the resulting ion charge of some groups of elements. The ion formed depends on the element's position in the periodic table and its number of outer electrons.

	Group 1	Group 2	Group 6	Group 7
outer electrons	1	2	6	7
electrons lost or gained	1 lost	2 lost	2 gained	1 gained
charge on ion	1+	2+	2–	1–
example	Li^+	Ca^{2+}	S^{2-}	F^-

D formation of ions by elements in groups 1, 2, 6 and 7

Diagram E shows the number of protons, neutrons and electrons in each atom and ion in the formation of the ionic bond in magnesium oxide.

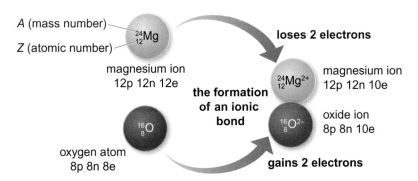

E ionic bond formation in magnesium oxide

5 An aluminium atom $^{27}_{13}Al$ loses three electrons when its ion is formed.

 a How many protons, neutrons and electrons are in the aluminium ion?

 b Write the symbol for the aluminium ion.

 6 Draw dot and cross diagrams to show the ions in diagram E.

3 Write the symbol for the ion formed by:

 a potassium (K) in group 1

 b selenium (Se) in group 6.

4 A sulfur atom contains 16 protons.

 a How many electrons does it contain?

 b Write out its electronic configuration.

 c Explain why it forms S^{2-} ions.

Checkpoint

How confidently can you answer the Progression questions?

Strengthen

S1 Describe what happens when lithium (group 1) and fluorine (group 7) react to form an ionic bond.

Extend

E1 Using dot and cross diagrams, explain what happens when aluminium and oxygen form an ionic bond.

Exam-style question

Bromine is in group 7 of the periodic table.

a Write the symbol for a bromide ion. *(1 mark)*

b State what the symbol tells you about the electrons in a bromide ion compared with a bromine atom. *(1 mark)*

CC5b Ionic lattices

Specification reference: C0.1, C1.25, C1.26, C1.27

Progression questions

- What is an ionic lattice?
- What do the endings –ide and –ate tell you about a substance?
- How do you work out the formulae of ionic compounds?

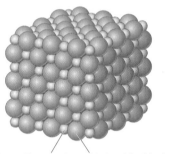

Na⁺ (a sodium ion)   Cl⁻ (a chloride ion)

A Sodium chloride forms a cubic lattice structure.

 2 Explain why the solid shown in photo B can be described as crystals.

B Sodium chloride crystals are shaped like cubes. These crystals are from a salt mine in Poland and the largest one has sides of 5 cm.

Ionic compounds, which are formed by the loss and gain of electrons, are held together by strong electrostatic forces of attraction between oppositely charged ions. These strong ionic bonds allow 'billions' of ions to be packed together in a regular repeating arrangement called a **lattice structure**. The lattice structure in sodium chloride is shown in diagram A.

 1 a What holds ions together in an ionic bond?

 b Why is the structure in diagram A described as a cubic lattice?

Ionic compounds will often form **crystals** when solid because of their regular lattice structure. Crystals are pieces of solid that have a particular regular shape, flat surfaces and sharp edges. Photo B shows crystals of sodium chloride.

Did you know?

The shapes of crystals are determined by the structure of the lattice. There are seven basic crystal or lattice structures.

cubic	tetragonal	hexagonal	trigonal

triclinic	monoclinic	orthorhombic

C the seven basic crystal structures

Positive ion	Ion formula	Negative ion	Ion formula
sodium	Na⁺	fluoride	F⁻
lithium	Li⁺	chloride	Cl⁻
potassium	K⁺	bromide	Br⁻
magnesium	Mg²⁺	oxide	O²⁻
calcium	Ca²⁺	sulfide	S²⁻
aluminium	Al³⁺	phosphide	P³⁻

D common ions

Working out ionic formulae

Ionic compounds are electrically neutral (they have no overall charge). So the formula of an ionic compound contains the same number of positive charges as negative charges. To work out ionic formulae we will need to use ion formulae, as shown in table D. Note that in two-element compounds the name ending of the non-metal ion is changed to –ide.

Worked example W1

Magnesium oxide contains the ions Mg^{2+} and O^{2-}.

A magnesium ion has two positive charges and an oxide ion has the same number of negative charges. One of each ion will balance the charges, and so the formula = MgO

Worked example W2

Sodium sulfide contains the ions Na^+ and S^{2-}.

Therefore two Na^+ ions are needed to balance the charges on the S^{2-} ion, and so the formula = Na_2S

Some ions contain more than one atom. For example, the sulfate ion, shown in diagram E, contains one sulfur atom bonded to four oxygen atoms with two added electrons. More examples of these **polyatomic ions** are shown in table F. An ion name ending '–ate' or '–ite' shows that the ion contains oxygen as well as another element.

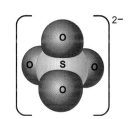

E The formula of a sulfate ion is SO_4^{2-}.

If an ionic formula contains two or more of the same polyatomic ions then the formula of the polyatomic ion must be written inside brackets.

Worked example W3

Calcium nitrate contains the ions Ca^{2+} and NO_3^-.

Therefore two NO_3^- ions are needed to balance the charges on the Ca^{2+} ion, and so the formula = $Ca(NO_3)_2$

Note that the brackets are needed around the polyatomic ion. Without brackets the formula becomes $CaNO_{32}$ and this compound is not possible.

5 Write the formulae for:

  a sodium carbonate **b** ammonium sulfate.

6 Li_3PO_4 is an ionic compound.

  a Suggest a name for this compound.

  b Write the formulae for both of the ions.

Exam-style question

Potassium iodide and potassium iodate, which contains the ion IO_3^-, are both used in health supplements.

a Give the formulae for both compounds. *(1 mark)*

b Compare and contrast these two compounds. *(2 marks)*

---

3 Write the formulae for:

  a sodium fluoride

  b calcium sulfide

  c magnesium bromide

  d aluminium oxide.

4 The formula of iron chloride is $FeCl_3$.

  a What is the charge on the iron ion?

  b Explain how you worked out your answer.

Polyatomic ion name	Ion formula
ammonium	NH_4^+
nitrate	NO_3^-
hydroxide	OH^-
carbonate	CO_3^{2-}
sulfate	SO_4^{2-}
sulfite	SO_3^{2-}

F Polyatomic ions are groups of two or more atoms, which have become charged.

Checkpoint

How confidently can you answer the Progression questions?

Strengthen

S1 Describe with the help of a diagram the type of structure you find in ionic compounds.

Extend

E1 What does the formula $Fe_3(PO_4)_2$ tell you about the compound and its structure?

CC5c Properties of ionic compounds

Specification reference: C1.33

Progression questions

- What particles and forces are present in ionic compounds?
- Why do ionic compounds have high melting points and boiling points?
- Why do ionic compounds conduct electricity when they are liquids or dissolved in water but not when they are solids?

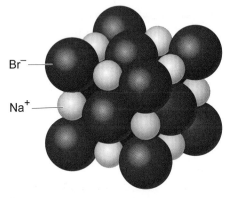

A the lattice structure of sodium bromide

All ionic compounds contain charged particles called ions. Ions have one or more positive charges or one or more negative charges. The oppositely charged ions in ionic compounds are held together by strong electrostatic forces of attraction, which we call ionic bonds. It is important to remember that ionic compounds contain *ions*, not atoms or molecules.

In ionic compounds, huge numbers of ions are arranged in a giant structure or lattice. This has a regular pattern and so ionic compounds form crystals.

1 State the type of particles present in an ionic compound.

2 State the type of forces found in an ionic bond.

Melting points and boiling points

The electrostatic forces of attraction between oppositely charged ions are strong. A lot of energy is needed to overcome these forces in order to separate the ions and cause the substance to melt. This is why ionic compounds must be heated to high temperatures before they change state. They have high melting points and boiling points.

Some ions have more than one charge (such as Mg^{2+} and O^{2-}). These highly charged ions will attract other ions more strongly than ions with one charge. More energy will be needed to overcome the electrostatic forces of attraction and so the melting points will be higher.

B molten sodium chloride

Ionic compound	Melting point (°C)	Boiling point (°C)
sodium bromide, NaBr	747	1390
sodium chloride, NaCl	801	1413
magnesium oxide, MgO	2852	3600

C Ionic compounds have high melting points and boiling points.

3 Explain why ionic compounds have high melting points.

4 Explain why magnesium oxide has a much higher melting point than sodium chloride.

Electrical conductivity

Ionic compounds conduct electricity when they are molten or dissolved in water. They do not conduct electricity when they are in the solid state.

Two conditions must be met for a substance to conduct electricity:

- it must contain charged particles
- these particles must be free to move.

5 Samples of sodium chloride and magnesium oxide are both heated to 1080 °C. State and explain how the properties of these two compounds will or will not change at this temperature compared to room temperature.

When an ionic compound conducts electricity, it is the charged *ions* that carry the current. Ionic compounds do not conduct electricity in the solid state as the ions are not free to move from place to place. When the ionic compound is molten or in **aqueous solution**, the ions are free to move and so it does conduct electricity. Most ionic compounds are soluble in water and form an aqueous solution.

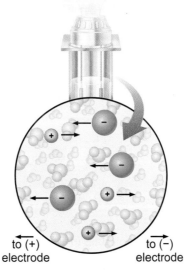

Positive and negative ions fixed in a solid do not conduct a current.

In solution, positive and negative ions move and conduct a current.

D Solid sodium chloride does not conduct electricity but aqueous sodium chloride does conduct.

The negative ions are also known as anions and they are attracted to the positive electrode, which is called the **anode**. The positive ions are also known as cations and they are attracted to the negative electrode, which is called the **cathode**.

It is important to remember that it is ions moving that enable ionic compounds to conduct electricity and that it is not *electrons* moving.

 6 Explain why ionic compounds conduct electricity when they are dissolved in water.

 7 Magnesium oxide is insoluble in water. State the condition needed for magnesium oxide to conduct electricity.

Exam-style question

Magnesium chloride is an ionic compound and has a high melting point. Explain why magnesium chloride has a high melting point. *(3 marks)*

Did you know?

Molten salts are used to store energy in some solar power stations. The salts are heated up by the Sun and release their thermal energy at night, allowing electricity to be generated when it is dark.

Checkpoint

How confidently can you answer the Progression questions?

Strengthen

S1 You are given a substance and asked to find out if it is an ionic compound. Describe the tests you would carry out in order to decide.

Extend

E1 Table E shows some properties of five compounds.

Compound	Melting point (°C)	Soluble in water?	Conducts when molten?
A	2072	no	yes
B	191	no	no
C	782	yes	yes
D	605	yes	yes
E	150	yes	no

E

Identify the compounds that have ionic bonding and explain your reasoning. Give reasons why the other compounds do not have ionic bonding.

CC6a Covalent bonds

Specification reference: C1.28; C1.29; C.1.30; C1.31

Progression questions

- What are the names of some covalent molecules?
- How are covalent bonds formed?
- How can dot and cross diagrams be used to explain the formation of covalent molecules?

Did you know?

A cup of tea will contain over 1 000 000 000 000 000 000 000 000 (10^{24}) water molecules. This is the same as the estimated number of stars in the Universe.

 1 a What is a molecule?

 b What does a molecular formula tell you about a substance?

Molecular substances contain groups of atoms that are held together by strong bonds called **covalent bonds**. The number of atoms of each element bonded together in a simple **molecule** is shown by its **molecular formula.**

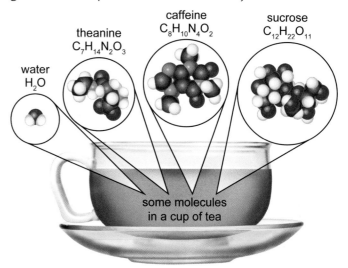

theanine $C_7H_{14}N_2O_3$
caffeine $C_8H_{10}N_4O_2$
sucrose $C_{12}H_{22}O_{11}$
water H_2O
some molecules in a cup of tea

A Most of the molecules in a cup of tea are water, which has the molecular formula H_2O.

Covalent bonds are usually formed between non-metal atoms and are produced by sharing pairs of electrons. By forming the bond the atoms become more stable, because they can use the shared electrons to complete their **outer electron shells**. The reason why noble gases are so stable is because they have full outer electron shells.

The **dot and cross diagrams** in diagram B show how covalent bonds are formed. Counting the shared electrons, each atom now has a complete outer shell of electrons. Sometimes atoms share more than one pair of electrons to fill their outer shells. In oxygen and carbon dioxide the atoms share two pairs of electrons, to form **double bonds**.

2 Oxygen molecules consist of two oxygen atoms.

 a Write the molecular formula for oxygen.

 b Explain why a noble gas, such as argon, exists as single atoms and not as molecules.

Dots show electrons from one atom and crosses show electrons from the other atom. This allows us to see which atoms the electrons in the bond originally came from. The electrons themselves are all identical.

single covalent bond

a hydrogen

H×Cl

single covalent bond

b hydrogen chloride

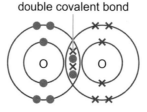

double covalent bond

c oxygen

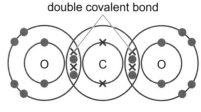

double covalent bond

d carbon dioxide

B Dot and cross diagrams can be used to explain how covalent bonds are formed.

3   **a** Describe how covalent bonds are formed.

   b Write the molecular formulae for the substances shown in diagram B.

 4 The electronic configuration of fluorine is 2.7. Draw a dot and cross diagram to show how fluorine molecules (F_2) are formed.

The atoms in molecules are held together by strong **electrostatic forces** of attraction between the positive nuclei and the negative electrons in the bonded atoms. There are also some forces of attraction *between* molecules but these are very weak in comparison. Atoms and molecules are extremely small, about 10^{-10} metres across, so we represent them using models, such as those shown in Diagram C.

 5 What holds the atoms together when a covalent bond has been formed?

Working out molecular formulae

The numbers of covalent bonds formed by atoms of different elements are shown in table D. This is called the **valency** of the element. It is the same as the number of electrons needed to obtain a complete outer shell.

Group number	Examples	Outer electrons	Bonds formed	Valency
4	C and Si	4	4	4
5	N and P	5	3	3
6	O and S	6	2	2
7	F and Cl	7	1	1

D valencies of some elements

Diagram E shows how molecular formulae can be worked out by matching up the valencies, so that all atoms have the correct number of bonds (and so a complete outer electron shell).

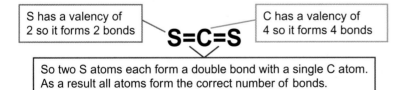

E working out the formula of carbon sulfide

 7 Work out the molecular formulae for:

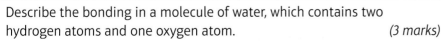   **a** oxygen fluoride   **b** hydrogen sulfide   **c** nitrogen chloride.

Exam-style question

Describe the bonding in a molecule of water, which contains two hydrogen atoms and one oxygen atom.   *(3 marks)*

CH₄
molecular formula

structural formula (stick bonds)

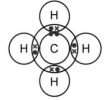

full dot and cross diagram

dot and cross (outer shell only)

3D space filling

ball and stick

C different representations of methane

6 Look at diagram C.

   a How are bonds represented in structural formulae?

   b Describe the covalent bonds in methane.

   c Draw four different models of a water molecule, including one dot and cross diagram.

Checkpoint

How confidently can you answer the Progression questions?

Strengthen

S1 What does diagram B tell you about hydrogen chloride?

Extend

E1 Describe the bonding in a molecule of ammonia, which contains three hydrogen atoms and one nitrogen atom. Use diagrams in your answer.

CC7a Molecular compounds

Specification reference: C1.34; C1.39

Progression questions

- Why do simple molecular compounds have low boiling and melting points?
- Why are simple molecular compounds poor electrical conductors?
- What is a polymer?

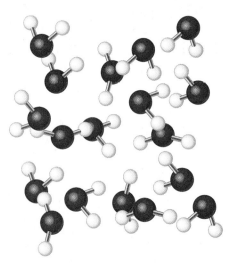

A 'ball and stick' models of H_2O molecules

All **compounds** contain atoms of more than one **element**, chemically joined together by **bonds**. The properties of a compound are influenced by its atoms and by its type of bonding.

Some compounds exist as molecules – distinct groups of atoms joined by **covalent bonds**. They have **covalent, simple molecular structures**. An example is water. One molecule of water always contains one atom of oxygen covalently bonded to two atoms of hydrogen.

 1 Look at diagram A.

 a What do the red and white spheres represent?

 b How are bonds represented in this model?

2 Why is the ratio of oxygen to hydrogen atoms the same in every glass of water?

Melting and boiling points

The covalent bonds in a water molecule are strong forces of attraction. However, there are also weak forces of attraction *between* molecules – **intermolecular forces**. These intermolecular forces hold water molecules together and must be overcome when turning liquid water into a gas. Small, simple molecules such as water often have low melting and boiling points, because it doesn't take much energy to overcome the weak intermolecular forces.

 3 Covalent bonds are strong, so why does water have a low melting point?

 4 What would you expect the strength of the bonds to be like between carbon and oxygen atoms in carbon dioxide, compared to the strength of the forces between neighbouring carbon dioxide molecules?

 5 **a** Methane consists of molecules (containing one carbon atom covalently bonded to four hydrogen atoms). Would you expect methane to have a high or low melting point?

 b Explain your reasoning.

Did you know?

Intermolecular forces can allow water in an open container to be higher than the top of the container.

B

Conduction of electricity

An electric current is a flow of charged particles. Simple molecules have no overall charge and so cannot carry an electric current. In a covalent bond, electrons are shared between two atoms. The strong forces between the negatively charged electrons and the positively charged nuclei hold the electrons in place. The electrons cannot flow and so cannot carry a current.

Polymers

Monomers are small, simple molecules that can be joined in a chain to form a **polymer**. Carbon atoms can form up to four covalent bonds with other atoms, and so monomers are usually linked together by covalent bonds between carbon atoms. Most polymers contain a chain of carbon atoms.

Poly(ethene) (or 'polythene') is a common polymer made of ethene monomers (as shown in diagram D).

Polymer molecules can have different lengths. Longer polymers have more intermolecular forces between them. The longer chains also tend to get tangled up with one another. For these reasons, longer polymers have higher melting and boiling points than shorter ones.

 6 Explain why water is a poor conductor of electricity.

C Poly(ethene) sheets are often used to protect things, such as plants. These are coffee beans being dried.

7 What is a polymer?

D two dimensional models of: (i) an ethene molecule (monomer) (ii) a poly(ethene) molecule

(i) ethene (ii) poly(ethene)

 8 **a** What monomer is used to make poly(butene)?

 b What polymer is formed by linking styrene monomers together?

 9 Explain why most polymers are solids at room temperature, whereas their monomers are liquids or gases.

Checkpoint

How confidently can you answer the Progression questions?

Strengthen

S1 You can ask three questions to find out if a substance consists of simple molecules or not. What questions would you ask?

Extend

E1 Propene melts at −185 °C. Explain how the melting point and electrical conduction will change if other propene molecules are added together to form a chain.

Exam-style question

Explain why small molecules have a lower melting point than large polymer molecules. *(3 marks)*

CC7b Allotropes of carbon

Specification reference: C1.35; C1.36; C1.37; C1.38

Progression questions

- How are simple molecular structures different from giant covalent structures?
- What are the differences in structure between the different allotropes of carbon?
- How do we explain the properties and uses of graphite, diamond and fullerenes?

Molecules are groups of atoms joined by covalent bonds. Molecules can be compounds (such as water, H_2O) or elements (such as oxygen, O_2).

The element carbon can form a number of different molecules. Different structural forms of the same element are called **allotropes**. The structure and bonding in different allotropes influences their properties and uses.

 1 What is an allotrope?

Fullerenes

Carbon can form simple molecules called **fullerenes**, in which each carbon atom is covalently bonded to three other carbon atoms. Fullerenes are often tubular molecules (nanotubes) or spherical. An example is buckminsterfullerene (or 'bucky ball'), which has 60 carbon atoms that form a ball with the formula C_{60}.

Fullerenes have weak intermolecular forces between the molecules and so have low melting points (or sublimation points). These weak forces also make them soft and slippery. However, the molecules themselves are very strong due to their covalent bonding.

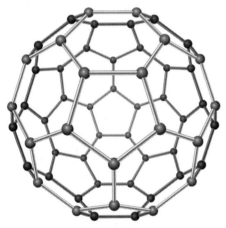

A Buckminsterfullerene is a simple molecule.

 2 A fullerene has the formula C_{60}. Describe its structure.

 3 Explain why fullerenes have low melting points.

Graphene

Graphene is similar to fullerenes but is not a simple molecule. It consists of a sheet of carbon atoms with no fixed formula. The sheet is just one atom thick, making it the lightest known material, but its covalent bonds make it extremely strong. It also allows free electrons to move across its surface and so is a good electrical conductor.

Did you know?

Buckminsterfullerene is named after an American architect called Richard Buckminster Fuller, who designed spherical buildings with a similar structure to C_{60}.

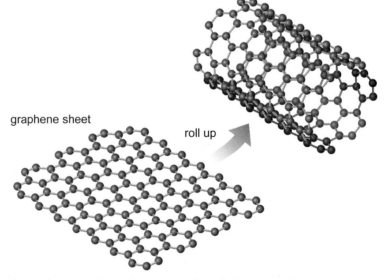

graphene sheet

roll up

 4 Explain why graphene is not a simple molecule.

B Graphene can be a sheet or can be rolled into a tube.

Giant structures of carbon

Diamond and graphite are two more allotropes of carbon that are not simple molecules. They are both examples of **covalent, giant molecular structures**, which have huge three-dimensional networks of carbon atoms linked by covalent bonds.

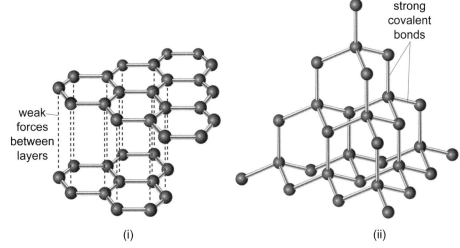

strong covalent bonds

weak forces between layers

(i)   (ii)

C small sections of (i) graphite and (ii) diamond to show the arrangements of atoms

 5 How many covalent bonds will most carbon atoms form in graphite, diamond and C_{60}?

 6 Describe how simple molecular structures are different from giant molecular structures.

Graphite and diamond both have high melting points because of the many strong covalent bonds that need to be broken to melt the solids.

However, graphite has three covalent bonds for each carbon atom, whereas diamond has four. This gives graphite a layered structure and means that not all of its electrons are held in covalent bonds. These **delocalised electrons** are free to move and can carry an electrical current. Since graphite conducts electricity well and is cheap and not very reactive, it is used as electrodes (in electrolysis).

 7 Explain why graphite conducts electricity but diamond does not.

The sheets of carbon atoms in graphite are held together by weak forces of attraction (purple dashed lines in diagram C). These weak forces allow the layers to slide past each other, which makes graphite quite soft and useful as a **lubricant**.

Diamond is very hard because it has a rigid network of carbon atoms in a tetrahedral arrangement, joined by strong covalent bonds. This property makes diamond useful for tools to cut things. It is also an electrical insulator because it has no free charged particles.

8 Explain why:

 a graphite is used as electrodes

 b diamonds are used on cutting heads when drilling through rocks

 c spherical fullerenes are used in some lubricants.

D This cutting head, used in mining, is studded with diamonds.

Checkpoint

How confidently can you answer the Progression questions?

Strengthen

S1 Describe how the structures of four allotropes of carbon cause their properties.

Extend

E1 Graphene sheets can be rolled into tubes. Predict the properties of these tubes.

Exam-style question

Explain why graphite is softer than diamond. *(4 marks)*

CC7c Properties of metals

Specification reference: C1.40; C1.42

Progression questions

- What are the typical physical properties of metals and non-metals?
- How are the particles arranged in metals?
- How can we explain the properties of a metal in terms of its bonding and structure?

The bucket is made of iron. Metals have some common properties:
- solids with high melting points
- shiny (when polished)
- malleable
- high density
- good conductors of electricity.

Sulfur is a non-metal. Non-metals have some common properties:
- solids, liquids or gases with low melting points
- not usually shiny (when solid)
- brittle (when solid)
- low density
- poor conductors of electricity.

A Sulfur being unloaded at a port in Darwin, Australia.

Chemists classify elements into **metals** and **non-metals**, depending on their properties. Just over three-quarters of the elements are metals.

A metal or a non-metal may not have all the common properties shown in photo A.

 1 Give two general properties of:

    a metals

     b non-metals.

 2 Name a form of the non-metal carbon that is a good conductor of electricity.

Metallic structure and bonding

The atoms in a metallic element are all the same size and are packed closely together in layers to form a giant **lattice**.

Metal atoms have one, two or three electrons in their outer shell. These outer shell electrons are lost from each atom and become free to move randomly throughout the metal. This leaves a giant lattice of positive metal ions surrounded by a 'sea' of delocalised electrons, which move randomly in all directions.

Metallic bonding is the electrostatic attraction between the positive metal ions and the negative delocalised electrons. This attraction is strong, so metals have high melting and boiling points.

 3 **a** Describe the structure of a metal.

     b Describe the bonding in a metal.

 4 Explain why most metals have high melting points.

B Metals consist of stacked layers of ions in a 'sea' of delocalised ('free') electrons.

Did you know?

Osmium is the most dense metal at room temperature (the mass of 1 cm³ is 22.6 g). A lump of osmium the size of an average smartphone has a mass of 1.5 kg (the same as one and a half bags of sugar)!

Metals are malleable

Metals are **malleable**. This means that they can be hammered or rolled into shape without shattering. When you hit a metal, the layers of ions slide over each other. The 'sea' of electrons holds the ions together and so the metal changes shape instead of breaking.

 5 Copper is used to make some saucepans. Explain why copper can be bent and shaped into a saucepan.

C When hit or bent, the layers of ions in a metal can slide over each other.

Metals conduct electricity

The delocalised electrons move randomly between the positive metal ions in all directions. When a potential difference (voltage) is applied between two points on a piece of metal, the electrons will flow towards the positive side. This flow of electrons transfers energy and forms an electrical current.

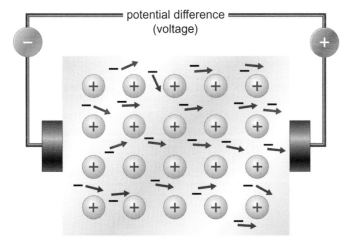

E When a voltage is applied to a piece of metal, an electrical current flows.

 6 Copper is used to make electrical wires. Explain why copper is a good conductor of electricity.

Substances that conduct electricity better than others have a higher **electrical conductivity**. The electrical conductivity of the metals increases as the number of delocalised electrons increases. Each sodium ion has one positive charge, Na^+, and contributes 1 electron to the 'sea' of delocalised electrons. Each magnesium ion has two positive charges, Mg^{2+}, and contributes 2 electrons to the 'sea' of delocalised electrons, and so magnesium has a higher electrical conductivity than sodium.

 7 Aluminium forms Al^{3+} ions. Explain why aluminium has a higher electrical conductivity than magnesium.

Exam-style question

Explain how metals conduct electricity. *(2 marks)*

D Copper conducts electricity well and so is used for electrical wiring.

Checkpoint

How confidently can you answer the Progression questions?

Strengthen

S1 You are given a solid substance and asked to find out if it is a metal or a non-metal. Describe the properties you would need to find out about.

Extend

E1 Elements A and B are solids at room temperature. Element A has a melting point of 98 °C, a density of 0.97 g/cm³ and conducts electricity. Element B has a melting point of 217 °C, a density of 4.81 g/cm³ and doesn't conduct electricity. Are these elements metals or non-metals? Explain your reasoning.

CC7d Bonding models

Specification reference: C1.32; C1.41

Progression questions

- What different types of structure and bonding models are used to describe substances?
- How do these models help explain the properties of substances?
- What are the limitations of the models that we use to show structure and bonding?

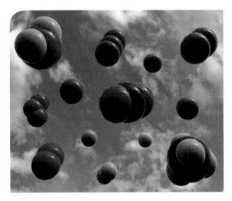

A 3D models of some gas molecules

Scientists have developed models to explain how different types of bonds and structures are formed. These models help us explain the properties of different substances. Most elements and compounds fit into one of the four main models summarised below.

Ionic

Where found: in most compounds containing metal and non-metal atoms.

Bonding: ionic bonds formed by the loss and gain of electrons to produce oppositely charged ions that attract one another.

Structure: billions of ions held together in a lattice structure.

Properties:
- high melting/boiling points
- many are soluble in water
- conduct electricity when liquid or in solution but do not when solid.

Simple molecular (covalent)

Where found: in most non-metal elements and compounds.

Bonding: covalent bonds formed when atoms share pairs of electrons.

Structure: small, distinct groups of atoms.

Properties:
- low melting/boiling points
- a few are soluble in water
- most do not conduct electricity.

Giant covalent

Where found: in a few non-metal elements and some compounds of non-metals.

Bonding: covalent bonds formed when atoms share pairs of electrons.

Structure: billions of atoms held together in a lattice structure.

Properties:
- high melting/boiling points
- insoluble in water
- most do not conduct electricity (except in carbon as graphite).

Metallic

Where found: in all metals.

Bonding: metallic bonds are the electrostatic attraction between positive metal ions and negative delocalised electrons.

Structure: billions of ions held together in a giant lattice structure of positive ions in a 'sea' of negative delocalised electrons.

Properties:
- high melting/boiling points
- insoluble in water
- conduct electricity when solid or liquid.

---

1 Look at the substances in the box below.

> potassium fluoride
> carbon dioxide
> diamond
> magnesium

Which substance:

5th a conducts electricity when solid

6th b is most likely to dissolve in water

6th c has the lowest melting point?

6th 2 a Name the type of bonding and structure that usually has a low melting point.

7th b Explain why the melting points of these substances are usually low.

The models help to explain some of the properties. For example:

- Substances with high melting points have many strong bonds that need to be broken during melting. Substances with low melting points have only weak forces that need to be overcome between molecules.
- Substances that conduct electricity have charged particles that can freely move. Substances that do not conduct electricity have charged particles that cannot move or particles that are not charged.

3 Explain why sodium metal conducts electricity when it is solid or liquid but sodium chloride conducts only when liquid.

4 A white solid with a melting point of 2614 °C does not dissolve in water.

 a Is the substance ionic or covalent or can you not tell? Explain your answer.

 b Describe a test you could do to help you answer part a.

 5 What do sodium ions and chloride ions have in common?

Problems with bonding models

The bonding models that we use to explain the properties of matter all have certain weaknesses or limitations.

- The dot and cross diagram for hydrogen chloride in diagram B shows how electrons are shared in covalent bonds. However, dot and cross diagrams do not show the structure formed and they suggest that the electrons in different atoms are different, when they are actually all the same.

- The metallic model in diagram C shows the metal ions held in a lattice and explains why it conducts electricity, but the model does not show that the ions will be vibrating all the time.

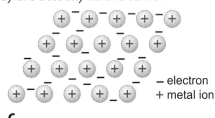

− electron
+ metal ion

C

- 3D ball and stick models, like diagram D for diamond, show which atoms are joined together and show the shape of the structure. However, they also show the atoms too far apart and there are not really 'sticks' holding the atoms together.

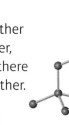

 6 **a** Draw a 3D structural ball and stick model of a sodium chloride lattice. **D**

 b Draw a dot and cross diagram for sodium chloride.

 c Explain one strength and one weakness of a dot and cross diagram for sodium chloride.

 7 Describe one strength and one weakness of the 3D models shown in photo A.

Exam-style question

Suggest why the melting point of silicon dioxide (1610 °C) is so much higher than the temperature at which solid carbon dioxide changes state (−78.5 °C), although both compounds contain covalent bonds. *(3 marks)*

Did you know?

Ideas about chemical bonds can be traced back to Roman times. The Roman poet Lucretius (*c.*95 BCE–*c.*55 BCE) imagined atoms as tiny spheres with fishhooks embedded in them. The atoms formed bonds when the fishhooks got tangled up with one another.

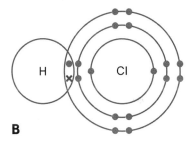

B

Checkpoint

How confidently can you answer the Progression questions?

Strengthen

S1 Draw up a summary table describing the four 'types of bonding and structure' under the headings: 'where it occurs'; 'how bonds form'; 'type of structure'; 'properties' and 'examples'.

Extend

E1 The models below show methane.

a Draw a dot and cross diagram for methane.

b Describe one strength and one weakness of your dot and cross diagram and the two models below.

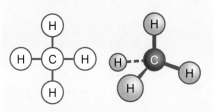

E

Bonding in compounds

Sodium chloride and hydrogen chloride are both compounds of chlorine. Sodium chloride has a boiling point of 1413 °C. Hydrogen chloride has a boiling point of −85 °C.

Explain this difference in boiling points in terms of the structure and bonding in the particles of the two compounds.

(6 marks)

Student answer

As it is a metal and a non-metal, sodium chloride contains ionic bonds with lots of oppositely charged ions attracting each other to form a giant lattice structure [1]. Ionic compounds contain lots of strong bonds which keep it solid [2].

[3]

Hydrogen chloride contains covalent bonds and is made up of molecules. The covalent bonds are strong bonds that hold the atoms together in the molecules. Substances which contain molecules have low boiling points [4].

[1] This is a good description of the bonding and structure of sodium chloride.

[2] The question asked for an explanation of the high boiling point, not why it was solid.

[3] The diagram will get no credit as it is not labelled or described.

[4] This part of the answer does not explain why hydrogen chloride has a low boiling point.

Verdict

This is an acceptable answer. It contains a good description of the bonding and structures of sodium chloride and hydrogen chloride. The answer has included information on both of the compounds in the question and uses correct scientific terminology.

This answer could be improved by explaining why the boiling points are low or high. The student should use scientific knowledge to explain the link between the structures of the compounds, the bonding within them and their boiling points.

Exam tip

You are more likely to get better marks in a question which requires extended writing if you plan your answer before you start. The plan can simply be a list of the keywords or phrases that you want to include. It is also useful to organise these keywords in a logical order to help structure your answer.

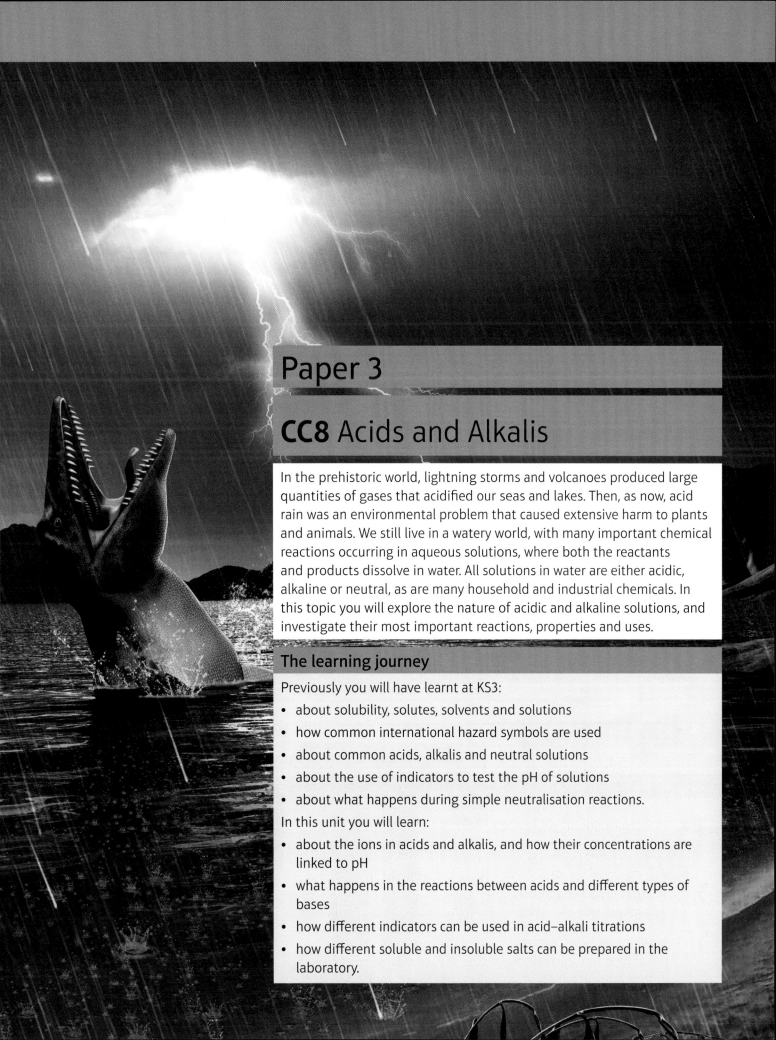

Paper 3

CC8 Acids and Alkalis

In the prehistoric world, lightning storms and volcanoes produced large quantities of gases that acidified our seas and lakes. Then, as now, acid rain was an environmental problem that caused extensive harm to plants and animals. We still live in a watery world, with many important chemical reactions occurring in aqueous solutions, where both the reactants and products dissolve in water. All solutions in water are either acidic, alkaline or neutral, as are many household and industrial chemicals. In this topic you will explore the nature of acidic and alkaline solutions, and investigate their most important reactions, properties and uses.

The learning journey

Previously you will have learnt at KS3:

- about solubility, solutes, solvents and solutions
- how common international hazard symbols are used
- about common acids, alkalis and neutral solutions
- about the use of indicators to test the pH of solutions
- about what happens during simple neutralisation reactions.

In this unit you will learn:

- about the ions in acids and alkalis, and how their concentrations are linked to pH
- what happens in the reactions between acids and different types of bases
- how different indicators can be used in acid–alkali titrations
- how different soluble and insoluble salts can be prepared in the laboratory.

CC8a Acids, alkalis and indicators

Specification reference: C0.5; C3.1; C3.2; C3.3; **H** C3.4

Progression questions

- Why are hazard symbols useful?
- What are the effects of acids and alkalis on some common indicators?
- What does the pH tell us about the ions in a solution?

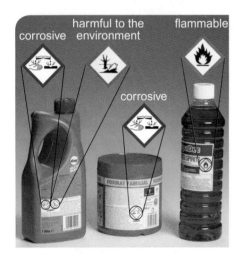

A International hazard symbols are used in all countries.

B Universal indicator can be used to find an approximate pH value.

All **aqueous solutions**, including those found in many household chemicals, are either **acidic**, **alkaline** or **neutral**. Some, including those that are neutral, can cause problems. For example, some acids and alkalis can be corrosive, toxic or harmful to the environment. The hazards associated with handling particular solutions are identified by international symbols, and they indicate the precautions that need to be taken when handling them.

 1 Name two acids and two alkalis used in the home.

 2 **a** Suggest an advantage of having internationally agreed hazard symbols.

b Suggest a safety precaution for each of the hazard symbols shown in photo A.

Indicators and pH

The **acidity** or **alkalinity** of a solution is measured on the **pH scale**. Most solutions lie between 0 and 14 on the scale. Solutions with a pH of 7 are neutral, while **acids** have a pH lower than 7 and **alkalis** have a pH greater than 7. The lower the pH, the more acidic the solution. The higher the pH, the more alkaline the solution.

The pH of a solution can be found by using **indicators** – substances that change colour depending on the pH. The **universal indicator** in photo B is made from a mixture of different indicators and produces a range of colours depending on the pH. Some other common indicators are shown in diagram C.

 3 Place the following pH values in order of increasing acidity. 4, 1, 7, 9, 6.

 4 **a** What pH is the solution in photo B?

 b What colour would this solution turn each of the indicators in table C?

indicator	litmus	methyl orange	phenolphthalein
colour in alkaline solutions	blue	yellow	pink
colour in acidic solutions	red	red	colourless

C the colours of litmus, methyl orange and phenolphthalein

Did you know?

Plant dyes can be used as pH indicators. The juice from cherries is bright red in acid solutions but turns blue/purple in alkalis. Curry powder contains the pigment curcumin, which changes from yellow at pH 7.4 to red at pH 8.6.

Ions in acids and alkalis

An ion is an atom that has become charged by losing or gaining electrons. Losing electrons forms positive ions (e.g. Na^+, H^+). Gaining electrons forms negative ions (e.g. Cl^-, Br^-, S^{2-}).

Polyatomic ions are formed when small groups of atoms, held together by covalent bonds, lose or gain electrons. Examples include OH^-, NO_3^- and SO_4^{2-}.

Acids produce an excess of hydrogen ions (H^+) when they dissolve in water. For example, hydrochloric acid is formed when hydrogen chloride gas dissolves in water and splits into H^+ ions and Cl^- ions as shown in diagram E.

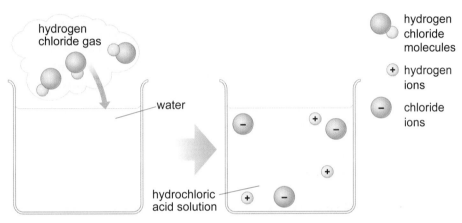

E Acids form hydrogen ions in water.

Alkalis produce excess hydroxide ions (OH^-) in water. For example, solid sodium hydroxide splits into Na^+ and OH^- ions when it dissolves.

H

The higher the number of hydrogen ions in a certain volume, the higher their **concentration**. The higher their concentration, the more acidic the solution and the lower the pH.

The higher the concentration of hydroxide ions, the more alkaline the solution and the higher the pH.

Neutral solutions, such as pure water, have a pH of 7 and contain low, equal, concentrations of hydrogen ions and hydroxide ions.

 8 Describe what happens to the acidity and pH of a solution, as more hydrogen ions are added.

Exam-style question

a Explain why the pH of a hydrochloric acid increases when pure water is added. *(2 marks)*

b What would happen to the pH of salt solution (pH 7) if pure water was added? Briefly explain your answer. *(2 marks)*

Common acids	Formula
hydrochloric acid	HCl
sulfuric acid	H_2SO_4
nitric acid	HNO_3

Common alkalis	Formula
sodium hydroxide	NaOH
potassium hydroxide	KOH
calcium hydroxide	$Ca(OH)_2$

D common laboratory acids and alkalis

 5 Describe what the pH scale tells us about acidity and alkalinity.

6 An acid is formed when hydrogen bromide dissolves in water.

 a Suggest a possible pH for the solution and explain your choice.

 b Write the symbols for the ions that form in this acidic solution.

 7 What ions will each of the substances in table D produce when they dissolve in water?

Checkpoint

How confidently can you answer the Progression questions?

Strengthen

S1 Describe the differences between an acidic and an alkaline solution.

Extend

E1 Explain how the nature of a solution is changing if the pH is: **a** increasing **b** decreasing.

CC8b Looking at acids

Specification reference: H C3.5; H C3.7; H C3.8

Progression questions

- H What is the difference between dilute and concentrated solutions?
- H How do changes in the concentration of hydrogen ions affect the pH of a solution?
- H What is the difference between strong and weak acids?

H

A **concentrated** solution contains a lot of dissolved solute per unit volume, while a **dilute** solution contains only a small amount of solute.

1 25 g of sulfuric acid is dissolved in water to make 200 cm³ of concentrated sulfuric acid solution.

 a What is a concentrated solution?

 b What is the concentration of this solution in g dm⁻³?

Worked example

$$\text{Concentration} = \frac{\text{amount dissolved}}{\text{volume of solution}}$$

Units: grams per decimetre cubed, g dm⁻³

For example, if 4 g is dissolved in 50 cm³

$$\text{Concentration} = \frac{4}{0.05} = 80\,\text{g dm}^{-3}$$

Note: the minus sign shows that g is divided by cm³. 1 dm³ is the same volume as 1 litre or 1000 cm³.

Note: divide cm³ by 1000 to change into dm³.

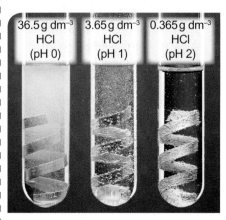

36.5 g dm⁻³ HCl (pH 0)   3.65 g dm⁻³ HCl (pH 1)   0.365 g dm⁻³ HCl (pH 2)

A More concentrated acids contain more hydrogen ions, so they react faster with magnesium metal.

Accurate measurements of the pH of different concentrations of acid show that the concentration of hydrogen ions in an acid is linked to the pH. Table B shows that if the concentration of hydrogen ions is increased by a factor of 10, the pH decreases by 1. If the concentration decreases by a factor of 10, the pH increases by 1.

pH	0	1	2	3	4	5	6	7
difference in concentration of H⁺ ions		×10	×10	×10	×10	×10	×10	×10

B pH and concentration

So, hydrochloric acid with a pH of 0 is 10 × 10 × 10 × 10 = 10 000 times more acidic than vinegar, with a pH of 4. This means that a solution with a pH of 0 has a concentration of H⁺ ions that is 10 000 times greater than a solution with a pH of 4.

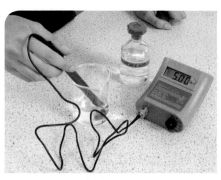

C Universal indicator only gives a rough estimate of acidity. A **pH meter** is used for accurate pH measurements.

 2 What does the pH of a solution measure?

 3 An acid with a pH of 3 is diluted by a factor of 10. What will the new pH be?

 4 The most acidic rain recorded in Britain had a pH of 2. How much more acidic is this than normal rainwater with a pH of 5?

 5 What is the pH of the solution formed when 10 cm³ of hydrochloric acid (pH 1) is made up to 1000 cm³ with distilled water?

The pH of an acid depends on the type of acid as well as its concentration. The acids in table D with low pH values are **strong acids**. Their molecules **dissociate** (break up) completely into ions when they dissolve in water and produce high concentrations of hydrogen ions. The other acids in the table are **weak acids**. They do not dissociate completely into ions in solution. Diagram E shows the difference between a strong and a weak acid.

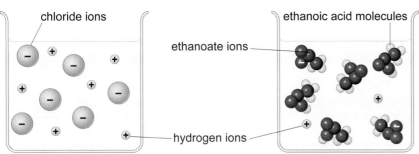

A strong acid like hydrochloric acid contains lots of hydrogen ions.

A weak acid like ethanoic acid contains only a few hydrogen ions.

E strong and weak acids

The chemical properties of an acid depend on both the type of acid and its concentration, as shown in photo F.

6 List the strong and the weak acids in table D.

7 About 1 in 60 000 butanoic acid molecules release hydrogen ions when they dissolve, while nearly all hydrogen iodide molecules do so.

a Explain which acid is a weak acid.

b Explain which acid will have the higher pH, if both are the same concentration.

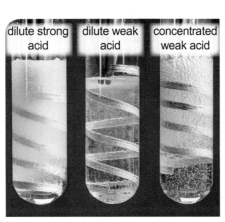

F A dilute solution of a strong acid can have a similar pH and reactivity as a concentrated solution of a weak acid. This is because they can have similar concentrations of hydrogen ions.

Acids (equal concentrations)	pH
carbonic acid	3.8
nitric acid	1.0
sulfuric acid	1.2
ethanoic acid	2.9
boric acid	5.2
hydrochloric acid	1.0

D the pH of acids of the same concentration

Did you know?

The pH scale was developed in 1909 by Søren Sørensen (1868–1939) who was the head chemist in the Carlsberg Brewery in Copenhagen. The letters pH stand for 'power of hydrogen' where 'p' is short for the German word for power, potenz, and H is the symbol for hydrogen.

Checkpoint

How confidently can you answer the Progression questions?

Strengthen

S1 What do the following terms tell you when they are used to describe an acid solution?
a concentrated **b** dilute
c strong **d** weak

Extend

E1 Explain how a concentrated solution of a weak acid could have the same pH and similar reactions to a dilute solution of a strong acid.

Exam-style question

The pH of five solutions (J–N) are described below.

J = pH 4 K = pH 12 L = pH 7 M = pH 3 N = pH 1

a Which two solutions have concentrations of hydrogen ions that differ by a factor of 10? *(1 mark)*

b State and explain which solution could be a concentrated solution of a strong acid. *(3 marks)*

Progression questions

- Why are metal oxides bases?
- What happens during neutralisation?
- How can a soluble salt be prepared from an acid and an insoluble base?

A Desulfurisation units attached to power station chimneys remove acidic sulfur-containing gases, by reacting them with the base calcium oxide.

Bases are substances that **neutralise** acids to form a **salt** and water only. All metal oxides are bases. For example, magnesium oxide is used to neutralise acids, like sulfuric acid, in industrial waste water.

$$MgO(s) \quad + \quad H_2SO_4(aq) \quad \rightarrow \quad MgSO_4(aq) \quad + \quad H_2O(l)$$

magnesium oxide + sulfuric acid → magnesium sulfate + water

Note the use of **state symbols** in brackets after the formulae in symbol equations: (s) – solid; (l) – liquid; (g) – gas; (aq) – dissolved in water.

All neutralisation reactions with metal oxides occur in a similar way:

metal oxide + acid → salt + water

During neutralisation, hydrogen ions in the acid combine with oxide ions to form water. This removes the hydrogen ions and so the pH increases (becomes more neutral).

The salts are produced by replacing the hydrogen ions with metal ions, as shown in diagram B. Different acids form different salts, as shown in table C.

 1 What is a base?

 2 Write a word equation and a symbol equation for the reaction of solid zinc oxide (ZnO) with sulfuric acid.

Acid	Salt formed
hydrochloric acid	chloride
sulfuric acid	sulfate
nitric acid	nitrate

C salts from acids

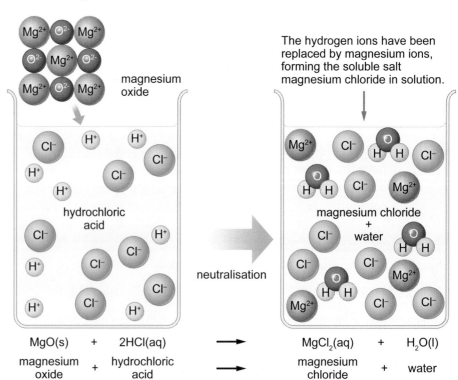

The hydrogen ions have been replaced by magnesium ions, forming the soluble salt magnesium chloride in solution.

$$MgO(s) \quad + \quad 2HCl(aq) \quad \longrightarrow \quad MgCl_2(aq) \quad + \quad H_2O(l)$$

magnesium oxide + hydrochloric acid → magnesium chloride + water

B how the salt magnesium chloride is formed

3 Write a word equation for the reaction between nitric acid and sodium oxide.

 4 Copy and complete the symbol equation below, including the missing state symbols.

$$Li_2O(s) \ + \ ....(..) \ \rightarrow \ Li_2SO_4(aq) \ + \ ....(..)$$

Preparing soluble salts

The reaction between an acid and an insoluble metal oxide can be used to prepare samples of different soluble salts. For example, tin chloride can be prepared by reacting tin(II) oxide with hydrochloric acid solution. The steps involved are shown in diagram D.

An excess of the base is always added, to make sure that all the acid is used up. To make sure the prepared salt is pure, the mixture is **filtered** to remove the residue (the unreacted metal oxide) from the filtrate, leaving only the salt and water. A solid sample of the salt is then obtained by allowing the water to evaporate so that **crystallisation** of the salt occurs. Allowing the water to evaporate slowly will form larger crystals.

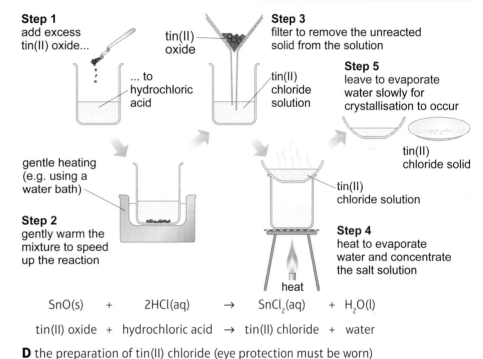

Step 1 add excess tin(II) oxide...

... to hydrochloric acid

Step 2 gently warm the mixture to speed up the reaction

gentle heating (e.g. using a water bath)

Step 3 filter to remove the unreacted solid from the solution

Step 5 leave to evaporate water slowly for crystallisation to occur

tin(II) chloride solution

tin(II) chloride solid

Step 4 heat to evaporate water and concentrate the salt solution

tin(II) chloride solution

heat

$$SnO(s) \ + \ 2HCl(aq) \ \rightarrow \ SnCl_2(aq) \ + \ H_2O(l)$$

tin(II) oxide + hydrochloric acid → tin(II) chloride + water

D the preparation of tin(II) chloride (eye protection must be worn)

5 Magnesium nitrate can be made by reacting magnesium oxide with an acid.

 a Name the acid used.

 b Why should the acid solution be warmed slightly?

 c Why is the magnesium oxide added in excess?

 d Why is the mixture filtered?

 e Why is the salt solution heated?

 6 Explain what happens to the hydrogen ions during the reaction between hydrochloric acid and tin(II) oxide.

Exam-style question

Explain, with reference to the ions present, how the pH of the acidic chimney gases in photo A will change as they pass over calcium oxide. *(3 marks)*

Checkpoint

How confidently can you answer the Progression questions?

Strengthen

S1 Draw a flowchart to explain the steps involved in preparing a soluble salt from an insoluble base.

Extend

E1 Aluminium nitrate, $Al(NO_3)_3$, can be made using aluminium oxide, Al_2O_3, and nitric acid, HNO_3. Describe the preparation of aluminium nitrate and explain each step of the process, including word and symbol equations.

CC8c Core practical – Preparing copper sulfate

Specification reference: C3.17

Aim

Investigate the preparation of pure, dry, hydrated copper sulfate crystals starting from copper oxide including the use of a water bath.

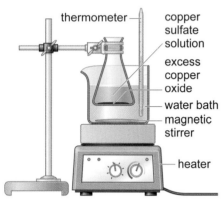

A Heating the acid makes the reaction between sulfuric acid and copper oxide faster.

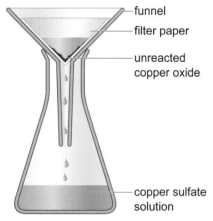

B Filtration separates the excess copper oxide (the residue) from the copper sulfate solution (the filtrate).

Salts, such as copper sulfate, are compounds formed by reacting an acid with a base. In the formation of a salt, the hydrogen ions in the acid are replaced by a positive ion (usually a metal ion) from the base. Different acids and bases produce different salts with a variety of properties and uses. For example, iron(III) oxide and hydrochloric acid form the salt iron(III) chloride ($FeCl_3$), which is used in water treatment. Copper sulfate ($CuSO_4$) is used by farmers and gardeners as a fungicide and herbicide. Skilled chemists can prepare, purify and obtain samples of many different salts.

Your task

Copper oxide reacts with warm sulfuric acid to produce a blue solution of the salt copper sulfate. You are going to use these reactants to prepare pure, dry hydrated copper sulfate crystals.

$$CuO(s) \quad + \quad H_2SO_4(aq) \quad \rightarrow \quad CuSO_4(aq) \quad + H_2O(l)$$

copper oxide + sulfuric acid → copper sulfate + water

Copper oxide (the base) is insoluble in water. So when all the sulfuric acid has been used up, the excess copper oxide remains. Excess copper oxide is added to make sure that all the acid is used up. The remaining copper oxide is then separated from the copper sulfate solution by filtration. If the water is allowed to evaporate, a pure, dry sample of copper sulfate can be obtained.

Method

Wear eye protection.

A Measure 20 cm³ of dilute sulfuric acid using a measuring cylinder and pour it into a small conical flask.

B Warm the acid in a water bath set at 50 °C. Use a thermometer to measure the temperature.

C Add a little copper oxide powder to the acid and stir.

D If all the copper oxide reacts, and disappears, add a little more. Stop when the copper oxide is in excess and no longer reacts.

E Filter the mixture and transfer the filtrate to an evaporating basin.

F Heat the evaporating basin by placing it over a beaker of water heated with a Bunsen burner as shown in diagram D on the previous page. Stop heating when crystals start to form.

G Pour the solution into a watch glass and leave for a few days to allow all the water to evaporate.

Exam-style questions

1   State why copper sulfate is described as a salt. *(1 mark)*

2   State why the sulfuric acid is heated in step B. *(1 mark)*

3   In step E, explain why the copper oxide gets stuck in the filter paper while the copper sulfate goes through it. *(2 marks)*

4   Explain why a water bath is used in step B rather than heating with a Bunsen burner. *(2 marks)*

5   Explain how you know a chemical reaction has occurred in step C. *(2 marks)*

6   State how you know when all the acid has been used up. *(1 mark)*

7   Give a reason why it is important to make sure the copper oxide is in excess in step D. *(1 mark)*

8   Describe one safety precaution that should be taken during this experiment and explain why it is necessary. *(2 marks)*

9   Nickel chloride ($NiCl_2$) is a soluble salt. It can be made by reacting insoluble nickel oxide (NiO) with hydrochloric acid (HCl).

   a   Write a word equation for this reaction. *(1 mark)*

   b   Write a balanced equation with state symbols. *(2 marks)*

   c   Briefly describe the three main stages involved in preparing a pure, solid sample of nickel chloride. *(3 marks)*

10 Two class groups prepared some zinc chloride. One group produced lots of very small crystals while the other group produced larger crystals. Suggest an explanation for the groups producing different-sized crystals. *(2 marks)*

C Large crystals of copper sulfate form if the water evaporates slowly from a concentrated solution of copper sulfate.

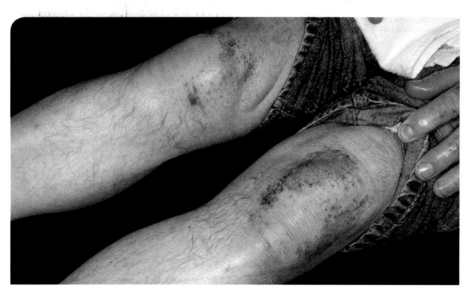

A These skin burns were caused by kneeling in wet cement, which contains an alkali called calcium hydroxide.

A base is any substance that reacts with an acid to form a salt and water only. Many bases are insoluble in water – they do not dissolve. A base that *can* dissolve in water, a *soluble* base, is called an **alkali**. Alkalis form alkaline solutions with pH values above 7.

 1 Explain why all alkalis are bases, but not all bases are alkalis.

Common alkalis

Copper(II) hydroxide and most other metal hydroxides are insoluble bases.

B

However, these bases are soluble and therefore also alkalis:

- sodium hydroxide, NaOH, and other group 1 hydroxides
- calcium hydroxide, $Ca(OH)_2$, and other group 2 hydroxides.

Notice that the chemical formulae for these alkalis look different. In general they are MOH for group 1 hydroxides, where M stands for the metal's chemical symbol, but $M(OH)_2$ for group 2 hydroxides. This is because the ions formed by group 2 atoms have a 2+ charge, but hydroxide ions have a 1– charge. The brackets show that two OH^- ions are needed to produce a neutral compound.

2 Write the formula for:

 a lithium hydroxide   **b** magnesium hydroxide.

Modelling reactions of alkalis with acids

Like other bases, alkalis react with acids to produce salts and water only. For example:

sodium hydroxide + hydrochloric acid → sodium chloride + water

During the neutralisation reaction, the reaction mixture becomes warmer. When an alkali is added to an acid, the pH increases and may go higher than 7 if enough alkali is added.

You can model the reaction using a **balanced equation**. In such equations, the numbers of atoms of each element must be the same on both sides of the arrow.

$NaOH(aq)$	+	$HCl(aq)$	→	$NaCl(aq)$	+	$H_2O(l)$
1			**Na**	1		
1			**O**			1
1		1	**H**			2
		1	**Cl**	1		

C There is one Na, one O, two H and one Cl atom on each side of this equation.

The water is formed from OH in the alkali and H in the acid.

You may need to write a number in front of one or more formulae to balance an equation. Remember that the formulae themselves cannot be changed. For example:

sodium hydroxide + sulfuric acid → sodium sulfate + water

$2NaOH(aq)$	+	$H_2SO_4(aq)$	→	$Na_2SO_4(aq)$	+	$2H_2O(l)$
(2 × 1) = 2			**Na**	2		
(2 × 1) = 2		4	**O**	4		(2 × 1) = 2
(2 × 1) = 2		2	**H**			(2 × 2) = 4
		1	**S**	1		

D The number 2 in front of NaOH and H_2O in the balanced equation shows that two units of these substances are needed.

Equations for the reactions of group 2 hydroxides with acids may look more complex. For example:

calcium hydroxide + nitric acid → calcium nitrate + water

$Ca(OH)_2(aq)$	+	$2HNO_3(aq)$	→	$Ca(NO_3)_2(aq)$	+	$2H_2O(l)$
1			**Ca**	1		
(1 × 2) = 2		(2 × 3) = 6	**O**	(3 × 2) = 6		(2 × 1) = 2
(1 × 2) = 2		(2 × 1) = 2	**H**			(2 × 2) = 4
		(2 × 1) = 2	**N**	(1 × 2) = 2		

E The number 2 outside the brackets for OH and NO_3 shows that there are two of these groups of atoms in the formulae for these substances.

8th **6** Balance this equation for the reaction between potassium hydroxide solution and phosphoric acid:

$$KOH(aq) + H_3PO_4(aq) \rightarrow K_3PO_4(aq) + H_2O(l)$$

Exam-style question

Magnesium hydroxide solution reacts with stomach acid, which is hydrochloric acid. Magnesium chloride solution is a product. Write a balanced equation for the reaction, including state symbols. *(3 marks)*

9th **3** Potassium hydroxide, KOH, reacts with hydrochloric acid in a similar way to sodium hydroxide. Write the balanced equation for this reaction, including state symbols.

9th **4** Explain why the equation in diagram D is *balanced*.

8th **5** Balance this equation for the reaction between barium hydroxide solution and sulfuric acid:

$$Ba(OH)_2(aq) + H_2SO_4(aq) \rightarrow BaSO_4(s) + H_2O(l)$$

Checkpoint

How confidently can you answer the Progression questions?

Strengthen

S1 What happens when metal hydroxides react with acids?

S2 How are chemical equations balanced?

Extend

E1 Evaluate the use of balanced equations to model the reactions of metal hydroxides with acids.

CC8d Core practical – Investigating neutralisation

Specification reference: C3.6

Aim

Investigate the change in pH on adding powdered calcium hydroxide or calcium oxide to a fixed volume of dilute hydrochloric acid.

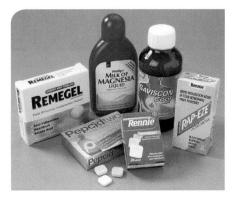

A Indigestion liquids and tablets contain different antacids.

Stomach acid contains hydrochloric acid. Acid indigestion causes a burning feeling in the chest and throat. Antacids are substances that neutralise stomach acid to relieve indigestion. Magnesium hydroxide is a white solid used in antacid tablets. It is sparingly soluble in water, so it is also used as a white suspension that some people find easier to swallow.

Magnesium hydroxide neutralises hydrochloric acid:

magnesium hydroxide + hydrochloric acid → magnesium chloride + water

$$Mg(OH)_2(aq) \quad + \quad 2HCl(aq) \quad \rightarrow \quad MgCl_2(aq) \quad + 2H_2O(l)$$

Your task

Calcium and magnesium are in group 2 of the periodic table. Calcium hydroxide has similar chemical properties to magnesium hydroxide, but it is more soluble in water. You will investigate the change in pH when you add powdered calcium hydroxide to dilute hydrochloric acid. You will add small portions of powder to the acid and record the pH of the mixture after each addition.

Method

Wear eye protection.

A Use a measuring cylinder to add 50 cm³ of dilute hydrochloric acid to a beaker.

B Estimate and record the pH of the contents of the beaker.
- Put a piece of universal indicator paper onto a white tile.
- Dip the end of a glass rod into the liquid, then tap it onto the universal indicator paper.
- Wait 30 seconds, then match the colour to the appropriate pH on a pH colour chart.
- Rinse the glass rod with water.

C Measure out 0.3 g of calcium hydroxide powder onto a piece of paper or a 'weighing boat'.

D Add the calcium hydroxide powder to the beaker and stir. Then estimate and record the pH of the mixture.

E Repeat steps B and C seven times so that you add a total of 2.4 g of calcium hydroxide powder to the acid.

F Plot a graph with pH on the vertical axis and mass of calcium hydroxide on the horizontal axis.

B A pH meter may also be used to measure pH.

Exam-style questions

1 **a** Name the soluble salt formed when hydrochloric acid reacts with calcium hydroxide. *(1 mark)*

    b Write the balanced equation, including state symbols, for the reaction between calcium hydroxide powder and dilute hydrochloric acid. *(3 marks)*

2 Diagrams C and D show part of the labels found on two laboratory containers.

    a Give *two* reasons why hazard symbols are used on chemical containers. *(2 marks)*

    b Explain why it may be more hazardous to handle calcium oxide than calcium hydroxide. *(3 marks)*

3 Give *two* reasons that explain why eye protection must be worn when using dilute hydrochloric acid. *(2 marks)*

4 A student investigates the change in pH when calcium hydroxide powder is added to 100 cm³ of dilute hydrochloric acid.

    a State *two* control variables in his experiment. *(2 marks)*

    b State the independent variable in his experiment. *(1 mark)*

    c Describe how the student could modify his experiment to investigate temperature changes instead of pH changes. *(1 mark)*

5 A student wants to find the mass of calcium oxide powder that produces a neutral solution when added to 75 cm³ of dilute hydrochloric acid. She adds 0.5 g portions of the powder to the acid, and measures the pH each time with a pH meter. Table E shows her results.

    a Predict the mass of calcium oxide that produces a neutral solution. *(1 mark)*

    b State and explain how the student could improve her experiment to obtain a more accurate result. *(3 marks)*

6 The pH of a solution may be determined using universal indicator paper or using a pH meter.

    a State why a pH meter must be calibrated using a solution with a known pH value. *(1 mark)*

    b Explain whether indicator paper or a pH meter has the higher resolution. *(2 marks)*

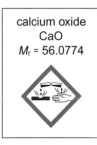

calcium oxide
CaO
M_r = 56.0774

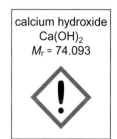

calcium hydroxide
Ca(OH)$_2$
M_r = 74.093

C   **D**

Mass of calcium oxide added (g)	pH of reaction mixture
0.0	0.3
0.5	0.6
1.0	2.8
1.5	12.3
2.0	12.5

E

CC8e Alkalis and neutralisation

Specification reference: C3.11; C3.14; C3.16; C3.18

Progression questions

- What happens to the ions from acids and alkalis during neutralisation?
- What is titration?
- How do we make a soluble salt using titration?

A Potassium sulfate, manufactured using sulfuric acid and a soluble reactant, is a soluble salt used in fertilisers.

Soluble bases or alkalis react with acids to form a salt and water only. The type of reaction involved is neutralisation.

Ions and neutralisation

Hydrochloric acid and other acids are a source of hydrogen ions, $H^+(aq)$, in solution:

$$HCl(aq) \rightarrow H^+(aq) + Cl^-(aq)$$

Sodium hydroxide and other alkalis are a source of hydroxide ions, $OH^-(aq)$, in solution:

$$NaOH(aq) \rightarrow Na^+(aq) + OH^-(aq)$$

In a neutralisation reaction, hydrogen ions from the acid react with hydroxide ions from the alkali. Water, a simple molecular substance containing covalent bonds, is formed in the reaction:

$$H^+(aq) + OH^-(aq) \rightarrow H_2O(l)$$

The other ions from the acid and alkali stay in the solution as ions of the dissolved salt. For example, $Na^+(aq)$ ions from sodium hydroxide and $Cl^-(aq)$ ions from hydrochloric acid remain after neutralisation. These ions combine to form solid sodium chloride, $NaCl(s)$, when the water evaporates.

Did you know?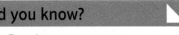

The Russian government imposed a high tax on table salt, sodium chloride, in the 17th century. This led to a 'salt riot' in Moscow in 1648.

 1 Explain how water is formed in neutralisation reactions.

2 Explain, in terms of ions, how potassium hydroxide solution reacts with sulfuric acid to form water and potassium sulfate.

Soluble salts from alkalis

You can obtain a dry soluble salt from its solution by crystallisation. It is important to have a neutral solution before evaporating the water, otherwise you will contaminate the salt with an excess of one reactant.

 3 Other than the hazards caused by hot liquids and solids, suggest a hazard caused by crystallising a salt from a solution that contains excess acid or alkali.

To obtain a neutral solution you need to mix an acid and an alkali in the correct proportions so that you end up with a solution that contains only water and the desired salt. You can do this using **titration**.

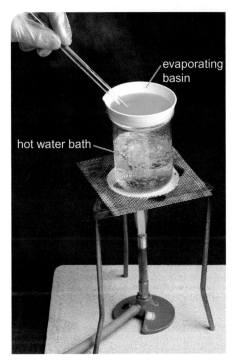

B producing a dry salt by crystallisation using a hot water bath

Titration

In a titration, acid is added from a **burette** to a fixed volume of alkali in a conical flask. The burette is a tall piece of glassware with 0.1 cm^3 graduations. You control the flow using a tap at the bottom. It is possible to add just one drop at a time.

You could use a measuring cylinder to measure out the alkali, but a **pipette** provides more accurate and repeatable measurements. A few drops of indicator are added to the alkali so you can follow the reaction. The **end-point** is when the indicator changes colour. Single indicators such as methyl orange or phenolphthalein are used because their obvious colour changes give you a sharp end-point.

To make a pure, dry salt:

- carry out a titration
- note the exact volume of acid needed to neutralise the alkali
- use the burette to add the correct volume of acid *without* the indicator
- evaporate the water from the solution formed.

 4 In a titration, name the most suitable apparatus to add alkali to the flask, and to add acid to the alkali.

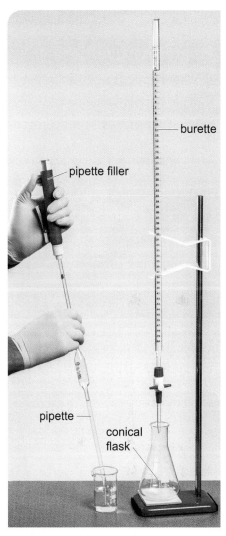

C This apparatus is used to carry out a titration. A white tile underneath the conical flask makes the end-point easier to see.

Checkpoint

How confidently can you answer the Progression questions?

Strengthen

S1 Describe how titration is used to prepare soluble salts.

Extend

E1 Evaluate the preparation of sodium and potassium salts using titration rather than by the reactions of the metals with acids.

Exam-style question

a Give a reason why universal indicator is not a good choice of indicator to use in a titration. *(1 mark)*

b Suggest a suitable indicator to use instead. *(1 mark)*

CC8f Reactions of acids with metals and carbonates

Specification reference: H C0.4; C3.11; C3.12

Progression questions

- What happens when an acid reacts with a metal?
- What happens when an acid reacts with a metal carbonate?
- What are the tests for hydrogen and carbon dioxide?

A Hydrogen gas is less dense than air and so was used to fill early air ships. Unfortunately it is also very flammable.

B Hydrogen gas is colourless and odourless. When hydrogen is mixed with air, it is highly flammable. To test for hydrogen, place a lighted splint in a hydrogen and air mixture. A squeaky pop is heard.

2 Zinc reacts with dilute hydrochloric acid. Write:

 a the word equation

 b the balanced equation

 H **c** the half equation to show what happens to the zinc atoms.

Acids and metals

Some metals, such as copper and silver, do not react with dilute acids. Metals such as potassium and sodium react explosively with dilute acids. Metals in the middle of the **reactivity series**, such as magnesium and zinc, react steadily with dilute acids. **Effervescence** is seen as hydrogen gas bubbles are produced. The reaction also produces a salt, giving the general reaction:

metal + acid → salt + hydrogen

Magnesium reacts with sulfuric acid to form magnesium sulfate, and with hydrochloric acid to form magnesium chloride. The first name of the salt comes from the metal and the second name comes from the acid.

$$Mg(s) + H_2SO_4(aq) \rightarrow MgSO_4(aq) + H_2(g)$$

$$Mg(s) + 2HCl(aq) \rightarrow MgCl_2(aq) + H_2(g)$$

 1 Explain why gold sulfate is not formed when gold is added to dilute sulfuric acid.

H

All acids form hydrogen ions, H^+, in aqueous solution. The metal atoms react with the hydrogen ions to form metal ions and hydrogen molecules. This can be summarised in an **ionic equation**, in which we only show the ions that change in the reaction. For example:

$$Mg(s) + 2H^+(aq) \rightarrow Mg^{2+}(aq) + H_2(g)$$

The other ions from the acid (e.g. sulfate, chloride) do not change during the reaction. They are known as **spectator ions**.

The hydrogen ions gain electrons to form hydrogen molecules. We can show what happens to electrons in a **half equation**:

$$2H^+(aq) + 2e \rightarrow H_2(g)$$

> e represents an electron. It is not necessary to include the negative charge.

The magnesium atoms lose electrons:

$$Mg(s) \rightarrow Mg^{2+}(aq) + 2e$$

A loss of electrons is an **oxidation** reaction. A gain of electrons is a **reduction** reaction. You can remember this using the mnemonic OILRIG. (Oxidation Is Loss, Reduction Is Gain).

Acids and carbonates

Acids react with metal carbonates to form a salt, water and carbon dioxide. Bubbles of carbon dioxide are produced and the solid metal carbonate disappears if there is enough acid to react with it.

metal carbonate + acid → salt + water + carbon dioxide

Copper carbonate reacts with sulfuric acid to form copper sulfate, with hydrochloric acid to form copper chloride, and with nitric acid to form copper nitrate.

$$CuCO_3(s) + H_2SO_4(aq) \rightarrow CuSO_4(aq) + H_2O(l) + CO_2(g)$$

$$CuCO_3(s) + 2HCl(aq) \rightarrow CuCl_2(aq) + H_2O(l) + CO_2(g)$$

$$CuCO_3(s) + 2HNO_3(aq) \rightarrow Cu(NO_3)_2(aq) + H_2O(l) + CO_2(g)$$

During these reactions, the hydrogen ions from the acids react with the carbonate ions to form water and carbon dioxide molecules.

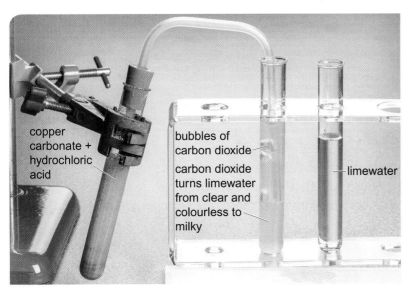

C Carbon dioxide is another colourless and odourless gas. To test for carbon dioxide, bubble the gas through limewater (calcium hydroxide solution). The limewater turns milky if carbon dioxide is present.

H

The sulfate, chloride and nitrate ions are spectator ions. The ionic equation is:

$$2H^+(aq) + CO_3^{2-}(s) \rightarrow H_2O(l) + CO_2(g)$$

 6 Write the ionic equation for the reaction between magnesium carbonate and hydrochloric acid.

Exam-style question

Describe a test to show that a gas is hydrogen.   *(2 marks)*

---

 3 Give the formula of the salt formed when solid calcium carbonate, $CaCO_3$, reacts with dilute hydrochloric acid.

 4 Explain the difference between the state symbols (aq) and (l).

 5 Write the balanced equation for the reaction between zinc carbonate, $ZnCO_3$, and nitric acid, HNO_3.

Checkpoint

How confidently can you answer the Progression questions?

Strengthen

S1 Describe a reaction to make:

a hydrogen

b carbon dioxide.

Include an equation for each reaction and a description of how to test for each gas.

Extend

E1 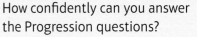 Dilute hydrochloric acid is added to zinc powder. Write word, balanced and ionic equations for the reaction that occurs. Include state symbols.

CC8g Solubility

Specification reference: **H** C0.4; C3.19; C3.20; C3.21

Progression questions

- What are the rules for solubility of common substances in water?
- How do you prepare a sample of a pure, dry insoluble salt?
- How do you predict whether a precipitate will be formed in a reaction?

A A red precipitate of silver chromate forms when sodium chromate solution is added to silver nitrate solution.

A **precipitation** reaction is one in which soluble substances in solutions cause an insoluble **precipitate** to form. Photo A shows an example. Table B shows some general rules that can be used to predict whether precipitates will form.

Soluble in water	Insoluble in water
all common sodium, potassium and ammonium salts	
all nitrates	
most chlorides	silver, lead chlorides
most sulfates	lead, barium, calcium sulfates
sodium, potassium and ammonium carbonates	most carbonates
sodium, potassium and ammonium hydroxides	most hydroxides

B some solubility rules

Solutions of lead nitrate and sodium chloride react to form soluble sodium nitrate and a white precipitate of lead chloride. The state symbols in the balanced equation show which substances are soluble and which are insoluble.

lead nitrate + sodium chloride → lead chloride + sodium nitrate

$$Pb(NO_3)_2(aq) + 2NaCl(aq) \rightarrow PbCl_2(s) + 2NaNO_3(aq)$$

The test for carbon dioxide using limewater (see CC8f) is also a precipitation reaction, in which insoluble calcium carbonate is formed:

calcium hydroxide (limewater) + carbon dioxide → calcium carbonate + water

$$Ca(OH)_2(aq) + CO_2(g) \rightarrow CaCO_3(s) + H_2O(l).$$

 1 Which of the following substances are soluble in water and which are insoluble? Sodium chloride, lead nitrate, calcium sulfate, potassium hydroxide, silver chloride, calcium carbonate, ammonium carbonate.

 2 Write a solubility rule for lead compounds.

Did you know?

The reaction between sodium chromate and silver nitrate is used to stain nerve cells for viewing under a microscope.

H

Ionic equations are also used to show the formation of precipitates. The formulae of the ions that react together to form the precipitate are shown on the left, and the formula of the precipitate is shown on the right. The ionic equation for the formation of lead chloride is:

$$Pb^{2+}(aq) + 2Cl^-(aq) \rightarrow PbCl_2(s)$$

The sodium and nitrate ions do not change, so they are spectator ions.

All salts are ionic. When two solutions containing soluble salts react together, the ions from the salts swap. For example:

copper sulfate + potassium carbonate → copper carbonate + potassium sulfate

We can predict whether a precipitate will form by checking the solubilities of the products. If both products are soluble, no precipitate will form.

In the word equation above, potassium sulfate does not form a precipitate because all potassium salts are soluble. However, copper carbonate is not in the list of soluble carbonates, so it should form as a precipitate:

$$CuSO_4(aq) \;+\; K_2CO_3(aq) \;\rightarrow\; CuCO_3(s) \;+\; K_2SO_4(aq)$$

H

The ionic equation is: $Cu^{2+}(aq) \;+\; CO_3^{2-}(aq) \;\rightarrow\; CuCO_3(s)$

Preparation of insoluble salts

A pure, dry sample of an insoluble salt can be prepared from two soluble salts in this way:

- Wear eye protection.
- Mix the two solutions in a beaker, then filter the mixture.
- Rinse the beaker with a little distilled water and pour this through the funnel.
- Pour a little distilled water over the precipitate in the funnel.
- Carefully remove the filter paper containing the precipitate and dry it in a warm oven.

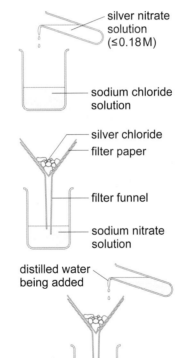

silver nitrate solution (≤0.18 M)

sodium chloride solution

silver chloride

filter paper

filter funnel

sodium nitrate solution

distilled water being added

C preparing an insoluble salt

 5 Explain:

a why the beaker is rinsed with a little distilled water and the washings are poured through the funnel

b why distilled water is poured over the precipitate in the funnel.

 6 Suggest two other ways of drying the precipitate.

Exam-style question

Zinc carbonate is an insoluble salt. Describe how you would use solutions of potassium carbonate and zinc chloride to produce a pure, dry sample of zinc carbonate. *(4 marks)*

3 Magnesium sulfate solution reacts with barium chloride solution.

 a Predict the name of the precipitate, if any.

 b Write the balanced equation. Include state symbols.

 H **c** Write the ionic equation for this reaction. Include state symbols.

4 Sodium chloride solution is added to copper nitrate solution.

 a Predict the name of the precipitate, if any.

 b Justify your answer.

Checkpoint

How confidently can you answer the Progression questions?

Strengthen

S1 Describe how to prepare a pure, dry sample of lead sulfate from two named solutions. Write a balanced equation for the reaction. Include state symbols.

Extend

E1 **H** The following aqueous solutions are available: sodium carbonate, copper sulfate, barium chloride. Any two of the solutions can be mixed together at a time. Predict which combinations of these solutions will produce a precipitate and name the precipitate. Write an ionic equation, including state symbols, for each reaction.

Magnesium sulfate

Soluble salts can be made by reacting an acid with an insoluble metal compound.

Plan an experiment to prepare pure, dry crystals of magnesium sulfate, $MgSO_4$, from a magnesium compound and a suitable acid. Start by choosing suitable reactants to use; you may wish to write a balanced equation to help you with your plan.

(6 marks)

Student answer

$Mg + H_2SO_4 \rightarrow MgSO_4 + 2H$ [1]

I will make magnesium sulfate from magnesium ribbon and sulfuric acid [2].

Place 25 cm³ of the acid in a beaker. Add magnesium ribbon a piece at a time until the bubbles of hydrogen stop. Filter the mixture and collect the solution in an evaporating basin [3]. Heat the basin until all the water has evaporated, leaving pure, dry crystals of magnesium sulfate [4].

[1] The balanced equation is incorrect. Hydrogen gas exists as H_2 molecules not separate hydrogen atoms.

[2] Sulfuric acid is correct, but the question asks for a magnesium compound (such as magnesium oxide). Magnesium is an element.

[3] The answer could also have explained that you need to filter the mixture to remove any excess magnesium.

[4] The last step is incorrect. If you evaporate all of the water, you will be left with a dry powder.

Verdict

This is an acceptable answer. It contains some correct chemistry, and the steps of the practical are written in a clear and logical order.

The answer could be improved by using a magnesium compound as mentioned in the question. The answer would also be better if it had a correct balanced equation, and described a suitable method for allowing crystals to form from the solution.

Exam tip

Make sure you revise the Core Practicals. The method asked for here is very similar to the preparation of copper sulfate which is a Core Practical.

Paper 3 and Paper 4

CC9 Calculations Involving Masses

In most chemical reactions it is important to mix the reactants in the correct amounts to form the maximum amount of product and to avoid waste. Iron is produced from iron ore in a blast furnace. Every tonne of iron ore needs to be mixed with 850 kg of limestone and 50 kg of coal. This should produce 350 kg of iron and 910 kg of a substance called 'slag' that can be used in concrete and for insulation. In this unit you will be learning how to calculate these amounts.

The learning journey

Previously you will have learnt at KS3:

- how to represent elements and compounds using symbols
- how mass is conserved during changes of state and chemical reactions
- how to show chemical reactions using equations.

In this unit you will learn:

- how to use relative atomic masses to calculate relative formula masses of elements and compounds
- how to work out empirical and molecular formulae of compounds
- how to calculate the mass of reactants or products in a reaction
- how to calculate the concentration of a solution
- **H** about the Avogadro constant and the quantity 1 mol of a substance
- **H** how to calculate the numbers of particles in a substance.

CC9a Masses and empirical formulae

Specification reference: C1.43; C1.44; C1.45; C1.46

Progression questions

- How do you calculate the relative formula mass of a compound?
- What is the difference between an empirical formula and a molecular formula?
- How do you determine the empirical formula of a compound?

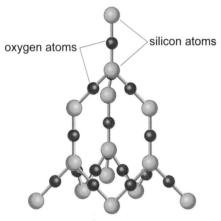

oxygen atoms — silicon atoms

A Silicon dioxide is a giant, covalent lattice structure (of billions of atoms). Its empirical formula is SiO_2 (the ratio of silicon atoms to oxygen atom is 1:2).

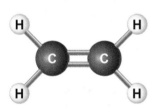

B Ethene has the molecular formula C_2H_4. CH_2 is its empirical formula.

Did you know?

The Galaxy Opal is the largest polished opal in the world. Opals consist mainly of silicon dioxide.

C

All substances have an **empirical formula**. This is the simplest whole number *ratio* of atoms or ions of each element in a substance.

Substances that are made of simple molecules also have a **molecular formula**. This represents the *actual* number of atoms of each element in one molecule.

Ethene has the molecular formula C_2H_4 but the empirical formula CH_2. Sometimes the empirical formula is the same as the molecular formula. For example, the formula for a molecule of water is H_2O and this cannot be simplified any further.

The 'formula' of a compound is its molecular formula if it is a simple molecule, or the empirical formula if it has a giant lattice structure.

1 Deduce the empirical formula of:

    a C_2H_6 **b** N_2H_4 **c** C_3H_8 **d** C_6H_6 **e** $C_2H_4O_2$.

Relative formula mass

The **relative formula mass** (M_r), of a substance is the sum of the relative atomic masses (A_r) of all the atoms or ions in its formula. Relative atomic masses are given in the periodic table.

Worked examples W1

Calculate the M_r of carbon dioxide (CO_2).

$$= A_r(C) + (2 \times A_r(O))$$
$$= 12 \quad + (2 \times 16)$$

So, M_r of $CO_2 = 44$

Calcium nitrate has a giant lattice structure. Its formula is $Ca(NO_3)_2$ (for each calcium ion there are two nitrate ions). Calculate the M_r of calcium nitrate.

$$= A_r(Ca) + 2(A_r(N) + (3 \times A_r(O)))$$
$$= 40 \quad + 2(14 + (3 \times 16))$$

So, M_r of $Ca(NO_3)_2 = 164$

2 Calculate the relative formula masses of:

    a N_2 **b** NaCl   **c** NH_3 **d** H_2SO_4 **e** $(NH_4)_2SO_4$.

Finding an empirical formula

The empirical formula of a compound can be calculated from the masses of the elements used to make it. Table D shows how this is done if 10.0 g of calcium reacts with 17.8 g of chlorine.

Symbol for element	Ca	Cl
Mass (g)	10.0	17.8
Relative atomic mass, A_r	40	35.5
Divide the mass of each element by its relative atomic mass	$\frac{10.0}{40} = 0.25$	$\frac{17.8}{35.5} = 0.5$
Divide the answers by the smallest number to find the simplest ratio	$\frac{0.25}{0.25} = 1$	$\frac{0.5}{0.25} = 2$
Empirical formula	$CaCl_2$	

D To calculate an empirical formula, each element needs its own column of working.

A *molecular* formula is determined from its empirical formula and its M_r.

Worked example W2

The empirical formula for glucose is CH_2O and its relative formula mass is 180. Determine the molecular formula for glucose.

- Find empirical formula mass
$$A_r(C) + (2 \times A_r(H)) + A_r(O)$$
$$= 12 + (2 \times 1) + 16 = 30$$

- Divide M_r by empirical formula mass $\frac{180}{30} = 6$

The molecular formula is six times the empirical formula, so the molecular formula is $C_6H_{12}O_6$.

Magnesium oxide can be made by heating magnesium ribbon in a limited oxygen supply, using the apparatus in diagram E. If the reactant and product are 'weighed', the empirical formula for magnesium oxide can be calculated.

 5 Magnesium ribbon with a mass of 0.576 g was heated in a crucible. It produced 0.960 g of magnesium oxide. Calculate the empirical formula of magnesium oxide.

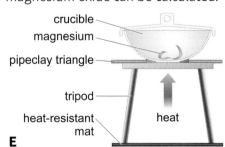

E

Exam-style question

5.6 g of iron react with 24.0 g of bromine to form iron bromide. Calculate the empirical formula of the iron bromide. (Relative atomic masses are given in the periodic table at the back of the book.) *(3 marks)*

3 Calculate the empirical formula of each of the following substances.

  a lithium oxide (1.4 g Li, 1.6 g O)

  b magnesium carbonate (1.2 g Mg, 0.6 g C, 2.4 g O)

  c butane (1.44 g C, 0.3 g H)

4 Determine the molecular formula of each of the following substances.

  a hydrogen peroxide, with empirical formula HO and M_r 34

  b hexene, with empirical formula CH_2 and M_r 84

  c pentane, with empirical formula C_5H_{12} and M_r 72

Checkpoint

How confidently can you answer the Progression questions?

Strengthen

S1 You are given some copper powder and a crucible. Describe an experiment to determine the empirical formula of copper oxide and explain how you would use the results to calculate the formula.

Extend

E1 A simple molecular compound contains 2.00 g of carbon, 0.33 g of hydrogen and 2.67 g of oxygen and has a relative formula mass of 60. Calculate the empirical and molecular formulae of this compound.

Progression questions

- How do you calculate the concentration of a solution?
- How does the law of conservation of mass explain why magnesium increases in mass when it is burned?
- How do you calculate the masses of reactants and products in a reaction?

1mg is 0.001g and 1l (1 litre) is the same volume as 1dm³

The concentration of calcium ions is 29.1mg/l or 0.0291g dm⁻³.

A Mineral water contains dissolved ions.

Concentrations of solutions

When a **solute** is dissolved in a **solvent** to make a **solution**, the mass of the solution is equal to the mass of the solvent *and* the mass of the solute. The overall mass of the substances does not change. This is the **law of conservation of mass**.

The amount of solute dissolved in a stated volume of a solution is its **concentration**. The units of concentration are usually 'grams per cubic decimetre', written as $g\,dm^{-3}$. 1 dm³ is the same volume as 1 litre or 1000 cm³.

You can calculate the concentration of a solution in $g\,dm^{-3}$ using this equation:

$$\text{concentration} = \frac{\text{mass of solute in g}}{\text{volume of solution in dm}^3}$$

If the volume of the solution is given in cm³, convert it to dm³ by dividing by 1000.

1 Calculate the concentration, in $g\,dm^{-3}$, of the solute in these solutions.

  a 20g of sodium chloride in 2 dm³ of solution

  b 0.5218g of sodium hydroxide in 250 cm³ of solution

B The total mass of the reactants always equals the total mass of products.

Conservation of mass in reactions

Lead nitrate solution reacts with potassium iodide solution to form a yellow **precipitate** of lead iodide and a colourless solution of potassium nitrate. This is an example of a **closed system** as no new substances are added or removed.

$$Pb(NO_3)_2(aq) + 2KI(aq) \rightarrow PbI_2(s) + 2KNO_3(aq)$$

The balanced equation shows that the number of atoms does not change, and so the mass cannot change. This is another example of the law of conservation of mass.

In the reaction shown in balanced equation C, the mass of the copper oxide left is less than the mass of copper carbonate at the start. Carbon dioxide gas escapes and so the mass appears to decrease. This is a **non-enclosed system** as the gas can escape.

Did you know?

Lead iodide was used as a yellow pigment in some 19th-century paintings, but it is not very stable so some of these paintings are changing colour.

$$CuCO_3(s) \rightarrow CuO(s) + CO_2(g)$$

C balanced equation for heating copper carbonate in air

Some solids appear to gain in mass when they are heated in a non-enclosed system. In the reaction shown in balanced equation D, the apparent gain is due to copper reacting with oxygen from the air. However, in all systems, the mass of the products is always the same as the mass of the reactants.

Calculating the masses of reactants or products

You can use relative masses and the balanced equation for a reaction to calculate the mass of a reactant or a product.

Worked example

Calculate the mass of chlorine needed to make 53.4 g of aluminium chloride.

Write the balanced equation	$2Al + 3Cl_2 \rightarrow 2AlCl_3$
Calculate relative formula masses of the substances needed	$M_r\ Cl_2 = 2 \times 35.5 = 71$ $M_r\ AlCl_3 = 27 + (3 \times 35.5) = 133.5$

Calculate ratio of masses (multiply M_r values by the balancing numbers shown in the equation).

$$3Cl_2 \quad makes \quad 2AlCl_3$$
$$so\ 3 \times 71 = \underline{213}\ g\ Cl_2 \quad makes \quad 2 \times 133.5 = \underline{267}\ g\ AlCl_3$$

Work out the mass for 1 g of reactant or product. (Here we want 1 g of the product because that's the mass we know already.)

$\div 267$

$$\frac{213}{267}g\ Cl_2 \quad makes \quad \frac{267}{267}g\ AlCl_3 \qquad \div 267$$

$$0.798\ g\ Cl_2 \quad makes \quad 1\ g\ AlCl_3$$

$\times 53.4$ $\times 53.4$

Scale up or down (*from 1 g to the mass you are given*) $42.6\ g\ Cl_2 \quad makes \quad 53.4\ g\ AlCl_3$

 4 Calculate the mass of hydrogen produced when 72 g of magnesium reacts with sulfuric acid.

$$Mg + H_2SO_4 \rightarrow MgSO_4 + H_2$$

 5 Calculate the mass of water produced when 500 g of methane burns.

$$CH_4 + 2O_2 \rightarrow CO_2 + 2H_2O$$

 6 Calculate the mass of sodium hydroxide needed to produce 42.6 kg of sodium sulfate.

$$2NaOH + H_2SO_4 \rightarrow Na_2SO_4 + 2H_2O$$

Exam-style question

Calculate the maximum mass of magnesium oxide that could be formed by reacting 1.56 g of magnesium with excess oxygen. *(3 marks)*

$$2Mg + O_2 \rightarrow 2MgO$$

$$2Cu(s) + O_2(g) \rightarrow 2CuO(s)$$

D balanced equation for heating copper in air

 2 12.4 g of copper carbonate was heated and formed 8.0 g of copper oxide. Calculate the mass of carbon dioxide produced.

 3 1.27 g of copper was heated in air and formed 1.59 g of copper oxide. Calculate the mass of oxygen that reacted with the copper.

Checkpoint

How confidently can you answer the Progression questions?

Strengthen

S1 Make notes so that you can explain to a friend who missed the lesson:

   a how to calculate the mass of sodium chloride formed when 5.3 g of sodium carbonate reacts with excess dilute hydrochloric acid
$$Na_2CO_3 + 2HCl \rightarrow 2NaCl + H_2O + CO_2$$

   b why there is a loss in mass during the reaction.

Extend

E1 Calculate the loss in mass when 2.96 g of magnesium nitrate decomposes.
$$2Mg(NO_3)_2(s) \rightarrow 2MgO(s) + 4NO_2(g) + O_2(g)$$

CC9c Moles

Specification reference: H C1.50; H C1.51; H C1.52; H C1.53

Progression questions

- H How do you calculate the number of moles and number of particles of a substance?
- H What controls the mass of product formed in a reaction?
- H How do you work out a balanced equation from the masses of reactants and/or products?

H

A Clockwise from top left: one mole (1 mol) each of iron(III) chloride, copper sulfate, potassium iodide, cobalt nitrate, potassium manganate(VII) and sodium chloride.

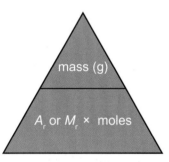

B To rearrange the equation with this triangle, cover up the quantity you want to calculate and what you can see gives you the calculation to use.

In everyday life we use special words to mean the amount of an item. A pair is two of that item and a dozen is 12 of them. In chemistry, a mole is 602 204 500 000 000 000 000 000 particles! This number is usually written in standard form as 6.02×10^{23} and is known as the **Avogadro constant.**

The SI unit symbol for 'mole' is **mol**. 1 mol of a substance contains the Avogadro constant number of particles. These can be atoms, molecules or ions and so you need to specify the type of particles.

The mass of one mole of a substance is the relative atomic mass (A_r) or relative formula mass (M_r) in grams. The relative atomic mass of magnesium is 24, so 1 mol of magnesium has a mass of 24 g and contains 6.02×10^{23} atoms.

You can calculate the number of moles of any substance using this equation:

$$\text{number of moles of substance} = \frac{\text{mass of substance (g)}}{A_r \text{ or } M_r}$$

1 Give the mass of the Avogadro constant number of:

  a carbon atoms   **b** sodium atoms.

2 Calculate the mass of:

  a 2 mol of nitrogen molecules, N_2

  b 0.1 mol of sulfur dioxide molecules, SO_2.

3 Calculate the number of moles of:

  a CO_2 molecules in 88 g of carbon dioxide

  b CH_4 molecules in 3.2 g of methane.

Reactions

A balanced equation shows the ratios of the substances in moles.

$$2Mg + O_2 \rightarrow 2MgO$$

This equation shows that 2 mol of magnesium reacts with 1 mol of oxygen to form 2 mol of magnesium oxide. In an experiment, we usually burn magnesium in excess oxygen to make sure that all the magnesium reacts.

In a chemical reaction, one of the reactants is often added in excess and is not completely used up in the reaction. The amount of product formed is determined by the amount of reactant that is *not* in excess (and so is used up completely in the reaction). This is called the **limiting reactant**.

H

Worked example W1

1.50 g of ammonium chloride and 4.00 g of calcium hydroxide are heated together to form ammonia.

$$2NH_4Cl + Ca(OH)_2 \rightarrow 2NH_3 + CaCl_2 + 2H_2O$$

a Which is the limiting reactant?

b Calculate the mass of ammonia formed.

a The equation shows that 2 mol of NH_4Cl reacts with 1 mol of $Ca(OH)_2$

number of moles of $Ca(OH)_2 = 4.00\,g/(40 + 2(16 + 1)) = 0.0541$ mol

We need: $2 \times 0.0541 = 0.108$ mol NH_4Cl to react with 0.0541 mol of $Ca(OH)_2$.

We have: $1.50\,g/(14 + (4 \times 1) + 35.5) = 0.0280$ mol

We have less than the 0.0541 mol of NH_4Cl needed; NH_4Cl = limiting reactant.

b The equation shows that the number of moles of NH_3 made equals the number of moles of NH_4Cl used.

So, 0.0280 mol of NH_4Cl forms 0.0280 mol of NH_3

mass of NH_3 formed = mol $\times M_r = 0.0280 \times (14 + (3 \times 1)) = 0.476\,g$

If you know the mass of each substance in a reaction, you can calculate the number of moles of each and deduce the balanced equation. The ratio of the moles of each substance is the **stoichiometry** of the reaction.

Worked example W2

10.8 g of aluminium reacted with 42.6 g of chlorine, Cl_2, to produce aluminium chloride, $AlCl_3$. Deduce the balanced equation for the reaction.

	Al	Cl_2
Calculate the number of moles (= mass/A_r or M_r)	$\frac{10.8}{27} = 0.4$	$\frac{42.6}{2 \times 35.5} = 0.6$
Divide by the smaller	$\frac{0.4}{0.4} = 1$	$\frac{0.6}{0.4} = 1.5$
Simplest whole number ratio	$1 \times 2 = 2$	$1.5 \times 2 = 3$

So 2 mol of Al react with 3 mol of Cl_2. The equation is completed by adding the formula of the product and balancing in the normal way.

$$2Al + 3Cl_2 \rightarrow 2AlCl_3$$

Exam-style question

Calculate the number of molecules in 90 g of water, H_2O. *(2 marks)*

4 Calculate the number of molecules in:

a 16 g of oxygen molecules, O_2

b 34 g of ammonia molecules, NH_3.

5 Calculate the maximum mass of magnesium oxide that can be made from 2.4 g of magnesium and 2.4 g of oxygen.

$$2Mg + O_2 \rightarrow 2MgO$$

6 15 g of hydrogen gas reacts exactly with 70 g of nitrogen gas to produce ammonia, NH_3. Deduce the balanced equation for the reaction.

Checkpoint

How confidently can you answer the Progression questions?

Strengthen

S1 5.00 g of iron and 5.00 g of sulfur are heated together to form iron(II) sulfide.

$$Fe + S \rightarrow FeS$$

a Calculate the number of moles of each reactant and state which one is the limiting reactant.

b Calculate the mass of iron(II) sulfide formed. Give your answer to 3 significant figures.

Extend

E1 Explain which of these contains the greatest number of particles.

4 g of hydrogen molecules, 16 g of oxygen molecules, 18 g of water molecules, 22 g of carbon dioxide molecules.

Empirical formula

A student carried out an experiment to determine the empirical formula of magnesium oxide using the apparatus shown.

Describe how you would use this apparatus and the results to show that the empirical formula of magnesium oxide is MgO.

(6 marks)

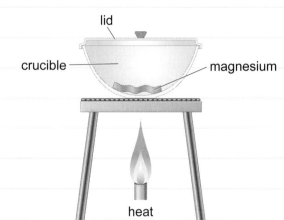

Student answer

Weigh an empty crucible, then add a piece of magnesium ribbon and weigh it again. Set up the apparatus as shown. Heat the crucible with a strong flame and lift the lid occasionally [1]. Stop heating when all the magnesium has reacted. Let the crucible cool and reweigh it [2].

Find the mass of magnesium used and the mass of oxygen that combined with it [3]. Divide the masses of magnesium and oxygen by their relative atomic masses. Then, divide these answers by the smaller of the numbers to find the simplest ratio. If the simplest ratio is 1:1, the empirical formula is MgO [4].

[1] It would be a good idea to explain why this is necessary.

[2] Overall, this is a good account of the experiment and the measurements that are needed.

[3] The correct masses are mentioned, but not how these masses are actually calculated.

[4] The explanation of the calculation is sufficient and the relationship between the simplest ratio and the empirical formula is given.

Verdict

This is a strong answer. The description of the experiment and the method of calculation are correct. The answer is written in a logical order with the description of the experiment first, and then a clear and well-ordered description of the calculations.

Exam tip

The examiner is looking for a 'well-developed, sustained line of scientific reasoning which is clear and logically structured'. When describing a process, make sure that you write down the steps in a logical order – in this case, the order that the experiment and the calculations would be carried out.

Paper 3

CC10 Electrolytic Processes /
CC11 Obtaining and Using Metals /
CC12 Reversible Reactions and Equilibria

The photo shows the Walt Disney Concert Hall in Los Angeles, which is clad in stainless steel. Buildings are made from large quantities of metals, including the steel frames and cladding, aluminium for window frames and copper for electrical wiring and water pipes. In this unit you will learn more about reactions, including some of the reactions involved in the extraction and purification of metals from their ores.

The learning journey

Previously you will have learnt at KS3:

- about oxidation and displacement reactions
- about the reactivity series.

You will also have learnt in *CC4 The Periodic Table*, *CC5 Ionic Bonding* and *CC8 Acids and Alkalis*:

- about anions and cations in ionic compounds
- to write balanced chemical equations with state symbols
- how the elements are arranged in the periodic table.

In this unit you will learn:

- more about reactivity, oxidation and reduction
- about the different ways in which metals can be extracted
- about the advantages of recycling metals
- about the factors involved in a life cycle assessment of a product
- to explain what happens during electrolysis
- about equilibria in chemical reactions
- about the Haber process
- **H** how to write half equations.

CC10a Electrolysis

Specification reference: C3.22; C3.23; C3.24; H C3.27; H C3.28; H C3.29

Progression questions

- What is an electrolyte?
- What happens to the ions during electrolysis?
- H How do you explain and represent the reactions taking place at the electrodes in electrolysis?

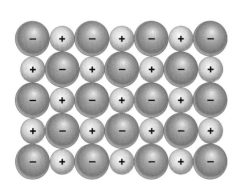

A (a) The ions cannot move in the lattice structure of solid sodium chloride.

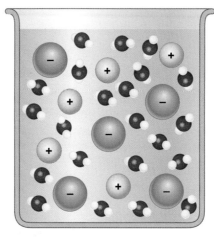

(b) The ions can move when sodium chloride is dissolved in water.

In 1800, Alessandro Volta invented the electric battery. English scientists William Nicholson and Anthony Carlisle soon discovered that electricity broke down acidified water into hydrogen and oxygen. This process is called **electrolysis** and today we use it to break down many substances.

When an ionic solid is melted or dissolved in water, its ionic bonds break. This allows the ions to move. An ionic substance with freely moving ions is called an **electrolyte** and can conduct electricity.

 1 Give the meaning of the following terms.

    a electrolysis

    b electrode

Electrolysis uses energy transferred by electricity to decompose electrolytes. Two **electrodes** are connected to a direct current (d.c.) electricity supply and placed into the electrolyte. The two types of ions carry opposite charges and so migrate (move) towards the electrode with the opposite charge.

- **Cations** are positive ions and are attracted to the negative **cathode**.
- **Anions** are negative ions and are attracted to the positive **anode**.

This can be shown by placing a purple potassium manganate(VII) crystal on a piece of damp filter paper attached to a microscope slide and connected to a d.c. electricity supply. The purple colour spreads towards the anode.

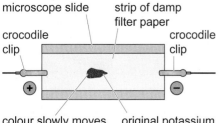

microscope slide   strip of damp filter paper

crocodile clip   crocodile clip

colour slowly moves towards the positive crocodile clip   original potassium manganate(VII) crystal

B Manganate(VII) ions are purple. Potassium ions are colourless.

 2 Give a reason why ionic solids cannot be electrolysed.

 3 State the type of charge on a manganate(VII) ion, giving a reason for your answer.

4 Look at these the formulae: Na^+, Cl^-, H_2O, OH^-, CO_2, SO_4^{2-}, Mg^{2+}

    a Identify the anions.

     b List the ions that will be attracted to the cathode during electrolysis.

H Reactions at the electrodes

At the anode, negative ions lose electrons (**oxidation**). At the cathode, electrons are transferred from the electrode to the positive ions (**reduction**).

Oxidation **I**s the **L**oss of electrons.

Reduction **I**s the **G**ain of electrons.

You can remember these by: OIL RIG.

This transfer of electrons changes charged ions into atoms or molecules, resulting in chemical changes at the electrodes. For example, in the electrolysis of molten zinc chloride, Zn^{2+} ions are attracted to the cathode, where they gain electrons and become zinc atoms. At the same time Cl^- ions migrate to the anode, where they lose electrons and become chlorine molecules.

These changes are represented by **half equations**, which show the change at each electrode.

Cathode reaction: $Zn^{2+} + 2e \rightarrow Zn$ reduction — ReduCtion takes place at the **C**athode.

Anode reaction: $2Cl^- \rightarrow Cl_2 + 2e$ oxidation — OxidAtion takes place at the **A**node.

Note that two Cl^- ions are needed to form one chlorine molecule.

5 The half equation for the reaction at the cathode during the electrolysis of molten lead bromide is:

$Pb^{2+} + 2e \rightarrow Pb$

 a Explain whether this half equation shows oxidation or reduction.

 b Write the half equation for the reaction of bromide ions, Br^-, at the anode.

 6 The following reaction takes place at an electrode:
$Cu \rightarrow Cu^{2+} + 2e$.
Identify the electrode at which the reaction occurs, giving a reason for your answer.

Did you know?

Metallic objects can be gold-plated using electrolysis. The anode is a strip of gold, the cathode is the object to be plated and the electrolyte contains gold ions.

C a gold-plated car

Checkpoint

How confidently can you answer the Progression questions?

Strengthen

S1 Give the meaning of each of the terms: electrolyte, anode, cathode, anion, cation.

S2 For each of the following ions, state which electrode it will move towards, during electrolysis: Mg^{2+}, OH^-. Give a reason for your answers.

Extend

E1 H Molten potassium bromide is electrolysed to form potassium and bromine. Write the half equations for the reactions at the electrodes, classify them as oxidation or reduction and state at which electrode they occur.

Exam-style question

Solid lithium chloride cannot be electrolysed, but molten lithium chloride can be electrolysed. Explain these observations. *(2 marks)*

Aim

Investigate the electrolysis of copper sulfate solution with inert electrodes and copper electrodes.

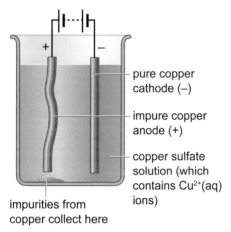

A In the purification of copper, the copper to be purified is used as the anode and some very pure copper is used as the cathode.

The copper needed for electrical wires must be very pure and this is achieved using the electrolysis of copper sulfate solution, as shown in figure A.

During electrolysis, the copper atoms in the anode lose two electrons each to become copper ions. These ions dissolve in the solution and migrate to the cathode, where they are deposited as pure copper. So, the impure copper anode loses mass and the pure copper cathode gains mass. Impurities from the anode do not form ions and collect below the anode as a 'sludge'. The anode sludge is collected because it may contain valuable metallic elements.

H

The half equation for the anode reaction is:

$$Cu(s) \rightarrow Cu^{2+}(aq) + 2e^-$$

The half equation for the cathode reaction is:

$$Cu^{2+}(aq) + 2e^- \rightarrow Cu(s)$$

Your task

You will set up an electrolysis cell to investigate the effect of changing the current on the mass of the copper electrodes used in the electrolysis of copper sulfate solution. You will also investigate the products formed during the electrolysis of copper sulfate solution using inert (graphite) electrodes.

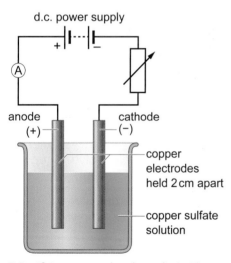

B Purifying copper by electrolysis. The copper to be purified is used as the anode and some very pure copper is used as the cathode.

Method

Using copper electrodes

Wear eye protection.

A Select two clean pieces of copper foil. Label one 'anode' and the other 'cathode'. Measure and record the masses of the two electrodes.

B Set up an electrolysis circuit as shown in diagram B.

C Turn on the power and adjust the variable resistor to give a current of about 0.2 A. Record the current and adjust the variable resistor to keep it constant. Leave the power on for 20 minutes.

D Turn off the power and remove the electrodes from the beaker. Gently wash the electrodes with distilled water then dip them into propanone. Lift the electrodes out and gently shake off the propanone. Allow the remainder of the propanone to evaporate.

E Measure and record the masses of the dry electrodes.

F Repeat the experiment using currents of 0.3 A, 0.4 A and 0.5 A.

Using graphite electrodes

G Set up the circuit as shown in diagram C.

H Turn on the power and observe what happens at each electrode.

Exam-style questions

1 Explain why a different product is formed at the anode when copper sulfate solution is electrolysed using graphite electrodes rather than copper electrodes. *(4 marks)*

2 Look at the method for electrolysis using copper electrodes.

   a State and explain *one* safety precaution *(1 mark)*

   b State why it is important to use clean copper electrodes. *(1 mark)*

   c Give a reason why a variable resistor is used in the electrolysis circuit. *(1 mark)*

   d Suggest a reason why the electrodes are washed at the end of the electrolysis. *(1 mark)*

   e Suggest a reason why propanone is used after washing the electrodes with distilled water. *(1 mark)*

3 The results of an investigation of the electrolysis of copper sulfate solution using copper electrodes are given in table D.

   a Calculate the changes in mass of the electrodes. *(2 marks)*

   b Plot a suitable graph to look for a correlation between the change in mass of each electrode and the current. *(4 marks)*

   c Describe the pattern in the change in mass at each electrode. *(2 marks)*

   d Explain the changes in mass of each electrode. *(4 marks)*

   e Explain the effect of increasing the current on these changes in mass. *(2 marks)*

   f Predict the change in mass at the anode when the current is 0.35 A. *(1 mark)*

   g Suggest a reason why the change in mass at the cathode is not the same as the change in mass at the anode when the same current is used. *(1 mark)*

   h Describe how you could improve the experiment to obtain more accurate results at the cathode. *(1 mark)*

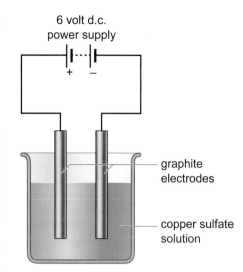

C electrolysis circuit for using graphite electrodes

Current (A)	0.2	0.3	0.4	0.5
Mass of anode at start (g)	2.77	2.68	2.53	2.36
Mass of anode at end (g)	2.69	2.55	2.36	2.15
Mass of cathode at start (g)	2.51	2.55	2.62	2.70
Mass of cathode at end (g)	2.58	2.66	2.76	2.87

D results of an electrolysis investigation

CC10b Products from electrolysis

Progression questions

- How do you predict the products formed in the electrolysis of molten zinc chloride?
- How do you explain the products formed in the electrolysis of sodium chloride solution?
- How is copper purified using electrolysis?

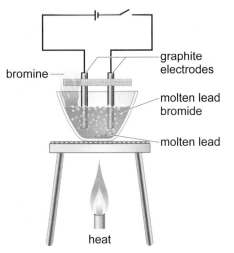

A Orange bromine gas is seen around the anode and a pool of grey liquid lead is seen under the cathode. This experiment must be carried out in a fume cupboard as bromine gas is toxic.

The electrolysis of molten or dissolved ionic salts is carried out using **inert** (unreactive) electrodes (usually graphite or platinum). When a molten salt is electrolysed, ions are **discharged** as atoms or molecules at the electrodes. When molten lead bromide is electrolysed, bromine is produced at the anode and lead is produced at the cathode.

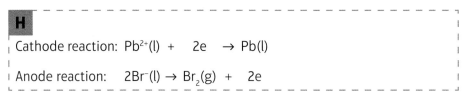

H

Cathode reaction: $Pb^{2+}(l) + 2e \rightarrow Pb(l)$

Anode reaction: $2Br^-(l) \rightarrow Br_2(g) + 2e$

You can predict the electrolysis products of any molten salt. The salt will always decompose into its elements. The metal is produced at the cathode and the non-metal is produced at the anode.

 1 Predict the products formed at the anode and cathode during the electrolysis of molten sodium chloride.

 2 **H** Explain which of the half equations in the electrolysis of molten lead bromide shows oxidation and which shows reduction.

Electrolysis of salt solutions

Water ionises to a very small extent, so in an aqueous solution of a salt there are some hydrogen ions (H^+) and hydroxide ions (OH^-), as well as the ions of the dissolved solid. Tables B and C show the electrolysis of two salt solutions, copper chloride solution and sodium chloride solution.

Ions	$Cu^{2+}(aq)$ and $Cl^-(aq)$ (from salt), $H^+(aq)$ and $OH^-(aq)$ (from water)	
cathode	$Cu^{2+}(aq)$ and $H^+(aq)$ ions are attracted. Copper ions are discharged more readily than hydrogen ions, so copper is formed as a brown solid.	**H** $Cu^{2+}(aq) + 2e \rightarrow Cu(s)$ (reduction)
anode	$Cl^-(aq)$ and $OH^-(aq)$ ions are attracted. Chloride ions are discharged more readily than hydroxide ions, so chlorine is formed as a pale green gas.	**H** $2Cl^-(aq) \rightarrow Cl_2(g) + 2e$ (oxidation)
Overall	The copper chloride decomposes but the water does not change. $CuCl_2(aq) \rightarrow Cu(s) + Cl_2(g)$	

B copper chloride solution electrolysis

 3 Describe what happens to the colour of the solution when copper chloride is electrolysed.

Ions	Na⁺(aq) and Cl⁻(aq) (from salt), H⁺(aq) and OH⁻(aq) (from water)	
cathode	Na⁺(aq) and H⁺(aq) ions are attracted. Hydrogen ions are discharged more readily than sodium ions, so hydrogen gas is formed.	**H** $2H^+(aq) + 2e \rightarrow H_2(g)$ (reduction)
anode	Cl⁻(aq) and OH⁻(aq) ions are attracted. Chloride ions are discharged more readily than hydroxide ions, so chlorine is formed as a pale green gas.	**H** $2Cl^-(aq) \rightarrow Cl_2(g) + 2e$ (oxidation)
Overall	The sodium chloride decomposes to form hydrogen and chlorine. The sodium and hydroxide ions remain in the solution. $$2NaCl(aq) + 2H_2O(l) \rightarrow H_2(g) + Cl_2(g) + 2NaOH(aq)$$	

C sodium chloride solution electrolysis

In the electrolysis of sodium sulfate solution, sodium ions (Na^+) and hydrogen ions (H^+) collect at the cathode, where hydrogen gas forms. At the anode, hydroxide ions (OH^-) are discharged more readily than sulfate ions (SO_4^{2-}), so oxygen gas is formed (along with water). Overall, water decomposes to form hydrogen and oxygen. The Na^+ and SO_4^{2-} ions stay in solution.

Water decomposes to form hydrogen and oxygen during the electrolysis of water acidified with dilute sulfuric acid (which contains $H^+(aq)$ and $SO_4^{2-}(aq)$).

 5 Use table C as a template to show the details of what happens in the electrolysis of:

a sodium sulfate   **b** acidified water.

 6 Explain why the electrolysis of acidified water produces twice as much hydrogen as oxygen.

Copper can be purified by the electrolysis of copper sulfate solution using copper electrodes. The copper atoms in the anode lose electrons to become copper ions. These dissolve in the solution and migrate to the cathode, where they are deposited as pure copper. Impurities from the anode do not form ions and collect below the anode as a 'sludge'.

7 **H** Write the half equations for the reactions at the electrodes when copper sulfate is electrolysed using copper electrodes and classify them as oxidation or reduction.

Exam-style question

The electrolysis of sodium chloride solution does not produce metallic sodium. State how you would change the electrolyte to obtain metallic sodium.

(1 mark)

 4 When sodium chloride solution is electrolysed, state why hydrogen is produced instead of sodium.

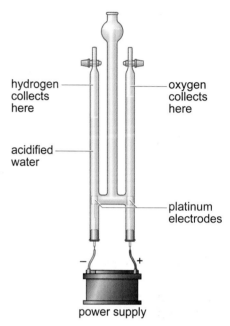

hydrogen collects here

oxygen collects here

acidified water

platinum electrodes

power supply

D Water is electrolysed in a Hofmann voltameter to collect the gases produced.

Checkpoint

How confidently can you answer the Progression questions?

Strengthen

S1 Explain the formation of the products during the electrolysis of molten zinc chloride.

S2 Predict the product formed at each electrode during the electrolysis of molten magnesium bromide. Justify your answers.

Extend

E1 Explain why the electrolysis of sodium chloride solution produces hydrogen and chlorine at the electrodes.

Progression questions

- What are the similarities and differences in the way different metals react with water, acids and salt solutions?
- What happens to metal atoms when they react with water and acids?
- **H** How do you explain displacement reactions as redox reactions?

A Caesium is more reactive than potassium, and so is placed above potassium in the reactivity series.

Did you know?

Caesium forms cations so easily that scientists think it could be used as a propellant in 'ion engines' for spacecraft.

 1 Name a metal that does not react with cold water or dilute acid.

 2 Write the word equation for the reaction of calcium with water.

 3 Write the balanced equation for the reaction of magnesium with dilute hydrochloric acid. Include state symbols.

The **reactivity series** is a list of metals in order of reactivity, with the most reactive at the top.

Metal	Reaction with water	Reaction with dilute acid	Tendency of metal atoms to form cations
potassium	react with cold water to form hydrogen and a metal hydroxide	react violently	increasing ability of metal atoms to form positive ions
sodium			
calcium		react to form hydrogen and a salt solution	
magnesium	react very slowly, if at all, with cold water but react with steam to form hydrogen and a metal oxide		
aluminium			
zinc			
iron			
copper	do not react with cold water or steam	do not react	
silver			
gold			

B the reactivity series for some metals

The metals that react with cold water form hydrogen and a metal hydroxide solution. For example:

$$2K(s) \quad + \quad 2H_2O(l) \quad \rightarrow \quad 2KOH(aq) \quad + \quad H_2(g)$$

The metals that react with steam form hydrogen and a solid metal oxide.

$$2Mg(s) \quad + \quad H_2O(g) \quad \rightarrow \quad 2MgO(s) \quad + \quad H_2(g)$$

The metals that react with dilute acids form hydrogen and a salt solution. Bubbles of gas will be seen. The more bubbles formed, the more reactive the metal.

$$Zn(s) \quad + \quad H_2SO_4(aq) \quad \rightarrow \quad ZnSO_4(aq) \quad + \quad H_2(g)$$

In all of these reactions, the metal atoms lose electrons to form positive ions (**cations**). The more easily a metal's atoms lose electrons, the higher the metal is in the reactivity series.

Displacement reactions

We can use the reactivity series to predict whether reactions will take place. Each metal will react with compounds of the metals below it in the series.

When zinc is dipped into copper sulfate solution, a copper coating forms on the surface of the zinc. Some of the zinc takes the place of the copper and forms zinc sulfate solution.

$$Zn(s) + CuSO_4(aq) \rightarrow Cu(s) + ZnSO_4(aq)$$

This is a **displacement reaction**. The zinc has displaced the copper.

Displacement reactions only work one way. Copper cannot displace zinc from its compounds because copper is less reactive.

C Blue copper sulfate solution changes to colourless zinc sulfate solution as zinc displaces copper.

 4 Use the reactivity series to predict whether a displacement reaction will take place in the reaction below. Either complete the equation or write 'no reaction'.

magnesium + copper sulfate →

 5 Write the balanced equation for the reaction between magnesium and zinc chloride.

H

Displacement reactions are also redox reactions. The reaction between zinc and copper sulfate can be written as an ionic equation:

$$Zn + Cu^{2+} \rightarrow Cu + Zn^{2+}$$

The sulfate ions have been left out as they do not change and are called **spectator ions**. The zinc atoms lose electrons to form zinc ions. This can be shown in a **half equation**. 2e represents the two electrons.

$$Zn \rightarrow Zn^{2+} + 2e \qquad \text{This is **oxidation** – the loss of electrons.}$$

The copper ions gain electrons to form copper atoms:

$$Cu^{2+} + 2e \rightarrow Cu \qquad \text{This is **reduction** – the gain of electrons.}$$

A reaction in which one substance is oxidised and another is reduced is called a **redox reaction**.

 6 Explain which substances are oxidised and reduced when:

$$Mg + Zn^{2+} \rightarrow Zn + Mg^{2+}$$

Checkpoint

How confidently can you answer the Progression questions?

Strengthen

S1 Describe the reactions you could carry out to find the order of reactivity for magnesium, tin, chromium and copper. You may use the metals and the metal nitrate solutions.

Extend

E1 **H** Magnesium reacts with dilute sulfuric acid and zinc nitrate solution, as shown:

$$Mg + H_2SO_4 \rightarrow MgSO_4 + H_2$$

$$Mg + Zn(NO_3)_2 \rightarrow Mg(NO_3)_2 + Zn$$

   a Write ionic equations for these reactions.

   b Explain, in terms of electrons, why these are redox reactions.

Exam-style question

Three metals are labelled **X**, **Y** and **Z**. Metal **X** displaces **Z** from **Z** sulfate solution. Metal **X** does not displace **Y** from **Y** sulfate solution.

State the order of reactivity of the three metals, giving a reason for your answer.

(3 marks)

CC11b Ores

Specification reference: C4.4; C4.7; **H** C4.8

Progression questions

- Which metals are found uncombined in the Earth's crust?
- How is the method of extraction of a metal related to its position in the reactivity series?
- **H** How are biological methods used to extract some metals?

A Gold occurs uncombined in the Earth's crust.

Very unreactive metals, such as gold and platinum, are found naturally in their **native state** (as uncombined elements). More reactive metals have reacted with other elements to form compounds in rocks. The process of obtaining a metal from these compounds is **extraction**.

An **ore** is a rock that contains enough of a compound to extract a metal for profit. Haematite is an ore containing iron oxide. Iron is extracted by heating the iron oxide with carbon. Carbon is more reactive than iron so it displaces it.

iron oxide + carbon → iron + carbon dioxide

This method is used for compounds of metals below carbon in the reactivity series shown in table B.

Malachite is an ore containing copper carbonate. Malachite is heated to convert it to copper oxide, which is then heated with carbon to produce copper.

Metals higher than carbon must be extracted using a more powerful method called **electrolysis**. This involves passing electricity through a molten ionic compound to decompose it into its elements. Aluminium is produced by electrolysis of aluminium oxide, found in an ore called bauxite:

aluminium oxide → aluminium + oxygen

A lot of energy is needed to keep metal oxides molten for electrolysis, making it extremely expensive. Electrolysis is only used to extract very reactive metals that cannot be obtained by heating their oxides with carbon.

7th 1 Write word equations for the two reactions needed to produce copper.

7th 2 State why copper can be produced by heating copper oxide with carbon.

5th 3 Name two metals that can only be extracted from their ores by electrolysis.

4 Zinc can be extracted from zinc oxide, ZnO, by heating with carbon.

9th a Write the balanced equation for this reaction.

9th b Explain why electrolysis is not used in the large-scale extraction of zinc.

Metal	Method of extraction
potassium	electrolysis of a molten compound
sodium	
calcium	
magnesium	
aluminium	
(carbon)	
zinc	heat an ore with carbon
iron	
copper	
silver	found as the uncombined element
gold	

increasing reactivity →

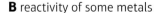

B reactivity of some metals

H Biological methods of metal extraction

Copper is traditionally extracted by heating copper sulfide (producing copper and sulfur dioxide). However, copper ores are running out and so we need to extract copper from ores containing much smaller amounts of copper compounds.

Bioleaching uses bacteria grown on a low grade ore. The bacteria produce a solution containing copper ions, called a **leachate**. Copper is extracted from the leachate by displacement using scrap iron, then purified by electrolysis. This method can also be used for metals such as nickel, cobalt and zinc.

Phytoextraction involves growing plants that absorb metal compounds. The plants are burnt to form ash, from which the metal is extracted.

Process	Advantages	Disadvantages
both bioleaching and phytoextraction	no harmful gases (e.g. sulfur dioxide) are produced causes less damage to the landscape than mining conserves supplies of higher grade ores	very slow
bioleaching	does not require high temperatures	toxic substances and sulfuric acid can be produced by the process, and damage the environment
phytoextraction	can extract metals from contaminated soils	more expensive than mining some ores growing plants is dependent on weather conditions

D some advantages and disadvantages of bioleaching and phytoextraction

 5 Suggest why bioleaching and phytoextraction are very slow.

 6 Copper ions, Cu^{2+}, are produced in solution during bioleaching. Write an ionic equation for the displacement reaction between these copper ions and iron. Include state symbols.

C The tree used for phytoextraction contains a nickel-rich sap, which makes it green.

Did you know?

When aluminium was first extracted by electrolysis in the late 19th century it was more expensive than gold.

Checkpoint

How confidently can you answer the Progression questions?

Strengthen

S1 Explain why iron is extracted from iron oxide using a different method to the one used to extract aluminium from aluminium oxide.

Extend

E1 H Compare and contrast biological and non-biological methods of metal extraction.

Exam-style question

Sodium is more reactive than aluminium. Describe a method to extract sodium from sodium chloride. Give a reason for your answer. *(3 marks)*

CC11c Oxidation and reduction

Specification reference: **H** C4.2; C4.5; C4.6; C4.9

Progression questions

- How do you explain oxidation and reduction in terms of oxygen?
- What types of reaction happen to ores when metals are extracted?
- How is the position of a metal in the reactivity series related to its resistance to corrosion?

A Iron oxide is reduced to iron in a blast furnace.

Many metals are extracted from metal oxide ores. In order to obtain the metal from its oxide, the oxygen must be removed. When oxygen is removed from a compound, the compound is said to be 'reduced'.

Metal extraction is reduction

Oxidation is the gain of oxygen by a substance. **Reduction** is the loss of oxygen from a substance. Oxidation and reduction always occur together. If one substance is oxidised, another will be reduced. Reactions in which oxidation and reduction occur are called **redox** reactions.

Iron is obtained by removing the oxygen from iron oxide by heating with carbon. The iron oxide is reduced to iron. Carbon is oxidised to carbon dioxide.

iron oxide + carbon → iron + carbon dioxide

Aluminium is obtained by removing oxygen from aluminium oxide by electrolysis.

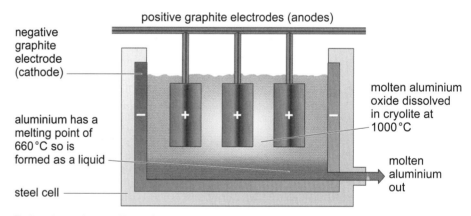

B the electrolysis cell used to extract aluminium

During electrolysis, aluminium ions (Al^{3+}) are attracted to the cathode, where they gain electrons to form aluminium. The oxide ions, O^{2-}, are attracted to the anodes, where they lose electrons to form oxygen. At the high temperature in the electrolysis cell, the oxygen reacts with the graphite (carbon) anodes to form carbon dioxide.

1. Metals are obtained by reduction of their ores. State the meaning of 'reduction'.

2. Zinc oxide reacts with carbon to form zinc and carbon dioxide in a redox reaction. Explain which substance has been oxidised and which has been reduced.

3. **H** Molten sodium chloride contains Na^+ and Cl^- ions. It is electrolysed to form sodium and chlorine.

   a. Write the half-equations for the reactions at the anode and the cathode.

   b. Explain whether the reaction at each electrode is oxidation or reduction.

H

The half-equations for the reactions occurring at the electrodes are:

cathode $Al^{3+} + 3e \rightarrow Al$ reduction (the ions have gained electrons)

anode $2O^{2-} \rightarrow O_2 + 4e$ oxidation (the ions have lost electrons)

Corrosion

Corrosion happens when a metal reacts with oxygen, making the metal weaker over time. The metal gains oxygen so is oxidised. The corrosion of iron requires water as well as oxygen and is called **rusting**.

The more reactive a metal is, the more rapidly it corrodes. Gold does not corrode at all, which is one of the reasons it is used in jewellery.

C The Grouville Hoard was found in a field in Jersey in 2012. It contains about 70 000 coins and pieces of gold jewellery, which are 2000 years old. The gold has not corroded.

Some metals, such as aluminium, are quite reactive and would be expected to corrode quickly. However, they do not corrode because their surfaces form a protective oxide layer (a **tarnish**), which prevents further reaction.

D The iron in the Angel of the North has reacted with oxygen and water.

Exam-style question

Iron oxide is reduced by heating it with carbon. Explain what is oxidised in this process. *(2 marks)*

The iron originally on Mars has rusted over billions of years, making the planet red. On the Moon, however, the dark areas on its surface are made of an iron-rich rock. The iron in these rocks has not rusted.

 4 Look at the Did you know? box. Explain what the different colours in the iron-rich rocks on Mars and the Moon tell us about their atmospheres.

Checkpoint

How confidently can you answer the Progression questions?

Strengthen

S1 Copper oxide reacts with hydrogen:
$CuO + H_2 \rightarrow Cu + H_2O$
State, with a reason, which substance has been:
a oxidised **b** reduced.

S2 Three metals were left outside for 1 month. Metal A did not corrode at all; metal B corroded a lot; metal C corroded a little. Put the metals in order of increasing reactivity and explain your reasoning.

Extend

E1 **H** The half-equation for the reaction taking place at one of the electrodes during the electrolysis of molten magnesium chloride is:
$Mg^{2+} + 2e \rightarrow Mg$. Explain: **a** at which electrode this reaction occurs **b** whether this is oxidation, reduction or neither.

235

Progression questions

- What are the advantages of recycling a metal?
- When might recycling a material not be worthwhile?
- What are the factors to consider in a life cycle assessment of a product?

A Artists have recycled the waste washed up on the coast of Kenya into sculptures.

Every UK household is estimated to produce 1 tonne of waste each year. About 45% of this waste is recycled but there is an EU target for **recycling** to reach 70% by 2030.

An estimated 2 million tonnes of waste electrical and electronic equipment (WEEE), such as phones, TVs and toasters, are thrown away in the UK each year. These items contain a lot of precious metals worth about £1 billion, including about £36 000 000 worth of aluminium.

Recycling metals

Many metals can be recycled by melting them down and making them into something new. Some of the main advantages of recycling are as follows:

- Natural reserves of metal ores will last longer.
- The need to mine ores is reduced. Mining can damage the landscape as well as create noise and dust pollution.
- Less pollution may be produced. For example, sulfur dioxide is formed when some metals are extracted from metal sulfide ores.
- Many metals need less energy to recycle them than to extract new metal from the ore.
- Less waste metal ends up in landfill sites.

However, there are some disadvantages of recycling – including the costs and the energy used in collecting, transporting and sorting metals to be recycled. Sometimes it can be more expensive, and require more energy, to recycle than to extract new metal.

B The WEEE man is made from over 3 tonnes of electrical and electronic equipment that the average person in the UK throws away in a lifetime.

 1 Describe what is meant by 'recycling metals'.

 2 Make a table to summarise the advantages and disadvantages of recycling metals compared to extracting more of the metals from ores.

Life cycle assessment

A life cycle assessment (LCA) can be carried out to work out the environmental impact of a product. An example is shown in diagram C.

The LCA also helps people to decide whether it is worthwhile to manufacture and recycle a product. LCAs can be used to compare the effect of using different materials for the same product, for example making a bottle from glass or plastic.

Some data that could be used as part of an LCA for the manufacture of a sample of 1 kg of aluminium is shown in the table below.

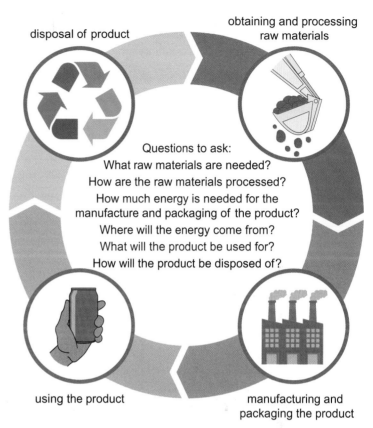

Questions to ask:
What raw materials are needed?
How are the raw materials processed?
How much energy is needed for the manufacture and packaging of the product?
Where will the energy come from?
What will the product be used for?
How will the product be disposed of?

disposal of product

obtaining and processing raw materials

using the product

manufacturing and packaging the product

C stages in an LCA

Data on the manufacture of aluminium

- 5.5 kg of bauxite produces 1.9 kg of aluminium oxide, which produces 1.0 kg of aluminium during electrolysis
- 0.3 kg of carbon is burnt from the anodes
- 285 000 kJ of energy is needed to produce 1 kg of aluminium from bauxite
- 14 000 kJ of energy is needed to produce 1 kg of aluminium from recycled aluminium

Did you know?

The Colossus of Rhodes, one of the Seven Wonders of the Ancient World, was completed in 280 BCE using bronze from abandoned weapons. It was destroyed by an earthquake in 226 BCE. About 800 years later, the metal was recycled again.

D the Colossus of Rhodes

 3 State the four stages that are considered in a life cycle assessment of a product.

 4 Give two reasons why a life cycle assessment should be carried out before deciding whether to make a new product.

Exam-style question

Describe two advantages of recycling copper, rather than obtaining it from its ores.
(2 marks)

Checkpoint

How confidently can you answer the Progression questions?

Strengthen

S1 a Outline how a broken aluminium saucepan is recycled to make an aluminium drinks can. **b** State the advantages and disadvantages of recycling aluminium.

Extend

E1 Discuss the life cycle assessment of aluminium, using the data shown in the data table and the extraction of aluminium in the previous topic. Include a description of other factors that need to be considered as part of the LCA.

CC12a Dynamic equilibrium

Specification reference: C4.13; C4.14; C4.15; C4.16; **H** C4.17

Progression questions

- What is meant by dynamic equilibrium?
- How is ammonia manufactured?
- **H** How do changes in temperature, pressure and concentration affect the equilibrium position?

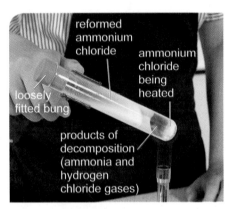

A Heating ammonium chloride is a reversible reaction.

In some chemical reactions the products react to reform the reactants. These are **reversible reactions**. In the equations for reversible reactions (such as the one shown in photo A), a double arrow '⇌' is used to show that both forward and backward reactions occur at the same time.

forward reaction

$$\text{ammonium chloride} \rightleftharpoons \text{ammonia} + \text{hydrogen}$$
$$NH_4Cl(s) \rightleftharpoons NH_3(g) + HCl(g)$$

backward reaction

 1 What is happening when a reaction reaches 'dynamic equilibrium'?

Graph B shows how the percentages of the reactants and products change during the reaction. At a certain point, the forward and backward reactions are still occurring but the percentages of the reactants and products are no longer changing. This is called a **dynamic equilibrium** because the reactions are still occurring (dynamic) but the substances remain in balance (equilibrium).

Although all reactions are reversible, dynamic equilibrium only occurs in **closed systems**, where there is no loss of reactants or products. In an **open system**, gases could escape and so equilibrium would not be achieved.

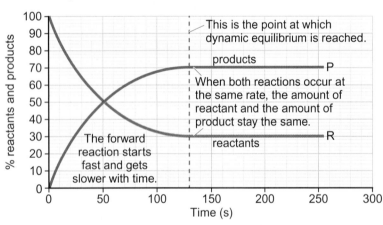

B In a reversible reaction, the backward reaction gets faster with time, and the forward reaction gets slower with time. When they are occurring at the same rate, dynamic equilibrium has been reached.

 2 When calcium carbonate is heated in an open test tube it decomposes to form calcium oxide and carbon dioxide.

 a Write a word equation to represent this change as a reversible reaction.

b Explain why equilibrium will not be achieved in this case.

$$N_2(g) + 3H_2(g) \rightleftharpoons 2NH_3(g)$$
nitrogen   hydrogen   ammonia

 3 What happens to the amount of ammonia after equilibrium is reached in the Haber process?

The manufacture of ammonia by the Haber process involves a reversible reaction between nitrogen (from the air) and hydrogen (from natural gas) that can reach a dynamic equilibrium. The 'equilibrium position' (the percentages of the products and reactants at equilibrium) is changed by the reaction conditions. In the Haber process, and all similar industrial reactions, the reaction conditions are chosen to favour the forward reaction and make a large amount of product as cheaply as possible. In the Haber process, these conditions are a temperature of 450 °C, a pressure of 200 atmospheres and the use of an iron catalyst.

H

The equilibrium position can be altered by changes in temperature, pressure and concentration. In general, the equilibrium position shifts to reduce the effects of any changes to the system, as described in table C.

Change by . . .	Equilibrium position shifts . . .
increasing temperature	in the **endothermic** direction (transferring energy from the surroundings, cooling them down)
decreasing temperature	in the **exothermic** direction (transferring energy to the surroundings, heating them up)
increasing gas pressure	in the direction that forms fewer gas molecules (as this reduces pressure)
decreasing gas pressure	in the direction that forms more gas molecules (as this increases pressure)
increasing a concentration	in the direction that uses up the substance that has been added
decreasing a concentration	in the direction that forms more of the substance that has been removed

C

Photo D shows how the equilibrium position of a mixture of nitrogen dioxide and dinitrogen tetroxide depends on temperature.

$$2NO_2(g) \quad \rightleftharpoons \quad N_2O_4(g) \quad \text{(forward reaction is exothermic)}$$
nitrogen dioxide (brown)   dinitrogen tetroxide (colourless)

As the temperature is decreased the equilibrium shifts to the right so the colour gets lighter.

This changes brown NO_2 molecules '●' into colourless N_2O_4 '○' molecules as this is the exothermic direction, which increases the temperature.

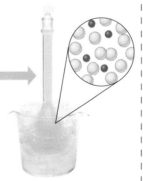

D As the temperature is decreased the equilibrium shifts in the exothermic direction.

---

 4 Explain why the equilibrium position in industrial reactions is often controlled.

 5 Describe the difference between exothermic and endothermic reactions.

6 The formation of methanol from carbon monoxide and hydrogen is a reversible reaction that is exothermic in the forward direction.

$$CO(g) + 2H_2(g) \rightleftharpoons CH_3OH(g)$$

Explain the effect on the position of equilibrium of increasing:

 a temperature

 b pressure

 c carbon monoxide concentration.

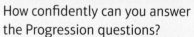

Checkpoint

How confidently can you answer the Progression questions?

Strengthen

S1 Use equations to explain the formation of ammonia in a reversible reaction that reaches a dynamic equilibrium.

Extend

E1 Explain how a dynamic equilibrium is reached in the formation of ammonia.

E2 **H** The formation of ammonia is exothermic. Describe three ways to increase the amount of ammonia at equilibrium.

Exam-style question

a Describe what happens in a reversible reaction.   *(1 mark)*

b **H** Look at the equilibrium between NO_2 and N_2O_4 in diagram D. Explain why the colour changes when the pressure is increased.

(3 marks)

Electrolysis

Lead bromide contains Pb^{2+} and Br^- ions and has the formula $PbBr_2$. The diagram shows the electrolysis of lead bromide. Explain what is happening at each electrode at the start of the experiment and as the electrolyte melts.   **(6 marks)**

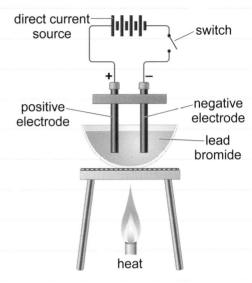

Student answer

Lead bromide contains Pb^{2+} ions and Br^- ions and has the formula $PbBr_2$ [1]. It is a compound and has ions, so it can be used for electrolysis [2]. During electrolysis, the ions move towards the oppositely-charged electrodes [3]. The products at each electrode are lead and bromine [4]. Heat is needed to melt the lead bromide so that the ions can move and conduct electricity. When the lead bromide is a solid, the ions can't move, so there is no flow of electricity.

[1] There are no marks for simply repeating information from the question.

[2] This is correct, but it is not relevant to the question which asks students to explain what is happening at the electrodes.

[3] The answer would be better if it explained what was happening at each electrode.

[4] These are the correct products, but the answer should state which product is formed at each electrode.

Verdict

This is an acceptable answer. It contains some correct chemistry, but is missing some information. There is a good explanation of why heat is needed for electrolysis, and the products of the electrolysis are given.

The answer could be improved by explaining which ions move towards which electrode and what happens at those electrodes. For example, it could explain that the positively-charged cations (Pb^{2+}) move towards the negatively-charged electrode (cathode), and once there, they gain two electrons to become lead. It would also have been more logical to have the last two sentences earlier in the explanation, starting with what happens in the circuit at the start of the experiment (when the lead bromide is still solid). There is also information that is copied from the question and some parts of the answer are not relevant.

Exam tip

Do not just repeat information from the question, and make sure that anything you write is relevant to the question that has been asked.

Paper 4

CC13 Groups in the Periodic Table / CC14 Rates of Reaction / CC15 Heat Energy Changes in Chemical Reactions

This light show, on the beaches of the Maldives, is generated by bioluminescent chemical reactions in tiny microorganisms called phytoplankton. Almost all of the energy transferred by the reaction is transferred by light, making it very efficient and of interest to scientists developing lighting systems that waste less energy. Understanding how chemical reactions occur and the energy transfers involved is fundamental to understanding our material world and the processes of life. This unit looks at some typical reactions of certain elements and general ideas about how chemical reactions can be controlled and used.

The learning journey

Previously you will have learnt at KS3:

- about elements, compounds and the periodic table
- what happens during chemical reactions.

You will also have learnt in *CC3 Atomic Structure, CC5 Ionic Bonds* and *CC8 Acids and Alkalis*:

- about the nature of atoms and ions
- how to write balanced chemical equations, including the state symbols.

In this unit you will learn:

- about the properties and reactions of the elements in groups 1, 7 and 0.
- how changes in conditions can affect the rates of reactions
- about the energy transfers that can occur during chemical reactions.

CC13a Group 1

Specification reference: C6.1; C6.2; C6.3; C6.4; C6.5

Progression questions

- What are the main properties of alkali metals?
- How do alkali metals react with water?
- Why do alkali metals have different reactivities?

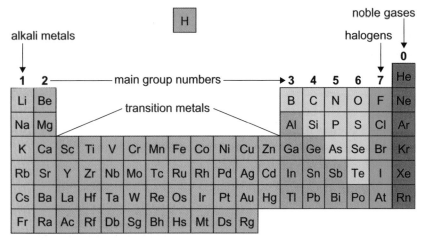

A Groups 1, 7 and 0 in the periodic table have special names.

The **periodic table** is arranged so that elements in the same vertical column or **group** have similar chemical and physical properties, and show trends in those properties.

The **alkali metals**, in group 1, have similar physical properties to other metals – they are all malleable and conduct electricity. However, they also have properties that are specific to this group. All alkali metals have relatively low melting points, are soft and easily cut. Alkali metals are also very reactive and readily form compounds with non-metals.

 1 Why are potassium and sodium placed in the same group of the periodic table?

 2 Describe two physical properties of alkali metals that make them different from other metals.

3 Write word equations for the reactions of sodium with:

 a oxygen

 b water.

All alkali metals are easily oxidised and burn brightly in air. For example, the reaction of potassium with oxygen can be shown as:

$$4K(s) + O_2(g) \rightarrow 2K_2O(s)$$
$$\text{potassium} + \text{oxygen} \rightarrow \text{potassium oxide}$$

The reactions of three alkali metals with water are described in table B. In each reaction, a metal hydroxide (an alkali) and hydrogen gas are the products. The **reactivity** of the alkali metals increases down the group.

$$2Li(s) + 2H_2O(l) \rightarrow 2LiOH(aq) + H_2(g)$$
$$\text{lithium} + \text{water} \rightarrow \text{lithium hydroxide} + \text{hydrogen}$$

reactivity		
	lithium + water	bubbles fiercely on the surface
	sodium + water	melts into a ball and fizzes about the surface
	potassium + water	bursts into flames and flies about the surface

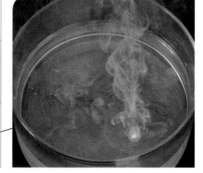

B reactions of alkali metals with water

Did you know?

Francium, discovered in 1939, was the last element to be discovered in nature. It is radioactive and extremely rare. Scientists think that only 20–30 g of francium exists on Earth at any one time.

 4 Caesium (Cs) is below potassium in the periodic table. Suggest how caesium might react with water.

To explain the trend in reactivity we need to look at the electronic configurations of alkali metal atoms. These atoms have one electron in their outer shells. When they react with non-metal atoms, the outer electrons are transferred from the metal to the non-metal. Diagram D shows an example. Each sodium atom loses its outer electron to form a positive (1+) ion, and each oxygen atom gains two electrons to form a negative (2–) ion.

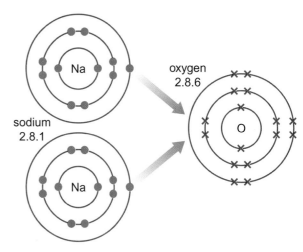

C dot and cross diagrams to show sodium reacting with oxygen to form sodium oxide (Na_2O, which contains Na^+ and O^{2-} ions)

 5 Draw diagrams, like the ones in diagram C, to show the electronic configurations of the sodium and oxide ions.

As we go down group 1, the atoms get larger because an extra electron shell is added in each period. The force of attraction between the positive nucleus and the negative outer electron decreases as they become further apart. This explains the trend in reactivity of alkali metals. Sodium is more reactive than lithium because it is easier to remove the outer electron from a sodium atom.

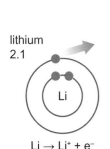 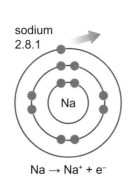 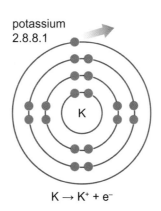

lithium 2.1   sodium 2.8.1   potassium 2.8.8.1

$Li \rightarrow Li^+ + e^-$ $Na \rightarrow Na^+ + e^-$ $K \rightarrow K^+ + e^-$

D As the distance between the outer electron and the nucleus increases, the alkali metals get more reactive.

 8 By referring to atomic structures, explain why potassium is more reactive than sodium.

 9 **H** Write an ionic equation for the reaction of potassium with water (hydroxide ion = OH^-).

 6 Why do alkali metals form an ion with a 1+ charge?

 7 a Why are alkali metals stored under oil?

 b How will the reactivity of rubidium (Rb) compare to potassium and caesium?

Checkpoint

How confidently can you answer the Progression questions?

Strengthen

S1 Name three alkali metals and describe their main physical and chemical properties.

Extend

E1 a Explain the difference in reactivity between rubidium and caesium.

b **H** Write ionic equations for the reactions of rubidium and caesium with water.

Exam-style question

a Write a balanced equation for the reaction of potassium with water. *(2 marks)*

b Explain why the reaction of caesium with water is not demonstrated in school laboratories. *(1 mark)*

CC13b Group 7

Specification reference: C6.6; C6.7; C6.8; C6.9; C6.10

Progression questions

- How do the physical properties of the halogens change, going down group 7?
- How can we test for chlorine gas?
- How do halogens react with metals and hydrogen?

A the three most common halogens

Elements in group 7 of the periodic table are called the **halogens**. They all share similar properties and show a pattern in the way their properties change through the group.

All halogens exist as **diatomic** molecules, with two atoms held together by a single covalent bond. They are all non-metallic elements, which are poor conductors of heat and electricity. Care has to be taken when handling halogens, as they are all toxic and corrosive.

 1 What pattern is there in the depth of colour of the halogens?

The physical properties of the three most common halogens are described in table B. As you go down the group the melting points, boiling points and densities increase.

Did you know?

The name halogen comes from the Greek words *hals*, meaning 'salt', and *gen*, meaning 'to make'. So halogens make salts – not just table salt (sodium chloride) but a range of metal halides that have a variety of uses.

Halogen	Melting point (°C)	Boiling point (°C)	Density (g/cm³)	Appearance
chlorine	−101	−34	0.0032	green gas
bromine	−7	59	3.12	brown liquid
iodine	114	184	4.95	purple/black solid

B halogen properties

Most halogens react with metals and non-metals in a similar way. Halogens react with metals forming ionic compounds called **salts**, which contain **halide** ions (X^-). For example:

$$Cl_2(g) \quad + \quad Mg(s) \quad \rightarrow \quad MgCl_2(s)$$
chlorine + magnesium → magnesium chloride

$$F_2(g) \quad + \quad 2Na(s) \quad \rightarrow \quad 2NaF(s)$$
fluorine + sodium → sodium fluoride

Halide salts have many uses. For example, common sodium halide salts include sodium chloride (table salt), sodium fluoride (found in many toothpastes), sodium bromide (used in a disinfectant for swimming pools) and sodium iodide (added to table salt to prevent iodine deficiency).

 2 Describe two ways that halogens are similar.

3 Look at photo A and table B.

 a What do you think fluorine, at the top of group 7, will look like?

b Estimate the melting point, boiling point and density of fluorine.

4 What ions are formed when sodium reacts with fluorine?

 5 a Name the product formed when calcium metal burns in fluorine.

 b Write a balanced equation for the reaction (calcium ion = Ca^{2+}).

All halogens can be used as **disinfectants** and **bleaches**, as they can kill microorganisms and remove the colour from materials. Chlorine is commonly used in swimming pools and many types of bleach. The test for chlorine, shown in photo C, depends on this bleaching action.

Halogens react with hydrogen to form hydrogen halides, which dissolve in water to form acidic solutions. For example, hydrogen and chlorine explode to form hydrogen chloride, which dissolves in water to make hydrochloric acid.

$$H_2(g) + Cl_2(g) \rightarrow 2HCl(g)$$
hydrogen + chlorine → hydrogen chloride

Hydrogen and chlorine molecules collide and the covalent bonds holding the atoms together break.

Covalent bonds form between hydrogen and chlorine atoms, making a new compound, hydrogen chloride.

When hydrogen chloride dissolves in water the molecules break up into two ions, H$^+$ and Cl$^-$.

The formation of H$^+$ ions makes the solution acidic.

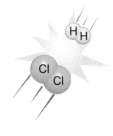

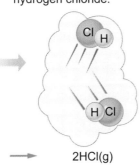

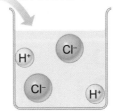

$$H_2(g) + Cl_2(g) \longrightarrow 2HCl(g)$$
hydrogen + chlorine ⟶ hydrogen chloride

dissolves in water to form hydrochloric acid

D making hydrochloric acid

C If damp blue litmus paper is placed in chlorine gas, it first turns red then bleaches white.

6 Describe for chlorine:

 a two uses

 b a safety precaution for its use

 c a test for the gas.

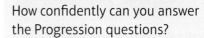

Checkpoint

How confidently can you answer the Progression questions?

Strengthen

S1 Describe how the halogens chlorine, bromine and iodine are similar, and how they show trends in properties down their group.

Extend

E1 Describe, using balanced equations where appropriate, how bromine can be converted into:

a sodium bromide

b hydrobromic acid.

7 In what state would each of the halogens in table B be at:

 a –50 °C   **b** 150 °C?

8 Write word equations for the reactions between:

 a lithium and chlorine   **b** hydrogen and fluorine.

 9 Explain how hydrogen fluoride can form an acidic aqueous solution and name the acid.

10 Write balanced equations for the reactions between:

 a sodium and iodine   **b** hydrogen and bromine.

Exam-style question

a Predict the state and appearance of astatine (At). *(1 mark)*

b Explain your answer. *(1 mark)*

245

CC13c Halogen reactivity

Specification reference: **H** C0.4; C6.11; **H** C6.12; C6.13

Progression questions

- How can displacement reactions be used to work out the reactivity of halogens?
- How can we explain the reactivity of halogens?
- **H** What happens to halogen atoms and halide ions during displacement?

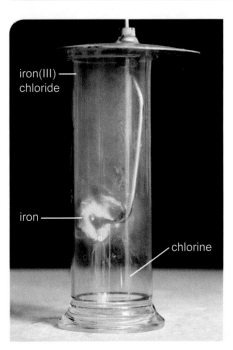

B $2Fe + 3Cl_2 \rightarrow 2FeCl_3$
iron + chlorine → iron(III) chloride

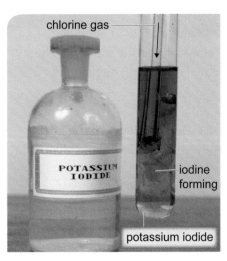

C Chlorine displaces iodine from potassium iodide solution.

Table A shows the order of reactivity of different halogens when heated with iron wool. In general the halogens become less reactive as you go down the group.

Halogen	Effect on iron wool
fluorine	bursts into flames
chlorine	glows brightly
bromine	glows dull red
iodine	changes colour

A halogens and heated iron wool

 1 Astatine, symbol At, is found below iodine in the halogen group.

   a Write a word equation for the reaction of astatine with iron wool.

   b How will this reaction compare with chlorine? Explain your answer.

 2 Write a balanced equation for the formation of magnesium iodide (MgI_2) from its elements.

The order of reactivity of halogens can also be worked out using **displacement reactions**. In a displacement reaction, a more reactive element takes the place of a less reactive element in an ionic compound. So, a more reactive halogen displaces a less reactive halogen from a halide compound. For example, chlorine displaces bromine from sodium bromide in solution, but bromine cannot displace chlorine from sodium chloride.

$Cl_2(aq) + 2NaBr(aq) \rightarrow Br_2(aq) + 2NaCl(aq)$
chlorine + sodium bromide → bromine + sodium chloride

 3 Which of the following pairs of substances do not react? Explain your choice.

   a $Br_2 + LiCl$ **b** $Cl_2 + NaI$

 4 Write a balanced equation, with state symbols, for the reaction that occurs in photo C.

 5 What would be observed if bromine gas were bubbled through potassium iodide solution?

To explain the trend in reactivity we need to look at the electronic configuration of the halogen atoms.

Group 7 atoms gain one electron when they react. Down the group, the distance between the outermost shell containing electrons and the nucleus increases. This means that the force of attraction between the positive nucleus and an incoming negative electron decreases, and so the ions do not form so easily and the reactivity decreases.

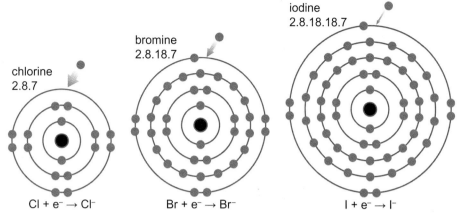

chlorine 2.8.7

bromine 2.8.18.7

iodine 2.8.18.18.7

$Cl + e^- \rightarrow Cl^-$ $Br + e^- \rightarrow Br^-$ $I + e^- \rightarrow I^-$

D Going down group 7, the outermost electron shell gets further from the nucleus and the ions are less readily formed.

 6 Explain why fluorine is the most reactive halogen and astatine is the least reactive halogen.

H Redox

When a metal reacts with oxygen it loses electrons and so we can define **oxidation** as a 'loss of electrons'. **Reduction** is the opposite and is a 'gain of electrons'. Use the mnemonic 'OILRIG' to remember that 'Oxidation Is Loss, Reduction Is Gain'. These two processes occur at the same time in displacement reactions, which makes them examples of reduction–oxidation or **redox** reactions.

Diagram E shows the reaction between fluorine atoms and chloride ions. As the fluorine atoms are **reduced**, by gaining electrons, the chloride ions are **oxidised**, by losing electrons.

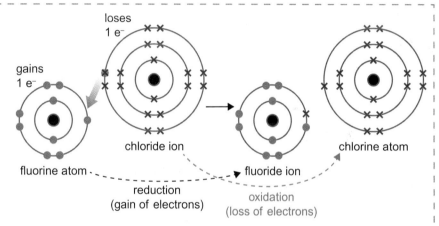

gains 1 e⁻

loses 1 e⁻

fluorine atom

chloride ion

fluoride ion

chlorine atom

reduction (gain of electrons)

oxidation (loss of electrons)

E Fluorine gains electrons more readily than chlorine. It displaces chlorine from chloride ions: $F_2(g) + 2Cl^-(aq) \rightarrow 2F^-(aq) + Cl_2(g)$

 7 a What happens in all redox reactions?

     b Identify the substances that are oxidised and reduced in the reaction below. Explain your choice.

$$2Na(s) + Br_2(g) \rightarrow 2NaBr(s)$$

8 Write an ionic equation with state symbols for the reaction that occurs in question 5.

Checkpoint

How confidently can you answer the Progression questions?

Strengthen

S1 Design a summary table or diagram to describe and explain the trend in reactivity of the halogens.

Extend

E1 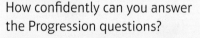 Use a displacement reaction to explain what is meant by 'redox reactions'.

Exam-style question

Compare the trends in melting point and reactivity of group 1 and group 7 elements. *(3 marks)*

CC13d Group 0

Specification reference: C6.14; C6.15; C6.16

Progression questions

- Why are the noble gases unreactive?
- How can noble gases be used?
- What trends are there in the physical properties of the noble gases?

Noble gas	Melting point (°C)	Boiling point (°C)	Density (g/cm³)
helium	−272	−269	0.00018
neon	−249	−246	0.0009
argon	−189	−186	0.0018
krypton	−157	−153	0.0038

A physical properties of noble gases

The **noble gases** are in group 0. They:

- are colourless
- have very low melting and boiling points
- are poor conductors of heat and electricity.

The data in table A clearly shows that there are trends in the physical properties of group 0 elements.

The unique property of the noble gas elements is that they are **inert**, which means they do not react easily with anything. Noble gases all exist as single atoms, because they do not form bonds easily with other atoms.

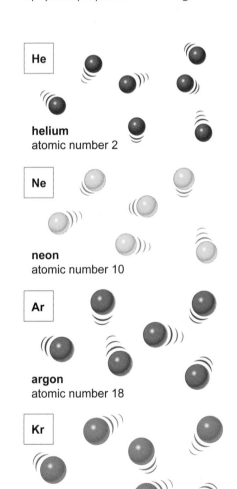

He
helium
atomic number 2

Ne
neon
atomic number 10

Ar
argon
atomic number 18

Kr
krypton
atomic number 36

B Noble gases exist as single atoms with no strong bonds between the atoms.

 1 a Describe the trend in density in group 0.

 b Predict the melting and boiling points of the fifth noble gas, xenon.

 c Explain how you made your prediction.

2 Nitrogen gas, formula N_2, is an inert gas. In what way is nitrogen:

 a similar to neon **b** different from neon?

 3 Explain which noble gas-filled balloons will float upwards in air. The density of air is about 0.0012 g/cm³.

The noble gas group was not known until the end of the 19th century. These elements were difficult to detect because they did not react with anything. There are only very small amounts of each noble gas in our atmosphere.

Noble gas	% in the atmosphere
helium	0.00052
neon	0.0018
argon	0.934
krypton	0.00011
xenon	0.000009

C noble gases in the atmosphere

 4 Suggest why the noble gases did not appear in Mendeleev's first periodic table.

5 Look at table C.

 a Place the noble gases in order of increasing abundance in the atmosphere.

 b Explain why it was easier to discover oxygen gas than argon.

The noble gases have a variety of uses because of their unique properties.

Krypton is used in photography lighting. It produces a brilliant white light when electricity is passed through it.

Argon is denser than air. It is added to the space above the wine in wine barrels to stop oxygen in the air reacting with the wine.

Helium has a very low density and is non-flammable, so it is used in weather balloons and airships.

Neon produces a distinctive red-orange light when electricity is passed through it. This property makes it useful for making long-lasting illuminated signs.

D helium-filled balloons

E a neon-filled advertising sign

To explain why noble gases are unreactive, we need to look at their electronic configurations. Diagram F shows that all noble gases have a complete outer shell of electrons. It has been shown that, when atoms form bonds, they can become more stable. They do this by gaining, losing or sharing electrons to get an electronic configuration like a noble gas. So noble gases are unreactive because their atoms already have a stable electronic configuration with a complete outer shell.

 6 a Explain how the properties of helium gas make it useful for weather balloons.

 b Explain why argon can be used in fire extinguishers.

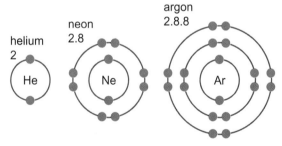

helium
2

neon
2.8

argon
2.8.8

He   Ne   Ar

F Noble gases do not react as they already have a complete outer shell of electrons.

 7 Explain why argon is very unreactive while potassium, with one more electron, is very reactive.

Checkpoint

How confidently can you answer the Progression questions?

Strengthen

S1 Explain how the electronic configuration of noble gases affects their properties.

Extend

E1 The noble gas radon is radioactive. Use the information on these two pages to predict other properties of radon.

Exam-style question

Neon is a colourless inert gas.

a Describe what the term inert tells you about neon.   *(1 mark)*

b Explain why neon exists as single atoms.   *(2 marks)*

CC14a Rates of reaction

Specification reference: C7.2; C7.5

Progression questions

- What changes can occur as a reaction proceeds?
- How can we investigate rates of reaction?
- How are graphs used to show rates of reaction?

A The combustion of the wood is a faster reaction than the baking of the pizzas.

New substances are always formed in chemical reactions. The **rate** of a reaction is the speed at which **reactants** are turned into **products**. Rates vary greatly, from very slow (e.g. the rusting of iron) to almost instantaneous (e.g. explosions, precipitation reactions). However, we can control rates of reaction by altering **variables**, such as the concentration of solutions and the size of pieces of solid reactant.

 1 Describe one example of a very fast and a very slow chemical reaction.

To investigate reaction rates, we need to be able to measure how the amount of reactants or products changes with time. Graph B shows how the concentrations change during a reaction. The gradient (slope) of the graph indicates the rate: the steeper the graph, the faster the reaction. Reaction rates are usually fastest at the start because that is when the concentration of the reactants is greatest.

Did you know?

Japanese scientists have developed a camera to observe extremely fast reactions. The camera records 4.4 trillion frames per second. A good smartphone would need over 1000 years to record as many frames as this camera records in the blink of an eye.

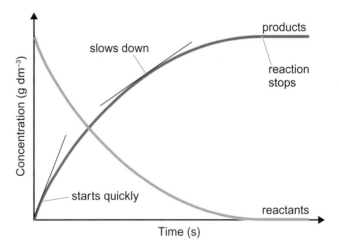

B Reactions are usually fastest at the start.

2 What happens to the concentration of reactants and products during a reaction?

We can also monitor rates by measuring changes in the mass or volume of reactants or products.

In the reaction between magnesium and sulfuric acid, shown in diagram C, we can follow the reaction by measuring the volume of hydrogen gas produced.

3 Why do most reactions slow down in time?

$$Mg(s) + H_2SO_4(aq) \rightarrow MgSO_4(aq) + H_2(g)$$

The results show the difference between using magnesium ribbon and magnesium granules. The graph for the granules is steeper and levels off more quickly. This shows that the granules, which are smaller pieces of solid than the ribbon, react more quickly.

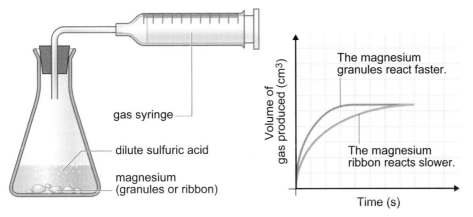

C In this experiment only the size of the pieces of magnesium is changed. All other variables are kept constant.

In the reaction between marble (calcium carbonate) and hydrochloric acid, shown in diagram D, we can follow the rate by measuring the change in mass. The mass decreases as carbon dioxide gas escapes from the flask.

$$CaCO_3(s) + 2HCl(aq) \rightarrow CaCl_2(aq) + H_2O(l) + CO_2(g)$$

6 Calcium carbonate is left at the end of the reaction shown in diagram D.

a Which reactant has been used up?

b How do you know when the reaction is complete?

c Sketch a graph to show how the mass of the flask will change as the reaction proceeds.

— cotton wool to stop acid 'spray' escaping

— dilute hydrochloric acid

marble chips —

balance

D As the reaction proceeds, the mass of the flask and contents will decrease.

7 Why would it be difficult to measure the reaction rate for the rusting of iron?

Exam-style question

When copper carbonate reacts with sulfuric acid, carbon dioxide gas is formed. Explain how an electronic balance could be used to investigate the rate of this reaction. *(2 marks)*

 4 **a** What piece of apparatus can be used to measure gas volumes accurately?

 b Explain why measuring gas volume can be used to monitor the rates of some reactions.

 5 How does the graph in diagram C show that magnesium granules react faster than ribbon?

Checkpoint

How confidently can you answer the Progression questions?

Strengthen

S1 Look at the reaction in diagram D.

a What is being measured in this experiment?

b What happens to the concentration of the acid as the reaction proceeds?

c What other change could be measured to follow this reaction?

Extend

E1 Describe, including diagrams, how you could use a gas syringe to investigate the correlation between temperature and the rate of the reaction between magnesium and hydrochloric acid.

CC14b Factors affecting reaction rates

Specification reference: C7.3; C7.4

Progression questions

- What has to happen for two particles to react?
- How does the speed of particles affect the rate of reaction?
- Why do changes in temperature, concentration, surface area and pressure affect rates of reaction?

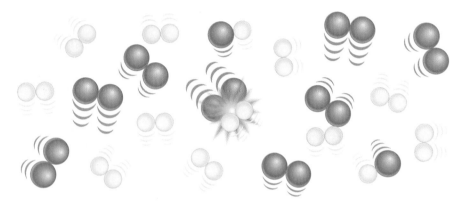

A The faster-moving hydrogen and chlorine molecules have more energy, and are more likely to react.

B The natural methane leaking out of these rocks has been burning for decades, having been set alight by lightning.

For chemical reactions to occur the reactant particles must collide or 'bump' together with enough energy to react. The minimum amount of energy needed for a reaction to occur is called its **activation energy**. During successful collisions, this energy helps to break bonds, so that the atoms can be rearranged to make new substances (the products of the reaction).

 1 What two things must happen before hydrogen and chlorine can react?

When methane and air are mixed the molecules collide, but no reaction occurs until a spark or flame provides the activation energy needed. The reaction then keeps going because the reaction releases energy, which then provides the activation energy needed. Reactions which release energy are described as **exothermic** changes.

A few chemical reactions need to take in energy to occur. These reactions, called **endothermic** changes, will not keep going unless energy is continually supplied. For example, the electrolysis of copper chloride needs a continuous supply of electrical energy.

 2 Why does a Bunsen burner not light as soon as you turn on the gas?

 3 What is the activation energy of a reaction?

 4 State two changes that would make the reaction in diagram A slower.

In general, reaction rates are increased when the energy of the collisions is increased, and when the frequency is increased (the number of collisions in a certain amount of time). More collisions occur if the particles are closer together or moving faster. The particles in any substance have a range of energies, but only those with enough energy can react. More collisions will be successful if more of the particles have the activation energy required.

Concentration and reaction rate

Change: Increasing the concentration of solutions increases the rate of reaction.

Explanation: There are more reacting particles in the same volume so collisions occur more often.

low concentration   higher concentration

C

Surface area and reaction rate

Change: Increasing the surface area to volume ratio, by decreasing the size of solid pieces while keeping the total volume of solid the same, increases the rate of the reaction.

Explanation: There is more surface for collisions to occur on, so collisions occur more often.

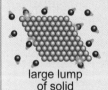 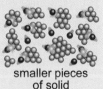

large lump of solid   smaller pieces of solid

D

Pressure of gases and reaction rate

Change: Increasing the pressure of gases increases the rate of reaction.

Explanation: The reactant particles are squeezed closer together so collisions occur more often.

lower pressure   higher pressure

E

Temperature and reaction rate

Change: Increasing the temperature increases the rate of reaction.

Explanation: The reactant particles speed up and have more energy. They therefore collide more often and more particles have enough energy to react when they collide.

lower temperature   higher temperature

F

 7 Suggest a reason why reactions between gases are often slower than reactions between liquids at the same temperature.

5 **a** Which of the following burns most quickly in air: wood chips, wood dust or wood shavings?

b Explain your answer to part **a**.

c Explain how using pure oxygen instead of air would affect the rate of burning.

6 The reaction between hydrogen (H_2) and chlorine (Cl_2) gases produces hydrogen chloride (HCl) gas. For this reaction:

a write a balanced chemical equation, with state symbols

b explain how and why decreasing the gas pressures affects the rate

c explain how and why increasing the temperature affects the rate.

Checkpoint

How confidently can you answer the Progression questions?

Strengthen

S1 Use ideas about collisions and energy to explain how the rate of a reaction can be increased by changes in concentration, temperature and the size of pieces of a solid reactant.

Extend

E1 Explain four ways in which the rate of reaction between iron lumps and oxygen from the air can be increased.

Exam-style question

Explain why acid reacts faster with powdered chalk than with lumps of chalk. *(3 marks)*

Specification reference: C7.1

Aim

Investigate the effects of changing the conditions of a reaction on the rates of chemical reactions.

The progress of a chemical reaction can be measured by how the amounts of reactant or product change with time, or by the time taken for the reaction to reach a certain point.

Your task 1 – measuring volumes of gases

You are going to investigate the reaction between hydrochloric acid and marble chips (calcium carbonate) and how the surface area of the marble chips affects the rate. You will monitor the progress of the reaction by measuring the volume of carbon dioxide produced.

Method 1

Wear eye protection.

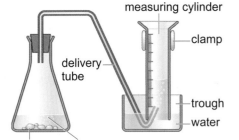

A investigating volumes of gas produced

A   Set up the apparatus as shown in diagram A.

B   Measure 40 cm³ of dilute hydrochloric acid into a conical flask.

C   Add 5 g of small marble chips to the flask.

D   Immediately stopper the flask and start the stop clock.

E   Note the total volume of gas produced after every 30 seconds until the reaction has finished.

F   Repeat the experiment using 5 g of larger marble chips.

Your task 2 – observing a colour change

You are going to investigate the effect of temperature on the rate of reaction between sodium thiosulfate and hydrochloric acid. You will monitor the progress of the reaction by observing a colour change (as shown in photo B).

Method 2

Wear eye protection.

B We can follow the rate of the reaction between sodium thiosulfate and hydrochloric acid by measuring the time taken for a 'cross' drawn beneath the reaction beaker to disappear.

G   Place 50 cm³ of sodium thiosulfate solution into a 300 cm³ conical flask.

H   Measure out 5 cm³ of dilute hydrochloric acid in a test tube.

I   Clamp the conical flask in place in a water bath at a certain temperature. Place the test tube in a rack in the same water bath. Record this temperature.

J   After 5 minutes, remove the flask and place it on a piece of white paper marked with a cross.

K   Add the acid to the thiosulfate and start the stop clock.

L Looking down from above, stop the clock when the cross disappears.

M Note this time and take the final temperature of the mixture.

N Repeat at three or four other temperatures, between 20 and 50 °C.

Exam-style questions

Look at Method 1.

1 Write a word equation and a balanced symbol equation for this reaction. *(4 marks)*

2 a State the dependent and independent variables in this investigation. *(2 marks)*

   b State two control variables. *(2 marks)*

3 a State why you must immediately stopper the flask in step D. *(1 mark)*

   b State the apparatus you would use to measure the mass of the marble chips. *(1 mark)*

4 Look at graph C.

   a State when the reaction is complete. Explain your answer. *(2 marks)*

   b Sketch graph C and add a curve that would be produced by smaller marble chips. *(2 marks)*

   c Use graph C to calculate the average reaction rate in cm^3/min between 45 and 105 seconds. Show your working. *(2 marks)*

   d Describe how you would use a tangent line to estimate the reaction rate in cm^3/min at 100 seconds. *(3 marks)*

5 Describe how you would modify Method 1 to investigate the effect of temperature on the rate of this reaction.

6 State one further variable that would effect the rate of this reaction. *(1 mark)*

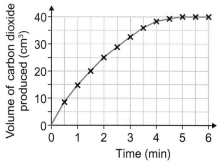

C volume of gas collected in the reaction between hydrochloric acid and marble chips

Look at Method 2.

7 State why the investigation would be improved by measuring the initial temperature of the reaction mixture (just after the acid is added) and then measuring the final temperature (when the reaction is finished). *(2 marks)*

8 Some results from the experiment in method 2 are shown in table D.

   a State why the cross disappears. *(1 mark)*

   b Sketch a graph of the results (no graph paper required) with temperature on the horizontal axis. *(3 marks)*

   c Explain what these results tell us about the effect of temperature on the rate of this reaction. *(2 marks)*

   d Describe one way of improving the results obtained from this investigation. *(1 mark)*

Average temperature (°C)	Time for cross to disappear (s)
20	165
30	81
40	42
50	21

D

CC14c Catalysts and activation energy

Specification reference: C7.6; C7.7; C7.8

Progression questions

- What is a catalyst?
- How do catalysts work?
- What are enzymes used for?

Add a small amount of the catalyst manganese dioxide.

Hydrogen peroxide decomposes very slowly at room temperature.

The catalyst makes the hydrogen peroxide decompose rapidly.

A The catalyst is not used up. So, if 1 g of manganese dioxide is added at the start, then 1 g will be recovered at the end.

Catalysts are substances that speed up chemical reactions without being permanently changed themselves and without altering the products of the reaction. Photo A shows the effect of a catalyst (manganese dioxide) on the decomposition of hydrogen peroxide.

Catalysts are often used in industry. For example, platinum is used as a catalyst in the manufacture of nitric acid from ammonia. These catalysts make industrial processes more profitable, by making products more quickly, and by allowing reactions to occur at lower temperatures, which saves costs. Catalysts also do not usually need to be replaced because they are not used up.

We can think about catalysts by using an analogy. In diagram B, the starting point and the finishing point are the same for all cars. However, those following the scenic route need more energy at the start to get over the hill. So, in terms of energy, most cars will use the road through the tunnel, which is the easier route.

 1 Explain how catalysts reduce the costs in industrial processes.

 2 Platinum is a very expensive catalyst. Why might this not matter?

 3 How could you show that the manganese dioxide in photo A was not used up?

B Not all cars have enough energy to go over the hill.

Like the tunnel, a catalyst provides an alternative reaction route, which requires less activation energy. **Reaction profiles** like graph C can be used to show the energy changes for a catalysed and an uncatalysed exothermic reaction. The catalyst does not alter the overall energy change. However, since less energy is needed to start the reaction, more reactant molecules have enough energy and so more collisions are successful. This means that the reaction is faster.

Did you know?

Many washing powders contain biological catalysts called enzymes to help break down different types of stains: proteases break down proteins like blood and egg, amylases break down starches and lipases break down fats and grease.

4 Explain whether a reaction with a high or low activation energy would be faster.

 5 In terms of energy changes, what is the same for catalysed and uncatalysed reactions?

In catalytic converters in car exhausts (shown in diagram D) the catalysts are platinum and palladium. Their presence lowers the activation energy needed to convert harmful gases into harmless gases. The metals used are expensive but don't need to be replaced as they are not used up.

6 Explain why the iron catalyst used in the manufacture of ammonia:

 a is in the form of small lumps

 b does not need to be replaced often.

Enzymes are large complex **protein** molecules that act as catalysts in biological reactions. Each enzyme molecule has a part with a specific shape called the **active site**. The reactant molecules (**substrates**) fit the shape of the active site, a bit like a 'lock and key'. So each enzyme only fits one substrate and only catalyses one specific reaction. Enzymes are sensitive to changes in temperature and pH as these can **denature** their molecules (make them change shape) so they will not work.

Enzymes are essential in living things and many industries. For example, alcoholic drinks are produced using an enzyme in yeast. This enzyme catalyses the reaction in which glucose is converted into ethanol (alcohol) and carbon dioxide.

 7 a Give an example of an enzyme and the reaction it catalyses.

 b Why will the enzyme not catalyse other reactions?

 8 Explain why heating a reaction involving a catalyst will usually make it faster but heating an enzyme-catalysed reaction can make it slower.

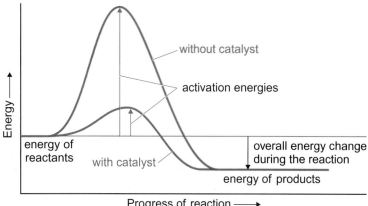

C This reaction profile shows that a catalyst lowers the activation energy.

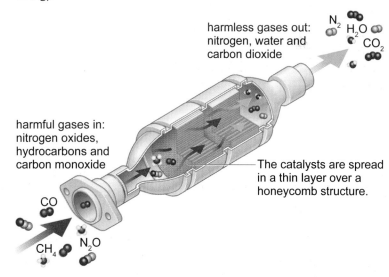

D The honeycomb structure gives the catalyst a large surface area.

Exam-style question

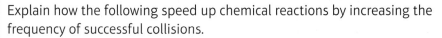

Explain how the following speed up chemical reactions by increasing the frequency of successful collisions.

a using a catalyst (2 marks)

b increasing the temperature (2 marks)

Checkpoint

How confidently can you answer the Progression questions?

Strengthen

S1 Explain, in terms of activation energy, how catalysts and enzymes work and why they are useful in industrial chemical reactions.

Extend

E1 Compare and contrast chemical catalysts and biological catalysts.

CC15a Exothermic and endothermic reactions

Specification reference: C7.9; C7.10; C7.11

Progression questions

- What are exothermic and endothermic reactions?
- What are some examples of exothermic and endothermic reactions?
- How can heat changes in solution be investigated?

A This self-heating can uses an exothermic reaction between sodium hydroxide pellets and water.

Energy is transferred between the surroundings and the reactants during chemical reactions. Energy is most often transferred by heating. Chemical reactions can be described as:

- **exothermic** – energy is transferred from stores of energy in chemical bonds to the surroundings.
- **endothermic** – energy is transferred from the surroundings to stores of energy in chemical bonds.

 1 Explain why combustion reactions are described as being exothermic.

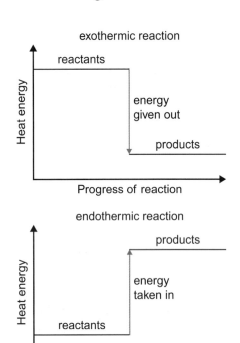

C simple reaction profiles

B Combustion reactions are exothermic.

You can use a **reaction profile** to model the energy change during a chemical reaction. In these diagrams, energy stored in bonds is represented as a horizontal line. The greater the energy stored, the higher the line.

 2 Explain how you can tell from its reaction profile whether a reaction is exothermic or endothermic.

 3 Sherbet sweets contain citric acid and sodium hydrogen carbonate. These react together to produce sodium citrate, water and carbon dioxide. The reaction makes your mouth feel cold. Draw a reaction profile for this reaction, labelling each horizontal line with the names of the substances involved.

Temperature changes during reactions

During a chemical reaction, energy is transferred between the reacting substances and their surroundings. This is usually by heating, particularly if a reaction takes place in solution. The stored thermal (heat) energy in the solution increases during an exothermic reaction, and it decreases during an endothermic reaction. This means you can determine whether a reaction in solution is exothermic or endothermic:

- the temperature increases in an exothermic reaction
- the temperature decreases in an endothermic reaction.

Diagram D shows a simple apparatus for these investigations.

 4 Explain why a lid and a *polystyrene* cup are used when investigating temperature changes in solution.

In **precipitation** reactions, an insoluble product forms from two solutions. For example:

$$AgNO_3(aq) + NaCl(aq) \rightarrow NaNO_3(aq) + AgCl(s)$$

Precipitation reactions can be exothermic or endothermic, depending on the substances involved. However, two types of reactions are always exothermic:

- **neutralisation**, the reaction between an acid and a base
- **displacement**, the reaction between a metal and a compound of a less reactive metal, or between a halogen and a compound of a less reactive halogen.

When a salt dissolves in water, the change is exothermic or endothermic, depending on the salt. The temperature increases as calcium chloride dissolves, but it decreases when ammonium chloride dissolves.

 5 Explain the temperature change you would expect when sodium hydroxide dissolves in water.

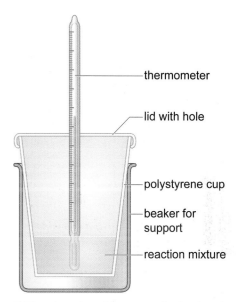

- thermometer
- lid with hole
- polystyrene cup
- beaker for support
- reaction mixture

D The air trapped between the beaker and the cup reduces energy transfers by heating, to and from the surroundings.

Checkpoint

How confidently can you answer the Progression questions?

Strengthen

S1 How can you work out whether a reaction in solution is exothermic or endothermic?

Extend

E1 The temperature changes in displacement reactions between metals and solutions of metal compounds can be used to determine a reactivity series. Explain which variables should be controlled to obtain valid results.

Exam-style question

Sodium carbonate solution reacts with calcium chloride solution. A precipitate of calcium carbonate forms. A student carries out an experiment to measure the temperature change in this reaction. These are her results:

temperature of reactants = 21 °C

final temperature of mixture = 12 °C

Explain what this shows about the type of energy change that happens.

(2 marks)

CC15b Energy changes in reactions

Specification reference: C7.12; C7.13; **H** C7.14; C7.15; C7.16

Progression questions

- How can exothermic and endothermic reactions be explained in terms of bonds?
- How are exothermic and endothermic reactions modelled?
- **H** How are energy changes in reactions calculated?

A These bikes are fuelled with pure methanol.

Reactions happen when reactant particles collide with each other with sufficient energy. The **activation energy** is the minimum amount of energy needed by colliding particles for a reaction to happen. Precipitation and neutralisation reactions have low activation energies, and start as soon as the reactants are mixed. Combustion reactions have higher activation energies.

 1 Explain why methanol needs a flame to start it burning.

You can model activation energy in a **reaction profile** by drawing a 'hump' between the reactants and products lines. Some reactions, such as combustion, have high activation energies and need energy from a spark or flame to start.

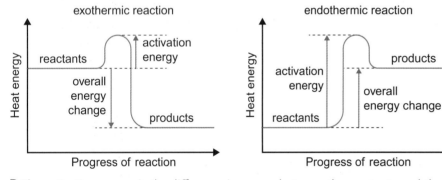

B The activation energy is the difference in energy between the reactants and the top of the 'hump'.

 2 Describe how the activation energy of a reaction is modelled on a reaction profile.

 3 Explain, in terms of bond breaking and bond making, why the combustion of methanol is an exothermic reaction.

Breaking and making bonds

During a chemical reaction, bonds in the reactants break and new bonds are made to form the products:

- energy is transferred to the reactants to break their bonds, so breaking bonds is endothermic
- energy is transferred to the surroundings as bonds form, so making bonds is exothermic.

A reaction is exothermic if more energy is given out making bonds than is needed to break bonds. A reaction is endothermic if less energy is given out making bonds than is needed to break bonds.

H Bond energy calculations

A **mole** of something is 6.02×10^{23} of them (see *CC9c Moles*).The energy needed to break one mole of a particular **covalent bond** is its **bond energy**, measured in kilojoules per mole (kJ/mol or kJ mol^{-1}). For example, the bond energy of a C–O bond is 358 kJ mol^{-1}. This means that 358 kJ must be taken in to break one mole of C–O bonds, and 358 kJ is given out when one mole of C–O bonds is made. Table C shows some bond energies.

You can use bond energies to calculate the energy change in a reaction, as shown in the worked example below.

Covalent bond	Bond energy (kJ mol^{-1})
C–O	358
C–H	413
H–H	436
O–H	464
O=O	498
C=O	805

C a selection of bond energies

Worked example

Methane burns completely in oxygen to form carbon dioxide and water:

$$H-\underset{H}{\overset{H}{C}}-H + 2(O=O) \longrightarrow O=C=O + 2\left(H\diagdown O \diagup H\right)$$

D

Calculate the energy change during this reaction.

Step 1 Calculate energy in (bonds broken)

4 × (C–H)	= 4 × 413	= 1652 kJ mol^{-1}
2 × (O=O)	= 2 × 498	= 996 kJ mol^{-1}
Total in	= 1652 + 996	= 2648 kJ mol^{-1}

Step 2 Calculate energy out (bonds made)

2 × (C=O)	= 2 × 805	= 1610 kJ mol^{-1}
4 × (O–H)	= 4 × 464	= 1856 kJ mol^{-1}
Total out	= 1610 + 1856	= 3466 kJ mol^{-1}

Step 3 Energy change = energy in – energy out

= 2648 – 3466 = –818 kJ mol^{-1}

The negative sign shows that the reaction is exothermic (endothermic reactions have a positive sign).

 4 Calculate the energy change when hydrogen reacts with oxygen:
2(H–H) + O=O → 2(H–O–H)

Did you know?

The strength of a given covalent bond differs between substances, and even between different places in the same molecule, so tables usually show mean bond energies.

Checkpoint

How confidently can you answer the Progression questions?

Strengthen

S1 What happens in exothermic and endothermic reactions when bonds are broken and made?

S2 What information do reaction profiles give us?

Extend

E1 Calculate the energy change when methanol undergoes complete combustion:
$CH_3OH + 1\tfrac{1}{2}O_2 \rightarrow CO_2 + 2H_2O$

Exam-style question

Explain, in terms of the energy involved in the breaking and making of bonds, why some reactions are endothermic. *(2 marks)*

Rates of reaction

Dilute hydrochloric acid reacts with solid calcium carbonate. A student carries out two experiments involving this reaction. She uses the same concentration of hydrochloric acid and the same mass of calcium carbonate each time. The table shows her results.

	Experiment 1	Experiment 2
calcium carbonate	lumps	powder
temperature of acid (°C)	22	45
reaction time (s)	225	25

Evaluate the student's results, explaining any difference in the rate of reaction between the two experiments in terms of particles.

(6 marks)

Student answer

I think the data shows that the reaction in experiment 2 is nine times faster than the same reaction in experiment 1 [1]. The greater rate of reaction in experiment 2 is for two reasons. Firstly, the particles in the powder have a greater surface area [2] than the particles in the lumps used in experiment 1. This means that more particles are exposed to the acid and there are more frequent collisions between reactant particles [3], so the rate of reaction is greater.

The increased rate of reaction is also due to the increased temperature of the acid. The reactant particles in experiment 2 have more energy than those in experiment 1. So, a greater proportion of them have the activation energy or more. This means that the frequency of successful collisions is greater, causing a greater rate of reaction.

It would have been better to vary the size of the particles and the temperature separately, but the data clearly shows that the rate of reaction in experiment 1 is greater than in experiment 2 [4].

[1] The reaction times given in the table are used to make a conclusion about the rates of reaction.

[2] An accurate answer should refer to the *surface area to volume ratio* of the particles, not just to their surface area.

[3] The answer should refer to *successful* collisions (as it does later), not just to collisions.

[4] The answer finishes by looking at the data and the experiment, and evaluating how strong the conclusion is.

Verdict

This is a strong answer. It comes to a clear conclusion about the data. The answer uses scientific knowledge to link the greater rate of reaction in experiment 2 to the energy and frequency of particle collisions.

Exam tip

When you are asked to evaluate data, you must use it to form a conclusion. This may include interpreting and explaining the information, or considering its strengths and weaknesses.

Paper 4

CC16 Fuels /
CC17 Earth and Atmospheric Science

Crude oil and natural gas are mostly used to provide fuels. However, burning oil and natural gas produces carbon dioxide, which is thought to be changing our atmosphere and climate. The photo shows a jet fighter, in which the fuel is kerosene (one of the 'fractions' that crude oil can be split into). The long flame is caused by its afterburner. Extra fuel is injected into the hot exhaust gases, producing additional thrust.

Crude oil also gives us the raw materials needed to make a huge range of products, including polymers such as polythene. Crude oil is, though, a finite resource and the substances we make from it are non-renewable. They will run out one day if we continue to use them.

The learning journey

Previously you will have learnt at KS3:

- that mixtures may be separated using fractional distillation
- about fuels and energy resources
- about the acidity of non-metal oxides
- about the production of carbon dioxide by human activity and the impact on climate.

In this unit you will learn:

- about the hydrocarbons found in crude oil and natural gas
- how crude oil is separated into useful fractions
- about the alkanes as an homologous series
- about the problems caused by some atmospheric pollutants
- how and why cracking of oil fractions is carried out
- about the advantages and disadvantages of different fuels for cars
- about how the Earth's atmosphere has changed in the past and how it is changing now
- more about the causes and effects of climate change.

CC16a Hydrocarbons in crude oil and natural gas

Specification reference: C8.1; C8.2; C8.15

Progression questions

- What are hydrocarbons?
- Why is crude oil so useful?
- Why is crude oil a non-renewable, finite resource?

A Hydraulic fracturing or 'fracking' is one way to obtain fossil fuels. A mixture of water, sand and other substances is injected into underground rock at high pressure. Natural gas or crude oil flows from cracks in the rocks to the well head at the surface.

Natural gas and **crude oil** are natural resources formed from the ancient remains of microscopic animals and plants that once lived in the sea. These remains became covered by layers of sediment. Over millions of years, the remains gradually turned into natural gas and crude oil. The sediments turned into rock, trapping the gas and oil. These resources are **finite resources** because they are not made any more (or are being made extremely slowly), which limits the amounts available to us.

Crude oil

Crude oil is a complex mixture of **hydrocarbons**. A hydrocarbon is a compound that contains hydrogen and carbon atoms only. Carbon atoms can each form four covalent bonds, so the carbon atoms in hydrocarbon molecules are able to join together in different ways, forming chains and rings. The number of carbon atoms in a hydrocarbon molecule can vary from just one carbon atom to many hundreds of them.

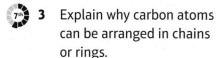 **1** Explain why natural gas and crude oil are finite resources.

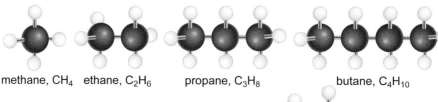

methane, CH_4 ethane, C_2H_6 propane, C_3H_8 butane, C_4H_{10}

methylbutane, C_5H_{12}

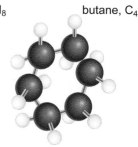

cyclohexane, C_6H_{12}

B These ball and stick models show some hydrocarbon molecules. The black spheres represent carbon atoms.

Hydrocarbons exist in different physical states, depending on the size and complexity of their molecules. Crude oil itself is liquid at room temperature, with hydrocarbons in the solid and gas states mixed with hydrocarbons in the liquid state.

2 Explain what is meant by the term hydrocarbon.

3 Explain why carbon atoms can be arranged in chains or rings.

Crude oil is an important source of useful substances, including:

- fuels for vehicles, aircraft, ships, heating and power stations
- **feedstock** or raw materials for the petrochemical industry.

Petrochemicals are substances made from crude oil, such as poly(ethene) and other polymers.

 4 Describe two reasons why crude oil is useful to us.

Fuels

Natural gas is a mixture of hydrocarbons in the gas state. Methane, the main hydrocarbon in natural gas, is useful for cooking.

Several different liquid fuels can be obtained from crude oil, including petrol and diesel oil for vehicles, and kerosene for aircraft. These **fossil fuels** are **non-renewable** – they are being used up faster than they are being formed. If we carry on using these fuels, they will run out one day.

C This oil industry engineer is pouring some crude oil into a container, ready for a test.

D Natural gas is used for domestic heating. This is a boiler with the cover taken off.

 5 Explain why diesel and methane are *non-renewable* fossil fuels.

Did you know?

The barrel is the unit of volume used by the oil industry. One barrel of oil is 159 litres. The world uses about 96 million barrels of oil each day – about 180 000 litres per second.

Checkpoint

How confidently can you answer the Progression questions?

Strengthen

S1 What are the main features of crude oil and the substances it contains?

S2 Why are crude oil and natural gas useful?

Extend

E1 Why is crude oil an important finite source of non-renewable substances?

Exam-style question

Octane, C_8H_{18}, is one of the substances found in petrol.

a Explain why octane is a hydrocarbon. *(2 marks)*

b State why petrol is non-renewable. *(1 mark)*

CC16b Fractional distillation of crude oil

Specification reference: C8.3; C8.4; C8.5

Progression questions

- How is crude oil separated into useful fractions?
- What are the names and uses of the main fractions from crude oil?
- What are the differences in the molecules found in different fractions from crude oil?

A Bitumen, a fraction obtained from crude oil, is mixed with small stones to make road surfaces.

Crude oil is usually not runny enough or ignited easily enough for it to be useful as a fuel. The different hydrocarbons it contains must be separated into simpler, more useful mixtures. This can be achieved using **fractional distillation** because the different hydrocarbons have different boiling points.

 1 State why crude oil can be separated using fractional distillation.

In the fractionating column

The industrial fractional distillation of crude oil happens in a tall metal **fractionating column**. Crude oil is heated strongly to **evaporate** it, and the hot vapours are piped into the bottom of the column, where:

- the column is hottest at the bottom and coldest at the top
- the vapours rise through the column and cool down
- the vapours **condense** when they reach a part of the column that is cool enough (below their boiling points)
- the liquid falls into a tray and is piped away
- the vapours with the lowest boiling points do not condense at all and leave at the top as a mixture of gases
- bitumen has the highest boiling point and leaves at the bottom as a hot liquid.

The separated liquids and gases are called oil **fractions** because they are only parts of the original crude oil.

B Fractional distillation of crude oil happens at oil refineries.

 2 Make a table to summarise the names and uses of the six main oil fractions.

 3 Explain where changes of state happen during fractional distillation of crude oil.

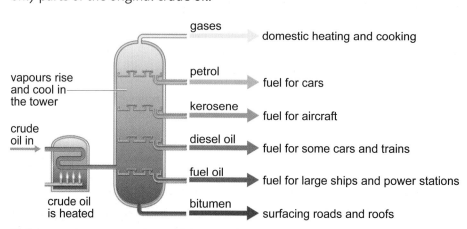

C These are the names and uses of the main fractions leaving an oil fractionating column.

Properties of fractions

Each fraction is a mixture of hydrocarbons, rather than a pure hydrocarbon. However, the hydrocarbons in a given fraction have similar numbers of carbon and hydrogen atoms in their molecules, and similar boiling points.

Different fractions have different uses because they have different properties. For example:

- the hydrocarbons in the gases fraction have the lowest **viscosity** (they flow easily) and are easiest to **ignite** (they are easily set alight), making them suitable for use as fuels
- bitumen is solid at room temperature, and waterproof, making it suitable for surfacing roads and roofs.

The other fractions are liquids at room temperature.

Fraction	Number of atoms in molecules	Boiling point	Ease of ignition	Viscosity
gases	smallest (1–4 carbon atoms)	lowest (<0 °C)	easy to ignite	lowest (flows most easily)
petrol				
kerosene				
diesel oil				
fuel oil				
bitumen	greatest (>35 carbon atoms)	highest (>350 °C)	difficult to ignite	highest (flows with difficulty)

D trends in the properties of the fractions leaving an oil fractionating column

 4 Describe the properties of kerosene that make it suitable for use as an aircraft fuel.

 5 Describe the relationships between the number of carbon atoms in a hydrocarbon molecule and the physical properties of the hydrocarbon.

Checkpoint

How confidently can you answer the Progression questions?

Strengthen

S1 How does fractional distillation of crude oil work?

S2 What do the substances in a crude oil fraction have in common?

Extend

E1 How is crude oil made into useful mixtures?

E2 Describe how the hydrocarbons in different fractions differ from each other.

Exam-style question

Petrol and fuel oil are different fractions separated from crude oil. Describe the difference in *one* physical property between these two fractions. *(2 marks)*

CC16c The alkane homologous series

Specification reference: C8.5; C8.6

Progression questions

- What is the main type of hydrocarbon found in crude oil?
- What are the features of an homologous series of compounds?
- Why do alkanes form an homologous series?

A Methane, CH_4, is the simplest alkane. It is transported in large amounts as liquefied natural gas (LNG). It is distributed as a gas to homes and businesses through a network of pipelines.

The compounds in crude oil fractions are mostly **alkanes**. Alkanes are hydrocarbons that only have single covalent bonds between the atoms in their molecules. The alkanes form a 'family' or **homologous series** of compounds. There are several different homologous series but the members of a series have these features in common:

- the molecular formulae of neighbouring compounds differ by CH_2
- they have the same general formula (see the next page)
- they show a gradual variation in physical properties, such as their boiling points
- they have similar chemical properties.

 1 Name the homologous series of compounds that make up most of crude oil.

Molecular formulae

The table shows information about the first three alkanes.

Name	Molecular formula	Structural formula
methane	CH_4	H H—C—H H
ethane	C_2H_6	H H H—C—C—H H H
propane	C_3H_8	H H H H—C—C—C—H H H H

B names and formulae of the first three alkanes

Going from ethane to propane, the number of carbon atoms increases by 1 and the number of hydrogen atoms increases by 2. You can see this in their **molecular formulae**, which show the actual numbers of atoms of each element in the molecules of these compounds. The molecular formula changes by CH_2 going from C_2H_6 to C_3H_8. You might find this easier to see in the **structural formulae** of ethane and propane. It looks as if an extra CH_2 group of atoms is fitted in between the two CH_3 groups of atoms.

 2 Describe the difference between the molecular formulae of methane and ethane.

General formulae

A **general formula** represents the formula for a whole homologous series. The general formula for the alkanes is: C_nH_{2n+2}. This means that the number of hydrogen atoms is twice the number of carbon atoms, plus two. For example, propane molecules have three carbon atoms, so:

- $n = 3$, and $2n+2 = (2 \times 3) + 2 = 8$
- the molecular formula is C_3H_8.

Trends in physical properties

The graph shows how the boiling points of alkanes change as the number of carbon atoms in the molecules increases. Notice that there is a gradual variation in this physical property. The difference in boiling points of the alkanes is the reason why alkanes in crude oil can be separated by fractional distillation.

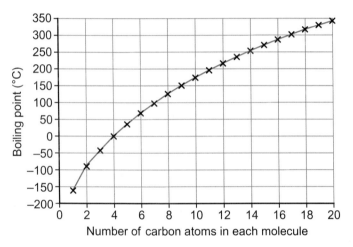

C The boiling point of a straight-chain alkane depends upon the size of its molecules.

Similar chemical properties

The alkanes have similar chemical properties. For example, they react with excess oxygen to produce carbon dioxide and water. These are the equations for propane, found in camping gas:

propane + oxygen → carbon dioxide + water

$$C_3H_8 + 5O_2 \rightarrow 3CO_2 + 4H_2O$$

5 Methane reacts with excess oxygen. For this reaction, write:

 a the word equation

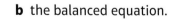 **b** the balanced equation.

Exam-style question

Ethene, C_2H_4, is a member of the alkene homologous series. The next two alkenes are propene, C_3H_6, and butene, C_4H_8. Explain why these three hydrocarbons are members of the same homologous series. *(2 marks)*

 3 Give the molecular formulae for:

a butane (an alkane with four carbon atoms)

 b hexadecane (an alkane with 16 carbon atoms).

Did you know?

The carbon atoms in alkanes can be arranged so there are branches as well as straight chains. There are only two ways to arrange the carbon atoms with butane but over 10 000 ways to do this with hexadecane.

 4 Describe how the boiling points of alkanes change as the number of carbon atoms in the molecules changes.

Checkpoint

How confidently can you answer the Progression questions?

Strengthen

S1 What are the features of an homologous series?

Extend

E1 Explain why the main components of crude oil fo an homologous series.

CC16d Complete and incomplete combustion

Specification reference: C8.7; C8.8; C8.9; C8.10

Progression questions

- What happens during the complete combustion of a hydrocarbon?
- What happens during the incomplete combustion of a hydrocarbon?
- What problems does incomplete combustion cause?

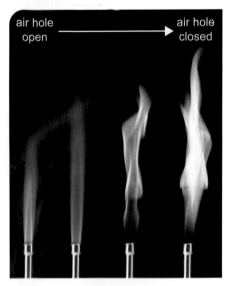

A Adjusting the air hole on a Bunsen burner alters the amount of air reaching the fuel, and changes the flame.

Hydrocarbon fuels react with oxygen in the air when they burn. This is an example of an **oxidation** reaction and is called **combustion**.

Complete combustion

Complete combustion of a hydrocarbon is a reaction in which:

- only carbon dioxide and water are produced
- energy is given out.

Complete combustion happens when there is a plentiful supply of air or oxygen, for example when the air hole on a Bunsen burner is fully open. Methane is the main hydrocarbon found in natural gas:

$$methane + oxygen \rightarrow carbon\ dioxide + water$$
$$CH_4 + 2O_2 \rightarrow CO_2 + 2H_2O$$

 1 Write the balanced equation for the complete combustion of pentane, C_5H_{12}.

The apparatus in photo B is used to investigate combustion. A pump draws combustion products from the Bunsen burner through the apparatus. Iced water cools and condenses water vapour passing through the U-shaped tube. White anhydrous copper sulfate in the U-shaped tube turns into blue hydrated copper sulfate, showing the presence of water. Limewater in the boiling tube turns milky, showing the presence of carbon dioxide.

2 Describe laboratory tests for water and for carbon dioxide.

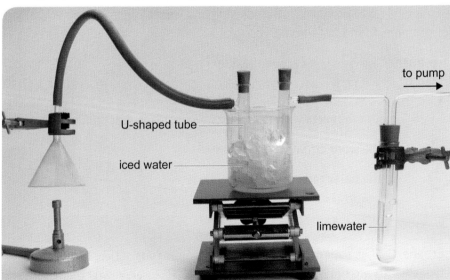

B This apparatus is used to investigate combustion products.

Incomplete combustion

Incomplete combustion happens when there is a limited supply of air or oxygen, such as when the air hole on a Bunsen burner is closed. During the incomplete combustion of a hydrocarbon:

- water is produced
- energy is given out (but less than with complete combustion)
- **carbon monoxide**, CO, and carbon are produced.

Some carbon atoms in the hydrocarbon may still be fully oxidised to carbon dioxide, but some are only partially oxidised to carbon monoxide. Some carbon atoms are released as smoke and **soot**.

Incomplete combustion problems

Incomplete combustion can cause problems in appliances that use hydrocarbon fuels, such as boilers and heaters, if they are poorly maintained or unventilated. Carbon monoxide is a **toxic** gas. It combines with **haemoglobin** in **red blood cells**, preventing oxygen combining. This reduces the amount of oxygen carried in the bloodstream, causing affected people to feel sleepy or to become unconscious. Severe carbon monoxide poisoning can even cause death.

Soot can block the pipes carrying away waste gases from an appliance. It blackens buildings, and it can cause breathing problems if it collects in the lungs.

D This wall has been blackened by soot from the exhaust pipe of an old boiler.

 5 Describe *one* problem caused by soot.

Exam-style question

Describe a problem caused by *one* product of the incomplete combustion of natural gas. *(2 marks)*

 3 Explain why incomplete combustion of hydrocarbons can produce carbon monoxide and carbon.

C Carbon monoxide is colourless and odourless, so electronic carbon monoxide detectors are used in homes using natural gas for heating or cooking.

 4 Explain why carbon monoxide is a *toxic* gas.

Did you know?

After hydrogen, carbon monoxide is the second most common molecule in interstellar space.

Checkpoint

How confidently can you answer the Progression questions?

Strengthen

S1 Why can burning fuels in a lack of oxygen cause problems?

Extend

E1 Explain why adequate ventilation is important when using appliances fuelled by hydrocarbons.

CC16e Combustible fuels and pollution

Specification reference: C8.11; C8.12; C8.13

Progression questions

- Why do some hydrocarbon fuels release sulfur dioxide when they are used?
- Why are oxides of nitrogen produced by engines?
- What problems are caused by acid rain?

A The trees in this forest have died because of the effects of acid rain.

Carbon dioxide, like other soluble non-metal oxides, forms an acidic solution with water. Rain water is naturally acidic because it contains carbon dioxide from the air. **Acid rain** has a pH lower than 5.2, making it more acidic than natural rain water. Sulfur dioxide is a major cause of this extra acidity.

1 Name a substance that causes acid rain.

B New stonework and similar stonework (on the right) damaged by years of acid rain.

2 Write a balanced equation for the reaction between sulfur and oxygen.

3 Describe two environmental problems caused by sulfur dioxide dissolving in rain water.

4 Write the balanced equation for the reaction between calcium carbonate, $CaCO_3$, and sulfuric acid.

Sulfur dioxide

Hydrocarbon fuels (such as petrol and diesel oil) may contain sulfur compounds. These occur naturally as **impurities** and are not deliberately added. On the contrary, most of these impurities are removed at oil refineries in an attempt to reduce the environmental problems they cause. When the hydrocarbon fuel is burnt, the sulfur reacts with oxygen to form sulfur dioxide gas, SO_2.

Sulfur dioxide dissolves in the water in clouds to form a mixture of acids, including sulfurous acid:

$$H_2O(l) + SO_2(g) \rightarrow H_2SO_3(aq)$$

Sulfurous acid is oxidised by oxygen in the air to form sulfuric acid:

$$2H_2SO_3(aq) + O_2(g) \rightarrow 2H_2SO_4(aq)$$

This mixture of sulfurous acid and sulfuric acid causes problems when it falls as acid rain. Crops do not grow well when the soil is too acidic. Excess acidity in rivers and lakes prevents fish eggs hatching, and it can kill fish and insects.

Acid rain increases the rate of **weathering** of buildings made of limestone or marble, and breaks down their structures. These rocks are almost pure calcium carbonate, which reacts with sulfuric acid:

calcium carbonate + sulfuric acid → calcium sulfate + water + carbon dioxide

Acid rain also increases the rate of corrosion of metals, such as the iron in steel, weakening them:

iron + sulfuric acid → iron(II) sulfate + hydrogen

Oxides of nitrogen

Car engines are 'internal combustion' engines – fuel is mixed with air and ignited *inside* the engine. This causes temperatures high enough for nitrogen and oxygen in the air inside the engine to react together. The reactions produce various **oxides of nitrogen**, or NO_x, which are atmospheric **pollutants**.

C Spreading powdered limestone on a field reduces the acidity of the soil.

NO_x are a cause of acid rain. Nitrogen dioxide, NO_2, forms dilute nitric acid when it dissolves in the water in clouds. Nitrogen dioxide is a toxic red-brown gas, and it can cause respiratory diseases such as bronchitis. Catalytic converters in cars convert most of the NO_x in exhaust gases to harmless nitrogen.

D In sunlight, oxides of nitrogen react with other pollutants to form a harmful 'photochemical smog'.

 6 Catalytic converters can reduce nitrogen dioxide, forming nitrogen and oxygen. Write a balanced equation for this reaction.

Exam-style question

Large ships use fuel oil, which contains sulfur as an impurity. Explain why this can cause environmental problems when ships travel the oceans.   *(3 marks)*

5 Explain why:

 a the use of some hydrocarbon fuels causes the production of sulfur dioxide

 b oxides of nitrogen may be produced when hydrocarbon fuels are used.

Checkpoint

How confidently can you answer the Progression questions?

Strengthen

S1 Why are some non-metal oxides produced when hydrocarbon fuels are used in cars?

S2 What problems are caused by acid rain?

Extend

E1 How does the use of hydrocarbon fuels produce pollutants?

E2 Why might the problems caused by acid rain vary over time?

CC16f Breaking down hydrocarbons

Specification reference: C8.14; C8.16; C8.17

Progression questions

- Why is cracking needed?
- What happens during the cracking of crude oil fractions?
- What are the advantages and disadvantages of hydrogen and petrol as vehicle fuels?

A This storage building has stockpiles outside because the supply of the products is greater than the customers' demand for them.

When crude oil is separated by fractional distillation, the volume of each fraction usually does not match the volume that can be sold. The supply of some fractions is greater than customer demand, while the demand for other fractions is greater than the supply. Oil refineries use **cracking** to match supply with demand. Cracking also produces hydrocarbons with C=C bonds. These hydrocarbons are used to make polymers.

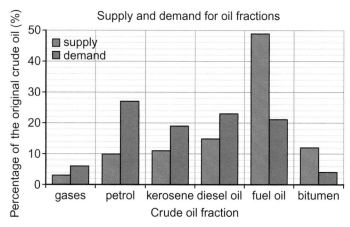

B example supply and demand for oil fractions

1 Use bar chart B to identify:

 a the fractions in higher supply than demand

 b the fractions in higher demand than supply.

Cracking

Cracking involves breaking covalent bonds in hydrocarbon molecules. Crude oil fractions are heated to evaporate them. The vapours are passed over a **catalyst** containing aluminium oxide and heated to about 650 °C. This speeds up reactions that break down larger hydrocarbon molecules. Smaller, more useful, hydrocarbon molecules form and these can be used as fuels or for making polymers. For example:

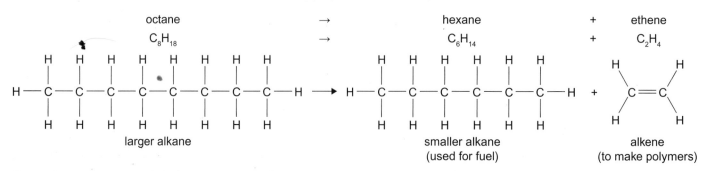

C a cracking reaction (modelled using structural formulae)

Notice that one of the products, ethene C_2H_4, is an **alkene**. Alkenes form a different homologous series to alkanes. Alkanes and alkenes are hydrocarbons, but:

- alkanes are **saturated** (their carbon atoms are joined by single bonds, C–C)
- alkenes are **unsaturated** (they contain a carbon–carbon double bond, C=C).

Fuels for cars

Petrol is in high demand for use as a fuel for cars. It is liquid at room temperature, so large amounts can be stored in the car's fuel tank and then pumped to the engine. Petrol is easily ignited, and its combustion releases large amounts of energy.

Hydrogen can also be used to fuel cars. It is a by-product of cracking and can also be produced by reacting methane (from natural gas) with steam. Unlike petrol and other hydrocarbon fuels, the combustion of hydrogen produces water vapour but no carbon dioxide. Hydrogen fuel has environmental benefits because carbon dioxide is a **greenhouse gas**, linked to global warming and climate change.

Like petrol, hydrogen is easily ignited and its combustion releases large amounts of energy. Unlike petrol, hydrogen is a gas at room temperature. This makes hydrogen difficult to store in large amounts unless it is compressed under high pressure or liquefied by cooling.

D In this car, electricity for an electric motor is generated by a fuel cell that uses hydrogen.

 5 Explain, in terms of hydrogen molecules, an advantage of storing hydrogen in the liquid state rather than in the gas state.

Exam-style question

Ethene, C_2H_4, is used to make poly(ethene). Ethene is produced by cracking crude oil fractions.

a Explain what is meant by the term cracking. *(2 marks)*

b Complete this equation: $C_8H_{18} \rightarrow 3C_2H_4 +$ .... *(1 mark)*

 2 Copy and complete this equation, which models a cracking reaction.

$$C_{16}H_{34} \rightarrow \text{.........} + C_2H_4$$

 3 Describe the difference between saturated and unsaturated hydrocarbons.

 4 Write a balanced equation, with state symbols, for the reaction between hydrogen and oxygen.

Did you know?

Scientists have discovered that graphene can store hydrogen. Roasted coconut or roasted chicken feathers work too.

Checkpoint

How confidently can you answer the Progression questions?

Strengthen

S1 How are crude oil fractions made more useful?

S2 What are the advantages and disadvantages of using hydrogen in cars, rather than petrol?

Extend

E1 How and why are relatively large alkanes broken down?

E2 What influences the choice of hydrogen or petrol as a fuel for cars?

CC17a The early atmosphere

Specification reference: C8.18; C8.19; C8.20

Progression questions

- What are the names of some common gases produced by volcanic activity?
- What evidence is there for the composition of the Earth's early atmosphere?
- How do scientists explain the formation of the oceans?

A Venus' atmosphere is 96.5% carbon dioxide and 3.5% nitrogen.

B Maat Mons (an 8 km high volcano on Venus) photographed by the NASA *Magellan* space probe

Did you know?

The largest volcano in the Solar System is on Mars. Called *Olympus Mons*, it is 27 km high (three times the height of Mount Everest).

Evidence indicates that significant changes have occurred to the **composition** of the Earth's **atmosphere** in its 4.5 billion year history. More recent changes are due to living organisms.

To investigate the atmosphere before life evolved, scientists look at evidence on Earth and study the atmospheres of other planets and moons. These bodies are unlikely to contain life, so their atmospheres may be similar to the Earth's early atmosphere.

 1 Explain why scientists study the atmospheres of other bodies in our Solar System.

Earth's early atmosphere

The Earth's early atmosphere is thought to have been mainly carbon dioxide, with smaller amounts of water vapour and other gases, and little or no oxygen.

Volcanoes affect the atmosphere by releasing large amounts of some gases, such as carbon dioxide and water vapour, and small amounts of other gases (including nitrogen). There was a lot of **volcanic activity** on the early Earth, so volcanoes probably helped form its atmosphere.

Earth, Venus and Mars are rocky planets with volcanoes. The atmospheres of Venus and Mars are mainly made of carbon dioxide, thought to have been released by volcanoes. This supports the idea that Earth's early atmosphere also contained lots of carbon dioxide.

Some scientists think that the Earth's early atmosphere was mainly nitrogen. Evidence for this comes from Titan, a moon of Saturn. Titan's atmosphere is 98.4% nitrogen, probably also released by volcanoes. However, space probes have shown that Titan has an icy interior, unlike Earth, Venus or Mars. So, Earth's early atmosphere is less likely to have been like Titan's.

 2 State how volcanoes affect the atmospheres of planets.

 3 a Give the name of the gas most likely to have formed most of the Earth's early atmosphere.

 b Explain why the discovery of Titan's icy interior does not support the idea that the Earth's early atmosphere was mainly nitrogen.

 4 Explain why scientists think that the early Earth had an atmosphere similar to Venus.

The oceans

About 4 billion years ago, the Earth cooled down. This caused water vapour in the atmosphere to condense to liquid water, which formed the oceans.

 5 Describe how the Earth's oceans may have formed.

Oxygen

While the exact composition of the Earth's early atmosphere is uncertain, there is much more direct evidence to support the idea that it contained little or no oxygen.

Oxygen is not produced by volcanoes. Further evidence comes from iron pyrite, a compound that is broken down by oxygen and so only forms if there is no oxygen. It is often found in very ancient rock.

About 2.4 billion years ago, rocks containing bands of iron oxide started to form. This oxidation of iron suggests that oxygen levels increased at this time. There is fossil evidence of microorganisms that may have produced this oxygen. So, scientists think that oxygen from these microorganisms reacted with iron in the early oceans, to produce insoluble iron oxides that formed layers on the seabed.

Some geologists suggest that it was only after microorganisms had produced enough oxygen to oxidise the iron in the ocean that atmospheric oxygen levels could rise.

 6 Explain the evidence that supports the idea that oxygen was not present in the early Earth's atmosphere.

 7 Why are scientists more certain about the oxygen content of the early atmosphere compared to other gases?

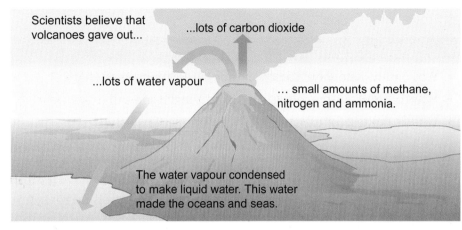

Scientists believe that volcanoes gave out...

...lots of carbon dioxide

...lots of water vapour

... small amounts of methane, nitrogen and ammonia.

The water vapour condensed to make liquid water. This water made the oceans and seas.

C Many scientists think that the gases in Earth's early atmosphere came from volcanoes.

D bands of iron oxide in an ancient rock

Checkpoint

How confidently can you answer the Progression questions?

Strengthen

S1 Describe two pieces of evidence that suggest that the composition of the Earth's early atmosphere was mainly carbon dioxide, with little or no oxygen.

Extend

E1 Explain why many scientists think that the Earth's early atmosphere was similar to that of Mars today (which is 95.3% carbon dioxide, 2.7% nitrogen, 1.6% argon and 0.13% oxygen).

Exam-style question

Describe how the Earth's cooling 4 billion years ago caused a change in the composition of the atmosphere. *(2 marks)*

Specification reference: C8.21; C8.22; C8.23

Progression questions

- Why did the amount of carbon dioxide in the atmosphere change?
- How did primitive organisms change carbon dioxide and oxygen levels?
- What is the test for oxygen?

A Shells from dead sea creatures form layers of sediment that turn into sedimentary rocks (e.g. limestone) over millions of years. Shells can often be seen in limestone.

B Stromatolites are caused by oxygen-releasing microorganisms called cyanobacteria.

As the young Earth changed, so did the atmosphere. Over hundreds of millions of years the amount of oxygen increased and carbon dioxide levels decreased. Scientists have put forward many **hypotheses** to explain this. There is strong evidence to support some of these.

Oceans

As the young Earth cooled, water vapour in the atmosphere condensed and formed oceans. Many scientists think that carbon dioxide then dissolved in the oceans, reducing the amount of carbon dioxide in the atmosphere. Sea creatures used the dissolved carbon dioxide to form shells made of calcium carbonate, $CaCO_3$. This then allowed more carbon dioxide to dissolve in the oceans.

 1 State what happened to the water vapour in the Earth's atmosphere when temperatures cooled.

Oxygen

Some organisms use energy from the Sun to make food by **photosynthesis**. These organisms change the atmosphere because photosynthesis uses up carbon dioxide and releases oxygen.

Some of the earliest photosynthetic organisms were cyanobacteria, which live in shallow waters. These bacteria grow in huge colonies and produce sticky mucus. The mucus traps a layer of sand grains and other sediments. The organisms need to move above the sediment layer in order to get sunlight. Over time, the sediment layers build up to form rocky shapes, called stromatolites.

 2 Explain why cyanobacteria need to move above the sediment as it collects in layers on a stromatolite.

Some stromatolites are over 3 billion years old. They provide evidence that photosynthetic organisms were living at this time. It is thought that microorganisms like these caused a rise in oxygen levels in the oceans and then the atmosphere.

Cyanobacteria evolved into other forms of life, including plants. When land plants evolved, about 500 million years ago, there was another jump in atmospheric oxygen levels.

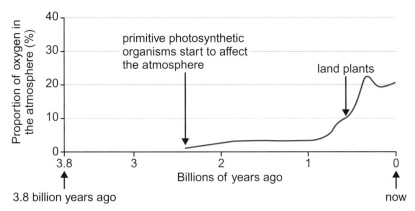

C Diagram showing how some scientists think that oxygen levels in the Earth's atmosphere may have changed over 3.8 billion years.

Today, oxygen makes up about 21% of the Earth's atmosphere. It is important for aerobic respiration in organisms. It also allows combustion (burning) to happen, and this property is used to test for the gas in the laboratory; pure oxygen will relight a glowing splint.

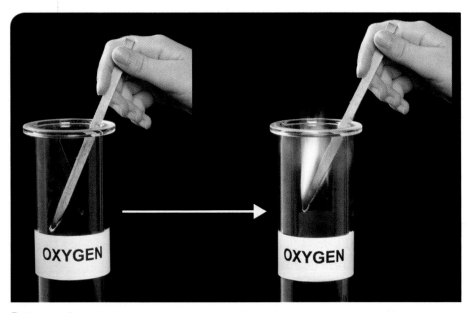

D the test for oxygen

 5 a State the laboratory test for oxygen.

 b Why does oxygen relight a glowing splint?

Exam-style question

Explain why the formation of oceans on Earth may have caused a decrease in atmospheric carbon dioxide levels. *(3 marks)*

 3 Explain why the presence of ancient stromatolites supports the idea of photosynthesis starting to occur over 3 billion years ago.

 4 Describe how the evolution of land plants changed the composition of the atmosphere.

Did you know?

Oxygen is very reactive and would soon disappear from the atmosphere without photosynthetic organisms. Space scientists are very interested in trying to find other planets that contain oxygen in their atmospheres.

Checkpoint

How confidently can you answer the Progression questions?

Strengthen

S1 Explain how carbon dioxide levels in the Earth's atmosphere decreased.

S2 Explain how oxygen levels in the Earth's atmosphere increased.

Extend

E1 Explain how the development of life on Earth influenced levels of carbon dioxide and oxygen in the atmosphere.

CC17c The atmosphere today

Specification reference: C8.24; C8.25

Progression questions

- What are the names of some greenhouse gases?
- How is the greenhouse effect caused?
- What is the link between fossil fuel combustion and climate change?

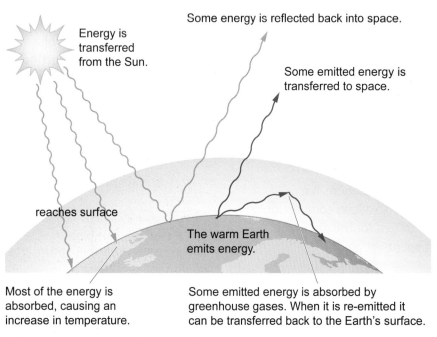

Energy is transferred from the Sun.

Some energy is reflected back into space.

Some emitted energy is transferred to space.

reaches surface

The warm Earth emits energy.

Most of the energy is absorbed, causing an increase in temperature.

Some emitted energy is absorbed by greenhouse gases. When it is re-emitted it can be transferred back to the Earth's surface.

A The greenhouse effect keeps the Earth warm.

Energy from the Sun is transferred to the Earth by waves, such as light and **infrared**. Some energy is absorbed by the Earth's surface, warming it up. The warm Earth **emits** (gives out) infrared waves. Some gases in the air **absorb** energy transferred by these infrared waves. When the gases re-emit the energy, some of it goes back to the Earth's surface and warms it. This is the **greenhouse effect**.

The gases in the atmosphere that absorb energy are called **greenhouse gases**, and include carbon dioxide (CO_2), methane (CH_4) and water vapour (H_2O). Without them, the mean surface temperature of the Earth would be about −18 °C (compared to about 14 °C, which it is today).

 1 List three greenhouse gases.

 2 State the influence of the greenhouse effect on the Earth.

Correlation and climate change

There is evidence to support the idea that human activity is increasing the greenhouse effect and causing **global warming**. This is thought to be causing **climate change** (changes to average weather conditions around the world).

Since about 1850, there has been a steady increase in the burning of fossil fuels for industry. During this period, carbon dioxide levels have increased. We know that combustion releases CO_2, and so this is good evidence that increased fossil fuel use has caused increased CO_2 levels.

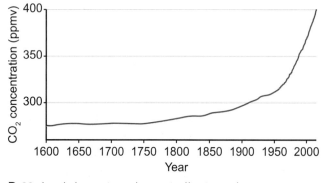

B CO_2 levels have risen dramatically since about 1850.

As CO_2 levels have risen, so has the average temperature of the Earth's surface. There is a strong **correlation** between CO_2 levels and surface temperature.

However, a correlation does not mean that there is a **causal link** (one thing causes the other). To show a causal link, scientists must collect evidence and explain *how* and *why* the correlation occurs. In this case, scientists want to know whether increasing CO_2 levels could actually cause global temperatures to rise, whether the reverse happens, or whether there is no causal link.

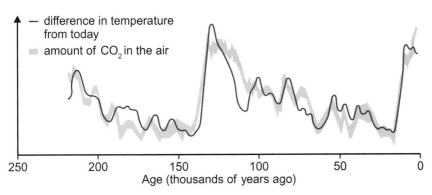

C Average global temperatures and atmospheric carbon dioxide levels are correlated.

Scientists can show in the lab that CO_2 absorbs infrared. Satellite data confirm that as CO_2 levels have increased, there has been a reduction in infrared waves from the Earth leaving the atmosphere. This supports the idea that CO_2 *causes* temperature rises because it shows how it could occur.

 3 Why might industrialisation have led to an increase in greenhouse gases?

 4 **a** Describe what global warming is.

 b Compare global warming with climate change.

 5 **a** What is a 'causal link'?

 b Explain why many scientists believe that there *is* a causal link between recent CO_2 level increases and a rise in temperature.

Evaluating the evidence

The amount of carbon dioxide in the air today is measured at monitoring stations around the world. Evidence for historical carbon dioxide levels comes from measuring concentrations of the gas trapped in ice cores. The oldest cores come from Antarctica and give data going back 800 000 years.

The oldest continuous temperature records are for central England and go back to 1659. However, these records cannot be used to assess global temperature changes because they are from only one place. Continuous temperature measurements from around the world exist from about 1880.

Earlier measurements were not very accurate. Modern thermometers are less prone to error and have a greater **resolution**. Today, we can also analyse huge amounts of data from around the world, including temperature measurements from many different sources (such as sensors and satellites).

 6 How do scientists measure carbon dioxide levels from the past?

D Gases are trapped in ice cores.

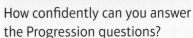

Checkpoint

How confidently can you answer the Progression questions?

Strengthen

S1 Describe the evidence to support the idea that increasing levels of greenhouse gases have caused increased average global temperatures.

Extend

E1 Describe how scientists would collect evidence to support a causal link between carbon dioxide levels and global temperatures.

Exam-style question

Describe why the greenhouse effect leads to increased average global temperatures.

(3 marks)

CC17d Climate change

Specification reference: C8.26

Progression questions

- What human activities influence the climate?
- What problems might climate change cause?
- How might we limit the impact of predicted climate change?

A Methane being released and burnt off on an oil rig.

The increased burning of fossil fuels has released more and more carbon dioxide (CO_2) into the atmosphere, which is thought to be causing global warming. However, CO_2 is not the only greenhouse gas produced by human activity.

Methane (CH_4) is a more powerful greenhouse gas than CO_2 because it is much better at absorbing infrared radiation from the Earth. Methane is the main component of natural gas, and is released into the atmosphere when oil and natural gas are extracted from the ground and processed.

Livestock farming (especially cattle) also produces a lot of methane. Cattle have bacteria in their stomachs to digest tough grass. Some of the bacteria produce methane. Soil bacteria in landfill sites and in rice 'paddy' fields also produce a lot of methane.

 1 State three human activities that cause climate change.

 2 How does livestock farming increase levels of greenhouse gases in the atmosphere?

 3 Describe why an increasing world population might lead to more greenhouse gases being released into the atmosphere.

B Rice paddy fields produce significant amounts of methane.

Effects of climate change

Rising average global temperatures will cause ice at the South Pole and glaciers to melt. The extra water will raise sea levels, which will lead to increased flooding in some areas. Higher average temperatures will also result in a loss of 'sea ice' at the poles.

Some animals may move away from their natural habitats to find cooler areas. Some animals and plants may become extinct if they cannot survive at warmer temperatures or find new places to live.

As weather patterns change, some areas will become drier and others will become wetter. Scientists predict that there will be more extreme weather events (such as heavy rainfall, powerful storms and heat waves). These changes will affect wildlife and the growth of crops that people depend upon.

Did you know?

Sea levels have been rising at a rate of over 3 mm per year since 1993.

As more CO_2 is released, more of this acidic gas will dissolve in seawater, lowering its pH. This can harm organisms living in the seas and oceans. Additionally, as ocean temperatures rise, it causes coral to push out the photosynthetic algae that live in their tissues. These algae provide the colour of coral and so coral 'bleaching' may occur.

 4 List four negative effects of climate change.

Limiting the impact

Using renewable energy resources can reduce greenhouse gas emissions, but there is a risk that this may not be enough to mitigate (lessen) the effects of climate change that we are already seeing.

Some people have suggested global engineering solutions, to reflect sunlight back into space or to capture CO_2 from the air and bury it underground. However, all countries will need to work together to reduce emissions and help pay for large-scale engineering. There is a risk that some countries will not help and that delicate ecosystems may be disrupted.

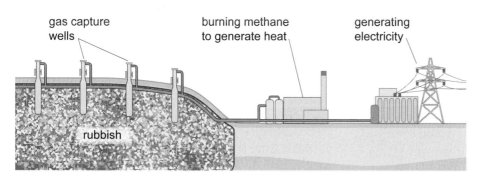

gas capture wells

burning methane to generate heat

generating electricity

rubbish

D Methane released from landfill sites can be captured and burnt to generate electricity.

Other ways of limiting the impact of climate change involve helping local people to adapt to new conditions. These include building flood defences, dams and irrigation systems. However, these ideas may destroy important habitats and there is a risk that they will not work.

 5 Explain why an increased use of renewable energy might help to limit the impact of climate change.

 6 Explain why international cooperation is important in dealing with climate change.

 7 a Identify a way of limiting the impact of climate change.

 b State one risk associated with your suggestion.

C If coral remain 'bleached' for too long they can die.

Checkpoint

How confidently can you answer the Progression questions?

Strengthen

S1 State an effect on the climate of increased carbon dioxide and methane levels, and identify whether the effect is global or local.

S2 Identify one way of reducing the harmful effect of your example above.

S3 State a risk associated with your suggested mitigation method.

Extend

E1 State the three most important policies you think the government should have for tackling climate change. Justify your choices.

Exam-style question

a State a problem caused by climate change. *(1 mark)*

b Describe what can be done to limit any harmful impact. *(1 mark)*

Fuels

Useful substances are separated from crude oil by fractional distillation. The diagram shows the column used and the fractions it produces. The bitumen fraction leaves from the bottom of this column.

Look at the heights at which the kerosene and fuel oil fractions are collected. Explain the properties and uses for kerosene and fuel oil using the information.

(6 marks)

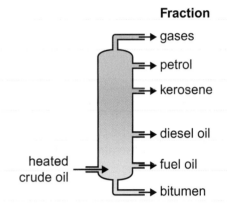

Fraction
- gases
- petrol
- kerosene
- diesel oil
- fuel oil
- bitumen

heated crude oil

Student answer

The top of the fractionating column is cooler than the bottom. Kerosene vapours condense higher up the column than fuel oil. Kerosene has a lower boiling point than fuel oil. This is because the hydrocarbon molecules in kerosene have fewer carbon atoms and hydrogen atoms than the hydrocarbon molecules in fuel oil [1]. Kerosene is more easily ignited than fuel oil [2]. It also has a lower viscosity than fuel oil, so kerosene flows more easily [3]. The differences in these properties make kerosene useful as a fuel for aircraft, [4] while fuel oil is used as a fuel for large ships and some power stations [5].

[1] The answer uses information given in the diagram, and the student's own knowledge and understanding, to link the size of the molecules in each fraction to its boiling point and position.

[2] This describes an important difference in the properties of the two fractions.

[3] It makes clear what low viscosity means – a less viscous substance flows more easily than a more viscous substance.

[4] It is important not to just describe kerosene as *used* in aircraft, but as a *fuel* for aircraft.

[5] More than one use of fuel oil is given, and both are correct.

Verdict

This is a strong answer. It shows good knowledge and understanding of the fractions obtained from crude oil, and uses correct scientific language. The answer uses scientific knowledge to link the size of the hydrocarbon molecules to their boiling points, and therefore the heights at which they are collected in the fractionating column. The answer is organised logically, explaining the differences in properties and then the difference in uses.

Exam tip

If you are given information in a question, make sure you use and refer to it in your answer. In this case, the question stated that you should use the information from the diagram.

Paper 5

CP1 Motion

Penguins cannot climb. They get onto the ice by accelerating to a high speed under the water. As they move upwards out of the water, gravity pulls on them and they slow down. But if they are swimming fast enough they land on the ice before they stop moving.

In this unit you will learn about quantities that have directions (such as forces). You will find out how to calculate speeds and accelerations, and how to represent changes in distance moved and speed on graphs.

The learning journey

Previously you will have learnt at KS3:

- what forces are and the effects of balanced and unbalanced forces
- how average speed, distance and time are related
- how to represent a journey on a distance-time graph.

In this unit you will learn:

- the difference between vector and scalar quantities
- how to calculate speed and acceleration
- how to represent journeys on distance/time and velocity/time graphs
- how to use graphs to calculate speed, acceleration and distance travelled.

CP1a Vectors and scalars

Specification reference: P2.1; P2.2; P2.3; P2.4; P2.5

Progression questions

- What are vector and scalar quantities?
- What are some examples of scalar quantities and their corresponding vector quantities?
- What is the connection between the speed, velocity and acceleration of an object?

A The person in the air stays there because of the force provided by the jets of water.

 1 Upthrust is a force that helps objects float. Sketch one of the boats in photo A and add arrows to show two forces on the boat acting in a vertical direction.

 2 Describe the differences between mass and weight.

 3 Explain why we say that displacement is a vector quantity.

 4 Runners in a 400 m race complete one circuit of an athletics track. What is their displacement at the end of the race?

The **force** needed to keep the person in photo A in the air depends on his **weight**. Weight is a force that acts towards the centre of the Earth. All forces have both a **magnitude** (size) and a direction, and are measured in newtons (N).

Quantities that have both size and direction are **vector quantities**. So forces are vectors. Forces are often shown on diagrams using arrows, with longer arrows representing larger forces.

The weight of the person in photo A depends on his **mass**. Mass measures the amount of matter in something and does not have a direction. Quantities that do not have a direction are called **scalar quantities**. Other scalar quantities include **distance**, **speed**, energy and time.

Displacement is the distance covered in a straight line, and has a direction. The displacement at the end of a journey is usually less than the distance travelled because of the turns or bends in the journey.

B The bend in the road means that the distance the cyclists cover is greater than their final displacement.

The speed of an object tells you how far it moves in a certain time. **Velocity** is speed in a particular direction. For example a car may have a velocity of 20 m/s northwards.

D These skaters maintain a constant speed around the bend, but their velocity is changing.

Other vector quantities include:

• **acceleration** – a measure of how fast velocity is changing
• **momentum** – a combination of mass and velocity.

Exam-style question

Weight and upthrust are both vector quantities.

a Name one other vector quantity that is not a force. *(1 mark)*
b Explain why you do not need to state a direction when describing a weight. *(1 mark)*

 5 Look at photo B. Explain why the cyclists' velocity will change even if they maintain the same speed.

 6 A student draws the diagram below. Explain what is wrong with it.

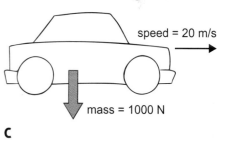

C

Checkpoint

How confidently can you answer the Progression questions?

Strengthen

S1 Sally walks 1 km from her home to school. When she arrives, she tells her science teacher 'My velocity to school this morning was 15 minutes'. What would her teacher say?

S2 Explain the difference between displacement and distance, and between speed and velocity. Give an example of each.

Extend

E1 A car is going around a roundabout. Explain why it is accelerating even if it is moving at a constant speed.

CP1b Distance/time graphs

Specification reference: P2.6; P2.7; P2.11; P2.12

Progression questions

- How do you use the equation relating average speed, distance and time?
- In metres per second, what are the typical speeds that someone might move at during the course of a day?
- How do you represent journeys on a distance/time graph?

A *ThrustSSC* broke the land speed record in 1997 at a speed of 1228 km/h (341 m/s). This was faster than the speed of sound (which is approximately 330 m/s).

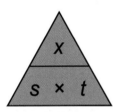

B This equation triangle can help you to rearrange the equation for speed (*s*), where *x* is used to represent distance and *t* represents time. Cover up the quantity you want to calculate and write what you see on the right of the = sign.

Worked example W1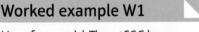

How far would *ThrustSSC* have travelled in 5 seconds during its record-breaking run?

distance = average speed × time

= 341 m/s × 5 s

= 1705 m

The speed of an object tells you how quickly it travels a certain distance. Common units for speed are metres per second (m/s), kilometres per hour (km/h) and miles per hour (mph).

The speed during a journey can change, and the **average speed** is worked out from the total distance travelled and the total time taken. The **instantaneous speed** is the speed at a particular point in a journey.

Speed can be calculated using the following equation:

$$\text{(average) speed (m/s)} = \frac{\text{distance (m)}}{\text{time taken (s)}}$$

The equation can be rearranged to calculate the distance travelled from the speed and the time.

$$\text{distance travelled} = \text{average speed} \times \text{time}$$
$$\text{(m)} \qquad\qquad \text{(m/s)} \qquad \text{(s)}$$

To measure speed in the laboratory you need to measure a distance and a time. For fast-moving objects, using **light gates** to measure time will be more accurate than using a stopwatch.

 1 A car travels 3000 m in 2 minutes (120 seconds). Calculate its speed in m/s.

 2 Look at diagram C. How far does a high speed train travel in 10 minutes?

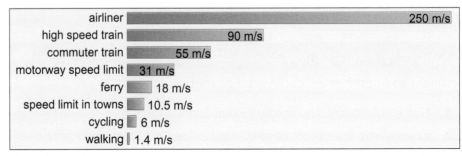

C some typical speeds

airliner 250 m/s
high speed train 90 m/s
commuter train 55 m/s
motorway speed limit 31 m/s
ferry 18 m/s
speed limit in towns 10.5 m/s
cycling 6 m/s
walking 1.4 m/s

Distance/time graphs

A journey can be represented on a **distance/time graph**. Since time and distance are used to calculate speed, the graph can tell us various things about speed:

- horizontal lines mean the object is stationary (its distance from the starting point is not changing)
- straight, sloping lines mean the object is travelling at constant speed
- the steeper the line, the faster the object is travelling
- the speed is calculated from the **gradient** of the line.

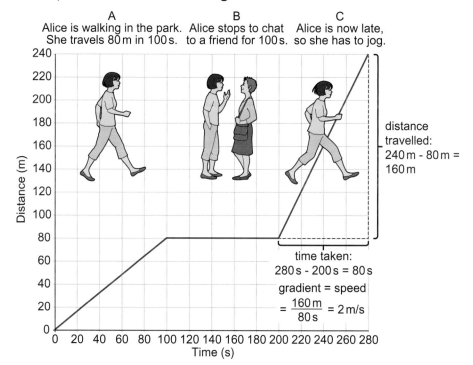

A
Alice is walking in the park. She travels 80 m in 100 s.

B
Alice stops to chat to a friend for 100 s.

C
Alice is now late, so she has to jog.

distance travelled:
240 m - 80 m = 160 m

time taken:
280 s - 200 s = 80 s

gradient = speed
$= \frac{160\,m}{80\,s} = 2\,m/s$

D The gradient of a distance/time graph gives the speed.

Worked example W2

In graph D, what is Alice's speed for part C of her walk?

gradient = $\frac{\text{vertical difference between two points on a graph}}{\text{horizontal difference between the same two points}}$

$= \frac{240\,m - 80\,m}{280\,s - 200\,s}$

Make sure you take the starting value away from the end value each time.

speed $= \frac{160\,m}{80\,s}$

speed $= 2\,m/s$

Exam-style question

A snail travels 300 cm in 4 minutes. Calculate the speed of the snail in m/s.

(3 marks)

3 Look at graph D. Calculate Alice's speed for:

 a part A on the graph

 b part B on the graph.

 4 If Alice had not stopped to chat but had walked at her initial speed for 280 s, how far would she have travelled?

Checkpoint

How confidently can you answer the Progression questions?

Strengthen

S1 A peregrine falcon flies at 50 m/s for 7 seconds. How far does it fly?

S2 Zahir starts a race fast, then gets a stitch and has to stop. When he starts running again he goes more slowly than before. Sketch a distance/time graph to show Zahir's race if he runs at a constant speed in each section of the race.

Extend

E1 Look at question S2. Zahir's speeds are 3 m/s for 60 seconds, 2 m/s for 90 seconds and his rest lasted for 30 seconds. Plot a distance/time graph on graph paper to show his race.

CP1c Acceleration

Specification reference: P2.8; P2.9; P2.13

Progression questions

- How do you calculate accelerations from a change in velocity and a time?
- How are acceleration, initial velocity, final velocity and distance related?
- What is the acceleration of free fall?

A A fighter plane can accelerate from 0 to 80 m/s (180 mph) in 2 seconds.

Fighter planes taking off from aircraft carriers use a catapult to help them to accelerate to flying speed.

A change in velocity is called acceleration. Acceleration is a vector quantity – it has a size (magnitude) and a direction. If a moving object changes its velocity or direction, then it is accelerating.

The acceleration tells you the change in velocity each second, so the units of acceleration are metres per second per second. This is written as m/s² (metres per second squared). An acceleration of 10 m/s² means that each second the velocity increases by 10 m/s.

Acceleration is calculated using the following equation:

 1 How are velocity and acceleration connected?

$$\text{acceleration (m/s}^2\text{)} = \frac{\text{change in velocity (m/s)}}{\text{time taken (s)}}$$

This can also be written as:

$$a = \frac{v - u}{t}$$

where a is the acceleration

v is the final velocity

u is the initial velocity

t is the time taken for the change in velocity.

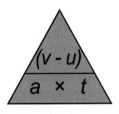

B This triangle can help you to rearrange the equation.

Worked example W1

An airliner's velocity changes from 0 m/s to 60 m/s in 20 seconds. What is its acceleration?

$$a = \frac{v - u}{t}$$

$$= \frac{60 \text{ m/s} - 0 \text{ m/s}}{20 \text{ s}}$$

$$= 3 \text{ m/s}^2$$

 2 Calculate the take-off acceleration of the fighter plane in photo A.

Acceleration does not always mean getting faster. An acceleration can also cause an object to get slower. This is sometimes called a **deceleration**, and the acceleration will have a negative value.

 3 A car slows down from 25 m/s to 10 m/s in 5 seconds. Calculate its acceleration.

Acceleration can be related to initial velocity, final velocity and distance travelled by this equation:

(final velocity)² – (initial velocity)² = 2 × acceleration × distance
  (m/s)²   (m/s)²   (m/s²)   (m)

This can also be written as $v^2 - u^2 = 2 \times a \times x$, where x represents distance.

 4 A cyclist accelerates from 2 m/s to 8 m/s with an acceleration of 1.5 m/s². How far did she travel while she was accelerating? Use the equation $x = \dfrac{v^2 - u^2}{2 \times a}$.

Acceleration due to gravity

An object in free fall is moving downwards because of the force of gravity acting on it. If there are no other forces (such as air resistance), the acceleration due to gravity is 9.8 m/s². This is represented by the symbol g, and is often rounded to 10 m/s² in calculations.

5 Look at photo C.

 a Calculate the acceleration on the ejecting pilot in m/s².

 b How does this compare to everyday accelerations?

CP1d Velocity/time graphs

Specification reference: P2.10

Progression questions

- How do you compare accelerations on a velocity/time graph?
- How can you calculate acceleration from a velocity/time graph?
- How can you use a velocity/time graph to work out the total distance travelled?

A Top Fuel dragsters can reach velocities of 150 m/s (335 mph) in only 4 seconds.

In a drag race, cars accelerate in a straight line over a short course of only a few hundred metres.

The changing velocity of a dragster during a race can be shown using a **velocity/time graph**.

On a velocity/time graph:

- a horizontal line means the object is travelling at constant velocity
- a sloping line shows that the object is accelerating. The steeper the line, the greater the acceleration. If the line slopes down to the right, the object is decelerating (slowing down). You can find the acceleration of an object from the gradient of the line on a velocity/time graph.
- a negative velocity (a line below the horizontal axis) shows the object moving in the opposite direction.

Graph C is a simplified velocity/time graph for a dragster. It shows the car driving slowly to the start line, waiting for the signal, and then racing.

B The graph shows a lift moving up at a constant speed (a), slowing to a stop (b) and waiting at a floor (c) then accelerating downwards (d) and then travelling downwards at a constant speed (e).

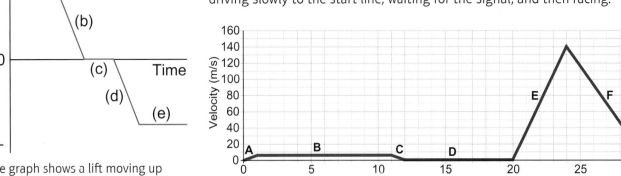

C simplified velocity/time graph for a drag race

 1 What does a horizontal line on a velocity/time graph tell you about an object's velocity?

2 a In which part of graph C is the dragster travelling at a constant velocity?

 b In which part of the graph does the dragster have its greatest acceleration?

 c Which part(s) of the graph show that the dragster is slowing down?

 3 Look at graph C. Calculate the acceleration during part F of the journey.

Calculating distance travelled from a graph

The area under a velocity/time graph is the distance the object has travelled (distance is calculated by multiplying a velocity and a time). In graph D, the distance travelled in the first 5 seconds is the area of a rectangle. The distance travelled in the next 5 seconds is found by splitting the shape into a triangle and a rectangle, and finding their areas separately.

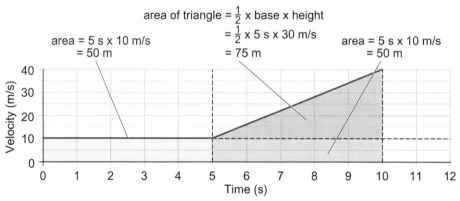

D

The total distance travelled by the object in graph D is the sum of all the areas.

total distance travelled = 50 m + 50 m + 75 m = 175 m

4 Look at graph C. The dragster travels at 5 m/s as it approaches the start line.

 a How far does it travel to get to the start line?

 b What is the distance travelled by the dragster during the race and slowing down afterwards?

 5 Mel draws a graph showing a bus journey through town. Explain why this should be called a speed/time graph, not a velocity/time graph.

Exam-style question

Explain why the area under part of a velocity/time graph gives you the distance covered. *(3 marks)*

Checkpoint

How confidently can you answer the Progression questions?

Strengthen

S1 Table E below gives some data for a train journey. Draw a velocity/time graph from this and join the points with straight lines. Label your graph with all the things you can tell from it. Show your working for any calculations you do.

Time (s)	Velocity (m/s)
0	0
20	10
30	30
60	30
120	0

E

Extend

E1 In a fitness test, students run up and down the sports hall. They have to run faster after each time they turn around. Sketch a velocity/time graph for 4 lengths of the hall, if each length is run at a constant speed.

Vectors and scalars

Explain the statements below, giving examples in each case.

- The speed of an object has the same value as its velocity.

- The displacement of an object from its starting point is often not the same as the distance travelled.

- The displacement of an object at the end of a journey can never be greater than the distance travelled. **(6 marks)**

Student answer

Speed is a scalar and velocity is a vector because it has a direction. So if a car goes around a corner at a constant speed, the magnitude [1] of the velocity does not change but the velocity is changing because the direction is changing [2].

Displacement is a vector, and is the distance in a straight line between the starting point and finishing point. Displacement has a direction [3]. Distance is a scalar, and is the actual distance moved during a journey including all the twists and turns [4].

[1] This is a good use of correct scientific terminology.

[2] This is a good explanation of the first statement, and includes an example.

[3] This is a good description of the meaning of displacement.

[4] Although the student has described distance, there isn't an example that illustrates the difference.

Verdict

This is an acceptable answer. It shows a good understanding of the differences between vectors and scalars. The answer also provides good descriptions of the terms speed, velocity, distance and displacement. The use of scientific language is good and the answer is arranged logically. However, there are some parts of the answer which are missing.

This answer could be improved by including information on the third statement and an explanation for the second statement.

Exam tip

Try to leave enough time to check through your answer. Make sure you have included everything that the question has asked for (in this example, the student should have covered all three statements).

Paper 5

CP2 Forces and Motion

The car crash in this image was staged for a photoshoot. Crashes like this are often used in films and tend to be more spectacular than real road accidents. For example, in films a piston on the road is often used to flip a car into the air. Stunt designers need to carefully calculate the force from a piston to make sure that a car flips in the way that they want it to.

Engineers designing cars also need to know about the forces on cars and about how these forces affect the car and its occupants. This information can help them to design cars that will reduce the harm to occupants in crashes. Knowledge about forces can also help the government to work out what the speed limits should be on different roads, and what safety advice to give drivers.

The learning journey

Previously you will have learnt at KS3:

- what forces are and the effects of balanced and unbalanced forces
- what a resultant force is
- about gravity as a non-contact force.

In this unit you will learn:

- about Newton's Laws of Motion
- how to calculate the weight of an object from its mass
- about the factors that affect the stopping distance of a vehicle
- about the dangers of large decelerations
- H how to calculate momentum, and apply ideas about momentum to collisions.

CP2a Resultant forces

Specification reference: P2.14

Progression questions

- What is the difference between the speed of an object and its velocity?
- How do we represent all the forces acting on an object?
- How do we calculate resultant forces?

A A 'wall of death' is a small arena with almost vertical sides. Motorcyclists ride around the walls, and won't fall as long as they keep moving!

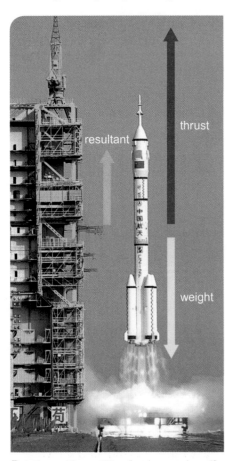

B A Chang Zheng 2F rocket has a take-off weight of approximately 5000 kN, and thrust of about 13 000 kN (1 kN = 1000 N).

Scalars and vectors

The motorcyclist in photo A is moving at a constant **speed** but his **velocity** is changing all the time. This is because velocity is a **vector quantity**. It has a direction as well as a magnitude (size). Speed is a **scalar quantity**. It only has a magnitude.

When an object changes its velocity, it is accelerating. As **acceleration** is a change in a vector quantity (velocity), acceleration is also a vector.

 1 A car is driving around a roundabout at 20 km/h. Explain whether or not:

 a its speed is changing

b its velocity is changing.

Representing forces

Forces are vector quantities. It is important to know the direction in which a force is acting, as well as how big it is. We can draw diagrams to show the forces on objects to help us to think about the effects the forces will have. The size of the force is represented by the length of the arrows.

The thrust on the rocket in photo B is the upwards force from its engines. You can easily see from the diagram that the thrust is greater than its weight. The weight cancels out part of the thrust, so the overall upwards force is 8000 kN. This is called the **resultant force** on the rocket.

To work out the resultant of two forces:

- if the forces are acting in the same direction, add them
- if they are acting in opposite directions (as in photo B), subtract one from the other.

 2 **a** A cyclist is riding along a flat road without pedalling. The air resistance is 10 N and friction is 5 N. What is the resultant force on the bike?

 b What is the resultant force if the cyclist is pedalling with a force of 25 N?

The aeroplane in photo C has two forces acting in the vertical direction and two in the horizontal. We do not have to think about all four forces at one time to work out a resultant, because the two sets of forces are at right angles to each other. We can think about the two sets of forces separately.

C

 3 Calculate the resultant force on the aeroplane in photo C in the:

 a vertical direction

 b horizontal direction.

4 In photo C, are the forces balanced or unbalanced in the:

 a vertical direction

 b horizontal direction?

If the resultant of all the forces on an object is zero, we say the forces are **balanced**. If there is a non-zero resultant force on an object, the forces are **unbalanced**.

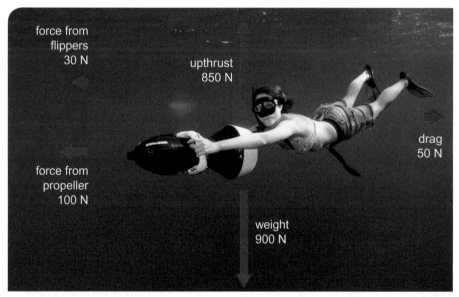

D What are the forces on this diver?

Checkpoint

How confidently can you answer the Progression questions?

Strengthen

S1 Draw a concept map to show what you know about forces.

Extend

E1 Calculate the resultant force on the diver in photo D in the vertical direction and in the horizontal direction.

E2 Draw a diagram of the diver and add force arrows to show the two resultant forces.

Exam-style question

The forces on a car are balanced. State and explain the size of the resultant force on the car. *(2 marks)*

CP2b Newton's First Law

Specification reference: P2.14; **H** P2.20; **H** P2.21

Progression questions

- What happens to the motion of an object when the forces on it are balanced?
- What can happen to the motion of an object when there is a resultant force on it?
- **H** What is centripetal force?

A Human cannonballs are propelled using unbalanced forces from compressed air or springs – not using explosives!

Sir Isaac Newton (1642–1727) worked out three 'laws' of motion that describe how forces affect the movement of objects.

Newton's First Law of motion can be written as:

- a moving object will continue to move at the same speed and direction unless an external force acts on it
- a stationary object will remain at rest unless an external force acts on it.

It is the overall resultant force that is important when you are looking at how the velocity of an object changes. Balanced forces (zero resultant force) will not change the velocity of an object. Unbalanced forces (non-zero resultant force) will change the speed and/or direction of an object.

 1 a What is the resultant force on the human cannonball in the vertical direction when she is flying through the air?

 b How will this resultant force affect her velocity?

2 Look at photo C on the previous page again. Explain how the velocity of the aeroplane will change in the:

 a vertical direction

 b horizontal direction.

The ice yacht in photo B is not changing speed in the vertical direction. Its weight is balanced by an upwards force from the ice.

B An ice yacht can go much faster than a sailing boat in the same wind conditions.

3 A sailing boat has a forwards force of 300 N from the wind in its sails. It is travelling at a constant speed.

a What is the total force acting backwards on the sailing boat? Explain your answer.

b The ice yacht in photo B has the same force from its sails. Explain why its velocity will be increasing.

H Circular motion

C This fairground ride is accelerating the people in the chairs.

An object moving in a circle has changing velocity, even though its speed remains the same. The resultant force that causes the change in direction is called the **centripetal force**, and acts towards the centre of the circle. In photo C, the centripetal force is provided by tension in the wires holding the seats. Other types of force that can make objects move in circular paths include friction and gravity.

centripetal force

D The centripetal force here is supplied by friction between the tyres and the road.

 9th **4** A satellite is in a circular orbit around the Earth. Explain how and why its velocity is continuously changing.

Exam-style question

A man is pushing a baby along the pavement in a pushchair. Friction is also acting on the pushchair. The pushchair is slowing down.
Compare the horizontal forces on the pushchair. *(2 marks)*

Checkpoint

How confidently can you answer the Progression questions?

Strengthen

S1 You are cycling along a flat road and your speed is increasing. Explain the resultant forces on you in the horizontal and vertical directions.

Extend

E1 Describe the forces on a human cannonball, from just before they are fired to when they land safely in a net, including how these forces affect their motion. You only need to consider forces and motion in the vertical direction.

E2 H Explain what a centripetal force is and describe three different kinds of force that can act as centripetal forces.

299

CP2c Mass and weight

Specification reference: P2.16; P2.17; P2.18

Progression questions

- What is the difference between mass and weight?
- What are the factors that determine the weight of an object?
- How do you calculate weight?

A The Huygens space probe used the air resistance from a parachute to balance its weight when it landed on Titan (one of Saturn's moons).

Mass is the quantity of matter there is in an object, and only changes if the object itself changes. For example, your mass increases when you eat a meal. **Weight** is a measure of the pull of gravity on an object and depends on the strength of gravity. The units for mass are kilograms. Weight is a force, so it is measured in newtons. Weight can be measured using a **force meter**, which has a scale in newtons. Many force meters contain a spring, which stretches as the force on it increases allowing the weight to be read off the scale.

 1 Suggest one way in which you can decrease your mass.

On Earth the **gravitational field strength** has a value of about 10 newtons per kilogram (N/kg). This means that each kilogram is pulled down with a force of 10 N. The gravitational field strength is different on other planets and moons.

The weight of an object can be calculated using the following equation:

$$\text{weight} = \text{mass} \times \text{gravitational field strength}$$
$$\text{(N)} \qquad \text{(kg)} \qquad \text{(N/kg)}$$

This is often written as: $W = m \times g$

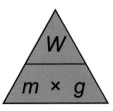

B This triangle can help you to change the subject of the equation. Cover up the quantity you want to find, and what you can see is the equation you need to use.

Worked examples

What is the weight of a 90 kg astronaut on the surface of the Earth?

$W = m \times g$

$W = 90 \text{ kg} \times 10 \text{ N/kg}$

$\quad = 900 \text{ N}$

A space probe has a weight of 3000 N on the Earth. What is its mass?

$m = \dfrac{W}{g}$

$\quad = \dfrac{3000 \text{ N}}{10 \text{ N/kg}}$

$\quad = 300 \text{ kg}$

Did you know?

Gravity is not the same everywhere on the Earth. Your weight is greater standing at the North Pole than it would be standing at the equator.

2 A 300 kg space probe lands on Titan, where the gravitational field strength is 1.4 N/kg.

 a What is its mass on Titan? Explain your answer.

 b What is its weight on Titan?

3 A Mars rover has a mass of 185 kg. Its weight on Mars is 685 N. What is the gravitational field strength on Mars?

Forces on falling bodies

On Earth, a falling object has a force of air resistance on it as well as its weight. Figure C shows how the forces on a skydiver change during her fall.

0.5 seconds after jumping, speed = 5 m/s

resultant

Air resistance increases with speed, so just after jumping the air resistance is much smaller than her weight. The large resultant force makes her accelerate downwards.

3 seconds after jumping, speed = 25 m/s

resultant

Her air resistance is larger but her weight stays the same. The resultant force is smaller, so she is still accelerating, but not as much.

12 seconds after jumping, speed = 55 m/s

resultant = 0

She is moving so fast that the air resistance balances her weight. She continues to fall at the same speed.

C

 4 Explain why the weight of the skydiver stays the same throughout the jump.

 5 When the skydiver opens her parachute her air resistance increases very suddenly. Explain how this affects the resultant force and her velocity.

Checkpoint

How confidently can you answer the Progression questions?

Strengthen

S1 Write glossary entries for 'mass' and 'weight'.

S2 A cat has a mass of 2 kg. Calculate its weight on Earth.

Extend

E1 Write an encyclopaedia entry that explains the difference between mass and weight.

E2 A space probe on Titan has a weight of 280 N. Calculate its mass and its weight on Earth.

Exam-style question

The mass of a spanner on Earth is 0.2 kg, and its weight is 2 N. The spanner is taken to the Moon as part of an astronaut's tool kit.

Compare the mass and weight of the spanner on the Moon and on the Earth. *(4 marks)*

Specification reference: P2.15; **H** P2.22

Progression questions

- What are the factors that affect the acceleration of an object?
- How do you calculate the different factors that affect acceleration?
- **H** What is inertial mass and how is it defined?

A The safety rules for building Formula 1® cars include a limit to the engine force and a minimum mass for the car.

The acceleration of an object is a measure of how much its velocity changes in a certain time. Sir Isaac Newton's Second Law of Motion describes the factors that affect the acceleration of an object.

The acceleration in the direction of a resultant force depends on:

- the size of the force (for the same mass, the bigger the force the bigger the acceleration)
- the mass of the object (for the same force, the more massive the object the smaller the acceleration).

Did you know?

B A bike with low mass is so important for track racers that their bikes do not even have brakes! Racing rules state that these bikes must have a minimum mass of 6.8 kg.

1 The resultant force on a ball is not zero. What will happen to the ball?

2 a The same force is used to accelerate a small car and a lorry. What will be different about their motions? Explain your answer.

b If you wanted to make the same two vehicles accelerate at the same rate, what can you say about the forces needed to do this? Explain your answer.

Calculating forces

The force needed to accelerate a particular object can be calculated using the equation:

force = mass × acceleration
  (N)   (kg)   (m/s²)

This is often written as $F = m \times a$

1 newton is the force needed to accelerate a mass of 1 kg by 1 m/s².

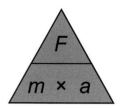

C This triangle can help you to change the subject of the equation. Cover up the quantity you want to find, and what you can see is the equation you need to use.

Worked example

A motorcycle has a mass of 200 kg. What force is needed to give it an acceleration of 7 m/s²?

$F = m \times a$
  = 200 kg × 7 m/s²
  = 1400 N

 3 A car has a mass of 1500 kg. What force is needed to give it an acceleration of 4 m/s²?

4 A force of 800 N accelerates the car in question 3. What is its acceleration?

D What do you need to know to work out whether the car or aeroplane has the greater acceleration?

H Inertial mass

The more massive an object is, the more force is needed to change its velocity (either to make it start moving or to change the velocity of a moving object). We define the **inertial mass** of an object as the force on it divided by the acceleration that force produces.

Calculating an object's inertial mass from values of force and acceleration gives the same mass value as that found by measuring the force of gravity on it.

 5 A force of 160 N on a bicycle produces an acceleration of 2 m/s². What is the total inertial mass of the bicycle and its rider?

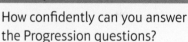

Checkpoint

How confidently can you answer the Progression questions?

Strengthen

S1 Look at photo A. Explain whether the Formula 1® rules are designed to set an upper or lower limit to the accelerations of the cars.

S2 Calculate the force needed to accelerate a 250 kg motorbike at 5 m/s².

Extend

E1 Look at photo D. Explain what you need to know to help you to work out which vehicle will have the greater acceleration.

E2 Explain why two objects dropped on the Moon will accelerate at the same rate, even when they have different masses.

Exam-style question

A car accelerates at 2 m/s². The resultant force acting on the car is 3000 N.

Calculate the mass of the car.   *(3 marks)*

CP2d Core practical – Investigating acceleration

Specification reference: P2.19

Aim

Investigate the relationship between force, mass and acceleration by varying the masses added to trolleys.

A

In drag racing, the aim is to get to the end of a straight track as quickly as possible, and so the most important feature of the bike is its acceleration. Drag racers can try to improve the performance of their bikes by changing the force produced by the engine and the tyres or by changing the mass of the bike.

Your task

You are going to use trolleys as a model of a motorbike to investigate the effects that mass and force have on acceleration. The force will be provided by masses hanging on a string. You can vary the mass of the trolley by adding stacking masses to it.

Method

A Prop up one end of the ramp. Place a trolley on the ramp. Adjust the slope of the ramp until the trolley just starts to move on its own. Keep the ramp at this slope for the whole investigation. Set up the light gates and the pulley and string as shown in diagram B.

B Stick a piece of card to the top of the trolley. Measure the length of the card and write it down.

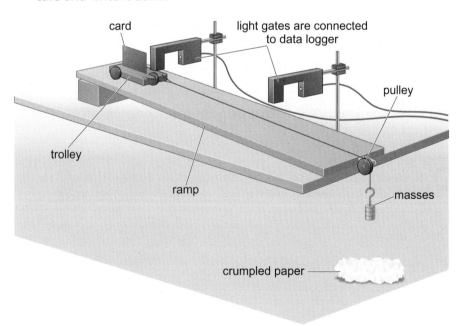

B apparatus for investigating acceleration

C Find the mass of the trolley and write it down.

D Put a mass on the end of the string. You will keep this mass the same for all your tests. You will have to decide what mass to use.

E Release the trolley from the top of the ramp and write down the speed of the trolley (from the datalogger) as it passes through each light gate. Also write down the time it takes for the trolley to go from one light gate to the other.

F Put a mass on top of the trolley. Keep the masses on the end of the string as they were before. Repeat step E.

G Repeat step E for other masses on top of the trolley. You will have to decide what masses to use, how many different masses you are going to test, and whether you need to repeat any of your tests.

H The steps above are investigating how the mass of the trolley affects the acceleration. If you wish to investigate the effect of force on acceleration, you need to keep the mass the same. However, the masses on the end of the string are also accelerating, along with the trolley, and it is the overall mass that you need to keep the same. You can do this by starting with a stack of masses on the trolley. Take one mass off the trolley and hang it on the end of the string. Then follow step E to measure the acceleration.

I Now transfer another mass from the trolley to the end of the string and find the acceleration again. Keep doing this until all the masses that started on the trolley have been transferred to the end of the string.

Exam-style questions

1 The light gates and datalogger record the speed of the trolley at the top of the ramp and at the bottom of the ramp, and also record the time the trolley takes to move between the two light gates. Describe how this information can be used to calculate the acceleration.

(2 marks)

2 State the difference between mass and weight. *(1 mark)*

3 Explain one way in which you would stay safe while doing the experiments. *(2 marks)*

4 Make a list of the apparatus you need to carry out the method.

(2 marks)

5 Explain why a light gate is needed at the top of the ramp as well as at the bottom. *(2 marks)*

6 Look at steps H and I. Explain why all the masses to be used in investigating the effect of the force on acceleration have to be on the trolley to start with. *(3 marks)*

7 Use the results shown in graph C to draw a conclusion for this part of the investigation. *(1 mark)*

8 Look at graph D.

    a Use graph D to draw a conclusion for this part of the investigation. *(1 mark)*

    b Explain how you would present the data in graph D to allow you to draw a better conclusion. *(2 marks)*

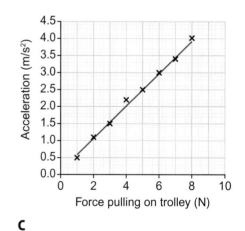

C

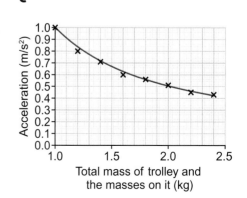

D

CP2e Newton's Third Law

Specification reference: P2.23; H P2.23

Progression questions

- What does Newton's Third Law tell us?
- How does Newton's Third Law apply to stationary objects?
- H How do objects affect each other when they collide?

A The dog is not moving. What are the forces acting here?

B The Earth attracts the Moon with the same force as the Moon attracts the Earth.

2 You are standing leaning on a wall. Draw a sketch to show this (a stick man will do) and add arrows to show an action–reaction pair of forces acting in the:

 a vertical direction

 b horizontal direction.

 3 For the situation in question 2, describe the balanced forces on you acting in the vertical direction.

Newton's Third Law is about the forces on two different objects when they interact with each other. This interaction can happen:

- when objects touch, such as when you sit on a chair
- at a distance, such as the gravitational attraction between the Earth and the Moon.

There is a pair of forces acting on the two interactive objects, often called **action–reaction forces**. The two forces are always the same size and in opposite directions. They are also the same type of force. In photo A the rope and the dog are both exerting pulling forces on each other. In photo B the two forces are both gravitational forces.

Photo A shows an **equilibrium** situation, because nothing is moving. A force in the rope is pulling on the dog but the dog is also pulling on the rope.

 1 Think about the vertical forces in photo A. One force is the weight of the dog pushing down on the ground. What is the other force in this pair?

The weight of a dog on the ground is equal to the force pushing up on the dog from the ground. In photo A there is another pair of action–reaction forces acting on the rope and the dog – there is a force from the dog on the rope and a force from the rope on the dog.

Action–reaction forces are not the same as balanced forces. In both cases the sizes of the forces are equal and act in opposite directions, but:

- action–reaction forces act *on different objects*.
- balanced forces all act *on the same object*

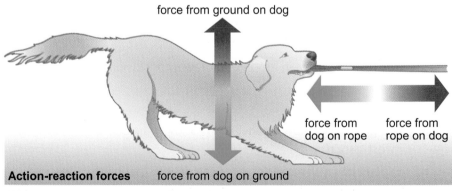

Action-reaction forces

force from ground on dog

force from dog on rope

force from rope on dog

force from dog on ground

Ci

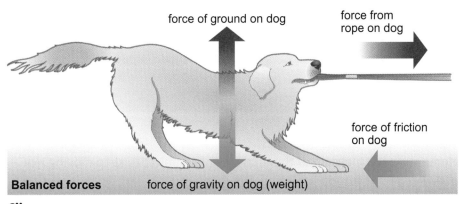

force of ground on dog

force from rope on dog

force of friction on dog

Balanced forces force of gravity on dog (weight)

Cii

H Collisions

We can apply the idea of action–reaction forces to what happens when things collide. In photo D, the ball will bounce off the footballer's head. His head exerts a force on the ball, but the ball also exerts a force on his head, as you can feel if you have ever tried heading a ball!

The action and reaction forces that occur during the collision are the same size, but they do not necessarily have the same effects on the two objects, because the objects have different masses.

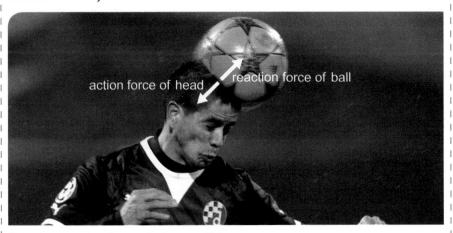

action force of head

reaction force of ball

D Action–reaction forces during a collision.

 4 Describe the action–reaction forces when a ball bounces on the ground.

 5 Look at photo D. The player's head and the ball both change velocity during the collision. Describe the effects on the two objects and explain why the effects are different.

Checkpoint

How confidently can you answer the Progression questions?

Strengthen

S1 Describe the action–reaction forces when you sit in a chair. Describe how these forces are different to a pair of balanced forces acting on you.

Extend

E1 Two teams are having a tug-of-war. Make a sketch and add labelled arrows to show three action–reaction force pairs and three pairs of balanced forces.

E2 H A ball is released a metre above the surface of the Earth. Describe the action–reaction forces due to gravity on the ball and the Earth. Describe the forces when the ball and the Earth collide. Explain how the effects on the two objects are different.

Exam-style question

A student is using a force meter to find the weight of an apple. Describe an action-reaction pair of forces in this situation. *(1 mark)*

CP2f Momentum

Specification reference: **H** P2.23; **H** P2.24; **H** P2.25; **H** P2.26

Progression questions

- **H** How is momentum calculated?
- **H** How is momentum related to force and acceleration?
- **H** What happens to momentum in collisions?

A The damage caused by a wrecking ball depends on its mass and how fast it is moving when it hits.

force, mass and acceleration	$F = m \times a$
change in velocity and time	$a = \dfrac{v - u}{t}$

C equations involving acceleration

Did you know?

The largest ships are oil tankers. It can take several miles for a moving oil tanker to come to a stop.

 4 A 1000 kg car accelerates from rest to 15 m/s in 15 seconds. What resultant force caused this?

Momentum is a measure of the tendency of an object to keep moving – or of how hard it is to stop it moving. The momentum of an object depends on its mass and its velocity. Momentum depends on a vector quantity (velocity), and is also a vector.

Momentum is calculated using this equation:

momentum = mass × velocity
(kg m/s)   (kg)   (m/s)

This can also be written as $p = m \times v$, where p stands for momentum.

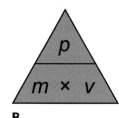

B

 1 Explain why a motorcycle travelling at 30 m/s has less momentum than a car travelling at the same velocity.

2 A 500 kg wrecking ball is moving at 10 m/s when it hits a building. What is its momentum?

3 The same ball at a different time has a momentum of 1500 kg m/s. What is its velocity?

Momentum and acceleration

Table C shows two equations involving acceleration. These can be combined to give:

$$\text{force} = \frac{\text{mass} \times \text{change in velocity}}{\text{time}} \quad \text{or} \quad \frac{m(v - u)}{t}$$

where v is the final velocity and u is the starting velocity.

As mass × velocity is the momentum of an object, this equation can also be written as:

$$\text{force} = \frac{\text{change in momentum}}{\text{time}} \quad \text{or} \quad \frac{mv - mu}{t}$$

Worked example

A 2000 kg car accelerates from 10 m/s to 25 m/s in 10 seconds. What resultant force produced this acceleration?

$$\text{force} = \frac{mv - mu}{t}$$

$$= \frac{2000 \text{ kg} \times 25 \text{ m/s} - 2000 \text{ kg} \times 10 \text{ m/s}}{10 \text{ s}}$$

$$= \frac{50\,000 \text{ kg m/s} - 20\,000 \text{ kg m/s}}{10 \text{ s}}$$

$$= 3000 \text{ N}$$

H Momentum and collisions

When moving objects collide the total momentum of both objects is the same before the collision as it is after the collision, as long as there are no external forces acting. This is known as **conservation of momentum**. Remember, momentum is a vector so you need to consider direction when you add the quantities together. If two objects are moving in opposite directions, we give the momentum of one object a positive sign and the other a negative sign.

before collision   after collision

E

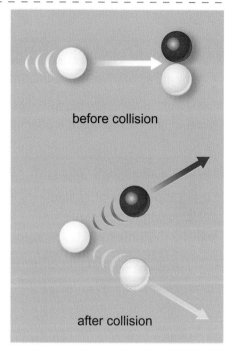

before collision

after collision

D The total momentum of the two coloured balls will be the same as the momentum of the white ball that hit them.

5 Look at diagram E.

 a Calculate the momentum of each penguin before they collide.

 b Calculate the total momentum before the penguins collide.

 c In which direction is the total momentum before the collision?

 d What is the total momentum after the collision and in which direction?

 e Explain whether momentum has been conserved.

Checkpoint

How confidently can you answer the Progression questions?

Strengthen

S1 Two 5000 kg railway trucks are travelling at 5 m/s in opposite directions when they collide. After the collision they are stationary. Show that momentum is conserved.

Extend

E1 A 1 g bullet is travelling at 300 m/s when it enters a stationary 1 kg block of wood. The impact of the bullet makes the wood move. What is the speed of the block immediately after the impact? Explain how you worked out your answer.

Exam-style question

A car has a mass of 1800 kg. It is moving with a velocity of 35 m/s.

Calculate the momentum of the car.   *(3 marks)*

CP2g Stopping distances

Specification reference: P2.27; P2.28; P2.29; P2.30

Progression questions

- How are human reaction times measured?
- What are typical human reaction times?
- What are the factors that affect the stopping distance of a vehicle?

Did you know?

Until 1896 all 'self-propelled' vehicles had to have a man walking in front with a red flag, to warn other road users that it was coming.

A More than 130 vehicles were involved in this crash and over 200 people were injured.

 1 Why is it important for drivers to know their stopping distances?

2 For a thinking distance of 5 m and a braking distance of 12 m, what is the overall stopping distance?

When a driver sees a problem ahead, their vehicle will travel some distance while the driver reacts to the situation. This is called the **thinking distance**. The vehicle will then go some distance further while the brakes are working to bring it to a halt. This is called the **braking distance**. The overall **stopping distance** for any road vehicle is the sum of the thinking and braking distances.

stopping distance = thinking distance + braking distance

Reaction times

A **reaction time** is the time between a person detecting a **stimulus** (such as a flashing light or a sound) and their **response** (such as pressing a button or applying the brakes in a car). Response times can be measured using computers or electric circuits that measure the time between a stimulus and a response.

The typical reaction time to a visual stimulus, such as a computer screen changing colour, is about 0.25 seconds. However this time can be much longer if the person is tired, ill or has been taking drugs or drinking alcohol. Distractions, such as using a mobile phone, can also increase reaction times.

 3 Explain why the thinking distance depends on:

    a the driver's reaction time   **b** the speed of the car.

 4 Suggest why the reaction time measured in a driving simulator might be longer than the time measured using a test on a computer.

B A driving simulator can be used to test reaction times in a realistic situation.

 5 Explain why there are legal limits for the amount of alcohol drivers are allowed in their blood.

Braking distances

Car brakes use friction to slow the car down. If the brakes are worn, they create less friction and do not slow the vehicle as effectively. Friction between the tyres and road is also important. If the road is wet or has loose gravel on it, or if the tyres are worn, there is less friction and the braking distance is increased.

If a vehicle has more mass, more force is needed to decelerate it. So if the same amount of friction is used to stop a vehicle, a heavier vehicle will travel further than a lighter one (it has a greater braking distance).

 6 Why are the overall stopping distances for cars less than for lorries?

 7 Look at photo D. Suggest why there are two separate speed limits.

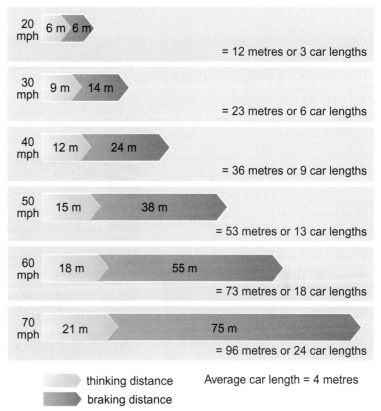

20 mph 6 m 6 m = 12 metres or 3 car lengths
30 mph 9 m 14 m = 23 metres or 6 car lengths
40 mph 12 m 24 m = 36 metres or 9 car lengths
50 mph 15 m 38 m = 53 metres or 13 car lengths
60 mph 18 m 55 m = 73 metres or 18 car lengths
70 mph 21 m 75 m = 96 metres or 24 car lengths

thinking distance
braking distance
Average car length = 4 metres

C The Highway Code shows typical stopping distances for a family car.

D This sign is from an autoroute (motorway) in France. The speed limits are in km/h.

Checkpoint

How confidently can you answer the Progression questions?

Strengthen

S1 List the factors that affect stopping distance. State whether each factor affects the thinking distance or the braking distance, and how they affect this distance.

Extend

E1 The crash in photo A happened in a sudden patch of fog. Write a paragraph for a road-safety website to explain why fog can be a hazard on the roads, and what drivers can do to avoid crashing in foggy conditions.

Exam-style question

Explain how thinking distance and braking distance depend on the speed of the vehicle. *(4 marks)*

CP2h Crash hazards

Specification reference: H P2.26; H P2.31

Progression questions

- What are the dangers caused by large decelerations?
- How can the hazards of large decelerations be reduced?
- H How can you use momentum to calculate the forces involved in crashes?

A The amount of damage caused by a collision depends on the mass of the lorry and on how fast it was travelling.

In a car crash, the vehicles involved come to a stop very quickly. Slowing down is a **deceleration** (or a negative acceleration). The force needed for any kind of acceleration depends on the size of the acceleration and on the mass of the object.

B The large forces in road collisions injure or kill people and damage cars.

1 Explain why the force on a vehicle in a crash is larger:

   a if the vehicle is moving faster before the crash

   b for a lorry than for a car travelling at the same speed.

Modern cars have lots of safety features built into them to help to reduce the forces on the occupants in a collision. **Crumple zones** are built into the front (and sometimes the back) of cars. If the car hits something it takes a little time for this crumpling to happen, so the deceleration of the car is less and the force on the car is also less than if it had a more solid front.

C Forces on humans can result from hitting the dashboard or steering wheel, or if other passengers hit them.

Photo C also shows that the passengers do not stop moving when the car stops! Seat belts hold the passengers into the car, so the effect of the crumple zone reduces the forces on the passengers as well as on the car. Airbags increase the time it takes for a person's head to stop in a collision.

D Airbags were used to help the Mars Pathfinder to land safely by increasing the time for the probe to hit the ground, and so reducing the force on it..

 2 Look at photo C. Explain why front *and* back seat passengers in a car should wear seat belts.

 3 Bubble wrap is a plastic covering with many air bubbles. How do you think bubble wrap protects fragile items?

H

The force in a road collision depends on the change of momentum as the car comes to a stop. You have seen (in Topic CP2f Momentum) that we can use the equation below to calculate the force:

$F = \dfrac{mv - mu}{t}$, where u is initial velocity and v is final velocity.

Worked example

A 1500 kg car is travelling at 15 m/s (just over 30 mph) when it hits a wall. It comes to a stop in 0.07 seconds. What is the force acting on the car?

force $= \dfrac{1500\,kg \times 0\,m/s - 1500\,kg \times 15\,m/s}{0.07\,s}$

$= \dfrac{-22\,500}{0.07}$

$= -321\,429\,N$

The negative sign shows that the force is in the opposite direction to the original motion.

 4 a **H** An 1800 kg car travelling at 20 m/s stops in 0.03 seconds when it hits a wall. What is the force on it?

 b **H** Explain why this force is different to the one in the worked example. Give as many reasons as you can.

Did you know?

Many people have survived falls from aeroplanes without parachutes. In 2004, skydiver Christine McKenzie's parachute failed – she escaped with only a cracked pelvis because she fell into some power lines which slowed her down before she hit the ground.

Checkpoint

How confidently can you answer the Progression questions?

Strengthen

S1 Describe two ways of reducing the forces in a collision, and explain how they work.

Extend

E1 **H** Use calculations to show the effects of velocity, mass and crumple zones on the forces acting in a road collision. You will need to find or estimate values for speed, mass and the change in length of a crumple zone in a crash.

Exam-style question

Explain why a crumple zone only reduces the force on vehicle passengers if they are wearing seat belts. *(4 marks)*

stopping distances

The stopping distance of a vehicle is affected by its mass, its speed and the state of its brakes.

Explain how these factors affect the stopping distance, using ideas about forces and acceleration.   (6 marks)

Student answer

The stopping distance is longer if the car is going faster or has a larger mass. If its brakes are working well, the stopping distance is shorter [1]. The deceleration of the car depends on the force applied, which depends on how good the brakes are, so if the brakes are good the deceleration is more and it can stop sooner [2]. The deceleration also depends on the weight [3], so if the brakes are the same [4] the deceleration will be less with a heavier car so it will go further while it is stopping.

[1] This part of the answer describes how each factor affects the stopping distance.

[2] This explains how the state of the brakes affects the stopping distance.

[3] The student should refer to mass here, not weight.

[4] This would have been clearer if the student had referred to the *force* from the brakes being the same.

Verdict

This is an acceptable answer. It shows a good understanding of some of the factors that affect stopping distances. The answer clearly states how each factor affects the stopping distance, and provides good explanations for two of the factors. The use of scientific language is generally good, although with a mistake about weight and mass.

This answer could be improved by including an explanation of how the speed of a vehicle affects the stopping distance, and making sure that correct scientific words are used.

Exam tip

In this example the command word is 'explain' so you need to say how *and why* each factor affects the stopping distance.

Paper 5

CP3 Conservation of Energy

This is a solar power station at Sanlúcar la Mayor in Seville, Spain. Rings of mirrors focus energy from the Sun into a central furnace where water is heated to make steam. The steam is used to turn turbines, which drive generators to make electricity in a similar way to a normal power station.

In this unit you will learn about the ways in which energy can be transferred and stored, how to reduce energy transfers, and the renewable and non-renewable resources we use in everyday life.

The learning journey

Previously you will have learnt at KS3:

- that temperature differences lead to energy transfers
- how energy can be transferred by conduction, convection and radiation
- ways of reducing energy transferred by heating
- that energy is conserved
- ways in which energy can be stored and transferred.

In this unit you will learn:

- how energy is stored and transferred
- how to represent energy transfers using diagrams
- how to calculate efficiency
- how to reduce transfers of wasted energy
- how to calculate the amount of gravitational potential energy or kinetic energy stored in objects
- about the different renewable and non-renewable resources we use to make electricity, for heating and cooking, and for transport.

Specification reference: P3.3; P3.4; P3.5; P3.6; P3.8

Progression questions

- How is energy transferred between different stores?
- How can we represent energy transfers in diagrams?
- What happens to the total amount of energy when energy is transferred?

A What energy stores and transfers are involved as the bullet goes through the egg?

Energy is stored in different ways. Energy stored in food, fuel and batteries is often called **chemical energy**. Energy can also be stored in moving objects (**kinetic energy**), hot objects (**thermal energy**), in stretched, squashed or twisted materials (**strain energy** or **elastic potential energy**) and in objects in high positions (**gravitational potential energy**). Energy stored inside atoms is called **atomic energy** or **nuclear energy**.

1 Describe the changes in energy stores when a car accelerates.

Energy can be transferred between different stores. In photo A, some of the kinetic energy stored in the moving bullet is transferred to the egg by forces. Some of this energy is stored in the moving fragments of the egg, and some will heat up the egg.

2 A ball thrown upwards has a store of kinetic energy as it leaves the person's hand. Describe the changes in energy stores as the ball rises and then falls again.

When an electrical kettle is used to heat water, energy transferred to the kettle by electricity ends up as a store of thermal energy in the hot water. As the hot water is at a higher temperature than the kettle and the surroundings, some energy is transferred to these things by heating. Energy can also be transferred by light and sound.

Conservation of energy

3 List the ways in which energy can be transferred that are mentioned on this page.

In physics, a **system** describes something in which we are studying changes. An electrical kettle and its surroundings form a simple system. Energy cannot be created or destroyed. It can only be transferred from one store to another. This is called the **law of conservation of energy**. This means that the total energy transferred by a system is the same as the energy put into the system. The units for measuring energy are **joules (J)**.

Although energy is always conserved, it is not always transferred into forms that are useful. Think of the kettle – the energy stored in the hot water is useful, but the energy stored in the kettle itself and in the surroundings is not.

Energy diagrams

We represent energy stores and transfers using diagrams, such as diagram B.

| energy stored in moving car (kinetic energy) | → energy transferred by forces during braking → | energy stored in hot brakes (thermal energy) |

B A flow diagram showing the energy transfers when a car brakes.

Did you know?

The energy transferred by the braking force can increase the temperature of brakes so much that they glow red.

C

A **Sankey diagram** shows the amount of energy transferred. The width of the arrows represents the amount of energy in joules.

energy transferred by electricity 12 J
5 J energy transferred by light
7 J energy transferred by heating

D energy transfers in a light bulb

 7 Sketch a Sankey diagram for a kettle using the energy values given in question 4.

Exam-style question

a Draw a diagram to represent the energy transfers in a television. *(3 marks)*
b Identify the useful energy transfers in the television. *(1 mark)*

 4 1000 J of energy is transferred to a kettle. 850 J ends up stored in the hot water in the kettle. Explain how much energy is transferred to the kettle itself and its surroundings.

 5 Look at diagram B. The car's brakes do not stay hot. Describe the final energy store in this system.

 6 a Draw an energy transfer diagram similar to diagram B for the bullet and egg in photo A.

 b Describe how your diagram would be different if it were a car hitting a wall.

Checkpoint

How confidently can you answer the Progression questions?

Strengthen

S1 Describe the energy stores and transfers when you climb up to a high diving board and then jump into a swimming pool.

Extend

E1 A light bulb has 25 J of energy transferred to it every second, and 10 J of energy are transferred to the surroundings by light. Draw a Sankey diagram to show the energy transfers and explain how you worked out the amount of energy transferred by heating.

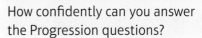

CP3b Energy efficiency

Specification reference: P3.7; P3.9; P3.11; **H** P3.12

Progression questions

* What does efficiency mean?
* How do we calculate the efficiency of an energy transfer?
* How can we reduce unwanted energy transfers in machines?

A Oiling the chain on a bicycle makes pedalling it much easier.

Did you know?

When two sticks are rubbed together the temperature rise can be used to start a fire. In this case the energy transferred by heating is useful!

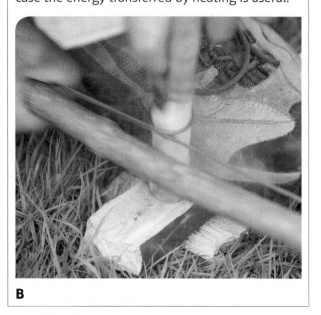

B

When a light bulb is switched on, most of the energy supplied to it by electricity is transferred to the surroundings by heating. This energy is **dissipated** (it spreads out) and cannot be used for other useful energy transfers – it is wasted.

Most machines waste energy when they get hot. Whenever two moving parts touch each other, friction causes them to heat up. The thermal energy stored in the hot machine is transferred to the surroundings by heating, which dissipates the energy. This energy is wasted energy.

Friction between moving parts can be reduced by **lubrication**. Oil or other liquids, and sometimes even gases, can be used as lubricants.

 1 a Explain why it is harder to pedal a bicycle if the chain needs oiling.

 b When you pedal a bicycle, how is wasted energy transferred to the surroundings?

Efficiency

Efficiency is a way of describing how good a machine is at transferring energy into useful forms. The efficiency of a machine is given as a number between 0 and 1. The higher the number, the more efficient the machine. This is shown in diagram C.

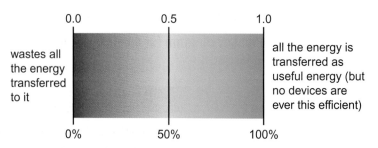

C The efficiency of a machine is sometimes given as a percentage.

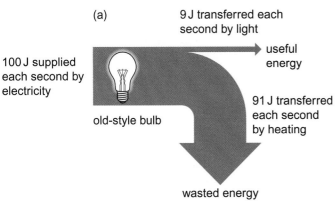

(a) 9 J transferred each second by light

100 J supplied each second by electricity

old-style bulb

useful energy

91 J transferred each second by heating

wasted energy

(b) 45 J transferred each second by light

100 J supplied each second by electricity

low-energy bulb

useful energy

55 J transferred each second by heating

wasted energy

D Modern low-energy bulbs are more efficient than old-style bulbs.

 2 Look at diagram D. How can you tell from these diagrams that modern low-energy bulbs are more efficient?

The efficiency of a device can be calculated using this equation:

$$\text{efficiency} = \frac{\text{(useful energy transferred by the device)}}{\text{(total energy supplied to the device)}}$$

Worked example

Calculate the efficiency of the old-style bulb shown in diagram D.

$$\text{efficiency} = \frac{\text{(useful energy transferred by the device)}}{\text{(total energy supplied to the device)}}$$

$$= \frac{9\,\text{J}}{100\,\text{J}}$$

$$= 0.09$$

The efficiency is a ratio so there are no units.

 3 Calculate the efficiency of the low-energy light bulb shown in diagram D.

 4 Look at diagram D in CP3a. Calculate the efficiency of the light bulb.

H

Reducing the amount of wasted energy can increase the efficiency of a device or a process. For mechanical processes, such as engines, this can mean reducing friction. It can also mean finding ways to make sure all the fuel going into an engine is burned, or finding a way of using the energy transferred by heating that would otherwise be wasted.

 5 Explain how the efficiency of a bicycle can be increased.

Exam-style question

Kettle A transfers 200 J of energy to boil some water. Kettle B transfers 250 J to boil the same volume of water. Explain which kettle is more efficient. *(3 marks)*

Checkpoint

How confidently can you answer the Progression questions?

Strengthen

S1 Explain why adding oil to door hinges makes the door easier and quieter to open.

S2 A radio is supplied with 50 J of energy and transfers 5 J of this by sound. Explain what happens to the rest of the energy and calculate the efficiency of the radio.

Extend

E1 A coal-fired power station has an efficiency of 0.4. Some of the energy wasted is stored in hot water that needs to be cooled down. The efficiency can be doubled if this hot water is used to heat nearby buildings. Explain how much useful energy is now transferred by electricity and how much is transferred by heating for each 1000 J of energy stored in the coal. Suggest what causes the remaining wasted energy and what happens to it.

CP3c Keeping warm

Specification reference: P3.9; P3.10

Progression questions

- What does thermal conductivity mean?
- What affects the rate at which buildings cool?
- How can insulation reduce unwanted energy transfers?

Did you know?

The best insulator is aerogel. This is a solid made from a silica or carbon framework with air trapped inside it. Aerogel is 99.8% air, and so it has an extremely low density. It has many uses, including insulation for space suits.

B The aerogel is protecting the hand from the heat of the flame.

1 A pan of water is heated on a cooker. Describe how:

 a energy is transferred from the cooker to the water

 b the energy spreads out through the water.

 2 Explain why bubble wrapping is a good insulating material.

It costs money to keep our houses warm. **Insulation** slows down the rate at which energy is transferred out of a house by heating.

A This house is being built from straw bales. Straw is around 10 times better as an insulator than bricks.

Energy can be transferred by heating in different ways.

- In **conduction** vibrations are passed on between particles in a solid. Metals are good **thermal conductors** and materials such as wood are poor thermal conductors (good **thermal insulators**).
- In **convection** part of a **fluid** that is warmer than the rest rises and sets up a convection current.
- **Radiation** is the only way in which energy can be transferred through a vacuum. **Infrared radiation** can also pass through gases and some solid materials. Infrared radiation is **absorbed** and **emitted** easily by dull, dark surfaces, and is absorbed and emitted poorly by light, shiny surfaces.

The straw bales in photo A have a low **thermal conductivity**. This means that energy is not transferred through them very easily by heating. Materials that contain air are good insulators because air has a very low thermal conductivity. When air is trapped it cannot form convection currents and so does not transfer much energy.

The rate at which energy is transferred through a material by heating depends on its thickness, on its thermal conductivity and also on the temperature difference across it. The rate of energy transfer is reduced by increasing thickness, decreasing thermal conductivity and decreasing temperature difference.

single wall

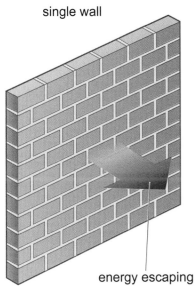

cavity wall

cavity

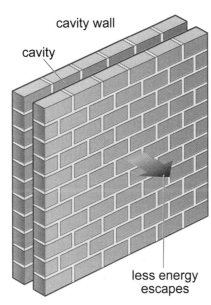

energy escaping

less energy escapes

C Modern brick walls are built from two layers with a cavity (air gap) between them, which helps to insulate a house.

D A 'vacuum flask' is often used to store hot or cold liquids and uses a combination of different materials to reduce energy transfer by heating.

 6 The container in diagram D keeps hot drinks hot but also keeps cold drinks cold. Explain how it can do this.

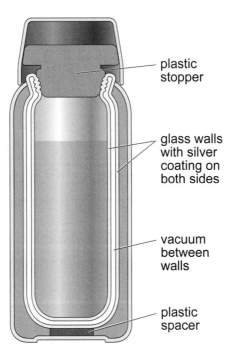

plastic stopper

glass walls with silver coating on both sides

vacuum between walls

plastic spacer

 3 a Look at photo B. Do you think the aerogel has a higher or lower thermal conductivity than straw bales?

 b Explain how you worked out your answer to part a.

 4 Straw bale houses have very thick walls. Give two reasons why the walls in the house in photo A are better insulators than normal brick walls.

5 Look at diagram C.

a Give two reasons why the cavity wall keeps a house warmer than a single wall.

 b Suggest why modern buildings have the cavity filled with foam or a similar material.

Checkpoint

How confidently can you answer the Progression questions?

Strengthen

S1 Explain two ways in which walls can be built to keep a house warmer.

S2 Explain two ways in which insulation is used at home to reduce energy transfers.

Extend

E1 Look at diagram D. Explain which features of the flask reduce energy transfer by radiation, by conduction and by convection.

Exam-style question

Energy is needed to keep homes warm in the winter. Explain how the thermal conductivity of the walls in a house affects the energy needed to keep a house warm. *(2 marks)*

CP3d Stored energies

Specification reference: P3.1; P3.2

Progression questions

- What factors affect the gravitational potential energy stored in an object?
- How do you calculate gravitational potential energy?
- How do you calculate the amount of kinetic energy stored in a moving object?

A There are three heavy 'weights' on steel cables inside the Big Ben clock tower. They are lifted up three times a week to store the energy needed to drive the clock and the bells.

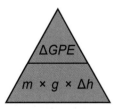

B This equation triangle can help you to change the subject of the equation. Δ is the Greek letter delta and stands for 'change in'.

Gravitational potential energy (GPE) is energy that is stored because of an object's position in a gravitational field. Any object that is above the surface of the Earth contains a store of gravitational potential energy. Every time something is moved upwards, it stores more gravitational potential energy.

The amount of GPE stored depends on the mass of the object, the strength of gravity and how far the object is moved upwards. It can be calculated using this equation:

$$\begin{matrix} \text{change in gravitational} \\ \text{potential energy} \\ \text{(J)} \end{matrix} = \begin{matrix} \text{mass} \\ \text{(kg)} \end{matrix} \times \begin{matrix} \text{gravitational} \\ \text{field strength} \\ \text{(N/kg)} \end{matrix} \times \begin{matrix} \text{change in} \\ \text{vertical height} \\ \text{(m)} \end{matrix}$$

This can be written as: $\Delta GPE = m \times g \times \Delta h$

where ΔGPE represents the change in gravitational potential energy

  m represents mass

  g represents gravitational field strength

  Δh represents change in vertical height.

The value for gravitational field strength on Earth is approximately 10 N/kg.

Worked example W1

A 5 kg box stores an extra 25 J of GPE when it is lifted onto a shelf. Calculate the distance it was lifted.

$$\Delta h = \frac{\Delta GPE}{m \times g}$$

$$= \frac{25\,J}{5\,kg \times 10\,N/kg}$$

$$= 0.5\ m$$

 1 The gravitational field strength on the Moon is about 1.6 N/kg. Explain why the GPE stored by an object lifted 1 metre above the Moon's surface is less than when it is lifted by 1 m on the Earth.

2 One 'weight' in the Big Ben clock tower has a mass of 100 kg.

 a Calculate the change in the GPE when it is raised by 5 metres.

 b How far does this 'weight' have to be lifted to store 3000 J of energy?

Did you know?

Some birds crack open the shells of nuts or animals they are going to eat by dropping them onto stones. The birds store gravitational potential energy in the shells by lifting them into the air.

Kinetic energy

Energy is stored in moving objects. We call this kinetic energy. The amount of kinetic energy stored in a moving object depends on its mass and its speed.

Kinetic energy can be calculated using this equation:

$$\text{kinetic energy (J)} = \tfrac{1}{2} \times \text{mass (kg)} \times \text{(speed)}^2 \text{ (m/s)}^2$$

This can be written as:

$$KE = \tfrac{1}{2} \times m \times v^2$$

where KE represents kinetic energy

m represents mass.

v represents speed.

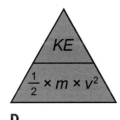

D

C The heavy disc at the bottom of this potter's wheel stores energy while it is spinning.

Worked example W2

A cricket ball with a mass of 160 g is bowled at a speed of 30 m/s. How much kinetic energy is stored in the moving ball?

$160 \text{ g} = 0.16 \text{ kg}$

$KE = \tfrac{1}{2} \times m \times v^2$

$\quad\quad = \tfrac{1}{2} \times 0.16 \text{ kg} \times (30 \text{ m/s})^2$

$\quad\quad = 72 \text{ J}$

3 Calculate the kinetic energy stored in the following.

 a A 2 kg toy robot dog walking at 2 m/s.

 b A boy on a bike riding at 8 m/s. The mass of the boy and his bike is 70 kg.

 4 A whale swimming at 7 m/s stores 98 000 J of kinetic energy. Calculate the mass of the whale.

Checkpoint

How confidently can you answer the Progression questions?

Strengthen

S1 A missile is flying at 220 m/s at 100 m above the sea. Its mass is 1000 kg. Calculate its:

    a gravitational potential energy

    b kinetic energy.

Extend

E1 A crow drops a 15 g walnut from 5 m above the ground. Calculate the amount of GPE stored in the nut just before it fell.

E2 Assume all the GPE stored in the walnut was transferred to kinetic energy just before it reached the ground. How fast was it moving when it hit the ground?

Exam-style question

Explain why a car moving at 20 m/s is storing more kinetic energy than a cyclist moving at 2 m/s. *(2 marks)*

CP3e Non-renewable resources

Specification reference: P3.13; P3.14

Progression questions

- What non-renewable energy resources can we use?
- How are the different non-renewable resources used?
- How is the use of non-renewable energy resources changing?

A The New Horizons space probe was launched in 2006 and flew past Pluto in 2015. Power for the spacecraft is provided by energy stored in a radioactive nuclear fuel.

Nuclear fuels such as **uranium** store a lot of energy in a small piece of material. This makes nuclear fuels very useful for spacecraft, where the mass of the fuel is important.

Most of the electricity used in the UK is generated using nuclear fuels or **fossil fuels** such as coal, oil and natural gas. These are all **non-renewable** energy resources, which means they will run out one day.

Petrol and diesel are fossil fuels made from oil. They are used in most vehicles, aeroplanes and ships because they store a lot of energy and they are easy to store and to use in engines. Another fossil fuel, natural gas, is burnt to heat homes or for cooking.

 1 Describe two reasons why fuels made from oil are used in vehicles.

Burning fossil fuels release carbon dioxide and other gases. Carbon dioxide emissions contribute to **climate change**. Other emissions from power stations and vehicles cause further pollution problems. There are various ways of reducing this pollution, but these cost money.

Burning natural gas causes less pollution than burning coal. Natural gas power stations also emit less carbon dioxide than other fossil-fuelled power stations producing the same amount of electricity.

 2 Describe two advantages of using natural gas instead of coal to generate electricity.

Nuclear power stations do not emit any carbon dioxide or other gases. However, the waste they produce is radioactive and some of it will stay radioactive for millions of years. This is expensive to dispose of safely. It is also very expensive to decommission (dismantle safely) a nuclear power station at the end of its life. It costs a lot more to build and to decommission a nuclear power station than a fossil-fuelled one.

There are not many accidents in nuclear power stations and the stations are designed to contain any radioactive leaks. However, if a major accident occurs it can have very serious consequences.

B Accidents with oil rigs or oil tankers can pollute large areas, harming wildlife.

C In 2011 a tsunami swept over a nuclear power station in Japan and damaged it. Radioactive materials were released into the atmosphere. Some of this polluted the sea nearby and then spread across the Pacific Ocean.

Most countries in the world are trying to cut down the use of fossil fuels. This will reduce pollution and also help to make supplies of the fuels last longer. **Renewable** resources are energy resources such as solar or wind energy that will not run out. Most renewable resources do not emit polluting gases.

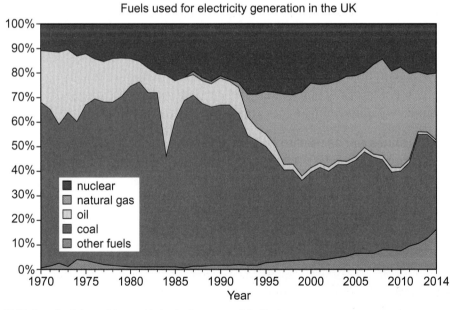

D 'Other fuels' on this graph include renewable fuels.

 6 Look at graph D. Describe how the energy resources the UK uses for generating electricity have changed since 1970.

Exam-style question

State two reasons why many countries are trying to reduce the amount of non-renewable fuel they use. *(2 marks)*

---

 3 a Write down one advantage of nuclear power over fossil-fuelled power stations.

 b Write down two disadvantages.

 4 a Why do you think a nuclear power station costs more to build?

 b Why is decommissioning it properly very important?

 5 How can a nuclear accident affect people in many different parts of the world?

Checkpoint

How confidently can you answer the Progression questions?

Strengthen

S1 Name four different non-renewable fuels and describe how they are used.

S2 Suggest why the use of renewable energy resources has been increasing in the UK in recent years.

Extend

E1 List three different ways in which non-renewable fuels are used. Describe the advantages and disadvantages of each fuel for each use.

325

CP3f Renewable resources

Specification reference: P3.13; P3.14

Progression questions

- What renewable energy resources can we use?
- How are the different renewable resources used?
- How is the use of renewable energy resources changing?

A In a solar chimney power station, solar energy heats the air under the glass. The hot air rises up the tower, turning turbines as it moves.

Renewable energy resources are resources that will not run out. Most renewable energy resources do not cause pollution or emit carbon dioxide when used to generate electricity because no fuel is burned.

 1 What advantage do almost all renewable energy resources have over fossil fuels for generating electricity?

Solar cells convert **solar energy** directly into electrical energy, in 'solar farms' or on house roof-tops. Solar energy can also be used in power stations such as the one in diagram A or the one on the opening page of this unit. Solar energy can also be used to heat water for use in homes. Solar energy is not available all the time.

 2 Describe two ways in which electricity can be produced using energy from the Sun.

Hydroelectricity is generated by falling water in places where water can be trapped in high reservoirs. It is available at any time (as long as the reservoir does not dry up). A hydroelectric power station can be started and stopped very quickly unlike fossil fuel power stations.

Wind turbines can be used to generate electricity as long as the wind speed is not too slow or too fast. A lot of wind turbines are needed to produce the same amount of energy as a fossil-fuelled power station and some people think they spoil the landscape.

Tidal power can generate electricity when turbines in a huge barrage (dam) across a river estuary turn as the tides flow in and out. Tidal power is not available all the time but is available at predictable times. There are not many places in the UK that are suitable for barrages and they may affect birds and other wildlife that live or feed on tidal mudflats. Underwater turbines can be placed in water currents in the sea to generate electricity, as seen in Figure B.

B artist's impression of tidal stream turbines

 3 Describe two ways in which electricity can be produced using tides.

Bio-fuels can be used in the same ways as fossil fuels. They are made from animal wastes or from plants. Bio-fuels can be made from waste wood or the parts of plants that are not used for food, but some crops are grown specifically to be made into bio-fuels. Bio-fuels are called carbon neutral because when they burn, they release the same amount of carbon dioxide that they took from the atmosphere when the plants grew. However, energy is also needed to grow and harvest the crops and to turn them into fuel, so most bio-fuels are not really carbon-neutral.

Electricity can also be generated from waves or from hot rocks underground.

C Some people object to growing crops for fuel because this reduces the land available for farming food and can increase food prices.

We cannot only use renewable resources to generate electricity because most are not available all the time. It also takes a lot of land to obtain energy from bio-fuels or other renewable resources such as solar farms.

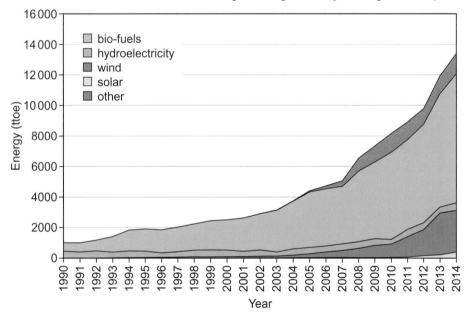

D On the graph, 'other' includes wave, tidal, geothermal and biofuel resources. The unit 'ttoe' (thousand tonnes of oil equivalent) is used to make fair comparisons between energy resources.

5 Look at graph D.

 a Describe how the use of renewable energy has changed since 1990.

 b Suggest two reasons for the changes you have described.

Exam-style question

State one advantage and one disadvantage of using renewable resources for generating electricity. *(2 marks)*

4 State which renewable resources:

 a are available all the time

 b are available at predictable times

 c can only be used in certain places

 d depend on the weather.

Checkpoint

How confidently can you answer the Progression questions?

Strengthen

S1 Describe five renewable energy resources and how they are used.

S2 State two advantages of a hydroelectric power station compared with a natural gas power station.

Extend

E1 Explain why we would need an efficient way of storing electricity before we could generate all our electricity from renewable resources. Give examples to support your answer.

Generating electricity

Hydroelectric power and solar power can be used as alternatives to fossil fuels.

Assess hydroelectric power and solar power as energy resources for the large-scale generation of electricity in the UK.

(6 marks)

Student answer

Both these resources are renewable, and they do not produce gases that harm the environment. Using these resources would help to reduce the gases put into the air by burning fossil fuels [1]. Hydroelectricity is available at any time, but solar energy is only available during the day and if the clouds are not too thick [2]. Not many places in the UK are suitable for building the reservoirs for hydroelectricity, and they can affect wildlife and habitats. Solar panels need to cover large areas of land to produce the same amount of electricity as a fossil-fuelled power station, and there is not enough sunshine in the UK to produce a lot of electricity [3]. So neither resource is really good enough to produce enough electricity to replace fossil fuels for generating electricity [4].

[1] The student has given some advantages that apply to both resources compared to using fossil fuels.

[2] This sentence considers the availability of hydroelectricity and solar power.

[3] This section explains the limitations of using hydroelectricity and solar power in the UK.

[4] The last sentence provides a final conclusion, and links this to the use of fossil fuels as mentioned in the question.

Verdict

This is a strong answer. It clearly lists the factors that affect the use of the two renewable resources and provides a conclusion. The ideas are presented clearly and in a logical order. The answer links scientific ideas together, for example, that burning fossil fuels produces gases and that these gases can harm the environment. The use of scientific language is good.

Exam tip

If a question asks you to 'assess' something, you need to consider all the factors that apply, and consider which are the most important. Most 'assess' questions require you to draw a conclusion.

Paper 5

CP4 Waves

This photo was taken as an aeroplane flew in front of the Sun. The dark lines show shock waves in the air made by the aircraft. The waves in the air cause light waves from the Sun to be refracted so we see brighter and darker areas.

The learning journey

Previously you will have learnt at KS3:

- about light waves and sound waves, and how they can be described
- how sound waves are produced and how they are detected by our ears
- some uses of sound waves
- how light can be absorbed, scattered and reflected
- different colours of light.

In this unit you will learn:

- that waves transfer energy and information
- how to describe the characteristics of waves
- how the speed of a wave is related to its frequency and wavelength
- how the speed of a wave is related to the time it takes to travel a certain distance
- how waves are refracted at boundaries between different materials.

CP4a Describing waves

Specification reference: P4.1; P4.2; P4.3; P4.4; P4.5

Progression questions

- What do waves transfer?
- How can we describe waves?
- What is the difference between a longitudinal wave and a transverse wave?

A Energy from waves demolished part of the railway line and road at Dawlish in Devon in 2014.

Sea **waves** transfer energy to the shore. When waves hit the land, the energy is transferred to the land and can wear it away.

Waves on the surface of water are **transverse** waves. Particles in the water move up and down as a wave passes – the particles are not carried to the shore.

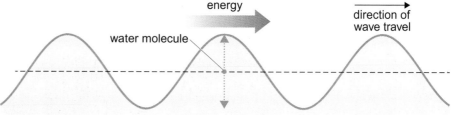

B In a transverse wave the particles move up and down at right angles to the direction the wave is moving.

 1 If the water in a wave moved in the same direction as the energy, what would happen to the water in a swimming pool if you made waves at one end?

Sound waves also transfer energy. Sound waves are **longitudinal** waves. Particles in the material through which the wave is travelling move backwards and forwards as the wave passes.

 2 Particles in a sound wave move in the same direction as the wave is travelling. Explain why loudspeakers do not move all the air in a room away from them.

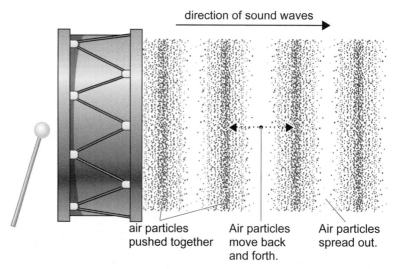

C Sound waves are longitudinal waves. The particles move back and forth in the same direction as the wave is travelling.

Earthquakes and explosions produce **seismic waves** that travel through the Earth. Solid rock material can be pushed and pulled (longitudinal seismic waves) or moved up and down, or side to side (transverse seismic waves).

Electromagnetic waves (such as light, radio waves, microwaves) are transverse waves and do not need a **medium** (material) through which to travel.

Describing waves

Wave **frequency** is the number of waves passing a point each second. It is measured in **hertz** (**Hz**). A frequency of 1 hertz means 1 wave passing per second. For sound, the wave frequency determines the pitch (how high or low it sounds) and for light the frequency determines the colour.

The **period** is the length of time it takes one wave to pass a given point.

The **wavelength** of a wave is the distance from a point on one wave to a point in the same position on the next wave, measured in metres.

The **amplitude** of a wave is the maximum distance of a point on the wave away from its rest position, measured in metres. The greater the amplitude of a sound wave, the louder the sound.

The **velocity** of a wave is the speed of the wave in the direction it is travelling. Waves travel at different speeds in different materials.

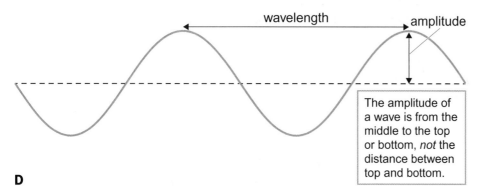

wavelength   amplitude

The amplitude of a wave is from the middle to the top or bottom, *not* the distance between top and bottom.

D

Changes in the frequency, wavelength or amplitude of a wave can be used to transfer information from one place to another. For example, when you listen to FM radio, the music is sent by variations in the frequency of the radio waves.

5 The tops of sea waves pass a stick twice every second.

 a What is the frequency?

b What is the period?

6 Write down two things that waves transfer and give an example of each.

Exam-style question

Compare and contrast the way particles move in a sound wave and in a wave on the surface of water. *(4 marks)*

3 List two types of wave that are:

 a transverse waves

 b longitudinal waves.

Did you know?

The Sun has 'sunquakes'. Huge explosions of gas, called solar flares, cause waves to spread through the Sun in a similar way to Earth movements causing earthquakes.

 4 Suggest how we see light change when the amplitude of light waves varies.

Checkpoint

How confidently can you answer the Progression questions?

Strengthen

S1 Draw a transverse wave and label the amplitude and wavelength.

S2 Describe the similarities and differences between longitudinal and transverse waves.

Extend

E1 Write glossary entries for the different terms used to describe waves, including examples of different types of wave.

E2 Explain the differences between waves on the surface of water and sound waves, in terms of what they transfer and the characteristics of the waves.

CP4b Wave speeds

Specification reference: P4.6; P4.7

Progression questions

- How can we calculate the speed (or velocity) of a wave?
- How can we measure the speed of sound in air?
- How can we measure the speed of waves on water?

A The sound waves from this volcano plume took time to reach the photographer. This time can be used to calculate how far away the lightning was.

The speed of a wave can be calculated from the distance it travels in a certain time. This is the same equation we use for calculating the speed of moving objects.

$$\text{speed (m/s)} = \frac{\text{distance (m)}}{\text{time (s)}}$$

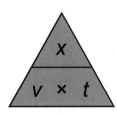

B You can rearrange the equation for speed using this triangle. v stands for speed and x stands for distance.

 1 Calculate the speed of light waves which travel 900 000 000 m in 3 s.

2 You hear thunder 5 s after you see lightning.

 a Sound travels at 330 m/s in air. How far away was the lightning strike?

 b Explain what assumption you made in your answer.

Worked example W1

A surfer travels 52 m on the front of a wave in 8 s. Calculate the wave speed.

$$\text{wave speed} = \frac{\text{distance}}{\text{time}}$$

$$\text{wave speed} = \frac{52\,\text{m}}{8\,\text{s}}$$

$$= 6.5\,\text{m/s}$$

Did you know?

Waves on the surface of water get slower as the water gets shallower. This is what causes waves to break as they reach the shore.

C

The wave speed is linked to the wave frequency and wavelength by this equation.

wave speed (m/s) = frequency (Hz) × wavelength (m)

Worked example W2

Some waves have a wavelength of 13 m and a frequency of 0.5 Hz. Calculate their speed.

$v = f \times \lambda$

= 0.5 Hz × 13 m

= 6.5 m/s

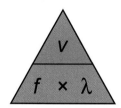

D You can rearrange the equation for wave speed using this triangle. *v* stands for speed and *f* stands for frequency. *λ* is the Greek letter lambda and represents wavelength.

 3 Calculate the speed of sound waves that have a wavelength of 2 m and a frequency of 170 Hz.

 4 Calculate the wavelength of seismic waves that travel at 5000 m/s and have a frequency of 100 Hz.

The speed of a wave depends on the medium through which it is travelling. Light always travels at 300 000 000 m/s in a vacuum but it travels more slowly in glass or water. When light goes from air into water its wavelength also reduces.

Measuring the speed of waves

You can find the speed of sound by measuring the time it takes for a sound to travel a certain distance. For example, if you stand in front of a large wall you can measure the time it takes for an echo of a loud sound to reach you. The speed can be calculated using the speed, time, distance equation.

One way of measuring the speed of waves on water is to measure the time it takes for a wave to travel between two fixed points such as buoys. The speed can be calculated from the time and the distance between the points.

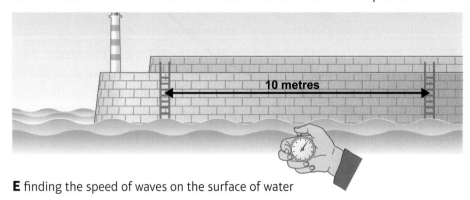

E finding the speed of waves on the surface of water

 6 Look at diagram E. It takes 7 s for a wave to move from one ladder to the other. Calculate the speed of the wave.

Exam-style question

Humans can hear sounds with a wavelength of 16 m. The speed of sound in air is 330 m/s. Calculate the frequency of these sounds. *(3 marks)*

 5 When light travels from air into water, its frequency does not change. Explain why its wavelength decreases.

Checkpoint

How confidently can you answer the Progression questions?

Strengthen

S1 An underwater sound wave travels 2000 m in 1.3 s. Calculate its speed.

S2 The frequency of the sound wave in **S1** is 3000 Hz. Calculate the wavelength of the sound wave.

Extend

E1 You are asked to find the speed of ripples on water using the equation linking speed, frequency and wavelength. Describe how to take the measurements you need and how you would work out the speed.

CP4b Core practical – Investigating waves

Specification reference: P4.17

Aim

Investigate the suitability of equipment to measure the speed, frequency and wavelength of a wave in a solid and a fluid.

A This photo shows a detailed image of the USS *Monitor* made using frequency sonar. The USS *Monitor* was an iron-hulled steamship that sank in 1862.

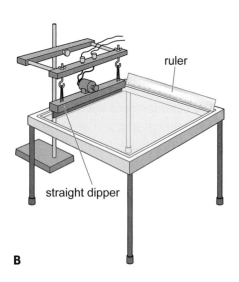

B

Light waves do not travel very far through sea water before being absorbed by the water or reflected by tiny particles in the water. This makes it impossible to take pictures of things that are deep down on the sea bed. Scientists and explorers use sonar equipment to send sound waves into the water and detect the echoes. The depth can be worked out from the speed of sound in the water and the time it takes for the echo to return.

Your task

You are going to use different pieces of equipment to measure the speed and wavelength of waves on the surface of water, and the speed and frequency of sound waves in solids.

Method

Measuring waves on water

A Set up a ripple tank with a straight dipper near one side of the tank. Fasten a ruler to one of the adjacent sides so you can see its markings above the water level.

B Vary the current to the motor until you get waves with a wavelength about half as long as the ripple tank (so you can always see two waves).

C Count how many waves are formed in 10 seconds and write it down.

D Look at the waves against the ruler. Use the markings on the ruler to estimate the wavelength of the waves. Use the wavelength and frequency to calculate the speed of the waves.

E Mark two points on the same edge of the ripple tank as the ruler. Measure the distance between your points. Use the stopwatch to find out how long it takes a wave to go from one mark to the other. Use this information to calculate the speed of the waves.

Measuring waves in solids

F Suspend a metal rod horizontally using clamp stands and rubber bands.

G Hit one end of the rod with a hammer. Hold a smartphone with a frequency app near the rod and note down the peak frequency.

H Measure the length of the rod and write it down. The wavelength will be twice the length of the rod.

I Use the frequency and wavelength to calculate the speed of sound in the rod.

Exam-style questions

1 A sound wave in air travels 660 metres in two seconds. Calculate the speed of the sound wave. *(2 marks)*

2 A sound wave travelling in water has a frequency of 100 Hz. The speed of sound in water is 1482 m/s. Calculate the wavelength of the wave. *(2 marks)*

3 Describe how to find the frequency of the waves in the ripple tank using the method in step C. *(2 marks)*

4 Luke estimated the wavelength of the waves in the ripple tank using the method described in step D. Emily took a photo of the waves in the ripple tank and estimated the wavelength using the photo.

Explain which method was likely to give the more accurate result. *(2 marks)*

5 Adanna is watching waves on the sea go past two buoys. She knows the buoys are 20 metres apart. Describe how she can find the speed of the waves. *(2 marks)*

6 Liwei measured the frequency and wavelength of waves in a ripple tank and calculated their speed as 0.4 m/s. Using the method in step E, she calculated the speed as 0.2 m/s.

Explain which result is likely to be more accurate. *(2 marks)*

7 The speed of sound in air can be measured by finding the time it takes for a sound to echo from a nearby wall, and measuring the distance to the wall.

Hitting the end of a metal rod with a hammer causes sound waves to travel along the rod. They reflect from the far end of the rod and continue to move up and down the rod until the energy dissipates.

Give a reason why the method used for finding the speed of sound in air cannot be used for finding the speed of sound in a metal. *(2 marks)*

8 Gina used the method described in step G to measure the frequency of sound in an aluminium rod 0.8 metres in length. She recorded a peak frequency of 4000 Hz. Sound inside a metal rod has a wavelength that is twice the length of the rod.

Use Gina's results to calculate the speed of sound in aluminium. *(3 marks)*

CP4c Refraction

Specification reference: H P4.10

Progression questions

- What happens when waves refract?
- When does refraction occur?
- H How does a change in the speed of a wave affect its direction?

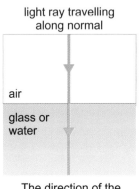

light ray travelling along normal

air

glass or water

The direction of the light does not change.

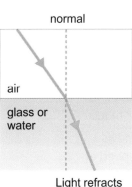

normal

air

glass or water

Light refracts towards the normal.

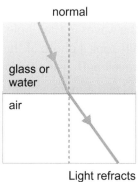

normal

glass or water

air

Light refracts away from the normal.

A Light is refracted when it goes from one material to another.

Most waves travel outwards from their source in straight lines. However, waves can change direction when they move into a different medium. The change in direction is called **refraction** and happens at the **interface** (boundary) between the two media. A line at right angles to the interface is called the **normal** line. Light travelling along the normal does not change direction when it goes into a different medium.

We see things when light reflected from them reaches our eyes. An object on the bottom of a swimming pool looks closer than it really is because light reflected by it changes direction when it leaves the water.

1 Describe how the direction of a light wave changes when it moves:

 a from glass into air

 b from air into glass.

 2 a Explain why archerfish (photo B) have to learn to compensate for refraction when aiming at insects.

b Draw a diagram to show how light reflected by the insect reaches the fish's eyes.

B Archerfish knock insects into the water by spitting at them. The fish have to learn to compensate for refraction when aiming at insects.

H

Waves can travel through many different media but with different speeds. For example, light travels faster in air than it does in glass or water. As light passes the interface between one medium and another it changes speed. This change in speed causes the direction of the light to change.

The bend depends on how fast the light travels in the two media and the angle of the light hitting the interface. The greater the difference in speed between the two media, the more the light is bent. The light bends towards the normal when it slows down.

We can use waves on water as a model to help us to understand what happens with light waves. The speed of waves on water depends on how deep the water is. Waves moving from deep water into shallow water slow down and change direction (diagram D). Lines on ray diagrams (diagram A) show the direction in which the waves are moving, not the waves themselves.

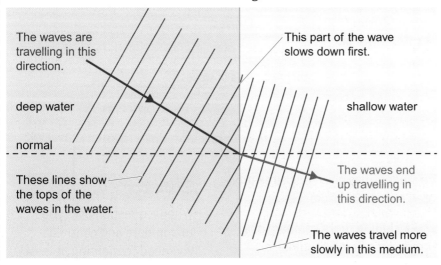

The waves are travelling in this direction.

This part of the wave slows down first.

deep water

shallow water

normal

These lines show the tops of the waves in the water.

The waves end up travelling in this direction.

The waves travel more slowly in this medium.

D Water waves change direction when the depth changes.

3 Look at diagram D. Explain what happens to the waves when they move into shallow water.

4 Explain why the waves do not change direction when they are travelling at right angles to the interface.

5 Explain what happens to waves on the surface of water when they cross an interface from shallow water into deeper water.

6 Explain how diagram A shows that light travels more slowly in glass and water than it does in air.

Exam-style question

Lane markings on the bottom of a swimming pool are straight lines. Explain why they do not usually look straight when you look at them from above the water.

(2 marks)

Did you know?

Refraction can also happen when the properties of a material change gradually. A mirage occurs when air near the ground is hotter than air higher up. In this photo, refraction is distorting the path of the light from the sky, making it appear to come from the ground and giving the impression of a puddle of water in the road.

C

Checkpoint

How confidently can you answer the Progression Questions?

Strengthen

S1 Describe how the direction of a light ray changes as it goes from air into water, and when it goes from water into air. Use the word 'normal' in your answer.

Extend

E1 **H** A ray of light shines through a thick piece of glass. Explain why the light ray emerges from the glass travelling in the same direction as originally, but not along the same line. You may use a diagram to help you to explain.

Waves

Waves on water in a ripple tank are often used as a model to help students to understand sound waves and light waves.

Compare and contrast waves on water, sound waves and light waves.

(6 marks)

Student answer

All waves move energy around [1]. We get big water waves on the sea and they can damage things in storms [2]. Light waves don't have particals, but waves on water and sound waves both have moving particals that make the waves [3]. Light can go through vacumes. We can use light waves and sound waves to send information, but we don't use waves on water for sending information [4].

[1] This is one similarity between all the types of waves mentioned.

[2] The statement about waves on the sea does not add any further scientific information.

[3] This is a difference between light waves and the other two types of waves.

[4] This is a difference between waves on water and the other two types of waves.

Verdict

This is an acceptable answer. The student has given one similarity between all the waves and pointed out some differences.

The answer could be improved by including more comparisons, such as whether the waves are transverse or longitudinal, or commenting on how fast they travel. A really good answer would also link facts together with scientific ideas – for example, by making it clear that light waves can travel through a vacuum *because* these waves do not need particles to pass them on.

The answer could also be improved by correcting the spelling of the scientific words.

Exam tip

When a question asks you to 'compare and contrast', you need to mention at least one similarity *and* at least one difference between *all* the things mentioned in the question.

Paper 5

CP5 Light and the Electromagnetic Spectrum

We see things when a form of radiation that we call visible light enters our eyes. But there are other forms of radiation similar to light that we cannot see.

Our skin can detect infrared radiation. All objects emit infrared radiation – the hotter the object the more infrared it emits. The thermogram of the penguins is an image made using a special camera that detects infrared radiation. White shows the warmest parts of the image, then red, orange and yellow, with green and blue showing the coldest areas.

In this unit you will learn about different forms of radiation that we cannot see, their uses and dangers.

The learning journey

Previously you will have learnt at KS3:

- that light transfers energy
- about colours and how different colours are absorbed and reflected differently.

In this unit you will learn:

- that light is part of a family of waves called the electromagnetic spectrum, which all have some properties in common
- about some uses of the waves in different parts of the electromagnetic spectrum
- about some of the harmful effects of the waves in different parts of the electromagnetic spectrum.

CP5a Electromagnetic waves

Specification reference: P5.7; P5.8; P5.12; **H** P5.14

Progression questions

- What are some examples of electromagnetic waves?
- What do all electromagnetic waves have in common?
- Which electromagnetic waves can our eyes detect?

A A marsh marigold flower seen in visible light (left) and ultraviolet light (right).

The distance from a point on one wave to a point in the same position on the next wave is the **wavelength**.

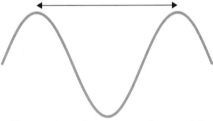

The number of waves passing a point each second is the frequency.

B Electromagnetic waves are transverse waves.

We see things when light travels from a source and is reflected by an object into our eyes. The light transfers energy from the source to our eyes. Light is a type of **electromagnetic wave**.

Our eyes can detect certain **frequencies** of light, and we refer to these frequencies as **visible light**. Different frequencies cause us to see different colours. Lower frequencies of visible light appear more red and higher frequencies appear more blue.

Some animals, such as birds, can also detect electromagnetic waves with frequencies that are higher than visible light. Electromagnetic waves with frequencies a little higher than visible light are called **ultraviolet** (**UV**).

 1 Look at the photos in A. Describe what a marsh marigold flower would look like to a bird.

All electromagnetic waves are **transverse** waves. This means that the electromagnetic vibrations are at right angles to the direction in which the energy is being transferred by the wave. All electromagnetic waves travel at the same speed (3×10^8 m/s) in a **vacuum**. Like all waves, electromagnetic waves transfer energy from a source to an observer.

 2 a What types of waves are electromagnetic waves?

 b State two ways in which electromagnetic waves differ from one another.

 3 We see visible light as a range of colours from red to green to violet. Explain whether red or violet light has the higher frequency.

Electromagnetic waves with frequencies slightly lower than visible light are called **infrared** (**IR**). All objects emit energy by infrared radiation. The hotter the object the more energy it emits. The photo on the opening page for this unit shows what penguins would look like if our eyes could detect infrared radiation. We can feel the effects of infrared radiation when energy is transferred from the Sun to our skin.

340

4 Write down two similarities and two differences between infrared radiation and ultraviolet radiation.

 5 Look at the opening page for this unit. Which parts of the penguins are the hottest?

Speed and refraction

Electromagnetic waves move at different speeds in different materials. Waves that pass an **interface** (boundary) between two materials get faster or slower. If waves meet an interface at an angle the change of speed also makes them change direction. This change of direction is called **refraction**. If they meet the interface at right angles they do not change direction.

H

Light waves slow down when they go from air into water or glass. Different frequencies of light slow down by different amounts, so they are bent by different angles. This is why a prism can be used to split up visible light into the colours of the spectrum.

 6 What happens to the speed of light when it goes from glass into air?

Discovering infrared

The first person to investigate infrared radiation was the British astronomer William Herschel (1738-1822). He put dark, coloured filters on his telescope to help him observe the Sun safely. He noticed that different coloured filters heated up his telescope to different extents and he wondered whether the different colours of light contained different 'amounts of heat'.

To test his idea he used a prism to split sunlight into a spectrum and then put a thermometer in each of the colours in turn. He also measured the temperature just beyond the red end of the spectrum, where there was no visible light.

7 Look at photo D.

 a Which colour of visible light caused the greater temperature rise?

 b Compare the energy transferred to the thermometer by infrared radiation and by visible light.

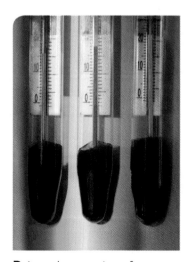

D A modern version of Herschel's experiment.

Exam-style question

State two characteristics that all electromagnetic waves have in common.

(2 marks)

C Light is refracted as it enters and leaves the goldfish bowl, and makes the cat look much bigger than it really is.

Did you know?

Some animals have special sense organs to detect infrared radiation. Many snakes, such as pit vipers, have these organs under their eyes, which help them to detect warm-blooded prey.

Checkpoint

How confidently can you answer the Progression questions?

Strengthen

S1 Describe how we can see a flower on a sunny day. Use the words 'energy' and 'transferred' in your answer.

S2 Explain why the image we see may not be the same as the image a bird sees.

Extend

E1 Compare and contrast infrared, visible light and ultraviolet radiation.

E2 Does photo D show that violet light transfers less energy than red light? Explain your answer.

CP5a Core practical – Investigating refraction

Specification reference: P5.9

Aim

Investigate refraction in rectangular glass blocks in terms of the interaction of electromagnetic waves with matter.

A This photo was taken through the wall of an aquarium. Light reflected by the parts of the turtle under the water changes direction when it enters air, and makes it look as if the animal has been cut in half!

Electromagnetic waves travel at different speeds in different materials. Light slows down when it goes from air into glass or water. If the light hits the interface at an angle, it changes direction. This is called refraction.

We can investigate refraction by measuring the angles between light rays and the **normal** (a line at right angles to the interface). The light ray approaching the interface is called the **incident ray**. The angle between this ray and the normal is called the **angle of incidence (*i*)**. The angle between the normal and the light ray leaving the interface (the **refracted ray**) is called the **angle of refraction (*r*)**.

Your task

Your task is to investigate how the direction of a ray of light changes as it enters and leaves a rectangular glass block.

Method

A Place a piece of plain paper on the desk. Set up the power supply, ray box and single slit so that you can shine a single ray of light across the paper on your desk. Take care, as ray boxes can become very hot.

B Place a rectangular glass block on the paper. Draw around the block.

C Shine a ray of light into your block. Use small crosses to mark where the rays of light go.

D Take the block off the paper. Use a ruler to join the crosses to show the path of the light, and extend the lines so they meet the outline of the block. Join the points where the light entered and left the block to show where it travelled inside the block.

E Measure the angles of incidence and refraction where the light entered the block, and measure the angles where it left the block.

F Repeat steps C to E with the ray entering the block at different angles.

G Move the ray box so that the light ray reaches the interface at right angles. Note what happens to the light as it enters and leaves the block.

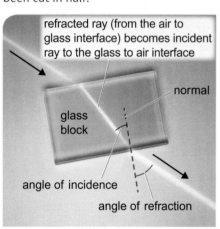

refracted ray (from the air to glass interface) becomes incident ray to the glass to air interface

normal

glass block

angle of incidence

angle of refraction

B

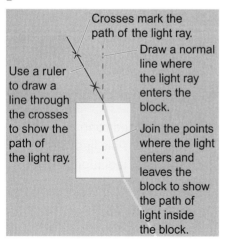

Crosses mark the path of the light ray.

Draw a normal line where the light ray enters the block.

Use a ruler to draw a line through the crosses to show the path of the light ray.

Join the points where the light enters and leaves the block to show the path of light inside the block.

C

Exam-style questions

1 Describe the difference between the way that light travels through glass compared with the way in which it travels through air? *(1 mark)*

2 State what the following terms mean:

  a normal *(1 mark)*

  b angle of incidence *(1 mark)*

  c angle of refraction. *(1 mark)*

3 Table D shows a student's results from this investigation.

  a Draw a diagram to show the glass block and a light ray going into the glass at an angle of incidence of 30°. *(2 marks)*

  b Draw in the refracted ray. *(1 mark)*

4 a Use the data in table D to plot a scatter graph to show the results for light going from air to glass. Put the angle of incidence on the horizontal axis, and join your points with a smooth curve of best fit. *(5 marks)*

  b Use table D and your graph to write a conclusion for this part of the investigation. *(3 marks)*

  c Use your graph to find the angle of refraction when the angle of incidence is 15°. *(1 mark)*

5 a Use the data in table D to plot a scatter graph to show the results for light going from glass to air. Put the angle of incidence on the horizontal axis, and join your points with a smooth curve of best fit. *(5 marks)*

  b Use your graph to write a conclusion for this part of the investigation. *(3 marks)*

  c Use your graph to find the angle of incidence when the angle of refraction is 45°. *(1 mark)*

6 If light passes through a glass block with parallel sides, the ray that comes out should be parallel with the ray that goes in. This means that the angle of incidence for air to glass should be the same as the angle of refraction from glass to air.

Look at table D. Suggest one source of random error that may have caused the differences in these angles. *(1 mark)*

Air to glass		Glass to air	
i	r	i	r
10°	6°	6°	9°
20°	13°	13°	20°
30°	20°	20°	31°
40°	25°	25°	40°
50°	30°	30°	50°
60°	34°	34°	58°
70°	38°	38°	69°
80°	40°	40°	78°

D

CP5b The electromagnetic spectrum

Specification reference: P5.10; P5.11; **H** P5.13

Progression questions

- What are the main groupings of waves in the electromagnetic spectrum?
- What characteristics of electromagnetic waves are used to group them?
- **H** What are some of the differences in the behaviour of waves in different parts of the electromagnetic spectrum?

A A rainbow shows the colours of the visible spectrum.

Visible light is part of a family of waves called electromagnetic waves. Our eyes can detect different colours in visible light. Scientists describe seven colours in the **visible spectrum**:

red, orange, yellow, green, blue, indigo, violet.

You can remember the order of the colours using a phrase such as ROY G BIV.

Did you know?

The colours in visible light were described by Sir Isaac Newton (1642–1727). He originally divided the spectrum into five colours, which were all that he could see. However, he thought there was a mystical connection between the colours, the days of the week and the number of known planets, so he ended up describing seven colours.

The colour of visible light depends on its frequency. If the frequency of an electromagnetic wave is lower than that of red light, human eyes cannot see it. Infrared, **microwaves** and **radio waves** have lower frequencies than red light.

 1 Name three different types of electromagnetic waves.

Ultraviolet radiation has a higher frequency than visible light. Even higher frequencies and shorter wavelengths are present in **X-rays** and then **gamma rays**.

The full range of electromagnetic waves is called the **electromagnetic spectrum**. The spectrum is continuous, so all values of frequency are possible. Higher frequency waves have shorter wavelengths, and lower frequency waves have longer wavelengths. It is convenient to group the spectrum into seven wavelength groups, as shown in diagram B.

 2 Which part of the electromagnetic spectrum has a higher frequency than X-rays?

 3 What type of electromagnetic wave has a wavelength between those of visible light and X-rays?

 4 How do we know that electromagnetic waves can travel through a vacuum, such as space?

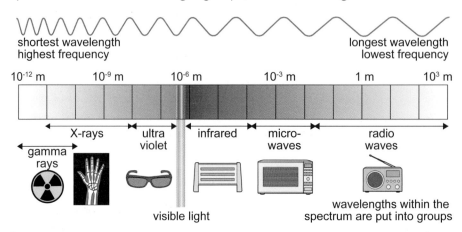

B the electromagnetic spectrum (not to scale)

H

Stars and other space objects can emit energy at all wavelengths. Astronomers use telescopes to study this radiation but they need to use different kinds of telescope to study different wavelengths. This is because different materials affect electromagnetic waves depending on the wavelength. For example, diagram C shows which wavelengths pass through the atmosphere and which are absorbed.

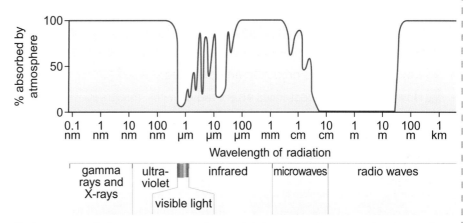

C Absorption of electromagnetic radiation by the atmosphere. You do not need to recall the details of this diagram.

Most telescopes use curved mirrors to focus the electromagnetic radiation onto a central sensor. The type of material used for the mirror and the size of the telescope depend on the wavelength of the radiation being studied.

5 Look at diagram C. Explain why telescopes that detect infrared radiation from objects in space are put into orbit around the Earth.

D The Arecibo telescope in Puerto Rico has a reflector dish that is over 300 m in diameter and contains nearly 40 000 aluminium panels.

Checkpoint

How confidently can you answer the Progression questions?

Strengthen

S1 List the seven parts of the electromagnetic spectrum in order and describe how the wavelength and frequency change from one end of the spectrum to the other.

Extend

E1 **H** Explain how the locations and types of instruments astronomers use depend on the wavelength of the electromagnetic waves that they study.

Exam-style question

State one way in which X-rays are similar to visible light, and one way in which they are different. *(2 marks)*

CP5c Using the long wavelengths

Specification reference: **H** P5.13; **H** P5.14; P5.22; **H** P5.23

Progression questions

- What are some uses of radio waves, microwaves and infrared?
- **H** How are radio waves produced and detected?
- **H** How do different substances affect radio waves, microwaves and infrared?

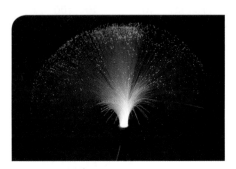

A This sculpture is made from optical fibres which act as 'light pipes'. Visible light and infrared can both be sent along optical fibres.

Did you know?

Microwave cooking was invented by Percy Spencer (1894–1970). The heating effects of radio waves had been known for years, but Spencer applied the idea to cooking after he noticed that waves from a radar apparatus he was working with had melted a chocolate bar in his pocket.

The uses for the waves in different parts of the electromagnetic spectrum depend on their wavelengths.

Visible light

Visible light is the part of the electromagnetic spectrum that our eyes detect. Light bulbs are designed to emit visible light, while cameras detect it and record images.

Infrared

Infrared radiation can be used for communication at short ranges, such as between computers in the same room or from a TV to its remote control unit. The information sent along optical fibres is also sent using infrared radiation.

A grill or toaster transfers energy to food by infrared radiation. The food absorbs the radiation and heats up. Thermal images show the amount of infrared radiation given off by different objects.

Security systems often have sensors that can detect infrared radiation emitted by intruders. Some buildings are fitted with systems of infrared beams and detectors – someone walking through one of these beams breaks it and sets off the alarm.

Microwaves

Microwaves are used for communications and satellite transmissions, including mobile phone signals. In a microwave oven, microwaves transfer energy to the food, heating it up from the inside.

Radio waves

Radio waves are used for transmitting radio broadcasts and TV programmes as well as other communications. Some radio communications are sent via satellites. Controllers on the ground communicate with spacecraft using radio waves.

B Pilots communicate with each other and with ground controllers using radio waves.

1 Which parts of our body can detect:

   a visible light

   b infrared radiation?

2 List three parts of the electromagnetic spectrum used for communication.

 3 Describe how two different parts of the electromagnetic spectrum are used for cooking.

 4 Suggest why security systems have sensors that detect infrared rather than other wavelengths of electromagnetic radiation.

H

Radio waves are produced by **oscillations** (variations in current and voltage) in electrical circuits. A metal rod or wire can be used as an aerial to receive radio waves. The radio waves are absorbed by the metal and cause oscillations in electric circuits connected to the aerial.

Waves travel in straight lines unless they are reflected or refracted. Refraction is the bending of the path of a wave due to a change in velocity. Some frequencies of radio waves can be refracted by a layer in the atmosphere called the ionosphere. If radio waves reach the ionosphere at a suitable angle, they may be refracted enough to send them back towards the Earth. Microwaves are not refracted in the Earth's atmosphere.

The oscillations cause radio waves to spread out from the aerial.

Radio waves cause an oscillating current in the receiving aerial.

Current moves up and down in the aerial.

transmitting aerial — receiving aerial

radio transmitter circuits / radio receiver circuits

C

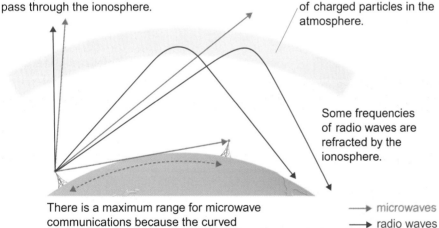

Some radio waves and all microwaves pass through the ionosphere.

The ionosphere is a region of charged particles in the atmosphere.

Some frequencies of radio waves are refracted by the ionosphere.

There is a maximum range for microwave communications because the curved surface of the Earth gets in the way.

→ microwaves
→ radio waves

D The maximum distance (range) of radio communication is much greater than for microwave communication.

 5 Microwaves and radio waves are both used for communication between different places on the Earth. Explain why a satellite is needed to give microwaves a similar range to radio waves.

Checkpoint

How confidently can you answer the Progression questions?

Strengthen

S1 Draw a table or make a list of bullet points to show the uses for visible light, infrared, microwaves and radio waves.

Extend

E1 Compare the uses for visible light, infrared, microwaves and radio waves.

Exam-style question

Compare the ways in which infrared and microwaves are used in cooking.
(2 marks)

Did you know?

Obtaining clean drinking water is a problem in many parts of the world. Microorganisms in water can be killed by putting the water in clear plastic bottles and leaving them in sunshine for several hours. Infrared energy from the sun heats up the water and the high temperature and the ultraviolet radiation both help to kill microorganisms.

A

Ultraviolet

Ultraviolet radiation transfers more energy than visible light. It is absorbed by most of the same materials that absorb visible light, including our skin. The energy transferred can be used to disinfect water by killing microorganisms in it.

 1 Why would there be UV lamps at a sewage works?

Some materials absorb ultraviolet radiation and re-emit it as visible light. This is called **fluorescence**. Fluorescent materials are often used in security markings – they are only visible when ultraviolet light shines on them.

Many low energy light bulbs are fluorescent lamps. A gas inside these lamps produces ultraviolet radiation when an electric current passes through it. A coating on the inside of the glass absorbs the ultraviolet and emits visible light.

 2 Why might someone write their postcode on a TV or computer using a pen with fluorescent ink that is not visible in normal light?

B Forged banknotes can be detected using UV light because they do not have markings that glow. These are real notes.

X-rays

X-rays can pass through many materials that visible light cannot. For example, they can pass through muscles and fat easily but bone absorbs some X-rays. This means X-rays can be used in medicine to make images of the inside of the body. X-rays can also be used to examine the insides of metal objects and to inspect luggage in airport security scanners.

 3 Suggest two reasons why security staff at airports use X-ray scanners to check luggage instead of looking inside the luggage.

Gamma rays

Gamma rays transfer a lot of energy, and can kill cells. For this reason, they are used to sterilise food and surgical instruments by killing potentially harmful microorganisms.

Gamma rays are used to kill cancer cells in **radiotherapy**. They can also be used to detect cancer. A chemical that emits gamma rays is injected into the blood. The chemical is designed to collect inside cancer cells. A scanner outside the body then locates the cancer by finding the source of the gamma rays. Gamma rays can pass through all the materials in the body.

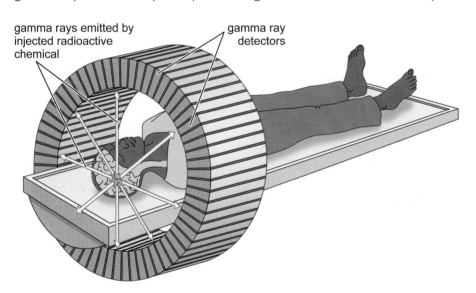

gamma rays emitted by injected radioactive chemical

gamma ray detectors

D a gamma ray medical scanner

 4 Describe two ways in which gamma rays can be used for medical purposes.

 5 H Describe the differences in the way muscle, fat and bone absorb or transmit X-rays and gamma rays.

Exam-style question

Describe three different ways in which electromagnetic radiation with frequencies greater than that of visible light can be used in medicine.

(3 marks)

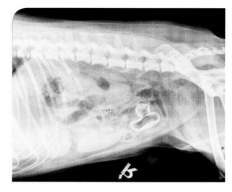

C This X-ray image shows that the dog has swallowed a toy duck.

Did you know?

Lenses, such as spectacle lenses, work because light travels more slowly in glass than in air and changes direction as it changes speed. The change of speed when X-rays enter different materials is very small, so X-rays can only be focused using several metal lenses together.

Checkpoint

How confidently can you answer the Progression questions?

Strengthen

S1 Describe three uses for:
  a ultraviolet radiation
  b X-rays
  c gamma rays.

Extend

E1 State two similarities and two differences between:
  a gamma rays and ultraviolet radiation
  b gamma rays and X-rays.

CP5e EM radiation dangers

Specification reference: P5.20; P5.21; P5.24

Progression questions

- What are the dangers of electromagnetic radiation?
- How is the danger associated with an electromagnetic wave linked to its frequency?
- How is electromagnetic radiation linked to changes in atoms and their nuclei?

A Mobile phone transmitters use different frequencies of microwaves compared with microwave ovens.

 1 Why should you be careful not to stand too close to a bonfire?

 2 Why do microwave ovens have shields in them to stop the waves escaping?

All waves transfer energy. A certain microwave frequency can heat water and this frequency is used in microwave ovens. This heating could be dangerous to people because our bodies are mostly water and so the microwaves could heat cells from the inside. Mobile phones use different microwave frequencies. Current scientific evidence tells us that, in normal use, mobile phone signals are not a health risk.

B The metal grid in the door of the microwave oven reflects microwaves but the holes allow visible light through.

Infrared radiation is used in grills and toasters to cook food. Our skin absorbs infrared, which we feel as heat. Too much infrared radiation can damage or destroy cells, causing burns to the skin.

Higher-frequency waves transfer more energy than low-frequency waves and so are potentially more dangerous. Sunlight contains high frequency ultraviolet radiation, which carries more energy than visible radiation. The energy transferred by ultraviolet radiation to our cells can cause sunburn and damage **DNA**. Too much exposure to ultraviolet radiation can lead to **skin cancer**. We can help to protect our skin by staying out of the strongest sunshine, covering up with clothing and hats, and using sun cream with a high SPF (sun protection factor).

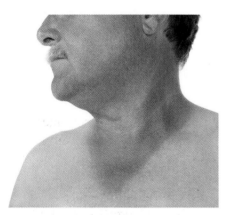

C Sunburn is caused by too much ultraviolet radiation being absorbed by the skin.

The ultraviolet radiation in sunlight can also damage our eyes. Skiers and mountaineers can suffer temporary 'snow blindness' because so much ultraviolet radiation is reflected from snow. We can protect our eyes using sunglasses.

D This photo was taken using ultraviolet light. The dark spots show parts of the skin that may have been damaged by exposure to lots of ultraviolet light from the Sun. Some of this damage could eventually turn into skin cancer.

 3 State three ways to protect your body against damage by UV radiation when in bright sunlight.

X-rays and gamma rays are higher frequency than ultraviolet radiation and so transfer more energy. They also can penetrate the body. Excessive exposure to X-rays or gamma rays may cause **mutations** in DNA that can kill cells or cause cancer.

 4 Why do people have hospital X-ray photographs taken if X-rays are so dangerous?

 5 Two different electromagnetic waves have frequencies of 10 000 Hz and 100 000 Hz. Explain which wave is likely to cause the most harm if absorbed by your body.

Radiation and atoms

Electromagnetic radiation is produced by changes in the electrons or the nuclei in atoms. For example, when materials are heated, changes in the way the electrons are arranged can produce infrared radiation or visible light. Changes in the nuclei of atoms can produce gamma radiation.

Radiation can also cause changes in atoms, such as causing atoms to lose electrons to become ions. You will learn more about this in Unit CP6.

 6 Explain why gamma radiation produces positive ions.

Exam-style question

Look back at diagram C on CP5b. Explain why changes in the composition of the atmosphere could cause an increase in skin cancer. *(2 marks)*

Checkpoint

How confidently can you answer the Progression questions?

Strengthen

S1 State one danger to your body of:

  a microwaves

  b infrared radiation

  c ultraviolet radiation

  d X-rays and gamma rays.

Extend

E1 Draw a table with a row for each part of the electromagnetic spectrum mentioned on these pages, with frequency increasing down the table. In the second column list any hazards that you know of for each part of the spectrum. Use your table to explain how the frequency relates to the potential danger.

Electromagnetic waves

Infrared and ultraviolet waves have different frequencies. Both types of wave can have harmful effects on humans. Compare and contrast the harmful effects of infrared and ultraviolet waves.

(6 marks)

Student answer

Infrared waves and ultraviolet waves can both damage our skin [1]. Infrared waves can cause skin burns, for example when we have been sunbathing [2]. Ultraviolet waves can damage our eyes and damage the cells in our skin which can lead to skin cancer [3]. Ultraviolet waves have higher frequencies than infrared waves, which is why they cause more harm [4].

[1] This is a similarity between the harm caused by the two types of radiation. This question asks you to 'compare and contrast', so you need to include both similarities and differences.

[2] The student has mentioned a harmful effect of infrared.

[3] This mentions harmful effects of ultraviolet, and so is contrasting the harm with the harm caused by infrared.

[4] This last part explains why ultraviolet causes more harm by linking its frequency with the danger.

Verdict

This is a strong answer. It mentions the different types of harm that can be caused by each type of wave, and mentions similarities between the waves. The answer also links ideas together by pointing out that the higher frequency waves are more harmful.

Exam tip

Once you have written your answer, read the question again to make sure you have answered all parts of the question. In this case, don't forget to relate the harm caused by the different types of wave to their frequency.

Paper 5

CP6 Radioactivity

In the first half of the twentieth century, radium paint was used to make objects such as watch hands and numbers glow in the dark. The paint was radioactive. The women who painted the watch faces used to 'point' their brushes by putting them in their mouths. The women did not know about the harmful effects of this until they noticed that their teeth were beginning to fall out and their jaw bones were collapsing. In this unit you will find out more about atoms and their structure, and how atoms can produce radioactivity when they change.

The learning journey

Previously you will have learnt at KS3:

- about the particle model of matter
- that atoms contain smaller charged particles called electrons.

In this unit you will learn:

- how the particles inside atoms are arranged
- how to represent atoms using symbols
- about the different types of radiation and how they affect atoms
- about the background radiation that is all around us
- about the dangers of radiation and how we can protect ourselves.

CP6a Atomic models

Specification reference: P6.1; P6.2; P6.17

Progression questions

- What particles make up atoms?
- How big are atoms?
- How has our model of the atom changed over time?

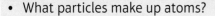
1.2 × 10⁻¹⁰ m
(0.00000000012 m,
or 0.12 millionths
of a millimetre)

a carbon dioxide
molecule modelled
using spheres

an oxygen atom
modelled as
a sphere

A Atoms and molecules are often modelled as spheres.

Particle theory (or **kinetic theory**) is a model that helps explain the properties of solids, liquids and gases. The particles are usually represented as spheres.

We can explain some of the properties of different **elements** by thinking about the particles that each contains. We call these particles **atoms**. Chemical reactions occur when the different atoms in substances become joined in different ways.

1 How does particle theory explain why solids have a fixed shape?

These ideas helped scientists throughout the 1800s. However, in 1897 J.J. Thomson (1856–1940) carried out some experiments that showed that atoms contain much smaller **subatomic particles** called **electrons**. These had a negative charge and hardly any mass.

In the 1900s, Thomson supported using a new model for atoms that could explain this new evidence. This new model described the atom as a 'pudding' made of positively charged material, with negatively charged electrons (the 'plums') scattered through it.

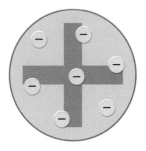

B the plum pudding model of the atom

2 Positive and negative charges cancel each other out. How does the plum pudding model explain that atoms have no overall charge?

3 Carbon atoms are roughly the same size as oxygen atoms. How long is the carbon dioxide molecule shown in diagram A?

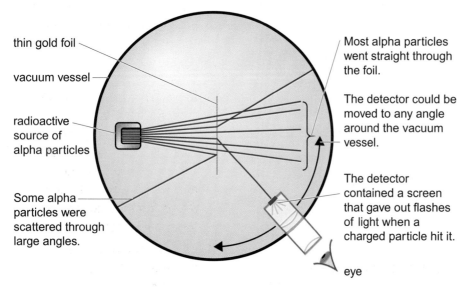

thin gold foil

vacuum vessel

radioactive source of alpha particles

Some alpha particles were scattered through large angles.

Most alpha particles went straight through the foil.

The detector could be moved to any angle around the vacuum vessel.

The detector contained a screen that gave out flashes of light when a charged particle hit it.

eye

C the design of one of Rutherford's experiments

Between 1909 and 1913, a team of scientists led by Ernest Rutherford (1871–1937) carried out a series of experiments that involved studying what happened when positively charged subatomic particles, called **alpha particles**, passed through various substances (such as gold foil).

In the experiment shown in diagram C, the scientists discovered that most of the alpha particles passed through the gold foil, but a few bounced back. The plum pudding model could not explain this result.

Rutherford suggested that atoms were mostly empty space, with most of their mass in a tiny central **nucleus** with a positive charge and electrons moving around the nucleus. Figure D shows how this model of the atom explains the results.

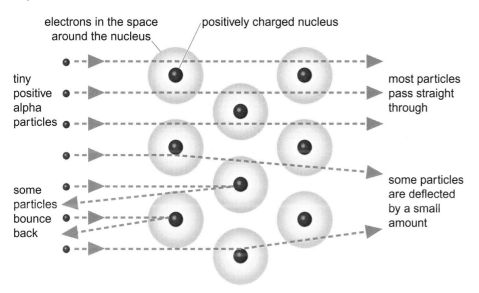

D The small nucleus in Rutherford's model explained why a small number of alpha particles were deflected by the gold foil.

Today, we know that the radius of a nucleus is about 1×10^{-15} m (0.000 000 000 000 001 m). The radius of an atom is about 1×10^{-10} m (0.000 000 000 1 m). So the atom itself is 100 000 times bigger than the nucleus inside it.

E If an atom had the same diameter as the dome of the O2, its nucleus would be the size of this dot ●.

 5 A dot one millimetre in diameter represents the nucleus of an atom. To the same scale, how far across would the whole atom be?

Exam-style question

Compare and contrast Rutherford's model of the atom with the plum pudding model.   *(4 marks)*

4 Which part of Rutherford's atomic model is responsible for some alpha particles bouncing back?

Checkpoint

How confidently can you answer the Progression questions?

Strengthen

S1 Describe Rutherford's model of the atom. Include these words in your description: charge, electron, mass, nucleus.

Extend

E1 Draw a labelled diagram to show Rutherford's model of the atom and explain why it is not drawn to scale. (Note that neutrons had not been discovered when Rutherford was carrying out his experiments.)

E2 Describe two pieces of evidence that support this model of the atom.

CP6b Inside atoms

Specification reference: P6.3; P6.4; P6.5; P6.6

Progression questions

- What are the relative masses and charges of the particles that make up atoms?
- What are isotopes of an element?
- How can isotopes be represented using symbols?

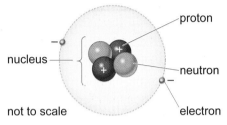

A the structure of an atom

The mass of an atom is concentrated in its nucleus. The nucleus itself is made up of smaller particles called **nucleons**. Nucleons can be **protons** or **neutrons**. All subatomic particles have very small masses so it is easier to describe their **relative masses**. We give the proton a mass of 1 and we compare the masses of the other subatomic particles relative to this. Table B summarises the subatomic particles within atoms.

Subatomic particle	Location in atom	Relative charge	Relative mass
proton	nucleus	+1 (positive)	1
neutron	nucleus	0	1
electron	around nucleus	−1 (negative)	$\frac{1}{1835}$ (negligible)

B The mass of an electron is so small that it is usually ignored when talking about the mass of an atom.

1 Which two subatomic particles:

 a are nucleons

 b have a charge

 c have a relative mass of 1?

2 What do these numbers tell you about the numbers of protons, neutrons and electrons in the atoms of an element?

 a the atomic number

 b the mass number

All atoms of a particular element have the same number of protons. This number is called the **atomic number** or **proton number** of the element. Atoms of different elements have different numbers of protons and so have different atomic numbers.

Neutrons have no charge and so it is the protons that give the nucleus its positive charge. Atoms have the same number of electrons as protons and so atoms are always electrically neutral (they have no overall charge).

The number of neutrons in an atom can vary. The **mass number** or **nucleon number** is the total number of protons and neutrons in the nucleus.

We can represent the atomic number and mass number of an element in symbol form, as shown in diagram C.

 protons + neutrons
= mass number
= 12

$^{12}_{6}\text{C}$

 protons
= atomic number
= 6

Worked example

An atom of nitrogen has 7 protons and 7 neutrons. Show this atom in symbol form, with its mass and atomic numbers.

mass number = 7 + 7 = 14

In symbols, this is written as $^{14}_{7}\text{N}$.

C In symbol form, the mass number is always above the atomic number in both value and position.

Isotopes

Two atoms of the same element will always have the same atomic number, but they can have different mass numbers if they contain different numbers of neutrons. Atoms of a single element that have different numbers of neutrons are called **isotopes**.

For example, carbon can occur naturally as carbon-12, carbon-13 or carbon-14. The number in the name is the mass number of the isotope. The atomic number of carbon is 6, so an atom of carbon-14 has 6 protons and 8 neutrons in its nucleus.

D a carbon-14 nucleus

Did you know?

The age of the remains of extinct animals such as this mammoth can be found by examining the different isotopes of carbon in them.

E

Exam-style question

Sam says that as two different atoms have the same mass number, they must be isotopes. Is Sam correct? Explain your answer.   *(2 marks)*

3 A helium nucleus has 2 protons and 2 neutrons. Write down the symbol for this isotope of helium.

4 The symbol for an isotope of beryllium is $^{9}_{4}\text{Be}$. How many of the following particles does it contain?

 a protons

 b neutrons

5 How many neutrons are there in the nucleus of an atom of:

 a oxygen-18

 b carbon-13?

Checkpoint

How confidently can you answer the Progression questions?

Strengthen

S1 Write glossary definitions for these terms: atomic number, electron, isotope, mass number, neutron, proton.

Extend

E1 Hydrogen has three isotopes, hydrogen-1, hydrogen-2 and hydrogen-3. The atomic number of hydrogen is 1. Explain what an isotope is and give the similarities and differences between these three isotopes.

CP6c Electrons and orbits

Specification reference: P6.7; P6.8; P6.9; P6.17

Progression questions

- How are electrons arranged in an atom?
- What happens to atoms when they absorb or emit electromagnetic radiation?
- How do atoms become ionised?

A The different colours in this sign are due to the different gases inside the tubes. The orange tubes contain neon gas.

These orbits (electron shells) are normally empty in neon atoms.

nucleus

If an atom absorbs energy, an electron can move to a 'higher' orbit.

When an electron returns to a lower orbit the atom emits energy as visible light of a particular wavelength.

Electrons can make all of these different orbit changes. Each different change produces a different wavelength of light.

B electronic configuration and energy level changes for neon

emission

absorption

C emission and absorption spectra for neon

The tubes in photo A produce light when an electrical voltage makes electrons move within atoms of a gas.

The electrons in an atom can only exist in certain **orbits** around the nucleus, called **electron shells**. Each electron shell is at a different energy level. Diagram B shows the **electronic configuration** for neon.

In a neon tube, the neon atoms absorb energy transferred by the electricity because the electrons jump to higher shells. When the electrons fall back again they emit energy as **electromagnetic radiation** that we can see. The top part of photo C shows the colours of visible light emitted by neon. Each colour is a different **wavelength** of light. This is called an **emission spectrum**. The emission spectrum is different for each element.

 1 Look at photo A. How do you know that several different gases are used in the sign?

 2 Look at diagram B. Explain why neon can emit light at lots of different wavelengths.

 3 Suggest an explanation for why neon tubes glow orange.

Gases can also absorb energy transferred by electromagnetic radiation, such as **visible light**. The bottom part of photo C shows the parts of the **visible spectrum** that neon gas absorbs when light passes through it. This is the **absorption spectrum** for neon. The wavelengths of light that neon gas absorbs are the same wavelengths that it emits.

Niels Bohr (1885–1962) amended Rutherford's model of the atom to explain observations like these by suggesting that electrons can only be in certain fixed orbits (electron shells) around the nucleus. They cannot be part-way between two orbits. This model could explain the lines in emission and absorption spectra.

Ionisation

Sometimes an atom gains so much energy that one or more of the electrons can escape from the atom altogether. An atom that has lost or gained electrons is called an **ion**. Radiation that causes electrons to escape is called **ionising radiation**.

An atom has the same number of protons and electrons, so overall it has no charge. If an atom loses an electron, it then has one more proton than it has electrons. It has an overall positive charge and is called a **positive ion**.

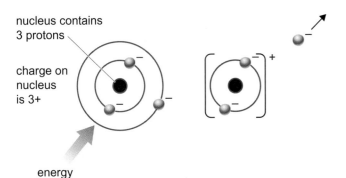

D ionisation of a lithium atom

 5 Describe what happens if an atom absorbs less energy than the amount needed to ionise it.

6 Sodium has an atomic number of 11 and loses 1 electron when it forms an ion. How many protons and electrons are in:

 a a sodium atom

b a sodium ion?

 4 a What is the Rutherford model of the atom? (You may need to look back at CP6a.)

 b How is Bohr's model different from Rutherford's model?

Did you know?

The different colours in fireworks are due to metal compounds. When the firework goes off, metal ions give out different coloured light as electrons change energy levels.

Checkpoint

How confidently can you answer the Progression questions?

Strengthen

S1 Draw a labelled diagram to describe the Bohr model of the atom.

S2 Describe how an atom becomes a positive ion.

Extend

E1 Describe the link between energy, the emission of light and the orbits of electrons in an atom.

CP6d Background radiation

Specification reference: P6.12; P6.13; P6.14

Progression questions

- What is meant by background radiation?
- What are the sources of background radiation?
- How is radioactivity detected and measured?

A This radon outlet pipe sucks air containing radon from beneath a solid concrete floor, stopping it from entering the house.

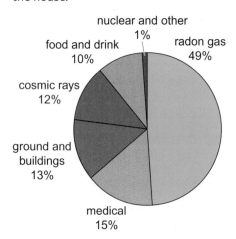

B sources of background radiation in the UK

We are constantly being exposed to ionising radiation at a low level, from space and from naturally radioactive substances in the environment. This is called **background radiation**.

Sources of background radiation

Chart B below shows the sources of background radiation averaged over the UK. The main source is radon gas. This radioactive gas is produced by rocks that contain small amounts of uranium. Radon diffuses into the air from rocks and soil and can build up in houses, especially where there is poor ventilation. The amount of radon in the air depends on the type of rock and its uranium content. Rock type and building stone vary around the country and so does the amount of radon.

 1 Explain why background radiation varies in different parts of the UK.

Some foods contribute to your exposure to background radiation because they naturally contain small amounts of radioactive substances. Hospital treatments, such as X-rays, gamma-ray scans and cancer treatments, also contribute to people's exposure to background radiation.

High-energy, charged particles stream out of the Sun and other stars. They are known as **cosmic rays** and are a form of radiation. Many cosmic rays are stopped in the upper atmosphere but some still reach the Earth's surface.

 2 Approximately how much background radiation in the UK comes from natural sources?

 3 Suggest how your food and drink become naturally radioactive.

 4 During a solar storm, the Sun's output of high-energy charged particles increases dramatically. Explain why some scientists suggest that aeroplanes should fly at lower altitudes during a solar storm.

Measuring radioactivity

Radioactivity can be detected using photographic film, which becomes darker and darker as more radiation reaches it. However, the film has to be developed in order to measure the amount of radiation (the **dose**). People who work with radiation often wear film badges (called dosimeters) to check how much radiation they have been exposed to. Newer dosimeters use materials that change colour without needing to be developed.

The radioactivity of a source can also be measured using a **Geiger-Müller (GM) tube**. Radiation passing through the tube ionises gas inside it and allows a short pulse of current to flow.

A GM tube can be connected to a counter, to count the pulses of current, or the GM tube may give a click each time radiation is detected. The **count rate** is the number of clicks per second or minute.

Did you know?

Henri Becquerel (1852–1908) discovered radioactivity when he put some substances he was investigating on top of a photographic plate in an envelope. When he developed the plate he found it had become dark and he suggested that some 'rays' emitted by the material had caused this effect.

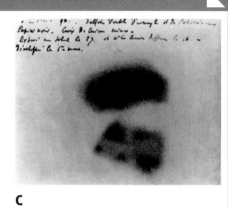

C

D using a GM tube and counter to measure radiation

When scientists measure the radioactivity of a source, they need to measure the background radiation first by taking several readings and finding the mean. This mean value is then subtracted from measurements.

 5 Tom records background counts of 15, 22 and 17 counts per minute. He then records a count rate of 186 counts per minute from a sample of granite. What is the corrected count rate for the sample's activity?

Exam-style question

The following was found on a blog: 'Natural radiation won't hurt you but human-made radiation will.' Comment on this statement. *(4 marks)*

Checkpoint

How confidently can you answer the Progression questions?

Strengthen

S1 List three sources of background radiation.

S2 Describe two ways of detecting radiation.

Extend

E1 Explain why the measurements of the activity of a radioactive source must be corrected.

CP6e Types of radiation

Specification reference: P6.5; P6.10; P6.11; P6.15; P6.16

Progression questions

- What are alpha particles, beta particles and gamma radiation?
- How do the different kinds of radiation compare in their ability to penetrate materials?
- How do the different kinds of radiation compare in their ability to ionise atoms?

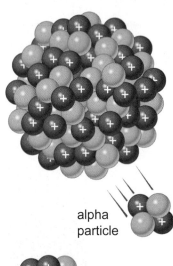

alpha particle

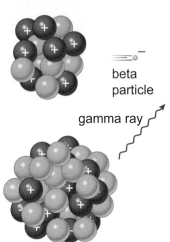

beta particle

gamma ray

A Three types of radiation that can be emitted by unstable nuclei.

The nucleus of a radioactive substance is **unstable**, which means it can easily change or **decay**. When decay occurs, radiation is emitted which causes the nucleus to lose energy and become more stable. You cannot predict when a nucleus will decay – it is a **random** process.

Types of radiation

There are different sorts of radiation that a nucleus can emit when it decays.

Alpha particles contain two protons and two neutrons, just like the nucleus of a helium atom. They have a relative mass of 4. They have no electrons and so have a charge of +2. They can be written as α or $^4_2$**He**.

> The electrons that are beta particles come from the *nuclei* of atoms when a neutron transforms into a proton. Beta particles do not ionise the atoms as they leave them.

Beta particles are high-energy, high-speed electrons. They have a relative mass of $\frac{1}{1835}$ and a charge of –1. They can be written as β^- or $^0_{-1}$**e**.

> This number represents charge.

Positrons are high-energy, high-speed particles with the same mass as electrons but a charge of +1. They can be written as β^+ or $^0_{+1}$**e**.

Gamma-rays (γ) are high-frequency electromagnetic waves (they travel at the speed of light). They do not have an electric charge.

Neutrons can also be emitted from an unstable nucleus. They have a relative mass of 1 and no electric charge.

 1 Draw a table to summarise the charges and relative masses of the five different types of radiation emitted from atomic nuclei.

 2 Carbon-12 is a stable isotope and carbon-14 is an unstable isotope. Explain which of these isotopes will decay.

Did you know?

Electrons are normal matter particles and positrons are antimatter particles. If a positron meets an electron, the two particles will annihilate each other, releasing energy. The energy released is far more than can be obtained from normal chemical fuels and NASA are carrying out research to see if antimatter can be used to power spacecraft.

B

Ionising and penetrating radiation

The types of radiation described above are all examples of ionising radiation, and they can all **penetrate** (pass through) materials.

Alpha particles are emitted at high speeds. Due to this and their high relative mass, they transfer a lot of energy and so are good at ionising atoms they encounter. However, each time they ionise an atom they lose energy. Since they produce many ions in a short distance, they lose energy quickly and have a short penetration distance.

Beta particles are much less ionising than alpha particles and so can penetrate much further into matter than alpha particles can. Gamma-rays are about ten times less ionising than beta particles and can penetrate matter easily.

(α) alpha particles
• will travel a few centimetres in air
• very ionising
• can be stopped by a sheet of paper

(β⁻) beta particles
• will travel a few metres in air
• moderately ionising
• can be stopped by 3mm thick aluminium

(γ) gamma rays
• will travel a few kilometres in air
• weakly ionising
• need thick lead or several metres of concrete to stop them

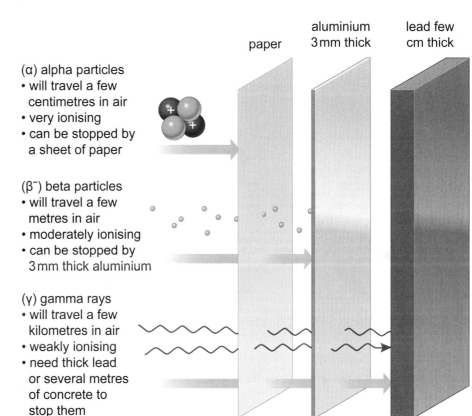

C the penetrating properties of alpha, beta and gamma radiation

D Gamma-rays can be used to check the inside of lorries, to help prevent the movement of illegal goods.

 3 What materials will absorb and stop beta particles?

 4 The reactor in a nuclear power station is surrounded by large amounts of concrete. Why is this necessary?

 5 Look at photo D. Explain why gamma radiation is used for checking lorries.

 6 Explain how an oxygen molecule in the air might become an ion by being near a radioactive source.

Checkpoint

How confidently can you answer the Progression questions?

Strengthen

S1 Describe alpha particles, beta particles and gamma radiation.

S2 Draw up a table to summarise the penetration and ionisation properties of the three types of radiation in question **S1**.

Extend

E1 Use the characteristics of alpha and beta particles to explain the differences in their abilities to ionise and penetrate.

Exam-style question

Compare and contrast the emission of an electron during the ionisation of an atom with the emission of an electron during β⁻ decay. *(4 marks)*

CP6f Radioactive decay

Specification reference: P6.18; P6.19; P6.20; P6.21; P6.22

Progression questions

- How does beta decay occur?
- How are atomic and mass numbers affected by different kinds of decay?
- How can radioactive decays be represented in nuclear equations?

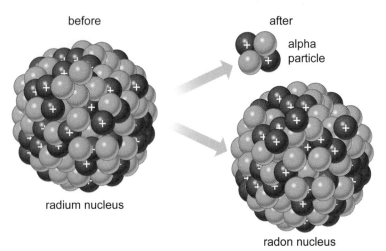

A Alpha decay turns a radium nucleus into a radon nucleus.

When an unstable nucleus changes and emits particles, the atomic number can change. If this happens, the atom becomes a different element. For example, when an alpha particle is emitted, the mass number of the nucleus goes down by 4 and the atomic number goes down by 2.

During β⁻ decay, a neutron changes into a proton and an electron. The electron is ejected from the atom. The atomic number increases by 1 but there is no change to the mass number.

In β⁺ decay a proton becomes a neutron and a positron. The atomic number goes down by 1 but the mass number does not change.

If a neutron is ejected from a nucleus, the mass number goes down by 1 but the atomic number does not change.

Nuclei may also lose energy as gamma radiation when the subatomic particles in the nucleus are rearranged. This helps to make them more stable.

 1 Carbon-14 decays by emitting a beta particle. How is the beta particle formed?

Did you know?

Long-lasting lights can be made using tritium, a radioactive isotope of hydrogen (hydrogen-3). The tritium is placed in a sealed glass tube coated on the inside with a material that glows when it is hit by the particles produced as the tritium decays.

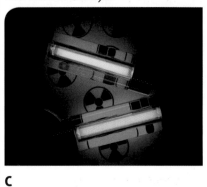

C

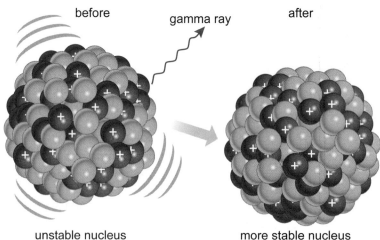

B gamma radiation

 2 Explain why the numbers of nucleons do not change if a nucleus emits only gamma radiation.

3 When a neutron is ejected, explain why:

    a the mass number drops   **b** the atomic number stays the same.

Nuclear equations

A **nuclear equation** shows what happens during radioactive decay. The equation must be balanced – the total mass number must be the same on each side and the total charges must be the same.

Table D shows the symbols used to represent the various particles. The atomic (proton) number for a nucleus or an alpha particle also represents the amount of positive charge. We give beta particles and positrons a –1 or +1 to indicate their charge.

Particle	Symbol	
alpha	α	^4_2He
beta	β^-	$^0_{-1}e$
positron	β^+	$^0_{+1}e$
neutron		n

D symbols used in nuclear equations

Worked example W1

Radium-226 emits an alpha particle. What is the other product?

$$^{226}_{88}Ra \rightarrow {}^4_2He + ?$$

On the right of the arrow the nucleus has an atomic number of 88 – 2 = 86. This is radon (Rn). (The atomic numbers also represent the positive charges.)

Mass numbers must also balance. The radon nucleus has a mass number of 226 – 4 = 222.

$$^{226}_{88}Ra \rightarrow {}^4_2He + {}^{222}_{86}Rn$$

Worked example W2

Iodine-131 undergoes β^- decay. What is the other product?

$$^{131}_{53}I \rightarrow {}^0_{-1}e + ?$$

The mass number stays the same. The atomic number goes up by 1 to 54. This is xenon (Xe). The atomic numbers represent positive charges and the –1 on the beta particle represents a negative charge.

$$^{131}_{53}I \rightarrow {}^0_{-1}e + {}^{131}_{54}Xe$$

4   Write balanced nuclear equations to show the following decays. You will need to use the periodic table at the back of the book.

   a Polonium-208 ($^{208}_{84}Po$) undergoes α decay.

   b Technetium-99 ($^{99}_{43}Tc$) undergoes β^- decay.

   c Potassium-37 ($^{37}_{19}K$) undergoes β^+ decay.

5   Explain the difference between radioactive decay and a chemical reaction in the way new substances are formed.

Exam-style question

Describe what happens when a nucleus undergoes β^+ decay and the effect this has on the nucleus.   *(2 marks)*

Checkpoint

How confidently can you answer the Progression questions?

Strengthen

S1 Draw up a table to summarise the different types of radioactive decay, and what effect each one has on the atomic number and mass number of the nucleus.

S2 Carbon-14 ($^{14}_6C$) undergoes β^- decay. Write a balanced nuclear equation to show this.

Extend

E1 Polonium-216 ($^{216}_{84}Po$) undergoes alpha decay and the product then undergoes β^- decay. Write two nuclear equations to show this sequence of decay.

CP6g Half-life

Specification reference: P6.23; P6.24; P6.25; P6.26; P6.27

Progression questions

- How does the activity of a substance change over time?
- What does the half-life of a radioactive substance describe?
- How can the half-life be used to work out how much of a substance decays?

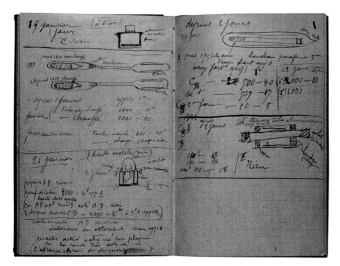

A one of Marie Curie's notebooks

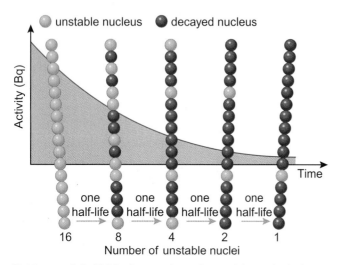

B After each half-life the number of unstable nuclei halves.

 2 What does the half-life of an isotope describe?

 3 A 10 kg sample of caesium-137 has a half-life of 30 years. What is the half-life of a 5 kg sample?

Marie Curie (1867–1934) made many important discoveries connected with radioactivity, before its dangers were known. Her laboratory notebooks are still radioactive and will be dangerous for at least another 1500 years.

When an unstable nucleus undergoes radioactive decay its nucleus changes to become more stable. The **activity** of any radioactive substance is the number of nuclear decays per second and is measured in **becquerels** (**Bq**). One becquerel is one nuclear decay each second.

 1 A sample of uranium-235 has a decay rate of 2 Bq. How many nuclei decay each second?

Radioactive decay is a random process – we cannot predict when it will happen. When you throw a die, sometimes you get a six and sometimes you don't. The **probability** of getting a six is $\frac{1}{6}$.

In a similar way, at any given moment there is a certain probability that a particular unstable nucleus will decay.

The **half-life** is the time taken for half the unstable nuclei in a sample of a radioactive isotope to decay. This is shown in diagram B. We cannot predict the decay of an individual nucleus because it is a random process. However, the half-life does allow us to predict the activity of a large number of nuclei. The half-life is the same for any mass of a particular isotope. Some half-lives are shown in table C.

Isotope	Half-life
uranium-235	700 million years
carbon-14	5730 years
caesium-137	30 years
radon-222	3.8 days

C half-lives of some isotopes

After decaying, a nucleus may become stable. The more stable nuclei a sample of a substance contains, the lower its activity. The half-life of an isotope is therefore also a measure of how long it takes for the activity to halve. It can be found by recording the activity of a sample over a period of time.

Worked example

In figure D, the activity at 3 minutes is 800 counts per second. After one half-life the count rate will have decreased to 400 counts per second.

This occurs at 9.5 minutes, so the half-life is 9.5 – 3 = 6.5 minutes.

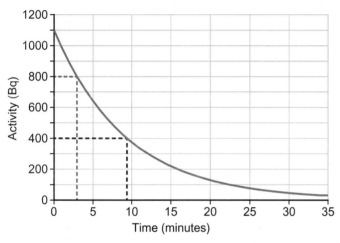

D graph of activity against time for a radioactive substance

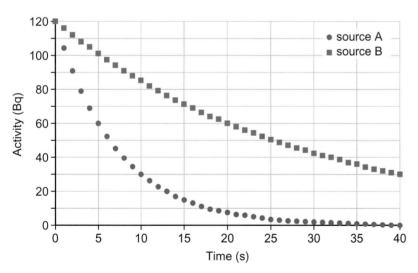

E graph showing the decay of two different radioactive substances

 6 Work out the half-lives of the two sources shown in Figure E.

Exam-style question

Describe how you could find the half-life of a newly discovered radioactive substance. *(2 marks)*

4 Strontium-90 has a half-life of 29 years. How many strontium-90 half-lives is:

 a 29 years **b** 58 years

 c 116 years **d** 14.5 years?

5 There are 10 million atoms in a sample of radon-222. How many undecayed nuclei are left after:

 a 3.8 days **b** 7.6 days

 c 11.4 days **d** 1.9 days?

Did you know?

When the Earth was formed around 4.5 billion years ago, most of it was molten. The Earth has been cooling down ever since but part of the core is still molten, partly because of the energy released by radioactive isotopes in the Earth.

Checkpoint

How confidently can you answer the Progression questions?

Strengthen

S1 A sample of caesium-137 has an activity of 100 Bq. What will its activity be in 90 years time?

Extend

E1 Explain what the half-life of a radioactive sample tells you about how its activity and the number of unstable nuclei change over time.

E2 A sample containing carbon-14 has an activity of 1.5 Bq. How long ago would it have had an activity of 24 Bq?

CP6h Dangers of radioactivity

Specification reference: P6.29; P6.31; P6.32

Progression questions

- What are the dangers of ionising radiation?
- What precautions should be taken to protect people using radiation?
- What is the difference between contamination and irradiation effects?

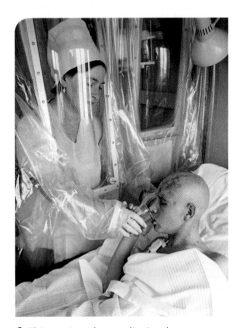

A This patient has radiation burns. He was among the first emergency personnel on the scene after the Chernobyl nuclear power plant disaster on 26 April 1986.

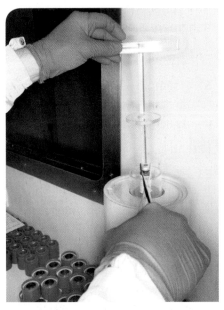

B Radioactive sources are handled with tongs.

A large amount of ionising radiation can cause tissue damage such as reddened skin (radiation burns) and also other effects that cannot be seen.

Small amounts of ionising radiation over long periods of time can damage the DNA inside a cell. This damage is called a **mutation**. DNA contains the instructions controlling a cell, so some mutations can cause the cell to malfunction and may cause cancer. Gene mutations that occur in gametes can be passed on to the next generation. However, not all mutations are harmful and cells are often capable of repairing the damage if the radiation **dose** is low.

 1 Describe two effects of ionising radiation on the human body.

Radiation is a hazard, because it can cause harm. We are exposed to background radiation all the time, but we are only exposed to small amounts so the risk of harm is low. However, people who work with radioactive materials could be exposed to more radiation and so must take precautions to minimise the risks from radiation.

Handling radioactive sources

The intensity of radiation decreases with distance from the source, so sources are always handled with tongs. The risk can also be reduced by not pointing sources at people and storing them in lead-lined containers.

2 Explain how the following precautions reduce exposure to radiation.

 a handling sources with tongs

 b storing sources in lead-lined containers

Radiation in hospital

Medical staff working with radioactive sources have their exposure limited in a number of ways, including increasing their distance from the source, shielding the source and minimising the time they spend in the presence of sources. Their exposure is also closely monitored using dosimeter badges (see CP6d).

Some patients may be exposed to a dose of radiation for medical diagnosis or treatment (such as detecting and treating cancer). This is only done when the benefits are greater than the possible harm the radiation could cause, and the minimum possible dose is used.

Nuclear accidents

Occasionally there is an accident in a nuclear power station, allowing radioactive materials to escape into the environment. Accidents such as this cause a hazard, as they may lead to people being irradiated or contaminated.

Someone is **irradiated** when they are exposed to alpha, beta or gamma radiation from nearby radioactive materials. Once the person moves away the irradiation stops.

Someone becomes **contaminated** if they get particles of radioactive material on their skin or inside their body. They will be exposed to radiation as the unstable isotopes in the material decay, and this will continue until the material has all decayed or until the source of contamination is removed (which is not always possible). Water and soils can also be contaminated, so contamination can spread into the food chain.

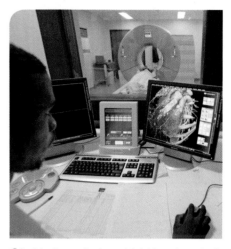

C behind a radiation shield in a hospital

D These workers are cleaning up after an accident at a nuclear reactor. The overalls stop their clothing becoming contaminated.

Dangers in perspective

It is important to understand that the dangers of radiation from medicine, industry and power generation are small compared with many other aspects of our modern lives. However, many people are concerned that accidents may happen in nuclear power stations.

 3 Look at photo D. Suggest why the workers are wearing breathing masks.

4 Explain whether an alpha or beta source is the most harmful if both sources are:

 a outside the body

 b inside the body (e.g. if breathed in or swallowed).

Exam-style question

Describe the difference between contamination and irradiation. *(2 marks)*

Did you know?

When radioactivity was first discovered, people did not know of the harm it could cause. Radioactive substances such as thorium and radium were put into face creams and other products because people thought they might have health benefits.

Checkpoint

How confidently can you answer the Progression questions?

Strengthen

S1 What are the hazards posed by radiation?

S2 Describe three ways of minimising the risk from radiation.

Extend

E1 Explain two precautions that should be taken by people:

a working with radioactive sources in industry

b using radioactive sources in hospitals

c cleaning up after a nuclear accident.

Background radiation

Some scientists carry out an experiment to measure the radioactivity from a source to be used in a factory.

They measure the background radiation before and after their experiment.

They take the background count at the same place they do their experiment.

Explain how this procedure helps to make sure that the results of the experiment are valid.   (6 marks)

Student answer

Background radiation is around us all the time and comes from natural and human sources. Up to half of it can come from radon gas and a lot of it also comes from the ground and from hospitals [1]. It is not the same in every place, so the background count needs to be measured at the place where you are doing an experiment [2]. If they don't measure the background count, their radiation measurements of the source will be wrong [3].

[1] The question did not ask for information about different sources of background radiation. Putting in information that is not asked for does not gain any extra credit and wastes time.

[2] This explains why the background count has to be measured in the same place as the experiment.

[3] This does not actually explain how the measurements of background radiation are used to make the results valid. Valid results would only be obtained if the values for radioactivity only came from the source – so the background count needs to be measured and subtracted from the counts in the experiment.

Verdict

This is an acceptable answer. The student has used scientific knowledge to explain that background radiation varies from place to place, and so measurements should be taken in the place where the experiment is carried out.

The answer could be improved by linking facts with scientific reasons. For example, explaining that the results are only valid if they are only measuring radioactivity levels from the source. This is why the background count needs to be subtracted from the radioactivity of the source. The answer also needs to link the fact that the background count varies with time to the idea that the background count needs to be taken both before and after the experiment is carried out.

Exam tip

You should be able to apply your knowledge of practical work to other contexts. In this example you should be able to explain what has to be measured and why, in order to make the data as useful as possible.

Paper 6

CP7 Energy – Forces Doing Work / CP8 Forces and their Effects

This base jumper is wearing a wing suit. As he falls, gravitational potential energy stored in his body will be transferred to a store of kinetic energy because of the force produced by the Earth's gravitational field. The wing suit will help him to fly away from the cliff.

In this unit you will learn more about how forces can transfer energy. You will also learn about force fields, and how to use vector diagrams to work out what happens when several different forces act on an object at the same time.

The learning journey

Previously you will have learnt at KS3:

- the different ways in which energy can be stored and transferred
- about using force arrows in diagrams, adding forces in one dimension, balanced and unbalanced forces
- the effects of balanced and unbalanced forces.

You will also have learnt in *CP1 Motion* and *CP3 Conservation of Energy*:

- the difference between vector and scalar quantities
- how to calculate changes in GPE and KE (also examined in this paper)
- about energy transfer diagrams and how to work out the efficiency of a transfer (also examined in this paper).

In this unit you will learn:

- how the energy in a system can be changed
- how to calculate power and work done
- how objects interact with each other, through force fields and contact forces
- **H** how to use vector diagrams to work out the effects of forces on an object.

CP7a Work and power

Specification reference: P8.1; P8.4; P8.5; P8.6; P8.7; P8.12; P8.13; P8.14

Progression questions

- How can the energy of a system be changed?
- What is work done and how can it be measured and calculated?
- What is power and how is it calculated?

A Animals are used instead of machines in many parts of the world.

Energy is transferred whenever things happen. Electricity transfers energy to an electric light bulb, which then transfers the energy to the surroundings by light and heating.

Energy can also be transferred when a force makes something move. The energy transferred by a force is called **work done**, and this amount of energy depends on the size of the force and on how far the force moved. We can calculate the work done using this equation:

 1 Give the scientific meaning for work done.

$$\underset{(J)}{\text{work done}} = \underset{(N)}{\text{force}} \times \underset{(m)}{\text{distance moved in the direction of the force}}$$

This can be written as:

$$E = F \times d$$

 2 The log in photo A weighs 1800 N and the elephant lifts it up 1.5 metres. How much work does the elephant do?

where E represents work done

F represents force

d represents distance.

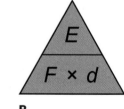

B

Worked example

Danny is moving a box weighing 300 N. He pulls it 3 m along a sloping ramp using a force of 200 N. Calculate the work Danny does.

$E = F \times d$

$= 200\,\text{N} \times 3\,\text{m}$ ⟶ The force must be in the direction of the movement.

$= 600\,\text{J}$

3 Calculate the work done when:

 a a weightlifter lifts a 280 N barbell weight 1.5 m straight up

 b a boy cycles 760 m against friction forces of 140 N.

 4 The total weight of the osprey and fish in photo C is 550 N. The osprey does 2200 J of work. Calculate how high it lifts the fish.

C An osprey does work when it lifts a fish.

Power

Power is the rate at which energy is transferred. When energy is being transferred by forces, then power is also the rate of doing work. Power is measured in **watts (W)**. 1 watt means 1 joule of work done per second.

If two ospreys lift the same sized fish 2 metres in the air, they will both have done the same amount of work. But if one lifts its fish in a shorter time, that bird has produced a greater power.

Power can be calculated using this equation:

$$\text{power (W)} = \frac{\text{work done (J)}}{\text{time taken (s)}}$$

This can be written as:

$$P = \frac{E}{t}$$

where E represents work done

P represents power

t represents time.

Did you know?

Some adverts still quote the power of vehicles in horsepower. This term was first used in the 1700s to compare the power of steam engines with the power of a horse. 1 horsepower = 746 watts.

D Horses are still used for ploughing in some parts of the world.

E

5   Iesha and Fran both weigh 500 N. Iesha runs up a 3 m high flight of stairs in 10 seconds. Fran takes 12 seconds.

 a Calculate the work done by Iesha in climbing the stairs.

 b Calculate the power of each girl.

 6   Explain how an electric motor can transfer energy to a system by heating. Include the word friction in your answer.

Checkpoint

How confidently can you answer the Progression questions?

Strengthen

S1 Explain what you would need to measure to find out how much work the horses in photo D do when they plough a field.

S2 A car has a weight of 10 000 N. A man takes 10 seconds to push it 5 m using a force of 1000 N.

    a Calculate the work done.

    b Calculate the power of the man.

Extend

E1 A 7800 W lift took 10 seconds to move a 5000 N weight. How far did the lift move this weight?

Exam-style question

Two children with the same mass run up the same flight of stairs. One child takes twice as long as the other. Compare the work done and the power of the two children.

(4 marks)

CP8a Objects affecting each other

Specification reference: P9.1; P9.2

Progression questions

- What forces are there when two objects are touching?
- How can objects affect each other without touching?
- How are pairs of forces represented?

A What forces are acting on the narrowboat and on the aqueduct?

weight of gymnast

normal contact force from beam

B The weight of the gymnast is balanced by the normal contact force from the beam acting upwards. The normal contact force acting on the gymnast is a reaction force due to the weight of the gymnast acting on the beam.

Objects can interact (affect each other) by exerting forces on each other. If the objects are touching, then the forces between them are **contact forces**. When you stand on the floor, there is an upwards force from the floor on you called the **normal contact force**. The narrowboat in photo A needs an engine to keep it moving because water resistance (a form of **friction**) slows it down. The force from the engine and water resistance are both contact forces.

The narrowboat is floating because of another contact force, called **upthrust**, from the water. The upthrust is balanced by a **non-contact force** called gravity. Gravity does not need to touch the boat to give it weight. The upthrust and the weight are both acting on the same object.

1 Look at photo A.

 a How is the water affecting the narrowboat?

 b How is the narrowboat affecting the water?

 2 Describe the forces caused by the interaction of the aqueduct with the ground below it.

Gravity is a force that occurs between any two objects that have mass. The Moon stays in orbit around the Earth because the two bodies are attracting each other. The force from the Moon on the Earth is the same size as the force from the Earth on the Moon, but in the opposite direction. The gravitational forces between two objects with mass can be represented as **vectors** (arrows that show both direction and magnitude). These two forces are **action–reaction forces** (pairs of forces acting on *different* objects, in opposite directions).

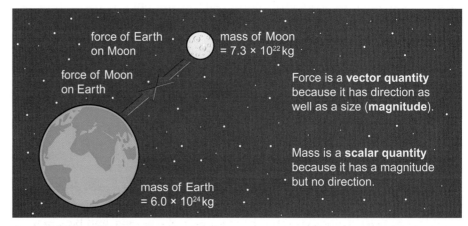

force of Earth on Moon

mass of Moon = 7.3×10^{22} kg

force of Moon on Earth

Force is a **vector quantity** because it has direction as well as a size (**magnitude**).

Mass is a **scalar quantity** because it has a magnitude but no direction.

mass of Earth = 6.0×10^{24} kg

C The gravitational forces between the Earth and the Moon can be shown using arrows, where the length of the arrow represents the size of the force.

The space around an object where it can affect other objects is called a **force field**. The Moon and the Earth affect each other because the Moon is within the Earth's **gravitational field** and vice versa.

Other forces that affect objects they are not in direct contact with are **magnetism** and **static electricity**. A **magnet** can attract objects made from **magnetic materials** including iron, nickel and cobalt. A magnet can attract or repel another magnet. The space around a magnet where it can affect other materials is called the **magnetic field**.

An object charged with static electricity has an **electric field (electrostatic field)** around it. The electric field can affect objects within it. Two objects with the same charge that are close to each other produce a pair of forces that are equal in size and acting in opposite directions.

D Foam packing pellets can pick up a charge of static electricity and become attracted to things around them.

5 Draw a diagram with arrows to show the forces between two charged objects that are:

 a attracting each other

b repelling each other.

Exam-style question

Two plastic rods with identical charges of static electricity are suspended near each other. Describe the forces between the two rods, and between the rods and the Earth. *(4 marks)*

 3 Describe the effect of the gravitational force from the Sun on the Earth.

 4 The force from the Sun on the Earth is 3.5×10^{22} N. What is the force of the Earth on the Sun?

Did you know?

The gravitational force between two people standing next to each other is about 0.000 003 N.

Checkpoint

How confidently can you answer the Progression questions?

Strengthen

S1 Name three contact forces and three non-contact forces.

Extend

E1 A heavy box is resting on a table. Describe how it interacts with the table and with the Earth.

E2 Describe one similarity and two differences between a gravitational field and a magnetic field.

CP8b Vector diagrams

Specification reference: **H** P9.3; **H** P9.4; **H** P9.5

Progression questions

- **H** What is a free body force diagram?
- **H** How and why do we resolve forces?
- **H** How do all the forces on a single body combine to affect it?

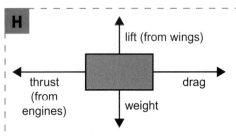

A A free body force diagram for an aeroplane. The arrows represent force vectors. The direction of the arrow shows the direction of the force and the length of the arrow represents its size. The simplest aeroplane to sketch is a box!

Every object usually has more than one force acting on it. If the forces are equal in size but in opposite directions, the **resultant force** (or **net force**) is zero. The forces on the object are said to be balanced.

When an aeroplane is flying at a constant velocity and height, the horizontal forces and vertical forces on it are balanced. The resultant (net) force on the aeroplane is zero. You can show the forces on the aeroplane using a **free body force diagram**, as shown in diagram A.

1 Describe the resultant force on a car that is slowing down.

2 Draw a free body force diagram to show:

a the vertical forces on a person sitting on a chair

b the forces on a car travelling at a constant speed.

The forces on an object are not always acting along the same line. When an aeroplane makes a cross-wind landing, the force from the aeroplane's engines is pushing it forwards, but there is also a force from the wind pushing it sideways. We can find the resultant force using a **scale diagram**.

Did you know?

Many airports have several runways pointing in different directions. This allows the pilot to use the one nearest to the wind direction to reduce the component of the wind acting across the runway.

3 In Figure B the force from the engines is 50 kN and the force from the wind is 15 kN at an angle of 150° from the direction the aeroplane is pointing. Draw a scale diagram to work out the resultant of these two forces.

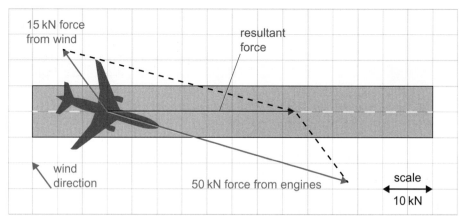

- Draw arrows at the correct angles to represent the forces. The length of each arrow should represent the size of the force.

- Draw lines to make a parallelogram.

- The resultant force is the diagonal of the parallelogram. Measure this arrow to work out the size of the resultant force.

B A scale diagram can be used to work out a resultant force.

H

The aeroplane in photo C is climbing at a steep angle. The thrust from its engines is helping it to climb. We can work out how much of the thrust is pushing the aeroplane upwards and how much is pushing it forwards by **resolving** the thrust force into two **component** forces at right angles to each other. This can be done using a scale diagram, as shown in diagram D.

C The aeroplane is at an angle of 30° to the ground. The engines generate 200 kN of thrust.

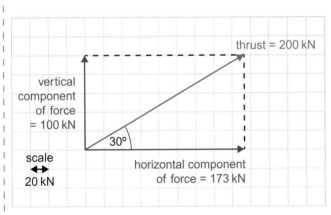

- Draw a force arrow to scale at the correct angle.

- Draw a rectangle with the sides in the directions you are interested in (e.g. horizontal and vertical).

- The resolved forces are the sides of the rectangle.

D A scale diagram can be used to resolve the forces on an aeroplane.

 5 An aeroplane is climbing at an angle of 50° to the horizontal, with 200 kN of thrust. Draw a scale diagram to find the vertical component of this thrust.

Exam-style question

Look at the aeroplane in photo C. Describe how the horizontal and vertical components of the force would change if the aeroplane were climbing at a shallower angle. *(4 marks)*

 4 a Which force, affecting the horizontal movement of the aeroplane, has not been included in diagram B?

 b The aeroplane is moving at a constant velocity. Explain how the size and direction of the force from part 4a compares to the resultant force you worked out in question 3.

Checkpoint

How confidently can you answer the Progression questions?

Strengthen

S1 There is a forwards force of 20 N on a toy car and a backwards force of 5 N.

  a Calculate the resultant force.

  b Explain the effect of the resultant force.

  c Draw a free body force diagram to represent all of the forces on the toy car.

Extend

E1 A model rocket takes off at an angle of 20° from the vertical. Its thrust is 50 N. Draw a scale diagram to work out the horizontal and vertical components of the thrust.

Walking uphill

Al walks directly up a hill and he takes 12 minutes to get to the top. Bev walks up the same hill on a shallower path that zig zags as it goes up. She takes 15 minutes to get to the top.

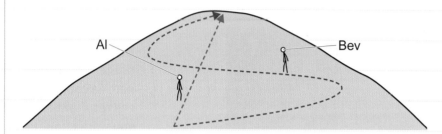

Explain who has exerted the greater power, and who has transferred more energy while getting to the top of the hill. Include any assumptions you make in your answer.

(6 marks)

Student answer

Power is the rate of doing work, and is measured in watts. In climbing the hill, they are doing work against gravity, and the energy transferred is the force (their weight) multiplied by the distance moved in the direction of the force (up the hill) [1]. If they both have the same weight, as they both have climbed the same distance, in theory they have both transferred the same amount of energy [2]. Al exerted the greater power because he gained the height in a shorter time [3].

However, this answer may not be correct if their weights are not the same. It also assumes that the human body is totally efficient, which it is not. As Bev was walking for longer, she will waste more energy and so will have transferred more energy altogether [4].

[1] The answer correctly describes what power and work mean.

[2] This states that both have transferred the same amount of energy if we make an assumption about their weights.

[3] This part of the answer explains who has transferred more power.

[4] The final section points out that the answer relies on certain assumptions that may not be correct.

Verdict

This is a strong answer. It answers all the points in the question and also explains the assumptions that had to be made in reaching the conclusion. The points in the answer are given in a logical order and linked together with scientific ideas.

Exam tip

Make sure you understand key terms and can use them correctly. In this example, the key terms are power and energy. It can be useful to circle the key terms in the question to help you think about what they mean as you prepare your answer.

Paper 6

CP9 Electricity and Circuits

An incubator has many circuits to keep a premature baby alive. It monitors the baby's temperature, blood oxygen concentration, heart rate and breathing rate. It can make automatic adjustments to the baby's environment and alert staff to problems.

In this unit you will learn how electricity is supplied to hospitals, homes and factories, and about its effects and uses in many different types of circuits.

The learning journey

Previously you will have learnt at KS3:

- that electric current is measured in amps and voltage is measured in volts
- that circuits can be connected with components in series or in parallel
- that conductors have low resistance and insulators have high resistance.

In this unit you will learn:

- about current, charge and potential difference
- how to calculate resistance, power and energy transferred
- about components with changing resistance
- about the UK domestic electricity supply and electrical safety features in homes.

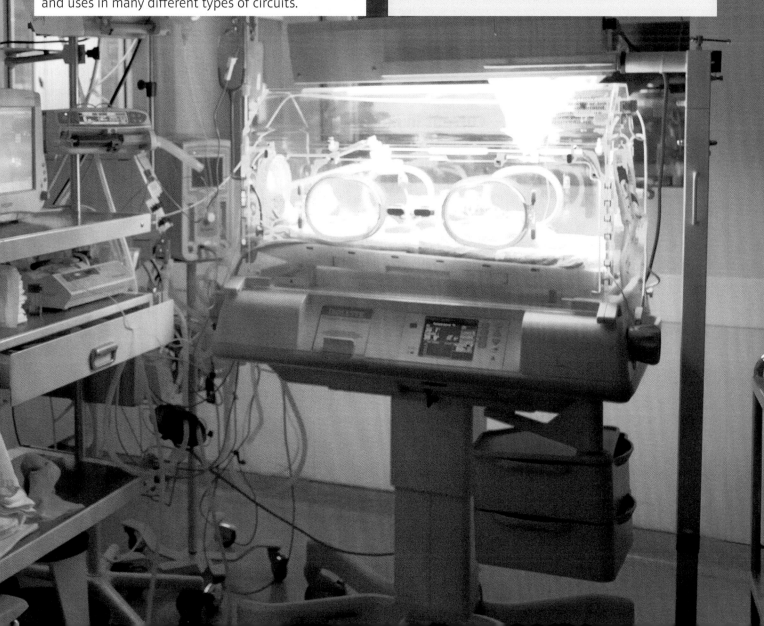

CP9a Electric circuits

Specification reference: P10.1; P10.2; P10.3

Progression questions

- How does the structure of atoms affect the flow of electric current?
- What are the names and symbols of components used in electric circuits?
- What are the differences between series and parallel circuits?

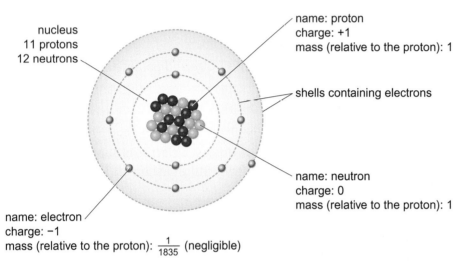

name: proton
charge: +1
mass (relative to the proton): 1

shells containing electrons

name: neutron
charge: 0
mass (relative to the proton): 1

nucleus
11 protons
12 neutrons

name: electron
charge: −1
mass (relative to the proton): $\frac{1}{1835}$ (negligible)

A the structure of a sodium atom (not to scale)

Diagram A shows a sodium **atom**. The atom has a central **nucleus** of positively charged **protons** and uncharged **neutrons**. Both these particles have a similar mass.

The **electrons** are found at different distances from the nucleus, in **shells**. Electrons are much smaller than protons or neutrons. Each electron has a negative charge, equal but opposite to the charge on a proton. The number of electrons is equal to the number of protons and so overall an atom is uncharged.

 1 Draw a table of the particles in the atom, giving their charge, mass (relative to the proton) and their location in the atom.

 2 Draw a diagram of a carbon-14 atom with 6 protons and 8 neutrons.

Current in metals

Sodium is a metal. Look at diagram A. There is one electron in the outer shell that is only weakly attracted to the nucleus. All metals have electrons like this, including copper which is used for electrical wiring. These electrons can easily be removed, so a metal wire has many 'free' electrons. When a battery is attached to the wire the voltage 'pushes' the free electrons around the circuit. The electrons are negatively charged so they move towards the positive terminal of the battery.

When working with circuits, however, the conventional direction of current is used. Conventional current direction goes from the positive terminal to the negative terminal of the battery.

Did you know?

The conventional direction of current is thanks to Benjamin Franklin, an American scientist. He chose the direction long before the electron was discovered.

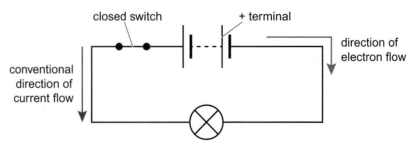

closed switch   + terminal

conventional direction of current flow

direction of electron flow

B electron flow and conventional current

Series and parallel circuits

Circuit diagrams are used to show the components and the junctions in a circuit. Table C shows some common circuit symbols.

Components in circuits can be connected in **series** or **parallel**. In series circuits there is just one route the current can take around the circuit. In parallel circuits there are junctions that allow the current to take different routes. Diagram D shows circuit diagrams for both series and parallel circuits.

Circuit symbol	Component	Circuit symbol	Component
switch (open)	switch (open)	lamp	lamp
cell	cell	ammeter	ammeter
battery	battery	voltmeter	voltmeter

C table of circuit symbols

In the series circuit, lamps cannot be switched on and off individually, and if one lamp fails they will all switch off. In the parallel circuit each lamp can be switched separately.

a) series   b) parallel

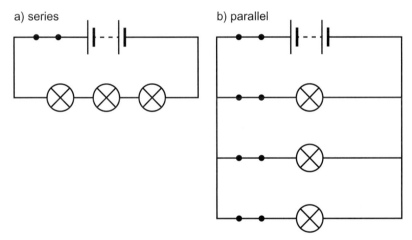

D three lamps connected in a) series and b) parallel

 3 Draw a series circuit with:

   a 2 lamps

   b a switch and 4 lamps.

 4 Draw a circuit with 2 lamps in parallel.

5 Draw a circuit containing 3 lamps, one in series and two in parallel. Include 3 switches (both open and closed) to show how two of the lamps could be lit and one of them unlit.

Exam-style question

Look at diagram D. Explain what happens in each circuit if all the lamps are on and then one lamp breaks.   *(4 marks)*

Checkpoint

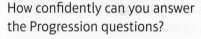

How confidently can you answer the Progression questions?

Strengthen

S1 Draw a circuit diagram with a cell, two lamps in parallel and two switches so that each lamp can be turned off separately.

S2 Add labelled arrows to your diagram from **S1** showing the directions of conventional current and electron flow.

Extend

E1 Describe the way that the protons, neutrons and electrons are arranged in an atom and explain why having free electrons means that metals can conduct electricity.

E2 Compare and contrast series and parallel circuits.

CP9b Current and potential difference

Specification reference: P10.4; P10.7; P10.10; P10.11

Progression questions

- How is electric current measured?
- What happens to the electric current at a junction in the circuit?
- What is potential difference and how do you measure it?

Current

Electric current is measured in units called **amperes** (often shortened to **amps**, A), using an **ammeter**. An ammeter is connected in series to measure the current passing through a component or circuit.

The total amount of current stays the same on its journey around the circuit. The current leaving the positive terminal of the battery is the same as the current arriving at the negative terminal. This is because current is **conserved**. In a parallel circuit, current splits at a junction to travel along different branches, but the total amount entering the junction is the same as the total amount leaving.

Did you know?

There are several different species of fish called electric rays. They can use electricity to stun or kill their prey. The voltage used can be as high as 220 V.

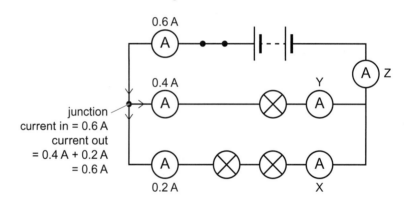

A Currents are conserved at the junctions.

 1 In the circuit in diagram A, what is the reading on ammeter:

 a X

 b Y

 c Z?

 2 A current of 2 A passes through a circuit with 5 identical lamps in parallel. What is the current through each lamp?

Potential difference

You need a **potential difference** to 'push' current around an electric circuit. Potential difference is also called **voltage**. Diagram B shows marbles on a ramp. This can be used as a model for potential difference. On a flat surface the marbles won't move but when there is a height difference, they can roll down the ramp. Similarly, electrons will flow when a potential difference is applied across a component.

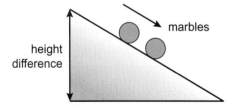

B A height difference applied to the ramp can make marbles roll.

A circuit contains electrons all the way round. For a current to flow, the circuit must be closed and contain a source of potential difference (such as a **cell** or **battery**). The electrons all move together when a current flows.

 3 Explain what happens to the marbles when the height difference in diagram B is increased.

4 For a current to flow, why must there be:

 a a potential difference

 b a closed circuit?

The bigger the potential difference across a component the bigger the current.

In a parallel circuit, the potential difference across each branch of the circuit is the same. When there is more than one component in a branch of a circuit, the potential differences across all the components add up to give the total potential difference supplied by the cell or battery.

Potential difference is measured in **volts**, V, using a **voltmeter.** A voltmeter is always connected in parallel to measure the potential difference across a component or circuit.

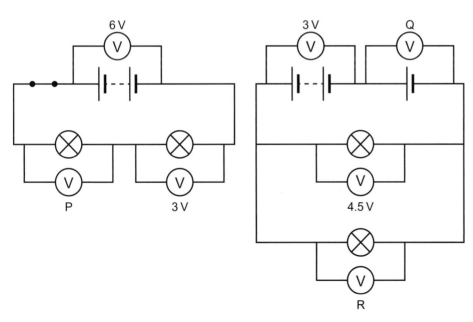

C A voltmeter is always connected in parallel with components.

 5 In the circuits in diagram C, calculate the potential difference measurements on voltmeters P, Q and R.

Exam-style question

Describe how you would measure the current and potential difference in a circuit with one lamp. You may draw a circuit diagram to help you. *(2 marks)*

Checkpoint

How confidently can you answer the Progression questions?

Strengthen

S1 List the symbols used in the circuits in diagram D.

S2 What are the readings on meters A and B?

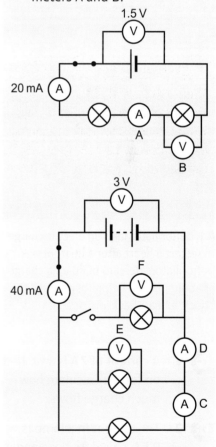

D Two circuits, in which the lamps are all identical.

Extend

E1 State and explain each of the meter readings A to F in diagram D.

383

CP9c Current, charge and energy

Specification reference: P10.5; P10.6; P10.8; P10.9

Progression questions

- What is a coulomb?
- What is the connection between the electric current and the amount of charge that flows in a circuit?
- What is the equation that relates electric charge, potential difference and the energy transferred in a circuit?

A A defibrillator uses an electric charge to restart a heart after a heart attack. Defibrillators need to build up a charge of about 160 mC before being used to 'shock' a heart back into action.

 2 A current of 2 A is switched on for 8 s. Calculate how much charge flows.

 3 The current in a lamp is 0.5 A. Calculate how long it will take for 10 C of charge to flow through the lamp.

Moving charged particles form an electric current. Electric **charge** is measured in **coulombs** (C). One coulomb is the charge that passes a point in a circuit when there is a current of 1 amp for 1 second.

In metals the current is a flow of electrons. Each electron has a very tiny negative charge, just -1.6×10^{-19} C (less than one millionth of a millionth of a millionth of a coulomb).

The size of the current at any point in a circuit tells you how much charge flows past that point each second. Electric current is the **rate** of flow of charge.

 1 Explain how a current flows in a metal (use the words electron and charge).

The charge that flows in a set time can be calculated using the equation:

$$\text{charge} = \text{current} \times \text{time}$$
$$\text{(C)} \qquad \text{(A)} \qquad \text{(s)}$$

This can also be written as:

$$Q = I \times t$$

where Q represents charge

     I represents current

     t represents time.

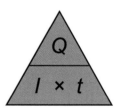

B This triangle can help you to rearrange the equation.

Worked example W1

The current in a lamp is 0.6 A. How much charge flows through it in 1 minute?

$$Q = I \times t$$
$$= 0.6\,\text{A} \times 60\,\text{s}$$
$$= 36\,\text{C}$$

Worked example W2

There is a current of 0.3 A in a circuit. How long will it take for 36 C to flow past a point in the circuit?

$$t = \frac{Q}{I}$$
$$= \frac{36\,\text{C}}{0.3\,\text{A}}$$
$$= 120\,\text{seconds}$$

Energy and charge

Diagram C shows how energy is transferred in a circuit. The cell transfers energy to the charge, and so the charge then has the potential to transfer energy to other components in the circuit. The charge has 'potential energy'.

The potential *difference* of a cell is the amount of potential energy the cell transfers to each coulomb of charge flowing through it. There is a potential difference of 1 volt when there is a transfer of 1 joule of energy to each coulomb of charge (1 volt = 1 joule per coulomb). These quantities are related by the following equation:

energy transferred = charge moved × potential difference
  (J)   (C)   (V)

This can also be written as:

$E = Q \times V$

where E represents energy transferred

  Q represents charge

  V represents potential difference.

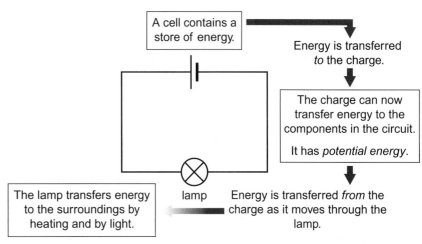

C how energy is transferred in a circuit

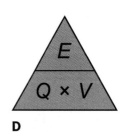

D

Worked example W3

The potential difference across a lamp is 1.5 V. When the circuit is switched on, 600 J of energy is transferred in the lamp. How much charge flowed through the lamp?

$$Q = \frac{E}{V}$$

$$= \frac{600\,J}{1.5\,V}$$

$$= 400\,C$$

 4 Calculate how much energy is transferred when 8 C of charge flows through a potential difference of 3 V.

 5 150 J of energy is transferred when 50 C of charge flows through a wire. Calculate the potential difference across the wire.

Checkpoint

How confidently can you answer the Progression questions?

Strengthen

S1 The current in a circuit is doubled and it is switched on for three times as long. Explain the change in the amount of charge that flows in the circuit.

S2 Explain what happens to the charge flowing in a circuit when the cell is replaced by a cell with double the potential difference.

Extend

E1 The label on a 12 V car battery says that it will give a current of 44 A for 1 hour. Calculate the charge and the potential energy stored in the battery.

Exam-style question

A mobile phone battery provides a potential difference of 4 V. Explain what is meant by 'a potential difference of 4 V'.   *(2 marks)*

CP9d Resistance

Specification reference: P10.12; P10.13; P10.14; P10.15; P10.16

Progression questions

- What is electrical resistance?
- What is the connection between voltage, current and resistance?
- What are the different effects of adding resistors in series and parallel?

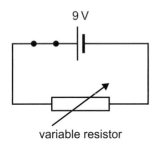

A When the variable resistor in this circuit is used to increase the resistance, the current decreases.

Some wires and components need a larger potential difference to produce a current through them than others. This is because they have a large electrical **resistance**. Resistance is measured in units called **ohms** (Ω). The resistance of a wire, a component or a circuit is calculated using the equation:

$$\text{potential difference} = \text{current} \times \text{resistance}$$
$$\text{(V)} \qquad\qquad \text{(A)} \qquad \text{(}\Omega\text{)}$$

This can also be written as:

$$V = I \times R$$

where V represents potential difference

I represents current

R represents resistance.

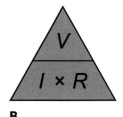

B

 1 In diagram A the resistance is 600 Ω. Calculate the current.

 2 In diagram A, explain what happens to the current when the resistance is decreased.

Worked example W1

Calculate the resistance in circuit A when the current is 0.3 A.

$$R = \frac{V}{I} = \frac{9\,V}{0.3\,A} = 30\,\Omega$$

Resistors in series

When resistors are connected in series the total resistance of the circuit is increased because the pathway becomes harder for current to flow through. The potential difference from a cell is shared between the resistors, but it may not be shared equally. There will be greater potential difference across resistors with higher resistances.

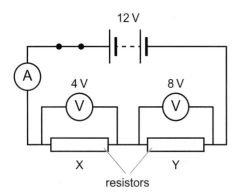

C Resistors X and Y are connected in series. Adding resistors in series increases the total resistance of the circuit.

Worked example W2

In circuit C, X has a resistance of 20 Ω. Calculate: **a)** the current in the resistors and **b)** the resistance of Y.

a)
$$I = \frac{V}{R}$$
$$= \frac{4\,V}{20\,\Omega}$$
$$= 0.2\,A$$

b)
$$R = \frac{V}{I}$$
$$= \frac{8\,V}{0.2\,A}$$
$$= 40\,\Omega$$

For Y the current is the same.

3 In diagram C, X and Y are changed for two 30Ω resistors. The potential difference across each is 6 V. Calculate:

 a the current

 b the total resistance.

 4 In diagram C, X is 20Ω and Y is changed to 100Ω. Compare and contrast the current through, and the potential difference across, X and Y.

Parallel circuits

When resistors are connected in parallel the total resistance of the circuit is less than the resistance of the individual resistors. This is because there are now more paths for the current.

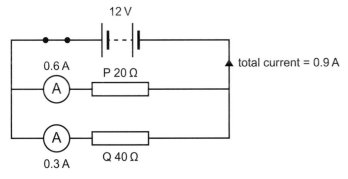

D Resistors P and Q have the same potential difference across them, but the current in resistor P is larger. This is because P has less resistance.

 5 Two 30Ω resistors are connected in place of P and Q in diagram D. Explain whether the total resistance of this circuit is larger or smaller than 30Ω.

Testing and measuring

The variable resistor in diagram E is used to change the current in the circuit. Measurements of the current and potential difference are recorded and the resistance of Z is calculated.

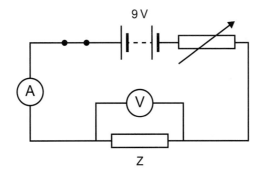

E A circuit like this one can be used to check whether a resistor has the correct value or to measure an unknown resistance.

Did you know?

When some metals are cooled to very low temperatures their resistance drops to zero and they become superconductors.

Checkpoint

How confidently can you answer the Progression questions?

Strengthen

S1 The resistance of the circuit in diagram A is increased. Use the equation for voltage, current and resistance to help you describe what will happen to the current in the circuit.

S2 You have three 100Ω resistors. Draw diagrams to explain how they should be connected to give the maximum and the minimum total resistance.

Extend

E1 In diagram C, X and Y are changed for two 200Ω resistors. Using $V = I \times R$, show that the total resistance of the circuit is 400Ω.

E2 Two 200Ω resistors are connected in place of P and Q in diagram D. Calculate the total resistance of the circuit. (*Hint*: work out the total current.)

Exam-style question

In diagram E the potential difference across the variable resistor is 3 V and the current is 0.05 A. Calculate the value of Z. *(3 marks)*

Specification reference: P10.18; P10.19; P10.20; P10.21

Progression questions

- How does potential difference affect current and resistance in fixed resistors, lamps and diodes?
- How do light intensity and temperature affect resistance in LDRs and thermistors?
- How are circuits used to explore resistance in lamps, diodes, thermistors and LDRs?

1 Look at graph A.

 a State what a fixed resistor is.

 b For a fixed resistor, if the potential difference increases by 20%, by what percentage will the current increase?

 2 How can you tell from the graph that, for a filament lamp current is not directly proportional to potential difference?

Did you know?

The first diodes were made over 100 years ago. They were called cat's-whisker diodes because they used a thin wire touching a crystal. In 2015 scientists reported making a diode from a single molecule.

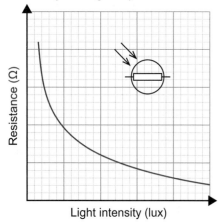

B The resistance of an LDR changes with light intensity.

Graph A shows that when potential difference changes across a fixed resistor, the current changes by the same percentage. The two variables are in **direct proportion**, and the graph forms a straight line going through the origin. This happens because the resistance stays the same.

Other components, such as filament lamps and **diodes** (also shown in graph A), have resistances that change when potential difference changes.

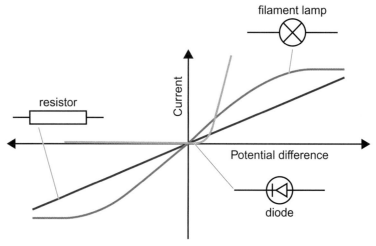

A graph of current against potential difference for a fixed resistor, filament lamp and diode

A potential difference across a filament lamp causes a current to flow through it. The current causes the filament to heat up and glow. The greater the potential difference, the more current flows and the hotter and whiter the filament gets. However, as it heats up, the filament's resistance increases. This means that when the potential difference changes, the current does not change by the same percentage (the two variables are not in direct proportion).

A **diode** has a low resistance if the potential difference is in one direction but a very high resistance if the potential difference is in the opposite direction. This means that current can only flow in one direction.

A **light-dependent resistor** (**LDR**) has a high resistance in the dark but the resistance gets smaller when the light intensity increases.

 3 Describe how the resistance of an LDR changes with increasing light intensity.

Thermistors have high resistances at low temperatures but as the temperature increases the resistance decreases.

 4 Write down the name and symbol of the five components mentioned so far on these two pages.

 5 Why does the current flowing through a thermistor increase with increasing temperature?

The circuit in diagram D can be used to explore how the resistance of the lamp changes as the potential difference across the lamp is changed. The current through the lamp, measured by the ammeter, is recorded for different values of the potential difference measured on the voltmeter.

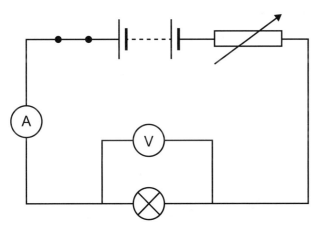

D A circuit used to explore variation in resistance of a lamp. It can easily be adapted to explore resistance in a diode, thermistor or LDR.

 6 a Explain how you would use the circuit in diagram D to find out how the resistance of a lamp changes with potential difference.

 b Predict what will happen.

7 You are going to explore how increasing temperature affects resistance in a thermistor.

 a List the apparatus you need.

 b Draw a circuit diagram of your set-up.

 c Suggest the measurements you would make.

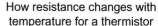

How resistance changes with temperature for a thermistor

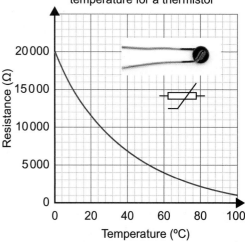

C The resistance of a thermistor changes with temperature.

Checkpoint

How confidently can you answer the Progression questions?

Strengthen

S1 Look at graph A. Compare and contrast the graph for the fixed resistor with that of:

   a the filament lamp

   b the diode.

S2 Explain which components could be used to switch a heater and a light on in an hospital incubator.

Extend

E1 For the thermistor shown in graph C, at what temperature is it most sensitive to changes in temperature? (*Hint*: find the biggest change in resistance for a 1 degree change in temperature that's one quarter of a square on the temperature axis.)

Exam-style question

A circuit similar to the one in diagram D is set up. This time the lamp in the circuit is replaced by an LDR. A light source which can be brightened and dimmed is shone onto the LDR. Explain what will happen when the light intensity of the light source is changed. *(2 marks)*

Aim

Construct electrical circuits to:

a investigate the relationship between potential difference, current and resistance for a resistor and a filament lamp

b test series and parallel circuits using resistors and filament lamps.

A Circuits are built up from different components.

B Older style light bulbs are filament lamps. They give out light when the electricity flowing through them makes the filament so hot that it glows white. The lamp shown in the photo is not quite so hot, but you can clearly see the filament.

Most machines around us rely on electricity in some way. The circuits inside computers, cars and phones can be quite complex, but they are all built up from simpler components. Engineers who design the circuits need to know the characteristics of different components. For example, resistors are used to control the amount of current flowing in part of a circuit, but not all components keep the same resistance if the potential difference across them changes.

Your task

You will construct a circuit to investigate the link between potential difference, current and resistance for a resistor and a filament lamp.

You will then find out what happens to the current through filament lamps when they are used in series and parallel circuits.

Method

Investigating resistance

A Set up circuit C. Use a power pack that can provide different potential differences. Ask your teacher to check your circuit before you switch it on.

B Set the power pack to its lowest voltage (potential difference) and switch on. Write down the readings on the ammeter and voltmeter and then switch the power pack off.

C Repeat step B for five different voltage settings, up to a maximum of 6 V.

D Replace the resistor in the circuit with two filament lamps, and repeat steps B and C.

Filament lamps in series and parallel circuits

E Set up circuit D. Ask your teacher to check your circuit before you switch it on.

F Set the power pack to its lowest voltage. Write down the readings on the ammeter and the voltmeters. Repeat with the power pack set to provide different voltages, up to a maximum of 6 V.

G Now set up circuit E and ask your teacher to check it. Repeat step F for several different voltage settings.

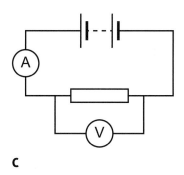

C

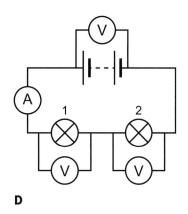

D

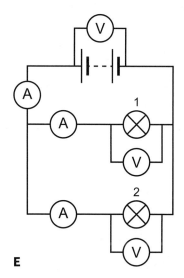

E

Exam-style questions

1 State the units for measuring resistance. *(1 mark)*

2 a Explain why the ammeter in diagram C is in series with the resistor (and not in parallel). *(2 marks)*

   b Explain why the voltmeter is in parallel with the resistor (and not in series). *(2 marks)*

3 Table F shows a set of results from the 'Investigating resistance' investigation. Plot a graph to present these results, showing both sets of results on the same axes. Draw a curve of best fit through the points for each component. *(6 marks)*

4 Use the readings at 1 V and at 6 V given in table F to calculate the resistance of:

   a the resistor *(3 marks)*

   b the filament lamp. *(2 marks)*

5 Use your graph from question 3 and your answers to question 4 to write conclusions for the investigation with:

   a the resistor *(3 marks)*

   b the filament lamp. *(3 marks)*

   c Describe how you could find out if your conclusions are applicable to all resistors or to all filament lamps. *(3 marks)*

6 Tables G and H show some results from the investigation on filament lamps in series and parallel circuits.

   a Explain what the current readings (x) and (y) would be. *(2 marks)*

   b Explain what the current reading (z) would be. *(2 marks)*

7 a Use the information in tables G and H to calculate the overall resistance of:

     i circuit D *(2 marks)*

     ii circuit E. *(2 marks)*

   b Describe how two bulbs can be put in a circuit to give the lowest possible overall resistance. *(1 mark)*

Potential difference (V)	Current (A)	
	resistor	filament lamp
0	0	0
1	0.2	0.12
2	0.4	0.23
3	0.6	0.33
4	0.9	0.41
5	1.0	0.47
6	1.2	0.53

F

	Potential difference (V)		
	power pack	lamp 1	lamp 2
Series (D)	4	2	2
Parallel (E)	4	4	4

G

	Current (A)		
	power pack	lamp 1	lamp 2
Series (D)	0.23	(x)	(y)
Parallel (E)	(z)	0.41	0.41

H

Progression questions

- What are the advantages and disadvantages of the heating effect of a current?
- How can the energy transfer that causes the heating effect be explained?
- **H** How can unwanted energy transfer be reduced in wires?

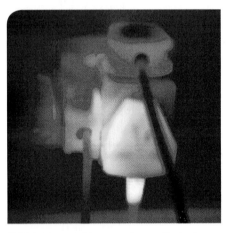

A This thermal image shows that plugs and wires are heated by the currents passing through them.

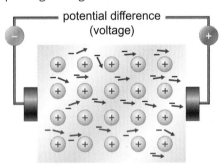

B Inside a resistor, free electrons (shown by –) move through a lattice of positive ions.

 3 Using the model of a lattice of ions, suggest why a larger current makes a resistor hotter.

 4 Explain why thick copper cables are used to carry electricity from electrical substations to homes.

All circuits have some resistance, so they warm up when there is a current. When a current passes through a resistor, energy is transferred because electrical **work** is done against the resistance. The energy is transferred by heating and the resistor becomes warm.

The heating effect is useful in an electric heater or a kettle. It is not useful in a computer or in plugs and wires because it means that useful energy is being transferred from the circuit by heating, and spread out or **dissipated**. The surroundings gain thermal energy.

 1 Name four appliances where the heating effect of a current is useful.

 2 Describe an example of when the heating effect of a current is not useful.

A model of resistance

Diagram B shows the structure inside a resistor. As the electrons flow through the lattice of vibrating ions, they collide with the ions. The more collisions they make with the ions, the harder it is for them to pass through, so the higher the electrical resistance. When the electrons collide with the ions, they transfer energy to them.

H Reducing resistance

Resistance in circuits can be reduced by using wires made from metals with low resistance, such as copper. Thicker wires also have lower resistance. Resistance can also be decreased by cooling metals so that the lattice ions are not vibrating as much.

C The wires carrying electricity in this photo are thick wires made of aluminium which has a low resistance. When the resistance is lower, less energy is transferred by heating and less energy is dissipated.

Calculating the energy transferred

energy transferred = current × potential difference × time
  (J)   (A)   (V)   (s)

This can also be written as:

$E = I \times V \times t$

Did you know?

Computer core chips are cooled by a fan. If the fan stops, the electric currents inside the chips overheat them. They can even catch fire.

Worked example W1

A 12 V battery supplies a current of 0.3 A to a heater for 8 minutes. Calculate the energy that is transferred in heating up the heater and the surroundings.

$E = I \times V \times t$

= 0.3 A × 12 V × 8 minutes

= 0.3 A × 12 V × (8 × 60 s)

= 1728 J

> Note: for the equation to work, time has to be in seconds and so minutes need to be converted to seconds here.

Worked example W2

The current in a lamp is 0.4 A when it is connected to a 230 V supply. Calculate how long it takes to transfer 2000 J of energy.

$t = \dfrac{E}{I \times V}$

$= \dfrac{2000\,J}{0.4\,A \times 230\,V}$

= 21.7 s

5 Calculate the energy transferred when a TV using a 230 V supply and current of 0.9 A is switched on for one minute.

6 Calculate the energy transferred when a 4.5 V battery is used to produce a 0.22 A current in a string of LED Christmas lights for 30 minutes.

7 900 J is transferred when there is a 0.5 A current in a circuit for 20 minutes. Calculate the potential difference across the circuit.

Checkpoint

How confidently can you answer the Progression questions?

Strengthen

S1 The label on an extension lead says '230 V max 13 A (unwound)'. Suggest why the lead must be unwound if it is carrying the maximum current.

Extend

E1 When the temperature of a material increases, the ions in the lattice vibrate more. Suggest what effect this will have on the electrical resistance of the material.

E2 Compare the energy transferred by a 3 V LED with a current of 20 mA and a 2.5 V filament lamp with current of 320 mA.

Exam-style question

To boil the water in a kettle requires 325 kJ of energy. The electric kettle transfers this energy in 1 minute and 49 s. Explain why it will actually take longer than this to boil the water. *(2 marks)*

CP9g Power

Specification reference: P10.28; P10.29; P10.30; P10.31

Progression questions

- What is power and what units are used to measure it?
- How is power related to the energy used in joules?
- How can you calculate power when you know current, potential difference and/or resistance?

A This oven takes an hour to roast a chicken. There are 28 halogen lights in the downstairs rooms of this house.

In photo A, it takes about an hour to roast the chicken. This transfers about the same amount of energy as using the 28 halogen ceiling lights for 2 hours.

The energy transferred by an electric current depends on the time taken, so it is often more useful to compare the **power** of the appliances. Power is the energy transferred per second. This is often shown on appliances as the **power rating**. Power is measured in **watts** (W). 1 W is a transfer of 1 joule per second.

To calculate the power, use the equation:

$$\text{power (W)} = \frac{\text{energy transferred (J)}}{\text{time taken (s)}}$$

This can also be written as:

$$P = \frac{E}{t}$$

where P represents power

E represents energy transferred

t represents time taken.

Worked example W1

Calculate the energy transferred by a 800 W microwave in 1 minute.

$$E = P \times t$$

$$= 800\,\text{W} \times 60\,\text{s}$$

$$= 48\,000\,\text{J}$$

1 The power rating of the oven in photo A is approximately 3 kW.

  7th   **a** Calculate the energy used by the oven in one hour.

  8th   **b** Calculate the energy used by one halogen light in 2 hours.

  8th   **c** Calculate the power of one halogen light.

  8th   2 A kettle transfers 540 000 J of energy in 3 minutes. Calculate the power of the kettle.

1952   2005

B The Blackpool Tower originally had 10 000 filament lights, but now has 25 000 LED lights because they use less power and decrease the electricity bill.

Calculating electrical power

The power transfer in a component or appliance is proportional to the potential difference across it and the current through it. This means that:

electrical power = current × potential difference
(W)   (A)   (V)

This can also be written as:

$P = I \times V$

where P represents power

       I represents current

       t represents voltage.

 3 Calculate the power of a wheelchair motor that has a current of 20 A and a potential difference of 12 V.

 4 Calculate the current in an electric kettle with a power rating of 3 kW and a potential difference of 230 V.

In *CP9d* you learned the equation $V = I \times R$. Using this to substitute for V in the equation $P = I \times V$ gives a new equation for power:

$P = I \times I \times R$ or $P = I^2 \times R$

electrical power = current² × resistance
(W)   (A²)   (Ω)

Worked example W2

An electric cable has a resistance of 900 Ω and a current of 3 A through it. Calculate the power transferred in kilowatts.

$P = I^2 \times R$

  $= (3\,A)^2 \times 900\,\Omega$

  $= 9\,A^2 \times 900\,\Omega$

  $= 8100\,W$

  $= 8.1\,kW$

 5 A 46 W electric blanket has a resistance of 1150 Ω. Calculate the current in the blanket.

Exam-style question

Calculate the energy transferred by a 5 W spotlight in 2 hours.　*(2 marks)*

Checkpoint

How confidently can you answer the Progression questions?

Strengthen

S1 Describe what is meant by the power of a 650 W electric toaster.

S2 State three ways the power of an appliance can be worked out.

Extend

E1 500 W of power can be supplied to a building at 250 V or at 1000 V. Calculate the current in the cable in each case.

E2 If the cable has a resistance of 100 Ω, calculate the energy transferred by heating the cable and the surroundings in each case. Compare your answers and suggest whether it is more efficient to use 250 V or 1000 V.

CP9h Transferring energy by electricity

Specification reference: P10.32; P10.33; P10.34; P10.35; P10.36; P10.42

Progression questions

- How is energy transferred from electrical cells or batteries to motors and heating devices?
- What is the difference between direct and alternating, for both current and voltage?
- What is the voltage and frequency of the UK domestic electricity supply?

In photo A some of the energy stored in the battery is transferred by electricity to the motor, where it is transferred to a store of kinetic energy in the fan. Some energy will also be transferred by heating the wires, the motor and the surroundings. In the end, all the energy will be dissipated by heating, making the surroundings a little warmer (increasing their store of **thermal energy**).

1 Describe how energy is transferred in:

    a a battery operated toothbrush

    b a battery operated cup that warms drinks.

The gloves in photo B contain wire that has a high resistance. Energy stored in the battery is transferred by electricity to the high resistance wire where it is transferred by heating to a store of thermal energy in the wire. The energy is then transferred by heating to the gloves and hands of the wearer, and eventually dissipates to the surroundings.

A This battery-operated fan contains an electric motor.

B These gloves warm your hands – they use a battery-operated heating circuit.

2 Describe the energy transfers in:

    a mains operated hair straighteners

    b a mains operated electric drill.

Appliances that need a large amount of power use **mains electricity**. In a power station energy is transferred from a store of kinetic energy (such as a turbine) by electricity. The electricity is carried to our homes through a network of wires and cables known as the **national grid**.

In our homes, appliances use the energy transferred by electricity in various ways. For example, the motor in a washing machine transfers energy to kinetic energy in the washing machine drum.

Direct voltage and alternating voltage

Cells and batteries have a positive and a negative terminal and the direction of the movement of charge stays the same. This is called **direct current** (d.c.).

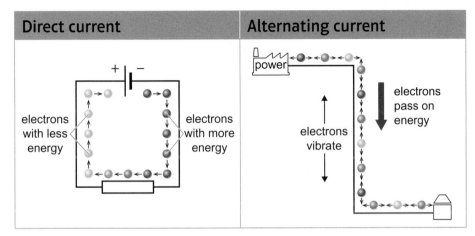

Direct current	Alternating current

C The direction of the current and the movement of charge stays the same in direct current but changes in alternating current.

Mains electricity is produced using generators that rotate, causing the direction of the current to keep changing. This is called **alternating current** (a.c.). The voltage also changes, increasing to a peak voltage then decreasing to zero. It then increases to a peak in the opposite direction before decreasing back to zero. This cycle then repeats. In the UK there are 50 of these cycles per second or, in other words, the frequency of the mains supply is 50 **hertz** (Hz). The voltage is constantly changing but the average effect is the same as a d.c. voltage of 230 V.

 4 Compare a.c. and d.c. in terms of:

   a the movement of charges   **b** the voltage.

Power rating of domestic appliances

The power rating of an appliance is measured in watts (W). A kettle with a power rating of 3 kW transfers 3000 joules of energy each second (from the mains electricity supply to a store of thermal energy in the water).

 5 What is the relationship between energy transferred and the power rating?

 6 A hairdryer has a power rating of 1200 W. Calculate the amount of energy it transfers every hour. Show your working.

Exam-style question

An electric deep fat fryer uses the UK mains electricity supply. Describe all the energy transfers that take place when the fryer is used.   *(3 marks)*

 3 A mobile phone is provided with 5 V d.c. using a charger plugged into the mains supply. State two changes the charger makes to the mains electricity.

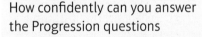

Checkpoint

How confidently can you answer the Progression questions

Strengthen

S1 Describe how energy is transferred in a battery operated hairdryer.

S2 Draw a table to compare the voltage and the movement of charge in UK mains electricity and a 12 V car battery.

Extend

E1 Explain an advantage of using the UK mains supply instead of a 12 V battery for an electric kettle.

CP9i Electrical safety

Specification reference: P10.37; P10.38; P10.39; P10.40; P10.41

Progression questions

- What is the difference between the live and the neutral wires?
- How do earth wires and fuses make circuits safer?
- What are the potential differences between the live, neutral and earth wires?

In the UK, appliances are connected to the mains electricity with a 3-pin plug as shown in photo A.

earth wire – connects the metal parts of the appliance to a large metal spike or metal tubing that is pushed into the ground. It is for safety and is at 0V if the circuit is correctly connected.

neutral wire – the return path to the power station. If the circuit is correctly connected it is at a voltage of 0V.

fuse – a safety device marked with the current it can carry. Usually 3A, 5A or 13A.

live wire – connects the appliance to the generators at the power station. The voltage on this wire is 230V.

A A 3-pin plug is designed to safely connect appliances to mains electricity.

 1 State the colours of each of the wires in a plug.

2 Calculate the potential difference between the following pairs of wires.

 a live and neutral

 b live and earth

 c neutral and earth

 3 An iron uses a current of 4A. Fuse ratings are usually 3A, 5A or 13A. Explain which fuse is best to use in the plug for the iron.

Did you know?

An a.c. electric current of just 0.1A through the heart is enough to stop it and kill you. The voltage needed to produce this current depends on the resistance of the path through your body. This resistance could be as low as 1 kΩ for wet skin but 500 kΩ for dry skin.

Safety features

Switches are connected in the live wire of a circuit. When they are off, no current goes through the appliance.

A fuse is a tube with a thin wire inside. The current passes through the wire and the wire gets hotter. If the current exceeds a certain value the wire melts. This breaks the circuit and stops the current.

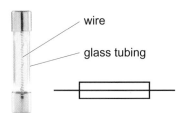

B The fuse melts before wiring or parts of an appliance can overheat. Once the fault is fixed, a new fuse can be fitted.

If a faulty appliance draws too much current, it can caused overheating of the wiring in either the walls or in the appliance. This can cause fires. A fuse stops this from happening. If an appliance develops a fault, its metal parts can be at a high voltage. If you touched the metal you might get dangerous electric shock – a current would flow through you into the ground (which is at 0 V). For this reason, the metal parts of appliances are connected to the earth wire so that this current goes into the ground instead of through you.

If a fault causes the live wire to touch a metal part, it makes a very low resistance circuit between 230 V and 0 V (the earth). This causes a very large current to flow to the earth, which heats up the wire and could cause a fire. If this happens, the current blows the fuse and cuts off the mains electricity supply.

Circuit breakers can be an alternative to fuses. They detect a change in the current and safely switch off the supply.

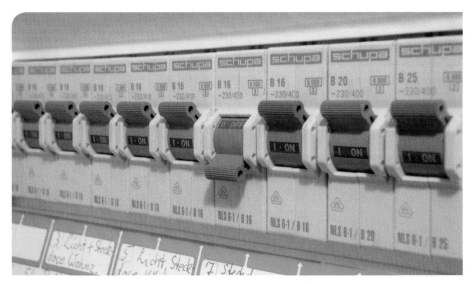

C Circuit breakers are a type of automatic switch that stop current flowing if there is a problem in the circuit, such as too much current or current flowing in the wrong wires.

One advantage of circuit breakers is that once a fault is fixed they can be switched back on again, whereas a fuse has to be replaced. Another advantage of some types is that they work very quickly, so can save lives. A fuse takes some time to melt and will not prevent you getting a shock if, for example, you touch a live wire.

 7 Compare and contrast circuit breakers and fuses as safety devices.

Exam-style question

Why is the earth wire needed in a plug?   *(2 marks)*

---

 4 Explain why a current would flow though you if you touched a metal part of a faulty appliance that did not have an earth wire.

 5 Explain why the fuse must be in the live wire and not the neutral wire of a circuit.

 6 Suggest what could happen if a fuse were replaced by a piece of ordinary wire and a fault caused the live wire to touch the metal case of an oven.

Checkpoint

How confidently can you answer the Progression questions?

Strengthen

S1 Describe the functions and voltage of the three wires found in a plug.

S2 Write a sentence or two for each of the following safely devices to explain how they work: fuses, the earth wire, circuit breakers.

Extend

E1 All appliances could be fitted with 13 A fuses. Explain the advantages of replacing them with lower value fuses and how you would work out which fuse to use.

Electrical safety

A 3-pin plug is used to connect a television to the mains electrical supply. In the plug there is a 5 amp fuse and an earth connection. Explain how these safety features work to make using the television safer.   **(6 marks)**

Student answer

The 5 amp fuse is made of thin wire which melts if a current greater than 5 amps passes through it [1]. The earth connection joins any metal parts of the television to a large metal spike in the ground, through the plug. If there is a fault which connects the metal parts of the television to a high voltage, then a high current passes through the earth wire to the ground [2]. The current also flows through the fuse and the wire melts [3]. This disconnects the television so that nobody can get an electric shock by touching it [4].

[1] This part of the answer describes how the fuse works, but the information about how this makes using the television safer is at the end of the answer. It would be better to have all the information about the fuse in one paragraph, and all the information about the earth wire in another.

[2] This explanation should have included the fact that the earth wire makes using the television safer by taking charge away from the metal parts of the television and so preventing someone getting an electric shock by touching it.

[3] This sentence would be clearer if the student had stated that the wire that melts is the one inside the fuse.

[4] The main purpose of a fuse is to protect against the wiring overheating and causing a fire. The fuse will protect people from electric shocks only if the live wire touches the outer casing of the television, in which case a large additional current flows and the fuse wire melts.

Verdict

This is an acceptable answer. It shows an understanding of how a fuse works and how the earth connection works. The use of scientific language is good with the terms current and voltage used correctly.

This answer could be improved by explaining that the earth wire is the primary safety feature for preventing electric shocks and does this by removing any build-up of charge (or current flowing through) the parts of the television that someone could touch. This answer could also be improved by including an explanation of how a fuse improves safety – if a fault causes a high current, it breaks the circuit so that overheating does not cause fire or damage to the television.

Exam tip

When a question asks for a series of points it is often a good idea to pull the question apart and make a list. In this question you are being asked about two safety features and how each one works. A planning list might look like this:

earth { how it works, how it makes the television safer } fuse

Paper 6

CP10 Magnetism and the Motor Effect /
CP11 Electromagnetic Induction

The aurora borealis occurs when charged particles flowing out from the Sun become trapped by the Earth's magnetic field and enter the Earth's atmosphere near the North Pole. These particles collide with atoms in the atmosphere, and the atoms gain energy. This energy is then emitted by the atoms as light.

In this unit you will learn about magnetic fields and how they are used to produce forces and to change the voltage of electricity supplies.

The learning journey

Previously you will have learnt at KS3:

- how to plot the shape of a magnetic field and that the Earth has a magnetic field
- that electric currents cause magnetic fields, including in electromagnets and motors.

In this unit you will learn:

- about permanent and induced magnets, and how to represent a magnetic field
- about the magnetic field around a current in a wire and the factors that affect it
- how the fields from the individual coils in a solenoid interact
- how to use the power equation for transformers
- how transformers are used in the national grid
- **H** how a current can be induced in a wire and the factors that affect it
- **H** how to calculate the size of the force on a wire carrying a current in a magnetic field
- **H** how to work out the direction of the force on a wire carrying a current in a magnetic field.

CP10a Magnets and magnetic fields

Specification reference: P12.1; P12.2; P12.3; P12.4; P12.5; P12.6

Progression questions

- How are magnets used?
- What shape are magnetic fields and how can they be plotted?
- What is the evidence that the Earth has a magnetic field?

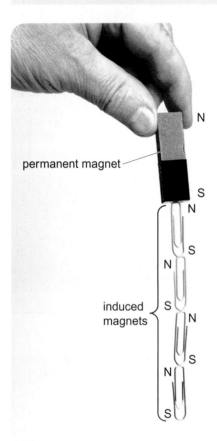

permanent magnet

induced magnets

A A permanent magnet can turn objects made from magnetic materials into induced magnets.

A bar magnet is a **permanent magnet** because it is always magnetic. A magnet can attract **magnetic materials**. These include the metals iron, steel, nickel and cobalt. The space around a magnet where it can attract these materials is called the **magnetic field**.

A bar magnet has two ends, one called a north-seeking pole and one called a south-seeking pole (usually called the north pole and south pole for short). If two magnets are placed close to each other, the north pole on one magnet attracts the south pole on the other. If two north poles or two south poles are put close together, the magnets repel each other.

1 Suggest what material the paper clips in photo A are made from. Explain your answer.

When a piece of magnetic material is in a magnetic field it becomes a magnet itself. This is called an **induced magnet**. It stops being magnetic when it is taken out of the field again.

2 In photo A, how would the induced magnetism in the paper clips be different if the magnet were held the other way up?

Magnets are used in electric motors, generators, loudspeakers and other electrical devices. They are also used for simpler things such as door latches and knife holders.

The shape of a magnetic field can be found using **plotting compasses**. We represent magnetic fields using lines that show how a single north pole would move (from north to south). The field is strongest where the lines are closest together.

3 Magnets are used to separate steel food cans from aluminium drinks cans in recycling plants. Explain why magnets can be used for this purpose.

4 Look at photo B. Describe how you can use a plotting compass to find the shape of the magnetic field of a bar magnet.

B You can draw lines to show the shape of a magnetic field using a plotting compass

Diagram C shows the shape of the magnetic field around a bar magnet. Diagram D shows how two magnets together can form a uniform magnetic field. This has the same strength and direction everywhere.

 5 Describe two differences between a uniform magnetic field and the field around a bar magnet.

Earth's magnetic field

The needle of a plotting compass is a very small magnet. Compasses can be used to help people to find their way, as the needle always points to a position near the Earth's North Pole. A magnet suspended on a string will tilt relative to the horizontal by different amounts in different places. Compass needles are weighted at one end to keep them level.

This behaviour of compasses is evidence that the Earth has a magnetic field, which is similar in shape to the magnetic field of a bar magnet. The Earth's magnetic field is thought to be caused by electric currents in the molten outer **core**, which is made from a mixture of iron and nickel.

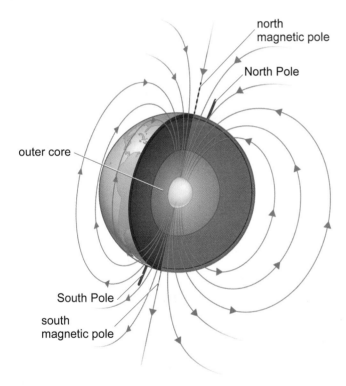

E The Earth's magnetic field has a similar shape to the magnetic field of a bar magnet.

6 Look at diagram D. Explain where the Earth's magnetic field is:

 a strongest **b** weakest.

Exam-style question

Describe the difference between a permanent magnet and an induced magnet. *(2 marks)*

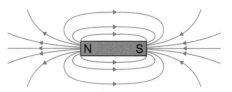

C The magnetic field occurs all around a bar magnet but we use a 2-dimensional diagram like this as a model.

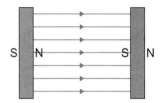

Two flat magnets produce a uniform magnetic field between them.

D These two magnets are producing a uniform magnetic field.

Did you know?

Magnetic compasses were invented in China in about 200 BCE, although at first they were only used for fortune-telling.

Checkpoint

How confidently can you answer the Progression questions?

Strengthen

S1 Explain why compasses point north. Use the words attract, repel, pole and magnetic field in your answer.

Extend

E1 Describe how a magnet suspended on a thread can be used to find the shape of the Earth's magnetic field. Explain why this works.

Specification reference: P12.7; P12.8; P12.9

Progression questions

- How is the magnetic field around a wire related to the current?
- What factors affect the strength of the magnetic field around a wire?
- How does the magnetic field around a wire change when the wire is made into a coil?

A Earphones and loudspeakers work because of the magnetic effect of an electric current.

A current flowing through a wire causes a magnetic field. Electric motors and many other devices depend on the magnetic effect of electric currents.

Photo B shows a wire passing through a piece of card. When a current flows through the wire, iron filings on the card make circular patterns. This shows that the current is causing a magnetic field because the iron filings are lining up with the direction of the magnetic field.

Did you know?

Hans Christian Ørsted (1777–1851) had been trying to show that electric currents had a magnetic effect for several years. He did not find any evidence until he was giving a lecture and noticed a compass needle move when current was switched on in a nearby wire. His previous experiments had been designed to find a magnetic field running in the same direction as the wire.

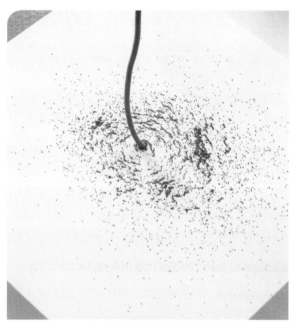

B The iron filings show the shape of the magnetic field around a wire carrying a current.

You can use plotting compasses to find the direction of the magnetic field. The direction of the magnetic field depends on the direction of the current. If the current changes direction, so does the direction of the magnetic field.

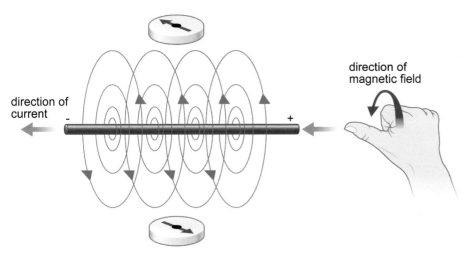

 C If you point your right thumb in the direction of the current (from + to –), the magnetic field goes in the direction your fingers are pointing.

 2 Look at diagram C. How does the diagram show that the magnetic field is strongest close to the wire?

The strength of the magnetic field depends on the size of the current – the higher current the stronger the field. The magnetic field is strongest closer to the wire and gets weaker with increasing distance.

You can think of the magnetic field as forming a series of cylinders around the wire. If the wire is made into a coil (called a **solenoid**), the magnetic fields of all the different parts of the wire form an overall magnetic field like the one shown in part b of diagram D. The fields from individual coils add together to form a very strong field inside the solenoid. Outside the solenoid the fields from one side of the coil tend to cancel out the fields from the other side to give a weaker field outside. This is shown in part a of diagram D.

A coil of wire with a current flowing through it is an **electromagnet**. The magnetic field of an electromagnet can be made stronger by putting a piece of iron (an iron core) inside the coil. This iron becomes a **temporary** magnet – it is only magnetic while the field from the electromagnet is affecting it.

 3 Where is the magnetic field around an electromagnet strongest? Explain your answer.

 4 a Suggest why iron, rather than a metal like copper, is needed to make the magnetic field of an electromagnet stronger.

 b Suggest one other way of making the field stronger.

c Suggest how you can reverse the direction of the magnetic field in an electromagnet.

Exam-style question

Describe two ways in which the magnetic field around a wire can be changed.

(2 marks)

 1 In photo B, the current is flowing down the wire. Draw a sketch to show the shape and direction of the magnetic field around the wire.

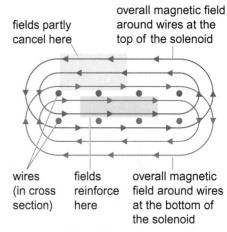

a cross section of a small coil of wire

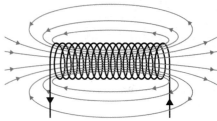

b The magnetic field inside the solenoid is almost uniform near the centre of the coil.

D

Checkpoint

How confidently can you answer the Progression questions?

Strengthen

S1 Describe two different shaped magnetic fields that can be made using current flowing through a wire.

Extend

E1 Describe how you could use a coil of wire and a plotting compass as a simple ammeter and explain how your idea will work.

Progression questions

- **H** How can electricity and magnetism combine to produce forces?
- **H** What is Fleming's left-hand rule?
- **H** How can we calculate the size of the force produced by a current in a magnetic field?

H

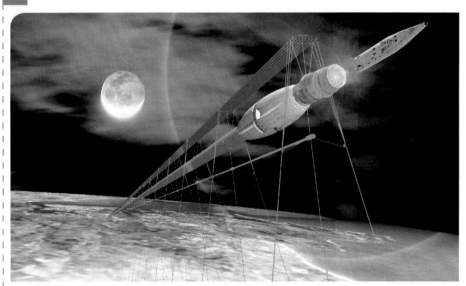

A an artist's impression of a rail gun launcher

Rockets are not the only way of getting spacecraft into orbit. Photo A shows an idea for a rail gun launcher, which uses a current flowing through the two rails to produce a force. The force produced by the rail gun is an example of the **motor effect**.

Did you know?

One of the earliest electric motors was demonstrated in 1838 by Moritz von Jacobi (1801–1874). His motor was strong enough to push a boatload of 14 people across a river.

Any wire carrying a current can experience a force near a magnetic field. The force occurs because the current in the wire creates a magnetic field around the wire and this interacts with the magnetic field between the magnets. The force is experienced as long as the wire is not in the same direction as the magnetic field (the force is zero if the wire lies in this direction). There is an equal and opposite force on the magnet or magnets. The greatest force on the wire occurs when it is at right angles to the magnetic field.

 1 What is the motor effect?

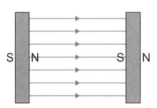

Two flat magnets produce a uniform magnetic field between them.

A magnetic field goes around a wire carrying a current.

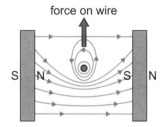

When the wire carrying a current is put between the magnets, the two fields interact to produce a force.

B Two magnetic fields can interact to produce a force on the wire.

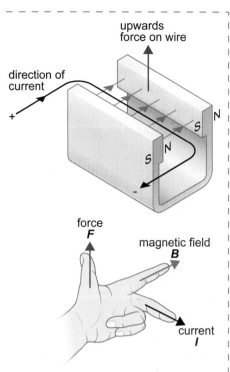

direction of current

upwards force on wire

force **F**

magnetic field **B**

current **I**

C Remember that the direction of the current is from + to − when using Fleming's left-hand rule.

H

The direction of the force depends on the directions of the magnetic field and the current. **Fleming's left-hand rule** shows how the directions are related, as shown in diagram C.

2 Look at diagram C. What will happen if the connections to the power supply are swapped over?

The size of the force on the wire depends on the magnetic field strength, the current and the length of the wire in the field. The strength of a magnetic field (the **magnetic flux density**) is measured in units of newtons per ampere metre (N/A m) (also called **tesla, T**) and is given the symbol B.

$$\begin{array}{l} \text{force on conductor carrying} \\ \text{current at right angles to} \\ \text{magnetic field (N)} \end{array} = \begin{array}{ccc} \text{magnetic flux density} & \times \text{ current} & \times \text{ length} \\ \text{(N/A m or T)} & \text{(A)} & \text{(m)} \end{array}$$

This can be written as $F = B \times I \times l$.

Worked example

A 200 m long wire carries a current of 3 A at right angles to the Earth's magnetic field. There is a force of 0.024 N on the wire. Calculate the strength of the magnetic field.

$$B = \frac{F}{I \times l}$$

$$= \frac{0.024\,\text{N}}{3\,\text{A} \times 200\,\text{m}}$$

$$= 0.000\,04\,\text{N/A m (or } 4 \times 10^{-5}\,\text{N/A m)}$$

3 Look at diagram C. What will happen if:

a the current is doubled

b the magnets are set further apart (weakening the field)?

4 The apparatus shown in diagram C is placed on a balance. The wire is held so that it cannot move. Explain how the reading on the balance changes when the current is switched on.

5 A 10 cm wire runs at right angles to a magnetic field of 0.5 T.

a Calculate the force on the wire when the current is 0.3 A.

b Calculate the current needed to produce a force of 0.02 N.

Exam-style question

Describe three factors that affect the force experienced by a current-carrying conductor in a magnetic field. Include the effect of each factor in your answer.

(3 marks)

Checkpoint

How confidently can you answer the Progression questions?

Strengthen

S1 a A 2 m long wire runs at right angles across a magnetic field with a strength of 0.2 N/A m. Calculate the force on the wire when the current is 0.5 A.

b Explain two ways in which the direction of the force could be reversed.

Extend

E1 Two wires are held in clamp stands so they run parallel to each other a few centimetres apart. When current flows through the wires they repel each other. Explain why this happens.

CP11a Transformers

Specification reference: P13.10

- How can you calculate the power of an electric current?
- How do transformers follow the law of conservation of energy?
- How can you calculate the current and voltage produced by a transformer?

A Shaver sockets used in bathrooms contain a transformer.

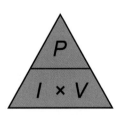

C

Transformers are used to change the **potential difference** (voltage) of an electricity supply. A transformer is usually made using two coils of wire wound onto an iron core. There is no electrical connection between the two coils of wire. An effect called **electromagnetic induction** means that a voltage in one coil causes (**induces**) a voltage in the second coil.

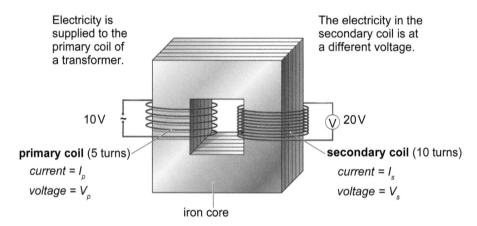

Electricity is supplied to the primary coil of a transformer.

The electricity in the secondary coil is at a different voltage.

10 V

20 V

primary coil (5 turns)
current = I_p
voltage = V_p

secondary coil (10 turns)
current = I_s
voltage = V_s

iron core

B the structure of a transformer

The potential difference (p.d.) is a measure of the energy transferred by each coulomb of charge that flows through a wire. The current measures the number of coulombs per second. So the **electrical power** (the energy transferred each second by an electric current) is calculated using this equation:

$$\text{electrical power (W)} = \text{current (A)} \times \text{potential difference (V)}$$

This can also be written as:

$$P = I \times V$$

Where P represents the electrical power

   I represents the current

   V represents the potential difference

1 What will the electrical power of a motor be if:

a the current is 0.2 A and the voltage is 12 V

b the potential difference across the motor is 9 V and the current is 0.1 A?

 2 A 20 W light bulb uses electricity from the mains supply (230 V). Calculate the size of the current.

Energy cannot be created or destroyed, so the power supplied to a transformer in the primary coil must be equal to the power transferred away from the transformer in the secondary coil. If the transformer is 100% efficient (no energy is wasted by heating), then the power in the secondary coil equals to the power in the primary coil.

potential difference across primary coil (V) × current in primary coil (A) = potential difference across secondary coil (V) × current in secondary coil (A)

This can also be written as:

$$V_P \times I_P = V_S \times I_S$$

Worked example

The primary coil of a transformer has a current of 0.5 A with a potential difference of 100 V. The current in the secondary coil is 25 A. What is the potential difference across the secondary coil?

$$V_P \times I_P = V_S \times I_S$$
$$100\,V \times 0.5\,A = V_S \times 25\,A$$
$$50 = V_S \times 25$$
$$V_S = \frac{50}{25} = 2\,V$$

3 A transformer receives 5000 W of energy by electricity.

 a How much power is transferred by the electricity coming out of the transformer?

 b Explain how the power output will be different if the transformer is not 100% efficient.

4 Calculate the missing values for these transformers.

 a $V_P = ?, I_P = 2\,A, V_S = 200\,V, I_S = 0.1\,A$

 b $V_P = 11\,000\,V, I_P = ?, V_S = 230\,V, I_S = 11\,A$

 c $V_P = 33\,kV, I_P = 2\,A, V_S = 230\,V, I_S = ?\,A$

 5 Part of an electricity supply system is designed to transfer power up to 4 MW. The input voltage is 33 kV and the output voltage is 230 V. Calculate the maximum input and output currents.

Exam-style question

A step-up transformer is a type of transformer used to increase the potential difference of an electricity supply. Explain why the current decreases at the same time. *(3 marks)*

Did you know?

An electric toothbrush contains the secondary coil of a transformer. The charger contains the primary coil, and the iron core sticks up from the base. Since there is no electrical contact between the toothbrush and the charger, it is safe to use in a bathroom.

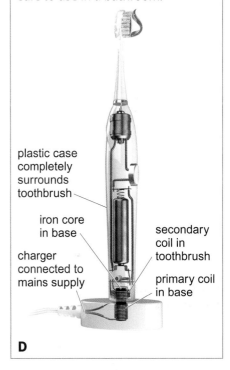

plastic case completely surrounds toothbrush

iron core in base

charger connected to mains supply

secondary coil in toothbrush

primary coil in base

D

Checkpoint

How confidently can you answer the Progression questions?

Strengthen

S1 Calculate the missing value:
$V_P = 500\,V, I_P = ?, V_S = 5\,V, I_S = 2\,A$

Extend

E1 Some types of halogen light bulbs need a 12 V supply. A transformer is used to convert the mains supply to run six 50 W bulbs. Use the equation $V_P \times I_P = V_S \times I_S$ to calculate the current drawn from the mains supply.

CP11b Transformers and energy

Specification reference: **H** P13.2; **H** P13.5; **H** P13.6; P13.8; P13.9

Progression questions

- How is electricity transmitted around the country?
- **H** How do transformers work?
- **H** What are the factors that affect the size and direction of an induced potential difference?

Did you know?

There are over 25 000 km of transmission lines in the national grid.

A Electricity sub-stations contain step-down transformers.

 1 Write these national grid voltages in the order that they occur in diagram B, starting with the voltage at the power station: 11 kV, 25 000 V, 33 kV, 0.23 kV, 400 kV.

 2 Look at diagram B. The transformers are labelled A, B and C. For each transformer, say whether it is a step-up or step-down transformer and explain why it is used.

The national grid

Electricity is sent from power stations to homes, schools and factories by a system of wires and cables called the **national grid**. When electricity flows through a wire, the wire gets warm. There is a significant amount of energy wasted by heating in the **transmission lines** of the national grid.

If the voltage of the electricity passing through a wire is increased, the current is decreased. The power transferred by heating depends on the current squared multiplied by the resistance of the wires (*see also CP9g Power*). So when the current is smaller, less energy is wasted by heating and the efficiency is improved. Power stations produce electricity at 25 kV. This is changed to 400 kV by transformers before the electricity is sent around the country. The voltage is reduced again before the electricity is sent to factories and other buildings.

A **step-up transformer** increases the voltage and decreases the current at the same time. A **step-down transformer** makes the voltage lower and the current higher.

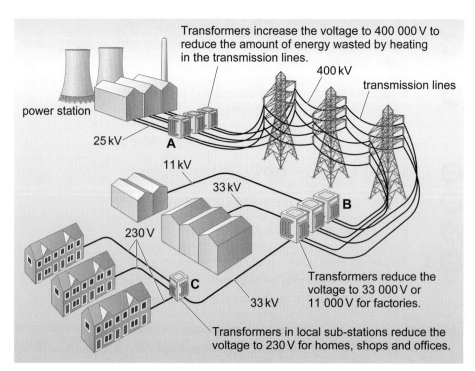

B the national grid

H Electromagnetic induction

Transformers work because a changing magnetic field induces a potential difference (p.d.) in a wire, which causes a current to flow.

A potential difference is also induced if a wire is moved in a magnetic field. The size of the induced potential difference depends on:

- the number of turns in a coil of wire
- how fast the magnetic field changes or moves past the coil.

Reversing the direction of the magnetic field reverses the direction of the induced current.

If the potential difference causes a current to flow in a wire, the magnetic field of this current opposes the original change.

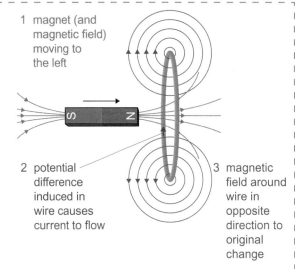

1 magnet (and magnetic field) moving to the left

2 potential difference induced in wire causes current to flow

3 magnetic field around wire in opposite direction to original change

C a magnet being moved through a loop of wire

Did you know?

The hoverboard in photo D works using rotating magnets that induce a current inside the metal ramp. A magnetic field caused by this current repels the magnets in the board.

D

3 Look at diagram C. The magnet is moved to the left.

a What will be the direction of the magnetic field inside the loop of wire?

b Explain how you could have worked out your answer without referring to the diagram.

How transformers work

Transformers only work with **alternating current**, when the direction of the potential difference (and so also the current) changes many times each second. The alternating current in the primary coil creates a continuously changing magnetic field, and the iron core of the transformer carries this magnetic field to the secondary coil.

The changing magnetic field induces a changing potential difference in the secondary coil. The potential difference is greater in the secondary coil if it has more turns than the primary coil.

4 Explain why the core of a transformer is made from iron.

5 The UK mains supply changes direction 100 times each second. How would increasing this rate of change affect the magnetic field induced in the core of a transformer?

Checkpoint

How confidently can you answer the Progression questions?

Strengthen

S1 Explain why different voltages are used in the national grid. Present your answer as a paragraph.

Extend

E1 Direct current always flows in the same direction. Explain why a transformer will not work with direct current.

Exam-style question

Electricity is transferred through the national grid at a voltage of 400 000 V. Explain why this high voltage is used. *(3 marks)*

Magnetic fields

An electric current in a wire produces a magnetic field around the wire. A straight wire can be coiled to form a solenoid.

Describe the shapes of the magnetic fields around a straight wire and a solenoid, and the factors that affect the direction and strength of the field.

(6 marks)

Student answer

The magnetic field around a straight wire is circular. The direction of the field depends on the direction of the current [1]. It [2] gets stronger if the current gets bigger, and is strongest close to the wire and weaker further away [3]. When the wire is wound up to make a solenoid, all the fields from all the coils join up and make a field that looks like a bar magnet. The field is the same all the way inside the coil [4].

[1] This is a good description of the shape of the field around a straight wire, and describes what affects its direction.

[2] 'It' can sometimes be misunderstood. This sentence would be better if it started with 'The magnetic field gets stronger if...'

[3] This is a good description of the factors affecting the strength of the field, including *how* each factor affects its strength.

[4] The student understands that the fields from the individual coils combine to form the field, and describes the shape.

Verdict

This is an acceptable answer. The student has described the shapes of the magnetic fields around a straight wire and around a solenoid, and has clearly described the effects of two factors that affect the strength of the field around a wire. The answer is well organised and includes links between scientific ideas, for example the field around a solenoid and the field around a bar magnet.

The answer could be improved by describing where the magnetic field of a solenoid is strongest and the factors that affect its strength.

Exam tip

The word 'describe' is often used in exam questions. You might be asked to describe a process, how something works or the effect of one thing on another. In a 'describe' question, you don't need to give reasons for *why* things happen. Instead, you need to write an account of *what* happens.

Paper 6

CP12 Particle Model / CP13 Forces and Matter

'Dry ice' is often used in theatres or concerts to produce fog that creeps along the floor. Dry ice is actually frozen carbon dioxide. When this becomes warmer than −78 °C it starts to sublimate (change directly from a solid to a gas). To make fog, the dry ice is put into warm water where it sublimates and makes bubbles of carbon dioxide gas. These bubbles are very cold, and when they escape from the water they cause water vapour in the air to condense and form very tiny droplets of water. These drops of liquid water form the fog that you can see.

In this unit you will learn how the particle model explains the properties of matter and what happens when energy is transferred to or from a substance. You will also learn about springs and the energy transfers in stretching them.

The learning journey

Previously you will have learnt at KS3:

- that mass is conserved during changes of state
- about the properties of solids, liquids and gases
- how particles are arranged in solids, liquids and gases, and how this is affected by temperature.

Previously you will have learnt in *CP2 Forces and Motion*:

- some of the effects that forces have on objects.

In this unit you will learn:

- how to explain different densities of substances and how to calculate density
- about specific heat capacity and specific latent heat and how to calculate them
- how changing the temperature of a gas affects its pressure
- about the Kelvin and Celsius temperature scales
- about elastic and inelastic distortion
- about the relationship between force and extension, and how to calculate the extension and spring constant
- how to calculate the work done when stretching a spring.

Progression questions

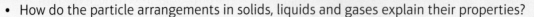

- How do the particle arrangements in solids, liquids and gases explain their properties?
- What happens to particles when a substance changes state?
- How can you calculate the density of a substance?

The ice in glaciers is added to by winter snowfall. Ice is lost from the top of a glacier by **sublimation**, when a solid turns straight into a gas without becoming a liquid first.

1 Describe two properties of:

 a solids

 b liquids

 c gases.

Ice, water and water vapour are three different **states of matter** with very different properties.

A a glacier in Greenland

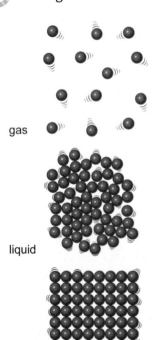

B Particles (e.g. **atoms**, **molecules**) are arranged differently in the three states of matter.

Kinetic theory

The **kinetic theory** states that everything is made of tiny particles.

In solids, forces of attraction hold particles closely together. The particles can vibrate but they cannot move around. This explains why solids keep their shape and usually cannot be **compressed**.

In liquids, the particles are moving faster and so the forces of attraction between the particles are not strong enough to hold them in fixed positions. The particles can move past each other so liquids flow and take the shape of their container. The particles are still very close together, so liquids usually can't be compressed.

In a gas, the particles are far apart and moving around quickly. Gases are compressible and expand to fill their container.

2 Explain why:

 a liquids and gases can flow but solids cannot

 b gases can be compressed but solids and liquids cannot.

When a substance undergoes a **change of state** the particles end up in a different arrangement. There are the same number of particles so the mass stays the same (mass is **conserved**). This is a **physical change**, because no new substances are formed and the substance recovers its original properties if the change is reversed. Mass is also conserved in **chemical changes**, but the change in the substances often cannot be reversed.

Density

The **density** of a substance is the mass of a certain volume of the substance. Almost all substances are most dense when they are solids and least dense when they are gases. The arrangement of particles can explain the differences in density between different states of matter. A solid is usually denser than the same substance as a liquid, because the particles in solids are closer together.

C Ice is less dense than liquid water. This is unlike most substances, which become more dense when they turn from liquid to solid.

Density can be calculated using the equation below. The units for density are usually kilograms per cubic metre (kg/m³).

$$\text{density} = \frac{\text{mass}}{\text{volume}} \qquad \rho = \frac{m}{V}$$

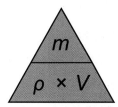

D You can rearrange the formula for density using this triangle. m represents mass and V represents volume. ρ is the Greek letter rho and represents density.

 5 A 500 kg block of aluminium has a volume of 0.185 m³. Calculate its density.

 6 The density of solid copper is 8960 kg/m³. Calculate the volume of a 5 tonne (5000 kg) delivery of copper.

Exam-style question

Use the kinetic theory model to explain *two* differences in the properties of solids and gases. *(4 marks)*

 3 Explain which beaker in photo C shows how the density of most substances changes when they freeze.

 4 Look at diagram B. Explain why a substance becomes less dense when it changes from a liquid to a gas.

CP12a Core practical – Investigating densities

Specification reference: P14.3

Aim

Investigate the densities of solids and liquids.

A Plimsoll line markings on the hull of a ship. TF stands for 'tropical fresh', F stands for 'fresh', T, S and W stand for Tropical, Summer and Winter seawater.

As ships are loaded they sink further down into the water. Ships have a 'Plimsoll line' marked on them to show how far into the water they can sink without becoming unsafe. The safe level depends on the density of the sea water. The density of sea water depends on its temperature and saltiness, so there are extra lines to show the safe level for different parts of the world and different times of the year.

Your task

To work out where to put the Plimsoll line markings on hulls, ship builders need to know the densities of different types of water. You are going to measure the densities of some different solids and liquids.

Method

Liquids

A Put an empty beaker on a balance, and set the balance to zero.

B Use a measuring cylinder to measure 50 cm³ of a liquid and then pour it into the beaker. Write down the reading on the balance. This is the mass of 50 cm³ of the liquid.

Solids

C Find the mass of the solid and write it down.

Diagram B shows how to find the volume of an irregular shape:

D Stand a displacement can on the bench with its spout over a bowl. Fill it with water until the water just starts to come out of the spout.

E Hold a measuring cylinder under the spout and carefully drop your object into the can. If your object floats, carefully push it down until all of it is under the water. Your finger should not be in the water.

F Stand the measuring cylinder on the bench and read the volume of water you have collected. This is the same as the volume of your object. Write it down.

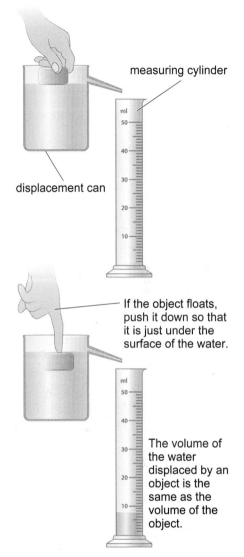

B how to use a displacement can

Exam-style questions

1 Solids and liquids are both made up of tiny particles. Compare solids and liquids in terms of:

  a how the particles move *(2 marks)*

  b the spacing between the particles. *(1 mark)*

2 **a** Write down the equation for calculating the density of a substance. *(1 mark)*

  b Give suitable units for each of the quantities in the equation. *(1 mark)*

3 You need to find the differences in density between different concentrations of salty water.

  a List the apparatus you would need to carry out this investigation. *(3 marks)*

  b Write a method for your investigation. *(3 marks)*

  c State how you would make sure your investigation was a fair test. *(1 mark)*

4 A student found that the mass of 50 cm³ (0.000 05 m³) of cooking oil was 46 g. Calculate the density of the cooking oil. Give your answer in kg/m³. *(3 marks)*

5 A large piece of wood is 2 m long, 50 cm wide and 2 cm thick. It has a mass of 12 kg. Calculate its density. *(3 marks)*

6 A student uses the method in steps E and F, and works out that the density of pure water is 980 kg/m³. A textbook gives a value of 1000 kg/m³.

  a Give a possible reason for the error in the student's result. *(1 mark)*

  b Describe a way of making the measurement of the density of fluids more accurate. *(1 mark)*

7 The values for the densities of substances given in reference books often state a temperature at which that density is correct. Explain why the density of a substance depends on its temperature. *(2 marks)*

Specification reference: P14.6; P14.7; P14.10

A A geyser shoots hot water into the air. Energy from hot rocks is transferred to the water, which gets hot enough to turn to steam and the water above this steam explodes out of the vent.

Energy transferred to a system by heating will be stored. The energy is stored in the movement of the particles that make up the substances in the system. Energy stored in this way is sometimes called **thermal energy**.

Temperature changes

When a solid stores more thermal energy, the vibrations of its particles increase. The speeds of the particles in liquids and gases increase when the liquid or gas is storing more energy. The **temperature** of a substance is a measure of the movement of the particles.

Temperature is not the same as thermal energy. For example, a kettle full of boiling water stores more energy than a cup full of water at the same temperature.

Did you know?

The temperature can affect the properties of a material. Flowers that are put into liquid nitrogen (about −196 °C) become very brittle and shatter if they are dropped.

B

To maintain a store of thermal energy, the amount of energy that is transferred to the surroundings by heating needs to be reduced. This can be done by surrounding the warm object with insulating materials such as wool, foam or bubble wrap. Insulation is also used in things like fridges, to stop energy from the surroundings being transferred to the inside of the fridge by heating.

The amount of thermal energy stored in something depends on:

- its temperature
- its mass
- the material it is made from.

The **specific heat capacity** of a material is the amount of energy it takes to increase the temperature of 1 kilogram of the substance by 1 °C.

 1 What are the units used for measuring:

a temperature

 b energy?

 2 Explain why a saucepan full of soup stores more energy than a spoonful of soup at the same temperature.

Changes of state

When enough energy is transferred to a solid it reaches its melting point. If energy continues to be transferred, the temperature stops rising because the extra energy is used to overcome the forces between the particles and turn the solid into a liquid.

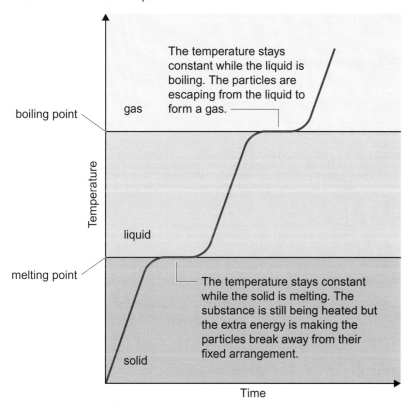

The temperature stays constant while the liquid is boiling. The particles are escaping from the liquid to form a gas.

The temperature stays constant while the solid is melting. The substance is still being heated but the extra energy is making the particles break away from their fixed arrangement.

C This heating curve shows how the temperature of a substance changes as it absorbs energy.

The amount of energy it takes to make 1 kg of a substance change state is called the **specific latent heat**. It takes more energy to evaporate 1 kg of a substance than it does to melt 1 kg of the same substance, so these quantities are sometimes called the specific latent heats of melting and of evaporation. This energy is given out again when a substance freezes or condenses.

5 Sketch a labelled graph similar to graph C to show how the temperature of a substance changes as it cools from a gas into a liquid then into a solid.

6 Explain why the specific latent heat of melting for butanol is less than its specific latent heat of evaporation.

Exam-style question

a Sketch a graph to show how the temperature changes when a block of ice is heated from −5 °C until the melted water is at 10 °C. *(2 marks)*

b Explain the shape of your graph. *(3 marks)*

3 A cook heats 1 kg of water and 1 kg of cooking oil. The cooking oil reaches 50 °C before the water.

a Explain which substance has the higher specific heat capacity.

b What assumption did you make in your answer to part a?

4 Look at graph C. Explain why the temperature stops rising when the liquid is boiling.

Checkpoint

How confidently can you answer the Progression questions?

Strengthen

S1 A bag of food is put into a freezer. Explain the factors that affect how much energy is transferred from the food to the air in the freezer as its temperature falls.

S2 Water put into a freezer cools down and then starts to turn to ice. Explain why the temperature stops falling while the water is freezing.

Extend

E1 Explain this energy-saving advice: 'When you are boiling potatoes, turn the heat down as soon as the water starts to boil. Leaving the heat turned up high will not make your potatoes cook any faster!'

CP12c Energy calculations

Specification reference: P14.8; P14.9

Progression questions

- How is a change in thermal energy related to the mass, specific heat capacity and temperature difference?
- How can we calculate the energy needed to make a substance melt or evaporate?
- How can we calculate the energy released when a substance condenses or freezes?

A A masonry heater can have a mass of around 800 kg. It is designed to store energy from a fire and continue radiating energy into the house long after the fire has stopped burning.

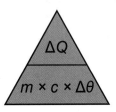

B This triangle can help you to rearrange the equation.

Changing temperature

The energy needed to heat a substance depends on the type of material, its mass and the temperature rise. These quantities are related by the following equation:

$$\text{change in thermal energy (J)} = \text{mass (kg)} \times \text{specific heat capacity (J/kg°C)} \times \text{change in temperature (°C)}$$

This can also be written as:

$$\Delta Q = m \times c \times \Delta\theta$$

where Δ (the Greek letter delta) represents the change in a quantity

Q represents energy

m represents mass

c represents the specific heat capacity of the material

θ (the Greek letter theta) represents the temperature.

Worked example W1

The specific heat capacity of water is 4182 J/kg°C. Calculate the energy needed to heat 2 kg of water from 10°C to 60°C.

$\Delta\theta = 60°C - 10°C$

$\quad = 50°C$

$\Delta Q = 2\,kg \times 4182\,J/kg°C \times 50°C$

$\quad = 418\,200\,J$

 1 a Explain why the heater in photo A has a large mass.

b Brick has a specific heat capacity of 840 J/kg°C. Calculate how much energy the 800 kg heater in photo A stores when the bricks are 40°C above the air temperature in the room.

 2 Calculate the temperature change when 25 000 J of energy is transferred to a 1 kg brick.

420

Changing state

Energy is needed to make a substance melt or evaporate. The amount of energy depends on the mass of the substance and on its specific latent heat. These quantities are related by the following equation:

$$\begin{array}{c} \text{thermal energy needed} \\ \text{for a change of state} \\ \text{(J)} \end{array} = \begin{array}{c} \text{mass} \\ \text{(kg)} \end{array} \times \begin{array}{c} \text{specific latent heat} \\ \text{(J/kg)} \end{array}$$

This can also be written as:

$Q = m \times L$

where Q represents energy

m represents mass

L represents the specific latent heat

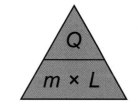

D This triangle can help you to rearrange the equation.

C Energy is transferred from the stag's body to evaporate water from its lungs. This energy is transferred to the surroundings when the water vapour condenses again.

Worked example W2

The specific latent heat of evaporation for water is 2257 kJ/kg. How much energy does it take to evaporate 5 kg of water at 100 °C?

2257 kJ/kg = 2 257 000 J/kg

energy for change of state = mass × specific latent heat

energy = 5 kg × 2 257 000 J/kg

= 11 285 000 J

Did you know?

Getting a scald from steam hurts more than spilling the same mass of boiling water on your skin. This is because the steam releases the latent heat of evaporation when it condenses.

 3 Look at Worked example W2. Explain why the question gives the temperature of the water.

 4 The specific latent heat of melting of water is 334 kJ/kg. How much energy does it take to melt 10 kg of ice at 0 °C?

 5 In an experiment, students transfer 100 000 J of energy to water at 100 °C. Calculate the mass of water that evaporates.

Exam-style question

A kettle is filled with 0.5 litres of water, which has a mass of 0.5 kg. The temperature of the water is 10 °C. Calculate how much energy is needed to bring the water to boiling point and then to evaporate all the water in the kettle.

(4 marks)

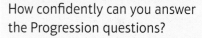

Checkpoint

How confidently can you answer the Progression questions?

Strengthen

S1 Calculate the temperature change when 8000 J of energy is transferred to 0.2 kg of water.

S2 10 000 J of energy is transferred to boiling water. Calculate the mass of water that evaporates.

Extend

E1 1 g of steam at 100 °C condenses on your hand and the water cools to your skin temperature (30 °C). Calculate how much energy this releases compared to spilling 1 g of boiling water onto your skin. (*Hint*: calculate the heat released during condensation and then as the water on your skin cools.)

Aim

Investigate the properties of water by determining the specific heat capacity of water and obtaining a temperature–time graph for melting ice.

A glaciologists drilling for an ice core sample in a glacier

The world is getting gradually warmer due to the effects of climate change. One effect of this is that glaciers in various parts of the world are melting and getting smaller. Glaciers can also get smaller due to sublimation. Scientists monitoring the changes in glaciers need to understand the properties of water in its solid (ice), liquid and gas forms.

Your task

You will find out what happens to the temperature of ice as it melts, and how much energy is needed to increase the temperature of a certain mass of water by 1 °C.

Method

Melting ice

Wear eye protection.

A Put a boiling tube full of crushed ice into a beaker. Put a thermometer in the ice and note the temperature.

B Put the beaker onto a tripod and gauze. Pour hot water from a kettle into the beaker, and keep it warm using a Bunsen burner.

C Measure the temperature of the ice every minute and record your results in a table. Stop taking readings three minutes after all the ice has melted.

D Note the times at which the ice starts to melt and when it appears to be completely melted.

Specific heat capacity

E Put a polystyrene cup in a beaker onto a battery-powered balance and zero the balance. Then fill the cup almost to the top with water and write down the mass of the water. Carefully remove the cup from the balance.

F Put a thermometer in the water and support it as shown in photo B. Put a 12 V electric immersion heater into the water, making sure the heating element is completely below the water level. Connect the immersion heater to a joulemeter.

G Record the temperature of the water, and then switch the immersion heater on. Stir the water in the cup gently using the thermometer.

H After five minutes record the temperature of the water again and also write down the reading on the joulemeter.

B

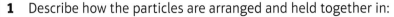

Exam-style questions

1   Describe how the particles are arranged and held together in:

   a   ice   *(2 marks)*

   b   liquid water.   *(2 marks)*

2   Table C shows a set of results from the melting ice investigation. Plot a graph to present these results. Draw a line through the points.   *(5 marks)*

3   Using ideas about kinetic theory:

   a   explain why the graph has a level section in the middle   *(2 marks)*

   b   state why the temperature of the ice increases at a different rate to the temperature of the water.   *(1 mark)*

4   What does the specific heat capacity of a substance tell us about the substance?   *(1 mark)*

5   Look at photo B.

   a   Describe the purpose of the glass beaker and the tripod.   *(1 mark)*

   b   Suggest why the water to be heated was put into a polystyrene cup instead of being put directly into the beaker.   *(3 marks)*

6   Sam heated 250 g of water in a polystyrene cup. The joulemeter reading was 11 kJ and the temperature change was 10 °C.

   a   Calculate the specific heat capacity of water using the following equation:

   specific heat capacity (J/kg °C) =

   $$\frac{\text{change in thermal energy (J)}}{\text{mass (kg)} \times \text{change in temperature (°C)}}$$

                                                                               (3 marks)

   b   A textbook gives the specific heat capacity of water as 4181 J/kg °C. Suggest why you would expect Sam's result to be higher than this.   *(3 marks)*

   c   Suggest how the method described above could be improved to reduce these errors.   *(1 mark)*

Time (min)	Temperature (°C)
0	−12
1	−8
2	−4
3	0
4	0
5	0
6	2
7	4
8	6

C

CP12d Gas temperature and pressure

Specification reference: P14.12; P14.13; P14.14; P14.15

Progression questions

- What causes gas pressure?
- How does the temperature of a gas affect its pressure?
- What is the difference between the kelvin and Celsius temperature scales?

The particles in a gas are far apart from each other and move around quickly. The temperature of a gas is a measure of the average **kinetic energy** of the particles in the gas. The faster the average speed of the particles, the higher the temperature. Heating a gas increases the kinetic energy of the particles, so they move faster and the temperature rises.

Did you know?

The Sun never shines on parts of these craters near the south pole of the Moon. The places in permanent shadow are the coldest recorded places in the Solar System and temperatures can get below −240 °C.

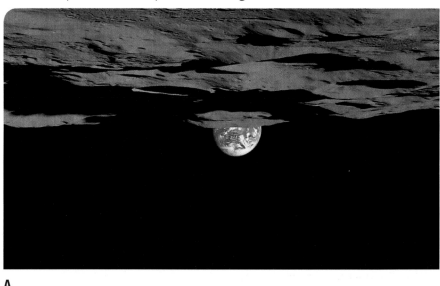

A

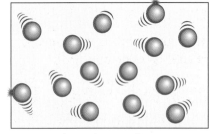

lower temperature

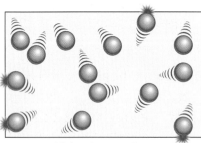

higher temperature

B The faster the average speed of the particles in a gas, the higher the temperature of the gas. The higher the temperature, the higher the pressure. This is because faster particles hit with more force and more often.

Particles and pressure

The **pressure** of a gas is due to forces on the walls of a container caused by the moving particles hitting the walls. The faster the particles are moving, the more frequent the collisions will be and the more force they will exert when they collide. Increasing the temperature of a gas increases the speed of the particles, so it also increases the pressure of the gas. For a fixed mass of gas in a fixed volume, the pressure increases when the temperature increases. The units for pressure are **pascals** (**Pa**), where $1\,Pa = 1\,N/m^2$.

 1 What causes pressure in a gas?

 2 Why does increasing the temperature of a fixed volume of gas increase its pressure? Give two reasons.

Absolute zero

Graph B shows how the pressure of a fixed volume of gas changes with temperature. The measurements cannot continue below the boiling point of the substance, as the gas will condense to form a liquid. However, the same graph is obtained for all gases, and if the lines are extended to colder temperatures they meet the horizontal axis at −273 °C. The temperature of −273 °C is called **absolute zero**. If a gas could be made this cold its pressure would be zero and the particles would not be moving.

The **kelvin temperature scale** measures temperatures relative to absolute zero. The units are **kelvin (K)**, and 1 K is the same temperature interval as 1 °C. Absolute zero is 0 K on this scale.

To convert from kelvin to degrees Celsius, subtract 273.

To convert from degrees Celsius to kelvin, add 273.

The average kinetic energy of the particles in a gas is directly proportional to the kelvin temperature of the gas.

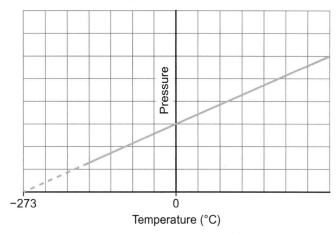

B the relationship between the pressure of a fixed volume of gas and the temperature of the gas (in degrees Celsius)

Worked example

What is the boiling point of water in kelvin?

boiling point = 100 °C + 273 = 373 K

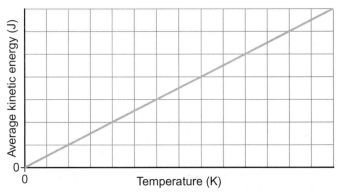

C the relationship between the average kinetic energy of gas particles and the kelvin temperature of the gas

3 Convert the following temperatures to the Celsius scale.

 a 500 K   **b** 100 K

4 Convert the following temperatures to the kelvin scale.

 a 500 °C   **b** −100 °C

 5 The temperature of a gas is increased from 200 K to 400 K. Explain what happens to the average kinetic energy of the particles.

Exam-style question

Look at graph C. Explain the significance of the point where the line crosses the horizontal axis.   *(2 marks)*

Checkpoint

How confidently can you answer the Progression questions?

Strengthen

S1 Explain what absolute zero is. Use the terms kinetic energy and absolute zero in your answer.

Extend

E1 Look at the graphs on this page.

   a Describe the relationship between the pressure of a gas and its temperature.

   b Explain what the relationship is between the pressure of a gas and the average kinetic energy of its particles.

CP13a Bending and stretching

Specification reference: P15.1; P15.2; P15.5

Progression questions

- How do forces cause objects to change shape?
- What is the difference between elastic and inelastic distortion?
- What is the relationship between force and extension when an object is deformed?

A This pole bends when forces are applied to both ends of it.

Forces can deform or change the shape of an object. It requires more than one force to stretch, bend or compress an object. For example, the weight of the pole vaulter in photo A is making the pole bend. But this only happens because there are also forces on the other end of the pole holding that end still.

The pole in photo A is **elastic**. This means that it will return to its original shape when the forces are removed. Some materials or objects are **inelastic**, which means that they will keep their new shape after the forces are removed.

B Metals are described as malleable, which means they can be hammered into shape. This hot iron is inelastic because it keeps its new shape after being hammered.

Some objects are elastic when the forces are small but behave inelastically if the forces are too big. Metals can be made into springs that behave elastically, but if the forces used to stretch them are too big they become permanently deformed.

 1 Suggest two materials that always deform inelastically.

2 A diving board usually bends when a diver stands on the end.

 a Is the deformation elastic or inelastic? Explain your answer.

 b Describe the two forces that cause the board to bend.

Did you know?

The tendons in our bodies that connect muscles to bones are springy. Tendons in our legs help us to save energy when we are running. The tendons store elastic potential energy as they stretch and this energy is transferred later in the stride to help to push us forwards.

426

Force and extension

The **extension** of a spring (or other object) is the change in length when forces are applied.

For a metal spring, there is usually a **linear relationship** between the force and the length. This means a graph of force against length will be a straight line. If force is plotted against *extension* the line passes through the origin, so the extension is **directly proportional** to the force. This means that the extension doubles if the force doubles. However, the relationship becomes **non-linear** if the spring is stretched too far. Other objects, such as rubber bands, have non-linear relationships between force and extension.

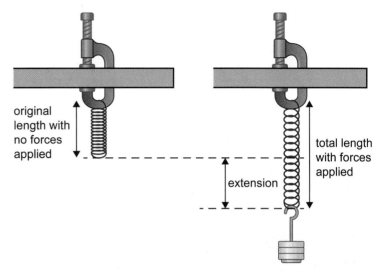

C The *extension* of a spring is not the same as its length.

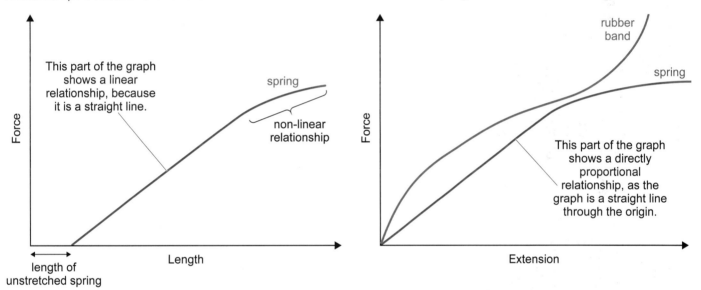

D force and extension relationships for springs and rubber bands

 3 Look at diagram D. A spring has an extension of 4 cm when a 2 N weight is hung from it.

 a What will the extension be when the weight is 6 N?

b Explain how you worked out your answer, including any assumptions you have made.

4 Look at diagram D. Describe how the force needed to produce greater and greater extensions changes for:

 a a spring   **b** a rubber band.

Exam-style question

Springs and rubber bands both stretch when forces are applied to them. Compare and contrast the way these items stretch.   *(3 marks)*

Checkpoint

How confidently can you answer the Progression questions?

Strengthen

S1 Write glossary entries for all the key terms on these pages.

Extend

E1 A piece of material is 10 cm long. As five weights of 1 N each are added, its length becomes: 10.5, 11.5, 13.0, 14.5, 15.5 cm. Explain how this data shows that the material is probably a rubber band.

CP13a Core practical – Investigating springs

Specification reference: P15.6

Aim

Investigate the extension and work done when applying forces to a spring.

A A spring in the top of this door bouncer lets the baby bob up and down.

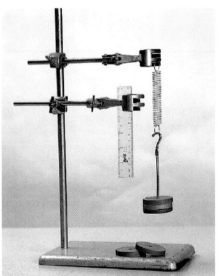

B

Photo A shows a baby in a door bouncer. The spring used in the door bouncer must be stretchy enough to allow the baby to bounce up and down, but not so stretchy that the weight of the baby stretches it too far and the baby ends up on the floor. Designers need to know the characteristics of springs so they can choose the type that best suits their purpose.

Your task

Investigate the force needed to stretch springs and calculate how much work is done when a spring is stretched.

The work done to stretch a spring is calculated using the following equation:

energy transferred in stretching = ½ × spring constant × (extension)²
(J)   (N/m)   (m)²

Method

Wear eye protection while you carry out this investigation.

A Set up the apparatus as shown in photo B. The zero on the ruler should be level with the bottom of the unstretched spring.

B Measure the length of the spring with no weights hanging on it and write it down.

C Hang a 1 newton weight on the spring. Record the extension of the spring (the length shown on the ruler).

D Repeat step C until you have found the extension of the spring with 10 different masses.

E Repeat steps A to D for a different spring.

F Use your results to calculate the spring constant for each spring.

Exam-style questions

1 **a** State what is meant by the spring constant of a spring. *(1 mark)*

    b State the equation that can be used to find the spring constant of a spring. *(1 mark)*

    c Give the units that should be used in the equation. *(1 mark)*

2 **a** When a force moves an object, the work done in moving the object can be calculated using the equation: work done = force × distance. Explain why this equation cannot be used to calculate the work done in stretching a spring. *(2 marks)*

    b A spring has an extension of 0.5 m when there is a force of 20 N pulling on it. Calculate the spring constant, and then calculate the energy transferred in stretching this spring. *(4 marks)*

3 Look at photo A.

    a Describe what happens to the spring in the door bouncer when the baby is first put into it. *(2 marks)*

    b The baby's father pulls the baby down by 20 cm, and then releases her. Describe what happens to the energy transferred by the father pulling the baby downwards. *(2 marks)*

4 Write a list of the apparatus you need to carry out an investigation like the one described in the method. *(1 mark)*

5 Table C shows the results of one group's investigation.

    a Draw a table of the results that shows the force and the *extension*, in metres. *(2 marks)*

    b Plot a graph of force against extension to show their results. Draw the lines for both springs on the same axes. *(5 marks)*

    c The readings for springs X and Y were taken by two different students. Use your graph to suggest which student has taken the more accurate readings for the length of the spring. *(1 mark)*

    d Read a pair of values for force and extension from your graph for spring X and use these values to find the spring constant. *(3 marks)*

    e Give a reason why you should use values read from the graph to find the spring constant, rather than taking data points from the table. *(2 marks)*

6 **a** Compare the two springs in terms of original length and how easily they stretch. *(2 marks)*

    b Explain which spring stores more energy when it has an extension of 20 cm. *(2 marks)*

7 A student carried out the investigation described, adding 10 N to the spring between each measurement. The spring stretched by only 1 mm with 10 N hanging on it.

    a Describe how this might affect the accuracy of the results. *(2 marks)*

    b Explain how the method could be modified to improve the accuracy of the student's results. *(2 marks)*

Weight (N)	Length (cm)	
	spring X	spring Y
0	6.0	4.0
1	9.4	8.8
2	13.0	14.2
3	16.2	19.2
4	19.1	23.1
5	22.9	28.8
6	26.5	34.3
7	29.5	39.5
8	33.0	45.5
9	36.0	48.8
10	39.5	55.0

C results for a spring investigation

CP13b Extension and energy transfers

Specification reference: P15.3; P15.4

Progression questions

- What is the spring constant of a spring?
- What is the equation that relates the force and extension of a spring?
- How do we calculate the work done in stretching a spring?

Did you know?

Very small springs are used in many things, including medical devices such as hearing aids and in miniature cameras. Some of the smallest springs have a diameter of 45 μm (1 μm = 1 × 10^{-6} m or 0.000 001 m or 0.001 mm).

B The spring used here needs a large spring constant.

Worked example W1

Calculate the spring constant for spring X in graph A.

$$k = \frac{F}{x}$$

$$= \frac{50\,N}{0.5\,m}$$

$$= 100\,N/m$$

> You can choose any point on the graph to read off a force and extension.

Graph A shows the force and extension for two different springs. Spring X needs a bigger force than spring Y to produce the same extension. The **spring constant** for a spring is the force needed to produce an extension of 1 metre. Spring X has a higher spring constant than spring Y.

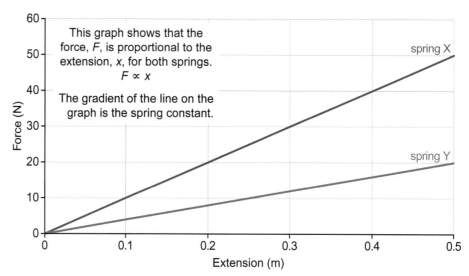

This graph shows that the force, *F*, is proportional to the extension, *x*, for both springs.
$$F \propto x$$
The gradient of the line on the graph is the spring constant.

A Force-extension graph for two springs. The ∝ symbol means 'directly proportional to'.

The spring used in a pogo stick (shown in photo B) needs to be much stiffer than a spring used in a force meter to measure very small forces. It needs a larger spring constant.

The force, extension and spring constant are related by this equation:

$$\text{force} = \text{spring constant} \times \text{extension}$$
$$\text{(N)} \qquad \text{(N/m)} \qquad \text{(m)}$$

This can be written as: $F = k \times x$

where *F* represents force
  k represents the spring constant
  x represents extension.

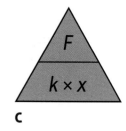

C

1 A spring has a spring constant of 400 N/m. Calculate the force needed to make it extend by:

　a 0.8 m　　**b** 10 cm.

　2 Show that the spring constant of spring Y in graph A is 40 N/m.

Energy transferred in stretching

Energy is needed to stretch a spring. The energy transferred when a force moves through a distance is calculated from the force multiplied by the distance. This is called the **work done** (see CP7a). However, when you stretch a spring the force needed increases as the extension increases, so the equation is a little more complicated.

The energy transferred in stretching a spring is calculated using this equation:

$$\text{energy transferred in stretching (J)} = \frac{1}{2} \times \text{spring constant (N/m)} \times (\text{extension})^2 \ (m)^2$$

This can be written as:

$$E = \frac{1}{2} \times k \times x^2$$

where E represents energy transferred
k represents the spring constant
x represents extension.

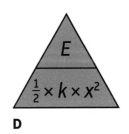

D

E Springs can also store energy when they are twisted. In this mousetrap, the spring is twisted to set the trap. When a mouse touches the pin the spring is released and the stored elastic potential energy is transferred to kinetic energy stored in the moving bar.

 3 Springs X and Y in graph A are stretched by the same amount. Explain which one needs the greater transfer of energy.

 4 Calculate the energy transferred when a spring with a spring constant of 200 N/m is stretched by 50 cm.

 5 It takes 5 J of energy to stretch a spring by 10 cm. Calculate the spring constant.

Exam-style question

Explain how a designer would use the spring constant to choose a type of spring to use in a force meter. *(2 marks)*

Worked example W2

Calculate the energy transferred when a spring with a spring constant of 100 N/m is stretched by 0.2 m.

$$E = \frac{1}{2} \times k \times x^2$$
$$= \frac{1}{2} \times 100\,N/m \times (0.2\,m)^2$$
$$= 2\,J$$

Checkpoint

How confidently can you answer the Progression questions?

Strengthen

S1 A spring has a spring constant of 400 N/m. A force of 20 N is applied to it. Calculate the extension.

S2 The same spring has an extension of 5 cm. Calculate the energy transferred to produce this extension.

Extend

E1 A spring stretches by 10 cm when a 50 N force is applied to it.

a Calculate the spring constant of the spring.

b Calculate how far the spring must be stretched to transfer 10 J of energy.

Electric storage heaters

Electric storage heaters use cheap night-time electricity to raise the temperature of a storage material. During the day, the stored energy is transferred to the surroundings to keep homes warm.

Water has a specific heat capacity of 4182 J/kg °C. Brick has a specific heat capacity of 900 J/kg °C, and is more dense than water.

Assess the suitability of these materials to store energy in a storage heater.

(6 marks)

Student answer

Specific heat capacity is the amount of energy it takes to raise the temperature of 1 kg of a substance by 1 °C [1]. It will take more energy to heat a storage heater full of water than one with the same mass of bricks, but this also means that the water will store more energy. So there will be more energy released when the water cools down again than if there is brick inside [2]. But if you damage a heater with water in it, the water will spill on to the floor [3].

[1] This shows that the student understands what specific heat capacity means.

[2] This is an advantage of using water inside the heater.

[3] This is a disadvantage of using water inside the heater.

Verdict

This is an acceptable answer. The student has explained what specific heat capacity means, and given one advantage and one disadvantage of using water compared to using brick.

The answer could be improved by linking some scientific ideas. For example, stating that the higher density of brick means that the same volume storage heater can hold a higher mass of brick, and how this will affect the energy stored. The command word for the question is 'assess', which means that the answer should include a conclusion about which material is best and which facts are important.

Exam tip

When a question asks you to assess something, you need to consider all the facts and explain which facts are the most important. Your answer also needs to make a judgement or reach a conclusion – in this case, which material is best.

Glossary

abiotic factors — Non-living conditions that can influence where plants or animals live (e.g. temperature, the amount of light)

absolute zero — The temperature at which the pressure of a gas drops to zero. It is −273 °C or 0 K.

absorb — To soak up or take in.

absorption spectrum — A spectrum of light (or electromagnetic radiation) that includes black lines. These are caused by some wavelengths being absorbed by the materials that the light (or radiation) passes through.

abundance — A measure of how common something is.

acceleration — A measure of how quickly the velocity of something is changing. It can be positive if the object is speeding up or negative if it is slowing down. Acceleration is a vector quantity.

acid — A solution that reacts with alkalis, turns litmus red and has a pH of less than 7.

acid rain — Rainwater that is more acidic than usual due to air pollution, usually caused by sulfur dioxide and nitrogen oxides dissolved in it.

acidic (adjective) — Containing or having the properties of an acid.

acidity — The amount of acid in a solution.

acquired characteristic — A characteristic of an organism that can change during its life due to a change in the environment.

acquired immune deficiency syndrome (AIDS) — When a person's immune system has been damaged by HIV, so they are more likely to get secondary infections.

acrosome — A cap-like structure on the head of a sperm cell that contains enzymes used to penetrate an egg cell.

action–reaction forces — Pairs of forces on interacting objects. Action–reaction forces are always the same size, in opposite directions, and acting on different objects. They are not the same as balanced forces (which act on a single object).

activated — To make active, such as when a lymphocyte is triggered by a pathogen to start dividing rapidly.

activation energy — The minimum amount of energy needed to start a reaction.

active site — The space in an enzyme where the substrate fits during an enzyme-catalysed reaction.

active transport — The movement of particles across a cell membrane from a region of lower concentration to a region of higher concentration (against the concentration gradient). This process requires energy.

activity — The number of emissions of ionising radiation from a sample in a given time. This is usually given in becquerels (Bq).

adaptation — The features of an organism that enable it to do a certain function (job).

adapted — If something has adaptations for a certain function (job), it is said to be adapted to that function.

adenine — One of the four bases found in DNA. Often written as A and pairs up with thymine.

adrenal gland — A gland located on top of a kidney that produces the hormone adrenalin. It can be referred to as 'an adrenal'.

adrenalin — A hormone that is released from the adrenal gland when you are nervous or excited.

adult stem cell — A stem cell found in specialised tissue that can produce more of the specialised cells in that tissue for growth and repair.

aerobic respiration — A type of respiration in which oxygen is used to release energy from substances such as glucose.

alkali — A solution which contains excess OH^- ions, turns litmus blue and has a pH greater than 7.

alkali metals — A group of very reactive metals found in group 1 of the periodic table.

alkaline (adjective) — Containing or having the properties of an alkali.

alkalinity — The amount of alkali in a solution.

alkane — A hydrocarbon in which all the bonds between the carbon atoms are single bonds.

alkene — A hydrocarbon in which there are one or more double bonds between carbon atoms.

allele — Most genes come in different versions called alleles.

allotrope — A different structural form of an element (e.g. graphite and diamond are allotropes of carbon).

alpha particle — A particle made of two protons and two neutrons, emitted as ionising radiation from some radioactive isotopes.

alternating current — Current whose direction changes many times each second.

alveoli — Small pockets in the lungs in which gases are exchanged between the air and the blood.

amplitude — The size of vibrations or the maximum distance a particle moves away from its resting position when a wave passes.

anaerobic respiration — A type of respiration that does not need oxygen.

anaphase — A stage of mitosis in which the separated chromosomes move away from each other.

ancestor — An organism from which more recent organisms are descended.

angle of incidence — The angle between an incoming light ray and the normal.

angle of refraction — The angle between the normal and a ray of light that has been refracted.

anion — A negatively-charged ion formed by gaining electrons (usually a non-metal ion).

anode — Positive electrode.

antibiotic — Medicine that helps people recover from a bacterial infection by killing the pathogen.

antibody — A protein produced by lymphocytes. It attaches to a specific antigen on a microorganism and helps to destroy or neutralise it.

antigen — A protein on the surface of a cell. White blood cells are able to recognise pathogens because of their antigens.

aqueous solution — A mixture that is formed when a substance is dissolved in water.

aquifer — An underground layer of rock containing groundwater which can be extracted using a well or pump.

A_r — The symbol for relative atomic mass (RAM).

Ardi — The nickname for a 4.4-million-year-old fossilised specimen of *Ardipithecus ramidus* that was discovered in Ethiopia.

artery — A blood vessel that carries blood away from the heart.

artificial selection — When people choose organisms with certain characteristics and use only those ones for breeding.

asexual reproduction — Producing new organisms from one parent only. These organisms are genetically identical to the parent.

assisted reproductive technology (ART) — Technology that helps increase the chance of pregnancy, such as the use of hormones to stimulate egg release.

atom — The smallest neutral part of an element that can take part in chemical reactions.

atomic energy — A term used to describe energy when it is stored inside atoms. It is another name for 'nuclear energy'.

atomic number — The number of protons in the nucleus of an atom (symbol Z). It is also known as the proton number.

atrium — An upper chamber in the heart that receives blood from the veins.

average speed — The speed worked out from the total distance travelled divided by the total time taken for a journey. Speed = distance travelled/time.

Avogadro constant — This is the number of particles in one mole of a substance $(6.02 \times 10^{23} \text{ mol}^{-1})$.

axon — The long extension of a neurone that carries an impulse away from the dendron or dendrites towards other neurones.

axon terminal — The small 'button' at the end of the branches that leave an axon.

background radiation	Ionising radiation that is around us all the time from a number of sources. Some background radiation is naturally occurring, but some comes from human activities.
balanced equation	Description of a reaction using the symbols and formulae of the reactants and products, so that the number of 'units' of each element to the left of the arrow is the same as those to the right of the arrow.
balanced forces	When the forces in opposite directions on an object are the same size so that there is a zero resultant force.
base	A substance that will react with an acid to form only salt and water.
base (in DNA)	A substance that helps make up DNA. There are four bases in DNA, often shown by the letters A, C, G and T.
becquerel (Bq)	The unit for the activity of a radioactive object. One becquerel is one radioactive decay per second.
belt transect	A line in an environment along which samples are taken to measure the effect of an abiotic factor on the distribution of organisms.
beta particle	A particle of radiation emitted from the nucleus of a radioactive atom when it decays. It is an electron.
binomial system	The system of naming organisms using two Latin words.
biodiversity	The variety of species in an area.
biofuel	A fuel made from plants or animal wastes.
biological catalyst	A substance found in living organisms that speeds up reactions, i.e. an enzyme.
biomass	The total mass in living organisms, usually shown as the mass after drying.
biotic factors	Living components (the organisms) in an ecosystem.
bleach	To bleach means to take the colour out of something.
blood	The fluid that carries oxygen and other substances from the heart to the body.
body mass index (BMI)	An estimate of how healthy a person's mass is for their height.
boiling point	The temperature at which a substance changes from a liquid to a gas.
bond	The force of attraction between atoms or ions holding them together.
bond energy	The energy needed to break one mole of a specified covalent bond. It is measured in kJ mol^{-1}.
braking distance	The distance travelled by a vehicle while the brakes are working to bring it to a halt.
breed	A group of animals of the same species that have characteristics that make them different to other members of the species.
burette	A piece of apparatus used to accurately measure the volume of solution that has been added during a titration.

cancer	A disease caused by the uncontrolled division of stem cells in a part of the body.
cancer cell	A cell that continues dividing, causing disease.
capillary	A tiny blood vessel with thin walls to allow for the transfer of substances between the blood and tissues.
captivity	Keeping something in unnatural surroundings, such as animals in a zoo.
carbon cycle	A sequence of processes by which carbon moves from the atmosphere, through living and dead organisms, into sediments and into the atmosphere again.
carbon monoxide	A poisonous gas produced from carbon burning without enough oxygen.
cardiac output	The volume of blood the heart can pump out in one minute. It is calculated using the equation cardiac output = stroke volume × heart rate
cardiovascular disease	A disease in which the heart or circulatory system does not function properly.

catalyst	A substance that speeds up the rate of a reaction without itself being used up.
cathode	Negative electrode.
cation	A positively-charged ion formed by losing electrons.
causation	The action of causing something to occur.
cell cycle	A sequence of growth and division that happens in cells. It includes interphase and mitosis, and leads to the production of two daughter cells that are identical to the parent cell.
cell (surface) membrane	The membrane that controls what goes into and out of a cell.
cell sap	The liquid found in the permanent vacuole in a plant cell.
cell wall	A tough layer of material around some cells which is used for protection and support. It is stiff and made of cellulose in plant cells. Bacteria have a flexible cell wall.
cellular respiration	Chemical processes by which living cells produce energy in the cell.
cellulose	Plant cell walls are made of tough cellulose which support the cell and allow it to keep its shape.
central nervous system (CNS)	The main part of the nervous system that includes the brain and spinal cord.
centripetal force	A force that causes objects to follow a circular path. The force acts towards the centre of the circle.
Chalara dieback	A disease of ash trees caused by a fungus called *Hymenoscyphus fraxineus*.
chamber	An enclosed space. A human heart has four chambers.
change of state	The changing of matter from one state to another e.g. from solid to liquid.
chemical analysis	Using chemical reactions or sensitive machines to identify and measure substances in a sample.
chemical defence	The use of chemical compounds to defend against attacks.
chemical energy	A term used to describe energy when it is stored in chemical substances. Food, fuel and batteries all store chemical energy.
chemical property	How a substance reacts with other substances.
Chlamydia	A bacterium that causes a sexually transmitted infection (STI).
chlorination	The process of adding chlorine to a substance, often to water.
chlorophyll	The green substance found inside chloroplasts that traps energy transferred by light.
chloroplast	A green disc containing chlorophyll found in plant cells. This is where the plant makes glucose through photosynthesis.
cholera	A bacterial infection of the small intestine.
chromatogram	The piece of paper showing the results of chromatography.
chromatography	A technique for separating the components of a mixture e.g. different food colouring agents
chromosomal DNA	The main bulk of DNA found in a cell. In humans, this DNA is found in chromosomes but the term is also used to describe the large loop of DNA found in bacteria.
chromosome	A thread-like structure found in the nuclei of cells. Each chromosome contains one enormously long DNA molecule packed with proteins.
ciliated (epithelial) cell	A cell that lines certain tubes in the body and has cilia on its surface.
cilium	A small hair-like structure on the surface of some cells. Plural is cilia.
circulatory system	The system that moves blood through the body. It consists of the heart, arteries, veins and capillaries.
cirrhosis	Damage to the liver caused by drinking large amounts of alcohol over a long period of time.
classification	The process of sorting organisms into groups based on their characteristics.
climate change	Changes that happen to the global weather patterns as a result of global warming.
clinical trial	The testing of a medicine on people.
clomifene therapy	A form of therapy used to stimulate ovulation.

clone The offspring from asexual reproduction. All the cells in a clone are genetically identical to each other and to the parent's cells.

closed system When substances cannot enter or leave an observed environment e.g. a stoppered test tube.

colony A cluster of microorganisms living closely together.

combustion A chemical reaction in which a compound reacts with oxygen.

communicable disease Any disease that can be spread directly from one person to another.

community All the different organisms living and interacting with one another in a particular area.

companion cell A specialised cell located in the phloem of plants.

compete When organisms interact to obtain a limited resource that they need.

competition When organisms need the same resources as each other, they struggle against each other to get those resources. We say that they 'compete' for those things.

complementary base pair Two DNA bases that fit into each other and link by hydrogen bonds.

complete combustion Combustion of hydrocarbons with enough oxygen present to convert all the fuel into carbon dioxide and water.

component A part of something e.g. a lamp might be a component of an electrical circuit.

compound A substance that can be split into simpler substances because it contains the atoms of two or more elements joined together.

compress To squash something together to make it shorter or smaller.

concentrated Containing a large amount of solute dissolved in a small volume of solvent.

concentration The amount of a solute dissolved in a certain volume of solvent.

concentration gradient The difference between two concentrations.

condense When a gas turns into a liquid.

conduction The way energy is transferred through solids by heating. Vibrations are passed on from particle to particle.

conservation The protection of an area or species to prevent damage.

conservation of momentum The total momentum of moving objects before a collision is the same as the total momentum afterwards as long as no external forces are acting.

conserved A quantity that is kept the same throughout e.g. momentum.

contamination An unwanted addition that makes something unsuitable or impure e.g. pure gold may become contaminated with another metal or, a person may be contaminated with a radioactive substance.

continuous variation Continuous data can take any value between two limits. Examples include length, mass and time. Continuous variation is when differences in a characteristic are continuous.

contraception The prevention of pregnancy by interfering with the process of ovulation.

contract To shorten.

control variable A variable that is kept the same in an investigation.

convection The movement of particles in a fluid (gas or liquid) depending on their temperature. Hotter, less dense regions rise, and cooler, denser regions sink.

core The innermost part of something e.g. the part of a nuclear reactor where controlled fission takes place.

corpus luteum A structure that develops in an ovary after an egg cell has been released. It secretes progesterone.

correlation A relationship between two variables, so that if one variable changes so does the other. This can be positive or negative.

cosmic rays Charged particles with a high energy that come from stars, neutron stars, black holes and supernovae.

count rate The number of alpha or beta particles or gamma rays detected by a Geiger-Müller tube in a certain time.

covalent bond The bond formed when a pair of electrons is shared between two atoms.

covalent, giant structure Three-dimensional lattice of carbon atoms linked by covalent bonds.

covalent, simple molecular structure Two or more atoms covalently bonded together to form a distinct unit.

cracking A chemical reaction in which large alkane molecules are split into two or more smaller alkanes and alkenes.

crop rotation Where a different crop is planted in the same field each year in a 3- or 4-year cycle, such as potatoes, oats, beans and cabbages. This helps to control the build-up of soil pests for each crop.

crude oil A mixture of hydrocarbons formed from dead microscopic organisms by heat and pressure over millions of years.

crumple zone A vehicle safety device in which part of the vehicle is designed to crumple in a crash, reducing the force of the impact.

crystallisation Separating the solute from a solution by evaporating the solvent.

crystals Solids that are made up of a regular repeated pattern of atoms, molecules or ions which form fixed shapes with flat surfaces and sharp edges.

cytokinesis When the cytoplasm of a cell is separated as the cell membrane becomes pinched to form two daughter cells.

cytoplasm The watery jelly inside a cell where the cell's activities take place.

cytosine One of the four bases found in DNA. Often written as C and pairs up with guanine.

daughter cell A new cell produced from the division of a parent cell.

decay (biology) A process in which complex substances in dead plant and animal biomass are broken down by decomposers into simpler substances.

decay (physics) When a radioactive isotope emits ionising radiation.

deceleration When an object is slowing down. A negative acceleration.

decomposer An organism that feeds on dead material, causing decay.

deficiency disease An illness due to insufficient supply of an essential dietary requirement.

delocalised electron An electron that is free to move and can carry an electrical current.

denatured A denatured enzyme is one where the shape of the active site has changed so much that its substrate no longer fits and the reaction can no longer happen.

dendrite A fine extension from a neurone which carries impulses towards the cell body.

dendron Large, long extension of a sensory neurone that carries impulses from dendrites towards the axon.

density The mass of a substance per unit volume. It has units such as g/cm^3.

deoxygenated Without oxygen.

dependent variable The variable that you measure in an investigation.

desalination A process that produces fresh drinking water by separating the water from the salts in salty water.

diabetes A disease in which the body cannot control blood glucose concentration at the correct level.

diarrhoea Loose or watery faeces.

diatomic Two atoms chemically bonded together.

differentiation The process by which a less specialised cell becomes more specialised for a particular function. The cell normally changes shape to achieve this.

diffusion The random movement and spreading of particles. There is a net (overall) diffusion of particles from areas of high concentration to regions of lower concentration.

digest	To break down large molecules into smaller subunits, particularly in the digestive system.
digestion	A process that breaks molecules into smaller, more soluble substances.
dilute	A low concentration of a solute in a solution.
diploid	A cell or nucleus that has two sets of chromosomes. In humans, almost all cells except the sperm and egg cells are diploid.
direct proportion	A linear relationship in which the percentage change in a variable occurs with an equal percentage change in another variable. A direct proportion is seen as a straight line through the origin when the two variables are plotted on a graph.
discontinuous variation	Data values that can only have one of a set number of options are discontinuous. Examples include shoe size and blood group. Discontinuous variation is when differences in a characteristic are discontinuous.
disease	An illness that prevents the body functioning normally.
disease resistance	Unaffected or less affected by a certain disease.
disinfectant	Something that destroys or neutralises disease-carrying microorganisms.
displacement	The distance travelled in a particular direction. Displacement is a vector, distance is not.
displacement reaction	When a more reactive element displaces a less reactive element from one of its compounds.
dissipated	Spread out.
dissociate	Breaking up of a compound in to simpler components.
distance	How far something has travelled. Distance is a scalar, and has no direction.
distance/time graph	A graph of the distance travelled against time for a moving object. The gradient of a line on a distance/time graph gives the speed.
distillation	The process of separating a liquid from a mixture by evaporating the liquid and then condensing it (so that it can be collected).
distribution	The places in which a certain organism can be found in an area.
DNA	Deoxyribonucleic acid. A polymer made of sugar and phosphate groups joined to bases.
DNA replication	When the DNA molecules are copied before cell division occurs.
domain	The three main groups that organisms are now sorted into: archaea, bacteria and eukarya.
dominant	Describes an allele that will always affect a phenotype as opposed to a recessive allele, whose effect will not be seen if a dominant allele is present.
dosage	The total amount of something received e.g. medicine, ionising radiation.
dot and cross diagram	A diagram to explain what happens when a bond is formed. It uses dots and crosses to represent the electrons of different atoms.
double bond	The covalent bond formed when two pairs of electrons are shared between the same two atoms.
double helix	The shape of a DNA molecule, consisting of two helices.
drought	Lack of water.
drug	A chemical substance that alters the functioning of part of the body.
dynamic equilibrium	When the forwards and backwards reactions in a reversible chemical reaction are occurring at the same rate.
ecosystem	An area in which all the living organisms and all the non-living physical factors in an area form a stable relationship that needs no input from outside the area to remain stable.
effector	A muscle or gland in the body that performs an action when an impulse from the nervous system is received.

effervescence	The formation of gas bubbles in a liquid due to a chemical reaction occurring.
efficiency	The proportion of input energy that is transferred to a useful form. A more efficient machine wastes less energy.
egg cell	The female gamete (sex cell).
egg follicle	Cells in the ovary that surround a developing egg. The follicle produces oestrogen.
elastic	An elastic material changes shape when there is a force on it but returns to its original shape when the force is removed.
elastic potential energy	A name used to describe energy when it is stored in stretched or squashed things that can change back to their original shape. Another name for 'strain energy'.
electric field/ electrostatic field	The space around an object with a charge of static electricity where it can affect other objects.
electrical conductivity	Allowing electricity to pass through.
electrical current	A flow of electrons around a circuit.
electromagnet	A magnet made using a coil of wire with electricity flowing through it.
electromagnetic induction	A process that creates a current in a wire when the wire is moved relative to a magnetic field, or when the magnetic field around it changes.
electromagnetic radiation	A form of energy transfer including radio waves, microwaves, infrared, visible light, ultraviolet, X-rays and gamma rays.
electromagnetic spectrum	The entire frequency range of electromagnetic waves.
electromagnetic waves	A group of waves that all travel at the same speed in a vacuum, and are all transverse.
electron	A tiny particle with a negative charge and very little mass.
electron shell	Areas around a nucleus that can be occupied by electrons and are usually drawn as circles. Also called an electron energy level or an 'orbit'.
electronic configuration	The arrangement of electrons in shells around the nucleus of an atom.
electrostatic force	The force of attraction between oppositely-charged particles, and force of repulsion between particles with the same charge.
element	A simple substance made up of only one type of atom.
elongation	When something gets longer such as a cell in a plant root or shoot before it differentiates into a specialised cell.
embryo	The ball of cells produced by cell division of the zygote. A very early stage in the development of a new individual.
embryonic stem cell	A cell from an early stage of division of an embryo that can produce almost any kind of differentiated cell.
emission spectrum	A set of wavelengths of light or electromagnetic radiation showing which wavelengths have been given out (emitted) by a substance.
emit	To give out.
empirical formula	The formula showing the simplest whole number ratio of atoms of each element in a compound.
endangered	An area or species that is at great risk of destruction.
endocrine gland	An organ that makes and releases hormones into the blood.
endothermic	A type of reaction in which energy from the surroundings is transferred to the products, i.e. photosynthesis.
end-point	When just enough solution has been added from the burette to react with all the solution in the flask in a titration experiment.
energy	Something that is needed to make things happen or change.
environmental variation	Differences between organisms caused by environmental factors such as the amount of heat, light and damage by other organisms. These differences are called acquired characteristics.
enzyme	A protein produced by living organisms that acts as a catalyst to speed up the rate of a reaction.

epidemic	When many people over a large area are infected with the same pathogen at the same time.
epithelial cell	A cell found on the surfaces of parts of the body.
equilibrium	When a situation is not changing because all the things affecting it balance out.
erythrocyte	Another term for red blood cell.
eukaryotic	A cell with a nucleus is eukaryotic. Organisms that have cells like this are also said to be eukaryotic organisms.
eutrophication	The addition of more nutrients to an ecosystem than it normally has.
evaporate	When a liquid turns in to a gas.
evolution	A change in one or more characteristics of a population over a long period of time.
excrete	To expel waste materials that have been produced inside an organism.
exothermic	A type of reaction in which energy is transferred to the surroundings from the reactants e.g. combustion.
extension	The amount by which a spring or other stretchy material has stretched. It is worked out from the stretched length minus the original length.
eyepiece lens	The part of the microscope you look down.
faeces	Undigested food that forms a waste material.
family pedigree chart	A chart showing the phenotypes and sexes of several generations of the same family, to track how characteristics have been inherited.
feedstock	Raw material. A substance used to make other substances.
fertilisation	Fusing of a male gamete with a female gamete.
field of view	The circle of light you see looking down a microscope.
fight-or-flight response	Several responses that prepare the body for sudden action, including increased heart rate, increased blood flow to muscles and the release of glucose into the blood.
filter	To separate out something e.g. separating insoluble substances from a liquid using filter paper.
filtrate	A solution that has passed through a filter.
filtration	Using a filter to separate insoluble substances from a liquid.
finite resource	Something useful that is no longer made or which is being made very slowly.
fish farming	Growing fish in a contained area, usually to supply humans with food.
flagellum	A tail-like structure that rotates, allowing a unicellular organism to move. Plural is flagella.
Fleming's left-hand rule	A way of remembering the direction of the force when a current flows in a magnetic field.
fluid	A liquid or a gas.
fluorescence	Absorbing radiation of one wavelength and re-emitting the energy at a different wavelength (usually so that it becomes visible).
food chain	A diagram that uses arrows to show the flow of energy through organisms that depend on each other for food.
food web	A diagram of interlinked food chains. It shows how the feeding relationships in a community are interdependent.
force	At the simplest level a force is a push, pull or twist. Forces acting on an object can cause it to accelerate. Force is a vector quantity.
force field	The space around something where a non-contact force affects things. Examples include magnetic fields and gravitational fields.
force meter	A meter, often containing a spring, which measures forces in newtons.
fossil fuel	A fuel formed from the dead remains of organisms over millions of years, i.e. coal, oil and natural gas.
fraction	A component of a mixture that has been separated by fractional distillation.

fractional distillation	A method of separating a mixture of liquids with different boiling points into individual components (fractions).
fractionating column	A long column used for fractional distillation. It is warmer at the bottom than at the top.
free body diagram	A diagram of an object showing all the forces acting upon it and the size and direction of those forces.
frequency	The number of cycles of a wave per second, measured in hertz (Hz).
friction	A force between two surfaces that resists motion and is always opposite to the direction of a moving object.
FSH	A hormone produced by the pituitary gland which causes eggs to mature in the ovaries.
fullerene	A molecule in which each carbon atom is covalently bonded to three other carbon atoms, forming spheres or tube shapes.
gamete	A haploid cell produced by meiosis used for sexual reproduction.
gamma ray (γ)	A high-frequency electromagnetic wave emitted from the nucleus of a radioactive atom. Gamma rays have the highest frequencies in the electromagnetic spectrum.
gas exchange	A process in which one gas diffuses across a membrane and another gas diffuses in the opposite direction.
Geiger-Müller (GM) tube	A device that can detect ionising radiation and is used to measure the activity of a radioactive source.
gene	A section of the long strand of DNA found in a chromosome which often contains instructions for a specific protein.
general formula	The formula showing the proportions of different atoms in molecules of a homologous series. For example, alkenes have the general formula C_nH_{2n}.
genetic diagram	A diagram showing how the alleles in two parents may form different combinations in the offspring when the parents reproduce.
genetic disorder	A disorder caused by faulty alleles.
genetic engineering	Altering the genome of an organism, usually by adding genes from another species. Also called genetic modification.
genetic modification	Another term for genetic engineering.
genetic variation	Differences between organisms caused by differences in the alleles they inherit from their parents, or differences in genes caused by mutation. Also called inherited variation.
genetically modified organism (GMO)	An organism that has had its genome artificially altered.
genome	All of the DNA in an organism. Each body cell contains a copy of the genome.
genotype	The alleles for a certain characteristic that are found in an organism.
genus	A classification group for closely-related species with similar characteristics. The genus name is the first word in the scientific name for a species (the second word is the 'species name').
glucagon	A hormone that increases blood glucose concentration.
glucose	A sugar produced by the digestion of carbohydrates and needed for respiration.
glycogen	A polymer storage material made from glucose.
gradient	A measurement describing the steepness of a line on a graph. It is calculated by taking the vertical distance between two points and dividing by the horizontal distance between the same two points. Also called the slope.
graphene	An allotrope of carbon consisting of a sheet that is one atom thick, with atoms arranged in a honeycomb shape.
gravitational field	The space around any object with mass where its gravity attracts other masses.
gravitational field strength	A measure of how strong the force of gravity is somewhere. The units are newtons per kilogram (N/kg).
gravitational potential energy	A term used to describe energy when it is stored in objects that can fall.

greenhouse gas	A gas that helps to trap 'heat' in the atmosphere. Carbon dioxide, methane and water vapour are greenhouse gases.
group	A vertical column of elements in the periodic table. Elements in the same group generally have similar properties.
growth	A permanent increase in the number and/or size of cells in an organism.
guanine	One of the four bases found in DNA. Often written as G and pairs up with cytosine.
guard cell	A pair of guard cells open and close plant stomata.

habitat	The place in which an organism lives e.g. woodland or sea shore.
haemoglobin	The red, iron-containing pigment found in red blood cells.
haemorrhagic fever	A disease which includes a fever (high body temperature) and internal bleeding, such as caused by the Ebola virus.
half equation	A chemical equation written to describe an oxidation or reduction half-reaction.
half-life	The average time taken for half of the radioactive nuclei in a sample of radioactive material to have decayed.
halide	A compound formed between a halogen and another element such as a metal or hydrogen.
halogen	An element in group 7 of the periodic table.
haploid	A cell or nucleus that has one set of chromosomes. Gametes are haploid.
hazard	Something that could cause harm.
health	A state of complete physical, social and mental well-being.
heart	A muscular organ in the circulatory system which pumps blood around the body.
heart attack	When the heart stops pumping properly due to a lack of oxygen reaching part of it.
heart rate	The number of heart beats in a unit of time, usually per minute (beats/min).
heart valve	A flap of tissue between the atria and ventricles of the heart that stops blood flowing in the wrong direction when the heart muscle contracts.
hertz (Hz)	The unit for frequency, 1 hertz is 1 wave per second.
heterozygous	When both the alleles for a gene are different in an organism.
homeostasis	Controlling the internal environment of the body at stable levels.
homologous series	A family of compounds that have the same general formula and similar properties, but have different numbers of carbon atoms.
homozygous	When both the alleles for a gene are the same in an organism.
hormonal system	The collection of glands in the body that release hormones.
hormones	Chemical messengers that are made in one part of the body and are carried in the blood to other parts, which they affect.
host	An individual that can be infected by a certain pathogen.
Human Genome Project	The project that mapped the base pairs in the human genome.
human immunodeficiency virus (HIV)	A virus that attacks white blood cells in the human immune system, often leading to AIDS.
hydrocarbon	A compound containing only hydrogen and carbon atoms.
hydroelectricity	Electricity generated by moving water, usually falling from a reservoir, to turn turbines and generators.
hydrogen bond	A weak force of attraction caused by differences in the electrical charge on different parts of different molecules.
hygiene	Keeping things clean by removing or killing pathogens.

ignite	To start burning.
immune	When a person does not fall ill after infection because their immune system attacks and destroys the pathogen quickly.

immune system	All the organs in the body that protect against disease. It includes organs that provide an external barrier e.g. skin and those that kill pathogens directly or produce substances that kill pathogens.
impulse	An electrical signal transmitted along a neurone.
impure	A substance that is not pure.
impurity	Unwanted substances found mixed into a useful substance.
Incident ray	A ray of light going towards an interface or object.
incomplete combustion	When a substance reacts only partially with oxygen, such as when carbon burns in air producing carbon dioxide, carbon monoxide and soot (unburnt carbon).
independent variable	The variable that is changed in an investigation and which affects the dependent variable.
index	A small raised number after a unit or another number to show you how many times to multiply that number together. For example, 10^3 means multiply 10 together 3 times ($10 \times 10 \times 10$).
indicator	A substance which can change colour depending on the pH of a solution.
indigenous	Organisms that have always been in an area. Another word for native.
induce	To create. For example, a wire in a changing magnetic field has a current induced in it.
induced magnet	A piece of material that becomes a magnet because it is in the magnetic field of another magnet.
inelastic	A material that changes shape when there is a force on it but does not return to its original shape when the force is removed.
inert	Does not react.
inertial mass	The mass of an object found from the ratio of force divided by acceleration. The value is the same as the mass calculated from the weight of an object and gravitational field strength.
infrared	Electromagnetic radiation that we can feel as heat.
inhibit	To stop or slow down a process.
insoluble	A substance that cannot be dissolved in a certain liquid.
instantaneous speed	The speed at one particular moment in a journey.
insulation	The method of reducing energy transfer (often using insulating materials).
insulin	A hormone that decreases blood glucose concentration. It is used in the treatment of type 1 diabetes.
interdependent	When organisms in an area need each other for resources e.g. for food and shelter.
interface	The boundary between two materials.
intermolecular force	A weak force of attraction between molecules.
interphase	The stage during which a cell prepares itself for cell division. DNA replication takes place and additional sub-cellular structures are produced.
inverse square law	A mathematical relationship in which a quantity varies in inverse proportion to the square of the distance from the source of the quantity.
ion	An atom or group of atoms with an electrical charge due to the gain or loss of electrons.
ionic bond	A strong electrostatic force of attraction between oppositely-charged ions.
ionic compound	A substance made up of ions of different elements.
ionising radiation	Radiation that can cause charged particles (ions) to be formed. It can cause tissue damage and DNA mutations.
irradiated	Something has been irradiated if it has been exposed to ionising radiation e.g. to sterilise food or medical equipment with gamma rays.
isotope	Atoms of an element with the same number of protons (atomic number) but different mass numbers due to different numbers of neutrons.

438

IVF	Fertilising an egg cell by placing it in a sterile container and then adding sperm cells.
joule (J)	A unit for measuring energy.
kelvin (K)	The unit in the Kelvin temperature scale. One kelvin is the same temperature interval as 1 °C.
Kelvin temperature scale	A temperature scale that measures temperatures relative to absolute zero.
kinetic energy	A term used to describe energy when it is stored in moving things.
kinetic theory	The model that explains the properties of different states of matter in terms of the movement of particles.
kingdom	There are five kingdoms into which organisms are usually divided: plants, animals, fungi, protists and prokaryotes.
lactic acid	The waste product of anaerobic respiration in animal cells.
lattice	An arrangement of many particles that are bonded together in a fixed, regular, grid-like pattern.
law of conservation of energy	The idea that energy can never be created or destroyed, only transferred from one store to another.
law of conservation of mass	The idea that mass is never lost or gained during a chemical reaction or physical change.
LH	A hormone produced by the pituitary gland which causes ovulation.
lifestyle	The way we live that can our affect bodies, such as what we eat, whether we smoke or do exercise.
ligase	An enzyme that joins two DNA molecules together.
light gate	A piece of apparatus containing an infrared beam that is transmitted from a source onto a detector. If the beam is cut, the light gate measures how long it is cut for, giving you a reading for time.
lignin	A type of polymer that is combined with cellulose in some plant cells to make them woody, i.e. in xylem cells.
limiting factor	A single factor that when in short supply can limit the rate of a process such as photosynthesis.
limiting reactant	The reactant that determines the amount of product formed in a chemical reaction. Any other reactants will be present in excess.
linear relationship	A relationship between two variables shown by a straight line on a graph.
lipid	A substance in a large group of compounds that includes fats and oils.
lock-and-key model	A model that describes the way an enzyme catalyses a reaction when the substrate fits within the active site of the enzyme.
longitudinal wave	A wave where the vibrations are parallel to the direction in which the wave is travelling, i.e. in a sound wave.
lubricant	A substance placed between two moving surfaces to reduce the friction between them.
lubrication	To reduce friction by putting a substance (usually a liquid) between two surfaces.
Lucy	The nickname for a 3.2 million-year-old fossilised specimen of *Australopithecus afarensis*.
lymphocyte	A type of white blood cell that produces antibodies.
lysozyme	An enzyme produced in tears, saliva and mucus that damages pathogens.
magnet	An object that has its own magnetic field around it.
magnetic field	The area around a magnet where it can affect magnetic materials or induce a current.
magnetic flux density	A way of describing the strength of a magnetic field. It is measured in teslas (T).
magnetic materials	A material, such as iron, that is attracted to a magnet.
magnetism	The force caused by magnets on magnetic materials.

magnification	The number of times larger an image is than the initial object that produced it.
magnitude	The size of something, such as the size of a force or the measurement of a distance.
malaria	A dangerous disease caused by a protist that causes serious fever, headaches and vomiting and can lead to death.
malleable	A substance that can be hammered or rolled into shape without shattering.
malnutrition	Health problems caused by a diet that contains too little or too much of one or more nutrients.
manure	A mixture containing animal waste that is added to soil to improve its fertility.
mass	A measure of the amount of material there is in an object. The units are kilograms (kg). Mass is a scalar quantity.
mass number	The total number of protons and neutrons in the nucleus of an atom (symbol A). It is also known as the nucleon number.
mean	An average calculated by adding up the values of a set of measurements and dividing by the number of measurements in the set.
median	The middle value in a data set.
medium	Material through which electromagnetic waves travel.
meiosis	A form of cell division in which one parent cell produces four haploid daughter cells.
melting point	The temperature at which a substance changes from the solid state to the liquid state when heated, or from the liquid state to the solid state when cooled.
memory lymphocyte	A lymphocyte that remains in the blood for a long time after an infection or vaccination.
menopause	When the menstrual cycle stops completely.
menstrual cycle	A monthly cycle involving the reproductive organs in women.
menstruation	The breakdown and loss of the lining of the uterus at the start of a woman's menstrual cycle.
meristem	A small area of undifferentiated cells in a plant where cells are dividing rapidly by mitosis.
meristem cell	A stem cell found in a plant meristem.
metabolic rate	The overall rate at which chemical reactions occur within the body.
metabolism	All the chemical reactions that occur in your body.
metal	Any element that is shiny when polished, conducts heat and electricity well, is malleable and flexible and often has a high melting point.
metallic bonding	The type of bonding found in metals. You can think of it as positively-charged ions in a 'sea' of negatively-charged electrons.
metaphase	The stage of mitosis when the chromosomes line up across the middle of the cell.
microvillus	A fold on the surface of a villus cell. Plural is microvilli.
mitochondrion	A sub-cellular structure (organelle) in the cytoplasm of eukaryotic cells where aerobic respiration occurs. Plural is mitochondria.
mitosis	The process of cells dividing to produce two diploid daughter cells that are genetically identical to the parent.
mixture	A substance containing two or more different substances that are not joined together.
mobile phase	In paper chromatography, this is when the solvent moves along the paper carrying the dissolved samples with it.
mode	The most common value in a data set.
mole	A mole of something is 6×10^{23} of it. The mass of a mole of a substance is the relative formula mass expressed in grams.
molecular	Refers to substances that are made up of molecules.
molecular formula	The formula showing the actual number of atoms of each element in a molecule of a compound.
molecule	A particle consisting of two or more atoms joined together by covalent bonding.

momentum	The mass of an object multiplied by its velocity. Momentum is a vector quantity measured in kilogram metres per second (kg m/s).
monohybrid inheritance	The study of how the alleles of just one gene are passed from parents to offspring.
monomer	A small molecule that can join with other molecules like itself to form a polymer.
motor effect	The force experienced by a wire carrying a current that is placed in a magnetic field.
motor neurone	A type of neurone that carries impulses to effectors.
mucus	A sticky substance secreted by cells that line many openings to the body.
multicellular	An organism that is made up of many cells.
mutation	A change to a gene caused by a mistake in copying the DNA base pairs during cell division, or by the effects of radiation or certain chemicals.
mutualistic	A relationship between individuals of different species where both individuals benefit.
myelin sheath	Fatty covering around the axons of many neurones.

national grid	The system of wires and transformers that distributes electricity around the country.
native	Another term for indigenous.
native state	The native state of an element is when it is not combined with other elements in compounds.
natural gas	A fossil fuel formed from the remains of microscopic dead plants and animals that lived in the sea.
natural selection	A process in which certain organisms are more likely to survive and reproduce than other members of the same species because they possess certain genetic variations.
negative feedback	A control mechanism that reacts to a change in a condition, such as temperature, by trying to bring the condition back to a normal level.
negative ion	An atom that has gained electrons and so has an overall negative charge.
nerve cell	Another term for neurone.
nervous system	An organ system that contains the brain, spinal cord and nerves and carries impulses around the body. This system helps you to sense and respond quickly to changes inside and outside of your body.
net force	Another term for resultant force.
neurone	A cell that transmits electrical impulses in the nervous system.
neurotransmission	Impulses passing from neurone to neurone.
neurotransmitter	A substance that diffuses across the gap between one neurone and the next at a synapse, and triggers an impulse to be generated.
neutral (chemistry)	A liquid that is neither acidic nor alkaline and has a pH of 7.
neutral (physics)	Something that has no overall charge.
neutralisation	A reaction in which an acid reacts with a base to produce a salt and water only.
neutron	A particle found in the nucleus of an atom having zero charge and mass of 1 (relative to a proton).
nitrate	A compound that contains nitrogen in the form of a nitrate ion.
nitrogen cycle	A sequence of processes by which nitrogen moves from the atmosphere through living and dead organisms, into the soil and back to the atmosphere.
nitrogen-fixing bacteria	Bacteria that can take nitrogen from the atmosphere and convert it to more complex nitrogen compounds such as ammonia.
noble gas	An unreactive gas in group 0 of the periodic table.
non-communicable	When a disease cannot be spread from animal to animal, or person to person.

non-indigenous	Organisms that have been introduced to an area where they haven't been before.
non-linear	A relationship between two variables that does not produce a straight line on a graph.
non-metal	An element that is not shiny and does not conduct heat or electricity well.
non-renewable	Any energy resource that will run out because you cannot renew your supply of it, e.g. oil.
normal	An imaginary line drawn at right angles to the surface of a mirror or lens where a ray of light hits it.
normal contact force	A force that acts at right angles to a surface as a reaction to a force on that surface.
normal distribution	When many individuals have a middle value for a feature with fewer individuals having greater or lesser values. This sort of data forms a bell shape on charts and graphs.
nuclear energy	A name used to describe energy when it is stored inside atoms. Another term for atomic energy.
nuclear equation	An equation representing a change in an atomic nucleus due to radioactive decay. The atomic numbers and mass numbers must balance.
nuclear fission	When the nucleus of a large atom such as uranium, splits into two smaller nuclei.
nuclear fuel	A radioactive metal such as uranium. Nuclear fuels are used in nuclear power stations to generate electricity.
nucleon	A particle found in the nucleus (neutron or proton).
nucleon number	Another term for mass number.
nucleus (biology)	The 'control centre' of a eukaryotic cell.
nucleus (chemistry)	The central part of an atom or ion.

obesity	A condition in which someone is overweight for their height and has a BMI above 30.
objective lens	The part of the microscope that is closest to the specimen.
oestrogen	A hormone produced by the ovaries that is important in the menstrual cycle.
open system	A system into or from which substances can enter or leave, such as a reaction inside an open test tube.
optimum pH	The pH at which an enzyme's rate of reaction is greatest, or at which a population of microorganisms grows most rapidly.
optimum temperature	The temperature at which an enzyme's rate of reaction is greatest, or at which a population of microorganisms grows most rapidly.
orbit	The path taken by a planet around the Sun, or a satellite around a planet. Sometimes also used to describe electron shells.
oscillation	Movement backwards and forwards
osmosis	The overall movement of solvent molecules in a solution across a partially permeable membrane, from a dilute solution to a more concentrated one.
outer electron shell	The electron shell (or energy level) that is furthest away from a nucleus but which still contains one or more electrons.
ovary	The organ in the female reproductive system that releases egg cells and the hormones oestrogen and progesterone.
overfishing	Taking more fish from a population than are replaced by the fish reproducing so that the population falls over time.
oviduct	A tube that carries egg cells from the ovaries to the uterus in females. Fertilisation happens here.
ovulation	The release of an egg from an ovary.
oxidation	A reaction in which oxygen is added to a chemical; loss of electrons by an atom or negative ion.
oxide of nitrogen	Any one of a variety of gaseous compounds consisting of only nitrogen and oxygen atoms. Together they are often represented as NO_x.
oxidised	When a substance gains oxygen (or loses electrons) in a reaction, it is oxidised.
oxygenated	With oxygen.

palisade cell	Tall, column-shaped cell near the upper surface of a plant leaf.
pancreas	An organ in the body that produces some digestive enzymes, as well as some hormones.
paper chromatography	Chromatography carried out by spotting drops of the samples onto paper and then allowing a solvent to move up the paper. Different components in the samples travel up the paper in the solvent at different rates.
parasite	An organism that lives on or in a host organism and takes food from it while it is alive.
parasitism	A feeding relationship in which a parasite benefits and its host is harmed.
partially permeable	Describes a membrane that will allow certain particles to pass through it but not others. Another term for semi-permeable.
particle	A tiny piece of matter that everything is made out of.
particle model or theory	Another term for kinetic theory.
pascal (Pa)	A unit of pressure. 1 Pa = 1 N/m^2.
passive	A process that does not require energy is passive.
pathogen	An organism (usually a microorganism) that causes disease.
penetrate	Go through.
penicillin	The first kind of antibiotic that was extracted from a mould.
percentile	The value of a variable below which a certain percentage of observations fall. For example, in an ordered set of data, the 20th percentile is the value at which 20% of the data points are the same or lower.
period (biology)	The 'bleed' that occurs during menstruation.
period (chemistry)	A horizontal row in the periodic table.
period (physics)	The time taken for one complete wave to pass a point. It is measured in seconds.
periodic table	The chart in which the elements are arranged in order of increasing atomic number.
permanent magnet	A magnet that is always magnetic such as a bar magnet.
petrochemical	A substance made from crude oil.
pH meter	An electronic device used to measure the pH of a solution.
pH scale	A scale going up to 14 showing acidity or alkalinity. Numbers below 7 are acids; numbers above 7 are alkalis; pH 7 is neutral.
phagocyte	A white blood cell that is capable of engulfing microorganisms such as bacteria.
phenotype	The characteristics produced by a certain set of alleles.
phloem	Living tissue formed of sieve tubes and companion cells that transports sugars and other compounds around a plant.
photosynthesis	A series of enzyme-catalysed reactions carried out in the green parts of plants. Carbon dioxide and water combine to form glucose. This process requires light energy from sunlight.
physical barrier	A structure that stops something from entering a certain area. For example, the body has physical barriers like the skin, which stop microbes from getting inside the body.
physical change	A change in which no new substances are formed, such as changes of state.
physical property	A description of how a material behaves and responds to forces and energy. For example, hardness is a physical property.
pipette	A piece of apparatus which can be used in a titration to accurately measure a set volume of a solution.
pituitary gland	An organ just below the brain that releases many different hormones. It can be referred to as 'the pituitary'.
plasma (biology)	The straw-coloured liquid component of blood.
plasmid	A small loop of DNA found in the cytoplasm of bacteria.
plasmid DNA	DNA found in plasmids.
platelet	Cell fragments that are important in the clotting mechanism of the blood.
plotting compass	A small compass used to find the shape of a magnetic field.
pollutant	A substance that harms living organisms when released into the environment.
pollution	Harm caused to the environment, such as by adding poisonous substances or by abnormally high amounts of a substance in the air.
polyatomic ions	A group of atoms that have a positive or negative charge due to the loss or gain of electrons e.g. nitrate NO^{3-}.
poly(ethene)	A common polymer made of ethene monomers.
polymer	A long-chain molecule made by joining many smaller molecules (monomers) together.
population	A group of one species living in the same area.
positive ion	An atom that has lost electrons and so has an overall positive charge.
positron	The anti-particle of an electron, having the same mass but opposite charge. Positron emission is a type of beta decay.
potable	Suitable for drinking.
potential difference (p.d.)	The difference in the energy carried by electrons before and after they have flowed through a component. Another term for voltage.
potometer	A device used for measuring the rate of water uptake by a plant.
power	The amount (rate) of energy transferred per second. The units are watts (W).
precipitate	An insoluble substance that is formed when two soluble substances react together in solution.
precipitation	A reaction in which a precipitate is formed.
pre-clinical	The testing of a drug before it is tried on humans, including testing on cells or tissues and on other animals.
predation	When one animal species kills and eats another animal species.
predator–prey cycle	The regular variation in numbers of predators and numbers of prey within a feeding relationship.
prediction	What you think will happen in an experiment (usually given with a reason of why you think this).
pregnancy	The time during which a fertilised egg develops in the uterus until the birth of the baby.
pressure	The force on a certain area. It is measured in pascals or N/m^2.
probability	The likelihood of an event happening. It can be shown as a fraction from 0 to 1, a decimal from 0 to 1 or as a percentage from 0% to 100%.
producer	An organism that makes its own food such as a plant using photosynthesis.
product	A substance formed in a reaction.
progesterone	One of the hormones released by the ovaries.
prokaryotic	A cell with no nucleus is prokaryotic. Organisms with cells like this are said to be prokaryotic organisms, i.e. bacteria.
prophase	The stage of mitosis in which the nucleus starts to break down and spindle fibres appear.
protein	A polymer made up of amino acids.
protist	An organism that belongs to a kingdom of eukaryotic and mainly single-celled organisms (also called 'protoctist').
proton	A particle found in the nucleus of an atom, having a positive charge and the same mass as a neutron.
proton number	The number of protons in an atomic nucleus. Another term for atomic number.
puberty	The stage of life when the body develops in ways that allow reproduction, e.g. the production of sperm cells in testes and the release of egg cells from ovaries.
pulmonary vein	A vein that carries oxygenated blood from the lungs to the left atrium.
pulse	A shock wave that travels through the walls of arteries leading from the heart.

Punnett square	A diagram used to predict the characteristics of offspring produced by two organisms with known combinations of alleles.
pure	A single substance with a fixed composition that does not have anything else mixed with it.
quadrat	A square frame of known area, such as 1 m², that is placed on the ground to get a sample of the organisms living in a small area.
quartiles	When an ordered set of data is divided into four equal groups, those groups are called quartiles.
radiation	A way of transferring energy. Often used to signify the transfer of energy by heating, which is better referred to as infrared radiation.
radioactive decay	When an unstable nucleus changes by giving out ionising radiation to become more stable.
radiotherapy	The use of ionising radiation to treat diseases, such as to kill cancer cells.
random	Any process that cannot be predicted and can happen at any time is said to be random.
range	In maths, this is the calculated difference between the highest and lowest values in a set of data, usually ignoring any outliers or anomalous results. In science, we often use the term as a statement of what the highest and lowest values are, without doing the calculation.
rate	How quickly something happens.
ratio	A relationship between two quantities, usually showing the number of times one value is bigger than the other.
reactant	A substance used up in a chemical reaction.
reaction profile	A diagram to show how the energy stored in substances changes during the course of a chemical reaction.
reaction time	The time taken to respond to a stimulus, which is affected by the speed of activity in the brain and nervous system.
reactivity series	A list of metals in order of reactivity with the most reactive at the top.
receptor cell	A cell that receives a stimulus and converts it into an electrical impulse to be sent to the brain and/or spinal cord.
recessive	Describes an allele that will only affect the phenotype if the other allele is also recessive. It has no effect if the other allele is dominant.
recombinant DNA	DNA made by joining two sections of DNA together.
red blood cell	A biconcave disc containing haemoglobin that gives blood its red colour and carries oxygen around the body to the tissues. Also known as erythrocyte.
redox reaction	A reaction in which both oxidation and reduction occur.
reduced	When a substance loses oxygen (or gains electrons) in a reaction, it is reduced (a reduction reaction).
reflex	A response to a stimulus that does not require processing by the brain. The response is automatic. Also called a reflex action.
reflex arc	A neurone pathway consisting of a sensory neurone passing impulses to a motor neurone, often via a relay neurone, which allows reflexes to occur.
reforestation	Planting new forests where old forests have been cut down.
refraction	The change in direction when a wave goes from one transparent material to another.
rejection	When the immune system attacks and kills cells and tissue that come from another person, such as blood (after transfusion) or stem cells.
relative atomic mass (RAM, A_r)	The mean mass of an atom relative to the mass of an atom of carbon-12, which is assigned a mass of 12. The RAM of an element is the mean relative mass of the isotopes in the element.
relative formula mass	The sum of the relative atomic masses of all the atoms in a formula.

relative mass	The mass of something compared to the mass of something else, which is often given the mass of 1.
relay neurone	A short type of neurone found in the spinal cord and brain. Relay neurones link with sensory, motor and other relay neurones.
renewable	An energy resource that will never run out, e.g. solar power.
replicate	When DNA replicates, it makes a copy of itself.
residue	Material remaining in the filter after a mixture has passed through it.
resistance (physics)	A way of saying how difficult it is for electricity to flow through something.
resistant	Unaffected or less affected by something.
resolution	The smallest change that can be measured by an instrument. For example, in a microscope it is the smallest distance between two points that can be seen as two points and not blurred into one point.
resolving	Representing a single force as two forces at right angles to each other.
resource (biology)	Something that an organism needs to stay alive such as food, water and space.
respiration	A series of reactions occurring in all living cells in which glucose is broken down to release energy.
response	An action that occurs due to a stimulus.
resting metabolic rate	The metabolic rate when the body is at rest.
restriction enzyme	An enzyme that cuts DNA molecules into pieces.
resultant force	The total force that results from two or more forces acting upon a single object. It is found by adding together the forces, taking into account their directions. Another term for net force.
reversible reaction	A chemical reaction that can work in both directions.
R_f value	The ratio of the distance travelled by a solute on a chromatogram to the distance travelled by the solvent under the same conditions.
ribosome	A tiny sub-cellular structure that makes proteins.
risk	The chance of a hazard causing harm.
risk assessment	Identification of the hazards of doing an experiment and ways of reducing the risk of harm from those hazards.
root hair cell	A cell found on the surface of plant roots that has a large surface area to absorb water and dissolved mineral salts quickly from the soil.
salt	A compound formed by neutralisation of an acid by a base.
sample	A small portion of an area or population.
Sankey diagram	A diagram showing energy transfers, where the width of each arrow is proportional to the amount of energy it represents.
saturated	A molecule that contains only single bonds between the carbon atoms in a chain.
saturated solution	Contains the maximum amount of solute that can dissolve in that amount of solvent at that temperature.
scalar quantity	A quantity that has a magnitude (size) but not a direction. Examples include mass, distance, energy and speed.
scale bar	A line drawn on a magnified image that shows a certain distance at that magnification.
scale diagram (physics)	A way of working out the resultant forces or component forces by drawing a diagram where the lengths of arrows represent the sizes of the forces.
scientific paper	An article written by scientists and published in a science magazine called a journal. It is like an investigation report, but usually shows the results and conclusions drawn from many experiments.
screening	Tests on samples of body fluids to check if people have a certain condition, e.g. an STI.
secondary infection	An infection due to the immune system being weakened previously by a different pathogen.

secondary response	The way in which the immune system responds on the second occasion that a particular pathogen enters the body.
sedimentation	The process in which rock grains and insoluble substances sink to the bottom of a liquid.
seismic wave	Vibrations in the rocks of the Earth caused by earthquakes or explosions. There are transverse and longitudinal seismic waves.
selective breeding	When humans choose an organism that has a certain characteristic and breed more of these organisms, making that chosen characteristic more and more obvious.
semi-permeable	Another term for partially permeable.
sense organ	An organ that contains receptor cells.
sensory neurone	A neurone that carries impulses from receptor cells towards the central nervous system.
sex chromosome	A chromosome that determines the sex of an organism.
sex hormone	Any hormone that affects reproduction.
sexually transmitted infection (STI)	A communicable disease that is passed from an infected person to an uninfected person during sexual activity.
side effect	Unintended harmful effect of a medicine.
sieve tubes (and cells)	Tubes formed of plant phloem sieve cells (so called because the cells have holes in their ends). The tubes carry sugars and other compounds around the plant.
simple distillation	The process of separating a liquid from a mixture by evaporating the liquid and then condensing it so that it can be collected.
skin cancer	A cancer or cancerous tumour on the skin.
solar cell	A flat plate that uses energy transferred by the light to produce electricity.
solar energy	Energy from the Sun.
solenoid	A coil of wire with electricity flowing in it. Also called an electromagnet.
soluble	Describes a substance that dissolves in a given solvent.
solute	Describes a substance that dissolves in a liquid to make a solution.
solution	Formed when a substance has dissolved in a liquid.
solvent	Describes the liquid in which a substance dissolves to make a solution.
soot	Tiny particles of solid carbon produced by incomplete combustion.
sound wave	Vibrations in the particles of a solid, liquid or gas, which are detected by our ears and 'heard' as sounds. Sound waves are longitudinal waves.
specialised cell	A cell that is adapted for a certain specific function (job).
species	A group of organisms that can reproduce with each other to produce offspring that will also be able to reproduce.
specific	A particular requirement e.g. an enzyme is specific and only reacts with one particular substrate.
specific heat capacity	The energy needed to raise the temperature of 1 kg of a substance by 1 °C.
specific latent heat	The energy taken in or released when 1 kg of a substance changes state.
speed	A measure of the distance an object travels in a given time. Often measured in metres per second (m/s), miles per hour (mph) or kilometres per hour (km/h). It is a scalar quantity.
sperm cell	The male gamete (sex cell).
spinal cord	The large bundle of nerves leading from the brain and down the back.
spindle fibre	A filament formed in a cell during mitosis which helps to separate chromosomes.
spring constant	A measure of how stiff a spring is. The spring constant is the force needed to stretch a spring by 1 m.
stain	A dye used to colour parts of a cell to make them easier to see.

standard form	A very large or very small number written as a number between 1 and 10 multiplied by a power of 10. Example: $A \times 10^n$ where A is between 1 and 10 and n is the power of 10.
starch	A polymer carbohydrate that is made by the joining together of glucose molecules.
state of matter	One of three different forms that a substance can have: solid, liquid or gas.
state symbol	A letter or letters to show the state of a substance.
static electricity	Electric charges on insulating materials.
stationary phase	The surface through which the solvent and dissolved substances move in chromatography.
stem cell	An unspecialised cell that continues to divide by mitosis to produce more stem cells and other cells that differentiate into specialised cells.
stent	A small mesh tube used to widen narrowed blood vessels and allow blood to flow more easily.
step-down transformer	A transformer that reduces the voltage.
step-up transformer	A transformer that increases the voltage.
sticky end	A short section of single-stranded DNA at the end of a piece of DNA that has been cut by a restriction enzyme.
still	A piece of apparatus used to carry out distillation or fractional distillation.
stimulus	A change in a factor (inside or outside the body) that is detected by receptors such as sight or sound. Plural is stimuli.
stoichiometry	The molar ratio of the reactants and products in a chemical reaction.
stoma	A tiny pore in the lower surface of a leaf which, when open, allows gases to diffuse into and out of the leaf. Plural is stomata.
stopping distance	The distance in which a car stops, which is the sum of the thinking and braking distances.
storage organ	A plant organ used to store energy-rich substances such as starch. For example, a potato.
strain energy	The name used to describe energy when it is stored in stretched or squashed things that can change back to their original shapes. Another term for elastic potential energy.
stroke volume	The volume of blood the heart can pump out with each beat.
strong acid	An acidic solute that dissociates completely into ions when it dissolves.
structural formula	The formula showing the symbols for each atom in a compound with straight lines joining them to represent the covalent bonds.
subatomic particle	A particle that is smaller than an atom, such as a proton, neutron or electron.
sublimation	When a solid changes directly to a gas without becoming a liquid first.
substrate	A substance that is changed during a reaction.
sucrose	The type of sugar found in the phloem of plants, and used as table sugar.
surface area : volume ratio (SA : V)	The total amount of surface area of an object divided by its volume.
synapse	The point at which two neurones meet. There is a tiny gap between neurones at a synapse.
synthesis	To build a large molecule from smaller subunits.
system	A set of things being studied. For example, a kettle, the water in it and its surroundings form a simple system.
target organ	An organ on which a hormone has an effect.
telophase	The stage of mitosis in which the chromosomes arrive at opposite ends of the cell and the nucleus membrane reforms.
temperature	A measure of how hot something is.
temporary magnet	A magnet that is not always magnetic, such as an electromagnet or an induced magnet.

tesla (T)	The unit for magnetic flux density, also given as newtons per ampere metre (N/A m).
testis	An organ in the male reproductive system that produces sperm cells and the hormone testosterone. Plural is testes.
thermal conductivity	A measure of how easily energy can pass through a material by heating. A material with a low thermal conductivity is a good insulating material.
thermal conductor	A material that allows energy to be transferred through it easily by heating.
thermal energy	A term used to describe energy when it is stored in hot objects. The hotter something is, the more thermal energy it has. It is sometimes called 'heat energy'.
thermal insulator	A material that does not allow energy to be transferred through it easily by heating.
thinking distance	The distance travelled by a vehicle while the driver reacts.
thymine	One of the four bases found in DNA. Often written as T and pairs up with adenine.
thyroid gland	A gland that releases the hormone thyroxine into the blood. Can be referred to as 'the thyroid'.
thyroxine	A hormone released by the thyroid gland which affects metabolic rate by changing how certain cells work, e.g. causes heart cells to contract more strongly.
tidal power	Generating electricity using the movement of the tides.
titration	A technique in volumetric analysis that is used to find the exact volumes of solutions which react with each other.
toxic	Poisonous.
transformer	A device that can change the voltage of an electricity supply.
translocation	The transport of sugars (mainly sucrose) in the phloem tissue of a plant.
transmission lines	The wires (overhead or underground) that take electricity from power stations to towns and cities.
transpiration	The flow of water into a root, up the stem and out of the leaves.
transverse wave	A wave where the vibrations are at right angles to the direction in which the wave is travelling.
tuberculosis (TB)	A communicable bacterial disease that infects the lungs.
tumour	A lump formed of cancer cells.
type 1 diabetes	A type of diabetes in which the pancreas does not produce insulin.
type 2 diabetes	A type of diabetes in which cells do not respond to insulin, or too little insulin is produced.
ulcer	A sore area in the stomach lining.
ultraviolet (UV)	Electromagnetic radiation that has a shorter wavelength than visible light but longer than X-rays.
unbalanced forces	When the forces in opposite directions on an object do not cancel out, so there is a non-zero resultant force.
universal indicator	A mixture of different indicators giving a different colour at different points on the pH scale.
unsaturated	A molecule that contains one or more double bonds between carbon atoms in a chain.
unstable	An unstable nucleus in an atom is one that will decay and give out ionising radiation.
uranium	A radioactive metal that can be used as a nuclear fuel.
urea	A waste product produced in the liver from excess amino acids.
vaccine	A substance containing dead or weakened pathogens (or parts of them), introduced into the body to make a person immune to that pathogen.
vacuole	The membrane-bound space in the cytoplasm of cells. Plant cells have a large permanent vacuole, which stores water and nutrients, and helps to support the plant by keeping the cells rigid.
vacuum	A place where there is no matter at all.

valency	The number of covalent bonds formed by an atom, or the charge number of the ion formed by an atom.
variable	A factor that can change.
variation	Differences in the characteristics of organisms.
variety	Group of plants of the same species that have characteristics that make them different to other members of the species.
vector (biology)	Something that transfers things from one place to another.
vector (physics)	A quantity that has both a size and a direction. Examples include force, velocity, displacement, momentum and acceleration.
vein	A blood vessel that transports blood towards the heart.
velocity	The speed of an object in a particular direction. Usually measured in metres per second (m/s). Velocity is a vector, speed is not.
velocity/time graph	A graph of velocity against time for a moving object. The gradient of a line on the graph gives the acceleration and the area under the graph gives the distance travelled.
vena cava	A major vein leading to the heart.
ventricle	A lower chamber in the heart that pumps blood out into the arteries.
virus	A particle that can infect cells and cause the cells to make copies of the virus.
viscosity	How thick or runny a liquid is. Low viscosity is very runny; high viscosity is thick.
visible light	Electromagnetic waves that can be detected by the human eye.
visible spectrum	The part of the electromagnetic spectrum that can be detected by our eyes.
voltage	The difference in the energy carried by electrons before and after they have flowed through a component. Another term for potential difference.
waist : hip ratio	A measure of the amount of the fat in the body, calculated by dividing the waist measurement by the hip measurement.
water cycle	A sequence of processes by which water moves through abiotic and biotic parts of an ecosystem.
watts (W)	The unit for measuring power. 1 watt = 1 joule of energy transferred every second.
wave	A way of transferring energy or information. Many waves travel when particles pass on vibrations.
wavelength	The distance between a point on one wave and the same point on the next wave.
weak acid	An acidic solute that does not dissociate completely into ions when it dissolves.
weathering	When rocks are broken up by physical, chemical or biological processes.
weight	The force pulling an object downwards. It depends upon the mass of the object and the gravitational field strength. The units are newtons (N). Weight is a vector.
white blood cell	A type of blood cell that forms part of the body's defence system against disease.
wilt	Drooping of parts of a plant caused by a lack of water.
wind turbine	A kind of windmill that generates electricity using energy transferred by the wind.
work done	A measure of the energy transferred when a force acts through a distance.
X-ray	Electromagnetic radiation that has a shorter wavelength than UV but longer than gamma rays.
xylem vessel (and cells)	A long, thick-walled tube found in plants, formed from many dead xylem cells. The vessels carry water and dissolved mineral salts through the plant.
yield	The amount of useful product that you can get from something.
zygote	A fertilised egg cell.

Index

A

A_r (relative atomic mass) 167
abiotic factors and
communities 126–127
absolute zero 425
absorption 280
absorption of radiation 320
absorption spectrum 359
abundance 125
acceleration 287, 290–291, 296, 308
acid rain 272
acidic solutions 196
acidity 196
acids 196–197, 198–199
 reaction with metals 210
 strong 199
 weak 199
acquired characteristics 52
acrosome 9
action–reaction forces 306, 374
activated 80
activation energy 252, 260
 catalysts 256–257
active site of an enzyme 14, 257
active transport of substances 21, 93
adaptations 8, 126
adenine 42
adrenal gland 98
adrenalin 101
adult stem cells 32
aerobic respiration 118
agricultural applications of
genetics 64–65
AIDS (acquired immune deficiency
syndrome) 75
alcohol and disease 71
alkali metals 242–243
alkaline solutions 196
alkalinity 196
alkalis 196–197, 204–205, 208–209
alkane homologous series 268–269
alkanes 268
alkenes 275
alleles 46–47, 64
allotropes of carbon 188–189
alpha particles 362
alternating current (a.c.) 397, 411
alveoli 113
ammeters 382
amperes 382
amplitude 331
amps 382
anaerobic respiration 112
 exercise 119
anaphase of mitosis 27
ancestors 58
animal cells 4–5
animal growth 28–29
anions 178, 224
anode 224
antibiotics 59, 82–83
antibodies 80, 115
antigens 80
aqueous solutions
 acids and alkalis 196
 ionic compounds 183

aquifers 159
Ardi (fossil remains) 56
arteries 114
artificial selection 62
asexual reproduction 27
Assisted Reproductive Technology
(ART) 105
atmosphere
 changing 278–279
 composition 276
 early 276–277
 present-day 280–281
atomic energy 316
atomic models 354–355
atomic number 164, 356
 periodic table 172–173
atomic structure 162–163
atoms 146, 162, 380
 electromagnetic
 radiation 351, 354
 structure 356–357
atrium 116
attractive forces 147
average speed 288
Avogadro constant 220
axon terminals 35
axons 35

B

background radiation 360–361
bacteria 10–11
 genetic engineering 65
 nitrates 142–143
balanced equations 205
balanced forces 297
bases 200
bases of DNA 42, 65
belt transect 126
bending 426–427
bequerels 366
beta particles 362
binomial system 56
biodiversity, preserving 136–137
biodiversity and humans 134–135
bio-fuels 327
bioleaching 233
biological catalysts 13
biology core practicals
 DNA extraction 44–45
 light intensity and
 photosynthesis 90–91
 osmosis in potato slices
 22–23
 pH and enzymes 18–19
 quadrats and transects
 128–129
 respiration rates 120–121
 using microscopes 6–7
biomass 86, 140
biotic factors and communities 130–131
bleaches 245
blood 114, 115
 deoxygenated 116
 glucose control 106–107
 oxygenated 116

body mass index (BMI) 72, 108–109
boiling point 147
 ionic compounds 182
 molecular compounds 186
bond energy 261
bonding 186
 covalent 184–185, 186, 192,
 261
 giant covalent 192
 ionic 178–179, 192
 metallic 190, 192
 models 192–193
bonds
 breaking and making 260
 energy calculations 261
brain 34
braking distance 310, 311
breeds 62–63

C

cancer tumours 27
capillaries 112
captivity 137
carbon allotropes 188–189
carbon cycle 140–141
carbon monoxide 271
carbon neutral operation 327
carbonates, reactions with acids 211
cardiac output 117
cardiovascular disease 72–73
 treatment 73
catalysts 13, 256–257
 cracking 274
cathode 224
cations 178, 224
causal links 280
cause (of effects) 69
cell cycle 26
cell differentiation 29, 30
cell sap 5
cell walls 5
cells (biological) 4–5
 specialised 8–9
cellular respiration 118–119
cellulose 86
central nervous system (CNS) 34
centripetal force 299
Chalara dieback 74, 76
chambers of the heart 116
change of state 414, 421
 energy 418–419
charge 384
 energy 385
chemical analysis, water for 158
chemical barriers against disease 78–79
chemical changes 414
chemical energy 316
chemical properties of substances 147
 elements 170
chemistry core practicals
 electrolysis of coppersulfate
 solution 226–227
 investigating inks 156–157
 investigating neutralisation
 206–207
 investigating reaction rates

254–255
 preparing copper sulfate
 202–203
Chlamydia infections 79
chlorination 159
chloroplasts 5, 86
cholera 74
chromatogram 152
chromatography 152
 paper 152–153
chromosomal DNA 10
chromosomes 4, 26, 40, 42
 replication 41
 sex chromosomes 48
cilia 9
ciliated cells 79
ciliated epithelial cells 9
circuit breakers 399
circular motion 299
circulatory system 112, 114–115
cirrhosis of the liver 71
classification of organisms 60–61
climate change 280–281, 282–283, 324
 effects 282–283
 limiting the impact 283
clinical trials 83
clomifene therapy 105
clones 27
closed systems 218, 238
collisions 307
 momentum 309
combustion 270–271
communicable diseases 69
communities of organisms 124
 abiotic factors 126–127
 biotic factors 130–131
companion cells 95
competition between organisms 58, 130
complementary base pairs 42
complete combustion 270
component forces 377
compounds 148
 ionic 180–183
 molecular 186–187
compression 414
concentrated solutions 198
concentration 20, 88, 197
concentration gradient 20, 92
condensation 154, 266
conduction of heat 320
conservation 136
conservation of energy, law of 316–317
conservation of mass, law of 218–219
conservation of momentum, law of 309
contact forces 374
contamination 369
continuous variation 52
contraception 103
contraction of heart muscles 116
convection 320
cores 403
corpus luteum 104
correlations 69, 108, 280
corrosion 235
cosmic rays 360
coulombs 384
count rate 361

covalent bonds 184–185, 186, 261
covalent, giant molecular structures 189
covalent, simple molecular structures 186
cracking 274
crash hazards 312–313
crop rotation 143
crude oil 264
    fractional distillation 266–267
crumple zones 312
crystallisation 150, 201
    laboratory practice 151
crystals 180
currents 382–383, 384
    metals 380
cytokinesis phase of mitosis 27
cytosine 42

D

Darwin's theory of evolution 58–59
daughter cells 26, 41
decay 141
deceleration 291, 312
decomposer organisms 141
deficiency diseases 70
denaturing of enzymes 15, 257
dendrites 35
dendrons 35
density 415
deoxygenated blood 116
desalination 139, 158
diabetes 106
diabetes (type 1) 65, 108
diabetes (type 2) 108–109
diarrhoea 74
diatomic molecules 244
diffusion 20, 92–93, 112
digestion, specialised cells for 8
dilute solutions 198
diodes 388
diploid cells 8, 26, 40
direct current (d.c.) 397
direct proportion 89, 388
directly proportional 427
discharged ions 228
discontinuous variation 52
disease 68–69
disease resistance 62
disinfectants 245
displacement (distance) 286
displacement reactions 231, 246, 259
dissipation of energy 318, 392
dissociation 199
distance 286
distance/time graphs 289
distillation
    fractional 155, 266–267
    simple 158
    water 139, 154–155, 158
distribution of organisms 126
DNA 4, 10, 40, 42–43, 350
    recombinant 65
DNA code 43
DNA replication 26, 41
domains 61

dominant alleles 46
dose of drugs 83
dot and cross diagrams 184
double bonds 184
double helix of DNA 42
drought 126
drugs 71
dynamic equilibrium 238–239

E

ecosystems 124–125
effectors 36
effervescence 210
efficiency 318–319
egg cells 8, 40
egg follicles 104
elastic materials 426
elastic potential energy 316
electric charge 384
electric circuits 380–381
electrical conductivity
    ionic compounds 182–183
    metals 191
    molecular compounds 187
electrical power 395, 408
electrical safety 398–399
electricity and energy transfer 396–397
electrodes 224
    reactions at 225
electrolysis 224–225
    products 228–229
    salt solutions 228–229
electrolytes 224
electromagnetic induction 408, 411
electromagnetic radiation 358
electromagnetic spectrum 344–345
electromagnetic waves 340–341
    dangers 350–351
electromagnetism 404–405
electromagnets 405
electron micrographs 5
electron orbits 358–359
electron shells 162, 174, 358
    outer 184
electronic configurations 174–175, 358
    noble gases 178
electronic shells 380
electrons 162, 354, 380
electrostatic field 375
electrostatic forces 178
elements 148, 162, 186, 354
    groups 173
    periodic table 170–171
elongation of cells 30
embryo 8
embryonic stem cells 32
emission 280
emission of radiation 320
emission spectrum 358
empirical formulae 217
endangered species 136
endocrine glands 98
endothermic reactions 252, 258–259
    equilibrium 239
    photosynthesis 86
end-point of a titration 209

energy 372
    changes of state 418–419
    charge 385
    conservation of 316–317
    stored 322–323
energy calculations 420–421
energy changes during reactions 260–261
energy diagrams 317
energy efficiency 318–319
energy stores and transfers 316–317
energy transfer 430–431
    stretching 431
energy transfers 392–393
    electricity 396–397
environmental variation 52
enzyme action 14–15
enzyme activity 16–17
enzymes 8, 12–13, 257
    denaturing 257
epidemics 77
epithelial cells 9
equations
    balanced 205
    half equations 210, 225, 231
    ionic 210
equilibrium, dynamic 238–239
equilibrium of forces 306
erythrocytes (red blood cells) 115
eukaryotic cells 4
eutrophication 135
evaporation 154, 266
evolution
    Darwin's theory 58–59
    faster evolution 59
    human evolution 56–57
excretion 112
exercise and anaerobic respiration 119
exothermic reactions 118, 252, 258–259
    equilibrium 239
extension 427, 430–431
extraction of metals 232
eyepiece lens of microscopes 2

F

faeces 140
family pedigree chart 49
feedstock 265
fertilisation 8, 40, 102
field of view of microscopes 4
fight-or-flight response 101
filtrate 151
filtration 150, 201
    laboratory practice 151
fish farming 134
flagellum 10
Fleming's left-hand rule 407
fluids 93, 320
fluorescence 348
food chains 86
food webs 125
force field 375
force meters 300
forces 286
    balanced 297
    calculating 303

    extension 427
    falling bodies 301
    resultant 296–297, 376
    unbalanced 297
fossil evidence for evolution 56
fossil fuels 141, 265
fractional distillation 155, 266–267
fractionating columns 266
free body force diagram 376
frequency 331, 340
friction 374
FSH (follicle-stimulating hormone) 104
fuels 265
    for cars 275
    pollution 272–273
fullerenes 188

G

gametes 8, 40
    production 41
gamma rays 344, 349, 362
gas exchange 87, 113
gases
    pressure 424
    temperature 424
Geiger–Müller (GM) tube 361
gene mutation 50–51
general formulae 269
genes 40, 63
genetic diagrams 47
genetic disorders 70
genetic engineering 63
    bacteria 65
    issues 64
genetic variation 46, 52, 58
genetically modified organisms (GMOs) 63
genetics in agriculture and medicine 64–65
genome 40, 51, 63
genotypes 47
genus 60
giant structures of carbon 189
global warming 280
glucagon 107
glucose 118
    control of blood levels 106–107
glycogen 101
gradients 289
graphene 188
gravitational field 375
gravitational field strength 300
gravitational potential energy (GPE) 316, 322
gravity 291
greenhouse effect 280
greenhouse gases 275, 280
groups (of the periodic table) 173
    group 0 elements 248–249
    group 1 elements 242–243
    group 7 elements 244–245, 246–247
    valency 185
growth in animals 28–29
growth in plants 30–31

guanine 42
guard cells 87

H

habitats 124
haemoglobin 115, 271
haemorrhagic fever 75
half equations 210, 225, 231
half-lives 366–367
halide ions 244
halogens 244–245
    reactivity 246–247
haploid cells 8, 26, 40
hazards 151
health 68–69
heart 114, 116–117
    cardiac output 117
heart attacks 72, 116
heart rate 117
heart valves 116
hertz (Hz) 331
heterozygous for alleles 46
hidden pathogens 75
homeostasis 107
homologous series 268
homozygous for alleles 46
hormonal system 98
    metabolic rate control
    100–101
hormones 98–99
    blood glucose 106–107
    menstrual cycle 104–105
hospital radiation 368
host of a parasite 132
human evolution 56–57
Human Genome Project 51
human immunodeficiency virus (HIV) 75
hydrocarbons 264–265
    breaking down 274–275
hydrochloric acid 79
hydroelectricity 326
hydrogen bonding 43
hygiene 76

I

ignition 267
immune system 69, 80–81
immunisation 81
immunity 81
impulses in nerves 34, 117
incomplete combustion 271
index number 11
indicators (pH) 196
indigenous species 134
induced magnets 402
inelastic materials 426
inert electrodes 228
inert substances 172
inertial mass 303
infrared (IR) radiation 280, 320, 340,
341, 346
inheritance 48–49
inhibition of cell processes 82
insoluble substances 150, 213
instantaneous speed 288
insulation of heat 320

insulin 65
interdependence of species 124
interface between media 336
intermolecular forces 186
interphase of cell cycle 26
inverse proportion 89
inverse square law 89
ionic bonds 178–179
ionic compounds 180
    properties 182–183
ionic equations 210
ionic formulae 180
ionic lattices 180–181
ionisation 359
ionising radiation 359, 363
ions 197, 359
    neutralisation 208–209
    spectator ions 210
irradiation 369
isotopes 166–167
isotopes 357
IVF (in vitro fertilisation) 105

J

joules 316

K

kelvin 425
Kelvin temperature scale 425
kinetic energy (KE) 316, 323
kinetic theory of matter 354, 414
kingdoms 60

L

lactic acid 119
lattices
    giant 190
    ionic 180–181
law of conservation of energy 316–317
law of conservation of mass 218–219
leachate 233
leaf adaptations 87
LH (luteinising hormone) 104
life cycle assessment (LCA) 237
lifestyles 69
ligase 65
light-dependent resistors (LDRs) 388
lignin 95
limiting factor 88
limiting reactant 220
linear relationships 89, 427
lipids 86
lock-and-key model of enzymes 15
long wavelength radiation 346–347
longitudinal waves 330
lubricants 189
lubrication 318
Lucy (fossil remains) 56
lymphocytes 80–81, 115
lysozyme 78

M

magnetic fields 375, 402–403
magnetic flux density 407
magnetic forces 406–407

magnetic materials 375, 402
magnetism 375
magnets 402–403
magnification 2
magnitude 286
mains electricity 396
malaria 74
malleability of metals 191
malnutrition 70
mass 216, 300–301
    conservation of 218–219,
    414
    inertial 303
mass number 165, 356
mean 53, 167
median 53
medical applications of genetics 64–65
medium for waves 331
meiosis 40–41
melting point 147, 149
    ionic compounds 182
    molecular compounds 186
memory lymphocytes 81
menopause 102
menstrual cycle 102–103
    hormonal control 104–105
meristem cells 32
meristems 30
metabolic rate control 100–101
metabolism 112
metals 190
    biological extraction
    methods 233
    corrosion 235
    electric currents 380
    electrical conductivity 191
    extraction as reduction 234
    malleability 191
    ores 232–233
    properties 190–191
    reaction with acids 210
    reaction with carbonates
    211
    reactivity series 210
    recycling 236
    structure and bonding 190
metaphase of mitosis 27
microscopes 2–3
microvilli 8
microwaves 344, 346
mineral ion absorption by plants 92
mitochondria 118
mitosis 24, 40
mixtures 148–149
    separation 154
mobile phase 152
mode 53
molecular compounds 186–187
molecular formula 184, 216
    working out 185
molecular formulae 268
molecular substances 184
molecules 146, 184
    diatomic 244
moles 220–221
momentum 287, 308–309
    conservation of 309

monohybrid inheritance 47
monomers 12, 187
motor effect 406
motor neurones 36, 37
mucus 78
multicellular organisms 26–27, 112
mutations 50–51, 351, 368
mutualism 133
mutualistic relationships 133
myelin sheath 35

N

national grid 396, 410
native species 134
native state metals 232
natural gas 264, 265
natural selection 58
negative feedback 100
nerve cells see neurones
nervous system 34–35
net force 376
neurones 35
    types 36, 37
neurotransmission 35
neurotransmission speeds 36–37
neurotransmitters 37
neutral solutions 196
neutralisation reactions 200, 204,
208–209, 259
neutrons 162, 356, 380
Newton's First Law 298–299
Newton's Second Law 302–303
Newton's Third Law 306–307
nitrates 142–143
nitrogen cycle 142–143
nitrogen oxides 273
nitrogen-fixing bacteria 143
noble gases 248–249
non-communicable diseases 69, 70–71
non-contact forces 374
non-enclosed systems 218
non-indigenous species 134
non-metals 190
non-renewable materials 265
non-renewable resources 324–325
normal contact force 374
normal distribution 53
normal line 336
nuclear accidents 369
nuclear atom 164
nuclear energy 316
nuclear equations 365
nuclear fission 166
nuclear fuels 324
nucleon number 356
nucleons 356
nucleus 162, 355, 380

O

obesity 72, 108
objective lens of microscopes 2
objects affecting each other 374–375
oceans 277, 278
oestrogen 103
ohms 386–387
oil fractions 266

OILRIG mnemonic 210, 225, 247
open systems 238
optimum pH for enzymes 17
optimum temperature for enzymes 16
oral route for pathogen transfer 77
ores 232–233
oscillations 347
osmosis 20–21
outer electron shells 184
ovaries 98
overfishing of wild fish 134
oviducts 9
ovulation 102
oxidation 210, 225, 231, 234–235
    OILRIG mnemonic 210, 225, 247
oxides of nitrogen 273
oxygen in the atmosphere 277, 278–279
oxygenated blood 116

P

pair reversals 173
palisade cells 87
pancreas 98
paper chromatography 152–153
papers, scientific 4
parallel circuits 381
    resistors 387
parasites 132
parasitism 132
particle model of matter 146, 354, 414–415
particles 146
passive processes 21
pathogens 69, 74–75
    hidden 75
    spreading 76–77
penetrating radiation 363
penicillin 82
percentiles 28
period (menstrual) 102
period (of a wave) 331
period (of the periodic table) 173
periodic table 164
    atomic number 172–173
    electronic configurations 174–175
    elements 170–171
    group 0 elements 248–249
    group 1 elements 242–243
    group 7 elements 244–245, 246–247
    valency 185
permanent magnets 402
petrochemicals 265
pH meters 198
pH scale 196
phagocytes 115
phenotypes 47
phloem 95
phloem tissue 95
photosynthesis 86–87, 278
    factors affecting 88–89
physical barriers against disease 78–79
physical changes 147, 414
physical properties of substances 149

elements 170
physics core practicals
    investigating acceleration 304–305
    investigating densities 416–417
    investigating refraction 342–343
    investigating resistance 390–391
    investigating springs 428–429
    investigating water 422–423
    investigating waves 334–335
phytoextraction 233
pituitary gland 98
plant cells 4–5
plant growth 30–31
plasma (of blood) 115
plasmid DNA 10
plasmids 10, 65
platelets 115
plotting compasses 402
pollutants 127
pollution 272–273
poly(ethylene) 187
polyatomic ions 181
polymers 12, 40, 86, 187
populations of species 124
positive ions 359
positrons 362
potable (drinkable) water 138, 158–159
potential difference 382–383, 408
potometers 94
power 373, 394–395
    electrical 395
power rating 394, 397
precipitates 158, 212, 218, 259
precipitation 212
pre-clinical stage of drug testing 83
predation 130
predator–prey cycle 131
predictions about elements 171
pregnancy 102
pressure of gases 424
probability 48, 366
producer organisms 86
products of a reaction 13, 250
    masses of 219
progesterone 103
prokaryotic cells 10
prophase of mitosis 27
proteins 86
protist 74, 86
proton number 356
protons 162, 356, 380
puberty 102
pulmonary vein 116
Punnett squares 48
pure substances 148

Q

quadrat 125, 126
quartiles 72

R

R_f values 152–153
radioactivity, dangers 368–369
radiation 320
radiation types 362–363
radio waves 344, 346
radioactive decay 364–365
radioactive sources, handling 368
radioactivity, measuring 360–361
radiotherapy 349
range of values 53
rate of photosynthesis 88
ratio of phenotypes 47
reactants 250
    limiting 220
    masses of 219
reaction profiles 256, 258, 260
reaction rates 250–251
    factors affecting 252–253
reaction times 310
reactions 220–221
    displacement 231, 246, 259
    energy changes 260–261
    neutralisation 259
    redox 231, 247
    reversible 238
    temperature changes 259
reactivity 230–231
reactivity series 210, 230
receptor cells 34
recessive alleles 46
recombinant DNA 65
recycling 236–237
red blood cells (erythrocytes) 115, 271
redox reactions 231, 234, 247
reduction 210, 225, 231, 234–235
    metal extraction 234
    OILRIG mnemonic 210, 225, 247
reflex arc 37
reflexes 37
reforestation 136
refraction 336–337, 341
relative atomic masses (RAM) 167, 170, 173
relative charges 162
relative formula mass 216
relative masses 162, 356
relay neurones 36, 37
renewable resources 326–327
reproduction
    asexual 27
    specialised cells for 8–9
residue 151
resistance 59, 83, 386–387, 388–389
    modelling 392
resistors
    parallel circuits 387
    series circuits 386–387
resolution 281
resolution of microscopes 3
resolving 377
resources 124
respiration 86
    cellular 118–119
response 34, 310

resting metabolic rate 100
restriction enzymes 65
resultant forces 296–297, 376
reversible reactions 238
risk 151
risk assessment 151
root hair cells 30, 92, 93
rusting 235

S

salts 200, 244
    insoluble 213
    soluble 201, 209
samples 125
saturated compounds 275
saturated solutions 150
scalars 286–287, 296
scale bars 5
scientific papers 4
screening for diseases 79
sea water purification 158
secondary infections 75
secondary response to infection 81
sedimentation 159
seismic waves 331
selective breeding 62
    risks 64
semi-permeable membranes 20, 93
sense organs 34
sensory neurones 35
series circuits 381
    resistors 386–387
sex chromosomes 48
sex hormones 99
sexual intercourse 103
sexually transmitted infections (STIs) 79
short wavelength radiation 348–349
SI units 3
side effects of drugs 83
sieve tubes 95
simple distillation 158
skin cancer 350
smoking and disease 73
solar cells 326
solar energy 326
solenoids 405
solubility 212–213
solutes 150, 218
solutions 150, 218
    concentrated 198
    dilute 198
    saturated 150
solvents 20, 150, 218
sound waves 330
specialised cells 8–9
    digestion 8
    reproduction 8–9
species 56, 60
    introducing to new habitats 134–135
specific heat capacity 418
specific latent heat 419
specific substrates 14
spectator ions 210, 231
speed 286, 296
speed of waves 331, 332–333, 341

sperm cells 8, 40
spinal cord 34
spindle fibres 27
spring constant 430
stains for microscope specimens 3
standard form for numbers 11
starch 86
state changes 147
state symbols 200
states of matter 146–147, 414
static electricity 375
stationary phase 152
stem cells 32–33
stents 73
step-down transformers 410
step-up transformers 410
sticky ends 65
still (distillation equipment) 154
stimulus 34, 310
stiochiometry 221
stomata (singular stoma) 87
stone tools 57
stopping distances 310–311
storage organs 86
stored energy 322–323
strain energy 316
stretching 426–427
   energy transfer 431
stroke 73
stroke volume of the heart 117
strong acids 199
structural formulae 268
subatomic particles 162, 354
sublimation 414
substance transportation 20–21
substances
  insoluble 150
  mixtures 148–149
  pure 148
substrates 13, 14, 257
sucrose 86
sulfur dioxide 272
surface area : volume (SA : V) ratio 112–113
synapses 37
synthesis 12–13

T
target organs 99
tarnishing 235
telophase of mitosis 27
temperature 418
  absolute zero 425
  gases 424
temperature changes 418, changes 420
temporary magnets 405
tesla 407
testes 98
thermal conductivity 320
thermal conductors 320
thermal energy 316, 396, 418
thermal insulation 320
thermistors 389
thinking distance 310
thymine 42
thyroid gland 98

thyroxine 100
tidal power 326
titrations 209
transformers 408–409
  energy transmission 410–411
translocation 95
transmission lines 410
transpiration 94–95
transporting substances 20–21, 112–113
transverse waves 330, 340
tuberculosis (TB) 74, 76

U
ulcers 75
ultraviolet (UV) radiation 340, 348
unbalanced forces 297
units 3
universal indicator 196
unsaturated compounds 275
uranium 324

V
vaccines 81
vacuoles 5, 87
vacuum 340
valency 185
valves of the heart 116
variables 250
variation 50, 52–53
varieties 62–63
vector diagrams 376–377
vector quantities 286, 296
vectors (disease transfer) 77
vectors (genetic) 65
vectors (mathematical) 286–287, 374
veins 114
velocity 287, 296
velocity/time graphs 292–293
vena cava 116
ventricles 116
viruses 75
viscosity 267
visible light 340, 346, 359
visible spectrum 344, 359
voltage 382–383
voltmeters 383
volts 383

W
waist to hip (waist : hip) ratio 72, 109
water
  distillation 154, 158
  for chemical analysis 158
  for drinking 158–159
water absorption in plants 92–93
water cycle 138–139
watts 373, 394
wavelength 331, 358
waves 330–331
  speed 332–333
weak acids 199
weight 286, 300–301

white blood cells 75, 115
wilting plants 92
wind turbines 326
work 372, 392
work done 372, 431

X
X-rays 172, 344, 349
xylem cells 30
xylem vessels 94, 95

Y
yield 62

Z
zygotes 40, 46

The Periodic Table of the Elements

Key

| relative atomic mass |
| **atomic symbol** |
| name |
| atomic (proton) number |

1
H
hydrogen
1

Group 1	Group 2											Group 3	Group 4	Group 5	Group 6	Group 7	Group 0
1	2											3	4	5	6	7	0
																	4 **He** helium 2
7 **Li** lithium 3	9 **Be** beryllium 4											11 **B** boron 5	12 **C** carbon 6	14 **N** nitrogen 7	16 **O** oxygen 8	19 **F** fluorine 9	20 **Ne** neon 10
23 **Na** sodium 11	24 **Mg** magnesium 12											27 **Al** aluminium 13	28 **Si** silicon 14	31 **P** phosphorus 15	32 **S** sulfur 16	35.5 **Cl** chlorine 17	40 **Ar** argon 18
39 **K** potassium 19	40 **Ca** calcium 20	45 **Sc** scandium 21	48 **Ti** titanium 22	51 **V** vanadium 23	52 **Cr** chromium 24	55 **Mn** manganese 25	56 **Fe** iron 26	59 **Co** cobalt 27	59 **Ni** nickel 28	63.5 **Cu** copper 29	65 **Zn** zinc 30	70 **Ga** gallium 31	73 **Ge** germanium 32	75 **As** arsenic 33	79 **Se** selenium 34	80 **Br** bromine 35	84 **Kr** krypton 36
85 **Rb** rubidium 37	88 **Sr** strontium 38	89 **Y** yttrium 39	91 **Zr** zirconium 40	93 **Nb** niobium 41	96 **Mo** molybdenum 42	[98] **Tc** technetium 43	101 **Ru** ruthenium 44	103 **Rh** rhodium 45	106 **Pd** palladium 46	108 **Ag** silver 47	112 **Cd** cadmium 48	115 **In** indium 49	119 **Sn** tin 50	122 **Sb** antimony 51	128 **Te** tellurium 52	127 **I** iodine 53	131 **Xe** xenon 54
133 **Cs** caesium 55	137 **Ba** barium 56	139 **La*** lanthanum 57	178 **Hf** hafnium 72	181 **Ta** tantalum 73	184 **W** tungsten 74	186 **Re** rhenium 75	190 **Os** osmium 76	192 **Ir** iridium 77	195 **Pt** platinum 78	197 **Au** gold 79	201 **Hg** mercury 80	204 **Tl** thallium 81	207 **Pb** lead 82	209 **Bi** bismuth 83	[209] **Po** polonium 84	[210] **At** astatine 85	[222] **Rn** radon 86
[223] **Fr** francium 87	[226] **Ra** radium 88	[227] **Ac*** actinium 89	[261] **Rf** rutherfordium 104	[262] **Db** dubnium 105	[266] **Sg** seaborgium 106	[264] **Bh** bohrium 107	[277] **Hs** hassium 108	[268] **Mt** meitnerium 109	[271] **Ds** darmstadtium 110	[272] **Rg** roentgenium 111							

Elements with atomic numbers 112-116 have been reported but not fully authenticated

*The lanthanoids (atomic numbers 58-71) and the actinoids (atomic numbers 90-103) have been omitted.

The relative atomic masses of copper and chlorine have not been rounded to the nearest whole number.